13 75/1

molecular
thermodynamics

JAMES A. FAY, Massachusetts Institute of Technology

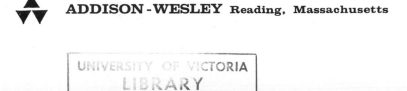

ADDISON-WESLEY Reading, Massachusetts

This book is in the Addison-Wesley Series in

ENGINEERING SCIENCES

Mechanics and Thermodynamics

Consulting Editors
HOWARD W. EMMONS · BERNARD BUDIANSKY

Addison-Wesley Publishing Company, Inc.
READING, MASSACHUSETTS · Palo Alto · London
NEW YORK · DALLAS · ATLANTA · BARRINGTON, ILLINOIS

PREFACE

It is now generally recognized that statistical thermodynamics and, to a lesser extent, the kinetic theory of gases are a valid part of the study of thermodynamics at the graduate level in an engineering as well as a science curriculum. There are some who include them in the engineering undergraduate curriculum. Wherever and whenever it is taught, however, statistical thermodynamics is invariably preceded by the traditional course in classical thermodynamics at the appropriate level, and in the former the emphasis is therefore placed on the determination of thermodynamic properties with which the student is expected to be familiar. The quantities work and heat, with which the initiate struggles so desperately in classical thermodynamics, play a subservient or even negligible role, although the statistical interpretation of entropy is, in the opinion of some, more clearly understood. Most statistical thermodynamics texts therefore presuppose a sufficient understanding of classical thermodynamics on the part of the student for him to have mastered the practical application of those properties he is now about to learn to determine from first principles.

The traditional approach to the teaching of thermodynamics, as outlined above, has several disadvantages. The great emphasis on the molecular structure of matter in the study of physics and chemistry at the high-school and college-freshman level forces the student to develop an ambivalent attitude toward the concepts of classical thermodynamics as they are commonly exposed. The macroscopic structure of matter must be handled in an ambiguous way if recourse to microscopic models is proscribed. Finally, the axiomatic approach of classical thermodynamics, in which definitions and postulates play the significant roles, leaves little room for physical intuition and insight and the rewards of experimental discovery. Even the subsequent teaching of the statistical thermodynamics is stunted: it appears to be an anticlimax, a sudden revelation of the preceding legerdemain.

This text constitutes an attempt to incorporate the major features of classical thermodynamics and statistical mechanics in a single treatment, giving equal

iii

emphasis to the macroscopic and microscopic aspects of the structure and behavior of matter. The basic approach is that of statistical mechanics, in which the thermodynamic and dynamic properties of matter and the laws of thermodynamics are seen to derive from the microscopic motion of the molecules of which macroscopic systems are composed. The laws of thermodynamics, as usually formulated, are found to be convenient means of expressing the mechanical conservation and nonconservation laws in macroscopic terms. Special emphasis is given to the distinction between work and heat in terms of a classical microscopic model. In some sections, such as Chapters 18 and 19 on heat engines and fluid flow, the treatment is nearly entirely macroscopic; in others, such as Chapter 14 on phase and chemical equilibrium, there is an equal admixture of both. In the remaining portions, such as Chapter 15 on crystals, the approach is based predominantly on a microscopic model.

This text is intended primarily for a first course in thermodynamics at the undergraduate level (usually the third or fourth year) but would also be suitable for a first-year graduate course in statistical thermodynamics, especially for students whose undergraduate preparation in thermodynamics was deficient. The requisite understanding of partial differentiation, integration, and vector operations is that commonly encountered at the third undergraduate year, and no wider acquaintance with phyiscs or chemistry is needed than that included in the usual freshman and sophomore courses. For the undergraduate course, two semesters would probably be sufficient to cover most, if not all, of the applications included in this text. At the graduate level, many of the applications could be treated in one semester when the conventional aspects of macroscopic thermodynamics, such as Chapters 18 and 19 on heat engines and fluid flows, are omitted. The problems have been devised to include a range of difficulty which is appropriate to students in the years indicated.

Certain aspects of classical thermodynamics and statistical mechanics which are conventionally included in most texts have been omitted, but where this has been done, appropriate references have been given for completeness. For example, only a few of the extensive Maxwell relations of thermodynamics are derived; they are so seldom used in practice that their inclusion serves primarily as a source of theoretical problems. In the development of statistical mechanics, the use of the canonical and grand ensembles has been omitted entirely since all the practical applications considered can be treated in terms of the microcanonical ensemble. It is not that the elegant treatment of Gibbs is not useful, but at the level of treatment we have chosen it is an unnecessary generalization which will probably distract the student from such simple concepts as the relation between entropy and volume in phase space. The instructor who wishes to discuss these topics will find that the conventional treatment as referenced will suitably fit into the scheme of development of this text.

Considerable emphasis has been given to wave mechanics, both quantum and continuum. While this follows the trend toward more wave mechanics in high-school and college-freshman physics courses, it is particularly appropriate here for two reasons. First, it is important to establish a credibility for the fundamentals of quantum statistics. Second, some applications of statistical mechanics, such as the phonon or photon systems, are concerned with systems of waves rather than particles. The duality of waves and particles is fundamental to modern physics and finds such useful applications in statistical mechanics that it deserves special prominence at an early stage.

Chapters 1 through 10 develop the basic ideas of statistical thermodynamics and the laws of thermodynamics after preparing the way by a survey of particle and wave mechanics, both classical and quantum. While some of this material deserves more or less emphasis, depending on the student's background, not much of it can be omitted. On the other hand, Chapters 11 through 19, which are concerned with applications to particular materials (perfect gas, crystal, radiation field, etc.) or to macroscopic systems (heat engines, fluid flow), need not be covered completely nor necessarily in the order in which they appear. A careful check of the equations and sections referenced in each of these chapters will reveal which antecedent development is required.

Chapter 20, which is an introduction to the kinetic theory of gases, is intended primarily to acquaint the student with one type of treatment of nonequilibrium systems. Because of the great emphasis in the early chapters on the use of phase space in statistical descriptions, only the concept of binary collisions needs to be introduced in order to develop the mean-free-path approach to transport properties.

References that appear throughout the text are collected in a list at the end of the book.

I wish to acknowledge the financial support of the Ford Foundation through its grant to the School of Engineering of the Massachusetts Institute of Technology. This financial aid and the encouragement of Dean Gordon S. Brown were instrumental in initiating the writing of this text. I am also indebted to many colleagues at M.I.T., especially J. H. Keenan, G. N. Hatsopoulos, S. W. Gouse, E. Carabateas, and S. Freedman, for stimulating and challenging discussions. The aid of Miss M. Gazan and Miss B. Wheatland in preparing the manuscript is gratefully acknowledged.

An especial debt is owed my former teachers, H. A. Bethe and A. R. Kantrowitz of Cornell University, and my students at Cornell and M.I.T., who have provided the stimuli so necessary for the writing of this book.

Cambridge, Mass.   J.A.F.
May 1965

CONTENTS

1   INTRODUCTION

1.1   Phenomenological thermodynamics   1
1.2   Molecular thermodynamics   2
1.3   Macroscopic and microscopic scales of measurement   4
1.4   Classical thermodynamics   5
1.5   Statistical mechanics   6
1.6   The kinetic theory of gases   11
1.7   Units   13
1.8   Notation   16

2   DYNAMICS OF PARTICLES

2.1   Kinematics of particle motion   17
2.2   Two-particle interactions   18
2.3   Interparticle forces   19
2.4   Angular momentum   21
2.5   Conservative forces and potential energy   21
2.6   Kinetic energy and energy conservation   23
2.7   The diatomic particle   24
2.8   Systems of particles   26
2.9   The interaction of systems of particles   29

3   PHASE SPACE

3.1   Conjugate coordinates   32
3.2   Canonical equations of motion   33
3.3   Phase space   34
3.4   Ensembles   37
3.5   Liouville's theorem   38
3.6   Stationary ensembles   41

4   WAVES

4.1   Properties of waves   44
4.2   Plane waves   46
4.3   Longitudinal waves in an elastic medium   47
4.4   Momentum and energy density in a wave   50
4.5   Group velocity   52
4.6   Modes of wave propagation   54
4.7   The usefulness of wave descriptions   56

5   QUANTUM MECHANICS

5.1   Quantum modifications of classical mechanics   58
5.2   Discreteness of energy and angular momentum   59
5.3   Wave-particle duality   62
5.4   The uncertainty principle   64
5.5   The Schrödinger wave equation   66
5.6   Probabilistic description of motion   67
5.7   Indistinguishability of molecular particles   69
5.8   Translational energies of particles in a box   70
5.9   Vibration of molecules   74
5.10   Rotational quantum states   78
5.11   Electronic and nuclear energy states   80
5.12   Quantum mechanics and phase space   82
5.13   Quantum statistics   83

6   STATISTICAL DESCRIPTIONS

6.1   Thermodynamic systems and ensembles   87
6.2   The state of a thermodynamic system   88
6.3   Discrete distribution functions   91
6.4   Continuous distribution functions   93
6.5   The state of an ensemble   96

7   THERMODYNAMIC PROBABILITY

7.1   The microcanonical ensemble and phase space   98
7.2   The basic postulate of statistical mechanics   99
7.3   Thermodynamic probability   103
7.4   Entropy   105
7.5   Absolute temperature   110
7.6   Chemical potential   112
7.7   Systems having several chemical components   113

8   THE MOST PROBABLE MACROSTATE

8.1   The thermodynamic probability of a system of independent particles   116
8.2   A simple example   119
8.3   The probability w of a macrostate   121
8.4   The most probable macrostate   124
8.5   The identification of α and β 128
8.6   The partition function Z 131
8.7   Boltzmann systems and the partition function Q 133
8.8   The classical Boltzmann partition function Q_{cl} 135
8.9   The difference between $\ln W$ and $\ln w_0$ 136

9   WORK AND HEAT

9.1   Interactions between a system and its environment   139
9.2   Short- and long-range intermolecular forces   140
9.3   Pressure in a gas   143
9.4   Body forces on charged particles in an electrostatic field   146
9.5   Microscopic work   147
9.6   Interaction energy   150
9.7   Macroscopic work and heat   151
9.8   The first law of thermodynamics   153
9.9   Forces in an equilibrium thermodynamic system   154

10   REVERSIBLE AND IRREVERSIBLE PROCESSES

10.1   Reversible and irreversible processes   156
10.2   Microscopic reversibility   157
10.3   Reversible and irreversible processes in thermodynamic systems   159
10.4   Changes in the most probable macrostate   160
10.5   Reversible work and heat in a closed system   166
10.6   Work and heat in irreversible processes   167

11   THE PERFECT GAS

11.1   The empirical perfect-gas law   171
11.2   The motion of gas molecules   172
11.3   The perfect-gas partition function   174
11.4   Perfect-gas thermodynamic properties   178
11.5   The perfect monatomic gas   181
11.6   The classical partition function   183
11.7   The imperfect gas   184
11.8   Specific extensive properties   187

12   POLYATOMIC PERFECT GASES

12.1	The rotation and vibration of polyatomic molecules	191
12.2	Rotation of diatomic molecules	194
12.3	Rotation of polyatomic molecules	196
12.4	Vibration of diatomic molecules	199
12.5	Vibration of polyatomic molecules	203
12.6	Electronic states of molecules	204
12.7	Thermodynamic properties of polyatomic molecules	206

13   MIXTURES OF PERFECT GASES

13.1	The homogeneous mixture of two perfect gases	211
13.2	The Gibbs-Dalton laws	214
13.3	The entropy of mixing and Gibbs' paradox	217
13.4	The perfect gas with constant specific heats	219

14   CHEMICAL AND PHASE EQUILIBRIUM

14.1	Changes in phase and chemical composition	223
14.2	Equilibrium in thermodynamic systems	225
14.3	Chemical equilibrium in a multicomponent phase	226
14.4	Thermochemical equilibrium of perfect gases	229
14.5	Some examples of gas-phase thermochemical equilibrium	232
14.6	The thermodynamic properties of a reacting mixture	235
14.7	The heats of reaction	237
14.8	Molecular structure of a phase	241
14.9	A phenomenological description of phase equilibrium	242
14.10	Thermodynamic properties of phases in equilibrium	247
14.11	Free energy	251
14.12	The equilibrium of a perfect-gas vapor and a condensed phase	253
14.13	The third law of thermodynamics	256

15   CRYSTALS

15.1	The motion of atoms in a solid	263
15.2	Binding forces in a solid	264
15.3	Crystal structure and waves	265
15.4	Quantum effects and Bragg reflection	268
15.5	Thermodynamic properties of a crystal	272
15.6	Thermal expansion of crystals	278
15.7	The motion of free electrons in a solid	280
15.8	The ideal Fermi gas	283
15.9	Thermionic emission	286

16 THERMAL RADIATION

16.1 The propagation of electromagnetic waves 290
16.2 Black-body radiation 291
16.3 The photon gas 293
16.4 Black-body emission 295
16.5 Emission from nonblack bodies 299
16.6 The interaction of photons with a gas 302
16.7 Thermal noise in electrical circuits 305

17 MAGNETIZATION

17.1 The magnetization of matter 311
17.2 The origin of the magnetic moment of a molecule 316
17.3 The perfect paramagnetic system 320
17.4 Magnetic cooling 326
17.5 Negative temperatures 328
17.6 Ferromagnetism 329
17.7 Superconductivity 332

18 HEAT ENGINES

18.1 The production of work from heat 337
18.2 The heat reservoir and heat engine 338
18.3 The performance of heat engines 340
18.4 Refrigeration 343
18.5 The Carnot cycle 344
18.6 The Rankine cycle 349
18.7 Other cycles 353
18.8 Open cycles with chemical change 357

19 FLUID FLOW

19.1 The fluid continuum 361
19.2 Field properties 362
19.3 The conservation of mass, momentum, and energy 365
19.4 The heating or cooling of fluids in ducts 370
19.5 Flow in rotating and reciprocating machines 373
19.6 Steady flow of an ideal fluid 378
19.7 Flow in a convergent-divergent nozzle 382
19.8 Shock waves 388
19.9 Flow of an ideal fluid with chemical change 392
19.10 The fuel cell 397

20 COLLISIONS IN A GAS

20.1   Transport and other rate processes 404
20.2   The velocity distribution function 406
20.3   The Maxwellian velocity distribution 409
20.4   The fluxes of mass, momentum, and energy 411
20.5   Binary collisions in a gas 417
20.6   Viscosity 420
20.7   Thermal conductivity 425
20.8   Diffusion 428
20.9   The Boltzmann equation 433

REFERENCES 440

BIBLIOGRAPHY 441

APPENDIX

Table A-1. Physical constants and defined units 444

Table A-2. Conversion of units of energy per molecule . . . 446

Table A-3. Conversion of units of energy/mass 447

Table A-4. Definite integrals 448

Table A-5. Series 448

Table A-6. Thermodynamic functions of the harmonic oscillator 449

LIST OF SYMBOLS 450

ANSWERS TO EVEN-NUMBERED PROBLEMS 460

INDEX 462

1

INTRODUCTION

1.1 Phenomenological thermodynamics

Thermodynamics is generally considered to be the study of the relationship between the energy which can be stored in a material body and its other properties, such as temperature, pressure, and structure, as well as the means whereby work and heat may be produced or consumed by virtue of changes in energy. It is distinguished from mechanics and fluid dynamics by the fact that motion and momentum and their changes with time are relatively unimportant. It is a paradox of thermodynamics that it makes no statement concerning the rates at which changes will occur in time, yet declares the one incontrovertible statement about the nature of a change, if any, which takes place in a physical system as time progresses. The relationships between heat and work and energy and structure are incorporated in the laws of thermodynamics in such a way as to be applicable to all systems with which one can experiment in the laboratory. In some applications, such as the production of electrical power from fuels, heat and work will be the most important quantities of interest. In others, such as the processing of chemicals, the structure of the material will be most important. Nevertheless, thermodynamics covers both situations equally well.

By *classical thermodynamics*, we mean a phenomenological study and application of the laws of thermodynamics in which observable properties can be related to one another in an operational manner. For example, the recording of the empirical relationship between pressure, volume, and temperature for a substance and its application to predicting the performance of an engine using this substance as a working fluid are both parts of classical thermodynamics. In terms of ultimate usefulness, almost all the results of thermodynamics will be couched in such empirical or phenomenological terms. On the other hand, classical thermodynamics makes no attempt to explain why one material will behave in one manner while another behaves differently. It merely states what can or cannot be done in a given thermodynamic experiment or application involving a given substance.

The historical development of thermodynamics was largely empirical rather than analytical. In the latter half of the 18th century and first half of the 19th century, there developed great controversies over the nature of heat and work, and their interconvertibility. The caloric theory of heat, which held heat to be a substance which passed from a hot to a cold body, was eventually discredited by Joule through his brilliant experiments on the conversion of work to heat. At the same time, the limitations on the production of work from heat were first realized by Carnot, a French engineer who was vitally interested in improving the performance of steam engines. The second law of thermodynamics was formulated in 1850 by Clausius in terms which were most appropriate to the experiments and applications scientists and engineers were most interested in at that time. According to this view, the second law of thermodynamics states that it is impossible to build a heat engine* which will completely convert heat to work, whereas the reverse is entirely possible. Despite the seeming simplicity of such phenomenological laws, their application is by no means trivial, and the operational definitions even of heat and work are, to this day, often confused or imprecisely understood.

In the latter half of the 19th century, the phenomenological approach to thermodynamics was extended to substances undergoing more complex physical and chemical changes. A secure foundation for the understanding of chemical equilibrium was established by Willard Gibbs. The behavior of systems at very low temperatures was also extensively studied, and the third law of thermodynamics, which deals with the properties of systems near the absolute zero of temperature, was also formulated.

The great importance of the phenomenological approach to thermodynamics was in providing quantitative relationships embodied in the laws of thermodynamics, as well as an empirical understanding of the irreversible processes we so often observe in nature. For these reasons, it is still an important subject of study for the engineer, who must still deal with situations which do not differ greatly in principle from those confronting the scientists of the 18th and 19th centuries. On the other hand, classical thermodynamics in no way recognizes or incorporates the advances in our understanding of the atomic structure of matter. It remains predominantly a 19th-century science, historically interesting, often practically useful, but of limited scope.

1.2 Molecular thermodynamics

Despite the fact that classical thermodynamics deals with quantities such as work and heat which are directly measurable in an experiment, it fails to satisfy our suspicion that the observable behavior of matter basically stems from its molecular structure. We might use the term *molecular thermodynamics* to describe the point of view which attempts to incorporate into the scheme of thermodynamics those ideas about the molecular structure of matter which constitute most of the advances in physics and chemistry of the last hundred years. The atomistic point of view is one which constructs a picture of the structure

---

* A heat engine is defined in Section 18.2.

of matter whose minutest details are not directly observable and are in fact, to some extent, uncertain, yet which correlates so many diverse phenomena on the laboratory scale as to make it highly unlikely that this point of view will be completely displaced in the near future. Considering the formidable place which the molecular theory of matter now holds in the physical sciences, one must be prepared to accept its validity as a working hypothesis and to consider all its implications in whatever area of science one is dealing with.

The means by which the molecular theory of matter can be incorporated into the study of thermodynamics is the science of *statistical mechanics*. This is primarily an analytical discipline in that it logically relates the behavior of individual atoms and molecules to the observable behavior of material systems composed of an extremely large number of such atoms and molecules. Its methods are mostly mathematical, although the information it provides is always given in terms of observable quantities in a laboratory experiment. More than this, however, it affords a deeper understanding of the reasons for the laws of thermodynamics and the relationship between them.

The molecular view of thermodynamics also has a history dating from the 18th century. In 1738 Daniel Bernoulli proposed that a gas consisted of individual molecules in a constant state of motion, colliding with one another and with the walls of the container which enclosed it. It was over 100 years later that Maxwell and Boltzmann developed this idea into what we now call the *kinetic theory of gases* and showed the connection between the total kinetic energy of all the gas molecules and the internal energy as used in phenomenological thermodynamics. The important contribution of Maxwell and Boltzmann, and later of Gibbs, was to develop statistical descriptions of thermodynamic systems and general methods of relating these descriptions to the quantities ordinarily used in classical thermodynamics. Even beyond this, the methods of Maxwell and Boltzmann could be applied to predicting the rate of heat transfer in a gas, a property which is outside the province of thermodynamics.

The full importance of statistical mechanics as a link between the molecular theory of matter and classical thermodynamics did not become apparent until the early part of the 20th century, for it was during this period that the quantum theory of matter was being propounded. In fact, it was the inability of statistical mechanics, as then understood, to properly predict the characteristics of thermal radiation from a body that first led Planck to propose his quantum theory of radiation. So complete has become our understanding of this field in the intervening years that the modern engineer and scientist relies entirely on the calculated properties of some substances for which the empirically determined properties are either nonexistent or difficult to obtain directly.

One way to contrast the points of view of classical and molecular thermodynamics is to consider a system at thermodynamic equilibrium, a sample of gas at fixed volume, for example. From the point of view of phenomenological thermodynamics, the pressure and temperature are constant and fixed in time if the system is in equilibrium. The situation might be termed 'static.' From the molecular point of view, however, the situation is far from static, for there is continual motion of the molecules which collide with one another and with the walls of the containing vessel. While each molecule undergoes radical changes in its motion in time, the average behavior of all the molecules is unchanging in time, if the system is at equilibrium. From this point of view, therefore, the condition of the system is hardly static and might truly be considered dynamic.

This idea of a dynamic molecular system, which under the proper circumstances might have an average behavior that is unchanging in time, is incorporated in the principle of detailed balancing. This principle states that for any particular molecular process, there will be a reverse process proceeding at such a rate as to produce no net change if the system is in equilibrium. For example, if air is heated to a sufficiently high temperature, some of the molecules of oxygen and nitrogen will dissociate into atoms. According to the principle of detailed balance, for each molecular collision which dissociates a molecule into two atoms there will be an inverse collision in which several atoms associate to form a molecule when the system is at equilibrium. If a system is not at equilibrium, then this principle can be applied in determining the rate at which the system tends toward equilibrium.

A basic hypothesis underlying the molecular theory of matter is the indestructibility of matter and energy (at least in nonrelativistic experiments). For example, if monatomic gas particles can possess only kinetic energy, then according to this picture they will remain in motion indefinitely if their total energy is not changed. We say that the ordinary frictional effects observable in large-scale objects such as billiard balls do not exist on the molecular scale. The first law of thermodynamics is the statement of the conservation of energy expressed in terms which are proper to phenomenological thermodynamics.

1.3 Macroscopic and microscopic scales of measurement

A quantity which can be measured directly in the laboratory through direct human observation or by means of appropriate instruments can be called a *macroscopic* quantity. On the other hand, a *microscopic* quantity is one whose dimension or character is essentially molecular and can only be inferred by measurement on a large number of molecules. For example, the macroscopic mass of a body can be measured in the laboratory scale while the microscopic mass of a molecule is measured in a mass spectrometer only through the charge-to-mass ratio and the collection of a large number of masses and hence charges. Because of the great disparity in mass, size, and energy between a piece of laboratory apparatus and a molecule, there is never any ambiguity in distinguishing between a macroscopic and a microscopic quantity.

From a conceptual point of view there is an important distinction between macroscopic and microscopic quantities. For the former we often consider in thought, if not in actual practice, the possibility of dividing the whole into as many parts as we please. We conceive of the idea of a continuum as an appropriate mode of description for a macroscopic body. In computing the mass or moment of inertia of a metal object we subdivide it into minute parts which contribute to the total mass or moment of inertia in proportion to their individual masses. On the other hand, molecular systems are discrete and indivisible except into their elementary particles. The basic mode of description of a macroscopic as opposed to a microscopic system will be different. It is one of the consequences of the modern quantum point of view that the discreteness of microscopic systems extends to their energies as well as to their masses and sizes. The consequence of this discreteness on macroscopically measurable quantities is one of the most striking results of statistical mechanics and will be encountered often in subsequent chapters.

One might be tempted to apply the terms macroscopic thermodynamics and microscopic thermodynamics in place of the names classical thermodynamics and molecular thermodynamics as we have used them above. This would be misleading, since thermodynamics as such can apply only to a macroscopic system. An individual molecule or atom has neither temperature nor entropy, for these are properties which apply only to systems composed of a very large number of molecules. It is true that a molecule or atom will have mass or energy, but these quantities are basic to dynamics and hence exist irrespective of thermodynamics. Thermodynamics always gives results in macroscopic terms even when a microscopic description is used as a starting point.

1.4 Classical thermodynamics

Like the laws of dynamics, the laws of thermodynamics restrict the possible changes in a material body (called a thermodynamic system) which is acted upon by other bodies. If the action of one body on another consists of a force exerted between them, then the motion of the bodies is governed by the laws of *dynamics*. If the action involves the transfer of heat or work, then the resultant behavior is circumscribed by the laws of *thermodynamics*. In order to predict the motion of bodies through use of the laws of dynamics, we must know all the details of the forces they exert on one another as well as the inertial properties of the bodies. Similarly, in thermodynamics we must know not only the nature of the interaction involved (i.e., the details of the heat and work) but also the thermodynamic properties of the bodies in question. Compared with dynamical properties like inertia and velocity, the thermodynamic properties such as entropy and temperature are more difficult to define and measure. Likewise we find it easier to understand the characteristics of forces than those of heat and work. For these reasons the application of the laws of thermodynamics requires a precise understanding of the nature of heat, work, and thermodynamic properties.

Seen in this way, classical thermodynamics is concerned with (1) the nature of heat and work, (2) the thermodynamic properties of matter, and (3) the laws which relate the changes in these properties to the amount of heat and work accompanying such a change. (In the usual development of thermodynamics,* the laws are so stated in terms of the heat and work involved in a cyclic process that new thermodynamic properties such as entropy and absolute temperature may be defined and measured.) In applying these laws to a particular thermodynamic system, we must not only determine the work and heat but also know the thermodynamic properties of the system. We usually are able to treat the system as a "black box" having a few measurable quantities such as pressure and temperature, whose changes can be related to the heat and work interactions through the laws of thermodynamics combined with the thermodynamic properties. This simplification is analogous to that used in particle dynamics, in which the change in the momentum and position of a point mass is determined by the laws of motion once the forces acting and the particle mass are known. In other cases we must treat the thermodynamic system as a continuum having local thermodynamic properties which vary with position and time. (The analogous dynamical example would be the flow of a fluid.) In this latter case, heat and work are more difficult to identify and measure just as the forces in a fluid are not so simple to describe as those, for example, which act on the planets. Regardless of the complexity of the description required in a given application, the laws of thermodynamics are always expressed in macroscopic terms which involve heat, work, and thermodynamic properties.

As previously mentioned, heat and work in classical thermodynamics are defined operationally in terms of specific kinds of changes observed in the bodies which interact with the system of interest. Heat and work are not properties, that is, quantities which may be measured at an instant of time (such as mass, force, pressure, etc.) and they are not stored or separately conserved in any way. The distinction between heat and work is made manifest only on the macroscopic scale. Because of the macroscopic and operational definitions of heat and work, the thermodynamic properties measured thereby will not reveal the microscopic structure of matter.†

1.5 Statistical mechanics

Despite the great simplicity of Newtonian dynamics, it is exceedingly difficult to solve the problem of the motion of three or more particles which exert forces on each other. With the advent of high-speed computers, the many-body

---

* For example, see Keenan. (The publication of an author listed in a footnote or table is given in the list of references at the back of the book.)

† In other words, microscopic constants such as Avogadro's number or Planck's constant cannot be determined from a thermodynamic experiment alone.

problem can be attacked numerically,* but even with their aid it is still impossible to determine the motion of the 10^{23} molecules in one gram-mole of gas. We must therefore adopt a different approach, statistical in nature, if we wish to obtain any information at all concerning the motion of systems composed of many particles. By a statistical approach we mean one in which the results of the analysis or experiment are presented only in a statistical form; that is, we can determine the average value of many successive measurements or calculations but cannot predict with certainty the outcome of a future measurement. *Statistical mechanics* is an analytical science by which the statistical properties of the motion of a very large number of particles may be inferred from the laws of motion governing the individual particles.

Let us illustrate the principle used in the statistical approach. Suppose a box contains N particles which move about, colliding with each other and with the wall. Let us further suppose that the total kinetic energy of two particles which collide is unchanged by the collision, even though the kinetic energy of one of the colliding partners may be changed. Also, let us suppose that a particle which reflects from the wall of the box suffers no change in kinetic energy. In the absence of any external forces, the laws of motion of a single particle predict that there is no way to change its kinetic energy except through a collision with another particle. Since the total kinetic energy of the colliding pair is conserved and since no energy is lost to the walls of the box, it therefore follows that the kinetic energy E of all of the particles in the box does not change with time. If we make a series of measurements of the kinetic energy of particles selected at random from the box, we would expect that the average value of this measurement would be E/N, that is, the average energy per particle in the box. We cannot say with certainty what would be obtained in one measurement in the future but only what we can expect from an average of many such measurements.

In the above example we have made use of one property of the laws of motion, namely, the conservation of kinetic energy in collisions between particles which exert conservative forces on each other. Now this is not all we know about the motion, for in principle we can predict how rapidly the dynamical properties of each particle will change with time. But however possible the latter is in principle, it is impossible in practice. We are therefore forced to utilize only a few properties of the motion and thereby to forgo any detailed knowledge of the behavior of a single particle as time progresses. On the other hand, if we are satisfied with information concerning average properties, then we can indeed learn much from a statistical approach.

---

* The prediction of the motion of three bodies, such as the earth, moon, and sun, for a long time into the future (or past) requires not only a great accuracy of numerical calculation but also a commensurate accuracy in the knowledge of the forces and the initial positions and velocities of the bodies involved. While it is possible to predict the occurrence of solar eclipses for the next several hundred years, the exact time of an eclipse one hundred years hence is not known so accurately as one which might occur one year from now.

As the word is usually construed, the study of statistical mechanics does not include the determination of the evolution in time of a dynamical system of great complexity. For example, in the hypothetical case of the particles in the box referred to above, suppose that all of the particles were initially injected into the box with the same speed. As more and more collisions occurred, their speeds would change, so that the average of the square of the speed and the square of the average speed would no longer be equal as they were initially.* To determine how rapidly the difference in these two statistical quantities would change with time is exceedingly difficult and can be estimated only on the basis of statistical models of the processes involved. One such model, called the kinetic theory of gases, we shall have occasion to discuss below in Section 1.6 and in Chapter 20.

Statistical mechanics would be irrelevant to thermodynamics if it were not for the fact that it is possible to find some statistical properties of systems of many molecules which are identical with the thermodynamic properties used in classical thermodynamics. Furthermore, in many cases these macroscopic thermodynamic properties may be easily calculated from the known dynamical properties of a single molecule. Equally significant, however, is the insight we gain into the laws of thermodynamics by studying from the statistical point of view the changes which can occur in a thermodynamic system. The greater fraction of this book is devoted to an exposition of these three aspects of statistical mechanics.†

It is not intuitively obvious how it is possible to relate the statistical properties of the molecules composing a thermodynamic system with such thermodynamic properties as temperature and entropy. Indeed, it will require the next nine chapters of this book to develop this connection adequately. In order to illustrate the statistical mechanical approach to this problem and to contrast this method with that used in the kinetic theory of gases, we shall briefly consider the determination of the thermodynamic property pressure for an ideal gas. In doing this we shall have to invoke some of the results of more involved arguments derived later in subsequent chapters, so our analysis is a demonstration of the principles used rather than a derivation or proof.

We wish to consider the force per unit area, or pressure, exerted on the wall of a vessel containing a gas. This force is caused by molecules striking the wall and then rebounding. From the dynamical point of view, which is adopted in the kinetic theory of gases as explained below in Section 1.6, the wall force is

---

* Suppose that three particles initially had equal speeds of 4. The square of the mean speed 4 is 16, while the mean of the squares of the speeds is $(4^2 + 4^2 + 4^2)/3 = 16$ also. If at a later time the speeds are 3, 4, and $\sqrt{23}$, then the mean of the squares of the speeds is $(3^2 + 4^2 + 23)/3 = 16$ as before, so that the kinetic energy is unchanged, but the mean speed squared is $[(3 + 4 + \sqrt{23})/3]^2 = 15.5$.

† Some authors use the term *statistical thermodynamics* to denote the application of statistical mechanics to thermodynamic systems.

determined from the change in momentum of the particles which strike the wall during a short interval of time. From the statistical point of view, which we shall use here, the wall pressure is determined by summing the forces exerted by all the molecules that at a given instant are close enough to the wall to feel the repulsive force which acts between the gas molecules and the wall molecules. In the first case the pressure is found in terms of the momentum of the incident molecules while in the latter case it is expressed in terms of the energy of these molecules.

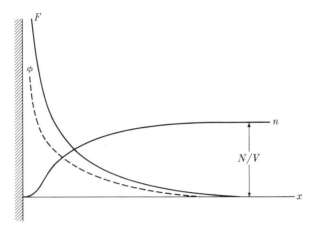

Fig. 1.1. The repulsive force F between a gas molecule and the wall of a container decreases with distance x from the wall. The potential ϕ of this force determines the number density n of molecules per unit volume according to Eq. (1.5–2).

Let us consider a small area ΔA of the surface of the vessel containing the gas. A molecule near the surface will be repelled by the wall, experiencing a force F which is a function of the distance x measured inward from the wall, as sketched in Fig. 1.1. Since the force F depends only on the distance x from the wall, a gas molecule located at x has a potential energy ϕ which equals the work required to move the particle from $x = \infty$ to x:

$$\phi = -\int_{\infty}^{x} F\, dx. \tag{1.5-1}$$

In Fig. 1.1, ϕ is also plotted. Because of the high potential energy near the wall, few incident molecules will have sufficient kinetic energy to penetrate close to the wall and will be reflected before reaching the surface. The number n of molecules per unit volume will therefore be less than that of the molecules far from the wall. If there are N molecules in the container of volume V, then as $x \to \infty$, we would expect that $n \to N/V$. A curve of n as a function of x is also sketched in Fig. 1.1.

At this point we shall introduce a result, later derived in Chapter 8, which relates the number density n to the potential energy ϕ:

$$n = (N/V)e^{-\phi/kT}, \tag{1.5-2}$$

in which k is Boltzmann's constant and T is the absolute temperature. This expresses quantitatively the statement previously made that fewer particles will penetrate closer to the wall where ϕ becomes very large.

We may now compute the pressure p by noting that the total force $p\,\Delta A$ acting on an area ΔA is just the sum of all the forces exerted on the molecules lying in elements of volume $\Delta A\,dx$, each of which contains $n\,\Delta A\,dx$ molecules experiencing a total force $Fn\,\Delta A\,dx$:

$$p\,\Delta A = \int_0^\infty Fn\,\Delta A\,dx$$

or

$$p = \int_0^\infty nF\,dx. \tag{1.5-3}$$

To perform this integration, we shall differentiate Eq. (1.5–1) to obtain

$$\frac{d\phi}{dx} = -F \tag{1.5-4}$$

and substitute into Eq. (1.5–3):

$$p = \int_{x=0}^\infty n\left(-\frac{d\phi}{dx}\right) dx = -\int_{\phi=\infty}^{\phi=0} n\,d\phi = \int_0^\infty n\,d\phi. \tag{1.5-5}$$

If we now replace n with its value given in Eq. (1.5–2), we find

$$p = (N/V)\int_0^\infty e^{-\phi/kT}\,d\phi = (NkT/V)\int_0^\infty e^{-\phi/kT}\,d(\phi/kT)$$

or

$$pV = NkT, \tag{1.5-6}$$

which is the usual perfect-gas law.

It is clear that this determination of the pressure, which is independent of the nature of the force F exerted on the molecules, depends on the variation of number density n with potential energy ϕ, as expressed in Eq. (1.5–2). Given this statistical information about the average number density of particles near the wall, we do not need to consider directly the dynamics of particle motion in order to determine the pressure.

In our subsequent discussion of the determination of thermodynamic properties and the elucidation of the laws of thermodynamics through the principles of statistical mechanics, we shall find it necessary to make much greater use of the properties of molecular motion, especially quantum-mechanical effects, than is evident from the illustration we have just considered. In some cases we shall find it more convenient to consider the motion of waves propagating through material systems rather than the motion of individual molecules. Even so, the general statistical approach is maintained throughout by concentrating our attention on those aspects of molecular or wave motion in which time does not enter explicitly.

1.6 The kinetic theory of gases

As mentioned above, the kinetic theory of gases is a dynamical theory in that time enters explicitly in determining such things as the rate of collisions of gas molecules or the rate of conduction of heat through a gas. It is also statistical in the sense that we forego the possibility of following the motions of all the molecules and consider only the average of the time-dependent behavior of the molecules. Thus kinetic theory goes beyond the statistical mechanics of gases and in so doing requires additional information about the behavior of colliding molecules.

The kinetic theory of gases is based on a model in which each gas molecule is assumed to move in a straight line, occasionally undergoing a collision with another molecule it meets at random, thereby changing its direction and speed. In each such binary collision the total energy of the molecules, which includes both the kinetic energy of translation and the energies of rotation, vibration, or other motions with respect to the mass center, is conserved. By means of such collisions, energy is transferred from one molecule to another, but the total energy is unchanged in a collision.

The principal physical property required by kinetic theory is the size of a molecule, that is, the minimum distance between the centers of two molecules which, upon colliding, are deflected through large angles away from their original lines of flight. If we picture the molecules as billiard balls, then two would collide and be deflected whenever their centers were one diameter apart. We may estimate the order of magnitude of a molecular diameter to be the same as the average distance between molecules in the liquid or solid phase, which for most solids is about 2×10^{-8} cm (or 2 angstrom units). At atmospheric pressure and temperature, the molecules of a gas occupy only $\frac{1}{1000}$ of the volume of the gas, this occupied volume having only a correspondingly small effect on the thermodynamic properties such as pressure, internal energy, etc. On the other hand, the conduction of heat through the gas from regions of high temperature to those of low temperature depends directly on the molecular diameter, small though it may be. Therefore we see that kinetic theory depends on a different aspect of molecular motion than does the statistical mechanics of a gas, namely the collision of two molecules rather than the motion of a single molecule.

It is comparatively easy to estimate the rate at which a molecule of speed v will undergo collisions with other molecules in a gas if we consider the molecule to be a sphere of diameter d. In the time t the molecule moves a distance vt.

If there are N/V molecules per unit volume, then we would expect $(N/V)\pi\, d^2 vt$ molecules to lie within a diameter of the flight path of the chosen molecule. Thus there are $\pi\, d^2 v N/V$ collisions per unit time for the molecule moving with a speed v. For a molecule in air at room temperature, this collision frequency is about 10^9/sec.

To illustrate more clearly the use in kinetic theory of the dynamical aspects of molecular motion, let us determine the pressure in a gas. When we consider the gas molecules near an area ΔA of surface enclosing a gas, we find that half will be moving toward the surface and the remaining half away from the surface if the gas is in equilibrium. If there are n molecules per unit volume having a component u of velocity directed toward the wall, then in a time t all of these molecules originally within a distance ut from the wall, or $nut\,\Delta A$ molecules in all, will have struck the surface area ΔA. Assuming that each molecule is specularly reflected from the wall, it will leave with the same velocity component u directed away from the wall. If m is the mass of a molecule, then each molecule will undergo a change in momentum of $2mu$. The total change in momentum of all the $nut\,\Delta A$ molecules striking the wall in the time t is therefore $2mnu^2 t\,\Delta A$. During the same time t, the impulse applied by the wall molecules exerting a pressure p is just $p\,\Delta A t$. We thus have

$$p = 2mnu^2. \tag{1.6-1}$$

Now all the molecules approaching the wall will not have the same value of u, since some will be moving slowly and others rapidly. We must therefore find the average value of nu^2, denoted by $\langle nu^2 \rangle$, in order to determine the pressure from Eq. (1.6–1). If there are N molecules in the total volume V, then we may replace $\langle nu^2 \rangle$ by

$$\langle nu^2 \rangle = (N/2V)\langle u^2 \rangle, \tag{1.6-2}$$

since only half the molecules are moving toward the wall. Hence

$$p = (N/V)m\langle u^2 \rangle. \tag{1.6-3}$$

The kinetic energy ϵ of a molecule is $m(u^2 + v^2 + w^2)/2$ if v and w are the other two components of the velocity, lying in a plane parallel to the wall. If the molecules have no preferred direction of motion, then $\langle u^2 \rangle = \langle v^2 \rangle = \langle w^2 \rangle$, so that

$$\langle \epsilon \rangle = m\{\langle u^2 \rangle + \langle v^2 \rangle + \langle w^2 \rangle\}/2 = 3m\langle u^2 \rangle/2, \tag{1.6-4}$$

with the result that the pressure p given by Eq. (1.6–3) becomes

$$p = (N/V)(2\langle \epsilon \rangle/3) = \tfrac{2}{3}\{N\langle \epsilon \rangle/V\}. \tag{1.6-5}$$

We therefore conclude from the kinetic-theory argument that the pressure p is two-thirds of the kinetic energy per unit volume, $N\langle \epsilon \rangle/V$. By comparing with Eq. (1.5–6), we would further conclude that $\langle \epsilon \rangle$, which is the average kinetic energy per molecule, is $3kT/2$. In Chapter 11 we shall see this same result derived directly from statistical mechanics.

In the above derivation we see the two aspects of kinetic theory being used: the dynamics of the momentum change upon reflection from the wall, which first requires the determination of the rate at which molecules strike the wall, and the averaging of the dynamical properties of all molecules colliding with the wall. These two features are present in all the fundamental developments of kinetic theory.

In Chapter 20 we shall present in more detail some of the elementary considerations of the kinetic theory of gases, together with some examples of its application to problems such as heat transfer and fluid flow. Our purpose is to illustrate the possibilities of kinetic theory and, at the same time, to indicate that the difficulty encountered in determining the rate at which thermodynamic changes take place is much greater than that involved in determining the properties themselves.

1.7 Units

The system of units most commonly used in dynamics is the mks-system for which the units of length, mass, and time are the meter (m), kilogram (kg), and second (sec), respectively. In this system, the unit for force, the newton (n), and unit of energy, the joule (j), are defined by

$$1 \text{ newton} \equiv 1 \text{ kilogram-meter/(second)}^2,$$
$$1 \text{ joule} \equiv 1 \text{ newton-meter} \tag{1.7-1}$$
$$= 1 \text{ kilogram-(meter/second)}^2,$$

so that a force of 1 n applied to a 1-kg mass produces an acceleration of 1 m/sec^2. An alternative system of units is the cgs-system, for which the fundamental units of length, mass, and time are the centimeter $(= 10^{-2} \text{ m})$, the gram $(= 10^{-3} \text{ kg})$, and the second. The corresponding units of force (dyne) and energy (erg) are defined by

$$1 \text{ dyne} \equiv 1 \text{ gram-centimeter/(second)}^2$$
$$= 10^{-5} \text{ newton};$$

$$1 \text{ erg} \equiv 1 \text{ dyne-centimeter}$$
$$= 1 \text{ gram (centimeter/second)}^2 \tag{1.7-2}$$
$$= 10^{-7} \text{ joule}.$$

Again, a unit force (dyne) applied to a unit mass (gram) results in a unit acceleration (cm/sec^2).

Most thermodynamic data are reported in a different energy unit than the joule or the erg: either the kilogram-calorie, or kilocalorie (kcal), or the gram-calorie, or calorie (cal). Although originally chosen as the amount of heat required to raise a unit mass of water 1 C°, these units are now defined in terms of the joule:

$$1 \text{ kilogram-calorie} \equiv 4.184 \text{ joules},$$
$$1 \text{ gram-calorie} \equiv 10^{-3} \text{ kilogram-calories}$$
$$= 4.184 \times 10^4 \text{ ergs}. \tag{1.7-3}$$

The kilogram-calorie or gram-calorie may be called the chemical unit of energy. Since it is a different unit from the mechanical (or dynamical) unit of the joule or erg, we must be careful to convert all quantities in an equation to identical units when applying the laws of thermodynamics.

The chemical unit of amount of matter is the kilogram-mole or the gram-mole. It is not a unit of mass in the dynamical sense but instead is a unit of measure of the number of molecules in a system. It is defined as the amount of matter having a mass (in kilograms or grams, respectively) equal to the molecular weight $\widetilde{M}$ of the substance involved:

$$1 \text{ kilogram-mole} = \widetilde{M} \text{ kilogram},$$
$$1 \text{ gram-mole} = \widetilde{M} \text{ gram}. \tag{1.7-4}$$

The molecular weight $\widetilde{M}$ of any substance is determined by setting the atomic weight of one element at a fixed value. (The units and physical constants given in the Appendix, Tables A–1 through A–3, are based on the choice of $\widetilde{M} = 12$ for the common isotope of carbon, C^{12}.) The reason for using a nondynamical unit of mass in chemical reactions lies in the tendency of molecules to combine chemically in proportion to their number rather than their masses. In an application where both chemistry and dynamics are important, such as the flow of propellant gases in a rocket nozzle, we must be careful to use appropriate units where each applies.

The number $\widetilde{N}$ of molecules in 1 kgm-mole (or 1 gm-mole), called *Avogadro's number*, is not a defined quantity and must be determined from experiment. The values of this and similar physical constants are listed in Table A–1 of the Appendix.

A *specific* property is the value of a property per unit mass, such as the energy per unit mass. The chemical unit of energy per unit mass is the kilocalorie/kilogram-mole (or calorie/gram-mole), which is related to the dynamical unit of joules/kilogram (or ergs/gram) by

$$1 \text{ kilocalorie/kilogram-mole} = (4.184/\widetilde{M})\text{joule/kilogram},$$
$$1 \text{ calorie/gram-mole} \equiv (4.184 \times 10^4/\widetilde{M})\text{erg/gram} \tag{1.7-5}$$
$$= 1 \text{ kilocalorie/kilogram-mole}.$$

Because the chemical unit of specific energy measures the energy of $\widetilde{N}$ molecules, it may be converted to other units of energy per molecule, such as the electron volt (ev).* (Table A–2 of the Appendix lists the conversion factors to other units of energy per molecule; the energy per unit mass needed for dynamical calculations may be converted to engineering units by means of Table A–3.)

The unit of temperature, called the kelvin degree (K°), is based on the absolute kelvin scale of temperature defined by the second law of thermodynamics and the arbitrary choice of a temperature of 273.16 °K for the triple point of water. This choice results in a 100-K° difference in temperature between the melting point of ice and the boiling point of water at atmospheric pressure. (The centigrade scale of temperature has the same unit as the kelvin scale but is shifted upward with respect to the latter by 273.16 degrees.) Physical constants, such as the universal gas constant and Boltzmann's constant, which depend upon the definition of the degree of temperature, are listed in Table A–1.

In Chapter 17 we shall discuss the magnetic properties of thermodynamic systems. The additional unit needed to determine electromagnetic properties is the unit of charge, the coulomb (coul). In terms of this unit, the units of current, voltage, power, capacitance, inductance, and magnetic induction are defined as

$$
\begin{aligned}
1 \text{ ampere} &\equiv 1 \text{ coulomb/second,} \\
1 \text{ volt} &\equiv 1 \text{ joule/coulomb,} \\
1 \text{ watt} &\equiv 1 \text{ joule/sec,} \\
1 \text{ farad} &\equiv 1 \text{ (coulomb)}^2/\text{joule,} \\
1 \text{ henry} &\equiv 1 \text{ joule (second/coulomb)}^2, \\
1 \text{ weber} &\equiv 1 \text{ joule (second/coulomb).}
\end{aligned}
\tag{1.7-6}
$$

The corresponding physical constants of a vacuum, the electric permittivity and the magnetic permeability, are given in Table A–1. (For simplicity we have avoided the use of cgs electromagnetic units in Chapter 17.)

There is still in common use a system of units called engineering units, having counterparts of those previously mentioned. The units of length, mass, and time are the foot (ft), the pound-mass (lbm), and the second. The unit of force, called the pound-force (lbf), is so defined as to produce a standard acceleration of g_0 feet/(second)^2 when applied to a unit mass:

$$
1 \text{ pound-force} \equiv g_0 \text{ pound-mass foot/(second)}^2, \tag{1.7-7}
$$

where g_0 has the numerical value given in Table A–1. For dynamical problems, these units are inconvenient because a unit force applied to a unit mass does not produce a unit acceleration. The engineering unit of energy is the foot-pound-force (ft-lbf), whose definition is obvious.

---

* The work required to move an electron through a potential drop of one volt is called one electron volt (ev).

The engineering unit of heat is the British thermal unit (Btu), which is defined in terms of the joule:*

$$1 \text{ Btu} \equiv 1.0551 \times 10^3 \text{ joules.} \tag{1.7–8}$$

The engineering temperature scale corresponding to the kelvin scale is called the rankine scale, for which the water triple point has the value of 491.69 degrees rankine (°R). This choice gives the following relationship between the temperature units:

$$1 \text{ rankine degree} \equiv \tfrac{5}{9} \text{ kelvin degree.} \tag{1.7–9}$$

(The fahrenheit temperature scale has the same unit as the rankine scale but is shifted upward with respect to the latter by 459.69°. As a consequence, the freezing and boiling points of water are 32° and 212°, respectively, on the fahrenheit scale.)

Engineering units are awkward to use, and when working problems, one will in general find it easier to convert them to mks units.

1.8 Notation

The mathematics used in the following chapters involves mostly differential and integral calculus. Vector quantities are printed in boldface, and the vector scalar and cross products are indicated by $\mathbf{a} \cdot \mathbf{b}$ and $\mathbf{a} \times \mathbf{b}$. Vector calculus, where used, is explained in a footnote.

A function f of several independent variables, say x, y, and z, is denoted by $f\{x, y, z\}$ whenever it is important to emphasize what are considered to be the independent variables. The partial derivative of f with respect to x is denoted by $(\partial f/\partial x)_{y,z}$ if it is necessary to emphasize what are the remaining variables that are held fixed in the differentiation. Thus $(\partial S/\partial E)_V$ implies that S is considered to be a function of the independent variables E and V; that is, $S = S\{E, V\}$, when this differentiation is performed.

---

* The Btu is actually defined in terms of the international steam-table calorie, which is then defined in terms of the joule. Originally, the Btu was defined as the amount of heat required to raise one pound-mass of water 1 F°.

2

DYNAMICS OF PARTICLES

2.1 Kinematics of particle motion

Kinematics is the description of how an identifiable particle moves through a three-dimensional space as time progresses. In a cartesian coordinate system (*xyz*-space), the position of a particle at any instant is determined by the three scalar components of its *position vector* **r**, which measures the distance and direction of the particle from the origin of the coordinate system. The *trajectory* is the path of the particle in space, and the position of the particle along its trajectory as a function of time t is given by $\mathbf{r}\{t\}$. The purpose of dynamics is to explain and predict the trajectories of particles in space as a function of time, that is, to find $\mathbf{r}\{t\}$ for each particle.

The *velocity* **v** is a vector defined as the time rate of change of position **r**. It is the limit of the ratio of the change in vector position **r** divided by the change in time t for two successive instants (Fig. 2.1):

$$\mathbf{v}\{t_1\} = \left(\frac{d\mathbf{r}}{dt}\right)_{t-t_1}$$

$$= \lim_{t_2 \to t_1} \left\{\frac{\mathbf{r}\{t_2\} - \mathbf{r}\{t_1\}}{t_2 - t_1}\right\}.$$

$$(2.1\text{--}1)$$

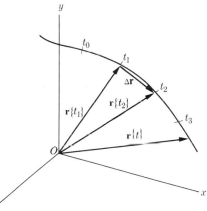

Fig. 2.1. The kinematical description of the motion of a point particle along the trajectory $\mathbf{r}\{t\}$.

Since **r** is a vector and t is a scalar, the ratio is still a vector quantity. The direction of **v** is measured in **r**-space, but the magnitude has a different dimension so that **v** cannot be plotted in **r**-space, even though it is conventional to draw velocity vectors tangent to the trajectory in **r**-space. For this reason, it is convenient to define a new space, called *phase space*, in which both velocity **v** and position **r** can be plotted simultaneously. This is discussed in Chapter 3.

17

In like manner, it is possible to construct the time rate of change of velocity, called the acceleration vector, which would be denoted by $d\mathbf{v}/dt$. While the time derivatives of the acceleration vector may be determined as a part of kinematics, it has been found neither necessary nor useful in the study of particle dynamics.

2.2 Two-particle interactions

The change in the motion of two bodies which collide, whether they be billiard balls, automobiles, or electrically charged pith balls which do not actually touch each other, is always found to observe a simple relation. *The change in velocity of particle 1 is opposite in direction to the change in velocity of particle 2, while the magnitudes of the velocity changes are in the same proportion to each other for all interactions between a given pair of particles.* If the velocity vectors of the two bodies before collision are denoted by $\mathbf{v}_1$ and $\mathbf{v}_2$, and those after collision by

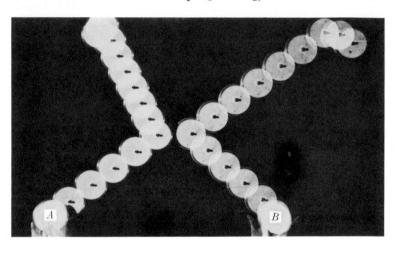

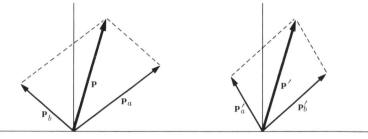

Fig. 2.2. Collision between two pucks, $m_a = 2.0$ kgm and $m_b = 1.5$ kgm, and a momentum vector diagram of the collision. Total momentum is conserved. (By permission from U. Ingard and W. Kraushaar, *Introduction to Mechanics, Matter and Waves*, Addison-Wesley, Reading, Mass., 1960.)

$\mathbf{v}_1'$ and $\mathbf{v}_2'$, respectively, then the mathematical statement of this law of motion is

$$\mathbf{v}_1' - \mathbf{v}_1 = -K_{21}(\mathbf{v}_2' - \mathbf{v}_2), \qquad K_{21} = \text{const.} \qquad (2.2\text{–}1)$$

A collision of two pucks whose velocity vectors are in agreement with Eq. (2.2–1) is shown in Fig. 2.2.

The scalar proportionality constant K_{21} is a property of both colliding particles. By experimenting with three sizes of particles, it is always found that

$$K_{21}/K_{31} = K_{23}. \qquad (2.2\text{–}2)$$

If this is universally true, it is possible to assign to each particle a scalar quantity m, called the mass, such that

$$m_2/m_1 \equiv K_{21}. \qquad (2.2\text{–}3)$$

Such a definition of the mass of a particle will obviously satisfy Eq. (2.2–2). With the mass so defined, Eq. (2.2–1) for the velocity change becomes

$$m_1(\mathbf{v}_1' - \mathbf{v}_1) = -m_2(\mathbf{v}_2' - \mathbf{v}_2). \qquad (2.2\text{–}4)$$

If the vector *momentum* $\mathbf{p}$ is defined as the product of scalar mass times vector velocity, then this equation may be rewritten and rearranged as

$$\mathbf{p}_1 + \mathbf{p}_2 = \mathbf{p}_1' + \mathbf{p}_2'. \qquad (2.2\text{–}5)$$

This is the statement of the conservation of linear momentum; that is, the sum of the momenta of the two particles before collision is equal in magnitude and direction to the sum of the momenta of the two particles after collision. Such a vector statement is equivalent to three scalar equations of conservation of the components of momentum along three mutually perpendicular directions.

2.3 Interparticle forces

The conservation of momentum in collisions where an abrupt change in velocity occurs, such as that of Fig. 2.2, is easy to ascertain experimentally. If two such pucks are connected by a light elastic string, and then given arbitrary initial motions, the resulting motion is more complex, as shown in Fig. 2.3. By carefully observing such a motion, one is led to conclude that *the total momentum is constant in time (and hence conserved)*, so that the time rate of change of momentum of particle 1 is equal and opposite in direction to that of particle 2.

$$\mathbf{p}_1 + \mathbf{p}_2 = \text{const,}$$

$$\therefore \frac{d}{dt}(\mathbf{p}_1 + \mathbf{p}_2) = 0$$

or

$$\frac{d\mathbf{p}_1}{dt} = -\frac{d\mathbf{p}_2}{dt}. \qquad (2.3\text{–}1)$$

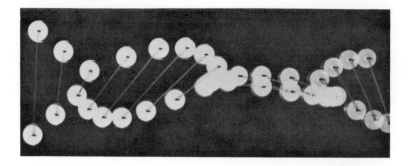

Fig. 2.3. Motion of two pucks connected by an elastic band. Prove that the total momentum is conserved. (By permission from U. Ingard and W. Kraushaar, *Introduction to Mechanics, Matter and Waves*, Addison-Wesley, Reading, Mass., 1960.)

By observing that the momentum of either particle 1 or 2 is changing in time only while the elastic string is taut, we invent the concept of a *force* acting between the particles as the cause of the change in momentum. By defining the force as equal to the time rate of change of momentum, it follows from Eq. (2.3–1) that the force $\mathbf{F}_{12}$ on particle 1 due to particle 2 must be equal and opposite to the force $\mathbf{F}_{21}$ on particle 2 due to particle 1. Thus the conservation of linear momentum is satisfied by the following set of equations:

$$\frac{d\mathbf{p}_1}{dt} = \mathbf{F}_{12},$$

$$\frac{d\mathbf{p}_2}{dt} = \mathbf{F}_{21},$$

$$\mathbf{F}_{12} = -\mathbf{F}_{21}. \tag{2.3–2}$$

The concept of a force is a very useful one. In the case of motion of the planets about the sun, or of a satellite about the earth, the force between the two bodies is related to their masses and the distance of separation by the universal law of gravitation. It then becomes possible to predict such motions from Eqs. (2.3–2), together with the gravitational force law. For charged particles moving in magnetic and electric fields, there are similar laws relating the force on a particle to its position and velocity, from which similar deductions can be made. Finally, if there is no change in position with time, then the net force on a particle must be zero, and the concept of balance of forces in static equilibrium leads to interesting deductions as to the stresses in structures. In all these cases, the concept of force, even if introduced as a primitive notion, is extremely useful to an understanding of the phenomena and to the prediction of the motion of the bodies involved.

2.4 Angular momentum

In the study of statics the moment of a force $\mathbf{F}$ about the origin of a fixed coordinate system is defined to be $\mathbf{r} \times \mathbf{F}$,* where $\mathbf{r}$ is the position vector of any point along the line of action of the force $\mathbf{F}$. One may similarly define the moment of momentum, or angular momentum, $\mathbf{L}$ as $\mathbf{r} \times \mathbf{p}$, where $\mathbf{r}$ is the instantaneous position and $\mathbf{p}$ is the instantaneous momentum of a particle.

For each particle, the time rate of change of angular momentum may be obtained by direct differentiation:

$$\frac{d\mathbf{L}_1}{dt} = \frac{d}{dt}(\mathbf{r}_1 \times \mathbf{p}_1) = \left(\frac{d\mathbf{r}_1}{dt}\right) \times \mathbf{p}_1 + \mathbf{r}_1 \times \left(\frac{d\mathbf{p}_1}{dt}\right). \tag{2.4-1}$$

Now $d\mathbf{r}_1/dt$ is the velocity of particle 1 and is a vector which is parallel to $\mathbf{p}_1$. Since the cross product of parallel vectors is identically zero, only the second term on the right-hand side of Eq. (2.4–1) remains. Adding to Eq. (2.4–1) a similar equation for particle 2, we find that the time rate of change of total angular momentum $\mathbf{L}$ is

$$\frac{d\mathbf{L}}{dt} = \frac{d\mathbf{L}_1}{dt} + \frac{d\mathbf{L}_2}{dt} = \mathbf{r}_1 \times \left(\frac{d\mathbf{p}_1}{dt}\right) + \mathbf{r}_2 \times \left(\frac{d\mathbf{p}_2}{dt}\right). \tag{2.4-2}$$

Replacing the time rate of change of linear momentum by the force as given in Eq. (2.3–2), we may rewrite this as

$$\frac{d\mathbf{L}}{dt} = (\mathbf{r}_1 - \mathbf{r}_2) \times \mathbf{F}_{12}. \tag{2.4-3}$$

If the force $\mathbf{F}_{12}$ acts in the same direction as the line joining the centers of the particles $(\mathbf{r}_1 - \mathbf{r}_2)$, then the vector product of Eq. (2.4–3) is zero, and the angular momentum does not change with time; that is, the angular momentum is conserved. Forces which act along the lines of centers are called *central forces*.

2.5 Conservative forces and potential energy

If a central force acting between two particles depends only on the relative position $\mathbf{r}_1 - \mathbf{r}_2$ of the two particles in such a way that the integral†

$$\int_{\mathbf{r}_1-\mathbf{r}_2}^{\mathbf{r}_1'-\mathbf{r}'} \mathbf{F}_{12} \cdot d(\mathbf{r}_1 - \mathbf{r}_2)$$

---

* If the cartesian components of a vector $\mathbf{a}$ are a_x, a_y, and a_z, and similarly for $\mathbf{b}$, then the components of $\mathbf{a} \times \mathbf{b}$ are $a_y b_z - a_z b_y$, $a_z b_x - a_x b_z$, $a_x b_y - a_y b_x$.

† The scalar product of $\mathbf{a}$ and $\mathbf{b}$ (denoted by $\mathbf{a} \cdot \mathbf{b}$) is the scalar sum $a_x b_x + a_y b_y + a_z b_z$.

depends only on the initial and final values of the relative positions of the two particles,* then the force is said to be *conservative*, for reasons to be explained in Section 2.6. For conservative forces this integral of the scalar product of the force and the increment in relative displacement may thus be written as

$$\int_{\mathbf{r}_1-\mathbf{r}_2}^{\mathbf{r}_1'-\mathbf{r}_2'} \mathbf{F}_{12} \cdot d(\mathbf{r}_1 - \mathbf{r}_2) = -[U\{\mathbf{r}_1' - \mathbf{r}_2'\} - U\{\mathbf{r}_1 - \mathbf{r}_2\}]. \quad (2.5\text{--}1)$$

The integral function U, defined by Eq. (2.5–1), is called the *potential energy*, and is a scalar function of the magnitude alone of the relative position of the two particles. It is not possible to ascribe an absolute value to the potential energy, for only changes in potential energy can be determined from the force integral. It is conventional to assign the value zero to the potential energy of a relative configuration which seems reasonable in the light of the nature of the forces involved. For example, for particles acted upon by a force inversely proportionate to the square of the distance between them, such as a Coulomb or gravitational force, the potential energy is usually taken to be zero for infinite separation. Thus, for a finite separation distance, the potential energy would be negative for particles which attract each other. For two masses connected by a spring, the potential energy may be taken as zero for a relative position in which there is neither tension nor compression in the spring. In this case the potential energy in all other positions will be positive.

It should be emphasized that the potential energy is a property not of either particle 1 or particle 2 but of the system of particles 1 and 2. The potential energy depends only on the relative displacement of the two particles, whether obtained by holding particle 2 fixed while moving particle 1 or vice versa. While it is customary, for example, to ascribe a potential energy to a body moving in the gravitational field of the earth, such an energy truly belongs only to the system of earth and body in question rather than to either one or the other. Only if one is careful about the misuse of such an erroneous potential energy function will no error be introduced.

An important noncentral force is that which acts on a charged particle moving through a magnetic field. Since this force acts perpendicular to the velocity (as well as to the magnetic field), it will also be perpendicular to the increment in displacement and thereby will not contribute to the integral of Eq. (2.5–1). There is no potential energy associated with such a force, and the motion may be treated as though it were a conservative system in the sense described in Section 2.6.†

---

* If x, y, z are the cartesian coordinates of the $(\mathbf{r}_1 - \mathbf{r}_2)$-space, then $\mathbf{F}_{12}$ is conservative if $(\partial/\partial x)(F_{12})_y = (\partial/\partial y)(F_{12})_x$, $(\partial/\partial y)(F_{12})_z = (\partial/\partial z)(F_{12})_y$, and $(\partial/\partial x)(F_{12})_z = \partial/\partial z(F_{12})_x$.

† For a treatment of the motion of charged particles in magnetic fields, see Goldstein, p. 19.

2.6 Kinetic energy and energy conservation

A scalar integral of the equation of motion (2.3–2) may be obtained by taking the scalar product of the equation of motion with an increment in displacement $d\mathbf{r}$, and integrating from the initial to final values of both the displacement and momentum:

$$\int_{\mathbf{p}_1}^{\mathbf{p}_1'} \left(\frac{d\mathbf{p}_1}{dt}\right) \cdot d\mathbf{r}_1 = \int_{\mathbf{r}_1}^{\mathbf{r}_1'} \mathbf{F}_{12} \cdot d\mathbf{r}_1. \tag{2.6–1}$$

The integration on the left may be performed by noting that $d\mathbf{r}_1/dt$ is by definition the velocity $\mathbf{v}_1$ and equal to $\mathbf{p}_1/m_1$. Thus, the left-hand side of Eq. (2.6–1) becomes

$$\int_{\mathbf{p}_1}^{\mathbf{p}_1'} (d\mathbf{p}_1) \cdot \frac{\mathbf{p}_1}{m_1} = \frac{(p_1')^2 - p_1^2}{2m_1} = \frac{m_1[v_1'^2 - v_1^2]}{2}. \tag{2.6–2}$$

By adding to Eq. (2.6–1) the corresponding equation for particle 2 (noting that $\mathbf{F}_{12} = -\mathbf{F}_{21}$) and using Eq. (2.5–1), which defines the potential energy U, we obtain

$$\frac{m_1}{2}[(v_1')^2 - (v_1)^2] + \frac{m_2}{2}[(v_2')^2 - (v_2)] = -U\{\mathbf{r}_1' - \mathbf{r}_2'\} + U\{\mathbf{r}_1 - \mathbf{r}_2\}. \tag{2.6–3}$$

This may be rewritten in the form of a conservation law:

$$T\{v_1', v_2'\} + U\{\mathbf{r}_1' - \mathbf{r}_2'\} = T\{v_1, v_2\} + U\{\mathbf{r}_1 - \mathbf{r}_2\},$$

where

$$T\{v_1, v_2\} \equiv \tfrac{1}{2}m_1 v_1^2 + \tfrac{1}{2}m_2 v_2^2$$
$$\equiv p_1^2/2m_1 + p_2^2/2m_2. \tag{2.6–4}$$

The function T is called the kinetic energy of the system and is necessarily always positive. *For systems acted upon by conservative forces only, Eq. (2.6–4) states that the sum of the kinetic and potential energy is a constant of the motion.*

It is important to realize that the conservation-of-energy statement contains less information about the motion of a system than does either of the other two conservation statements, that of conservation of linear momentum or angular momentum. The energy conservation law is a scalar equation and hence provides less information than either of the momentum laws, which are vector statements. It is impossible to determine the motion of a system from a statement of energy conservation alone, except in the case where the motion is restricted to one dimension. Furthermore, time does not enter explicitly into the law of conservation of energy, and thus the temporal behavior of a system can be determined only by returning to the momentum conservation condition.

Despite the limited usefulness of the energy conservation principle, it can help us to determine what motions are or are not possible even though we may not be clever enough to determine all the characteristics of the motion in question. For example, a satellite leaving the surface of the earth with a velocity less than the "escape velocity" has insufficient kinetic energy to move infinitely far from the earth, but when and where the satellite will return to the earth, if ever, cannot be determined from energy considerations alone.

2.7 The diatomic particle

A two-particle system which is useful in understanding perfect gases is the classical model of the diatomic molecule. It consists of two particles, of mass m_1 and m_2, held together by a linear spring which exerts an attractive or repulsive force when the interparticle distance exceeds or is less than a distance d (see Fig. 2.4). The tension in the spring per unit extension beyond the distance d is called the stiffness K. The force acting on particle 1 is in the direction of $\mathbf{r}_2 - \mathbf{r}_1$ and has a magnitude equal to K times the stretch in the spring:

$$\mathbf{F}_{12} = \frac{-K(\mathbf{r}_1 - \mathbf{r}_2)}{|r_1 - r_2|} \{|\mathbf{r}_1 - \mathbf{r}_2| - d\}. \tag{2.7-1}$$

The potential energy found by integration is

$$U\{\mathbf{r}_1 - \mathbf{r}_2\} = \tfrac{1}{2}K[|\mathbf{r}_1 - \mathbf{r}_2| - d]^2, \tag{2.7-2}$$

where U is arbitrarily zero when there is no stretch in the spring.

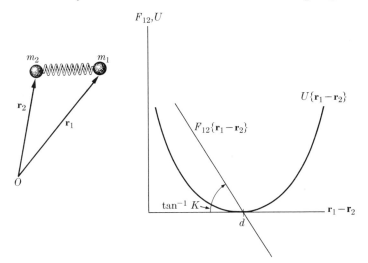

Fig. 2.4. Model of a diatomic molecule. The force between the atoms is proportional to the displacement from the equilibrium distance d (see Eq. 2.7–1) and depends only on the relative position $\mathbf{r}_1 - \mathbf{r}_2$.

The conservation of linear momentum for the two particles leads to the relation

$$\mathbf{p}_1 + \mathbf{p}_2 = m_1 \frac{d\mathbf{r}_1}{dt} + m_2 \frac{d\mathbf{r}_2}{dt} = \text{const}$$

or

$$\frac{d}{dt} (m_1\mathbf{r}_1 + m_2\mathbf{r}_2) = \text{const.} \tag{2.7-3}$$

Since the position of the mass center of the system is defined as

$$(m_1\mathbf{r}_1 + m_2\mathbf{r}_2)/(m_1 + m_2),$$

the conservation of momentum requires that the mass center move with a constant velocity.

For the motion of the system relative to the mass center, we return to the equations of motion (2.3–2). Dividing each equation by the mass of the particle in question and subtracting the second from the first, we obtain

$$\frac{d}{dt} (\mathbf{v}_1 - \mathbf{v}_2) = \mathbf{F}_{12} \left(\frac{1}{m_1} + \frac{1}{m_2} \right). \tag{2.7-4}$$

The harmonic mean of the masses is called the *reduced mass* μ,

$$\frac{1}{\mu} \equiv \frac{1}{m_1} + \frac{1}{m_2}, \tag{2.7-5}$$

and is always smaller than either of the masses. If $\mathbf{g}$ denotes the relative velocity $\mathbf{v}_1 - \mathbf{v}_2$ and $\mathbf{r}$ denotes the relative position $\mathbf{r}_1 - \mathbf{r}_2$, then Eq. (2.7–4) for the relative motion of the two particles, combined with Eqs. (2.7–1) and (2.7–5), becomes

$$\frac{d}{dt} (\mu\mathbf{g}) = -K \frac{(r - d)}{r} \mathbf{r}. \tag{2.7-6}$$

The relative motion is equivalent to that of a single particle of reduced mass μ acted upon by an external force equal to the tension in the spring and with the position vector of the equivalent single particle equal to the relative position vector of the two particles.

There are two simple modes of motion possible for the diatomic particle: the system may rotate with constant angular velocity at a fixed value of r (pure rotation), or $\mathbf{r}$ may remain fixed in direction and the two particles vibrate (pure vibration). In the more general case some of each type of motion will be present.

For pure rotation with constant angular velocity ω the magnitude of the time rate of change of the velocity $\mathbf{g}$ is just ωg, and the equilibrium radial distance r_e is determined from Eq. (2.7–6):

$$\mu g\omega = K(r_e - d). \tag{2.7-7}$$

If ω is replaced by its value g/r_e and Eq. (2.7–7) is solved for r_e, one obtains

$$r_e = d\{\tfrac{1}{2} + (\tfrac{1}{4} + \mu g^2/Kd^2)^{1/2}\}. \tag{2.7–8}$$

If the kinetic energy of rotation ($\tfrac{1}{2}\mu g^2$) is much smaller than the potential energy ($\tfrac{1}{2}Kd^2$) required to stretch the spring an amount d, then the interparticle distance in pure rotation is not very much different from d.

For pure vibration, we can apply the principle of conservation of energy to the equation of motion (2.7–6). Multiplying both sides by $d\mathbf{r}$ and integrating, as was done in Section 2.6, we find

$$\tfrac{1}{2}\mu g^2 + \tfrac{1}{2}K(r - d)^2 = \text{const.} \tag{2.7–9}$$

This equation is identical to the energy equation for a single-degree-of-freedom vibrating system. The motion consists of a harmonic variation in time with angular frequency ω, or total frequency ν, given by

$$r - d = A \sin \omega t,$$
$$\omega \equiv 2\pi\nu = \{K/\mu\}^{1/2}. \tag{2.7–10}$$

In this case, neither the kinetic nor potential energies are constant, but the sum is. As in the case of rotation, if the maximum kinetic energy is small compared with the potential energy needed to separate the particles by a distance d, then the average stretch in the spring is small compared with the distance d.

Although it will not be shown here, it can be seen that when the maximum value of $r - d$ is much less than d, the total motion can be quite accurately considered to be the sum of a simple rotation plus a vibration, as outlined above.

2.8 Systems of particles

The dynamics of two-particle systems which has been considered heretofore may be extended to systems with many particles. Since the ultimate purpose of statistical mechanics is to explain the behavior of systems of very many particles, say 10^{20}, one would like to understand to what extent the particle dynamics so far discussed could be useful in such a study. While it will be found that the conservation of linear momentum, angular momentum, and energy will also apply to many-particle systems, it will become clear that it would be hopeless to determine the time history of every particle of a system containing very many particles. However, in subsequent chapters it will be seen that a statistical approach to the solution of this problem can yield additional information beyond the three conservation laws derived below.

Consider a system composed of a large number N of particles. Identifying each particle by the subscript j, where j is an integer between 1 and N, the momentum of the jth particle will be denoted by $\mathbf{p}_j$. The force on the jth particle due to particle k will be denoted by $\mathbf{F}_{jk}$. Thus, the force on the kth particle due to particle j is $\mathbf{F}_{kj}$ and equals $-\mathbf{F}_{jk}$. To be most general, we will assume that a net force $\mathbf{F}_j^0$ acts on the jth particle because of the presence of other particles (called the environment) outside of the system under consideration. For example, the particles might be the molecules of a liquid which exert strong forces on one another while each may be subject to the gravitational attraction of the earth, the latter being an external force exerted by the environment. Using this notation, the vector equation of motion for each particle becomes

$$\frac{d\mathbf{p}_j}{dt} = \sum_k \mathbf{F}_{jk} + \mathbf{F}_j^0. \tag{2.8-1}$$

There are N such vector equations, or $3N$ scalar equations in all.

If the equations of motion for all the particles are added together vectorially, then the sum of all the internal forces $\mathbf{F}_{jk}$ will be zero because they appear in equal but opposite pairs:

$$\sum_j \left(\frac{d\mathbf{p}_j}{dt}\right) = \sum_j \left\{\sum_k \mathbf{F}_{jk} + \mathbf{F}_j^0\right\},$$

$$\frac{d}{dt}\left\{\sum_j \mathbf{p}_j\right\} = 0 + \sum_j \mathbf{F}_j^0. \tag{2.8-2}$$

Thus, *the time rate of change of the total momentum of the system equals the sum of all the external forces acting on the system. If there are no such external forces, the total linear momentum of the system is constant in time.*

A similar statement may be derived concerning the total angular momentum of the system. For each particle, the time rate of change of angular momentum is given in Eq. (2.4–1) as

$$\frac{d\mathbf{L}_j}{dt} = \mathbf{r}_j \times \frac{d\mathbf{p}_j}{dt}. \tag{2.8-3}$$

Substituting the equation of motion (2.8–1), this becomes

$$\frac{d\mathbf{L}_j}{dt} = \mathbf{r}_j \times \left\{\sum_k \mathbf{F}_{jk} + \mathbf{F}_j^0\right\}. \tag{2.8-4}$$

Summing this over all the particles of the system, the total time rate of change of angular momentum becomes

$$\frac{d}{dt}\left(\sum_j \mathbf{L}_j\right) = \sum_j \left[\mathbf{r}_j \times \left(\sum_k \mathbf{F}_{jk}\right)\right] + \sum_j (\mathbf{r}_j \times \mathbf{F}_j^0). \tag{2.8-5}$$

The first term on the right-hand side of Eq. (2.8–5) may be rewritten by grouping together the terms in the double sum containing the equal but opposite internal forces to give

$$\sum_j \left[\mathbf{r}_j \times \left(\sum_k \mathbf{F}_{jk}\right)\right] = \tfrac{1}{2} \sum_k \sum_j [(\mathbf{r}_j - \mathbf{r}_k) \times \mathbf{F}_{jk}], \tag{2.8-6}$$

where the factor $\frac{1}{2}$ arises because, in the following sum, each pair term is counted twice. If the internal forces are central forces, then this sum is identically zero, as in the previous case for two particles, since the internal force acts in the same direction as the relative position vector $\mathbf{r}_j - \mathbf{r}_k$. For central forces, Eq. (2.8–5) becomes

$$\frac{d}{dt}\left(\sum_j \mathbf{L}_j\right) = \sum_j (\mathbf{r}_j \times \mathbf{F}_j^0). \tag{2.8–7}$$

This is a statement that *the time rate of change of angular momentum is equal to the moment of all external forces acting on the system.* Again, *if no external forces act, then the total angular momentum is constant in time.*

The corresponding statement of energy conservation is obtained by taking the scalar product of the equation of motion and the increment of displacement $d\mathbf{r}_j$ and integrating:

$$\int_{\mathbf{r}_j}^{\mathbf{r}_j'} \frac{d\mathbf{p}_j}{dt} \cdot d\mathbf{r}_j = \int_{\mathbf{r}_j}^{\mathbf{r}_j'} \sum_k \mathbf{F}_{jk} \cdot d\mathbf{r}_j + \int_{\mathbf{r}_j}^{\mathbf{r}_j'} \mathbf{F}_j^0 \cdot d\mathbf{r}_j. \tag{2.8–8}$$

Summing this scalar equation over all particles of the system and performing the integration on the left-hand side as in Eq. (2.6–2), we obtain

$$\sum_j \frac{1}{2m_j} (p_j'^2 - p_j^2) = \frac{1}{2} \sum_j \sum_k \int_{\mathbf{r}_j - \mathbf{r}_k}^{\mathbf{r}_j' - \mathbf{r}_k'} \mathbf{F}_{jk} \cdot d(\mathbf{r}_j - \mathbf{r}_k) + \sum_j \int_{\mathbf{r}_j}^{\mathbf{r}_j'} \mathbf{F}_j^0 \cdot d\mathbf{r}_j. \tag{2.8–9}$$

As before, the double summation in the first term on the right-hand side contains the factor $\frac{1}{2}$ because the sum extends over all the values of j and k; that is, the force times the increment in relative displacement is counted twice. For conservative forces this integral depends only on the initial and final values of the position vectors $\mathbf{r}_j$ and can again be denoted by a scalar function of these position vectors called the potential energy U:

$$U\{\mathbf{r}_1, \mathbf{r}_2, \ldots, \mathbf{r}_j, \ldots, \mathbf{r}_N\} - U\{\mathbf{r}_1', \mathbf{r}_2', \ldots, \mathbf{r}_j', \ldots, \mathbf{r}_N\}$$

$$\equiv \frac{1}{2} \sum_j \sum_k \int_{\mathbf{r}_j - \mathbf{r}_k}^{\mathbf{r}_j' - \mathbf{r}_k'} \mathbf{F}_{jk} \cdot d(\mathbf{r}_j - \mathbf{r}_k). \tag{2.8–10}$$

Denoting the initial and final values of potential energy by U and U', respectively, the scalar equation of energy conservation becomes

$$T' + U' - (T + U) = \sum_j \int_{\mathbf{r}_j}^{\mathbf{r}_j'} \mathbf{F}_j^0 \cdot d\mathbf{r}_j, \tag{2.8–11}$$

where T denotes the total kinetic energy of the system. Thus the increase in the kinetic plus potential energies as the system undergoes a displacement from

$\mathbf{r}_j$ to $\mathbf{r}'_j$ is equal to the work* done by all the external forces in such a displacement. *If no external forces act on the system, then there will be no change in the total energy (kinetic plus potential) of the system.*

The only restriction on the use of the energy conservation equation is that the internal forces must be conservative. If this were not the case, then it would be impossible to define a potential energy for the system. However, the external forces need not be conservative; that is, they do not necessarily depend only upon the position of the particle on which they act. If the external forces are conservative, then the work done in the actual displacement of the system can be determined as a function of the initial and final positions by integrating the right-hand side of Eq. (2.8–11). In this connection, one should be careful not to confuse the work done by the external forces on the system with the potential energy of the system plus the environment. Only in special circumstances will the latter two quantities be numerically equal to each other.

Starting with $3N$ scalar equations of motion, we have deduced seven scalar equations (three equations of linear momentum, three equations of angular momentum, and one equation of energy) which are applicable to the system as a whole. There is thus the possibility that one might find $3N - 7$ additional combinations of the original equations of motion which might have some of the simplicity and generality of the three conservation laws. Despite this possibility, no one has yet obtained by direct deduction any other equations of the general usefulness of the conservation laws. By introducing additional hypotheses concerning the behavior of systems with large numbers of particles, it has been possible to derive additional statements which are as general as the conservation laws. These statements are derived through statistical mechanics and are embodied in the laws of thermodynamics. They give rise to properties other than linear momentum, angular momentum, and total energy, which are much more subtly related to the position and momenta of all the particles in the system.

2.9 The interaction of systems of particles

We shall have occasion in Chapter 9 to discuss the interaction of a thermodynamic system with its environment. For that purpose it is useful to find a special form of the scalar equation of energy conservation, Eq. (2.8–11), for the case in which the external forces $\mathbf{F}_j^0$ are conservative and are determined by the relative positions of the particles j of the system and the particles e outside the system. The particles outside a thermodynamic system are said to comprise its *environment*. We thus wish to describe the interaction of a system of j particles with e particles in which the interaction forces, as well as the forces between j particles, are conservative.

---

* We are using the conventional definition in dynamics that $\mathbf{F}_j \cdot d\mathbf{r}_j$ is the "work" done by the force $\mathbf{F}_j$ in the displacement $d\mathbf{r}_j$. The concept of work is extensively discussed in Chapter 9.

The external force $\mathbf{F}_j^0$ is thereby the sum of all the forces $\mathbf{F}_{je}$ exerted on the particle j by all the particles e:

$$\mathbf{F}_j^0 = \sum_e \mathbf{F}_{je}. \tag{2.9-1}$$

The integral on the right-hand side of Eq. (2.8–11) may therefore be decomposed in the following manner:

$$\sum_j \int_{\mathbf{r}_j}^{\mathbf{r}_j'} \mathbf{F}_j^0 \cdot d\mathbf{r}_j = \sum_j \int_{\mathbf{r}_j}^{\mathbf{r}_j'} \left\{ \sum_e \mathbf{F}_{je} \cdot (d\mathbf{r}_j - d\mathbf{r}_e) - \sum_e \mathbf{F}_{ej} \cdot d\mathbf{r}_e \right\}, \tag{2.9-2}$$

where use has been made of the fact that $\mathbf{F}_{je} = -\mathbf{F}_{ej}$.

Since the forces $\mathbf{F}_{je}$ are conservative, we can define an interaction potential energy ϕ by

$$\phi'\{\mathbf{r}_j' - \mathbf{r}_e'\} - \phi\{\mathbf{r}_j - \mathbf{r}_e\} \equiv -\sum_j \sum_e \int_{\mathbf{r}_j - \mathbf{r}_e}^{\mathbf{r}_j' - \mathbf{r}_e'} \mathbf{F}_{je} \cdot d(\mathbf{r}_j - \mathbf{r}_e). \tag{2.9-3}$$

Substituting Eqs. (2.9–3) and (2.9–2) into Eq. (2.8–11), we have the alternate form of the energy equation for conservative forces:

$$T' + U' + \phi' - (T + U + \phi) = -\sum_j \sum_e \int_{\mathbf{r}_e}^{\mathbf{r}_e'} \mathbf{F}_{ej} \cdot d\mathbf{r}_e. \tag{2.9-4}$$

This form of the energy equation states that the kinetic energy plus the potential energies associated with *all* the forces acting on the particles j of the system can be changed only if the particles e outside the system undergo a displacement. As will be seen in Chapter 9, it is the mechanical equivalent of the first law of thermodynamics.

PROBLEMS

2.1 A bullet of mass m and velocity v is fired into a stationary wood block of mass M. (a) What is the velocity of the block (and bullet) after impact? (b) Has there been a net loss or gain in kinetic energy as a result of the impact? (c) How much?

2.2 An electron makes a head-on elastic collision with a stationary proton. (An elastic collision is one for which the total kinetic energy of translation is conserved.) What fraction of the kinetic energy of the electron is imparted to the proton?

2.3 Show that the equation for the conservation of angular momentum of the diatomic particle considered in Section 2.7 is $(d/dt)(\mathbf{r} \times \mathbf{g}) = 0$, where $\mathbf{g}$ is the relative velocity and $\mathbf{r}$ is the relative position of the atoms.

2.4 If a diatomic molecule consists of two atoms of mass m_1 and m_2 separated by a fixed distance d, show that the moment of inertia about the mass center is μd^2, where μ is the reduced mass.

2.5 A motionless diatomic molecule is struck end-on by an atom of equal atomic mass m and speed v (see Fig. 2.5). Describe the resulting motion of the molecule and the atom if energy is conserved in the collision and determine their respective total energies.

m $\qquad$ m $\qquad$ m

Figure 2.5

2.6 A 100-kgm satellite is placed in a circular polar orbit 300 miles above the surface of the earth. Find (a) its kinetic energy and (b) its increase in potential energy above that for the same body on the surface of the earth. (Radius of the earth is 4000 miles.)

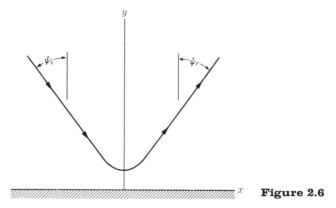

Figure 2.6

2.7 A particle is reflected from a smooth surface by a repulsive force whose potential $U\{y\}$ depends only on the distance y normal to the wall (see Fig. 2.6). (a) Show that the angle of reflection ψ_r is equal to the angle of incidence ψ_i, with ψ the angle between the trajectory and the y-axis far from the wall where the repulsive force is negligible. (b) If $U\{y\} = a/y^2$, find the equation $y = y\{x\}$ of the trajectory.

3

PHASE SPACE

3.1 Conjugate coordinates

The study of dynamics begins with kinematics, the description of the motion of a system. For systems composed of many particles, the kinematics is necessarily complex. We shall devise a description which is useful for all systems and is conceptually an extension of the methods used with simple systems.

Consider a system composed of N particles. If the positions and momenta of all the particles are known at any given time, and if the forces acting on the particles are conservative, then the positions and momenta of all the particles at any future time can be found by integration of the equations of motion. A complete history of the motion of the system consists of specifying all the momenta and positions at each instant of time. (This specification is redundant in that the momenta are proportional to the time derivatives of the positions; nevertheless, it is a convenient description because it contains all the information required at any instant to permit a forward integration on time.)

There are $3N$ scalar position coordinates which define the instantaneous position in space of all N particles. These position coordinates (which are not necessarily measured in a cartesian reference frame) will be denoted by q_i, where i is an integer between 1 and $3N$. Corresponding to each position coordinate q_i there is a momentum p_i which for cartesian coordinates is simply $m(dq_i/dt)$, where m is the mass of the particle whose position coordinate is q_i.* The momentum and position coordinates will always appear in pairs (p_i, q_i) and are called *conjugate coordinates*. For the N-particle system, there will be $3N$ pairs of such coordinates.

The choice of position coordinates is arbitrary and may be selected to suit our convenience. For example, if a single particle moves in the xy-plane, the following choice of cartesian position and momentum coordinates may be made:

$$q_x \equiv x, \qquad p_x \equiv m\,\frac{dx}{dt} = m\,\frac{dq_x}{dt}\;;$$

$$q_y \equiv y, \qquad p_y \equiv m\,\frac{dy}{dt} = m\,\frac{dq_y}{dt}\,.$$

$$(3.1\text{--}1)$$

---

* For a treatment of more general coordinate systems, see Goldstein, Chapter 1.

On the other hand, it may be more profitable to describe the motion in terms of polar coordinates r, θ. The choice of conjugate coordinates would be

$$q_r \equiv r, \qquad p_r \equiv m \frac{dr}{dt} = m \frac{dq_r}{dt} \; ;$$

$$q_\theta \equiv \theta, \qquad p_\theta \equiv r\left(mr \frac{d\theta}{dt}\right) = mr^2 \frac{dq_\theta}{dt} . \tag{3.1-2}$$

In this latter case, the conjugate pairs are radial position and radial momentum, and angular position and angular momentum.

3.2 Canonical equations of motion

If one uses cartesian coordinates to define the positions of the particles, then the equation of motion and the definition of the momentum give, respectively, the following pair of equations for the time rate of change of the conjugate coordinates (p_i, q_i):

$$\frac{dp_i}{dt} = F_i\{q_1, q_2, \ldots, q_i, \ldots, q_{3N}\}, \qquad \frac{dq_i}{dt} = \frac{p_i}{m_i}, \tag{3.2-1}$$

in which F_i is the force component in the direction of q_i acting on the particle whose position coordinate is q_i and whose mass is m_i. For an isolated system, this force is a function of the position of the particle in question and all the other particles, that is, a function of all the coordinates q_i. There are $3N$ pairs of equations like (3.2–1). If all the p_i and q_i are known at any instant, then their time rates of change can be computed from this set of equations and the new values of these coordinates established for the next instant of time; that is, the equations may be integrated on time.

For an isolated conservative system, the total energy (kinetic energy plus potential energy) is a function of the momenta and positions of all the particles of the system, except for an arbitrary additive constant in the potential energy. Denoting this total energy function of p_i and q_i by $\mathcal{H}\{p_i, q_i\}$, it can be written as the sum of the potential and kinetic energies for a cartesian coordinate system:

$$\mathcal{H}\{p_i, q_i\} \equiv \sum_i \frac{p_i^2}{2m_i} + U\{q_1, \ldots, q_i, \ldots, q_{3N}\}. \tag{3.2-2}$$

Considering all the p_i and q_i as independent variables, the partial derivatives of the function $\mathcal{H}$ may be determined by differentiating both sides of Eq. (3.2–2):

$$\frac{\partial \mathcal{H}}{\partial q_i} = \frac{\partial U}{\partial q_i} = -F_i, \qquad \frac{\partial \mathcal{H}}{\partial p_i} = \frac{p_i}{m_i}, \tag{3.2-3}$$

in which Eq. (2.8–10) was used in relating the partial derivative of the potential energy to the force component F_i in the q_i-direction. By substituting these relations in Eq. (3.2–1), one obtains the *canonical form* of the equations of motion:

$$\frac{dp_i}{dt} = -\frac{\partial \mathcal{H}}{\partial q_i}, \qquad \frac{dq_i}{dt} = \frac{\partial \mathcal{H}}{\partial p_i}. \tag{3.2–4}^*$$

The function $\mathcal{H}$ of p_i and q_i which is the total energy is called the *Hamiltonian function*. Equations (3.2–4) are called Hamilton's equations of motion. As well as being useful in Newtonian mechanics, the Hamiltonian function forms a starting point for determining the quantum-mechanical wave equation for any molecular system being studied.

3.3 Phase space

Since it is desirable to keep track of both position and momentum of N particles as a function of time, it is convenient to construct a $6N$-dimensional *phase space* composed of the $3N$ position coordinates q_i and their $3N$ conjugate momentum coordinates p_i. In this space a single point defines the instantaneous values of the $3N$ pairs of conjugate coordinates p_i, q_i. As time proceeds, this *representative point* follows a *trajectory* in phase space which defines the course of events in the system in question.

A $6N$-dimensional space can be described only by an extension of our understanding of three-dimensional space. Since the $6N$ coordinates are mutually perpendicular to each other, we can select a coordinate plane containing the axes of the conjugate pair p_i and q_i and project the trajectory of the representative point onto this $p_i q_i$-plane. Figure 3.1 shows the projection of a trajectory along which the projection of the representative point will travel as time increases. (This is like the projection of a trajectory of a particle moving on xyz-space upon the xy-plane.) As in the case of a particle moving in xyz-space, an instantaneous velocity of the representative point in phase space may be found by determining the time rates of change of the position coordinates p_i, q_i in phase space. By Eq. (3.2–1), the components of phase-space velocity in the directions p_i and q_i are F_i and p_i/m_i, respectively, as indicated in Fig. 3.1.

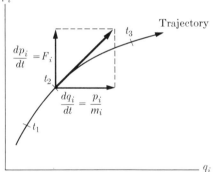

Fig. 3.1. The projection of the phase-space trajectory onto the $p_i q_i$-plane. The phase-space "velocity" vector diagram is drawn for the time t_2 and shows the components of the "velocity" in the directions p_i, q_i.

---

* For noncartesian coordinate systems Eq. (3.2–4) is still valid if p_i is properly defined. See Goldstein, p. 215.

Since $p_i = m_i(dq_i/dt)$, p_i and q_i cannot be varied independently in time. Thus, not any arbitrary curve in the p_iq_i-plane can be a trajectory but only those in which the velocity component in the q_i-direction is equal to p_i/m_i (see Fig. 3.2). It is this restriction on the trajectories which is formulated in a more elegant form in *Liouville's theorem* (Section 3.5).

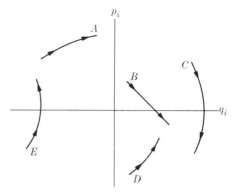

Fig. 3.2. Not just any trajectory in the phase plane is possible, only those for which $p_i = m(dq_i/dt)$. Which of the trajectories on the right are impossible?

As a simple example of motion in phase space, consider a linear spring-mass system which can move in one direction only. The mass of the system is m and the spring stiffness (force per unit displacement) is K. Since there is only one degree of freedom, namely, the displacement q, the phase space of the system consists of the two dimensions p and q and it degenerates to a plane (see Fig. 3.3).

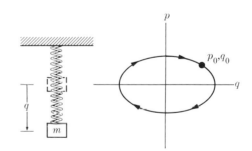

Fig. 3.3. The phase-space trajectory (Eq. 3.3–4) of a single-degree-of-freedom system composed of a mass m and a linear spring of stiffness K. The displacement from the equilibrium position is q and the momentum, $m(dq/dt)$, is p. As time progresses, the representative point moves clockwise along the trajectory. Why cannot the point move counterclockwise?

The total energy of this system at any instant is the sum of the kinetic energy $p^2/2m$ and the potential energy $Kq^2/2$. Thus, the Hamiltonian function is

$$\mathcal{H}\{p,\, q\} = \frac{p^2}{2m} + \frac{Kq^2}{2}. \tag{3.3–1}$$

The equations of motion in phase space (Eq. 3.2–4) are found by performing the appropriate partial differentiation of $\mathcal{H}$:

$$\frac{dp}{dt} = -Kq, \qquad \frac{dq}{dt} = \frac{p}{m}. \tag{3.3–2}$$

It is easy to prove by substitution that these equations have the solution

$$q = q_0 \cos \omega t + (\omega p_0/K) \sin \omega t,$$
$$p = p_0 \cos \omega t - m\omega q_0 \sin \omega t, \qquad (3.3\text{–}3)$$
$$\omega \equiv (K/m)^{1/2},$$

in which q_0 and p_0 are the values of p and q at $t = 0$.

To determine the shape of the trajectory in the phase plane, it is actually unnecessary to solve the equations (3.3–2). Since the spring-mass system is conservative, the total energy is constant and equal to its value at $t = 0$. The trajectory will then be determined by setting $\mathfrak{K}$ equal to this constant value:

$$\frac{p^2}{2m} + \frac{Kq^2}{2} = \frac{p_0^2}{2m} + \frac{Kq_0^2}{2}. \qquad (3.3\text{–}4)$$

This trajectory is an ellipse in the pq-plane, passing through the point p_0, q_0 as shown in Fig. 3.3.

It is sometimes convenient to divide phase space into two halves: *momentum space* and *configuration space*. The former is composed of the coordinates p_i, and the latter, the coordinates q_i. This is conceptually convenient, for example, in the case of a single particle moving in three dimensions, because each subspace has three dimensions and can easily be visualized. As an example, consider a single particle inside a cubical box of side L, which rebounds without loss of kinetic energy from the walls of the box. In configuration space, the projection of the trajectory consists of straight lines entirely within the volume L^3 enclosed by the box. In momentum space, since the kinetic energy T is constant, the projection of the trajectory consists of points on the sphere:

$$(1/2m)(p_x^2 + p_y^2 + p_z^2) = T. \qquad (3.3\text{–}5)$$

The representative point jumps from place to place on this sphere at each collision with the wall.

If phase space is considered to be a volume of infinite extent, then for conservative systems there are surfaces of constant energy E whose equation is determined from the Hamiltonian function:*

$$\mathfrak{K}\{p_i, q_i\} = E. \qquad (3.3\text{–}6)$$

These constant-energy surfaces (E_1, E_2 in Fig. 3.4) can never intersect, since it is impossible for the system to have the same set of coordinates (p_i, q_i) and yet different total energies. The constant-energy surfaces fill the phase volume in nonintersecting layers just like the leaves of an onion. On each energy surface lie lines of different trajectories. No two trajectories can intersect, for at each

---

* The equation of a surface in xyz-space has the form $f(x, y, z) = \text{const.}$ For example, a sphere is $x^2 + y^2 + z^2 = r^2$, and a plane is $ax + by + cz = d$.

point in phase space there is a unique direction to the phase-space velocity vector given by Eq. (3.2–4) and thus to the tangent to the trajectory.

Two trajectories on the same energy surface might be distinguished by different values of the linear or angular momentum. For systems of large N the specification of total energy, angular momentum, and linear momentum is insufficient to determine the trajectory uniquely, and additional information must be given, such as some of the p_i and q_i at a given time. Since statistical mechanics deals more with energy than momentum, surfaces of constant linear or angular momentum are usually ignored although they could be described in phase space.

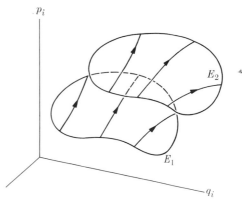

Fig. 3.4. Sections of constant-energy surfaces (E_1, E_2) in phase space, showing typical nonintersecting trajectories on each surface. Constant-energy surfaces also do not intersect.

In the preceding we have considered systems of N particles which need not be identical to each other (such as having different masses), giving rise to $6N$ coordinates in phase space. The phase space so defined is called Γ-*space*. If the system were composed of N identical particles, then an alternative description in phase space is possible. If a phase space is constructed of the three pairs of conjugate coordinates for each particle, then N representative points in this space would define the instantaneous state of the system of N identical particles. As time increases, the swarm of points moves about in this six-dimensional phase space called μ-*space*. If the particles are replaced by molecular models having more degrees of freedom, such as rotation and vibration, then the number of dimensions of μ-space would be correspondingly increased.

Both Γ-space and μ-space are used in statistical mechanics and kinetic theory: Γ-space is used entirely as an aid to theoretical reasoning, while μ-space is actually used in solving practical problems.

3.4 Ensembles

An *ensemble* is a collection of identically constructed systems, each of which at a given instant is usually in a different state (that is, has a different set of p_i, q_i). An ensemble is primarily a conceptual aid in understanding the physical behavior of a system which is a member of the ensemble. For example, 1 m^3 of copper can be considered an ensemble of 10^9 mm^3 of copper, each identical with the other. In actual practice, we do not assemble 1 m^3 of copper in this manner, although it could be done. The assembly of an ensemble is primarily a thought experiment.

If the systems composing the ensemble can exchange neither energy nor mass with each other, then the ensemble is called a *microcanonical ensemble*. For example, if the 10^9 mm^3 of copper are distributed throughout a barrel of insulating material so that no two touch each other, then this would constitute a microcanonical ensemble. As another example, N identical systems of the spring-mass type illustrated in Fig. 3.2 might be suspended from the ceiling of a large room and set into motion with arbitrary amplitudes and phases. Each system would continue its motion independently of the others and the collection of systems would again be a microcanonical ensemble.

If the elements of the ensemble are permitted to exchange energy but not mass with each other, they form a *canonical ensemble*. If the 10^9 mm^3 of copper are assembled to form a volume of 1 m^3, then heat may be conducted from one system of the ensemble to another, and they form a canonical ensemble. Gas molecules which can collide and exchange kinetic energy with each other also form a canonical ensemble.

A third type of ensemble is the *grand ensemble*, composed of systems which can exchange both energy and mass with each other. One cubic meter of gas which is mentally subdivided into 10^9 mm^3 would be composed of elements that exchange both energy and gas molecules with neighboring elements and would thus constitute a grand ensemble. A mixture of gaseous H_2, O_2, and H_2O would also be a grand ensemble since upon collision the molecules can exchange atoms as well as energy.

Each type of ensemble has a physically meaningful counterpart and can be used to discuss the statistical behavior of the corresponding physical system. We shall deal mostly with the microcanonical ensemble, being careful to call attention to this fact when appropriate.

3.5 Liouville's theorem

Consider a microcanonical ensemble of M identical systems, each composed of N particles. The Γ-space of a system consists of $6N$ dimensions, and a single point in this Γ-space represents the instantaneous state of one system of the ensemble. A cloud of M points in this Γ-space would then represent the instantaneous state of all the members of the ensemble. Since the ensemble is microcanonical, that is, no energy is exchanged between the members of the ensemble, each representative point in Γ-space moves independently of the others along its own trajectory. (The Γ-space of the system is the μ-space of the ensemble.)

If there is a sufficiently large number M of systems composing the ensemble, it is possible to define a *density* of representative points in phase space in a manner similar to the definition of the density of molecules in a gas. The density of representative points at a given location in phase space would be found by circumscribing this point by a small volume, counting the number of representative points within this small volume and then finding the ratio of the number of points to the volume. As the volume is made smaller, the ratio approaches a limiting value denoted by ρ. In this limiting process, the volume must not be taken too small, for then no representative points would be found inside it. The situation is entirely analogous to that of a gas, for if the physical volume chosen is much smaller than the average volume per gas molecule, there will be no molecules inside it and the limiting ratio cannot be determined. However, for the ensemble there is no limit to the number of elements which may be considered, so that, in principle, no matter how small a volume in phase space is chosen, the ensemble may be made sufficiently large to ensure that many representative points will be found within any given volume element in phase space.

The density ρ of representative points in phase space will be a function of the position in phase space and the time t just as is the density of the gas in a room a function of position in the room and time. Furthermore, the total number of points in phase space cannot change with time, for our ensemble consists of a fixed number of systems. Thus, if the density decreases at one point in phase space, there is a general tendency for it to increase in other points in order that the total number of representative points in phase space shall be constant in time. We shall attempt to express this idea of conservation of points, or continuity, in phase space in a quantitative form.

Consider first an ensemble of systems each of which has one degree of freedom, so that Γ-space is a plane. A volume element of phase space then becomes an element of area $dp\,dq$ (see Fig. 3.5). Fixing our attention on such a volume element, as time proceeds representative points drift along different trajectories, crossing into and then out of this volume element. If the density of points at a given location in phase space should happen to increase as time increases, it must be due to an inflow of such representative points in excess of the outflow across the surface enclosing a small volume element.

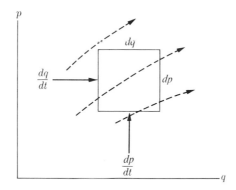

Fig. 3.5. The flux of representative points in phase space through a volume element $dp\,dq$ is equivalent to the flow of fluid particles through a volume element in physical space. The trajectories (streamlines) are shown by dotted lines; the "velocity" components normal to the surface of the volume element, by solid arrows.

The flux of points crossing a surface (number of points per second) is the product of the density of points ρ, the area of the surface, and the component of velocity normal to the surface. Thus the flux of particles Γ_q in the direction of q normal to the surface of "area" dp in Fig. 3.5 is

$$\Gamma_q = \rho \left(\frac{dq}{dt}\right) dp = \left(\rho\, \frac{\partial \mathcal{H}}{\partial p}\right) dp, \tag{3.5-1}$$

where Eq. (3.2–4) was used to determine the velocity dq/dt. The excess of the outflow in the q-direction over the inflow is the increase in the flux Γ_q over the distance dq, or

$$\left(\frac{\partial \Gamma_q}{\partial q}\right) dq = \frac{\partial}{\partial q}\left(\rho\, \frac{\partial \mathcal{H}}{\partial p}\right) dq\, dp. \tag{3.5-2}$$

The corresponding flux Γ_p in the p-direction normal to the surface dq is

$$\Gamma_p = \rho \left(\frac{dp}{dt}\right) dq = -\left(\rho\, \frac{\partial \mathcal{H}}{\partial q}\right) dq \tag{3.5-3}$$

by Eq. (3.2–4). The net outflow from the element in this direction becomes

$$\left(\frac{\partial \Gamma_p}{\partial p}\right) dp = -\frac{\partial}{\partial p}\left(\rho\, \frac{\partial \mathcal{H}}{\partial q}\right) dp\, dq. \tag{3.5-4}$$

Since the number of points within the volume element at any instant is $\rho\, dp\, dq$, the time rate of change of this quantity must equal the excess of the inflow over the outflow in order that there be no loss of the number of points in phase space:

$$\frac{\partial}{\partial t}\,(\rho\, dp\, dq) = -\left\{\left(\frac{\partial \Gamma_q}{\partial q}\right) dq + \left(\frac{\partial \Gamma_p}{\partial p}\right) dp\right\},$$

$$\frac{\partial \rho}{\partial t} = -\frac{\partial}{\partial q}\left(\rho\, \frac{\partial \mathcal{H}}{\partial p}\right) + \frac{\partial}{\partial p}\left(\rho\, \frac{\partial \mathcal{H}}{\partial q}\right) = \frac{\partial \rho}{\partial p}\, \frac{\partial \mathcal{H}}{\partial q} - \frac{\partial \rho}{\partial q}\, \frac{\partial \mathcal{H}}{\partial p}. \tag{3.5-5}$$

Replacing the partial derivatives of the Hamiltonian by the time derivatives of p and q as given in Eq. (3.2–4), we may rewrite this equation of continuity in phase space as

$$\frac{\partial \rho}{\partial t} + \left(\frac{\partial \rho}{\partial p}\right) \frac{dp}{dt} + \left(\frac{\partial \rho}{\partial q}\right) \frac{dq}{dt} = 0. \tag{3.5-6}$$

If ρ is considered a function of p, q, and t, then by the rules of partial differentiation the left-hand side of Eq. (3.5–6) is the total time derivative of ρ, that is, the rate of change of ρ with time which would be measured by an observer in phase space traveling along with the group of points that were at the position p, q at the time t. Equation (3.5–6) thus states that the density of representative points in phase space does not change for an observer moving with a small group of representative points along their own trajectories.

Although this result has been shown only for the case of a system having one degree of freedom, the proof can readily be extended to systems having any number of degrees of freedom.* The conclusion that the density of representative points of a microcanonical ensemble in the Γ-space of a member of that ensemble is unchanging with time along a trajectory is called *Liouville's theorem.* In Fig. 3.6, a volume element of arbitrary shape in phase space is shown at two successive times, the bounding surface of the volume element being composed of the same set of points. Liouville's theorem is the statement that the volume of this element is the same for all times, no matter how much the shape of the element may be distorted.

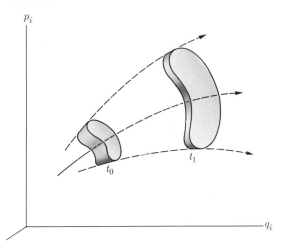

Fig. 3.6. The volume occupied by a given set of representative points in Γ-space does not change with time, according to Liouville's theorem. The volume element shown at time t_0 moves along the trajectories (dashed lines) as time progresses, changing its shape but not its volume.

3.6 Stationary ensembles

With the aid of Liouville's theorem, we can construct ensembles with the interesting property that, no matter how long we wait, there will be no change with time in the state of the ensemble as a whole, although any one member of the ensemble may undergo changes with time. Such an ensemble, called a *stationary ensemble*, is one for which the density of the representative points in phase space is everywhere independent of time. Stationary ensembles are interesting because they correspond to our notion of thermodynamic equilibrium, that is, a situation in which on the large (ensemble) scale nothing is changing in time, while on the micro (system) scale there are rapid and drastic changes with time.

---

* See Goldstein, p. 226.

If a microcanonical ensemble is prepared in such a way that the density of points in phase space is a function of the energy E alone, that is, on each energy surface ρ is everywhere constant (although a different constant value on different energy surfaces), then the ensemble will be stationary. This is a necessary consequence of Liouville's theorem, for trajectories lie in constant-energy surfaces, and once such a surface is uniformly populated no further changes in density can ensue.

Despite the great simplicity of Liouville's theorem, it has limited usefulness in physical problems. No such theorem exists for canonical and grand ensembles since these are composed of systems exchanging energy or mass with one another, and there exists no Hamiltonian function for a member of the ensemble. Nevertheless, the concept of a stationary canonical or grand ensemble is a physically attractive one, for it corresponds to an equilibrium situation in the physical systems in which we are interested. It is a principal problem of statistical mechanics to determine the stationary character of canonical or grand ensembles.

PROBLEMS

3.1 Using as conjugate coordinates the pairs p_r, q_r and p_θ, q_θ given in Eq. (3.1–2), find the canonical form of the equations of motion, Eq. (3.2–4), for a particle moving in a plane and subject to a central force whose potential function is $U\{r\} = -a/r$.

3.2 For a particle moving in one dimension, which trajectories shown in Fig. 3.2 are not possible?

3.3 Starting from rest, a ball of mass m drops downward [$(+x)$-direction] due to the gravitational attraction of the earth. (a) Derive and sketch its trajectory in phase space, indicating by an arrow the direction of motion. Mark off equal time intervals on the trajectory. (b) After falling a distance d, the same ball rebounds elastically from the floor, returning to its original starting point. Sketch its complete orbit in phase space.

3.4 A particle is injected into a rectangular box of dimensions $L'_x \times L'_y \times L'_z$. Initially the particle has momentum components p'_x, p'_y, and p'_z and rebounds specularly and elastically from the walls. (a) Draw the projection of the trajectory in the $p_x x$-plane. (b) Sketch the trajectory in momentum space (p_x, p_y, p_z). (c) If the particle rebounded elastically from a rough wall (diffuse reflection), describe in words the trajectory in momentum space and configuration space (xyz-space).

3.5 A simple pendulum consists of a mass m attached to a string of length R. (a) Find the total energy of the pendulum when oscillating in a vertical plane in a gravitational field of acceleration g. (Use as conjugate coordinates the angular displacement θ from the vertical and the angular momentum $mR^2\dot{\theta}$.) (b) Find the canonical form of the equations of motion, Eq. (3.2–4). (c) Sketch a trajectory in phase space for a small amplitude ($\theta \ll 1$) oscillation. (d) If the pendulum is initially given a sufficiently large angular velocity, it continues to rotate at a nonuniform angular velocity. Sketch such a trajectory in phase space. (Note that $-\pi < \theta < \pi$.)

3.6 The potential energy $U\{r\}$ of two hydrogen atoms in a hydrogen molecule is shown in the lower curve of Fig. 12.7 as a function of internuclear distance. For pure vibrational motion, sketch the orbits in the phase space (p_r, r) of the relative motion for a total energy (a) $E > 0$, (b) $E = 0$, and (c) $0 > E > U_0$, where U_0 is the minimum (negative) value of the potential energy.

3.7 The potential energy of an electron and proton is $-e^2/4\pi\epsilon_0 r$, in which e is the electronic charge and r is the distance between the particles. For motion having the velocity directed along the line of centers, sketch the trajectory in phase space (r, p_r) if the total energy is (a) greater than, (b) equal to, and (c) less than the potential energy for $r = \infty$. If a trajectory crosses an axis, indicate the value of the ordinate or abscissa.

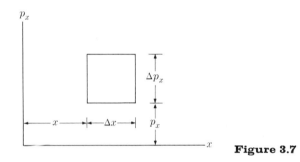

Figure 3.7

3.8 A group of particles moves freely (i.e., no forces act on them) in the x-direction. At $t = 0$, a group of them have positions between x and $x + \Delta x$ and momenta between p_x and $p_x + \Delta p_x$, so that their representative points in xp_x-phase space lie within the rectangle of area $\Delta x \, \Delta p_x$ (see Fig. 3.7). (a) At a time t later, show the area of phase space occupied by these same points. (b) State Liouville's theorem as it applies to this example and prove it directly from Part (a).

3.9 Derive Liouville's theorem for a system having two degrees of freedom for which the conjugate coordinates are p_1, q_1, and p_2, q_2.

4

WAVES

4.1 Properties of waves

Although matter is composed of atoms or molecules which continually exchange momentum and energy with each other by virtue of the forces they exert on one another, we find that there are two modes of transmitting the energy of a large number of molecules from one location to another in a material body. One mode consists of the slow diffusion of kinetic and potential energy in a step-by-step random process involving the interaction of pairs or groups of molecules. This method of energy propagation is called heat transfer and is characterized by a tendency for the energy to become evenly distributed throughout a body after a sufficiently long time. On the other hand, we recognize that both energy and momentum can be propagated very rapidly by means of waves, which are large-scale orderly or regular variations in the average energy or momentum of a group of atoms and molecules large enough so that these quantities can be measured on a laboratory scale. Waves can distribute energy and momentum throughout a material body and can possess some of the characteristic randomness (noise) of molecular motions. Perhaps a more important aspect of the study of waves, however, is the understanding it provides for the interpretation of dynamical experiments with atoms and molecules, which is embodied in the theory of quantum wave mechanics. Since the understanding of the dynamical behavior of atoms and molecules is essential to the interpretation of the behavior of very large systems of such molecules, and since in some cases this molecular behavior is best depicted in terms of waves, it will be useful to develop in some detail certain aspects of wave motions that are pertinent to these studies.

Wave propagation is characterized by the speed of a disturbance which, although large, may sometimes be detected by the senses without the aid of special instrumentation. Our eyes can follow the waves spreading from a point where a stone was thrown into a pond, and we notice that the noise of a jet fighter comes from a direction which is well behind the location of the plane at the time our ears detect the sound. On the other hand, it requires high-speed electronic measuring instruments to measure the velocity of the pulse of light emitted by the sudden discharge of a spark. However, in all these cases there is a measurable speed of propagation of a pulse or disturbance which is generally different for the various kinds of waves propagating in different media.

There is an important distinction between most of the waves we observe, such as sound waves, water waves, waves in a string or spring, or seismic waves and light waves. The former exist only by virtue of the medium through which they propagate, whereas the latter can spread even through a vacuum. Although electromagnetic waves can propagate through, and are affected by, transparent media (such as light waves passing through glass, or radio waves through the ionosphere), the effect of the medium is to couple slightly with the electromagnetic waves, thereby changing their propagation characteristics. The essential characteristics of a medium for the propagation of a wave (which includes a vacuum, in the case of electromagnetic radiation) is the ability to store energy and momentum. It is this aspect of waves which interests us most.

Another dominant characteristic of wave propagation is that the medium does not move with the wave but has its own motion. A cork floating on the surface of the water merely bobs up and down as the wave passes by, and only minute motions of a loud-speaker cone are needed to send a sound wave a great distance. The motion of the medium may be either transverse to the direction of propagation of the wave (transverse wave), as in a water wave or stretched string, or in the same direction as the wave propagates (longitudinal wave), as in a sound wave in air. In the absence of gravity, gases and liquids can propagate only longitudinal (sound) waves, while solids can propagate both longitudinal (dilatation) and transverse (shear) waves. In the latter case, these two different modes propagate with different speeds. (The difference in these speeds is used to help locate the source of earthquakes.) The absence of shear waves in liquids and gases stems from the fact that these substances lack any shear rigidity.

Generally speaking, there is a mode of wave propagation corresponding to each of the principal means of storing energy in the medium. Longitudinal waves are due to the energy stored in bulk compression of the medium, whereas transverse waves in a solid arise from the energy stored in shear deformation. The transverse wave in a stretched spring comes from the energy stored in the increased stretch of the spring. Surface waves on a body of water arise from the change of gravitational potential energy produced by the vertical motion of the fluid. In an electromagnetic wave, energy is stored in the coupled electric and magnetic field accompanying the wave propagation. A fisherman's line in a moving stream generates capillary, or surface, waves because of the energy stored in the surface tension of the liquid. A given medium may propagate many of these different kinds of waves; for example, water may simultaneously propagate sound waves, gravity waves, surface tension waves, and electromagnetic waves.

The ordinary properties of waves, such as their reflection or refraction at the interface between two media or their dispersion and diffraction by obstacles, are not of great interest in our study. However, the phenomenon of wave dispersion, which is caused by the variation of wave speed with wave frequency or wave length, is of some importance since it reflects the relationship between energy and momentum in a wave; so it will be dealt with in some detail below.

Any discussion of wave mechanics requires an acceptance of a wavelike description of the behavior of atomic-size particles. Such an acceptance is made easier by an understanding of the nature of wave propagation, the relationship between energy and momentum in waves, and the notion of group velocity. The purpose of this brief study of waves, then, is to make these concepts more meaningful as well as to derive the basic quantitative relationships which are needed for certain applications of statistical mechanics.

4.2 Plane waves

A source of sound in air sends out waves which are spherical in shape since the disturbance tends to propagate with equal speed in all directions. On the other hand, a sound wave propagating inside a long tube will very soon become plane because of reflections from the wall; that is, the wave front will lie in a plane normal to the tube axis. For the spherical wave the amplitude will decrease with distance from the origin, since the finite energy in the wave is being spread over a larger and larger volume as the wave propagates outward. However, for the plane wave the amplitude will remain constant because there is no increase in the volume occupied by each wavelength as the wave moves down the tube. Since the plane wave is easier to understand, we shall treat its properties exclusively.

For the time being, consider a medium of infinite extent with a plane wave traveling in an arbitrary direction with respect to a coordinate system fixed in the medium. If the wave is an acoustic wave, for example, of constant frequency ν and wavelength λ, then the points in the fluid of maximum pressure will consist of a series of parallel planes spaced a distance λ apart and moving normal to themselves with the wave speed c. If we denote the unit vector normal to these planes by $\mathbf{n}$, then we can describe the pressure in the wave at a position $\mathbf{r}$ by

$$p = p_0 + (\Delta p) \sin \left(2\pi \left\{ \frac{\mathbf{r} \cdot \mathbf{n}}{\lambda} - \nu t \right\} \right), \tag{4.2-1}$$

in which p_0 is the average undisturbed pressure in the medium and Δp is the pressure amplitude in the wave. The scalar product $\mathbf{r} \cdot \mathbf{n}$ is the projection of the position vector $\mathbf{r}$ on the wave normal, which is the proper distance to be compared with the wavelength λ in determining the change of amplitude of the wave as a function of position. An alternative way of writing this description is

$$p = p_0 + \Delta p \sin (\boldsymbol{\kappa} \cdot \mathbf{r} - \omega t), \tag{4.2-2}$$

in which

$$\boldsymbol{\kappa} \equiv \kappa \mathbf{n} = \frac{2\pi}{\lambda} \mathbf{n}, \tag{4.2-3}$$

$$\omega \equiv 2\pi \nu. \tag{4.2-4}$$

The reciprocal of the wavelength times 2π is called the *wave number* and is denoted by κ. The vector $\boldsymbol{\kappa}$ has the magnitude of the wave number and the direction of the wave normal and is called the *wave vector;* ω is called the *angular frequency* and is to be distinguished from the *total frequency* ν, which is the reciprocal of the wave period.

At any given position in space, the pressure change varies sinusoidally with time with a total frequency ν or an angular frequency ω. At any given instant of time, the pressure change varies sinusoidally with a wavelength λ in the direction of the wave normal. If we look for a point on the wave of constant phase, that is, a point for which the argument of the sine function in Eq. (4.2–2) is a constant, we find that

$$\mathbf{r} \cdot \mathbf{n} = (\nu\lambda)t + \text{const} = \left(\frac{\omega}{\kappa}\right) t + \text{const}; \qquad (4.2\text{–}5)$$

that is, we must select a point which moves in the direction of the wave normal at a velocity $\nu\lambda$ or ω/κ. This velocity is called the *phase velocity* and is denoted by c:

$$c \equiv \nu\lambda = \omega/\kappa. \qquad (4.2\text{–}6)$$

In most cases, the phase velocity is not a constant but depends both on the properties of the medium, the kind of wave being transmitted (such as transverse, longitudinal, or gravity), and the frequency or wavelength of the wave. When the phase velocity depends on frequency or wavelength, the medium is said to be *dispersive*.

4.3 Longitudinal waves in an elastic medium

As a simple example of wave propagation, consider the propagation of a plane wave in a tube filled with gas. For the gas in a tube, a wave of total frequency ν can be generated by moving a piston at one end of the tube at this same frequency and with a displacement amplitude $\Delta\xi$. This displacement of the piston will be propagated down the tube so that the displacement of any element of the fluid in the direction of the tube axis will have the same frequency as the piston but a different phase. The displacement ξ of any fluid element from its neutral position could then be described by

$$\xi = (\Delta\xi) \sin (\kappa x - \omega t), \qquad (4.3\text{–}1)$$

where the x-axis is chosen coincident with the tube axis. The relative displacements of the fluid elements are shown in Fig. 4.1.

The phase velocity may be determined by studying the kinematics and the dynamics of a fluid element. Referring to Fig. 4.2, we see that a fluid element of width dx is displaced from its original position in the direction of $+x$. The right side of the element is displaced more than the left side, thereby causing a decrease in the density ρ of the element. The fractional decrease in density

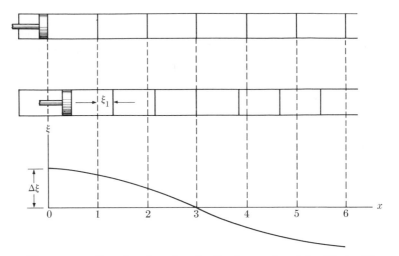

Fig. 4.1. The propagation of a plane longitudinal wave in a tube filled with gas. The upper sketch shows the undisturbed fluid divided into equal volume elements. The middle sketch shows the same elements distorted by the displacement of the piston at the left end of the tube. The displacement ξ of the edges of the volume elements is plotted as a function of position in the lower graph.

must be equal to the fractional stretch of the fluid element in the x-direction:

$$\frac{\rho_0 - \rho}{\rho_0} = \frac{(\partial\xi/\partial x) \cdot dx}{dx} = \frac{\partial\xi}{\partial x}. \tag{4.3-2}$$

This is a kinematical equation of continuity, or conservation of mass, for it states that an increase in volume of the element is accompanied by a decrease in density in order that the mass of the element remain unchanged.

The acceleration of the fluid element $(\partial^2\xi/dt^2)$ times its mass $(\rho_0\, dx)$ equals the difference in pressure on the two sides of the fluid element:

$$(\rho_0\, dx)\frac{\partial^2\xi}{\partial t^2} = -\left(\frac{\partial p}{\partial x}\right) dx, \tag{4.3-3}$$

in which the minus sign results from a force in the negative x-direction caused by the increase in pressure. By differentiating Eq. (4.3–2) partially with respect to x and then multiplying by the equation of motion (4.3–3), one obtains the *wave equation*

$$\frac{\partial^2\xi}{\partial t^2} = \left(\frac{\partial p}{\partial \rho}\right)\frac{\partial^2\xi}{\partial x^2}. \tag{4.3-4}$$

By substituting Eq. (4.3–1) into this wave equation, the phase velocity is found to be

$$c^2 \equiv \left(\frac{\omega}{\kappa}\right)^2 = \left(\frac{\partial p}{\partial \rho}\right). \tag{4.3-5}$$

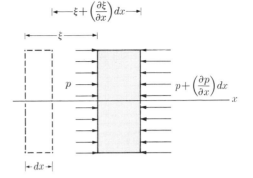

Fig. 4.2. The displacement of a volume element (solid line) from its undisturbed position (dotted line) in a plane longitudinal wave is accompanied by a difference in pressure on the faces normal to the direction of displacement.

The partial derivative $\partial p / \partial \rho$ is the rate of change of pressure with density for the medium when disturbed by the wave. Since such disturbances occur very rapidly, there is insufficient time for transfer of energy by heat conduction and this derivative should be evaluated for an *adiabatic** change. For a perfect gas, this derivative is computed in Chapter 19. For an elastic solid the change in pressure is the stress σ while the change in density is the strain ϵ times the initial density. Thus for a narrow bar this derivative becomes

$$c^2 = \left(\frac{\partial p}{\partial \rho}\right) = \frac{\sigma}{\epsilon \rho_0} = \frac{E}{\rho_0}, \tag{4.3-6}$$

in which E is the longitudinal, or Young's, strain modulus. [For an infinite solid the phase velocity is given in Eq. (15.3–2).]

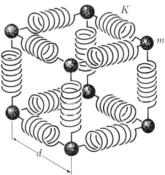

Fig. 4.3. A model of a cubic element of a solid in which atoms of mass m are arranged on the corners of a cubic lattice of spacing d and are connected along the edges of the lattice by springs of stiffness K, which replace the interatomic forces.

A simple model for propagation of a wave in a solid may be devised by assuming that atoms of mass m are regularly spaced in a cubic array and are connected by springs of stiffness K to their nearest neighbors, as shown in Fig. 4.3. If a plane of atoms is displaced an amount ξ with respect to the neighboring plane a distance d away, then the stress σ (force per unit area) would be

$$\sigma = K\xi/d^2. \tag{4.3-7}$$

---

* In macroscopic thermodynamics, *adiabatic* means the absence of heat transfer.

Since the strain is ξ/d, the ratio σ/ϵ would be

$$\frac{\sigma}{\epsilon} = \frac{\sigma}{\xi/d} = \frac{K}{d}. \tag{4.3-8}$$

Noting that the density ρ_0 is m/d^3, we find the phase velocity given by Eq. (4.3–6) to be

$$c^2 = (K/m)d^2 = (\omega_0 d)^2, \tag{4.3-9}$$

where ω_0 is a characteristic frequency ($\sqrt{K/m}$) of the lattice structure and d is the lattice spacing. Thus the wave proceeds at a speed at which the adjacent layers of atoms can transmit energy and momentum to one another by virtue of the interparticle forces.

Returning to the general equations for the plane wave, we can determine the density and pressure from Eqs. (4.3–2) and (4.3–3) if the displacement is given by Eq. (4.3–1):

$$\rho = \rho_0 - \rho_0 \kappa (\Delta \xi) \cos (\kappa x - \omega t),$$

$$p = p_0 - \rho_0 c^2 \kappa (\Delta \xi) \cos (\kappa x - \omega t)$$
$$= p_0 + (\rho - \rho_0)c^2. \tag{4.3-10}$$

The velocity $u \equiv (\partial \xi/\partial t)$ of any element of the fluid is found by differentiating (4.3–1):

$$u \equiv \frac{\partial \xi}{\partial t} = -\omega(\Delta \xi) \cos (\kappa x - \omega t) = \frac{c(\rho - \rho_0)}{\rho_0}. \tag{4.3-11}$$

In those regions where the material is compressed ($\rho > \rho_0$), the pressure is higher than average ($p > p_0$) and the particles are moving in the direction of wave propagation ($u > 0$).

4.4 Momentum and energy density in a wave

Let us determine the momentum of all the fluid within a prismatic volume of length λ in the direction of wave propagation and of unit area normal to this direction. Any element of this volume of thickness dx is filled with a medium of density ρ having a velocity u in the direction of propagation. Thus the total momentum of this medium divided by the volume under consideration will give the momentum density P:

$$P = \frac{1}{\lambda} \int_0^\lambda u\rho \, dx. \tag{4.4-1}$$

Making use of the particle velocity of Eq. (4.3–11), the momentum-density integral can be rearranged in the form

$$P = \frac{1}{\lambda} \int_0^\lambda \frac{\rho c(\rho - \rho_0)}{\rho_0} \, dx = \frac{c}{\lambda} \int_0^\lambda \frac{(\rho - \rho_0)^2 + \rho_0(\rho - \rho_0)}{\rho_0} \, dx. \tag{4.4-2}$$

Now, the first term in this expression is always positive since the integrand is the square of a quantity, while the second term will always be zero when integrated over one wavelength. Hence the momentum density P will be

$$P = \frac{c}{\rho_0 \lambda} \int_0^\lambda (\rho - \rho_0)^2 \, dx. \tag{4.4-3}$$

To determine the energy density, we must add together the kinetic and potential energies of an element of length dx. The kinetic energy will be the mass $\rho \, dx$ times one-half of the square of the velocity, while potential energy will be the average pressure (one-half the peak pressure p) times the total decrease in volume, $(-\partial \xi / \partial x) \, dx$. The energy density E is found by summing these two contributions over the whole volume and then dividing by the volume:

$$E = \frac{1}{\lambda} \int_0^\lambda \left[\left(\frac{u^2}{2} \rho \, dx \right) + \tfrac{1}{2}(p - p_0) \left(-\frac{\partial \xi}{\partial x} \cdot dx \right) \right]. \tag{4.4-4}$$

Using Eqs. (4.3-1), (4.3-10), and (4.3-11), we can evaluate this integral and obtain

$$E = \frac{1}{2\lambda} \int_0^\lambda \left[\frac{\rho c^2 (\rho - \rho_0)^2}{\rho_0^2} + \frac{(\rho - \rho_0) c^2 (\rho - \rho_0)}{\rho_0} \right] dx$$

$$= \frac{c^2}{\rho_0 \lambda} \int_0^\lambda (\rho - \rho_0)^2 \, dx, \tag{4.4-5}$$

where use has again been made of the fact that only squared terms will contribute to an integral over one wavelength.

By comparing Eqs. (4.4-3) and (4.4-5), we see that the energy density and momentum density are related by

$$E = Pc$$

or

$$E = (\omega / \kappa) P. \tag{4.4-6}$$

In determining the momentum density, we have summed the particle momentum in the direction of wave propagation. So the momentum density is truly a vector quantity and should be denoted by $\mathbf{P}$. Thus, the most general form of Eq. (4.4-6) is

$$E\boldsymbol{\kappa} = \omega \mathbf{P} \tag{4.4-7}$$

since both $\mathbf{P}$ and $\boldsymbol{\kappa}$ have the same direction.

It will be seen in Section 5.3 that the same relation holds for the quantum-mechanical behavior of a single particle if the energy density and momentum density in a wave are replaced by the energy and momentum of a single particle, and if a frequency and wave number are appropriately identified.

4.5 Group velocity

A pulse, or disturbance which is concentrated in a small region, can be considered to be a superposition of plane waves of different frequencies. If $A\{\kappa\}$ is the amplitude of a wave of wave number κ, then a pulse may be formed by performing a summation or integration over all wave numbers:

$$\xi(x, t) = \int_0^\infty A\{\kappa\} \cos (\kappa x - \omega t) \, d\kappa. \qquad (4.5\text{–}1)$$

If the phase velocity c is the same for all wavelengths, then this integration or summation is easily performed. For example, if $A\{\kappa\}$ is chosen as

$$A\{\kappa\} = e^{-a\kappa}, \qquad (4.5\text{–}2)$$

then the pulse shape is found to be

$$\xi(x, t) = \int_0^\infty e^{-a\kappa} \cos \kappa(x - ct) \, d\kappa = \frac{a}{a^2 + (x - ct)^2}, \qquad (4.5\text{–}3)$$

which is a symmetric pulse of constant shape propagating with a phase velocity c.

On the other hand, if c varies with wave length or frequency, then the energy or momentum in the wave propagates not with the phase velocity but with the *group velocity* v_g. To determine the group velocity, consider the superposition of two plane waves of slightly different wave number and frequency. Let the wave number and angular frequency be given by $\kappa + \Delta\kappa$, $\omega + \Delta\omega$, and $\kappa - \Delta\kappa$, $\omega - \Delta\omega$, respectively, where $\Delta\kappa$ and $\Delta\omega$ are very small compared with κ and ω. If both waves have the same amplitude, then the total amplitude will be

$$\begin{aligned} \xi &= \Delta\xi\{\sin[(\kappa + \Delta\kappa)x - (\omega + \Delta\omega)t] + \sin[(\kappa - \Delta\kappa)x - (\omega - \Delta\omega)t]\} \\ &= 2\Delta\xi \sin(\kappa x - \omega t) \cos[(\Delta\kappa)x - (\Delta\omega)t]. \end{aligned} \qquad (4.5\text{–}4)$$

Because of the smallness of $\Delta\kappa$ and $\Delta\omega$ compared with κ and ω, the variation in space or time of the cosine term in Eq. (4.5–4) is much more gradual than that of the sine term. Thus the superposition consists of a wave of wave number κ and frequency ω whose amplitude is slowly modulated in space and time by the cosine factor. Since the energy and momentum in the wave depend on the square of the amplitude, this energy and momentum will be propagated with the velocity of the amplitude rather than the phase of the wave. This velocity is determined by setting the argument of the cosine term equal to a constant and then finding dx/dt for the amplitude or group velocity v_g:

$$v_g = \Delta\omega/\Delta\kappa = d\omega/d\kappa. \qquad (4.5\text{–}5)$$

If the phase velocity is a constant, then the group velocity is identical to the phase velocity:

$$v_g \equiv \frac{d\omega}{d\kappa} = \frac{d(c\kappa)}{d\kappa} = c \qquad \text{if} \quad c = \text{const.} \qquad (4.5\text{–}6)$$

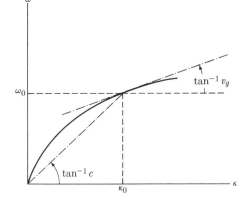

Fig. 4.4. The graphical determination of the phase velocity c and the group velocity v_g from the dispersion relation $\omega\{\kappa\}$ is accomplished by drawing the chord and tangent at the point corresponding to the desired wave number κ_0 or frequency ω_0.

One of the simpler methods of differentiating between the group and phase velocities is to plot a curve of frequency ω as a function of wave number κ, as shown in Fig. 4.4. Such dispersion curves can be obtained either from experiment or from theory. A wave of wave number κ_0 and frequency ω_0 has a phase velocity ω_0/κ_0 which is the same as the slope of the straight line connecting the point on the dispersion curve with the origin of the ω-,κ-axes. The tangent to the dispersion curve has the slope $d\omega/d\kappa$ which is just equal to the group velocity of waves having a wave number very close to κ_0.

An interesting example of such a dispersive wave propagation is that of the propagation of gravity waves on the surface of a liquid. For these waves, the relation between frequency and wavelength is the same as that for a simple pendulum of length $\lambda/2\pi$ in the same gravitational field:

$$\omega = \sqrt{2\pi g/\lambda}, \tag{4.5-7}$$

in which g is the local acceleration due to gravity. In terms of wave number κ the dispersion relation, the phase velocity, and the group velocity become

$$\omega = \sqrt{\kappa g},$$
$$c = \omega/\kappa = \sqrt{g/\kappa},$$
$$v_g = d\omega/d\kappa = \tfrac{1}{2}\sqrt{g/\kappa} = c/2. \tag{4.5-8}$$

Thus the group velocity is one-half of the phase velocity.

This phenomenon of group velocity being less than phase velocity for gravity waves is easily discernible in many instances. The ripple which spreads from a pebble dropped into a pond appears to move more slowly than the waves which compose it, for there is a continual streaming of waves from behind the major disturbance to in front of the disturbance. As each such wave passes through the disturbance, it grows in amplitude and then decays. A similar effect can be noted at the seashore where a particularly large group of waves approaches the shore more slowly than the regular waves which compose the group.

4.6 Modes of wave propagation

We have already pointed out the two principal types of waves: longitudinal waves, in which the particles of the medium oscillate back and forth in the same direction as the wave propagates (such as in sound waves in air), and transverse waves, in which the particle motion is perpendicular to the direction of the wave propagation (such as a gravity wave on the surface of a liquid, or a vibrating violin string). It is useful to enumerate in more detail the kinds of waves that may be expected to propagate in solids, liquids, and gases.

In a pure crystal, there will be one longitudinal and two transverse modes of wave propagation corresponding to the three degrees of freedom of each atom in the crystal. If the crystal is completely symmetric, the two transverse modes will have the same characteristics, that is, the same dispersion relation. One way to distinguish the two transverse modes is to notice that they correspond to two different directions of polarization. In a circularly polarized transverse wave, the particles of the medium move in small circles in a plane normal to the wave propagation. The polarization is said to be right or left, depending on whether the motion is clockwise or counterclockwise when viewed while we are looking in the direction of wave propagation. In an anisotropic or asymmetrical crystal, the three wave modes are not purely longitudinal and purely transverse with right and left polarization, but each mode is a combination of three such motions with one motion predominating over the other, and the modes are still named longitudinal and transverse.

The crystal modes considered above arise from the displacement of layers of atoms with respect to each other. They are called acoustic modes since they can propagate at low (audio) frequencies. In ionic crystals there are three additional modes, two transverse and one longitudinal, in which the alternate layers of positive and negative ions are displaced in opposite directions. These are called optical modes because they are accompanied by electric fields and can be excited by interaction with an electromagnetic wave of the appropriate (usually infrared) frequency.

A typical set of dispersion curves for an ionic crystal is shown in Fig. 4.5. For low frequencies and small wave numbers, the acoustic modes all become tangent to a line whose slope is the corresponding low-frequency phase velocity of the longitudinal and transverse (shear) waves. These waves have group and phase velocities which are approximately equal over the whole of the frequency spectrum. There is a maximum wave number which is determined by the fact that a wavelength smaller than the interatomic spacing is impossible. The optical modes have a much different dispersion relation, having small (and sometimes negative) group velocities but very high phase velocities for small wave number or long wavelength. The phase velocity for the optical modes of long wavelength is much greater than that for the acoustic modes of the same wavelength.

In liquids and gases, the modulus of shear rigidity is zero and there are no transverse modes of wave propagation (except when there are transverse forces acting, such as gravity or centrifugal forces). In a liquid, the forces tending to oppose the compression of the fluid in a longitudinal wave arise from the intermolecular repulsion. In a gas, the interparticle forces are negligible, and the macroscopic resistance to compression comes from the increased kinetic energy, rather than potential energy, of the particles in a fluid element which is compressed. The fact that the sound velocity in a gas depends on the temperature alone and is independent of the density, whereas the sound velocity in a liquid depends principally on the density and only slightly on the temperature, is indicative of the difference in behavior on the molecular scale even though on a macroscopic scale the wave propagation phenomena are identical.

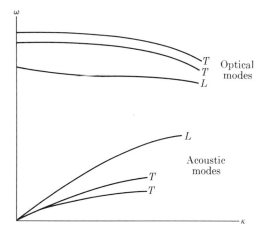

Fig. 4.5. Typical dispersion curves for a crystal. The letters T and L denote longitudinal and transverse waves, respectively. The two transverse modes are distinguishable when the crystal is anisotropic.

Much of what has been said concerning wave propagation is true for waves of sufficiently small amplitude. If the wave amplitude of an ocean wave becomes too large, the wave crest breaks down and forms a "whitecap." Waves breaking on a shelving beach illustrate the tendency of the wave amplitude to increase as the wave energy is concentrated in a shallower thickness of fluid and then to break down when the amplitude, or steepness, of the wave becomes too great. A similar phenomenon in a longitudinal wave in a gas is called a shock wave. A strong sound wave proceeding into a channel that becomes smaller and smaller will steepen just as does the ocean wave approaching a beach. However, the shock wave which is formed appears to be a smooth but discontinuous front with none of the evidence, at least to the naked eye, of the turbulence to be seen in a breaking wave. On a molecular scale, however, the shock wave is equally turbulent and violent as an ocean wave crashing against a rocky shore.

Even if the wave amplitude is sufficiently small, there may be a tendency for the wave amplitude to decrease with distance or time due to internal damping.

For example, imperfections or impurities in a crystal will cause a gradual scattering and attenuation of a low-frequency sound wave. A similar effect can occur in a gas due to the failure of molecules to adjust their vibrational and rotational kinetic energies sufficiently rapidly to respond to the changes required by the wave. These effects may be important in determining the ability to propagate a coherent wave through the medium, that is, one which sends a signal or carries information. For waves which merely disperse energy and momentum uniformly throughout a body, these damping characteristics have no significance.

An upper limit on the wave number, or lower limit on the wavelength, is seen to be a characteristic of waves in a crystal caused by the finite interatomic spacing. For a fluid there will be a similar upper limit on the wave number. For a liquid this is again the intermolecular spacing. However, for a gas the appropriate relative distance is not the average distance between particles but the average distance a particle moves between collisions (called the *mean free path*). Since the mean free path is invariably larger than the average distance between particles in a gas and since the latter is greater for gases than for liquids, the minimum wavelength is much greater for a gas than for either a liquid or solid.

4.7 The usefulness of wave descriptions

We have seen that it is possible to consider waves as a mechanism for spreading energy and momentum very rapidly throughout a system. In later chapters we will find it convenient to consider that the energy and momentum of a system composed of a large number of particles are contained in sets of waves of different amplitudes, frequencies, and wavelengths. From the point of view of mechanics, it is immaterial whether we use the $3N$ coordinates of the N particles to describe the configuration of a system or $3N$ modes of wave motion for the same purpose. The only question is whether the latter is a simpler or more useful description for the problem to be studied. As will be seen later, the wave description is best suited to the study of crystals and liquids, and the radiation field, while the particle description is most suited to the study of gases. In some cases, such as gaseous plasmas in strong magnetic fields, both types of descriptions are used simultaneously.

One reason for emphasizing the wave-type description of motion is that the mechanics of molecular or atomic-size particles requires such a description. The existence of quantum wave mechanics as a science is due to the fact that the wave phenomena we observe on a macroscopic scale embody ideas and principles which were found to explain most successfully the experiments conducted with molecules and atoms. An understanding of wave properties is essential to the understanding of molecular mechanics and the sciences which are built on such mechanics.

PROBLEMS

4.1 A proposed space propulsion engine operates on the principle of obtaining thrust by emitting a narrow beam of electromagnetic radiation at a single frequency. If the emitted power is one megawatt, what thrust will be obtained?

4.2 A point source of sound waves of fixed frequency ν sends out a signal of constant power. Show that the amplitude of the wave decreases inversely with the distance from the source. [*Hint:* The energy density in a wave is proportional to the square of the amplitude.]

4.3 A string of mass m per unit length is subject to a tension T. (a) For small displacements y normal to the distance x along the string, show that the equation of motion is $\partial\{T\,\partial y/\partial x\}/\partial x = m\,\partial^2 y/\partial t^2$. (b) For a sinusoidal wave propagating along the string, having an angular frequency ω and wave number κ, show that $\omega^2 = (T/m)\kappa^2$. (c) Show that the kinetic energy per wavelength is equal to the potential energy per wavelength. (d) A circularly polarized wave is one in which small displacements y and z in the xy-plane and xz-plane are out of phase by a quarter cycle; that is, $y = a\sin(\kappa x - \omega t)$ and $z = a\cos(\kappa x - \omega t)$. For a circularly polarized wave propagating along the string, show that the total energy per wavelength is ω times the angular momentum per wavelength about the x-axis.

4.4 A cylindrical bar of circular cross section can propagate a torsion wave. If $\theta\{x,t\}$ is the angular displacement of a section of the bar about the axis, the torque in the bar is $(\pi R^4 G/2)\,\partial\theta/\partial x$ and the angular momentum per unit length is $(\pi R^4 \rho/2)\,\partial\theta/\partial t$, where R is the radius of the bar, G the shear modulus of elasticity, and ρ the mass density. (a) Show that the equation of torsional motion of the bar is $G\,\partial^2\theta/\partial x^2 = \rho\,\partial^2\theta/\partial t^2$. (b) What is the phase velocity? (c) For a sinusoidal wave, show that the kinetic energy per wavelength is equal to the potential energy per wavelength.

4.5 The dispersion relation between frequency ω and wave number κ for a plane wave propagating in the model of Fig. 4.3 is $\omega = 2\omega_0\sin\{\kappa d/2\}$, provided $\kappa d \leq \pi$, that is, provided the wavelength is greater than $2d$. (a) Sketch curves of the phase velocity and group velocity as a function of κ for $0 < \kappa < \pi/d$. (b) Show that Eq. (4.3–9) is correct only if $\kappa d \ll \pi$.

4.6 An oceanographic station measures the period of an ocean swell and finds that the total frequency $\nu = \nu_0 + 10^{-7}t$, where t is the time in seconds since the measurements commenced (at which time the measured frequency was ν_0 sec^{-1}). Assuming that the wave pattern originated from a storm at a distant point at an unspecified time, compute the distance to the source of the disturbance. [*Hint:* A group of waves of frequency ν travels with the constant group velocity v_g, given by Eq. (4.5–8), from source to measuring station.]

4.7 The dispersion equation for gravity waves propagating in a fluid of depth h is given by $\omega^2 = g\kappa\tan h(\kappa h)$. (a) Show that this reduces to Eq. (4.5–7) for waves whose wavelength is small compared with h. (b) Derive a formula for the group velocity as a function of g, h, and κ. (c) Construct a dimensionless dispersion curve by plotting $(h/g)^{1/2}\omega$ versus κh. (d) Determine the maximum group velocity for waves in an ocean 2 km deep.

5

QUANTUM MECHANICS

5.1 Quantum modifications of classical mechanics

The theories of atomic physics developed in the 20th century had their genesis in a profound hypothesis concerning the nature of energy suggested by Max Planck in connection with the study of the thermal properties of radiation—an hypothesis that required the abandonment of some of the firmly held concepts of Newtonian mechanics in dealing with atomic and molecular systems. With the advantage of hindsight we can enumerate the principal departures from classical concepts which were laboriously developed in the early years of this century:

(1) The energy and momentum of molecular systems are not continuously variable but can have only *discrete* values which are determined by the structure of the molecular system and the forces exerted on it. Like matter, energy and angular momentum exist only in discrete quantities.

(2) Particles exhibit effects which are similar to those observed for waves, and waves (such as light waves) exhibit effects similar to those observed in particle experiments. *Wave-particle duality* is a universal phenomenon in molecular experiments.

(3) There is a fundamental limitation on the preciseness with which we can measure the motion of the molecule. This restriction on experimental accuracy is embodied in the *uncertainty principle* of Heisenberg.

(4) We must adopt a *probabilistic description* of the motion of molecules and atoms; that is, we can predict the results of an experiment only in terms of the probability of various outcomes from the repetition of identical experiments.

(5) Molecules of identical chemical structure *cannot be distinguished* from each other when undergoing an interaction. It is impossible to attach an identification to a particle of molecular size.

There are other modifications which might be listed but are not pertinent to the things we shall study. Furthermore, our list is already redundant; for example, it can be seen that the indistinguishability of particles is a direct result of the uncertainty principle. The purpose of this list is to emphasize the major aspects of quantum mechanics which enter as essential ingredients in the study of statistical mechanics and thermodynamics. While certain results of statistical mechanics can be obtained for systems of particles obeying classical Newtonian mechanics, by and large the most interesting and most useful applications require the introduction of quantum-mechanical phenomena. Because of the practical importance of these effects, and their direct confirmation on a laboratory scale through the measurement of thermodynamic properties, we shall consider them in some detail.

5.2 Discreteness of energy and angular momentum

The light emitted by an atomic gas when subject to bombardment of electrons in a gaseous discharge tube can be decomposed into its component wavelengths by a spectroscope. This spectrum, a typical example of which is shown in Fig. 5.1, is always found to contain sharp lines, indicating that the radiation consists of the superposition of waves of several discrete frequencies. Since the image recorded on the film is formed by light from many different atoms, each atom evidently radiates in precisely the same way as do other atoms of the same atomic structure. A classical hydrogen atom composed of a nuclear proton and a satellite electron could have an infinite number of states of motion correspond-

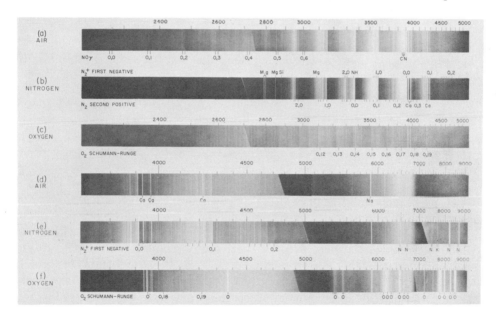

Fig. 5.1. Emission spectra of oxygen, nitrogen, and air heated to a high temperature (about 8000°K) in a shock tube. Atomic lines of O, N, K, Ca, Na, Mg, and Si are indicated, the latter four being prominent in the spectrum even though "clean" oxygen and nitrogen were used in the experiment. Molecular band systems are also prominent. The wavelength scale (angstroms) is shown above each spectrum. [By permission from J. Keck, J. Camm, B. Kivel, and T. Wentink, *Ann. Phys.* **7,** 13, Academic Press, N.Y., 1959.]

ing to any total energy and angular momentum we might wish to specify (provided only that the electron is bound to the proton). The fact that a large number of different atoms behave in precisely the same way indicates that there must be a discrete set of states of motion of an individual atom that would be the same for all atoms of like atomic structure. If we accept this point of view, we can explain the structure of the spectrum of an atom by assuming that the light emitted has a characteristic frequency governed by the change in the motion of an electron in passing from one discrete state of motion to another. (Even on classical grounds, an electron should emit radiation whenever its motion is changed.)

If an atomic electron can have only discrete values of energy, then the energy of the emitted radiation occasioned by the change of motion of an electron must also have a discrete value. The magnitude of this energy ϵ_p and the frequency ν of the light emitted by a gas composed of such atoms is related through the hypothesis suggested by Bohr, based on the Einstein relation that

$$\epsilon_p = h\nu = \hbar\omega,$$
$$\hbar \equiv h/2\pi, \tag{5.2-1}$$

in which h is a universal constant (called Planck's constant) having the dimensions of energy times time with the experimental value of 6.626×10^{-27} erg·sec.* The pulse of radiation emitted during this transition from one electronic state of the atom to another is called a *photon*. Since the energy of the photon is equal to the loss of energy of the atom, we would have

$$\epsilon_p = \epsilon_i - \epsilon_j = h\nu, \tag{5.2-2}$$

where the subscripts i and j identify the energies ϵ of the two states of motion of the atomic electron making the transition.

The states of motion of an atomic or molecular system, changes between which may be observed as lines in the spectrum, are called *quantum states*. For each pair of quantum states of different energy there would be one line in the spectrum (not necessarily in the visible spectrum, but somewhere within the whole electromagnetic spectrum). If there are N quantum states of an atom, each of different energy, there would be $N(N-1)/2$ pairs of states or lines in the spectrum.† For the heavier elements there are a large number of electronic states because of the large number of electrons, and even in the limited region of the visible spectrum there are a very large number of lines. One of the objectives of the spectroscopist is to construct a table listing the values of the energies ϵ_i of the electronic quantum states such that each line visible in the

---

* Because it is often convenient to use the angular frequency ω ($\equiv 2\pi\nu$) rather than the total frequency ν, the constant $\hbar \equiv h/2\pi$ is commonly used.

† Not all possible pairs of states give rise to a prominent line in the spectrum since some transitions are very unlikely to occur.

spectrum can be associated with a pair of quantum states in this table in accordance with the quantitative relation of Eq. (5.2–2).

It was discovered by Zeeman that if a discharge tube were placed in a strong magnetic field, some of the lines of the spectrum would split into two or more lines separated by a distance proportionate to the applied magnetic field. The Zeeman effect could be explained by assuming that for the transition in question, in the absence of the magnetic field there were several quantum states with the same energy but in the presence of a magnetic field the corresponding energies were actually different. Just as in the case of classical motion for which there may be two different motions with the same total energy but different angular momenta, it was proposed that in the absence of a magnetic field there could be different quantum states having the same total energy but different angular momenta. If an electron rotating about a nucleus has a constant angular momentum, it will, according to classical electromagnetic theory, have a magnetic dipole moment. Placed in a magnetic field, such an atomic system will have an energy which depends on the orientation of the magnetic moment with respect to the direction of the applied magnetic field. If one equates this energy to the energy change, computed from Eq. (5.2–1), corresponding to the change in frequency of the line in the Zeeman spectrum, then it is found that the angular momentum of the electron rotating about the nucleus would have a component L_z in the direction of the magnetic field equal to

$$L_z = \pm m\hbar, \tag{5.2–3}$$

where m is an integer called the *magnetic quantum number*. Thus it was concluded that the angular momentum is also quantized; that is, it exists only in discrete quantities.

As further experimental results were obtained, it became clear that they could be interpreted only by assigning to the electron and to the nucleus a certain intrinsic angular momentum, called *"spin."* The *spin quantum number* measures the intrinsic angular momentum in units of $\hbar$.

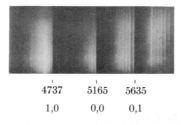

4737	5165	5635
1,0	0,0	0,1

Fig. 5.2. A high-dispersion spectrum of the Swan bands of C_2. The wavelength λ (angstroms) of the band head and the vibrational quantum numbers (v', v) of the upper and lower electronic states are shown below. The fine lines in each band are due to differences in the rotational quantum number (and hence rotational energy) of the electronic states. (Courtesy Avco-Everett Research Laboratory, Everett, Mass.)

A complete description of the quantum state of an atomic system involves more than a specification of the energy of such a state. In addition, the angular momentum of the electrons about a nucleus and the intrinsic angular momentum of the electrons and the nucleus all enter into a specification of the quantum state. The spectroscopist uses a shorthand notation to specify the states of the electron and lists both the states and their energies in appropriate tables.

For molecules the situation is more complex, but the same general rules apply. The motions of rotation and vibration of the heavy nuclei involve energy changes which are smaller than those associated with the motion of the binding electrons. Nevertheless, there will still appear sets of discrete lines in the spectrum (see Fig. 5.2) corresponding to the various possible changes of vibrational and rotational energy. However, the interpretation of these lines in terms of an energy-level diagram is much simpler than for the case of electronic states; it will be discussed further in Sections 5.9 and 5.10.

5.3 Wave-particle duality

If a beam of light falls on some conducting materials, electrons may be emitted. The number of electrons emitted in this *photoelectric effect* can be counted by collecting them at an anode and can be used to generate an electrical signal proportionate to the light intensity, as is done in ordinary phototubes and photomultiplier tubes. As the intensity of the incident light beam is decreased, the photoelectric count decreases until one observes, at very low intensity, the emission of single electrons at more or less random intervals. Since it requires a finite energy to eject an electron from the surface, it must be that the energy in the incident radiation arrives in small bunches rather than continuously. In this respect the incident radiation acts like a beam of particles striking the surface, much like rain striking an umbrella. A decrease in intensity corresponds to fewer particles arriving per unit time rather than to a decrease in the energy per particle, just as a decrease in the intensity of rain corresponds to fewer raindrops rather than smaller rain drops. Furthermore, if the frequency of the light is too low, the energy $h\nu$ is insufficient to eject an electron and no photoelectric emission takes place, irrespective of the intensity of the light (that is, the number of photons hitting the surface per unit time).

Photons carry momentum as well as energy and thereby exert a pressure on any surface they hit. This pressure can actually be measured in the laboratory, and it is known that part of the long-time drift of the orbit of a very light satellite of large surface is due to the absorption of photons emitted by the sun. While the transport of momentum in an electromagnetic wave is accounted for by classical electromagnetic theory, the concept of a beam of light as a stream of photons is an equally acceptable explanation for this momentum transport.

If a beam of electrons impinges on the smooth surface of a crystal at a very slight angle, most of the beam is reflected with an angle of reflection equal to the angle of incidence, as shown in Fig. 5.3. The intensity of the beam as a

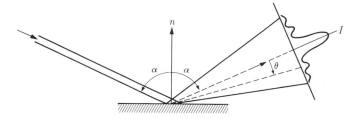

Fig. 5.3. The diffraction of a monoenergetic beam of particles reflecting from a smooth crystal surface is caused by the irregularity of the surface on the atomic scale. While the average angle of reflection equals the angle of incidence, the deviation θ from the mean in the reflected beam produces an intensity pattern I, which is similar to that of light from a diffraction grating.

function of the angle of reflection can be measured from the current collected by a small wire anode placed in the reflected beam. Since the crystal surface consists of a regular array of atoms, one would expect a spreading of the reflected beam because the force which reflects the electrons is not always normal to the surface, as would be the case for a perfectly smooth, plane surface. If the electrons behaved like classical particles, there would be a monotonic decrease in intensity of the beam to either side of its center line (a stream of sand reflected from a rough surface shows the same scattering behavior). However, what is actually observed is an angular distribution of intensity which has peaks and hollows reminiscent of the variation in light intensity in a beam diffracted by a grating. It is impossible to invent a regular surface which could cause classical particles to be deflected in this manner. Instead, a more fruitful approach is to assume that particles possess certain wavelike characteristics which in some way make themselves felt in experiments of this type. From our understanding of the optical diffraction experiment, we can relate the angle between two peaks in the diffraction pattern with the wavelength of the light and the spacing of the rulings on the diffraction grating. Using this same relationship for our molecular beam diffraction experiment and assuming the atomic spacing in the crystal as equivalent to the grating spacing, we can determine a wavelength λ to be associated with the beam of particles. As was predicted by de Broglie, the connection between this wavelength and the momentum of the particle in the beam is found from experiment to be

$$\lambda = h/p \qquad \text{or} \qquad \mathbf{p} = \hbar\boldsymbol{\kappa}, \qquad\qquad (5.3\text{-}1)$$

in which the wave number $\kappa \equiv 2\pi/\lambda$. This relation holds universally for all beam experiments involving any type of particle and for any type of diffraction having an optical equivalent by means of which the particle wavelength λ may be computed. As in optical diffraction, no diffraction effects can be observed unless the wavelength λ (called the *de Broglie wavelength*) is not too large compared with the grating spacing. For a de Broglie wavelength of 1 A (comparable to atomic spacing in a crystal) we find that an atomic particle must have a velocity of about 10^4 cm/sec in order to exhibit diffraction effects. This is about the average speed of a molecule in the air.

If for a particle having an energy ϵ and a momentum $\mathbf{p}$ we associate a frequency ν which is equal to ϵ/h and a wavelength λ which is equal to h/p, then the ratio of momentum to energy would be given by

$$p/\epsilon = 1/\nu\lambda = \kappa/\omega. \tag{5.3–2}$$

This relation is identical to that for the ratio of momentum to energy density in a classical wave, Eq. (4.4–6). Thus, the two general relationships expressed in Eqs. (5.2–1) and (5.3–1) are consistent with a wavelike description of the transport of energy and momentum. At the same time, they incorporate the concept of quantization of energy and angular momentum. The angular momentum quantization of Eq. (5.2–3) is identical in form to the linear momentum relationship of (5.3–1), for angular momentum is a vector quantity and m can be considered to be an *angular wave number*.

There are many examples of wave-particle duality which can be used to show the advantage of interpreting experiments in light of this concept. It is sufficient for our purposes that the connection between energy and frequency and between momentum and wavelength be made clear enough so that these relationships can be used with confidence in a closer examination of the dynamics of molecular systems.

5.4 The uncertainty principle

In the electron-beam diffraction experiment described above, the diffraction pattern observed is the result of some particles' being deflected through a different angle than other particles. Each electron remains a small, localized particle, but all electrons do not follow the same trajectory. Except for the pattern of the reflected beam, this situation is identical to that which exists when a gun is fired repeatedly at the same target; namely, the bullets scatter about a mean position in a random way because of small variations from round to round.

One way to interpret the beam experiment is to assume that the process of reflection has introduced a random component of momentum normal to the reflected beam. For a particle scattered through the angle θ of Fig. 5.3 the ratio of perpendicular momentum $p_\perp$ to the momentum $p_{||}$ parallel to the beam is simply

$$p_\perp/p_{||} = \theta. \tag{5.4–1}$$

Now, for any diffraction experiment the angular width of the diffraction pattern is approximately related to the wavelength λ and grating spacing d normal to the beam by

$$\theta \sim \lambda/d. \tag{5.4–2}$$

By combining Eqs. (5.4–1) and (5.4–2) with the de Broglie relationship (Eq. 5.3–1) for wavelength and momentum parallel to the beam, we find that

$$p_\perp d \sim h. \tag{5.4–3}$$

We thus conclude that the random momentum perpendicular to the beam times the grating spacing in the same direction is approximately equal to Planck's constant. By forcing the particles to be reflected from a surface with a roughness of scale d, we thereby introduce a randomness or uncertainty in the corresponding momentum.

This is a particular case of the general principle first enunciated by Heisenberg; it is called the *uncertainty principle*. If we measure the position of a particle and its conjugate momentum (in the sense of the conjugate coordinates introduced in Chapter 3), then the principle states that the product of the uncertainty, or randomness, in these two values can never be smaller than about Planck's constant. A more accurate statement is

$$(\Delta p_i)(\Delta q_i) \geq \hbar/2, \tag{5.4–4}$$

in which Δp_i and Δq_i are the uncertainties of the conjugate coordinates p_i and q_i.

The uncertainty principle has an important implication in the application of the phase-space description to quantum-mechanical systems. If we cannot specify with complete accuracy both the position and momentum of a particle, then we cannot truthfully represent it by a point in phase space. Rather, we must say that it is located within some small element of volume about equal to h^f, where f is the number of degrees of freedom, or number of pairs of conjugate coordinates required to specify the location and momentum of the particle or system in question. There is a fundamental unit of volume of phase space, namely h^f, which cannot be determined from classical mechanics alone. It will be found convenient to divide phase space into volume elements of this size, called cells, in such a way that each cell corresponds to a quantum state of the system under study. Thus phase space also takes on a discreteness; that is, its volume consists of a collection of cells rather than a continuous distribution of volume, much as a brick or concrete-block wall might be distinguished from a poured-concrete wall. This subdivision of phase space into unit cells will be considered in more detail in Section 6.2.

There is an alternative expression of the uncertainty principle which is very informative. If a molecular system remains at constant energy for a period Δt, then the uncertainty $\Delta \epsilon$ in the measurement of the energy it has during this period is limited by

$$(\Delta \epsilon)(\Delta t) \geq \hbar/2. \tag{5.4–5}$$

As an example, an electronically excited atom spontaneously emits a photon after a period of about 10^{-7} sec. Thus, there is an uncertainty in the energy which can be calculated from Eq. (5.4–5) and a corresponding uncertainty in the frequency of the emitted light as given by the relation of Eq. (5.2–1). This gives rise to a finite width of the line in the spectrum of this element. Usually this width is much smaller than can be resolved except by the finest spectroscopes. However, if interatomic collisions become more frequent, which happens when the gas pressure in the discharge tube is raised, then the life time Δt may become shorter. There is a corresponding increase in the uncertainty of the energy and a broadening of the line in the spectrum. This is called *collision broadening* and is more easily observed than the natural line width.

5.5 The Schrödinger wave equation

If we must abandon the Newtonian description of motion, that is, the Newtonian kinematics in which a particle has a precise location and momentum at any instant of time, we must devise both a suitable wavelike kinematics and equation of motion. To do this we will first assume that the appropriate description will be that of a *wave function* ψ which is a continuous function of space and time and which must somehow contain the information as to the location, momentum, and energy of a moving particle. One such possible wave function is that of the plane wave used in Section 4.2:

$$\psi\{\mathbf{r}, t\} = A \sin (\boldsymbol{\kappa} \cdot \mathbf{r} - \omega t). \tag{5.5–1}$$

If we replace the angular frequency and wave number by the values given by the Bohr and de Broglie relationships of Eqs. (5.2–1) and (5.3–1), then the wave function would be

$$\psi\{\mathbf{r}, t\} = A \sin \left\{\frac{1}{\hbar} (\mathbf{p} \cdot \mathbf{r} - \epsilon t)\right\}. \tag{5.5–2}$$

In this form, the wave function ψ certainly includes the energy and momentum as parameters. With the benefit of some hindsight, we will make the trial wave function somewhat more general by assuming it to be a complex function with real and imaginary parts* which are wavelike:

$$\psi\{\mathbf{r}, t\} = A \exp \left\{\frac{i}{\hbar} (\mathbf{p} \cdot \mathbf{r} - \epsilon t)\right\}. \tag{5.5–3}$$

If we differentiate this wave function with respect to time, we obtain

$$\frac{\partial \psi}{\partial t} = - \frac{i\epsilon}{\hbar} A \exp \left\{\frac{i}{\hbar} (\mathbf{p} \cdot \mathbf{r} - \epsilon t)\right\} = - \frac{i\epsilon}{\hbar} \psi. \tag{5.5–4}$$

By a similar double differentiation with respect to the cartesian coordinates x, y, and z, we also find

$$\frac{\partial^2 \psi}{\partial x^2} + \frac{\partial^2 \psi}{\partial y^2} + \frac{\partial^2 \psi}{\partial z^2} = - \frac{p^2}{\hbar^2} \psi. \tag{5.5–5}$$

---

* The real part of e^{ix} is $\cos x$, and the imaginary part is $\sin x$.

Now, if we have a freely moving particle, the energy and momentum are related by

$$\frac{p^2}{2m} = \epsilon. \tag{5.5-6}$$

If we multiply this classical relation by ψ, obtaining

$$\frac{p^2}{2m}\psi = \frac{1}{2m}(p_x^2 + p_y^2 + p_z^2)\psi = \epsilon\psi, \tag{5.5-7}$$

and then replace the quantities on both sides with those given in Eqs. (5.5-4) and (5.5-5), we obtain

$$\frac{1}{2m}\left\{\left(-i\hbar\frac{\partial}{\partial x}\right)^2 + \left(-i\hbar\frac{\partial}{\partial y}\right)^2 + \left(-i\hbar\frac{\partial}{\partial z}\right)^2\right\}\psi = \left(i\hbar\frac{\partial}{\partial t}\right)\psi. \tag{5.5-8}$$

This is the *Schrödinger wave equation* which corresponds to Newton's law of motion for molecular-scale particles. To make its form more general, we notice that the quantity $p^2/2m$ in Eqs. (5.5-6) and (5.5-7) is just the Hamiltonian function for a freely moving particle. Thus, a more general form of Eq. (5.5-7) would be

$$[\mathcal{H}\{p_i, q_i\}]\psi\{\mathbf{q}, t\} = \epsilon\psi\{\mathbf{q}, t\}. \tag{5.5-9}$$

Noting that the differential operator $-i\hbar(\partial/\partial x)$ in Eq. (5.5-8) appears in place of the momentum component p_x in Eq. (5.5-7), we see that the general form of the Schrödinger wave equation would be

$$\left[\mathcal{H}_{\text{op}}\left\{-i\hbar\frac{\partial}{\partial q_i},\, q_i\right\}\right]\psi\{\mathbf{q}, t\} = i\hbar\frac{\partial\psi\{\mathbf{q}, t\}}{\partial t}. \tag{5.5-10}$$

The Hamiltonian function becomes a differential operator in part, giving rise to a second-order partial differential equation in $\mathbf{q}$ and t, where $\mathbf{q}$ is the position vector in the configuration space (not necessarily cartesian space) that is deemed appropriate for the problem.

Although we have arrived at a wave equation which will certainly exhibit wavelike characteristics as well as account for momentum and energy, we must still place some interpretation on the wave function ψ.

5.6 Probabilistic description of motion

In interpreting the electron-beam diffraction experiment, we concluded that there was a certain randomness in the behavior of a particle as a result of its collision with the crystal surface. Any prediction we might wish to make could only involve the specification of the probability of various possible outcomes. Thus we are forced to describe the motion of a molecular system in terms of the relative probability of various events taking place. If we wish to interpret ψ as being related to the probability of finding the particle in question at a position $\mathbf{r}$

at the time t, then our description would include the notion of both wavelike and probabilistic behavior. Since ψ is in general a complex function, whereas probability must be a real and positive quantity, we first multiply ψ by its complex conjugate ψ^* (the same function of $\mathbf{r}$ and t as ψ, except that i is replaced by $-i$), obtaining a product which will always be real and positive. For example, if ψ were $a + ib$, then ψ^* would be $a - ib$, and the product $\psi^* \cdot \psi$ would be $a^2 + b^2$ and therefore positive. If $\psi^* \cdot \psi$ is proportionate to the probability of finding a particle at a position $\mathbf{r}$ at the time t, then since the particle must be found somewhere in space at each instant of time, the wave function must satisfy the normalization condition

$$\iiint\limits_{0}^{\infty} \psi^*\{\mathbf{r}, t\}\psi\{\mathbf{r}, t\}\, dx\, dy\, dz = 1. \tag{5.6-1}$$

For this reason, $\psi^*\psi$ is called the *probability density*, that is, the probability per unit volume of configuration space that the particle will be found at location $\mathbf{r}$ at time t.

If a plane electromagnetic wave can be considered to be a stream of photons, let us propose that a stream of particles can be represented by a plane wave function ψ as given in Eq. (5.5–3). If there are n particles per unit volume in the beam, then in any volume V which is large compared with the cube of the wavelength we would expect to find nV particles. If $\psi^*\psi$ is the probability of finding a particle per unit volume, then the normalization condition on ψ would be

$$n = \frac{1}{V} \iiint\limits^{V} \psi^*\psi\, dx\, dy\, dz. \tag{5.6-2}$$

Using hindsight again, let us evaluate the following integral:

$$\frac{1}{V} \iiint\limits^{V} \psi^* \left(i\hbar\, \frac{\partial \psi}{\partial t} \right) dx\, dy\, dz = \frac{1}{V} \iiint\limits^{V} \psi^*(\epsilon\psi)\, dx\, dy\, dz = n\epsilon, \tag{5.6-3}$$

where the derivative has been evaluated by use of the wave function in Eq. (5.5–3). Since $n\epsilon$ is the energy density of the particles in the beam, we can define $\psi^*i\hbar(\partial\psi/\partial t)$ as the *energy probability density*, that is, the energy per unit volume which, if integrated over all volume of configuration space, would give the energy of the system being studied. In a similar manner, it is easy to show that

$$\frac{1}{V} \iiint\limits^{V} \psi^* \left(-i\hbar\, \frac{\partial \psi}{\partial x} \right) dx\, dy\, dz = np_x \tag{5.6-4}$$

so that $-\psi^*i\hbar(\partial\psi/\partial x)$ could be called the *x-momentum probability density*. Again this quantity integrated over all volume would give the x-component of momentum of the system under consideration.

There is a remarkable similarity between these expressions for energy and momentum density and those previously derived in Section 4.4 for classical waves. It is this omnipresent correspondence which gives rise to the term *wave mechanics*. Actually, wave mechanics has been devised to incorporate the characteristics of waves, and we should not be surprised to find such a correspondence. One of the important properties of wave mechanics, which we will not consider here, is that in the limit of large mass or large scale certain integrals of the wave equation are identical to Newton's laws.

5.7 Indistinguishability of molecular particles

In creating a phase space (Γ-space) for a system of N particles, we assumed that each particle could be considered distinct from any other particle since the position and momentum coordinates of each particle were used to create the $6N$ dimensions of phase space. As a simple example, suppose we have two particles, each of which can move only along the x-axis. The location of the representative point in configuration space would have the coordinates q_1, q_2. If particles 1 and 2 are physically distinguishable, then the point 0, 1 in configuration space is clearly distinguishable from the point 1, 0, for these two states represent an interchange in physical space of the two particles in question. There is even a possible trajectory connecting these two points in phase space, representing the time evolution of the change from one state to another.

If the two classical particles are identical in mass, shape, and color, we could still follow their motions (see Fig. 2.3) and thereby trace the trajectory of the representative point in phase space during the time it takes for them to interchange their positions. So long as we can follow the motion of physically identical particles, distinguishing each one from instant to instant, such as we might do by examining a motion-picture film frame by frame, then identical particles can always be assigned separate identities. Now, to follow the motion of a single particle requires measuring its position at successive small instants of time and hence position and momentum. However, according to the uncertainty principle there is a limited accuracy with which we can make these measurements on molecular particles. After a sufficiently long period of time, because of the accumulated uncertainties, we would not be able to determine which of two identical molecules corresponded to which of the same two molecules at an earlier period of time; that is, the molecules would have lost their original identity.

The uncertainty principle can be thought of as requiring that the representative point in phase space be a fuzzy blob rather than a sharply defined point. Following the motion of a group of identical particles would be equivalent to taking a moving picture of a group of identical marbles or billiard balls moving rapidly about on a table top, using a moving-picture camera which was badly out of focus. When two such spheres collided, the image would be so blurred that it would be impossible to detect which sphere was which before the collision.

[Note that for particles of identical mass the momentum-conservation relation for a collision, Eq. (2.1–5), is unchanged by permuting the identity of the particles after collision or before collision. Thus, we cannot distinguish particles by momentum balance unless they have different masses or other distinguishable characteristics such as charge, etc.]

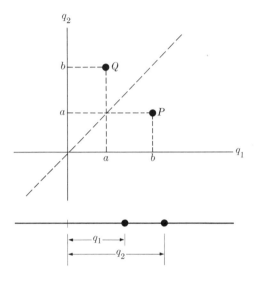

Fig. 5.4. The upper figure is the configuration space (plane) for two particles moving along a line with positions q_1 and q_2 as shown in the lower figure. For indistinguishable particles, points P and Q are identical and therefore only one half of the plane (lying to either side of the dashed line) is used in defining Γ-space.

This fundamental impossibility must be taken into account in any description of the motion of a system composed of identical particles, whether it be the motion of a representative point in phase space or the wave function itself. In the case of phase space, this may mean that there are several regions of phase space whose representative points define states of the system which are physically indistinguishable from each other, and therefore all but one of these regions should be excluded as being meaningless. For example, in Fig. 5.4, which shows configuration space for two identical particles, the points P and Q are physically indistinguishable configurations of the system. By simple construction, it can be seen that only one-half of this phase plane lying to one side or the other of the bisector of the q_1-, q_2-axes would be physically meaningful. In a similar manner, only wave functions possessing a certain symmetry can be used in describing the motion of diatomic molecules with identical atoms.

5.8 Translational energies of particles in a box

The quantization of energy applies even to particles moving about as do gas molecules confined to a volume V. To find these energies, we will look for a solution to the wave equation that describes particles which remain inside the box. For this to be so, the wave function ψ must be zero everywhere outside the box, and if we expect it to be a continuous function of position, it should certainly be zero on all the walls of the box. We cannot use a function of the form given in Eq. (5.5–3), for then $\psi^*\psi$ cannot be zero at any point. Instead, the dependence on $\mathbf{r}$ must be such that ψ has zero amplitude at the walls of the box. Consequently, we choose the following trial form for the wave function:

$$\psi\{\mathbf{r}, t\} = (\sin \kappa_x x)(\sin \kappa_y y)(\sin \kappa_z z)e^{-i\epsilon t/\hbar}, \tag{5.8–1}$$

in which κ_x, κ_y, and κ_z are the components of a wave vector $\boldsymbol{\kappa}$. This function can certainly be made zero for appropriate values of x, y, and z. Substituting this into the wave equation (5.5–8), we find

$$(\hbar^2/2m)(\kappa_x^2 + \kappa_y^2 + \kappa_z^2)\psi = \epsilon\psi. \tag{5.8–2}$$

This result should not surprise us, for the energy ϵ and the momentum p are related by

$$\epsilon = p^2/2m = (\hbar\kappa)^2/2m. \tag{5.8–3}$$

If our box consists of a cube of side L, then its faces are the planes $x = 0, L$; $y = 0, L$; and $z = 0, L$. The wave function of Eq. (5.8–1) will be zero on all these faces simultaneously, provided the following three conditions hold:

$$\kappa_x L = n_x \pi, \qquad \kappa_y L = n_y \pi, \qquad \kappa_z L = n_z \pi, \tag{5.8–4}$$

in which the *translational quantum numbers* n_x, n_y, n_z are any three positive integers. Using these values for the components of $\boldsymbol{\kappa}$ in Eq. (5.8–2), the energy is found to be

$$\epsilon_t = \frac{1}{2m}\left(\frac{\hbar\pi}{L}\right)^2 (n_x^2 + n_y^2 + n_z^2)$$

$$= \frac{h^2}{8mV^{2/3}} (n_x^2 + n_y^2 + n_z^2), \tag{5.8–5}$$

in which the volume V of the box has been substituted for L^3.

The quantum states of translation found above are each defined by a wave vector whose components are given by Eq. (5.8–4) and an energy ϵ given by Eq. (5.8–5). We note that there may be several sets of integers giving rise to the same value of ϵ. Such quantum states are called *degenerate* and may not be distinguished by the value of their energy but only by the set of quantum numbers, which is a shorthand method of characterizing the whole wave function.

By substituting the wave function of Eq. (5.8–1) into the integral for momentum density, Eq. (5.6–4), it can be seen that the momentum of all the particles in the box described by this wave function is zero. This is a natural result of the wave function we have chosen and means merely that it is equally probable that a particle is moving to the right as to the left. A wave vector κ, whose components are given by Eq. (5.8–4), does not define the direction of propagation of a plane wave, but its components do specify the wavelength in three mutually perpendicular directions of the *standing wave** described by ψ in Eq. (5.8–1). The quantum states described by wave functions of this type are called *stationary states* and are the quantum-mechanical equivalent of standing waves.

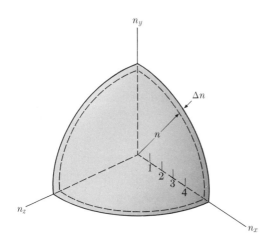

Fig. 5.5. The method of counting translational quantum states of nearly identical energy involves constructing an octant of a spherical shell in n-space of radius n and thickness Δn. Each cubic element of volume one corresponds to a translational quantum state.

It is now possible to show that a very simple proportionality exists between the volume in classical phase space between two constant-energy surfaces and the number of quantum states having an energy lying between these two limits. Let us first compute the number of translational quantum states whose energy lies between ϵ and $\epsilon + \Delta\epsilon$, where $\Delta\epsilon$ is a small increment in energy. To do this, construct the translational quantum-number space, shown in Fig. 5.5, composed of the three mutually perpendicular axes n_x, n_y, and n_z. If this space is divided into unit cubes of volume 1 each, then there is a one-to-one correspondence between the cubes and the quantum states. If we form a volume in this space enclosed between two spherical surfaces of inner radius n and of outer radius $n + \Delta n$, then the volume of this shell in the first octant will equal the number of quantum states whose quantum points lie within the shell. Furthermore, according to Eq. (5.8–5) the energy of each quantum state is proportionate to the square of the distance n from any cube to the origin of this space, that is, $n_x^2 + n_y^2 + n_z^2$. Thus, a spherical shell in this space would be a surface of constant energy, and the quantum states enclosed between the two shells lie

---

* A standing wave is one in which energy and momentum do not propagate, as in a vibrating violin string. It can be considered to be the superposition of two traveling waves moving in opposite directions. A quantum-mechanical standing wave would describe two molecular beams of particles moving in opposite directions.

between clearly defined energy limits. Because only positive integers are used, the volume included would be one-eighth that of a complete spherical shell, or

$$\text{volume} = \tfrac{1}{8}(4\pi n^2)\,\Delta n. \tag{5.8-6}$$

From Eq. (5.8–5) we have

$$n^2 = \frac{8mV^{2/3}\epsilon}{h^2}$$

and

$$\Delta n = (dn/d\epsilon)\,\Delta\epsilon = \tfrac{1}{2}\sqrt{(8mV^{2/3}/h^2\epsilon)}\,\Delta\epsilon. \tag{5.8-7}$$

When we substitute these into Eq. (5.8–6), the volume, and hence number of quantum states, becomes

$$\text{number of states} = (2\pi V/h^3)(2m)^{3/2}\epsilon^{1/2}\,\Delta\epsilon. \tag{5.8-8}$$

Let us now turn our attention to classical phase space for a translating particle. If the particle has a momentum lying between p and $p + \Delta p$, then in momentum space its representative point must lie between two complete spherical shells having these values for the inner and outer radii. The volume included between these two shells is thus $4\pi p^2\,\Delta p$. The volume in configuration space within which the particle must lie is just V. Thus, the total volume in phase space is the product of these two volumes, or

$$\text{phase-space volume} = 4\pi p^2 V\,\Delta p. \tag{5.8-9}$$

The relationship between p and Δp and ϵ and $\Delta\epsilon$ is given by

$$p = \sqrt{2m\epsilon},$$
$$\Delta p = (dp/d\epsilon)\,\Delta\epsilon = \tfrac{1}{2}\sqrt{2m/\epsilon}\,\Delta\epsilon. \tag{5.8-10}$$

Inserting these values into Eq. (5.8–9), the phase-space volume between two energy surfaces of energy ϵ and $\epsilon + \Delta\epsilon$ becomes

$$\text{phase-space volume} = 2\pi V(2m)^{3/2}\epsilon^{1/2}\,\Delta\epsilon. \tag{5.8-11}$$

Comparing this with Eq. (5.8–8), we see that the volume in classical phase space is related to the number of quantum states having energies within the same limit by the general relation

$$\text{number of quantum states} = \frac{\text{volume of phase space}}{h^f}, \tag{5.8-12}$$

where f is the number of pairs of conjugate coordinates defining the phase space and hence the motion whose energy is being considered. For the case of translation only, $f = 3$. It will be seen subsequently that this general relation holds for other types of motion as well.

The "unit" of translational energy is the coefficient $\hbar^2/8mV^{2/3}$ appearing in Eq. (5.8–5). We might compare this with the magnitude of an energy per unit mass which we can easily measure in the laboratory, say 1 cal/gm, by dividing this unit by the mass m of the particle to obtain an energy per unit mass of $\hbar^2/8m^2V^{2/3}$. If we evaluate this for a hydrogen atom in a box of 1-m³ volume, it is found to be approximately 10^{-10} cal/gm, an exceedingly small quantity. The increments in translational energy are so small that they are undetectable in any experiment. The practical importance of the translational energy quantization lies in the phase-space relationship of Eq. (5.8–12).

5.9 Vibration of molecules

In Section 2.7 we considered the classical motion of two particles joined together by a linear spring (that is, one for which the tensile or compressive force is linearly proportional to the stretch or compression of the spring). In the absence of any rotation, that is, for the case in which the angular momentum about the mass center is zero, it was found that the two masses vibrate back and forth in the direction of the line joining their centers with an angular frequency ω which is equal to $\sqrt{K/\mu}$, where μ is the reduced mass defined by Eq. (2.7–5) and K is the spring constant. This frequency is independent of the amplitude of the motion since there is no rotation of the system to which the vibration may couple. The corresponding quantum-mechanical system which represents the vibrating motion of a diatomic molecule is called an *harmonic oscillator*.

To determine the wave equation for this pure vibrational motion uncoupled to rotation, we must first find the Hamiltonian function for the classical motion. Since this is the function of momentum and position whose value at each instant equals the total energy of the system, it is given by the left-hand side of Eq. (2.7–9). Defining a new momentum p equal to μg, where g is the relative velocity of the two particles, and a corresponding displacement q equal to $r - d$, which is the stretch in the spring, the Hamiltonian function becomes

$$\mathcal{H}\{p, q\} = \frac{1}{2\mu} p^2 + \frac{1}{2} Kq^2 = \frac{p^2}{2\mu} + \frac{\mu\omega^2 q^2}{2}, \qquad (5.9–1)$$

where the spring constant has been replaced by the reduced mass times the square of the angular frequency, in accordance with Eq. (2.7–10). The corresponding wave equation, obtained by replacing p in the Hamiltonian function by the differential operator $-i\hbar(\partial/\partial q)$, is

$$-\frac{\hbar^2}{2\mu} \frac{\partial^2 \psi}{\partial q^2} + \frac{\mu\omega^2 q^2}{2} \psi = i\hbar \frac{\partial \psi}{\partial t}. \qquad (5.9–2)$$

While this is not a particularly easy equation to solve, there do exist solutions expressible in closed form which have the desirable property that the wave function ψ becomes zero for large values of q, a necessary restriction if we wish to describe a motion in which the two atoms do not pull apart, i.e. dissociate. These solutions are found to be

$$\psi_0 = \exp\left\{\frac{i\omega t}{2} - \frac{\mu\omega}{2\hbar}q^2\right\},$$

$$\psi_1 = q\exp\left\{\frac{3i\omega t}{2} - \frac{\mu\omega}{2\hbar}q^2\right\},$$

$$\psi_2 = \qquad\qquad \vdots \qquad\qquad\qquad\qquad\qquad (5.9\text{--}3)$$

The energy ϵ is determined from the energy operator $i\hbar(\partial/\partial t)$ as in Eq. (5.5–4) and is found to have the value

$$\epsilon\psi = i\hbar\frac{\partial\psi}{\partial t},$$

$$\epsilon_v = (v + \tfrac{1}{2})\hbar\omega = (v + \tfrac{1}{2})h\nu, \qquad v = 0, 1, 2, \ldots \qquad (5.9\text{--}4)$$

The integer v is called the *vibrational quantum number*, and is the shorthand index for specifying the particular vibrational quantum state of the molecule. In contrast with the translational quantum states, there is a distinct and different energy $(v + \tfrac{1}{2})h\nu$ for each quantum state of vibrational motion. There are no degenerate vibrational quantum states.

As for translational motion, the state of minimum energy $(v = 0)$ is a state of finite positive total energy $\tfrac{1}{2}h\nu$ when measured on the classical scale for which zero energy corresponds to no motion and no stretch in the spring. This finite energy again results from the fact that a particle confined to a finite region of space must have a finite wavelength, a finite momentum (by the de Broglie relationship), and therefore kinetic energy. A particle of zero kinetic energy would have zero momentum and its wave function would have an infinite wavelength, making it impossible to localize the particle in any small region of space.

It is relatively simple to make an approximate calculation of the energy of the vibrational quantum states if we suppose that the effect of the spring is to confine the motion of the particles to a one-dimensional box whose length is equal to the maximum amplitude of the vibrational motion. To determine the length L of this box, we will set the total energy ϵ equal to the maximum potential energy of the system when the spring has stretched a distance L:

$$\epsilon = \tfrac{1}{2}KL^2 = \tfrac{1}{2}\mu\omega^2 L^2. \qquad (5.9\text{--}5)$$

For a particle of mass μ moving in a one-dimensional box of length L, the translational energy would be given by Eq. (5.8–5) in which n_y and n_z are set equal to zero:

$$\epsilon = \frac{\pi^2\hbar^2}{2\mu}\frac{n_x^2}{L^2}, \qquad n_x = 1, 2, \ldots \qquad (5.9\text{--}6)$$

Eliminating L between these two equations results in

$$\epsilon = (\pi/2)n_x\hbar\omega. \tag{5.9--7}$$

This approximate result is not exactly correct, for it is not proper to replace the spring force by a box with impenetrable walls. Nevertheless, this simple calculation illustrates the point that approximate calculations of the energy can be made by determining a characteristic length describing the classical motion and then requiring that the quantum-mechanical wavelength equal this characteristic length divided by an integer. The solution of the wave equation is merely the exact and more elegant way of making this calculation.

As for translational motion, the constant-energy surfaces in classical phase space corresponding to the discrete vibrational energies of the quantum states can be shown to divide phase space into cells of volume h. To prove this, we first notice that a constant-energy surface in the two-dimensional phase space (p, q) is an ellipse given by

$$\frac{p^2}{2\mu} + \frac{\mu\omega^2 q^2}{2} = (v + \tfrac{1}{2})\hbar\omega. \tag{5.9--8}$$

The semiaxes of this ellipse may be found by setting either p or q equal to zero and solving for the maximum value of q or p:

$$\begin{aligned}
p_m^2 &= 2\mu(v + \tfrac{1}{2})\hbar\omega, \\
q_m^2 &= \frac{2(v + \tfrac{1}{2})\hbar}{\mu\omega}.
\end{aligned} \tag{5.9--9}$$

The area enclosed by this elliptical "surface" is $\pi p_m q_m$ and is the volume of the two-dimensional phase space we are considering:

$$\text{volume} = \pi p_m q_m = 2\pi(v + \tfrac{1}{2})\hbar = (v + \tfrac{1}{2})h. \tag{5.9--10}$$

The volume enclosed between energy surfaces whose v differs by one integer is just the volume difference between the two corresponding ellipses. From Eq. (5.9–10) this volume difference between adjacent vibrational quantum states is exactly h. Thus, once again we see that Eq. (5.8–12) is satisfied for this single-degree-of-freedom ($f = 1$) motion.

While the ideal harmonic oscillator is a useful model from which to determine the quantum-mechanical vibrational energy levels, it fails to take into account the real fact of life that such a molecule will break apart into two atoms if it is given sufficient vibrational energy. There appears to be no upper limit to the vibrational energy given in Eq. (5.9–4), but actually only a finite energy is required to dissociate a diatomic molecule. The reason for this is that our ideal model has a potential energy which becomes too large for large separation dis-

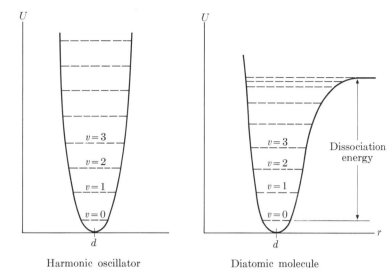

Harmonic oscillator   Diatomic molecule

Fig. 5.6. A comparison of the potential energy U as a function of the internuclear separation distance r for the harmonic oscillator and the actual diatomic molecule with finite dissociation energy. The total energy of the vibrational quantum states, $v = 0, 1, 2, \ldots$, is shown by dashed lines. Note the similarity for states of low vibrational energy.

tances between the atoms, as shown in the ideal curve of Fig. 5.6. A more realistic potential energy curve for two atoms is also shown in Fig. 5.6 for comparison. This latter curve has a finite energy for dissociating the molecule and a very large potential energy for pushing them very close together. This is a natural result of the fact that it requires a much larger force to push two nuclei together, because of the Coulombic repulsion, whereas the attractive forces between two atoms separated by a large distance are very weak indeed.

On the same diagrams of potential energy versus internuclear spacing one can draw horizontal lines whose ordinate is the total vibrational energy ϵ_v. For the ideal harmonic oscillator, these lines are equally spaced on the energy scale, a distance $h\nu$ apart. For the real diatomic molecule, these lines are equally spaced for the lower vibrational energies but become more closely spaced as the dissociation energy limit is reached. In this case, the quantum-mechanical vibrational states can still be distinguished by the quantum number v but the vibrational energy for large v will no longer be $(v + \frac{1}{2})h\nu$. However, for small v, the energies will be correctly given by the harmonic oscillator formula, because for small amplitudes of the motion there is no difference between the ideal and the real potential energy curve, provided both have the same curvature (and hence frequency) for small amplitude motion.

Polyatomic molecules (those with more than two atoms) can vibrate in several different modes, depending on the number of atoms in the molecule, and each mode will have a characteristic frequency ν. For small amplitudes of motion, the vibrational energy in each mode will be $(v + \frac{1}{2})h\nu$. Since the total vibrational motion is the sum of the motions in each mode of vibration, the total energy in vibration will be the sums of the energies corresponding to each vibrational mode. If there are m modes of vibration, then the vibrational energy will be

$$\epsilon_v = (v_1 + \tfrac{1}{2})h\nu_1 + (v_2 + \tfrac{1}{2})h\nu_2 + \cdots + (v_m + \tfrac{1}{2})h\nu_m, \quad (5.9\text{--}11)$$

where v_i is any integer. Of course, for large vibrational energies the molecule will tend to dissociate into atoms or polyatomic fragments and the vibrational energy spectrum will become quite complicated. A further discussion of the influence of vibrational modes on the specific heats of polyatomic gases will be given in Chapter 12.

The "unit" of vibrational energy, $h\nu$, is experimentally found to be of the order of 10^4 cal/gm or 10^{14} times the "unit" of translational energy. Since it is so large compared with an easily measured quantity like 1 cal/gm, it directly affects the specific heats of diatomic gases at ordinary temperatures, causing them to vary with temperature, as described in Chapter 12.

5.10 Rotational quantum states

As for vibration, one can idealize the rotational motion of a diatomic molecule by considering it to be a pure rotation without any vibration, as in Section 2.7. After defining the classical Hamiltonian function for such a motion and solving the corresponding wave equation, the rotational energies are found to be

$$\epsilon_r = j(j+1)[h^2/8\pi^2(\mu r_e^2)], \quad j = 0, 1, 2, \ldots, \quad (5.10\text{--}1)$$

where the rotational quantum number j is any integer (including 0), and μr_e^2 is the moment of inertia of the molecule measured about its mass center.

The total angular momentum L of a rotating rigid body is related to the kinetic energy of rotation ϵ by

$$\epsilon = L^2/2I, \quad (5.10\text{--}2)$$

where I is the moment of inertia of the rigid body about its mass center. Therefore the quantized angular momentum L of a rotating diatomic molecule would be

$$L^2 = j(j+1)\hbar^2, \quad j = 0, 1, 2, \ldots \quad (5.10\text{--}3)$$

This is an example of the quantization of angular momentum which was discussed in Section 5.2.

Another aspect of the solution of the wave equation for rotation of an ideal diatomic molecule is that there exist several wave functions, and thus several quantum-mechanical rotational states, for the same energy ϵ_r. These degenerate rotational quantum states are distinguished from each other by different wave functions and different values of one component of angular momentum L_z, given by

$$L_z = m\hbar, \qquad m = -j, -j+1, \ldots, j-1, j, \qquad (5.10\text{--}4)$$

in which the quantum number m is an integer lying between j and $-j$. Thus the quantum number j determines ϵ_r and also L^2, while the quantum number m fixes the value of L_z. For any given value of j, and hence rotational energy ϵ_r, there are $2j + 1$ values of m and thus $2j + 1$ rotational states of the same energy. The existence of these degenerate rotational states is connected with the fact that for the classical motion of given rotational energy, the plane of rotation of the molecule can have an arbitrary orientation in space. While the classical motion can have an infinite variety of energies, as well as orientations, the quantum-mechanical motion can have only discrete energies and discrete orientations.

It is interesting to note that the expression for the rotational energy given exactly by Eq. (5.10–1) is not much different from that for the translational energy given in Eq. (5.9–6) for one-dimensional motion in a box of length L, provided we equate L to the equilibrium internuclear distance r_e. In both cases the energies are proportionate to the square of the quantum number n_x or j (at least for j large compared with unity), as contrasted with energies proportional to the first power of the quantum number v for vibration. The difference is due to the fact that the size of the box (L or r_e) for translation or rotation is fixed, whereas for vibration the size of the box increases as the energy of vibration increases. In all these cases the solution of the wave equation is merely a more sophisticated and exact method of fitting the wave function into the appropriate box.

For *symmetric* diatomic molecules (such as O_2 or H_2), also called *homonuclear* molecules, that are composed of identical atoms, the principle of indistinguishability requires that only wave functions which would remain unchanged by interchange of the two atoms can be used. If one takes into account the intrinsic angular momentum (spin) of the atomic nuclei, this restricts the rotational states to either even values or odd values of j, depending on the relative orientation of the nuclear spins. There are therefore half as many quantum states of rotation for a symmetric diatomic molecule as there are for an asymmetric diatomic molecule having the same moment of inertia.

From the classical point of view, one consequence of the indistinguishability of particles is a reduction of the volume of phase space required to specify the state of the system. For a diatomic molecule, if we use the angular momentum p_θ and the angular position θ as conjugate coordinates to define a phase space for rotation, then the limits of θ are $0 \leq \theta \leq 2\pi$. If the molecule is symmetric, a rotation of 180° does not result in a distinguishably different configuration, so that θ must be restricted to $0 \leq \theta \leq \pi$. Since this reduces the range of variation of the angular displacement coordinate by a factor of 2, it also halves the appropriate volume in phase space. In accordance with the general correspondence of the volume in phase space enclosed between two energy surfaces to the number of quantum-mechanical states having energies lying between the two limiting values, the effect of molecular symmetry is to reduce this volume, and thus the number of quantum states, by a factor of 2. There is a direct equivalence between the restriction of j to either even or odd values and the halving of the corresponding volume in phase space.

For polyatomic molecules the rotational quantum states form a more complicated system than that for the diatomic molecule. If all the atoms lie in a straight line (such as for CO_2, C_2H_2, and NO_2), the molecule is called a *linear molecule* and the rotational energy states are identical to those of a diatomic molecule (including the symmetry characteristics). For the general polyatomic molecule there are three principal moments of inertia, each usually having a different value, which will all enter into the determination of the rotational energies. Furthermore, the principle of indistinguishability requires that for any symmetries with respect to rotation about the three principal axes, there must be a corresponding reduction in the number of rotational quantum states and the corresponding volume in phase space. The effect of this symmetry on certain thermodynamic functions is discussed further in Chapter 12.

5.11 Electronic and nuclear energy states

We have been considering so far the motion of atoms as single particles and of molecules as point particles held together by interatomic forces. The momenta and energies of these motions are those of the systems of atomic masses. An atom composed of a nucleus and its surrounding cloud of electrons was considered to be a point mass located at the center of the nucleus, at least insofar as a classical picture of the motion was required in formulating the appropriate wave equation. We will now consider the energies and angular momenta associated with the motion of the electrons with respect to the nuclei.

For atoms the only exact determination of the quantum states of an electron is that for a single electron bound to a charged nucleus (the hydrogen atom, the singly ionized helium atom, etc.). For the hydrogen atom, the discrete electronic energies are

$$\epsilon_e = -\mu_e e^4/8\epsilon_0^2 h^2 n^2, \qquad n = 1, 2, \ldots, \tag{5.11-1}$$

where μ_e is the reduced mass of the electron and proton (practically, the electron mass), e is the charge of an electron, ϵ_0 is the electric permittivity of a vacuum, and the integer n is called the *principal quantum number*. The total electronic energy ϵ_e is measured on the same scale as the classical potential energy between two charged particles; namely, the energy is zero for infinite separation of the particles. Since the electron and nucleus attract each other, the potential energy and total energy are negative for finite separation. For these negative energies, then, the electron is bound to the nucleus.

As in the case of the rigid rotating diatomic molecule, there are several quantum states of the same total energy ϵ_e which are distinguished by different wave functions. Some of these wave functions possess different values of total angular momentum L, whose square is given by

$$L^2 = l(l + 1)\hbar^2, \tag{5.11-2}$$

in which the *orbital quantum number* l is an integer lying between 0 and $n - 1$ inclusive. For each of the n possible values of l, there are $2l + 1$ different wave functions (quantum states) having a component of angular momentum L_z given by

$$L_z = m\hbar, \tag{5.11-3}$$

in which the *magnetic quantum number* m is an integer lying between $-l$ and l inclusive. In addition the electron has an intrinsic angular-momentum component $s\hbar$ which adds to the angular-momentum component L_z; s is called the *spin quantum number*. Thus there are four quantum numbers specifying the quantum state, one for each of the three degrees of freedom of the electron about the nucleus, and a fourth for its intrinsic rotation. There will be a different wave function for each possible set of the four quantum numbers, although the total energy ϵ_e will depend only on the value of the principal quantum number n if there are no magnetic or electric fields present.* The number of quantum states g_n having the same value of n and hence total energy turns out to be

$$g_n = 2n^2. \tag{5.11-4}$$

For atoms with several electrons we must expect a more complicated structure of quantum states and energies. Because the electrons interact with each other and with the nucleus, the energies will no longer be given so simply as those of Eq. (5.11–1). In fact, the energies are determined empirically from spectroscopic observations and must be tabulated. However, the quantum states may still be delineated by ascribing to each electron a set of four quantum numbers of the same type and meaning as those for the single electron. As in the case of a single electron, there may be several quantum states, each having the same energy but a different set of electron quantum numbers (or electron configuration).

An interesting result of the determination of the quantum numbers and quantum states of a single electron is that the number of quantum states corresponding to each value of the principal quantum number n is the same as the number of elements in the corresponding row of the periodic table. If we suppose that each electron in a many-electron atom is characterized by a different set of the four quantum numbers and we construct a table of all possible sets of

---

* For a discussion of the electronic energy of an atom in a magnetic field, see Section 17.2.

these numbers,. we would see a close correspondence between this table and the periodic chart. The basic requirement for such a table is that each electron have a different set of four quantum numbers; that is, each electron should be in a different quantum state. This empirical deduction is called the *Pauli exclusion principle*. If one deals with the wave functions themselves, then an alternative statement of this principle is that the total wave function of all the electrons in a many-electron atom must be antisymmetric. This is an empirical, not a fundamental, rule of quantum mechanics and does not apply to all many-particle systems.

The electronic states of molecules are also complex. Since the atomic nuclei are bound together by virtue of the electrons they share, a change in electron configuration may produce appreciable changes in the internuclear forces and thus change the vibrational frequency ν and the moment of inertia I of the molecule. A removal of an electron may even cause a molecule to dissociate, or conversely, it may be possible to form a stable molecular ion which has no neutral counterpart. (H_3O^+ is a stable ion, whereas H_3O does not exist.) Despite these complications, some of the electronic states of common molecules have been determined spectroscopically, and their energies have been tabulated.

In the absence of nuclear reactions, the only aspect of the motion of nucleons which affects the thermodynamic properties of a substance is the presence of a very weak magnetic moment due to the rotation of charged particles in the nucleus. This motion and the energy associated with it are ordinarily neglected except in the case of a solid at extremely low temperatures in the presence of a very strong magnetic field. The nuclear motion may be characterized by a *nuclear spin quantum number*, which measures the component of nuclear angular momentum in units of $\hbar$ and is an integer or half integer. The nuclear motion also affects the possible rotational states in homonuclear diatomic molecules, as discussed in Section 12.2.

5.12 Quantum mechanics and phase space

The quantization of energy and angular momentum has its counterpart in the quantization of phase space. For any molecular system with f degrees of freedom, the corresponding μ-space of $2f$ coordinates can be divided into cells of volume h^f in such a way that each cell corresponds to an individual quantum state. The general correspondence between the cells in phase space and the quantum states can usually be established by energy considerations alone through the general rule (Eq. 5.8–12) previously formulated. To each quantum state and its corresponding cell in phase space we can assign a unique combination of the f quantum numbers required to specify the motion of the molecular system under study. Thus, the state of motion of a molecular system can be represented by a cell number in μ-space. This identifying cell number in the phase space of any system will be denoted by the subscript i.

5.13 Quantum statistics

The term *quantum statistics* is commonly used to denote the rules to be followed in describing the quantum states of many-particle systems. In all the foregoing cases, we have considered only simple molecular systems except for the many-electron atom. For very large systems, such as a crystal, or a container filled with gas molecules, there will also be distinct quantum states, which are necessarily very complex. Most of our analyses of such systems are based on the approximation that the quantum state of these large systems can be described in terms of the quantum states of single particles. The details of this connection are included in the term quantum statistics.

There are two general rules for determining the quantum states of a system composed of a large number of molecules:

(a) *Fermi-Dirac statistics.* For systems in which the over-all wave function must be antisymmetric with respect to the spatial interchange of two like particles, no two such particles of the system may exist in the same quantum state. This type of restriction is applicable to the electron "gas" in a metal as well as to the electrons surrounding a nucleus.

(b) *Bose-Einstein statistics.* For systems in which the over-all wave function is symmetric, any number of identical particles may exist in the same quantum state. Bose-Einstein statistics apply to most normal gases and to systems in which the energy and momentum are considered to exist in the form of waves.

The importance of the symmetry of the wave function derives from the empirical fact that not all solutions of the wave equation correspond to physical situations found in nature. The classification of which quantum states are observed is most easily made in terms of the symmetry of the wave function. For a single particle, a symmetrical wave function is one which is unchanged by changing the sign of the space coordinates; that is, $\psi\{r\} = \psi\{-r\}$. An asymmetrical wave function, or odd wave function, is one for which the algebraic sign of the wave function is changed when the algebraic sign of the position coordinates are changed; that is, $\psi\{r\} = -\psi\{-r\}$. Now, any solution to the wave equation we might obtain is not necessarily either symmetric or antisymmetric but can be made so by a simple trick. If $\psi\{r\}$ is such a wave function, then $\psi\{r\} + \psi\{-r\}$ is a symmetrical wave function and $\psi\{r\} - \psi\{-r\}$ is an antisymmetrical wave function. It is therefore always possible to work with either symmetrical or antisymmetrical wave functions.

The connection between the symmetry character of the wave function and the type of statistics is best illustrated by considering only two particles. If $\psi_i\{r_1\}$ is the wave function of one particle in the quantum state i and $\psi_j\{r_2\}$ is the wave function of a second particle in the quantum state j, then $\psi_i\{r_1\}\psi_j\{r_2\}$ is the wave function for particles 1 and 2 considered together as a system. (The multiplicative character of the wave function stems from the fact that it is interpreted as a probability, so that the probability of one particle's being at position r_1 while another particle is at position r_2 is the product of the separate probabilities.) We may now form a symmetric wave function ψ_+ of the system by adding to the above wave function a similar one with interchanged arguments $\mathbf{r}_1$ and $\mathbf{r}_2$,

$$\psi_+\{\mathbf{r}_1, \mathbf{r}_2\} = \psi_i\{\mathbf{r}_1\}\psi_j\{\mathbf{r}_2\} + \psi_i\{\mathbf{r}_2\}\psi_j\{\mathbf{r}_1\}, \tag{5.13–1}$$

and an antisymmetric wave function ψ_- by subtracting the same,

$$\psi_-\{\mathbf{r}_1, \mathbf{r}_2\} = \psi_i\{\mathbf{r}_1\}\psi_j\{\mathbf{r}_2\} - \psi_i\{\mathbf{r}_2\}\psi_j\{\mathbf{r}_1\}. \tag{5.13–2}$$

It can be readily seen that ψ_+ is symmetric and ψ_- antisymmetric with respect to the interchange of $\mathbf{r}_1$ and $\mathbf{r}_2$; that is,

$$\psi_+\{\mathbf{r}_2, \mathbf{r}_1\} = \psi_+\{\mathbf{r}_1, \mathbf{r}_2\},$$
$$\psi_-\{\mathbf{r}_2, \mathbf{r}_1\} = -\psi_-\{\mathbf{r}_1, \mathbf{r}_2\}. \tag{5.13–3}$$

The antisymmetrical wave function of the two particles will be identically zero if $i = j$, that is, if the two particles are in the same quantum state.* This is the origin of the Fermi-Dirac statistics, which state that it is impossible to find an antisymmetric wave function for a system of particles whenever two of the particles are in the same quantum state. On the other hand, it can be seen that for the two-particle case no such restriction applies to the even wave functions, which is in agreement with the Bose-Einstein statistics.

The importance of quantum statistics in statistical mechanics will become more apparent in the studies of Chapters 7 and 8 and the special applications covered in Chapters 15 and 16. There are many examples that could be cited in which thermodynamic properties clearly reflect this fundamental difference in the quantum-mechanical properties of the individual particles. Whether we accept these differences as a statistical rule or as a reflection of the symmetry character of the motion has no effect on the validity of the subsequent development of statistical mechanics.

PROBLEMS

5.1 Compute the wavelength of an x-ray having an energy of 10,000 ev.

5.2 The total energy ϵ of a freely moving atom is $p^2/2m$. Noting that a wave frequency ω and wave number κ are defined by $\epsilon = \hbar\omega$ and $p = \hbar\kappa$, sketch a curve of ω as a function of κ. Find the phase velocity and group velocity as a function of p/m.

5.3 If the electron in the hydrogen atom were a classical particle rotating in a circle about the stationary nucleus with an angular momentum $\hbar$, show that the radius of the circle (Bohr radius) would be $4\pi\epsilon_0\hbar^2/me^2$. Find this radius in centimeters.

---

* A discussion of the general method of constructing antisymmetrical wave functions for many-particle systems is given by Davidson, pp. 35–39.

5.4 An electron with a velocity **v** moving in a plane normal to a magnetic field of intensity **B** is subject to a force $e(\mathbf{v} \times \mathbf{B})$, where e is the electronic charge. Thus the electron moves in a circle with a constant tangential velocity. (a) By equating the magnetic and centrifugal forces, find the angular frequency ω. (b) If the angular momentum can only be $n\hbar$, where n is an integer, find the kinetic energy of the electron in terms of ω.

5.5 Find the wave function $\psi\{\mathbf{r}, t\}$ of a particle in a rectangular box of dimensions L_x, L_y, and L_z, and determine the translational energy ϵ_t.

5.6 A box of volume V is filled with moving particles. Each particle exists in a different translational quantum state, and there is one particle for each quantum state of energy less than ϵ_m. Find the average energy of the particles expressed as a fraction of ϵ_m.

5.7 A standing sound wave in a cubical room of side L has wave number components $\kappa_x = n_x\pi/L$, $\kappa_y = n_y\pi/L$, and $\kappa_z = n_z\pi/L$, where n_x, n_y, and n_z are integers. For a room 10 ft on a side, find the number of standing waves of frequency between 10 and 11 kc/sec when the velocity of sound is 1000 ft/sec.

5.8 The potential energy of two H-atoms in the H_2-molecule is shown in Fig. 12.3, and the actual vibrational quantum levels are also shown. The measured values of $h^2/8\pi^2 I$ and $h\nu$ are 1.21×10^{-14} erg and 8.72×10^{-13} erg. (a) Compute the equilibrium distance d between the atoms. (b) Compute the width of a harmonic-oscillator potential curve (having the same frequency ν) at the energy corresponding to dissociation of the hydrogen molecule, i.e. 7.2×10^{-12} erg above the $(v = 0)$-vibrational level.

5.9 An approximate model of the potential energy of two atoms in a symmetric diatomic molecule is the "square-well" potential shown in Fig. 5.7. (a) For motion along the line of centers joining the atoms, sketch the trajectories in phase space for (i) vibratory motion in which the maximum kinetic energy is less than ϵ_d and (ii) a collision in which the maximum kinetic energy exceeds ϵ_d. (b) Find the approximate number of vibrational states in terms of ϵ_d, b, and the atomic mass m.

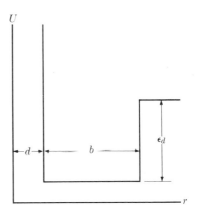

Figure 5.7

5.10 (a) A diatomic molecule radiates energy by changing from a vibrational state of quantum number v to a state of lower quantum number v'. If the frequency of the emitted light is the same as the vibrational frequency of the molecule, show that $v' = v - 1$. (b) A diatomic molecule radiates by changing from a rotational state of quantum number j to a state of lower quantum number j'. If the angular frequency ω of the emitted light is the same as the average angular velocity of the rotating molecule in the states j and j' (provided $j \gg 1$), show that $j' = j - 1$.

5.11 A diatomic molecule, whose equilibrium internuclear distance is d, rotates about its mass center with an angular velocity ω. (a) From classical mechanics, compute the relative increase in the internuclear distance $\Delta d/d$ in terms of ω and the vibrational frequency ν.   (b) For a hydrogen atom, what value of rotational quantum number j would make $\Delta d/d = 0.1$?   (See Problem 5.8 for H_2 data.)

5.12   The Lennard-Jones potential function $U\{r\}$ for the force between two identical atoms is given by $U\{r\} = \epsilon_0\{(d/r)^{12} - 2(d/r)^6\}$, in which ϵ_0 is the depth of the potential well and d is the distance between atoms at the potential minimum. (a) Make the dimensionless plot, U/ϵ_0 versus r/d.   (b) Determine the vibrational frequency ν of small amplitude oscillations about the equilibrium position $r = d$, in terms of the parameters d, ϵ_0, and the reduced mass μ.   (c) For the H_2 molecule, $\epsilon_0 = 7.62 \times 10^{-12}$ erg and $d = 7.42 \times 10^{-9}$ cm.   Compare your calculated value of ν for H_2 with the measured value of 1.82×10^{12} sec^{-1}.

5.13   The Morse potential function $U\{r\} = \epsilon_0\{1 - e^{-\beta(r-d)/d}\}^2$, in which d is the internuclear separation at the potential minimum, is frequently used to represent the potential energy of two atoms in a diatomic molecule.   (a) Plot U/ϵ_0 versus r/d for $\beta = 4$.   (b) From classical mechanics determine the vibrational frequency ν of small oscillations about the equilibrium position $r = d$, in terms of the parameters β, ϵ_0, d and the reduced mass μ.   (c) Using the Morse function, we find that the solution of the wave equation for vibrational motion results in a vibrational energy $\epsilon_v = h\nu\{v + \frac{1}{2} - (h\nu/4\epsilon_0)(v + \frac{1}{2})^2\}$.   Assuming $h\nu \ll \epsilon_0$, what is the largest value of v for a bound state?

6

STATISTICAL DESCRIPTIONS

6.1 Thermodynamic systems and ensembles

A *thermodynamic system* is a collection of matter or material objects whose behavior depends on its intrinsic molecular structure. A rocket engine, a block of copper, or an electromagnet are all thermodynamic systems in this sense, yet they differ considerably from each other in degree of complexity. Of the three, the block of copper is easiest to understand and might be termed a *simple thermodynamic system* because it consists of a sample of matter which is homogeneous and invariable in chemical composition. The behavior of the more complex systems can usually be described or understood in terms of the properties of simple thermodynamic systems. For example, we understand how a rocket engine works, provided we understand how the fuel and oxidant can combine to form the products of combustion and hence increase in temperature, how the gaseous products can increase in flow velocity by flowing out through a carefully shaped nozzle, and how the metallic structure of the rocket engine itself can withstand the high bursting pressures of the combustion gases inside and be cooled by a flow of liquid fuel or oxidant on the outside. Many aspects of these processes, such as the temperature increase in a chemical reaction, the decrease of temperature and density in a gas when the pressure is reduced, and the variation of strength and elasticity in a solid subjected to heating, can be studied by experimenting with simple thermodynamic systems subjected to elementary changes. A complex thermodynamic system, then, can be described in terms of the behavior of its elementary parts, which inherently determine the thermodynamic behavior of the system as a whole. Therefore, most of our attention will be devoted to understanding the thermodynamic behavior of simple thermodynamic systems.

The concept of an ensemble, a collection of identical simple thermodynamic systems, was introduced in Section 3.4 primarily to help us understand the connection between mechanical and thermodynamic behavior of a simple thermodynamic system composed of an extremely large number of molecules. In the language of algebra, an ensemble is to a thermodynamic system as a thermodynamic system is to a molecule. The types of ensembles, microcanonical,

canonical, and grand, have been previously defined. Each type of ensemble is useful in describing the statistical behavior of elementary thermodynamic systems under different conditions.

6.2 The state of a thermodynamic system

A *microstate* of a thermodynamic system is the most complete description of the motion of all the molecules of the system which can possibly be given. From a classical point of view, this would require specifying the positions and momenta of all the particles of the system by locating the representative point in the Γ-space of the system. From the quantum-mechanical point of view, it would require the specification of the quantum state of the whole system or the location of the corresponding quantum cell in Γ-space. If the molecules of the system interact only slightly with each other, the motion of each molecule will be describable by a single-particle quantum state and the state of the system could be described by the number of representative points in each quantum cell in μ-space.

Irrespective of the mode of description of a microstate, we must observe the fundamental law of indistinguishability of identical molecules. If two molecules exist in the same quantum state, we must record this fact by the statement, "There are two molecules in quantum state i," rather than by the statement, "Molecule 1 and molecule 2 are both in the quantum state i." The specification of a microstate therefore requires giving the number of identical molecules in each molecular quantum state in which such a molecule might be found when moving under the influence of the forces that act on the system.

From either a classical or quantum-mechanical point of view, it is manifestly impossible to record even one quantum state of a simple system such as a mole of gas. For a classical description, we would have to give the positions and momenta of the 10^{23} particles. If one could record a million such coordinates per second, it would still take the age of the universe to record the entire amount of data necessary. The situation for the quantum-mechanical description is similar, for the number of quantum states of translation with energies within a factor of two of the mean energy of all the molecules is even larger than the number of particles, and we are obliged to record the number of particles in each of these quantum states. It is the utter impossibility of dealing with such large numbers which forces us to seek a less complete description of a thermodynamic system.

How much information must we give in order to describe adequately the state of a thermodynamic system? The answer to this question depends on the use we make of whatever information we can obtain concerning the condition of the system at any instant of time. For example, we might wish to know where the molecules of a system are located so that we could determine the distribution of mass within the system. To do this, we might merely divide the volume of the system into a million equal elements and then specify the number of molecules in each element. An acceptable, and in fact a very accurate, description of the distribution of mass would therefore consist of specifying 10^6 numbers, each to three or four significant figures. Such a *number-density distribution* would define a *macrostate*.

The variables (such as density or energy) which enter into the description of a macrostate are just those to which we can ascribe a physical significance, and the accuracy with which they must be prescribed is entirely at our disposal. Since our aim is to reduce the frightful amount of information required to define a microstate, yet still to retain a fairly complete description of the system at hand, we will choose an amount of information that might be handled, for example, by a modern computing machine with perhaps 10^4 four-digit numbers. In any case, the number of such quantities will be much less than the number of molecules in our system, yet considerably greater than one could conveniently record with a paper and pencil.

As a partial description of a macroscopic state, or macrostate, we have previously considered the number-density distribution of molecules. Another important element of a macrostate would be the specification of how the energy is distributed among the various molecules. We might devise a suitable scale for measuring molecular energies by dividing the average energy per particle in the system into a sufficiently small number of parts, say 1000, and then specifying the number of molecules having energies which lie within each of the divisions on such an energy scale. Such a description would be an *energy distribution*; that is, it would describe how the total energy in the system is divided among the various molecules.

In addition to the number-density and energy distribution, we could also describe the macrostate in terms of the distribution of linear and angular momentum among the various molecules of the system. All of these are properties which are derived from an understanding of the dynamics of the molecules themselves. For each such property of a particle there is a conservation law: the conservation of mass, linear momentum, angular momentum, and energy. From the mechanical point of view there are no other particle properties that enter into the dynamics of particle motion, and these distributions should suffice for a complete description of a macrostate.

An alternative way to visualize a macrostate is to consider a division of μ-space into a large number of cells (say 10^6) of small but arbitrary size. The size of the cell is determined partly by the limited information we can record (this determines the number of cells) and partly by the volume of μ-space in which we expect to find the representative points of most of the molecules of the system. The size of such cells will have nothing to do with h^f, except that they cannot be smaller than the cell volume for a single quantum state, but will usually be much larger. Now specifying the number of molecules in each cell is a complete description of the macrostate (see Fig. 6.1). Corresponding to the center of each cell is a set of coordinates p_i, q_i, which is practically the same for all molecules whose representative points lie within such a cell and from which

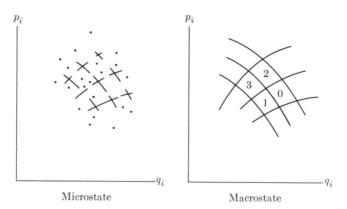

Fig. 6.1. A graphical illustration of the difference between a microstate and a macro-state. Left: The representative points in μ-space completely define the microstate of the system. Right: The number of representative points in each cell is used to denote the macrostate.

the number density, linear momentum, angular momentum, and total energy of the particles in the cell may be determined. If the cell volume in μ-space is made sufficiently small, this description will constitute a specification of a continuous distribution of number density of representative points in μ-space defining a macrostate of the thermodynamic system. (This is analogous to the continuous distribution of the representative points of the systems of an ensemble in Γ-space, used in deriving the Liouville theorem.)

The least amount of information which is required to describe the state of a system would be the values of those quantities that are conserved in an isolated thermodynamic system, namely, the number of atoms, the total energy, and the linear and angular momenta. When an isolated system has reached *thermodynamic equilibrium, that is, when no further macroscopic changes are found to occur with time,* then it will be found that there are additional properties such as temperature and pressure which characterize the system. Both conserved quantities and equilibrium properties can be used to characterize the *thermodynamic state* of the system. Those properties which apply to the system as a whole are called *thermodynamic variables,* despite the fact that some are clearly definable from particle mechanics alone and are applicable even if a system is not in thermodynamic equilibrium, while others are as yet unrelated to the dynamics of the system and can be found only when thermodynamic equilibrium exists. The former would better be termed *dynamical variables* and the latter *equilibrium variables.*

The hierarchy of descriptions, microstate, macrostate, and thermodynamic state, involves greatly decreasing amounts of information but increasing simplicity. The microstate description is impossible to deal with; the macrostate description will be most useful in understanding how the molecular structure of the system affects its gross properties in both a quantitative and a qualitative way. The thermodynamic-state description most succinctly relates the laboratory-scale observations of the characteristics of an elementary thermodynamic system to a more complex system of which it is only a part. The ability to adjust one's point of view in accordance with the experiment or problem at hand and to select the appropriate mode of description, or combination of modes, is an important asset to an engineer or a scientist.

Before proceeding further, it might be wise to consider an analogy which points out the differences between these methods of specifying the state of a system. Suppose it were desired to portray the characteristics of the population of a city of 100,000 people. The least detailed description would be a specification of the number of people living in the city. This would be the population's "thermodynamic state," consisting of a single property, namely, number of persons. A more detailed description would consist in specifying the number of people living in each of the various election districts of the city. This specification of the geographical distribution of the population would then define a "macrostate" of the population. Finally, the complete census of the population, listing each individual by name, age, residence, and other pertinent information, would describe the "microstate" of the population.

The ultimate use of information contained in the census will determine the appropriate variables to be used in specifying the "macrostate." For example, the Board of Education would be interested in the number of children in each year of school age and preschool age in order to estimate the need for new school buildings. Similarly, the Board of Public Welfare would be interested in knowing the number of people in or near retirement age, while the draft board is obviously concerned with those of military age. All of this information could be conveniently given in terms of an age distribution, that is, a specification of the number of people in each age interval of one year. One can easily see the usefulness of other descriptions such as geographical distributions, income distributions, etc.

6.3 Discrete distribution functions

In specifying the macrostate of a system, we are asked to determine the number of molecules whose representative points lie in each of the arbitrarily selected cells in μ-space. If the cells are selected so that each has a different energy ϵ_i, the set of numbers N_i which specify the number of points in each cell then defines the macrostate of the system. In many instances, it is possible to relate the numbers N_i with their corresponding energies ϵ_i by means of a distribution function; that is, N_i can be considered to be a dependent variable whose value is determined by the independent variable ϵ_i. We might write this statement mathematically as

$$N_i = N\{\epsilon_i\}. \tag{6.3-1}$$

The distribution function $N\{\epsilon\}$, while it may be a continuous function of ϵ, gives the discrete set of N_i when evaluated for the discrete set of ϵ_i.

A distribution function is useful when we are examining cause-and-effect relationships (dependent and independent variables). For example, in a population we expect that there will be a relationship between the number of people of a given age and the value of that age. We would expect that the number of people of a given age would decrease as the age increases because we understand something about the dynamics of population; that is, people are born young and die old.

Distribution functions enable us to determine totals and averages. The total number N of particles in the system whose energy-distribution function is given by Eq. (6.3–1) is

$$N = \sum_i N_i, \tag{6.3–2}$$

while the total energy E would be

$$E = \sum_i \epsilon_i N_i. \tag{6.3–3}$$

The average energy per particle, $\langle \epsilon \rangle$, which is the total energy divided by the total number of particles, is thus

$$\langle \epsilon \rangle = \frac{\sum_i \epsilon_i N_i}{\sum_i N_i} = \frac{1}{N} \sum_i \epsilon_i N_i. \tag{6.3–4}$$

In the language of mathematics, the total energy E is the first moment of the energy-distribution function of Eq. (6.3–1).

If we select a molecule at random from among all the molecules of the system, what will be the chance that it has an energy ϵ_i? If this molecule is selected without bias, the probability P_i of selecting such a molecule is just the ratio of the number of molecules N_i having this energy to the total number of molecules N:

$$P_i \equiv N_i/N. \tag{6.3–5}$$

In this sense we can consider the distribution function as defining a *probability distribution function* $\mathcal{P}$:

$$\mathcal{P}\{\epsilon_i\} \equiv (1/N)N\{\epsilon_i\}. \tag{6.3–6}$$

In either Eq. (6.3–5) or (6.3–6) the probability so defined is said to be normalized; that is, the sum of all the probabilities equals unity.

So far we have discussed only the simplest kind of distribution function, namely, one which is a function of one independent variable only, such as energy in a thermodynamic system or age in a population. It may be that we wish a more complete description which would require the introduction of several independent variables. For example, we might wish to describe a population in terms of age and height by counting the number of people corresponding to each possible combination of age in years and height in inches. For a system of gas particles in a box, we might wish to classify them according to the three scalar components of momentum, p_x, p_y, and p_z, by dividing momentum space into a suitable large number of cells and counting the number of representative points in each cell. For this latter case, the cell would be identified by the three components of momentum and the number of particles in each cell would be given by the distribution function

$$N_{ijk} = N\{(p_x)_i, (p_y)_j, (p_z)_k\}. \tag{6.3–7}$$

The total number of particles N would be the sum over all the cells of the number of particles N_{ijk} in each cell:

$$N = \sum_i \sum_j \sum_k N_{ijk}. \tag{6.3–8}$$

The average values of the momentum components are found by taking the first moments of the distribution

$$\langle p_x \rangle = \frac{1}{N} \sum_i \sum_j \sum_k (p_x)_i N_{ijk}. \tag{6.3–9}$$

As for a single independent variable, a probability P_{ijk} that a single particle selected at random from the system will fall within the cell ijk can be defined by

$$P_{ijk} \equiv N_{ijk}/N. \tag{6.3–10}$$

In all the cases of discrete distribution functions we have considered, the cell is identified by one or more subscripts i, j, k, etc., and the values of the independent coordinates such as ϵ, or p_x, p_y, p_z, which distinguish one cell from another, are also indicated by the same subscript. This general system of counting has great flexibility because it does not restrict us to choosing cells of equal size if this should be inconvenient. We usually do select cells of equal size, such as the age in years when counting a population, but this is not a necessity; our scheme of counting is completely general and can be made to serve many different purposes.

6.4 Continuous distribution functions

We learn in calculus that it is sometimes useful to replace the sum of a very large number of terms in a series by an integral when each term of the series differs only slightly from the preceding or succeeding term. It may also be convenient to replace a discrete distribution function by a continuous one, so that the summation over the whole population may be replaced by an integration. On the other hand, we must be very careful never to replace a discrete sum by a continuous sum, or integral, until we are sure that it satisfies the criterion stated above.

To define a continuous distribution function, we determine the density n of points in each cell by dividing the number N_i of points in each cell by a "volume" which is equal to the change in the independent variable from one cell to the next. For example, the density of points for an energy distribution would be

$$n\{\epsilon_i\} \equiv \frac{N\{\epsilon_i\}}{\epsilon_{i+1} - \epsilon_i}. \tag{6.4-1}$$

If we think of ϵ as defining a space of one dimension, then $n\{\epsilon\}$ is the density of points in this space. The total number of points N would become

$$N = \sum_i N_i = \sum_i n\{\epsilon_i\}[\epsilon_{i+1} - \epsilon_i] \simeq \int_0^\infty n\{\epsilon\} \, d\epsilon, \tag{6.4-2}$$

where the integral is an approximate representation of the sum. The average energy per particle, $\langle \epsilon \rangle$, would be

$$\langle \epsilon \rangle = \frac{1}{N} \int_0^\infty \epsilon n\{\epsilon\} \, d\epsilon. \tag{6.4-3}$$

Furthermore, we can again define a probability density $\rho\{\epsilon\}$ by

$$\rho\{\epsilon\} \equiv n\{\epsilon\}/N. \tag{6.4-4}$$

This is related to the probability P_i of finding a particle in the cell i by

$$P_i = \frac{N_i}{N} = \frac{n\{\epsilon_i\}(\epsilon_{i+1} - \epsilon_i)}{N}$$

$$= \rho\{\epsilon_i\}(\epsilon_{i+1} - \epsilon_i). \tag{6.4-5}$$

Thus the probability density ρ times the "volume" of the cell is the probability that a single particle selected at random from the system will lie within the specified cell of that volume. The probability of finding a particle in any cell is proportional to the size of the cell. By substituting Eq. (6.4–4) into (6.4–3), the average energy may be determined in terms of the probability density:

$$\langle \epsilon \rangle = \int_0^\infty \epsilon \rho\{\epsilon\} \, d\epsilon. \tag{6.4-6}$$

The definition of a continuous distribution function may be extended to include the use of any number of independent variables. For the case of momentum coordinates considered above, the continuous distribution of density of points in momentum space would be

$$n\{(p_x)_i, (p_y)_j, (p_z)_k\} \equiv \frac{N\{(p_x)_i, (p_y)_j, (p_z)_k\}}{[(p_x)_{i+1} - (p_x)_i][(p_y)_{j+1} - (p_y)_j][(p_z)_{k+1} - (p_z)_k]}. \tag{6.4-7}$$

The total number of particles would then be

$$N = \sum_i \sum_j \sum_k N_{ijk}$$

$$= \sum_i \sum_j \sum_k n\{(p_x)_i, (p_y)_j, (p_z)_k\}$$

$$\times [(p_x)_{i+1} - (p_x)_i][(p_y)_{j+1} - (p_y)_j][(p_z)_{k+1} - (p_z)_k]$$

$$\simeq \iiint n\{p_x, p_y, p_z\}\, dp_x\, dp_y\, dp_z, \tag{6.4-8}$$

and the average x-momentum would be

$$\langle p_x \rangle = \frac{1}{N} \iiint p_x n\{p_x, p_y, p_z\}\, dp_x\, dp_y\, dp_z. \tag{6.4-9}$$

In a similar manner, the probability density in momentum space would be defined as

$$\rho\{p_x, p_y, p_z\} \equiv (1/N)n\{p_x, p_y, p_z\}. \tag{6.4-10}$$

Let us examine further the restrictions placed on the definition of a continuous distribution function, namely, that the differences in the terms of a sum be small compared with the terms themselves. As an example consider the sum of the first n integers:

$$1 + 2 + 3 + \cdots + n = n(n + 1)/2. \tag{6.4-11}$$

If the sum on the left-hand side were replaced by an integral, its value would be

$$\int_0^n x\, dx = \frac{n^2}{2}. \tag{6.4-12}$$

If n is 4, then the exact sum is 10, while the approximate integral would be 8, not a very good approximation. The reason for this is that the difference between the terms in the series, which is always 1, is not small compared with the size of the average term of the series.

On the other hand, consider the following sum:

$$51 + 52 + 53 = 156. \tag{6.4-13}$$

Now, evaluate the integral

$$\int_{50}^{53} x\, dx = \tfrac{1}{2}(53^2 - 50^2) = 154.5, \tag{6.4-14}$$

which is very close to the sum. In this case, the difference between successive terms, 1, is small compared with the magnitude of any term in the series. Thus a general criterion for replacing a discrete distribution function with a continuous one would be

$$N_{i+1} - N_i \ll N_i. \qquad (6.4\text{–}15)$$

Perhaps at this point the distinction between a discrete and continuous distribution function describing a macrostate of a system would appear not to be very important. Nevertheless, we shall see that in many instances the distinction between classical and quantum-mechanical behavior of individual molecules is incorporated in the distinction between a continuous and discontinuous distribution function. The importance of this can hardly be overestimated, for it is the consequences of quantum-mechanical behavior of molecules as expressed in the thermodynamic properties which is one of the most convincing proofs of the necessity of the quantum point of view of molecular motions. Therefore, if we accept this point of view, we should consider the discrete description as the physically basic one and the continuous description as useful only under certain circumstances. Whenever there is any doubt as to its validity, its use should be justified. For this reason we will use the continuous description only in applications to particular situations, where the justifying criterion of Eq. (6.4–15) may be evaluated numerically.

6.5 The state of an ensemble

So far, we have been discussing the instantaneous descriptions of a thermodynamic system, each of whose molecules can be considered to exist in a definite quantum state. This is the case for molecules which are interacting weakly with each other, as the molecules of a gas, for example. For a liquid, whose molecules interact strongly, it is no longer possible to consider the wave function of a single particle, and hence its quantum state, to be independent of the wave functions of the other molecules. One must work with the wave functions of clusters of molecules, and the description of the state of the system must be correspondingly altered. The most general way to handle this problem is to work not with the molecules composing a thermodynamic system, but with a collection of identical thermodynamic systems comprising an ensemble.

The various possible descriptions of a thermodynamic system which were proposed above, namely, the microstate, the macrostate, and the thermodynamic state, can be applied as easily to an ensemble of identical systems as to a system of identical molecules. Each system of the ensemble, no matter how complex its structure, can exist in discrete quantum states and can have only discrete energies. Specifying the number of systems of the ensemble which exist in each of these quantum states would therefore specify a microstate. The other modes of description of the state of an ensemble would be entirely analogous to those for describing the state of a system.

Most of the applications that we shall consider can be treated adequately in terms of a system of slightly interacting molecules (or waves), and one need not resort to ensemble theory. The latter approach is more elegant and also more general but does not incorporate so directly the molecular point of view. In the next chapter we will find that ensembles still play a role in clarifying the fundamental postulates which underlie statistical mechanics.

PROBLEMS

6.1 The infinite series $1 + x + x^2 + x^3 + \cdots$ has the sum $(1 - x)^{-1}$, provided $x < 1$. Given that the sum is approximated by the integral $\int_0^\infty x^n \, dn$, find the smallest value of x for which the integral is greater than 90% of the sum.

6.2 A system consists of particles with energies $\epsilon_i = \epsilon, 2\epsilon, 3\epsilon, \ldots, 100\epsilon$. The number of particles with energy ϵ is one, the number with energy 2ϵ is two, etc., up to 100 particles each with energy 100ϵ. (a) What is the exact value of the average energy per particle? (b) What is its approximate value if the sums are replaced by integrals? [*Hint:* $1 + 2 + 3 + \cdots n = n(n + 1)/2$ and $1 + 2^2 + 3^2 + \cdots + n^2 = n(n + 1)(2n + 1)/6$.]

6.3 The probability density $\rho\{p_x, p_y, p_z\}$ in momentum space for a system is given by $\rho = 3/4\pi p_m^3$ if $p_x^2 + p_y^2 + p_z^2 \leq p_m^2$, and $\rho = 0$ if $p_x^2 + p_y^2 + p_z^2 > p_m^2$. Find $\langle p_x \rangle$, $\langle p_x^2 \rangle$, and $\langle p_x^2 + p_y^2 + p_z^2 \rangle$.

7

THERMODYNAMIC PROBABILITY

7.1 The microcanonical ensemble and phase space

In Section 3.4 we defined a microcanonical ensemble as one composed of physically identical systems which do not exchange energy with each other or with their surroundings. By "physically identical" we mean that each member of this ensemble consists of the same number of molecules, occupies the same volume V, and is subject to the same set of external forces, if to any. The Γ-space of a system is formed from fN pairs of conjugate coordinates, if f is the number of degrees of freedom of each of the N molecules in a system of the ensemble. A single point in this phase space represents the instantaneous microstate of one system of the ensemble, while a microstate of the ensemble is represented by a cloud of such points in Γ-space, one point for each member of the ensemble.

For each quantum-mechanical microstate of a member of the ensemble, there is a corresponding cell in Γ-space of volume h^{fN}. The portion of Γ-space "available" to the system consists of all values of p_i (that is, from $-\infty$ to $+\infty$ on each p_i-axis) but only those values of q_i lying within the volume V. This available volume in Γ-space is packed solid with cells, one for each quantum-mechanical microstate of a system. It is also possible to define surfaces of constant energy which divide Γ-space into successive layers of cells, just as the rings of a tree divide the volume into recognizable layers, each composed of many cells.

We wish to consider a special kind of microcanonical ensemble for which the energy of each system of the ensemble lies between E and $E + \delta E$, where δE is very much smaller than E. Each member of this ensemble has practically the same total energy E at least within any accuracy we might specify. (If $\delta E/E$ is 10^{-6}, then all members of the ensemble would have the same energy within one part in a million which, from a practical point of view, are essentially identical energies.) The two constant-energy surfaces $E + \delta E$ and E would enclose in Γ-space a layer of cells such as one might find in the leaf of a plant (see Fig. 7.1). We will denote by $\mathcal{V}$ the volume in Γ-space occupied by this layer of cells and by W the number of cells contained within this volume. From our previous argument, (Eq. 5.8–12), connecting a volume in phase space with the number of quantum cells occupying this volume, we would have

$$W = \mathcal{V}/(h)^{fN}. \qquad (7.1\text{-}1)$$

Since a volume in Γ-space will have the dimensions of (momentum $\times$ position)^{fN}, and since Planck's constant has the dimensions of momentum times length or energy times time, we see that W is truly dimensionless.

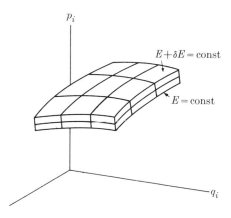

Fig. 7.1. The volume $\mathcal{V}$ of Γ-space included between two constant-energy surfaces which differ in energy by an amount δE can be divided into W cells for the purpose of describing a microcanonical ensemble.

In Section 3.6 it was proved from Liouville's theorem that if the density of representative points in Γ-space of a microcanonical ensemble were to be a function of the total energy alone at any instant of time, then this density at every point in phase space would always remain unchanging with time. Our particular microcanonical ensemble will therefore be stationary if the representative points of all the systems are uniformly distributed throughout the volume $\mathcal{V}$. While any one system of the ensemble changes its microstate from time to time, the ensemble macrostate, which is determined by the distribution of the representative points within the volume $\mathcal{V}$, will be unchanging with time. We thereby define a *stationary macrostate* of the ensemble.

7.2 The basic postulate of statistical mechanics

The purpose of an ensemble is to provide us with a population of identical thermodynamic systems from which we may compute average properties of the systems of physical interest. For example, if our system were a one-degree-of-freedom spring-and-mass system, that is, a harmonic oscillator, we could compute the average value of the potential energy of all the members of the ensemble at any instant. If the ensemble is stationary, this average would be the same, irrespective of what time we choose for making the computation. However, more important than this is the supposition that the properties of the ensemble can be easily related to the properties of the single system with which we experiment in the laboratory. If this were not so, the ensemble would be of hypothetical interest only.

The importance of stationary ensembles can be easily illustrated by returning to our ensemble of oscillators. If all the oscillators were in phase, that is, all reach maximum extension at one and the same time, then the average potential energy of such an ensemble would change with time. To compute this average potential energy, we would therefore have to completely understand the motion of our system in order to trace the trajectory of its representative point in phase space. On the other hand, if the ensemble is stationary, we need only to know how to draw surfaces of constant energy and to populate volumes in phase space with points of equal density in order to determine an ensemble average. Since to do this is easier than to solve for a time dependence of the motion of each member of the ensemble, stationary ensembles are clearly much easier to work with and much more is known about their properties.

While the properties of a stationary ensemble may be studied abstractly, for the ensemble is a purely mathematical construction, we must establish a connection between these properties and the experimentally measurable properties of a single thermodynamic system if we wish to profit from our understanding of ensembles. It is mathematically difficult, if not impossible, to establish such a connection, and we shall be content with postulating this relationship and then subsequently showing its plausibility. However, before doing this, we must discuss what we mean by the measurement of a property of a system.

As a simple example, suppose that we wish to determine the mass M of air which exists in a given volume V when the pressure and temperature have given values. To determine the mass M, we might weigh a container of volume V filled with air at the given pressure and temperature and from this weight subtract that of the evacuated container. To ascertain the reproducibility of the measurement, we repeat the experiment n times, measuring the masses $M_1, M_2, \ldots, M_i, \ldots, M_n$. The average value of M, denoted by $\langle M \rangle$,

$$\langle M \rangle \equiv \frac{1}{n} \sum_{i=1}^{n} M_i, \tag{7.2-1}$$

and the average of the deviation δM,

$$(\delta M)^2 \equiv \frac{1}{n} \sum_{i=1}^{n} (M_i - \langle M \rangle)^2, \tag{7.2-2}$$

are *statistical averages* of the measured property M which indicate to us what values of the mass M we would expect to record if further experiments were performed. As a result of the experiments, we would say that the mass of the gas under the given conditions is $\langle M \rangle$ and that the relative accuracy of this measurement is $\delta M / \langle M \rangle$. In other words, the properties of the system under investigation can be given only in terms of their statistical averages as ascertained from the measurements made in experiments repeated in identical fashion.

In the averaging processes defined in Eqs. (7.2–1) and (7.2–2), we gave equal importance to each measurement because we had no reason to expect one experiment to be more significant than the next. (Naturally we do not include measurements which we know to be faulty because of broken instruments, etc.) Faced with a lack of more definitive information, we place equal emphasis on equal experiments because there is no more logical alternative. Contrary to the rule often proposed for humans, some experiments are not more equal than others.

We now wish to postulate a connection between the interpretation of the results of experiments on a single system and the properties of the stationary ensemble of such systems. This fundamental postulate may be stated as follows:

As we increase the number of measurements of a property of a system made in repeated experiments, the statistical averages of this property approach those for the systems of a stationary ensemble, provided that the ensemble statistical averages are determined by assigning equal weight to each member system of the ensemble.

For example, this postulate states that the average pressure of a gas of fixed mass, energy, and volume, as measured in repeated experiments, would approach the average pressure of the systems of the corresponding stationary microcanonical ensemble as the number of measurements was increased. (For the microcanonical ensemble to be stationary, the representative points must fill with uniform density the volume in Γ-space between surfaces of energy E and $E + \delta E$, as explained above in Section 7.1.) The postulate not only makes it possible to calculate the limit of the mean value of a property, but also the deviation from the mean,* provided we can determine the corresponding averages of the stationary ensemble.

The specification of equal importance to each system of the ensemble in determining statistical averages is as logical as the same rule adopted for averaging the experimental measurements. Since there is no reason for preferring one member of the ensemble to another, we treat them all as equally important in defining an average. In a stationary microcanonical ensemble, representative points are distributed uniformly inside an energy shell in Γ-space, so that equal volume elements within this region of Γ-space contain the same numbers of representative points. It is therefore just as correct to define the ensemble average by assigning to equal volumes in Γ-space the same weight in the averaging process; i.e., we may average over the appropriate volume of Γ-space.

---

* In this book we shall be concerned primarily with mean values. *Fluctuation theory* treats the problem of deviations from the mean. (See, for example, Hirschfelder, Curtiss and Bird, pp. 121–128.)

Furthermore, since the number of quantum states of a system is proportional to the volume element in Γ-space, we could also perform an ensemble average by assigning equal weight to the system quantum states.* The ensemble statistical averages are therefore identical whether we average over systems of the ensemble, the available volume in Γ-space, or the quantum states of a system.

Because some member systems of the stationary ensemble will have properties different from the average of the whole ensemble, there will be an average deviation from the mean value for the ensemble and, by postulate, for the measurements performed on a single system. This deviation is inherent in the system and is not to be confused with experimental uncertainties introduced by instrumental inaccuracies or human error. The deviations are not simply those predicted for microscopic systems by the uncertainty principle, but they can be observed even in macroscopic systems such as dust particles in Brownian motion. It therefore appears that the fundamental postulate stated above incorporates a wider range of observable phenomena than we might have at first supposed.

A measurement of a property of a system at equilibrium, such as its pressure, which is repeated at equal time intervals could be considered a time history of that property, and the average value of the measurements would be a time average. From a dynamical point of view it is utterly impossible to predict as a function of time the behavior of a thermodynamic system composed of 10^{20} molecules so that time averages may be subsequently determined. However, if it is supposed that a time average approaches the ensemble average as the duration of the experiment is extended, then the ensemble average may be used in determining the property in question. This supposition, which follows from what is called the *ergodic hypothesis*,† has a long and fascinating history because it attempts to connect the dynamical evolution of a single system and the properties of the ensemble. However, like all statements of thermodynamic (as opposed to dynamic) content, it does not establish the time rate at which property changes take place, only the average values.

From an empirical point of view, the postulate is justified (but not necessarily proven) if the results of the postulate are shown not to be in disagreement with experiments. The ultimate justification of all hypotheses is not that they are mathematically satisfying but that they are useful; that is, they correlate existing experimental results and correctly predict new ones. Furthermore, this basic postulate is not physically unreasonable. In any series of measurements, a given system will be found in many different microstates. If the average of any property, averaged over the microstates in which the system is

---

* For this reason the averaging rule is often referred to as the "equal *a priori* probability of quantum states."

† The ergodic hypothesis states that the representative point of a system will, after sufficient time, pass through all the available volume in Γ-space, spending an equal time in equal volume elements.

found, is indistinguishably different from that of the whole ensemble, then we are justified in using the ensemble average to determine such properties. Because of the stationary character of the ensemble, this latter average is much easier to perform than that of an individual system.

7.3 Thermodynamic probability

From our study of mechanics we were able to find some quantities (such as energy, linear momentum, and angular momentum) which were properties of the system as a whole and which either were conserved or their changes could be related to the forces applied to the system. From our consideration of the stationary ensemble we see that there is another property of a system, namely, the volume $\mathcal{V}$ in phase space within which the representative point of the system must always be found. If this volume is measured by the number W of cells contained within it, as defined in Eq. (7.1–1), we then have a new dimensionless property of the system, which is called the *total thermodynamic probability*. (Strictly speaking, the use of the term *probability* in this connection is incorrect. If we ask what is the probability that a system selected at random from those of a stationary ensemble will have its representative point located within some given volume element $\Delta\mathcal{V}$ within the volume $\mathcal{V}$ of phase space, we would conclude that this probability would be proportional to $\Delta\mathcal{V}$ since the representative points fill the possible volume $\mathcal{V}$ with equal density everywhere. It is in this sense that we may term $\Delta\mathcal{V}$, or better the dimensionless quantity $\Delta\mathcal{V}/(h)^{fN}$, as a nonnormalized probability and hence W as a total probability.)

On what will the thermodynamic probability W depend? For a given chemical substance the number of coordinates in Γ-space will be proportional to the number of molecules, and hence W will certainly depend on N. If we change the total energy E of the system, we will most likely change W also. For a fixed E and N, we can certainly increase $\mathcal{V}$ by increasing the volume V of our system, for this increases the possible range of the position coordinates q_i of all the particles. Thus, we may write that the thermodynamic probability is a function of the energy, volume, and number of particles of our system:

$$W = W\{E, V, N\}. \tag{7.3–1}$$

The quantities energy, volume, and number of particles are dynamical variables in that they are the quantities which arise naturally in the study of dynamics and can be measured directly in a physical experiment. On the other hand, W, as we have defined it, cannot be measured directly, but at this stage can be computed only from an appropriate geometry of phase space. Nevertheless, W is just as much a property of our system as the energy, volume, or number of particles. Equation (7.3–1) is the statement that the construction of the volume $\mathcal{V}$ in phase space is uniquely related to the energy, volume, and number of particles of our system.

Let us make a rough estimate of the magnitude of W for a simple system composed of gas molecules in a box. To estimate υ crudely, we will multiply the average momentum $\langle p \rangle$ of a particle by the length L of the side of the box to obtain the component of this volume in any $p_i q_i$-plane. We then multiply this area over the $3N$ pairs of coordinates in Γ-space to obtain

$$\upsilon \sim (\langle p \rangle L)^{3N}. \tag{7.3-2}$$

Inserting this in Eq. (7.1-1), the thermodynamic probability becomes

$$W \sim \left(\frac{\langle p \rangle L}{h} \right)^{3N} = \left(\frac{L}{\lambda} \right)^{3N}, \tag{7.3-3}$$

where λ is the de Broglie wavelength for a particle of average momentum. For 1 gm-mole of gas at room temperature and pressure ($N \sim 10^{23}$, $L \sim 10$ cm, $\langle p \rangle / m \sim 10^4$ cm/sec), L/λ is about 10^{10}. Thus we see that W is truly an enormous number, about $10^{10^{24}}$, a number which is so large compared with countable things (such as the 10^{80} particles in the universe) that we find it difficult to understand what it means.

When numbers become too large to deal with easily, we usually work with their logarithms; that is, we keep track of the first few significant figures and the number of decimal places. If we take the logarithm of W in our last example, it would still be very large (10^{24}) but certainly no larger than the other numbers we deal with, such as N. Now, it is a curious property of a very large number that an appreciable change in its magnitude may make a very small change in its logarithm. For example, if our estimate of W in the case considered above were wrong by a factor of one million (a truly enormous factor, if we were counting our dollars in the bank), then logarithm W would be changed only by six parts in 10^{24}, an utterly negligible amount. Thus, the use of $\ln W$ instead of W itself makes it possible to use smaller numbers and reduces the accuracy which is required in computing υ.

It is this property of large numbers which makes it unnecessary to define the ratio $\delta E / E$ with any great precision. The volume υ in phase space will certainly increase if $\delta E / E$ is increased, yet this will make a negligible difference in $\ln W$. Thus, the mathematics itself assures us that the quantity of physical significance must be $\ln W$ rather than W itself.

It is worth noting here that our intuitive notions of volumes and areas in phase space, derived from experience in three-dimensional space, must be aided by mathematical analysis if we are to see more clearly the implications of the foregoing discussion. For example, let us show how the whole volume enclosed by a constant energy surface in the $6N$-dimensional Γ-space is almost entirely concentrated near the surface, that is, a very small change in energy will produce an enormous change in volume. We shall show this simple property of a hyperspace by considering a gas of N molecules for which the total energy

E is related to the $3N$ momentum coordinates $p_1, p_2, \ldots, p_{3N}$ by

$$E = \frac{p_1^2 + p_2^2 + \cdots p_{3N}^2}{2m}. \tag{7.3--4}$$

The constant-energy surface in momentum space is a hypersphere of $3N$ dimensions, having a radius p given by

$$p = (p_1^2 + p_2^2 + \cdots p_{3N}^2)^{1/2} = (2mE)^{1/2}, \tag{7.3--5}$$

in accordance with Eq. (7.3–4). The volume of this hypersphere can be computed with some difficulty but is probably not very different from the volume of a hypercube of side dimension $\bar{p}$, namely $\bar{p}^{3N}$, where $(\bar{p})^2/2m$ is the average energy E/N. Thus, the total volume $\mathcal{V}_e$ in Γ-space enclosed by this surface is the product of the volume $\bar{p}^{3N} = (2mE/N)^{3N/2}$ in momentum space and the volume V^N in configuration space:

$$\mathcal{V}_e \simeq \{(2mE/N)^{3/2} V\}^N. \tag{7.3--6}$$

If the energy E is changed by an amount dE, then the enclosed volume $\mathcal{V}_e$ changes by an amount $d\mathcal{V}_e$ given by

$$\frac{d\mathcal{V}_e}{\mathcal{V}_e} = \left(\frac{\partial \ln \mathcal{V}_e}{\partial \ln E}\right)_{V,N} \frac{dE}{E} = \left(\frac{3N}{2}\right) \frac{dE}{E} \tag{7.3--7}$$

so that the fractional change in enclosed volume is N times as large as the fractional change in energy. This means that the volume $\mathcal{V}$ between the energy surfaces E and $E - dE$ is practically the same as the total volume $\mathcal{V}_e$ enclosed by the surface E, provided $dE/E > 1/N$. It is for this reason that the volume $\mathcal{V}$ for a microcanonical ensemble does not depend on the ratio dE/E when the latter is not too small. This is equally true of $\ln \mathcal{V}$ and also of $\ln W$.

7.4 Entropy

Rather than work with the dimensionless property $\ln W$, we define a dimensional property proportional to it called the *entropy* S by using a proportionality constant k:

$$S \equiv k \ln W. \tag{7.4--1}$$

Since k is a universal constant, called *Boltzmann's constant*, having the value 1.3805×10^{-16} erg/K°, entropy has the same units, energy/degree of temperature.

The use of the dimensional property entropy rather than the dimensionless property $\ln W$ is the result of a historical process in which entropy was defined and measured empirically before there was a corresponding understanding of statistical mechanics. The empirical entropy was later found to be related to $\ln W$ in the simple manner of Eq. (7.4–1) with the same universal constant k

for all substances. However, empirical measurements always determine changes in entropy, whereas the statistical mechanical definition gives an absolute value to the entropy, which has implications that will be discussed in later chapters.

At first it might seem surprising that there is an experimental way of measuring the volume $\mathcal{U}$ in phase space. However, there is no direct way of measuring the entropy empirically, in the manner that a thermometer measures temperature or a scale measures mass. The entropy is calculated from experimental measurements of energy, temperature, etc., in a special kind of way which we shall review later on. Naturally, in such a calculation the units of energy and temperature will appear and will therefore determine a dimension for the entropy. A similar situation exists in dynamics, where the kinetic energy may be computed theoretically from the mass and velocity of a particle or measured empirically by finding the distance through which the particle would rise in a gravitational field. In the absence of a theoretical understanding of kinetic energy and how it is defined, one could develop from such empirical measurements and rules a restricted science of dynamics, which would be analogous to the historical development of classical thermodynamics.

The proportionality between entropy S and the logarithm of the volume $\mathcal{U}$ in phase space enables us to make some important deductions of a very general type concerning entropy. Consider, for example, two systems denoted by subscripts a and b, each with fixed and known values of energy, volume, and number of particles and hence with a known value of the thermodynamic probability W_a and W_b, respectively. So long as the two systems are not exchanging energy or particles with each other, the microstates of one system are entirely independent of the microstates of the other. If we consider systems a and b to be the two parts of a combined system ab, then the number of microstates available to system ab is just the product of the number of microstates of system a times the number of microstates of system b:

$$W_{ab} = W_a W_b \tag{7.4-2}$$

because of the independence of part a from part b. It follows that the entropy S_{ab} of the entire system is therefore the sum of the entropies of its parts:

$$\begin{aligned} S_{ab} &= k \ln W_{ab} = k\{\ln W_a + \ln W_b\} \\ &= S_a + S_b. \end{aligned} \tag{7.4-3}$$

The entropy, like the energy and number of particles, is an additive or *extensive property* of a system; that is, the entropy of the whole is the sum of the entropies of its parts.

One of the most important properties of entropy is that, unlike the energy and number of particles, it is not conserved in an isolated system but can only increase, if it changes at all. To show that this follows from the definition of entropy, we will consider two examples.

Consider the two systems shown in Fig. 7.2, each of which has the same total energy E and the same number of particles, N. In system a all the particles are confined by a partition to occupy one-half of a container, whose total volume is the same as that of system b, in which the same number of particles may move freely about the whole container. Now the entropy of system b is certainly greater than that of system a because all the microstates of the latter are certainly some of the microstates of the former, whereas those microstates of system b in which there are some particles in the right-hand half of the container certainly cannot be microstates for system a. From another point of view, the volume $\mathcal{U}_b$ in phase space which is available to system b can be divided into two parts. In one part all the coordinates q_i correspond to particles lying in the left half of the volume V_b, and in the other part at least one or more of these coordinates will correspond to particles located in the right half of V_b. The first part of this volume is just the phase-space volume $\mathcal{U}_a$ available to system a and is clearly smaller than the whole phase-space volume $\mathcal{U}_b$. From either point of view, system b has a greater entropy than a.

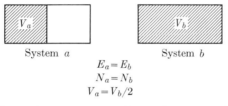

$$E_a = E_b$$
$$N_a = N_b$$
$$V_a = V_b/2$$

Fig. 7.2. A comparison of two systems of equal energy and number of particles but unequal volumes shows that there is a difference in entropy. In system a, all the particles are confined in the left half of the container, but in system b they are free to move about the whole of the volume.

If we remove the partition separating the two halves of the container of system a, the gas particles will fill the whole volume as they do in system b, and the entropy of system a will increase to that of system b. The removal of the partition in system a makes available to its particles a whole new class of microstates corresponding to those having some particles in the right-hand portion of the container. This removal of an inhibition to the motion of the molecules can only result in an increase in entropy if there is any change at all, because it makes available to the system a larger volume in phase space.

We can readily compute the difference in entropy between the systems and, hence, the increase in entropy of system a when the partition is removed, if the system is composed of gas particles whose total potential energy is very small compared with the total kinetic energy. For this special case, the total energy E depends only on the momenta of all the particles and is the same surface in momentum space for either system. However, for system b each of the N particles moves throughout a volume in configuration space (q_x, q_y, q_z) which is twice that for any particle in system a. Since the total volume $\mathcal{U}$ in phase space is the product of the volume in momentum space times the volume in configuration space of each particle multiplied over all the particles and since the volume in momentum space is the same for both systems, the ratio of the thermodynamic probability W for systems a and b becomes

$$\frac{W_b}{W_a} = \frac{(V_b)^N}{(V_a)^N} = \left(\frac{V_b}{V_a}\right)^N = 2^N. \tag{7.4-4}$$

The corresponding entropy difference is therefore

$$\begin{aligned} S_b - S_a &= k(\ln W_b - \ln W_a) \\ &= Nk \ln 2. \end{aligned} \tag{7.4-5}$$

It is seemingly a paradox that the introduction of a partition dividing system b into two parts results in no decrease of its entropy. The reason for this is that approximately half of all the particles will be found on either side of this partition, so that by virtue of the left-right symmetry of the two halves of the container, the phase volume of the divided system is about one-half the value of that of the undivided system. Whereas removing the diaphragm of system a increases the phase volume by a factor of 2^N, interposing the diaphragm in system

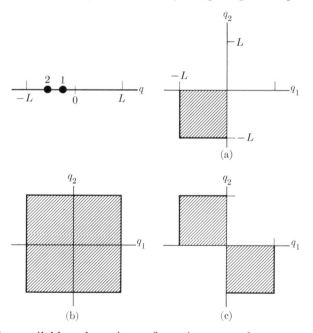

Fig. 7.3. The available volume in configuration space for a two-particle system confined in a one-dimensional box of length $2L$ is shown in (a) if the particles are confined to the left half of the box by a barrier, (b) if they are free to move anywhere within the box, and (c) if the barrier at the center maintains one particle in either half.

b reduces the phase volume of b by a factor of only 2. This results in a negligible decrease in entropy compared with the increase caused by the removal of the diaphragm of system a.

A simple example of the changes in phase-space volume occasioned by the removal and replacing of a diaphragm arises if we consider a system of only two particles, each of which can move in only one dimension. Let the "box" of total dimension $2L$ be divided into two halves, for which the left half has a position coordinate $-L \leq q \leq 0$ and the right half has the position coordinate $0 \leq q \leq L$, as shown in Fig. 7.3. If a partition keeps both particles in the left-hand side of the box, then the corresponding configuration-space volume will be the shaded area shown in Fig. 7.3(a). When the partition is removed, then either particle may traverse the whole length of the box and the corresponding configuration volume is increased by a factor of 2^2, or 4, as shown in Fig. 7.3(b). The corresponding entropy increase is therefore $2k \ln 2$, in agreement with Eq. (7.4–5). If the diaphragm is reinserted when one particle, say particle 1, is on the right-hand side and the other is on the left, then the corresponding configuration-space volume is shown in Fig. 7.3(c). Because of the indistinguishability of the particles, we must also include the configuration-space volume corresponding to particle 2 on the right and particle 1 on the left. The entropy of the system in this state is less than that of the undivided system by an amount $k \ln 2$, since the phase volume is half as large, again in agreement with our previous argument. If one had used three particles moving in the same box, the contrast between the phase volume for the different situations would be more striking.

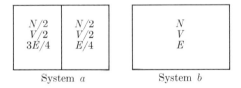

System a System b

Fig. 7.4. A comparison of two systems with the same total volume, energy, and number of particles shows that system a, which has an unequal distribution of energy between its halves, will have less entropy than b.

A similar argument may also be propounded for the increase in entropy in a system for which an inhibition to the sharing of energy among its parts has been removed. Consider the systems a and b of Fig. 7.4, with total energy, volume, and number of particles identical in both. However, system a is divided into halves with equal volume and equal number of particles but with more energy on the left-hand side than on the right-hand side. The diaphragm dividing the system prevents the sharing of energy or particles between the two sides. As in our previous argument, the microstates of system a are part of, but certainly not all of, the microstates of system b. Thus, the latter has a greater entropy than system a. The removal of the partition of system a, permitting the energy to be distributed among all the particles in the system, thereby results in an increase in entropy. We are again forced to conclude that the removal of an inhibition to the sharing of energy can result only in an increase in entropy. Likewise, an interposition of a diaphragm in system b will not cause any appreciable reduction of the entropy.

We are forced to conclude from our phase-space arguments that *the removal of an inhibition to the sharing of particles or energy among the parts of an isolated system* $(E, V, N$ *fixed) can result only in an increase in entropy. Similarly, interposition of an inhibition in an equilibrium system will not reduce its entropy.* If δS is the change in entropy of an isolated system, then

$$\delta S \geq 0 \qquad \text{(isolated system)}. \tag{7.4–6}$$

This principle of the increase of entropy does not apply to systems which are not isolated, that is, systems for which the energy, volume, or number of particles is being changed. For example, it is possible to return the system b of Fig. 7.2 to the state of system a by interposing a diaphragm and then pumping the gas from the left side into the right while also cooling it to reduce its temperature to that of system a.

The nonconservation of entropy in an isolated system distinguishes entropy from mass, linear momentum, angular momentum, and total energy, which are all conserved in an isolated system. Entropy is a quantitative measure of the number of quantum states available to the system with fixed values of the conserved quantities but with restrictions on the motion or sharing of energy of the molecules, such as the impervious walls of the confining container or internal partitions within the system. The entropy is a quantitative measure of the effect of these restrictions on the motion of the molecules.

7.5 Absolute temperature

The entropy of a simple thermodynamic system depends on its energy, volume, and number of particles, since they were the variables which determined the thermodynamic probability W. By the laws of partial differentiation, the total differential dS of the entropy would be

$$dS = \left(\frac{\partial S}{\partial E}\right)_{V,N} dE + \left(\frac{\partial S}{\partial V}\right)_{E,N} dV + \left(\frac{\partial S}{\partial N}\right)_{E,V} dN. \tag{7.5–1}$$

Now consider two systems a and b, not necessarily identical, brought into contact and allowed to exchange only energy with each other. If dE_a is the change in energy of system a and dE_b is the corresponding change in energy in system b, then because the total energy of the two systems is a constant, we have

$$dE_a = -dE_b. \tag{7.5–2}$$

If we keep the volume fixed ($dV = 0$) and the number of particles fixed ($dN = 0$) in both systems, then the corresponding changes in entropy of systems a and b will be

$$dS_a = \left(\frac{\partial S_a}{\partial E_a}\right)_{V,N} dE_a,$$

$$dS_b = \left(\frac{\partial S_b}{\partial E_b}\right)_{V,N} dE_b. \tag{7.5-3}$$

Adding these two entropy changes to find the total increase in entropy and using the conservation of energy given in Eq. (7.5-2), we find

$$dS_a + dS_b = \left\{\left(\frac{\partial S_a}{\partial E_a}\right)_{V,N} - \left(\frac{\partial S_b}{\partial E_b}\right)_{V,N}\right\} dE_a. \tag{7.5-4}$$

Since a and b together form an isolated system, we know that this total entropy change must be either zero or positive. If system a gains energy so that dE_a is positive, then the term in braces on the right-hand side of Eq. (7.5-4) must also be positive, so that

$$\left(\frac{\partial S_a}{\partial E_a}\right)_{V,N} \geq \left(\frac{\partial S_b}{\partial E_b}\right)_{V,N} \quad \text{if} \quad dE_a > 0, \tag{7.5-5}$$

and vice versa.

Since entropy and energy are both properties, the partial derivative $(\partial S/\partial E)_{V,N}$ is also a property. However, both entropy and energy are extensive properties. Their ratio, or the partial derivative, will be independent of the size of the system, for if we double S and double E by doubling the size of the system, we will not change the magnitude of the partial derivative. A property of this type is called an *intensive* property.

If this property is higher in system a than in system b, then the energy of a can only increase, and vice versa. If this property is the same in both systems, then there could be an exchange of energy either way. The property commonly used to measure the tendency of systems to exchange energy when brought into contact with each other is called the *temperature*. If we define an *absolute thermodynamic temperature* T by

$$\frac{1}{T} \equiv \left(\frac{\partial S}{\partial E}\right)_{V,N}, \tag{7.5-6}$$

then we can see that if T_a is greater than T_b, the energy of system b can increase while that of system a can only decrease, and vice versa. This temperature is called absolute because it does not depend on the peculiar properties of any particular substance, such as the expansion of liquid mercury when heated or the increase in pressure of a gas confined in a fixed volume.

Once a system of units is chosen for entropy and energy, then the absolute value of the temperature scale is fixed and can be determined in principle by use of any substance for which entropy and energy can be determined. Boltzmann's constant k in Eq. (7.4–1), which has the dimension of energy divided by temperature, has been so chosen that the absolute temperature of a mixture of water and ice at atmospheric pressure will be 273.16°. (The otherwise arbitrary number 273.16° was selected so that the temperature difference between the ice point and boiling point of water would be 100°. The division of the temperature scale between any two fixed points into an arbitrary number of divisions is purely a convention, and has no physical significance.) However, a given choice of the constant k automatically defines an absolute temperature scale, while the choice of an arbitrary temperature scale thereby fixes the constant k.

There is nothing unique about the choice of the functional form of the relationship between temperature and $\partial S / \partial E$ in Eq. (7.5–6). Any monotonically increasing function of the temperature would automatically satisfy the inequalities of Eq. (7.5–5). A linear function is the simplest monotonic function and was first suggested for this use by Kelvin. For this reason, the temperature, defined by Eq. (7.5–6), for which the ice point is 273.16°K is called the *Kelvin scale of absolute temperature*.

7.6 Chemical potential

Suppose the two systems considered above are brought into contact and permitted to exchange both energy and number of particles only with each other. Not only will the energy be conserved so that Eq. (7.5–2) still holds, but so will the number of particles:

$$dN_a = -dN_b. \tag{7.6–1}$$

If the volume of each system is not changed, then the entropy change of each will be

$$dS = \frac{1}{T}\, dE + \left(\frac{\partial S}{\partial N}\right)_{V,E} dN, \tag{7.6–2}$$

where the reciprocal of the absolute temperature now replaces the corresponding partial derivative. Summing the entropy changes of both systems, we obtain

$$dS_a + dS_b = \left(\frac{1}{T_a} - \frac{1}{T_b}\right) dE_a + \left\{\left(\frac{\partial S_a}{\partial N_a}\right)_{V,E} - \left(\frac{\partial S_b}{\partial N_b}\right)_{V,E}\right\} dN_a. \tag{7.6–3}$$

If the temperatures of systems a and b are identical, then only the second term on the right-hand side of Eq. (7.6–3) can contribute to an increase in entropy.

By an argument similar to that used above, we find

$$\left(\frac{\partial S_a}{\partial N_a}\right)_{V,E} \geq \left(\frac{\partial S_b}{\partial N_b}\right)_{V,E} \qquad \text{if} \quad dN_a \geq 0. \tag{7.6-4}$$

The partial derivative $(\partial S/\partial N)_{V,E}$ is also an intensive property. If this property is different in two systems with the same temperature, then a flow of particles can occur only to the system having the higher value of this property. By convention a new intensive property, called the *chemical potential* μ, is defined as

$$\frac{\mu}{T} \equiv -\left(\frac{\partial S}{\partial N}\right)_{E,V}. \tag{7.6-5}$$

The introduction of the absolute temperature, another intensive property, in the definition of chemical potential is simply a convention that makes the dimensions of the chemical potential equal to energy/particle. The negative sign in Eq. (7.6-5) then provides that particles can move only from regions of high chemical potential to low.

We shall see that the two intensive properties, absolute temperature and chemical potential, which follow from the definition of entropy, always appear quite naturally when one attempts to obtain numerical values for the entropy, as we shall do in the next chapter.

7.7 Systems having several chemical components

For the sake of simplicity, in all the foregoing we have considered a simple thermodynamic system having N molecules of a given chemical species. If our system were composed of N_1 molecules of species 1, N_2 molecules of species 2, etc., then its thermodynamic probability, and thereby its entropy, would depend on the total energy E, volume V, and numbers of molecules N_1, N_2, etc.:

$$S = S\{E, V, N_1, N_2, \ldots\} \tag{7.7-1}$$

because these quantities determine the volume $\mathcal{V}$ in phase space. If we consider the exchange of energy between two such systems, a and b, for each of which the volume and numbers N_1, N_2, etc., are held fixed, then the argument of Section 7.5 is still valid; that is, the condition for no increase of entropy is that the temperature T is the same for both systems, where T is defined by

$$\frac{1}{T} \equiv \left(\frac{\partial S}{\partial E}\right)_{V,N_1,N_2,\ldots} \tag{7.7-2}$$

If we further consider the exchange of energy and molecules of species 1 between two such systems, while preventing the change of volume or exchange of species 2, 3, etc., then the argument of Section 7.6 will also hold with respect to the exchange of species 1, namely, that the chemical potential μ_1, defined by

$$\frac{\mu_1}{T} \equiv -\left(\frac{\partial S}{\partial N_1}\right)_{E,V,N_2,N_3,\ldots}, \qquad (7.7\text{--}3)$$

must be the same in both systems if there is to be no increase in total entropy. By next considering the exchange of only species 2 under conditions of no volume change and equal temperature, we can define the chemical potential of species 2 as

$$\frac{\mu_2}{T} \equiv -\left(\frac{\partial S}{\partial N_2}\right)_{E,V,N_1,N_3,\ldots}, \qquad (7.7\text{--}4)$$

and so on for the other species. Our general conclusion would be that the difference in chemical potential for each species determines the possible exchange of each species between the two systems having equal temperatures.

The presence of several chemical components in a system provides little more complication than the introduction of the additional macroscopic variables N_1, N_2, etc. However, if the chemical species can react with each other to form new components, as H_2O is formed from O_2 and H_2, then the numbers N_1, N_2, etc., may not be constant for the exchanges contemplated above. This more complicated situation is treated in Chapter 14.

PROBLEMS

7.1 Using the argument followed in Section 7.3, estimate the number of particles in a gas for which the volume $\mathcal{U}$ enclosed between the surfaces E and $E - \delta E$ differs only by one part in 10^6 from that enclosed by the surface E, provided that $\delta E/E$ is 10^{-6}.

7.2 A hypersphere of n dimensions has a surface whose equation is $r_1^2 + r_2^2 + \cdots + r_n^2 = R^2$, in which R is the radius and $r_1, r_2, \ldots, r_n$ are the cartesian coordinates of the space. (a) Show that the volume of the hypersphere is

$$(2R)^n \prod_{s=2}^{n} \int_0^{\pi/2} (\cos \theta)^s \, d\theta.$$

(b) Given that

$$\prod_{s=2}^{n} \int_0^{\pi/2} (\cos \theta)^s \, d\theta = \frac{(\pi/4)^{n/2}}{(n/2)!},$$

find an expression for the volume in momentum space of a system of N gas particles of mass m whose total energy is E.

7.3 Give examples of a change which occurs because of a removal of an inhibition in an isolated system.

7.4 Consider a system of three particles confined to the one-dimensional box of length $2L$ shown in Fig. 7.3. (a) Sketch the volume in the three-dimensional configuration space (i) if the three particles are confined to the left half of the box and (ii) if they are free to move anywhere within the box. (b) Compute the entropy increase from the volumes determined in (a).

7.5 Over a restricted range of temperatures near T_0, the energy E of a system of fixed volume V_0 and number of particles N_0 can be approximated by $E = E_0 + c(T - T_0)$, where c is a constant. Starting with Eq. (7.5–6), show that $S\{E, V_0, N_0\} = S\{E_0, V_0, N_0\} + c \ln \{1 + (E - E_0)/cT_0\}$.

7.6 Two systems, a and b, of identical composition are brought together and permitted to exchange both energy and particles, the volumes remaining constant. Determine the minimum value of the ratio dE_a/dN_a in terms of T_a, T_b, μ_a, and μ_b.

8

THE MOST PROBABLE MACROSTATE

8.1 The thermodynamic probability of a system of independent particles

In Chapter 7 we found that the logarithm of the thermodynamic probability was proportional to a new thermodynamic property called entropy, and that from a knowledge of the entropy as a function of the energy of the system we could find its absolute temperature. The existence of entropy as a property was deduced from our understanding of the dynamics of molecular motion, including quantum-mechanical effects. The only uses of entropy so far touched upon have been the determination of the absolute temperature and chemical potential and the connections between possible changes in an isolated system with increases in entropy. We shall find that there are many more uses of entropy, provided we are willing to make a more extensive study of the connection between changes in entropy and changes in other thermodynamic properties of a system. However, before engaging in these studies we will show how to determine the entropy quantitatively in terms of the characteristics of the motion of individual molecules. But in doing so, we must restrict our analysis to a *system of independent particles*, that is, a system in which the characteristics of the motion of one particle* are independent of the presence of other particles.

Our principal problem is to determine the volume $\mathcal{U}$ in Γ-space available to a system of total energy E or, what is equivalent, to determine the total number of microstates of a system of total energy E, volume V, and total number of particles, N. Considering the complexity of Γ-space, it is unlikely that we can determine the volume $\mathcal{U}$ as simply as we can find, for example, the volume of a sphere or ellipsoid. Instead, we shall try an indirect approach which makes use of some physical intuition but can be justified *a posteriori*.

Even though a system is in thermodynamic equilibrium, we know that each molecule is constantly changing its state of motion and the system is very rapidly passing through different microstates. Nevertheless, the most detailed

---

* In this context the particle may be a photon or phonon (see Section 15.4) as well as a molecule.

measurements which we can make on the laboratory scale, such as the distribution of energy among the various molecules or even gross measurements of temperature or pressure, show very little or no change with time. The macrostate, as well as the thermodynamic state, is found to be unchanging in time for an isolated system at thermodynamic equilibrium. (In fact, this is essentially our criterion for thermodynamic equilibrium.) Even though there are many possible macrostates of an equilibrium system with given E, V, and N, we are forced to conclude that we always observe only one of them. For this reason this macrostate is called the *most probable macrostate*. The thermodynamic properties in which we are interested should all be determinable from this most probable macrostate since they are but simple numbers and contain even less information than the macrostate description. We shall therefore attempt to determine the properties of the most probable macrostate.

Our basic postulate of statistical mechanics required that upon observing a system at a given instant of time, it be equally probable that it will be observed in one microstate as in another (just as it is as likely that we draw the jack of spades as the queen of hearts when picking a card at random from a deck of playing cards). Why is it that we always observe only one macrostate? It can only be that the number of microstates which belong to the most probable macrostate is so much greater than all the other possible microstates combined that it is highly unlikely we shall ever observe any of the latter group of microstates. The observation of only one macrostate is perfectly consistent with the assumption of equal likelihood of microstates as soon as we recognize that each macrostate corresponds to a class of microstates and that some classes may involve many more individuals than others.

There are many simple illustrations of this basic principle. The probability of drawing any ace from a deck of cards is four times as great as drawing the ace of spades. The probability of drawing any spade from a deck of cards is thirteen times as great as drawing the ace of spades. The more detailed the specification of an event, the less likely it is to be observed. The specification of a certain card corresponds to a microstate, while the specification of a class of cards (such as fives or spades) corresponds to a class of microstates or a macrostate. The different probabilities of drawing card hands (macrostates) is exactly the difference which makes card playing so interesting.

In defining a macrostate in Section 6.2, we divided μ-space (in which the location of N points determines a microstate of the system) into a large number of cells, each of which can be identified by an integer subscript j. Since the cells are of small dimension in phase space, all the N_j particles in each cell will have practically the same conjugate coordinates p_i, q_i. Furthermore, for a system of independent particles, the energy of each particle will be determined solely by its conjugate coordinates, so that all particles in the cell j will have nearly the same energy ϵ_j. If we specify the set of numbers N_j and thereby define a macrostate, there will be a volume v in Γ-space comprising all the microstates of the system which will satisfy this prescription of a macrostate. The probability w

of a macrostate can be defined in the same way as the total thermodynamic probability, namely, as the volume v in Γ-space divided by h^{fN}:

$$w \equiv v/h^{fN}, \qquad (8.1\text{–}1)$$

where w is the number of microstates of the system corresponding to a given macrostate or set of integers N_j. For each given set of integers, there will be a different value of w. We shall denote each possible set by the index k and the corresponding value of w by w_k.

The correspondence between a macrostate which is described by the distribution of representative points among arbitrary cells in μ-space and the volume v in Γ-space is most easily seen by considering a very simple example. Consider a system of three distinguishable particles, each of which can move in one dimension only. Let us ignore their momenta and consider Γ-space to be composed of the three position coordinates only. The μ-space consists of only one coordinate but has three points representing the three particles. This coordinate may be divided into equal parts or cells, as shown in Fig. 8.1. One possible macrostate, called A, would consist of all three particles in a single cell in μ-space. The corresponding cell in Γ-space shown in Fig. 8.1 is the three-dimensional cube A, whose coordinates correspond to the limiting coordinates of the three particles in the same cell. A second macrostate, B, having two particles in one cell and a third in another, is also shown in Fig. 8.1 with the corresponding cell in Γ-space. The probabilities w_A and w_B are the number of microstates or quantum cells of the system contained within the volumes v_A and v_B in Γ-space.

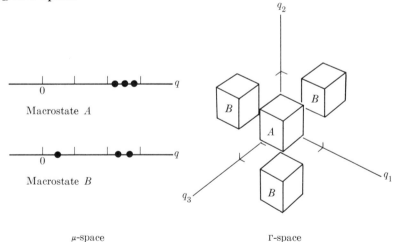

μ-space Γ-space

Fig. 8.1. The configuration volumes in Γ-space corresponding to macrostates defined by representative points in μ-space are shown for a system of three distinguishable particles which move along a line. The volume in Γ-space of macrostate B is not contiguous since it incorporates several different microstates.

Since there is a simple correspondence between a given macrostate and a corresponding volume in Γ-space, we might consider all of the accessible volume $\mathcal{V}$ in Γ-space to be divided up into portions, v_k, corresponding to each of the possible macrostates k. Each such subdivision will contain a very large number of the quantum-mechanical cells which are the basic building blocks of Γ-space. The number of such cells in each v_k is w_k. We might summarize this situation by saying that for each microstate of a system there is a cell in Γ-space of volume h^{fN}, while for each macrostate of a system there is a volume $w_k h^{fN}$. The largest of these latter volumes corresponds to the most probable macrostate and will be denoted by $k = 0$.

Of course, in defining a macrostate we must be careful to observe the restrictions (if any) on the coexistence of two molecules in the same quantum state, as discussed in Section 5.13. We shall therefore have to distinguish between results applicable to molecules obeying Bose-Einstein (B-E) statistics, in which any number of particles may exist in the same quantum state, and Fermi-Dirac (F-D) statistics, in which no more than one particle may exist in the same quantum state.

8.2 A simple example

For systems composed of only a few particles it is relatively easy to enumerate all the microstates and to classify them according to the macrostate to which each belongs. By so doing we can find the most probable macrostate as well as its thermodynamic probability w_0. In addition, the method of counting the number of microstates for systems with a larger number of particles will also become apparent.

Suppose we begin with a system composed of three identical particles, for each of which there is one quantum state of energy 0, another of energy 1, a third of energy 2, etc. Let us divide the μ-space into cells corresponding to the energies 0, 1, 2, etc., so that each cell contains only one quantum-mechanical state of a single particle. A macrostate will therefore be defined by specifying the number of particles in each energy cell which will be denoted by the subscripts 0, 1, 2, etc. Further, let us specify that the total energy of the system is 3. Within the restrictions of three particles and a total energy of 3, we would like to determine the various possible macrostates and their corresponding number, w_k, of microstates. In Table 8.1 are listed the three possible ways of distributing the particles among the various quantum states while still satisfying these restrictions. It can be seen that there are only three macrostates for each of which there is only one microstate, so that each macrostate is equally probable. The total thermodynamic probability is therefore 3.

In constructing Table 8.1, we have assumed it possible for two particles to exist in quantum state 0 for the distribution $k = 1$ and three in quantum state 1 for $k = 2$. The table is therefore correct only for a (B-E)-system. If (F-D)-statistics are applicable, then only the distribution $k = 0$ is permitted

Table 8.1. Microstates corresponding to macrostates k for a system of three particles having total energy 3 and one quantum state per cell j. Fermi-Dirac systems denoted by *.

	k			$\langle N_j \rangle$	$\langle N_j \rangle$*
	0*	1	2		
N_3	0	1	0	0.33	0
N_2	1	0	0	0.33	1.0
N_1	1	0	3	1.33	1.0
N_0	1	2	0	1.00	1.0

and the system will have a thermodynamic probability $W = 1$. Therefore, for a given energy and number of particles, (F-D)-systems will have fewer macrostates and microstates and hence smaller entropy than (B-E)-systems.

The results of Table 8.1 are not too interesting because we have restricted our example to a case in which there is but one particle-quantum state in each cell in μ-space. In our next example, suppose that for each energy 0, 1, 2, etc., there are two particle-quantum states. In this case, specifying the number of particles in each cell does not distinguish between different microstates because each particle within the cell can be in either of two quantum states which will correspond to a different microstate of the system. In Table 8.2 are listed all the possible microstates of our second system composed of three particles with total energy 3. The number of particles in each cell is given as the sum of two integers corresponding to the number of particles in each quantum state of the cell. There are 8 microstates in distribution $k = 0$, which has one particle in each of the first three cells; 6 microstates in the macrostate $k = 1$, for which one particle has energy 3 and the other two particles have energy 0; and 4 microstates in the macrostate $k = 2$, for which three particles have energy 1. Thus $k = 0$ is the most probable macrostate of the system, for which $w_0 = 8$. The total probability W is now 18, which is considerably greater than for the first case, having only one particle-quantum state per cell. For an (F-D)-system, only the microstates labeled with an asterisk are allowed, and therefore this W is less than that for a (B-E)-system.

The value of N_j averaged over all the microstates is called the *occupation number* of the cell j and is denoted by $\langle N_j \rangle$. To obtain this value for the systems in Tables 8.1 and 8.2, we sum the N_j in each row over all the columns and divide by the number of columns. The corresponding occupation numbers, starting with the lowest level, are also listed in Tables 8.1 and 8.2. The occupation numbers for the two cases considered are not very different even though the total number of microstates is considerably different. Also, the occupation number tends to decrease as j increases, that is for cells of higher energy. This is a particular example of a result which will later be found to be generally true.

Table 8.2. Microstates i corresponding to macrostates k for a system of three particles having total energy 3 and two quantum states per cell j. Fermi-Dirac systems denoted by *.

i	$k = 0$							
	1*	2*	3*	4*	5*	6*	7*	8*
N_3	0	0	0	0	0	0	0	0
N_2	$1 + 0$	$0 + 1$	$1 + 0$	$0 + 1$	$0 + 1$	$1 + 0$	$1 + 0$	$0 + 1$
N_1	$1 + 0$	$0 + 1$	$0 + 1$	$1 + 0$	$1 + 0$	$0 + 1$	$1 + 0$	$0 + 1$
N_0	$1 + 0$	$0 + 1$	$1 + 0$	$0 + 1$	$1 + 0$	$0 + 1$	$0 + 1$	$1 + 0$

i	$k = 1$							
	9	10	11	12	13*	14*		
N_3	$1 + 0$	$0 + 1$	$1 + 0$	$0 + 1$	$1 + 0$	$0 + 1$		
N_2	0	0	0	0	0	0		
N_1	0	0	0	0	0	0		
N_0	$2 + 0$	$2 + 0$	$0 + 2$	$0 + 2$	$1 + 1$	$1 + 1$		

i	$k = 2$						$\langle N_j \rangle$	$\langle N_j \rangle$*
	15	16	17	18				
N_3	0	0	0	0			0.33	0.2
N_2	0	0	0	0			0.44	0.8
N_1	$3 + 0$	$2 + 1$	$1 + 2$	$0 + 3$			1.11	0.8
N_0	0	0	0	0			1.11	1.2

We can see that it would be hopeless to continue an approach of this type for systems with many particles. Instead, we must seek a method of counting the number of microstates w_k for each macrostate by developing a general algebraic formula relating this number with the set of numbers N_j.

8.3 The probability w of a macrostate

Once we have divided μ-space arbitrarily into cells j of energy ϵ_j, we shall call the number of particle-quantum states within each cell C_j. This number depends on both the range of energies which are grouped together to form one energy cell and the nature of the particle in question, and its motion. However, having once fixed the mode of description of a macrostate, the ϵ_j and C_j are fixed quantities and only the N_j can be changed to specify different macrostates.

In order to find w, let us begin by concentrating our attention on one cell with N_j particles, each of which can be in any one of C_j quantum states. (We are assuming a (B-E)-system for the present.) In how many different ways, ω_j, can we assign the N_j indistinguishable particles to the C_j different quantum states? If we think of the C_j quantum states as boxes and the N_j particles as identical balls, then ω_j is the number of different ways of distributing the N_j identical balls among the C_j boxes.

In order to calculate ω_j, let us try the following thought experiment. Let us assign different numbers to all the boxes but one and to all the balls and then lay the boxes and balls down at random in a straight line. Since there are $C_j + N_j - 1$ differently numbered objects in this line, there are $(C_j + N_j - 1)!$ different ways in which this lineup may be accomplished.* Now the balls (molecules) are really indistinguishable so that their labels may be erased in this experiment by dividing the total number of ways of arranging the line by the smaller number of ways, $N_j!$, of arranging the N_j numbered balls among themselves. If we now consider the balls which follow any particular box in the line as the indistinguishable particles in that particular quantum state, then we have assigned all the particles to the quantum states, provided the first balls in the line are assigned to the odd box. Having put all the balls in their respective boxes, we notice that rearranging two boxes in the line does not correspond to a different microstate but only to a different order of the boxes in the line. We are therefore obliged to divide the total number of arrangements by the number of ways of rearranging the $C_j - 1$ boxes in the line, or $(C_j - 1)!$ Therefore, the corresponding value of ω_j is

B-E:
$$\omega_j = \frac{(C_j + N_j - 1)!}{(C_j - 1)!N_j!}. \tag{8.3–1}$$

The total number of microstates w will be the product of all the ω_j since each distinguishable assignment of the particles among the quantum states of a single cell gives rise to a new microstate:

B-E:
$$w = \omega_1 \cdot \omega_2 \cdot \omega_3 \cdots = \prod_j \omega_j$$

$$= \prod_j \left\{ \frac{(C_j + N_j - 1)!}{(C_j - 1)!N_j!} \right\}. \tag{8.3–2}$$

For an (F-D)-system there can never be more than one particle in each quantum state, so that N_j can never exceed C_j. To compute ω_j for this case, let us try the following thought experiment. Let us select N_j boxes from among

---

* There are $N_j + C_j - 1$ ways of placing the first object, $N_j + C_j - 2$ ways of placing the second, etc. The product of all these numbers is $(N_j + C_j - 1)!$

the C_j distinguishable ones and lay them down in a line. These will be the quantum states with one particle while the remainder will have no particles in them. The number of ways of accomplishing this line-up is just the number of combinations of C_j things taken N_j at a time, or $C_j!/(C_j - N_j)!$ Again we recognize that interchanging the identifiable boxes among one another in the line will not result in a different microstate. Therefore, this number must be divided by the number of ways of interchanging the N_j chosen boxes, or $N_j!$ Thus, for an (F-D)-system, ω_j becomes

F-D:
$$\omega_j = \frac{C_j!}{(C_j - N_j)!N_j!},$$
(8.3–3)

while the probability w is therefore

F-D:
$$w = \prod_j \left\{ \frac{C_j!}{(C_j - N_j)!N_j!} \right\}.$$
(8.3–4)

It has already been pointed out that for any practical description of a macrostate, the numbers N_j will be very large. For most practical systems, the number of quantum states of a particle within even the smallest cell which we might wish to define will also be very large. For these reasons, we can neglect the term 1 in Eqs. (8.3–1) and (8.3–2). Furthermore, the probability w will itself be very large and it will be much more convenient to use $\ln w$ rather than w itself. Consequently, we might write Eqs. (8.3–2) and (8.3–4) as

B-E:
$$\ln w = \sum_j [\ln (C_j + N_j)! - \ln C_j! - \ln N_j!],$$
(8.3–5)

F-D:
$$\ln w = \sum_j [\ln C_j! - \ln (C_j - N_j)! - \ln N_j!].$$
(8.3–6)

Now, the logarithm of the factorial of a very large number can be approximated in the following way. If we expand $\ln x!$ as a sum of logarithms, we obtain
$$\ln x! = \ln [x(x - 1)(x - 2) \cdots 3 \cdot 2 \cdot 1]$$
$$= \ln x + \ln (x - 1) + \cdots + \ln 3 + \ln 2.$$
(8.3–7)

The terms in this series contributing most to its sum are the leading terms. For these the difference in successive terms is very small, and we may approximate the series by replacing it by the integral

$$\ln x! \simeq \int_1^x \ln x \, dx \qquad (x \gg 1)$$

$$\simeq x \ln x - x.$$
(8.3–8)

A more accurate approximation is given by Stirling's formula:

$$\ln x! = x \ln x - x + \tfrac{1}{2} \ln x + \tfrac{1}{2} \ln (2\pi) + \cdots, \tag{8.3-9}$$

where each successive term on the right-hand side is smaller than the preceding term. In general, we will find that we need use only the first two terms to obtain sufficient accuracy.

By making use of this simplification for the logarithm of the factorial of a number, Eqs. (8.3–5) and (8.3–6) may be written as

B-E: $\quad \ln w = \displaystyle\sum_j \{(C_j + N_j) \ln (C_j + N_j) - C_j \ln C_j - N_j \ln N_j\}$

$$= \sum_j \{C_j[\ln (C_j + N_j) - \ln C_j] + N_j[\ln (C_j + N_j) - \ln N_j]\}$$

$$= \sum_j \left\{C_j \ln \left(1 + \frac{N_j}{C_j}\right) + N_j \ln \left(\frac{C_j}{N_j} + 1\right)\right\}; \tag{8.3-10}$$

F-D: $\quad \ln w = \displaystyle\sum_j \{C_j \ln C_j - (C_j - N_j) \ln (C_j - N_j) - N_j \ln N_j\}$

$$= \sum_j \left\{-C_j \ln \left(1 - \frac{N_j}{C_j}\right) + N_j \ln \left(\frac{C_j}{N_j} - 1\right)\right\}. \tag{8.3-11}$$

In this form $\ln w$ is nearly the same for either (B-E)- or (F-D)-systems except for the difference in algebraic sign of some terms. We shall therefore write $\ln w$ as

$\dfrac{\text{B-E}}{\text{F-D}}$: $\quad \ln w = \displaystyle\sum_j \left\{\pm C_j \ln \left(1 \pm \frac{N_j}{C_j}\right) + N_j \ln \left(\frac{C_j}{N_j} \pm 1\right)\right\}$

$$= \sum_j \left\{\pm C_j \left[\left(1 \pm \frac{N_j}{C_j}\right) \ln \left(1 \pm \frac{N_j}{C_j}\right) \mp \left(\frac{N_j}{C_j}\right) \ln \left(\frac{N_j}{C_j}\right)\right]\right\},$$

$$\tag{8.3-12}$$

where the upper sign in $\pm$ or $\mp$ refers to the (B-E)- and the lower to the (F-D)-system.

8.4 The most probable macrostate

The most probable macrostate is the one for which w is larger than for any other macrostate. We would like to determine the set of numbers N_j which will make w as large as possible for a system with given E, V, and N. Because the total energy E and number of particles N are fixed, we cannot choose the set N_j in any manner we please but only in such a way that

$$\sum_j N_j = N, \qquad (8.4\text{--}1)$$

$$\sum_j \epsilon_j N_j = E. \qquad (8.4\text{--}2)$$

To determine the maximum of a function we ordinarily set its differential equal to zero. In order to find the maximum of w or, what is just as good, the maximum of $\ln w$, we first find the differential of Eq. (8.3–12):

$$
\begin{aligned}
d(\ln w) &= \sum_j \left\{ \frac{\partial (\ln w)}{\partial N_j} \right\} dN_j \\
&= \sum_j \left\{ \pm \frac{C_j(\pm 1/C_j)}{1 \pm (N_j/C_j)} + \ln\left(\frac{C_j}{N_j} \pm 1\right) - \frac{C_j/N_j}{(C_j/N_j) \pm 1} \right\} dN_j \\
&= \sum_j \ln\left(\frac{C_j}{N_j} \pm 1\right) dN_j. \qquad (8.4\text{--}3)
\end{aligned}
$$

If we were to choose the changes dN_j at will, then $\ln w$ would be a maximum when each term in the series on the right-hand side of Eq. (8.4–3) is made zero by setting the coefficient of each dN_j equal to zero. However, the dN_j are restricted by the constancy of the total number of particles and energy as given by Eqs. (8.4–1) and (8.4–2). By differentiating each one of these equations, we find that the dN_j are restricted by

$$\sum_j dN_j = 0, \qquad (8.4\text{--}4)$$

$$\sum_j \epsilon_j \, dN_j = 0. \qquad (8.4\text{--}5)$$

For example, if the macrostate were specified by a set of 100 numbers N_j, then only 98 of them could be varied at will because of the two restrictive conditions on the total number of particles and energy.

There is a simple mathematical trick, due to Lagrange, by which we can find the maximum of $\ln w$ subject to the restrictions of Eqs. (8.4–1) and (8.4–2). If we multiply Eq. (8.4–4) by a constant α and (8.4–5) by a constant β and then subtract both from Eq. (8.4–3), we obtain

$$d(\ln w) = \sum_j \left\{ \ln\left(\frac{C_j}{N_j} \pm 1\right) - \alpha - \beta\epsilon_j \right\} dN_j. \qquad (8.4\text{--}6)$$

Let us now select the numbers α and β so that the first two terms in the series on the right-hand side are always zero.* If the derivative of the logarithm of w is to be zero, then the coefficient of the differentials dN_j in all the remaining terms must also be zero, since each of the remaining dN_j can be varied independently of each other. Thus, the requirement for every value of j is

$$\ln \left(\frac{C_j}{N_j^0} \pm 1 \right) - \alpha - \beta \epsilon_j = 0$$

or

$$\frac{\text{B-E}}{\text{F-D}} : \qquad\qquad \frac{N_j^0}{C_j} = \frac{1}{e^{\alpha + \beta \epsilon_j} \mp 1} , \qquad\qquad (8.4\text{--}7)$$

in which N_j^0 is the number of particles in the jth cell for the most probable distribution.

The numbers α and β, called the Lagrangian multipliers, can be found by specifying the number of particles in any two cells or, what is more pertinent to the problem at hand, they must be so chosen that the total number of particles and total energy have the assigned values N and E. Thus, if we substitute the most probable distribution, Eq. (8.4–7), into Eq. (8.4–1) and (8.4–2), we have

$$N\{\alpha, \beta\} = \sum_j \frac{C_j}{e^{\alpha + \beta \epsilon_j} \mp 1} , \qquad\qquad (8.4\text{--}8)$$

$$E\{\alpha, \beta\} = \sum_j \frac{\epsilon_j C_j}{e^{\alpha + \beta \epsilon_j} \mp 1} . \qquad\qquad (8.4\text{--}9)$$

While these equations are mathematically correct, they are, practically speaking, inconvenient because it appears to be hopeless to find α and β if E and N are given, whereas the reverse would be very simple. In Section 8.5, we shall attempt to find a physical interpretation for α and β, which, so far, are only mathematical quantities arising naturally in the determination of the most probable macrostate.

The difference in the most probable macrostates for (B-E)- and (F-D)-systems can best be shown by rearranging Eq. (8.4–7) in the form

$$e^\alpha \left(\frac{N_j^0}{C_j} \right) = \frac{1}{e^{\beta \epsilon_j} \mp e^{-\alpha}} , \qquad\qquad (8.4\text{--}10)$$

which is plotted in Fig. 8.2. For (B-E)-systems, α must always be positive if the right-hand side of Eq. (8.4–10) is not to become infinite or negative (if we assume for now that $\beta \epsilon_j$ is always positive). The upper unshaded area in Fig. 8.2 shows the region for all (B-E)-systems, since it is bounded by $\alpha = 0$ and ∞. However, for (F-D)-systems all values of α from $+\infty$ to $-\infty$ are permissible and lie within the lower shaded area of Fig. 8.2.

---

* This is a simpler procedure than solving Eqs. (8.4–4) and (8.4–5) for dN_1 and dN_2 and then substituting these values into Eq. (8.4–3) to eliminate dN_1 and dN_2 explicitly.

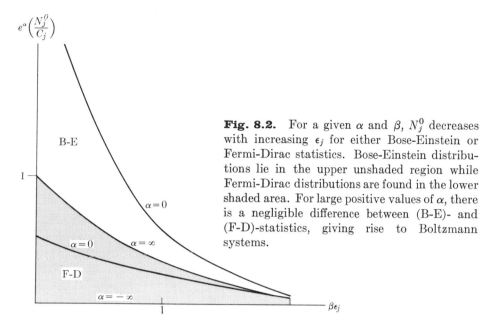

Fig. 8.2. For a given α and β, N_j^0 decreases with increasing ϵ_j for either Bose-Einstein or Fermi-Dirac statistics. Bose-Einstein distributions lie in the upper unshaded region while Fermi-Dirac distributions are found in the lower shaded area. For large positive values of α, there is a negligible difference between (B-E)- and (F-D)-statistics, giving rise to Boltzmann systems.

When α is very large and positive, the term $\pm e^{-\alpha}$ in the denominator of the right-hand side of Eq. (8.4–10) is very small compared with $e^{\beta\epsilon_j}$ and may be neglected. The distribution of particles in the most probable macrostate then becomes

$$N_j^0/C_j \simeq e^{-\alpha-\beta\epsilon_j}. \qquad (8.4\text{–}11)$$

Thus there is no distinction between (F-D)- and (B-E)-statistics when $\alpha \gg 0$. According to Eq. (8.4–11), $N_j^0/C_j \ll 1$, so that it is very unlikely that more than one particle will be found in the same quantum state, making the distinction between these statistics unnecessary. Systems for which $\alpha \gg 0$ are called *Boltzmann systems* because the distribution law of Eq. (8.4–11) was first derived by Boltzmann. We shall treat them as a separate class of systems because of the mathematical simplicity which ensues from the form of Eq. (8.4–11). For such systems, we do not need to know whether the particles conform to (B-E)- or (F-D)-statistics because the behavior of the system does not depend on such distinctions. Of course, we recognize that a Boltzmann system is simply a limiting case of an (F-D)- or (B-E)-system and does not belong to a different class of physical systems. For example, for perfect gases we shall be able to show that $\alpha \gg 0$ for all physically realizable situations and we therefore find it convenient to dispense with the problem of (B-E)- versus (F-D)-statistics and treat gases as Boltzmann systems.

Knowing what the numbers N_j^0 are for the most probable macrostate, we can now evaluate the logarithm of the probability w_0 for this macrostate by inserting Eq. (8.4–7) into Eq. (8.3–12) and using Eqs. (8.4–8) and (8.4–9) to replace the sums:

$$\ln w_0 = \sum_j \left\{ \pm C_j \ln \left[\frac{e^{\alpha+\beta\epsilon_j}}{e^{\alpha+\beta\epsilon_j} \mp 1} \right] + \frac{C_j \ln (e^{\alpha+\beta\epsilon_j})}{e^{\alpha+\beta\epsilon_j} \mp 1} \right\}$$

$$= \sum_j C_j \left\{ \frac{\alpha + \beta\epsilon_j}{e^{\alpha+\beta\epsilon_j} \mp 1} \mp \ln (1 \mp e^{-\alpha-\beta\epsilon_j}) \right\}$$

$$= \alpha N + \beta E \mp \sum_j C_j \ln (1 \mp e^{-\alpha-\beta\epsilon_j}). \qquad (8.4\text{--}12)$$

If we are given E and N, we can in principle determine α and β from Eqs. (8.4–8) and (8.4–9) and, by substituting this value of α and β into Eq. (8.4–12), we can then determine $\ln w_0$. Mathematically speaking, our problem is solved, yet, practically speaking, this is a very unsatisfactory state of affairs which we shall be obliged to resolve in Section 8.5.

However, before doing this, let us return to our original conjecture that the number of microstates, w_0, corresponding to the most probable macrostate is probably not very much different from the total number of microstates, W. If this is so, then there would be an even smaller difference between $\ln w_0$ and $\ln W$. As we pointed out in Section 7.3, this is a characteristic of the very large numbers with which we are dealing. In Section 8.9, we shall attempt to justify the assumption we now make, namely, that $\ln w_0$ and $\ln W$ are the same to any reasonable degree of accuracy. We may therefore determine the entropy S from the most probable distribution alone to be

$$S = k \ln w_0 = k \left[\alpha N + \beta E \mp \sum_j C_j \ln (1 \mp e^{-\alpha-\beta\epsilon_j}) \right]. \qquad (8.4\text{--}13)$$

8.5 The identification of α and β

As a result of our calculations so far, we have found the most probable macrostate and its thermodynamic probability but only at the expense of introducing two new parameters, α and β, which as yet bear no easily comprehended relation to the physical properties E, N, and S. While α and β were the result of a mathematical calculation, they may be interpretable in terms of physically measurable quantities. It is this interpretation for which we shall look. In so doing, we should bear in mind that the determination of the most probable macrostate was a mathematical operation that did not require the introduction of new physical laws, and we should therefore not expect α and β to be some hitherto undiscovered conserved quantities like mass, momentum, or energy but, rather, properties which are determinable only if the system is in thermodynamic equilibrium, i.e. in its most probable macrostate.

Let us now consider a change from one most probable macrostate to another in which only infinitesimally small changes dE, dN, and dS occur in the energy, number of particles, and entropy of the system. Accompanying this change there will probably be changes, $d\alpha$ and $d\beta$, in the unknown properties α and β. The changes in these five properties are not independent of one another, because the three equations, (8.4–8), (8.4–9), and (8.4–13), so relate these five quantities that only two of them may be varied independently.

If we consider the volume of our system and the forces acting on it to be fixed, then the quantum states of a molecule will be unchanged even though the system undergoes a change in thermodynamic state, since they depend only on the volume within which a molecule moves and the forces applied to it by particles outside the system. For this reason C_j and ϵ_j will remain unchanged.

Let us first determine the change in entropy accompanying this infinitesimal constant-volume change of state. To do this, we compute the total differential of Eq. (8.4–13), remembering that C_j and ϵ_j are constant in this process:

$$dS = k \left\{ \alpha \, dN + N \, d\alpha + \beta \, dE + E \, d\beta - \sum_j \frac{C_j e^{-\alpha - \beta \epsilon_j}(d\alpha + \epsilon_j \, d\beta)}{1 \mp e^{-\alpha - \beta \epsilon_j}} \right\}.$$

$$(8.5\text{–}1)$$

If we compare the last term on the right-hand side of this equation with Eqs. (8.4–8) and (8.4–9), we see that it is simply $-N \, d\alpha - E \, d\beta$ and therefore cancels the second and fourth terms of the right-hand side, leaving

$$dS = \beta k \, dE + \alpha k \, dN \qquad (V = \text{const}). \qquad (8.5\text{–}2)$$

In Section 7.6, we discussed the change in entropy due to a change in energy and number of particles for a system whose volume was fixed and found it to be

$$dS = \left(\frac{\partial S}{\partial E} \right)_{V,N} dE + \left(\frac{\partial S}{\partial N} \right)_{V,E} dN \equiv \frac{1}{T} \, dE - \frac{\mu}{T} \, dN, \qquad (8.5\text{–}3)$$

where the absolute temperature T and the chemical potential μ were defined in Eqs. (7.5–6) and (7.6–5). By comparing the preceding two equations, it is easy to see that β depends only on the temperature:

$$\beta = 1/kT, \qquad (8.5\text{–}4)$$

while α depends on both chemical potential and temperature:

$$\alpha = -\mu/kT. \qquad (8.5\text{–}5)$$

At this point, it is perhaps worth noting again that the intensive properties absolute temperature and chemical potential were first defined through the study of classical thermodynamics and their use has continued to this day through force of convention. The intensive properties α and β would be more convenient to use, together with the dimensionless entropy $\ln w_0$. That this is not done is a tribute to the powerful influence which historical processes exert even in such a rapidly changing field as science or engineering. We will bow to convention and consider temperature and chemical potential rather than α and β as the appropriate intensive thermodynamic properties defined in this change of state.

We may now rewrite Eqs. (8.4–7) through (8.4–9) and (8.4–13) in terms of T and μ as follows:

$$\frac{N_j^0}{C_j} = \frac{1}{\{e^{(\epsilon_j - \mu)/kT} \mp 1\}}, \tag{8.5–6}$$

$$N\{T, \mu; V\} = \sum_j \frac{C_j}{e^{(\epsilon_j - \mu)/kT} \mp 1}, \tag{8.5–7}$$

$$E\{T, \mu; V\} = \sum_j \frac{\epsilon_j C_j}{e^{(\epsilon_j - \mu)/kT} \mp 1}, \tag{8.5–8}$$

$$S\{T, \mu; V\} = \frac{E - \mu N}{T} \mp k \sum_j C_j \ln\left(1 \mp e^{(\mu - \epsilon_j)/kT}\right). \tag{8.5–9}$$

In these formulas, the temperature and chemical potential appear explicitly on the right-hand side, whereas the volume V appears implicitly in the C_j and ϵ_j. On the left-hand side, in listing the variables on which the quantity E, N, or S depends, the explicit variables appear first and the implicit follow the semicolon.

While we have succeeded in finding that α and β are related to temperature and chemical potential, we have not succeeded in reversing the form of Eqs. (8.5–7) and (8.5–8) so that the temperature and chemical potential would be given explicitly as functions of E, N, and V. We began by considering a system of fixed energy, volume, and number of particles and found that for an equilibrium system there were additional properties, namely, entropy, temperature, and chemical potential, which could be determined if the first three were known. The formulas we have developed require that a trial-and-error calculation be used to find μ and T if E and N are given. This is accomplished by guessing values of μ and T, inserting them in the right-hand side of Eqs. (8.5–7) and (8.5–8), computing E and N, and then making new and hopefully better guesses until the desired values of E and N are obtained. However, we will find that in certain simple cases, such as that of a monatomic perfect gas, it will be possible to evaluate these sums in closed form and then to solve for T and μ in terms of E and N.

It has been previously pointed out that the absolute value of the energy cannot be determined because one part of it, namely the potential energy, contains an arbitrary additive constant. It is easy to show that this arbitrariness will not affect any of the thermodynamic properties except E and μ.

Suppose we arbitrarily decide to measure the molecular energies from a new base line such that the new energy, ϵ_j', is greater than the old by a fixed amount, ϵ^0:

$$\epsilon_j' = \epsilon_j + \epsilon^0. \tag{8.5–10}$$

The total energy will therefore be increased by an amount $\epsilon^0 N$, or

$$E' = E + \epsilon^0 N. \tag{8.5-11}$$

Now, the chemical potential μ also has the dimensions of energy and should be increased by the same amount ϵ^0 if the N_j^0 given by Eq. (8.5–6) are to be unchanged by the redefinition of ϵ_j. Like energy, the absolute value of μ is unimportant, since only differences in μ cause the transfer of particles just as differences in temperature cause the transfer of energy. We therefore would have

$$\mu' = \mu + \epsilon^0. \tag{8.5-12}$$

By combining Eqs. (8.5–11) and (8.5–12), we also see that $E - \mu N$ remains unchanged:

$$E' - \mu' N = E - \mu N. \tag{8.5-13}$$

There will therefore be no change at all on the right-hand side of Eq. (8.5–9) so that the entropy is unaffected by the arbitrary choice of ϵ^0. The entropy has an absolute value (since it is a measure of the volume in phase space which can contain no arbitrary constant) whereas the energy does not. While only changes in energy will be seen to be important in practical applications, the absolute value of the entropy will be important in some problems, as shown in Chapter 14.

8.6 The partition function Z

There is a somewhat neater and more convenient way of writing the sums which appear on the right-hand side of Eqs. (8.5–7) through (8.5–9). This involves the definition of a *partition function Z* which is a sum similar to those appearing in these equations but with the special property that E, N, and S may be determined from it by partial differentiation. Such a function is called a potential function or generating function.

A word might be said here about the difference between a potential function and a potential. The first is a mathematical concept, while the second is a physical one. For example, the gravitational potential function is one such that its derivative gives the gravitational force exerted on a particle at that position:

$$F_x\{x\} = -\frac{\partial \phi\{x\}}{\partial x}. \tag{8.6-1}$$

There is a similar electrostatic potential function. On the other hand, a potential is a physically measurable quantity whose differences determine the direction of the transport of mass, energy, or momentum from one point in a system to another. For example, the temperature is a potential whose differences cause heat to flow; the voltage is a potential whose differences cause charge to flow. Similarly, the chemical potential is one whose differences cause particles to flow.

Potentials are useful because we can usually relate the rates of transport with the magnitude of the difference in potential, such as the rate of transport of charge, or current, with electric potential difference, or voltage. In thermodynamics, the practical significance of temperature and chemical potential is that they tell us when a system will remain at equilibrium. The rate at which the system approaches equilibrium can be determined only from much more extensive arguments than we have used heretofore.

Some of the thermodynamic functions themselves can be considered potential functions, provided they are expressed in terms of the proper independent variables. For example, the entropy S considered as a function of energy, volume, and number of particles, can be used to find the temperature:

$$\frac{1}{T} = \left(\frac{\partial S\{E, V, N\}}{\partial E}\right)_{V,N}. \tag{8.6-2}$$

For this reason, entropy can be called a thermodynamic potential function.

By pure trial and error, we can find a thermodynamic potential function Z from which E, N, and S may be obtained by differentiation:

$$Z\{T, \mu; V\} \equiv \mp \sum_j C_j \ln\left(1 \mp e^{(\mu-\epsilon_j)/kT}\right). \tag{8.6-3}$$

For example, if we hold V and T fixed, and allow only μ to change, we find

$$\left(\frac{\partial Z}{\partial \mu}\right)_{T,V} = \frac{1}{kT} \sum_j \frac{C_j e^{(\mu-\epsilon_j)/kT}}{1 \mp e^{(\mu-\epsilon_j)/kT}}$$

$$= \frac{N}{kT}, \tag{8.6-4}$$

where the sum has been recognized as the same as that in Eq. (8.5–7). By this means we find the following expressions for the thermodynamic properties:

$$N\{T, \mu; V\} = kT \left(\frac{\partial Z}{\partial \mu}\right)_{T,V}, \tag{8.6-5}$$

$$E\{T, \mu; V\} = kT^2 \left(\frac{\partial Z}{\partial T}\right)_{\mu,V} + \mu kT \left(\frac{\partial Z}{\partial \mu}\right)_{T,V}, \tag{8.6-6}$$

$$S\{T, \mu; V\} = kT \left(\frac{\partial Z}{\partial T}\right)_{\mu,V} + kZ. \tag{8.6-7}$$

The partition function has no physical significance whatsoever. It is simply a mathematical quantity which aids us in determining the thermodynamic functions more quickly and neatly in any practical case. It holds the same relation to thermodynamics as the velocity potential function holds to the fluid mechanics of incompressible flow; namely, it is a quantity of mathematical significance only, which enables us to find those quantities of direct physical significance. In contrast, the thermodynamic potential function $S\{E, V, N\}$ has both mathematical and physical significance, for it is both a potential function and a thermodynamic property, just as the gravitational potential function is both a potential function and a property (potential energy of a particle located at that point).

8.7 Boltzmann systems and the partition function Q

We have seen in Section 8.4 that if α is sufficiently large, and hence if μ/kT is a sufficiently large negative number, then the difference between (F-D)- and (B-E)-statistics is negligible.   Under such conditions the system is called a Boltzmann system, and its partition function Z may be found from Eq. (8.6–3) by making use of the fact that $\ln(1 + x) \simeq x$ when x is very small:

$$Z\{T, \mu; V\} = \mp \sum_j C_j \ln(1 \mp e^{(\mu-\epsilon_j)/kT})$$

$$= \sum_j C_j e^{(\mu-\epsilon_j)/kT} \qquad \text{if } \mu \ll -kT$$

$$= e^{\mu/kT} \sum_j C_j e^{-\epsilon_j/kT}. \tag{8.7–1}$$

The sum which appears on the right-hand side of Eq. (8.7–1) is now a function of temperature and volume alone, since the quantity $\exp(\mu/kT)$ can be factored from each term in the series.   The Boltzmann partition function $Q\{T; V\}$ is therefore defined as

$$Q\{T; V\} \equiv \sum_j C_j e^{-\epsilon_j/kT} \tag{8.7–2}$$

so that the relation between Z and Q is

$$Z\{T, \mu; V\} = e^{\mu/kT} Q\{T, V\}. \tag{8.7–3}$$

The corresponding approximations for Eqs. (8.5–7) through (8.5–9) are

$$N\{T, \mu; V\} = e^{\mu/kT} \sum_j C_j e^{-\epsilon_j/kT}, \tag{8.7–4}$$

$$E\{T, \mu; V\} = e^{\mu/kT} \sum_j \epsilon_j C_j e^{-\epsilon_j/kT}, \tag{8.7–5}$$

$$S\{T, \mu; V\} = \frac{E - \mu N}{T} + k e^{\mu/kT} \sum_j C_j e^{-\epsilon_j/kT}. \tag{8.7–6}$$

In terms of the Boltzmann partition function Q these become

$$N\{T, \mu; V\} = e^{\mu/kT}Q, \tag{8.7-7}$$

$$E\{T, \mu; V\} = e^{\mu/kT}kT^2 \left(\frac{\partial Q}{\partial T}\right)_V, \tag{8.7-8}$$

$$S = \frac{E - \mu N}{T} + ke^{\mu/kT}Q. \tag{8.7-9}$$

For Boltzmann systems it is possible to rearrange these formulas so that the roles of μ and N as independent and dependent variables are interchanged. To do this, we solve Eq. (8.7–7) for μ to obtain

$$\mu(N, T; V) = kT \ln\left(\frac{N}{Q}\right). \tag{8.7-10}$$

Substituting this expression into Eqs. (8.7–8) and (8.7–9), we find the energy and entropy as functions of the variables N, T, and V:

$$E\{N, T; V\} = \left(\frac{N}{Q}\right)kT^2 \left(\frac{\partial Q}{\partial T}\right)_V = NkT^2 \left(\frac{\partial \ln Q}{\partial T}\right)_V, \tag{8.7-11}$$

$$S\{N, T; V\} = \frac{E - NkT \ln (N/Q)}{T} + kN = \frac{E}{T} + Nk \ln\left(\frac{eQ}{N}\right)$$

$$= Nk \left(\frac{\partial}{\partial T}\left[T \ln\left(\frac{eQ}{N}\right)\right]\right)_V. \tag{8.7-12}$$

We shall have occasion to use these expressions for E and S when we study the properties of a perfect gas.

For the most probable macrostate of a Boltzmann system, the number N_j^0/C_j of particles per quantum state in the cell j was given in Eq. (8.4–11). By making use of Eqs. (8.5–4), (8.5–5) and (8.7–10), this may be put in the form

$$N_j^0/C_j = (N/Q)e^{-\epsilon_j/kT}. \tag{8.7-13}$$

By definition of a Boltzmann system, the ratio N_j^0/C_j is much less than unity. We may therefore simplify the expression for $\ln w$ given in Eq. (8.3–12) by noting that $\ln (1 + x) \simeq x$ for $x \ll 1$ and write the entropy of a Boltzmann system in the form

$$S = k \ln w_0 = k \sum_j \{N_j^0 + N_j^0 \ln (C_j/N_j^0)\}$$

$$= -k \sum_j C_j\{(N_j^0/C_j) \ln (N_j^0/eC_j)\}, \tag{8.7-14}$$

where terms as small as $(N_j^0/C_j)^2$ have been ignored. If Eq. (8.7–13) is substituted into the above, the resulting sum is found to equal the right-hand side of Eq. (8.7–12).

8.8 The classical Boltzmann partition function Q_{cl}

In the definition of Q, Eq. (8.7–2), we recall that C_j is the number of molecular quantum states in the cell j of μ-space. Since each quantum state in the cell j is considered to have the same energy ϵ_j, the sum Q can also be considered the sum of the quantity $e^{-\epsilon_j/kT}$ over all the quantum states of a single molecule; that is,

$$Q \equiv \sum_j C_j e^{-\epsilon_j/kT} = \sum_i e^{-\epsilon_i/kT}, \qquad (8.8\text{–}1)$$

where the subscript j identifies a cell in μ-space having C_j quantum states within it, while the subscript i identifies each of the possible quantum states in the same phase space.

If the differences in energies between adjacent quantum states of a molecule are sufficiently small compared with kT, then the successive terms in the sum of Eq. (8.8–1) will not be much different from each other and the sum could be replaced by an integral. The integral would cover the whole volume of μ-space, and its integrand would be simply $e^{-\epsilon/kT}$. The coordinates of μ-space are the f pairs of coordinates $p_1q_1; p_2q_2; \ldots ; p_fq_f$. The volume element for integration in μ-space would therefore be $dq_1\, dp_1\, dq_2\, dp_2 \cdots dq_f\, dp_f$, and the number of quantum states within this volume element would be its volume divided by h^f. Furthermore, the energy ϵ expressed as a function of the coordinates of μ-space is the Hamiltonian function $\mathcal{H}\{q_1, q_2, \ldots, q_f; p_1, p_2, \ldots, p_f\}$. The partition function evaluated from this integral under the assumption that it can replace the sum is called the *classical partition function** Q_{cl} and is given by

$$Q_{cl} = \frac{1}{h^f} \int \cdots \int \exp\left[-\mathcal{H}\{q_1, q_2, \ldots, q_f, p_1, p_2, \ldots, p_f\}/kT\right]$$
$$\times\, dq_1\, dp_1\, dq_2\, dp_2 \cdots dq_f\, dp_f. \qquad (8.8\text{–}2)$$

If we use this method of finding Q, we must be certain to check that the basic assumption

$$\epsilon_{i+1} - \epsilon_i \ll kT \qquad (8.8\text{–}3)$$

has not been violated.

In Chapter 12 we shall use this method for evaluating the partition function of a perfect monatomic gas. Furthermore, it is also helpful in treating imperfect gases.

---

* The modifier "classical" indicates that the same result could be obtained from classical mechanics, except for the factor h^{-f}.

8.9 The difference between ln W and ln w_0

In Section 8.4, we made the assumption that ln W and ln w_0 were numerically the same to a high degree of accuracy for systems with a large number of particles even though the number of microstates w_0 corresponding to the most probable macrostate is only a fraction of the total number of microstates W. Although there is a general method of proving the practical equality of ln w_0 and ln W, it is too complicated and lengthy to introduce here. Instead, we shall use a simple example which illustrates the principle.

Consider a simple system having a large number of particles, N, for which there is an even larger number of quantum states available, but each quantum state has the same energy. Thus the most probable distribution will have an equal number of particles per quantum state; that is, the ratio N_j^0/C_j is the same for each quantum state.

Let us now divide μ-space into two cells, each with an equal number C of quantum states. We will define a macrostate by saying that there are x particles in one cell and $N - x$ particles in the second cell. Using Eq. (8.3–12) and making use of the fact that C_j is much greater than N_j, we find

$$\ln w = \sum_j \{\pm C_j \ln (1 \pm N_j/C_j) + N_j \ln (C_j/N_j \pm 1)\}$$

$$\simeq \sum_j \{C_j(N_j/C_j) + N_j \ln (C_j/N_j)\} \simeq \sum_j N_j \ln C_j \simeq N \ln C, \qquad (8.9\text{–}1)$$

which is independent of x. For $x = N/2$, we would therefore have

$$\ln w_0 = N \ln C. \qquad (8.9\text{–}2)$$

Now there are in all only N possible macrostates, these being the ones whose number of particles in the respective cells are $0, N; 1, N - 1; \ldots; N, 0$. Since each macrostate has the same probability, $w = w_0$, the total probability W is the sum of all the w:

$$W = Nw_0$$

or

$$\ln W = \ln w_0 + \ln N. \qquad (8.9\text{–}3)$$

Dividing this equation by Eq. (8.9–2), we find

$$\frac{\ln W}{\ln w_0} = 1 + \frac{\ln N}{N \ln C}. \qquad (8.9\text{–}4)$$

It can be seen that the last term is always very small for large N and there is therefore very little difference between ln w_0 and ln W for this special case.

For a perfect monatomic gas, it is possible to compute ln W exactly because the constant-energy surface in momentum space is a hypersphere whose volume may be computed as in Section 7.3. For this case also, ln w_0 and ln W are negligibly different.

PROBLEMS

8.1 (a) Construct a table similar to Table 8.1 for a system of three particles having a total energy of 4 and one quantum state per cell j. (b) What is the difference in entropy of the system of part (a) and that of Table 8.1, assuming Bose-Einstein statistics hold for both? (c) If the spacing between energy levels is 10^{-15} erg, what is the average temperature of the two systems being compared?

8.2 (a) If the first three terms in the expansion of Eq. (8.3–9) are used to evaluate the terms in Eq. (8.3–5), find the corresponding expression for $\ln w$. (b) If $N_j \ll C_j$, what is the order of magnitude of the additional terms compared with those given in Eq. (8.3–10)?

8.3 By differentiating $\partial \ln w/\partial N_j$ in Eq. (8.4–6), show that $\ln w$ is a maximum (and not a minimum) for $N_j = N_j^0$, that is, for the most probable macrostate.

8.4 For each macrostate k shown in Tables 8.1 and 8.2, calculate w_k for the (B-E)-system from Eq. (8.3–2) and for the (F-D)-system from Eq. (8.3–4), and show that it agrees with the tabulated number of columns. (*Note:* $0! = 1$.)

8.5 (a) For the (B-E)-system treated in Table 8.2 for which $N = 3$, $E = 3$, and $C_j = 2$, show that $\alpha = 0.81$ and $\beta = 0.57$ satisfy the restrictions on N and E given by Eqs. (8.4–8) and (8.4–9). (b) For these same values of α and β, find from Eq. (8.4–7) the numbers N_1^0, N_2^0, ... for the most probable macrostate, and compare with the values for state $k = 0$ in Table 8.2. (c) Compute $\ln w_0$ from Eq. (8.4–13), and compare with the value obtained from Table 8.2.

8.6 A box of volume V contains N monatomic gas particles with total energy E and total momentum $\mathbf{P}$. (a) If the cell j in μ-space is characterized by a momentum $\mathbf{p}_j$ and an energy $p_j^2/2m$, find the most probable distribution for a Boltzmann system. [*Hint:* Use the scalar product of $\mathbf{P}$ and a vector Lagrange multiplier $\boldsymbol{\gamma}$ as an additional constraint in maximizing $\ln w$.] (b) Write the equations from which α, β, and $\boldsymbol{\gamma}$ may be found from the given E, N, and $\mathbf{P}$. (c) Show that the most probable distribution $N_j^0\{\mathbf{p}_j'\}$, expressed as a function of the momentum $\mathbf{p}_j' \equiv \mathbf{p}_j - \mathbf{P}/N$ measured relative to the motion of the mass center of the box, is the same as that for a stationary box (i.e., one for which $\mathbf{P} = 0$).

8.7 The constant-volume specific heat C_v is defined in Eq. (10.4–12) as $(\partial E/\partial T)_V$. (a) For a Boltzmann system, show that $C_v/Nk = \{\langle\epsilon^2\rangle - (\langle\epsilon\rangle)^2\}/(kT)^2$ in which the average energy per particle $\langle\epsilon\rangle \equiv \sum_j N_j^0\epsilon_j/N$ and the average square of the energy $\langle\epsilon^2\rangle \equiv \sum_j N_j^0\epsilon_j^2/N$. (b) Does the same relationship hold for (B-E)- or (F-D)-systems? (c) Using the results of part (a), compute the ratio $\{\langle\epsilon^2\rangle - (\langle\epsilon\rangle)^2\}^{1/2}/\langle\epsilon\rangle$ in terms of the thermodynamic properties C_v, N and E.

8.8 Show that

$$kZ = S + (\mu N - E)/T \quad \text{and} \quad Q = N\exp\left[-\{1 + E/NkT - S/Nk\}\right].$$

8.9 Obtain Eqs. (8.7–11) and (8.7–12) by substituting Eq. (8.7–3) into Eqs. (8.6–6) and (8.6–7).

8.10 Show that $\mu = \{\partial(E - TS)/\partial N\}_{T,V}$ by (a) using Eqs. (8.7–10) through (8.7–12) for Boltzmann systems and then (b) using Eqs. (8.6–5) through (8.6–7) for any system. [*Hint:* In part (b), $(\partial Z/\partial N)_{T,V} = (\partial Z/\partial\mu)_{T,V}/(\partial N/\partial\mu)_{T,V}$.]

8.11 Assuming that the partition function Q can be approximated by the integral of Eq. (8.8–2), find an integral expression for E.

8.12 Develop an integral expression for Z which is valid whenever the differences in energy between adjacent quantum states is very small compared with kT.

8.13 The macrostate of a system of slightly interacting particles may be described by the number of representative points per unit volume of μ-space, denoted by $\rho\{q_1, p_1, q_2, p_2, \ldots, q_f, p_f\}$, provided that ρ may be considered a continuous function. (a) For a Boltzmann system, show that $\ln w = \int \cdots \int \rho \ln (e/h^f \rho)\, dq_1\, dp_1 \cdots dq_f\, dp_f$. (b) Find an equivalent expression for $\ln w$ for a (B-E)- or (F-D)-system. (c) Write N in terms of an integral over μ-space.

8.14 A system of volume V consists of N particles for each of which there are only two quantum states having energies 0 and ϵ, respectively. (a) For a Boltzmann system find the partition function Q and energy E as a function of ϵ, T, and N. Plot curves of Q and $E/N\epsilon$ as a function of kT/ϵ. (b) For a (B-E)-system, find N and E as functions of μ, ϵ, and T. Sketch a curve of $E/N\epsilon$ as a function of $e^{\mu/kT}$.

9

WORK AND HEAT

9.1 Interactions between a system and its environment

In Chapter 2 we dealt with systems of particles. When the forces exerted on each particle of the system were due only to other particles in the system (isolated system), then it was found that the linear momentum, angular momentum, and total energy were unchanging in time. The total energy, which was the sum of the kinetic energy and the potential energy, was determined entirely by the coordinates and momenta of all the particles in the system. If the linear and angular momenta are zero, this energy is called the *internal energy* of the system. Our determination of the most probable macrostate was predicated upon the conservation of mass and internal energy of an isolated system.

If there are forces which are exerted on the molecules of a system by molecules outside the system, then we must consider the possibility of interactions between the system and its environment. One of the important aspects of thermodynamics is the study of such interactions. When the system is (or can be considered to be) composed of only one or two particles, then its interaction with other systems or its environment can be treated from the point of view of particle dynamics. Thus we can study the motion of the planets about the sun, the collision of two molecules, the motion of a ball rolling down an inclined plane, or the motion of a projectile. If the system is composed of a very large number of molecules, then its motion is studied separately from (but not independently of) the study of its energy. A study of the motion, such as fluid mechanics, is concerned primarily with the changes in momentum of groups of particles, whereas a study of the energy of such systems, which is included in thermodynamics, is concerned with the relationship between changes in internal energy and in other thermodynamic properties of the system. For example, in studying the motion of propellant gases in a rocket engine, fluid mechanics will relate the changes in velocity of the fluid flow to its density and changes in pressure, while thermodynamics will relate the changes in pressure and density to those of chemical composition and temperature. We must therefore be prepared to understand how a system composed of a very large number of particles can interact with its environment.

Since our interest is primarily in thermodynamics, we shall be concerned with interactions which produce changes in thermodynamic properties such as internal energy, temperature, entropy, and chemical composition. We shall find it convenient to specify quantitatively and qualitatively the amount of an interaction in terms of two quantities, *work* and *heat*. We shall also find that work and heat are distinguishable only on the laboratory scale but become identical when dealing with single particles. The distinction between work and heat is fundamental to classical thermodynamics and is absolutely essential to any application of thermodynamics to practical problems such as the generation of electrical power from the combustion of fuels. Since work and heat are so important, we will spend considerable time relating them to what we have discussed in previous chapters. We shall do this by beginning with a study of interactions from the microscopic point of view, that is, one in which we deal with the forces between individual molecules. By averaging over large groups of molecules, the results of this study may be extended to the macroscopic, or laboratory, scale. We shall use the adjectives "microscopic" and "macroscopic" wherever necessary to differentiate these points of view.

9.2 Short- and long-range intermolecular forces

In the study of dynamics, we become familiar with the concepts of body forces and contact forces. The former are those which are exerted on a body from a distance, such as the gravitational attraction of the earth by the sun, or the attraction of iron filings by a magnet. The latter are those which occur when two bodies collide with each other or are in contact with each other, as when a ball bounces on the floor or rolls along a table. This intuitive classification corresponding to observably different types of interaction can be related to a classification on the microscopic scale of *short-* and *long-range* forces. A long-range force acting between two molecules is one such that a large collection of one type of particle will be found to exert a force at a distance comparable with the size of the collection. A short-range force is one for which an effect is felt only at much smaller distances.

Another way to understand the distinction between short-range and long-range forces is to consider the force on a type-A particle, which is a fixed distance a away from the surface of a sphere composed of many type-B particles, as shown in Fig. 9.1. If the sphere is made larger and larger, while the density of particles remains the same, then the force on particle A will tend to increase. If the force exerted on A by a type-B particle is a long-range force, then the total force exerted by the B-particles will become infinite as the radius of the sphere also becomes infinite. On the other hand, if the force is a short-range one, then the total force on particle A will approach a fixed value as the radius of the sphere becomes infinite. An example of a long-range force is the gravitational

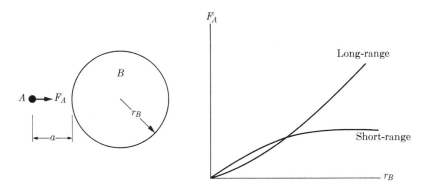

Fig. 9.1. The force between a particle, A, held at a fixed distance a from the surface of a sphere, B, of given density, can be called a long-range or short-range force, depending on whether it approaches a finite limit as the sphere radius approaches infinity.

attraction which varies inversely with the square of the distance between the particles. The more massive the planet on which a man stands, the greater the force of gravity which he feels. A typical short-range force, on the other hand, is the force on a gas molecule striking the wall of a container. No matter how thick the wall of the container, the force is felt only while the molecule is very close to the surface and not while it is in the center of the container.

It is relatively easy to demonstrate the difference between short-range and long-range forces by considering inverse-power forces, that is, forces between two particles whose magnitude is inversely proportionate to some power of the distance between them. For example, let the repulsive force between two particles be given by

$$F_r = \mathfrak{F}(l/r)^s, \tag{9.2-1}$$

where F_r is the magnitude of the repulsive force which has the value $\mathfrak{F}$ when the particles are a distance l apart. If s is large, then the repulsion dies off rapidly with distance, and the force will be short-range. If s is small, then the force extends out to a considerable distance and will be a long-range force. We shall try to determine the value of s which distinguishes a long-range from a short-range force.

Consider an A-molecule which is a distance a from an infinite sphere having n type-B molecules per unit volume. Using the coordinate system of Fig. 9.2, let us sum the force on molecule A due to all the molecules B. First, all the B-molecules in the ring of radius $r \sin \theta$ and cross section $r\, d\theta\, dr$ are an equal distance r from the molecule A and therefore exert the same force as given by Eq. (9.2–1). The net force exerted by all the particles in this ring is therefore the number of particles in the ring times the force of Eq. (9.2–1) times $\cos \theta$, since only the component normal to the surface of the sphere will not cancel out

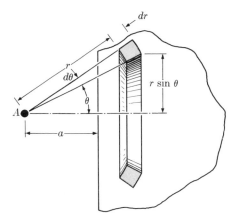

Fig. 9.2. The element of volume of a semi-infinite solid which exerts a force on particle A is a ring of radius $r \sin \theta$ and cross-sectional area $r\, d\theta\, dr$, having a volume $(2\pi r \sin \theta)r\, dr\, d\theta$.

in the vector addition of the forces. Thus, the total force of repulsion will be

$$
\sum F_r = \int_{\theta=0}^{\pi/2} \int_{r=a/\cos\theta}^{r=\infty} \left[\mathfrak{F}\left(\frac{l}{r}\right)^s \cos\theta \right] n(2\pi r \sin\theta) r\, d\theta\, dr
$$

$$
= 2\pi n \mathfrak{F} l^s \int_0^{\pi/2} \cos\theta \sin\theta \left[\int_{a/\cos\theta}^{\infty} r^{2-s}\, dr \right] d\theta, \qquad (9.2\text{--}2)
$$

where the lower limit of the integration on r depends on the angle θ. Now unless s is larger than 3, the integration on r will diverge, since the indefinite integral is proportional to r^{3-s} (or $\ln r$, if $s = 3$), which has an infinite value at $r = \infty$. Thus, if s is greater than 3, we would have a short-range force, whereas for $s \leq 3$, the force would be considered long-range. Since $s = 2$ for gravitational and electrostatic forces, these are necessarily long-range.

For the short-range forces ($s > 3$), Eq. (9.2–2) may be integrated to give

$$
\sum F_r = \frac{2\pi}{(s-3)(s-1)} \left(\mathfrak{F}\left(\frac{l}{a}\right)^s \right) \cdot (na^3). \qquad (9.2\text{--}3)
$$

Except for the small factor in front, the total force equals the force between two particles separated by a distance a times the number of B-particles in a volume a^3. For the short-range inverse power forces, only the molecules nearest particle A will contribute to the repulsion or attraction. However, for long-range forces even the particles far away have a cumulative effect which overpowers that of the nearby particles.

Since short-range forces are felt only over very small distances, we may sum all the forces acting on the molecules of a system very close to its surface due to nearby molecules outside the system and consider them to be a macroscopic surface force, or *stress*. In Fig. 9.3 is shown a volume element of a system at the surface. The particles within this volume element near the surface feel the stronger repulsive force, whereas those farther away from the surface feel a

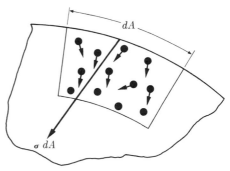

Fig. 9.3. The surface stress σ is determined by summing all the forces acting on particles within a volume near the surface and dividing by the surface area of the volume element. The surface stress is not necessarily normal to the surface.

much smaller force. If we sum all the forces within the volume element, the net force will be proportionate to the surface area. We can define a *surface stress* σ as the ratio of total force to area. The surface stress is a macroscopic quantity, since it is the force per unit area of surface averaged over a large number of molecules near the surface. In Section 9.3, we will consider in greater detail the determination of the surface stress, or pressure, for a gas. The surface stress is an example of a contact force, since it is applied to those particles at or near the contact surface between two different bodies (the gas and its container, for example).

Long-range forces are usually found by utilizing the concept of a *force field*. For example, we say that the particles outside the system cause an electrostatic or gravitational field and that the particles inside the system are acted upon by a force which is proportionate to the local value of the field. Because of the great usefulness of the concept of a field of force, this is undoubtedly a convenient way to treat long-range forces. We shall deal with an example of such a force in Section 9.4 when we consider a case of an electrostatic body force.

9.3 Pressure in a gas

As an example of the calculation of a surface stress resulting from short-range forces between the molecules inside and outside of a system, let us compute the pressure, or normal force per unit area, exerted on a gas by its container. To simplify our calculation, we will assume that the forces between the gas particles are so small that the average potential energy of these forces is everywhere negligible compared with the average kinetic energy of the gas particles. A gas of this type is called an *ideal* or *perfect gas*.

Consider a cylindrical element of volume of the gas whose base, of area dA, is the inner surface of the container and which extends inward into the gas. For any gas molecule inside this cylinder, the repulsive force exerted by the wall molecules will depend only on the distance x from the surface of the wall.

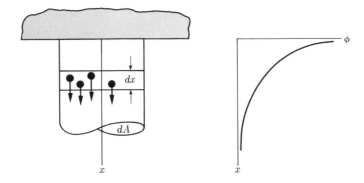

Fig. 9.4. The total force on the particles of a gas within a volume $dx \, dA$ located at a distance x from the surface of the container can be determined if the potential energy ϕ of a single particle is known as a function of the distance from the surface.

If F_x is this force and ϕ is the corresponding potential energy, then

$$F_x = -d\phi/dx. \tag{9.3-1}$$

A typical potential energy curve is shown in Fig. 9.4.

Now consider a slab of the cylinder of base area dA and thickness dx, situated at a distance x from the wall. If $n\{x\}$ is the number of molecules per unit volume in this slab, then the total force $\sum F$ exerted by the wall on all the molecules within this slab will be

$$\sum F = F_x n \, dx \, dA. \tag{9.3-2}$$

If this force is summed over the whole cylinder, the sum will be the surface stress, or pressure p, times the area, dA:

$$p \, dA = \int_{x=0}^{\infty} F_x n \, dx \, dA$$

or

$$p = -\int_{x=0}^{\infty} n \frac{d\phi}{dx} \, dx = -\int_{\infty}^{0} n \, d\phi = \int_{0}^{\infty} n \, d\phi, \tag{9.3-3}$$

where Eq. (9.3-1) has been used to replace the force by the derivative of potential energy and the integration has been changed from an integration on x to an integration on ϕ.

We must next determine the number of particles per unit volume $n\{\phi\}$ at a point in space where the potential energy is ϕ. If our system may be considered a Boltzmann system (and we shall see later that this is always possible for a perfect gas), then the number of particles dN in an element of volume $dx \, dy \, dz \, dp_x \, dp_y \, dp_z$ in μ-space is found from Eq. (8.7-13) to be $(N/Q)e^{-\epsilon/kT}$

times the number of quantum states in the element, namely its volume divided by h^3. Since ϵ is $(p_x^2 + p_y^2 + p_z^2)/2m + \phi$, we have

$$dN = h^{-3} \frac{N}{Q} \exp\left[-\frac{\{(p_x^2 + p_y^2 + p_z^2)/2m + \phi\}}{kT} \right] dx\, dy\, dz\, dp_x\, dp_y\, dp_z.$$

$$(9.3\text{-}4)$$

The number density $n\{\phi\}$ can be found by integrating dN over all values of the momentum components and dividing by the configuration volume $dx\, dy\, dz$ to obtain

$$n = h^{-3} \frac{N}{Q} e^{-\phi/kT} \iiint \exp\left[-\frac{p_x^2 + p_y^2 + p_z^2}{2mkT} \right] dp_x\, dp_y\, dp_z. \quad (9.3\text{-}5)$$

Except in a thin layer near the wall, ϕ is zero. If we integrate Eq. (9.3–5) over the whole volume V of configuration space, assuming ϕ to be zero everywhere, we obtain

$$N = h^{-3} \frac{N}{Q} V \iiint \exp\left[-\frac{p_x^2 + p_y^2 + p_z^2}{2mkT} \right] dp_x\, dp_y\, dp_z. \quad (9.3\text{-}6)$$

Dividing Eq. (9.3–5) by Eq. (9.3–6), we therefore find

$$n = (N/V)e^{-\phi/kT}. \quad (9.3\text{-}7)$$

Thus the local particle number density n is everywhere the same in the bulk of the gas but becomes less near the wall where ϕ is no longer zero. Because of the repulsive forces at the wall, fewer particles have the kinetic energy necessary to penetrate this repulsive field and the local density is therefore less.

We are now able to evaluate the pressure given in Eq. (9.3–3) by using the number density given by Eq. (9.3–7):

$$p = \int_0^\infty \left(\frac{N}{V}\right) e^{-\phi/kT}\, d\phi = \frac{NkT}{V} \int_0^\infty e^{-\phi/kT}\, d\left(\frac{\phi}{kT}\right) = \frac{NkT}{V}$$

or

$$pV = NkT. \quad (9.3\text{-}8)$$

We thus arrive at the well-known equation of state of a perfect gas, which embodies the empirical laws of Boyle and Charles.

For the particular case of a perfect gas, we have found the surface stress by summing all the repulsive forces over all the molecules of the gas lying within a small layer near the surface. The thickness of this layer is approximately the distance away from the solid wall at which the repulsive potential ϕ becomes small compared with kT, which at room temperature would be a distance of several angstroms. Furthermore, the pressure is independent of the form of $\phi\{x\}$ for this case; that is, the type of wall molecule does not affect the pressure of the gas. We will be able to show this in a more general way in Section 9.5.

9.4 Body forces on charged particles in an electrostatic field

As an example of long-range forces, consider the Coulomb repulsion between two charged particles of charge q_1 and q_2 separated by a distance r:

$$F_r = \frac{q_1 q_2}{4\pi\epsilon_0 r^2},\qquad(9.4\text{–}1)$$

in which ϵ_0 is the electric permittivity of free space.

As a particular example, suppose we have two large parallel plates separated by a small distance d, each plate having equal but opposite charge of q/A per unit area uniformly distributed over the surface. We shall first determine the force on a charge q_1 located between the plates at a distance a from the right-hand plate (see Fig. 9.5).

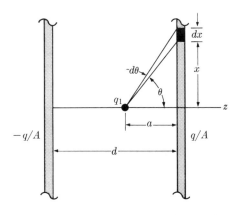

Fig. 9.5. The force on a charge q_1 at a distance a from one of two parallel infinite plates of equal but opposite charge, q/A, per unit area is found by summing the contributions of concentric rings of radius x and width dx.

If we first consider all the surface charge lying on a ring of radius x and width dx, all these charges will be at the same distance r from the charge q_1 and will therefore exert equal repulsive forces. Since only the component of the repulsive force in the z-direction will not cancel out due to symmetry, the repulsive force from all these charges will be

$$dF_r = \frac{q_1(q/A)(2\pi x\, dx)}{\epsilon_0 r^2}\cos\theta,\qquad(9.4\text{–}2)$$

in which $2\pi x\, dx$ is the area of the ring and the factor $\cos\theta$ accounts for the component of the repulsive force in the z-direction. Now x, r, and θ are related by

$$x = a\tan\theta,$$
$$dx = a\sec^2\theta\, d\theta,\qquad(9.4\text{–}3)$$
$$r = a\sec\theta.\qquad(9.4\text{–}4)$$

Inserting these into Eq. (9.4–2) and integrating over the whole plate, we obtain the net repulsive force:

$$F_r = \int_0^{\pi/2} \frac{q_1(q/A)(2\pi a^2 \tan\theta \sec^2\theta)\cos\theta \, d\theta}{4\pi\epsilon_0 a^2 \sec^2\theta}$$

$$= \frac{q_1}{2\epsilon_0}\left(\frac{q}{A}\right)\int_0^{\pi/2} \sin\theta \, d\theta$$

$$= \frac{q_1 q}{2\epsilon_0 A}. \tag{9.4--5}$$

The total repulsive force is independent of the distance between the charge q_1 and the plate. It does not decrease rapidly with distance from the plate because of the long-range nature of the Coulomb repulsive force.

There will be an equal force of attraction toward the opposite plate, so that the total force acting on the charge q_1 in the z-direction would be

$$F_z = -\left(\frac{q}{\epsilon_0 A}\right)q_1, \tag{9.4--6}$$

which is independent of where the particle is located between the two plates. The corresponding potential energy ϕ would therefore be

$$\phi\{z\} = \left(\frac{q_1 q}{\epsilon_0 A}\right)z. \tag{9.4--7}$$

It is customary to treat electrostatic problems of this type by means of field theory. The electric field **E** is determined from the distribution of charges on the plates and then the force on the charge q_1 is equal to the product of q_1 and **E**. For the reader familiar with electrostatic field theory, the coefficient of q_1 in Eq. (9.4--6) can be seen from Gauss' theorem to be simply the electric field between the two parallel plates of equal but opposite charge q and area A. For our purposes it is immaterial which method is used to determine the force on a particle of a system provided the distinction between long-range and short-range forces is clearly understood.

9.5 Microscopic work

In the study of particle dynamics, some ambiguity concerning the definition of work usually arises because it is not always clear which forces are to be included in the integral $\int \mathbf{F} \cdot d\mathbf{r}$. To illustrate this ambiguity, let us consider the simple case of a particle moving in the gravitational field of the earth. If the particle drops freely, the only force acting on the particle is the gravitational force directed downward. If we integrate the equation of motion, as was done in Section 2.6, we can then say that the increase in kinetic energy of the particle is equal to the work done by the gravitational force. From this point of view, we consider the particle as a system subject to a force produced by particles outside the system (the earth) and in the interaction the energy of the system can be changed by virtue of these forces. However, another point of view can be adopted if we realize that the gravitational force is a potential force and that the system of the particle plus the earth has a potential energy depending only on the relative positions of the particle and the earth. Considering the earth and the particle as a system, we would then state that since no forces are exerted on our system by particles outside the system, there is no work done and the sum of the kinetic plus potential energies is a constant. Both of these points of view are equally valid; they arise from the difference in choice of the system to which an energy statement is to be applied.

The ambiguous use of the word "work" arises only when we begin to introduce the common or everyday meaning for the word. If a man lifts a 20-lb weight from the floor to a table, he says he has done some work in lifting the weight. If we consider the weight as a system, the force required to lift it is equal and opposite to the gravitational force so that the net force is zero. Therefore, the integral of the net force exerted on the system by all matter external to it times the displacement of the system is zero. From the point of view of mechanics, we would say that there is no work done and no change in kinetic energy. (The potential energy is a property of the weight and the earth and should not be ascribed to the weight alone.) If we consider the weight as the system, then dynamics would properly say that work is done when the weight falls freely and work is not done when the weight is lifted from the floor to the table, which is exactly the opposite of what our intuitive notion of work would tell us concerning these two processes. From a practical point of view, the intuitive notion of work is often the more interesting to us.

We might attempt to remove this ambiguity by differentiating between the work done by the various kinds of forces acting on a system. For the freely falling weight, we could say that there is work done by the gravitational force. For the weight lifted from the floor, we could say that there is work done by the gravitational force and work done by the contact force which is exerted by our fingers on the weight. We might then be tempted to identify the intuitive notion of work with contact forces, or short-range forces, as distinct from long-range forces, yet we know that we could lift a nail from the floor with a magnet so that we can indeed do ordinary work with long-range forces. This certainly cannot be the distinction we are trying to discover.

If you stretch a spring by grasping one end in your left hand and one end in your right hand and extending both arms, our understanding of mechanics would tell us that the work done in stretching the spring does not depend on how far each end of the spring was stretched, but only on the total extension of the spring. Nevertheless, we know that there is a difference between holding the left end fixed while moving the right end and holding the right end fixed while moving the left end. In the first case, we say our right arm does the work; in the second case, our left arm. It would seem useful to so define work that this distinction can be made.

In order to define work in a way which will conform most closely with our intuitive notion, let us first return to the discussion of the interaction of a system of particles with other particles outside the system, as developed in Section 2.9. For the case where all the forces are conservative, we were able to show that the energy integral of all the particles in the system was given by

$$\left\{ T'\{v'_j\} + U'\{r'_j\} + \Phi'\{r'_j - r'_e\} \right\} - \left\{ T\{v_j\} + U\{r_j\} + \Phi\{r_j - r_e\} \right\}$$

$$= -\sum_j \sum_e \int_{r_e, r_j}^{r'_e, r'_j} \mathbf{F}_{ej} \cdot d\mathbf{r}_e. \qquad (9.5\text{--}1)$$

Here $T\{v_j\}$ was the total kinetic energy of all the particles in the system and therefore depended on the velocities of the particles; $U\{r_j\}$ was the potential energy due to the conservative forces acting between the particles of the system and therefore depended on the position vectors r_j of all the particles; and $\phi\{r_j - r_e\}$ was the interaction potential energy due to the conservative forces acting between the particles of the system and those outside the system whose positions were given by the vectors r_e. If we fix the positions of all the particles external to the system, then this equation would state that the sum of the kinetic energy plus internal potential energy plus interaction potential energy was constant. On the other hand, if there is some motion in the environment, then there will be in general some change in the total energy, $T + U + \phi$. Denoting this total sum by E, we could write the above equation in differential form:

$$E(v_j, r_j, r_e) \equiv T + U + \phi, \qquad (9.5\text{--}2)$$

$$dE = -\sum_e \sum_j \mathbf{F}_{ej} \cdot d\mathbf{r}_e. \qquad (9.5\text{--}3)$$

We will take as the fundamental definition of *microscopic work* W_μ the following:

$$dW_\mu \equiv \sum_e \sum_j \mathbf{F}_{ej} \cdot d\mathbf{r}_e. \qquad (9.5\text{--}4)$$

The microscopic work is therefore defined as the scalar product of the force exerted by the system on the environment times the displacement of the environment. This is in accordance with a long-standing thermodynamic convention that work done by a system is positive, while work done on a system is negative.

If we adopt this definition of work, we are now able to resolve the ambiguities previously raised. If a weight falls in a gravitational field, there is no motion of the molecules outside the system and therefore no work is done. By Eq. (9.5–3), the sum of the kinetic plus interaction potential energy must therefore be constant. If you lift a weight, the product of the force on your hand times the distance it moves gives a finite negative work and the potential energy U increases by a like amount. Finally, if you stretch a spring between your two hands, the work done by your right and left hand is easily distinguished in the sum of Eq. (9.5–4).

The microscopic work defined above is the sum of all the work done on the molecules of the environment. It is related to the change in total energy E of the system by

$$E' - E = -\int dW_\mu$$

or

$$dE = -dW_\mu. \tag{9.5–5}$$

Now the change in total energy E depends only on the initial and final values of the momenta and positions of all the molecules in the system and the positions of all the molecules in the environment and is therefore independent of the details of the process by which these changes come about. On the other hand, $\mathbf{F}_{ej} \cdot d\mathbf{r}_e$ cannot be evaluated between the initial and final values of $\mathbf{r}_e$ unless we know the point-by-point pair of position vectors $\mathbf{r}_j$ and $\mathbf{r}_e$, for it is this pair that determines the force $\mathbf{F}_{ej}$. Any one term in the sum of dW_μ can therefore be determined only if we know all the details of the motion of the molecules inside the system and in the environment. Nevertheless, Eq. (9.5–5) states that the sum of all the parts of the microscopic work is the same for any given change of microstate of the system and its environment, independent of the process by which this change was brought about.

A macroscopic example of this statement is the stretching of a spring. The change in total energy E depends only on the total stretch in the spring. The work done by the left hand and the right hand depends on the process used to stretch the spring, that is, the respective movements of the right and left hands. Nevertheless, the sum of the work done by the right and left hands is always the same for a given total stretch in the spring. Thus it is the difference in the parts of the total work which distinguishes one process from another producing the same net change in the system.

9.6 Interaction energy

The part of the total energy E which is due to the forces exerted between the molecules of the system and the molecules of the environment is the interaction potential energy ϕ in Eq. (9.5–1). This potential energy depends only on the relative positions of the particles inside and outside the system. It is that portion of the total energy which depends on the nature and position of the particles outside the system that distinguishes it from the remaining portions of the total energy, namely, the kinetic energy T and the potential energy U of all the molecules of the system interacting with each other. The interaction energy may be a small or large effect, depending on the system and the nature of the forces acting between the system and its environment. For short-range forces the interaction potential energy is appreciable only for those molecules very close to the surface of the system. If the number of these molecules near the surface is very small compared with the total number of molecules in the system, then their potential energy or surface energy will be small compared with the kinetic and potential energies of all the molecules in the system. In studying bulk thermodynamic properties, surface energies are usually neglected for this reason. (Surface energy that is due to the interaction of the surface molecules of a system with its container or environment should not be confused with surface tension which is due to the interaction of the surface molecules with each other. The potential energy of the surface tension forces is contained in the term U.) On the other hand, long-range forces such as electrostatic or gravitational forces can contribute appreciably to the total energy E because all the particles of a system will be affected by such forces instead of only those near the surface. Therefore, in the case of long-range forces it is very important not to neglect the interaction energy.

The interaction energy ϕ is a part of the total energy ϵ_i determined from the solution of the Schrödinger wave equation. For example, in determining the motion of a molecule in a box we must define the location of the walls of the box, that is, the position in space where the repulsive potential ϕ becomes infinite. Thus the force between the molecule and its environment ultimately appears in ϵ_i in terms of the volume V of the box (see Eq. 5.8–5). If we solve the wave equation for a repulsive potential between the molecule and the wall of the box having the shape of that shown in Fig. 9.4, then there would be slight changes to the ϵ_i which would depend on the shape of this potential function. We can therefore conclude that the shape and material of the environment influence the molecular quantum states and, hence, microstates of the system in a way which in principle is determinable from quantum mechanics. As in the case of classical mechanics, the effect of short-range forces may be negligible while that of long-range forces may be important.

9.7 Macroscopic work and heat

The microscopic work defined in Eq. (9.5–4) is not a very useful quantity since it must be summed over the motion of all the molecules of the environment that interact appreciably with the system. Like the molecules of the system, those of the environment are in continual rapid motion, exchanging energy with each other and with the system, and it is impossible to keep track of their motions. On the other hand, the average motion of a group of molecules in the environment is easily measurable on the macroscopic scale. As we blow up a balloon, we can easily follow the motion of any element of the surface of the balloon even though the motion of an individual rubber molecule in the surface may be quite complex.

For this reason, let us consider a group of molecules of macroscopic size which occupy a small volume element, denoted by K, of the environment. Let us denote the average displacement of the molecules in this volume element by $d\boldsymbol{\xi}_K$ and the total force on all the molecules in the cell by $\mathbf{F}_K$. The microscopic work done by all the particles in the cell K can be written:

$$
\begin{aligned}
(dW_\mu)_K &= \left(\sum_e \sum_j \mathbf{F}_{ej} \cdot d\mathbf{r}_e \right)_K \\
&= \left\{ \sum_e \sum_j \mathbf{F}_{ej} \cdot d\boldsymbol{\xi}_K - \sum_e \sum_j \mathbf{F}_{ej} \cdot (d\boldsymbol{\xi}_K - d\mathbf{r}_e) \right\}_K \\
&= \mathbf{F}_K \cdot d\boldsymbol{\xi}_K + \left\{ \sum_e \sum_j \mathbf{F}_{ej} \cdot (d\mathbf{r}_e - d\boldsymbol{\xi}_K) \right\}_K .
\end{aligned}
\qquad (9.7\text{–}1)
$$

Now the first term on the right-hand side of Eq. (9.7–1) is the work done by the total force $\mathbf{F}_K$ acting through the average displacement $d\boldsymbol{\xi}_K$. Both the total force and average displacement are macroscopic quantities, and we will call this term the *macroscopic work*. The second term is the work done by the microscopic forces acting on each molecule through a displacement which is the difference in the motion of the molecule and the average motion of the surrounding molecules. This latter quantity will be called *heat;* it is that portion of the microscopic work which results from the fact that the motion of a single molecule is different from the average motion of its neighbors.

The distinction between work and heat is a vital one in thermodynamics. Heat and work are similar quantities in that they are a quantitative measure of the amount and kind of interaction of a system with its environment. They differ in that each corresponds to a different macroscopic process by which the energy of the system can be changed. If there is a total force $\mathbf{F}_K$ acting on an element of the environment which displaces an amount $d\boldsymbol{\xi}_K$, then the energy E of the system can be reduced by doing the macroscopic work $\mathbf{F}_K \cdot d\boldsymbol{\xi}_K$ on the environment. On the other hand, if either the total force or the average displacement is zero, it is still possible for the system to dos ome microscopic work, that is, to exchange heat with its environment because the remaining terms on the right-hand side of Eq. (9.7–1) are not necessarily zero. This effect is easier to understand if we consider the special case of two molecules of the environment, one of which is attracted by the system and the other repelled, with equal forces, giving a zero net force. If these molecules should undergo equal but opposite displacements, there would also be a net average displacement of zero. Although the forces and displacements are equal and opposite, the microscopic work terms $\mathbf{F}_{ej} \cdot d\mathbf{r}_e$ are the same and do not add to zero.

Because we wish to understand the macroscopic consequences of the microscopic motion of the molecules of a system, we are forced to portray our findings in macroscopic terms. Since we can measure only total forces and average displacements of large groups of molecules, these quantities should certainly be used in describing part of the interaction between a system and its environment, thereby giving rise to the macroscopic work. The remainder of the interaction, or heat, cannot be measured directly in terms of force and displacement because its connection with these quantities is on the microscopic scale, which is much too detailed for practical purposes. Instead, the quantity of heat must be measured by other effects in the environment. However, we see that both work and heat can be measured only if there is an interaction between the system and its environment, and both are measured in terms of what happens in the environment. Both work and heat are measures of the changes brought about in the environment when it interacts with a system.

9.8 The first law of thermodynamics

Although the total microscopic work done by a system undergoing a certain change of state was independent of the detailed steps in the process by which this change was effected, we can no longer claim that the same is true of the two parts of the microscopic work, namely, the macroscopic work and the heat. It is relatively easy to think of many cases in which the same change of state in a system is accompanied by different amounts of macroscopic work and heat. For example, the temperature of a glass of water can be raised a given amount either by heating over a bunsen burner or by stirring with a paddle. In the first case only heat is involved and in the second case only macroscopic work, yet the change in state of the system is the same. To emphasize the fact that both heat and work depend on the details of the process, we will rewrite Eq. (9.7–1) in the form

$$dW_\mu \equiv dW - dQ, \qquad (9.8\text{--}1)$$

where dW is the macroscopic work and dQ is the heat. The symbol d indicates that the differential quantities can be added together only if the process is carefully described. The heat is arbitrarily defined (again according to convention) as the *negative* of the sum of all the microscopic work terms involved in the forces acting on the molecules times the respective displacements in excess of the local average. If we insert this into Eq. (9.5–5), we obtain the *first law of thermodynamics:*

$$E' - E = \int dQ - \int dW,$$

$$dE = dQ - dW, \qquad (9.8\text{--}2)$$

which states that the energy E of a system is increased by the heat added to the system and decreased by the work done by the system on its environment. This is a macroscopic statement of the conservation of energy in the interaction of a system with its environment. It applies to all changes in the system, even those in which the system is not in equilibrium. It is a direct consequence of the fact that all forces between molecules are conservative, and one can therefore relate changes in kinetic plus potential energy to the microscopic work done on the environment.

9.9 Forces in an equilibrium thermodynamic system

If a system is in thermodynamic equilibrium, that is, if it exists in the most probable macrostate, then there is a simple relationship between the long- and short-range forces acting on the system and the partition function Z (or Q). If $\phi_j\{\mathbf{r}_e\}$ is that additive portion of ϵ_j which is due to the energy of interaction of the particles of the system with its environment and which depends on all the coordinates $\mathbf{r}_e$ of the molecules in the environment, then the partial derivative of the partition function with respect to one of these coordinates is

$$\frac{\partial Z}{\partial \mathbf{r}_e} = \frac{\partial}{\partial \mathbf{r}_e}\left\{\mp\sum C_j \ln\left(1\mp e^{(\mu-\epsilon_j)/kT}\right)\right\}$$

$$= -\frac{1}{kT}\sum_j\left(\frac{\partial\phi_j}{\partial\mathbf{r}_e}\right)\left\{\frac{C_j}{e^{(\epsilon_j-\mu)/kT}\mp 1}\right\}$$

$$= \frac{1}{kT}\sum_j\left(-\frac{\partial\phi_j}{\partial\mathbf{r}_e}\right)N_j^0. \qquad (9.9\text{--}1)^*$$

Now $-\partial\phi_j/\partial\mathbf{r}_e$ is just the force acting on the particle whose position coordinate is $\mathbf{r}_e$ due to one of the N_j^0 particles in the jth cell of μ-space. The summation in Eq. (9.9–1) is therefore the summation over all particles of the system so that the net force $\mathbf{F}_e$ acting on the particle e of the environment is

$$\mathbf{F}_e = kT\left(\frac{\partial Z}{\partial\mathbf{r}_e}\right). \qquad (9.9\text{--}2)$$

For short-range forces we can sum this equation over all the particles near the surface of the environment which interact with the system. If an element of the surface having an area A is chosen, then the sum of all the forces acting on the particles within this layer will be just the surface stress $\boldsymbol{\sigma}$ times the area A:

$$\boldsymbol{\sigma}A \equiv \sum_e \mathbf{F}_e = \sum_e kT\left(\frac{\partial Z}{\partial\mathbf{r}_e}\right). \qquad (9.9\text{--}3)$$

If all the particles in the environment were to undergo the same displacement $d\boldsymbol{\xi}$ normal to the surface, then the work done by these forces would be

$$A\boldsymbol{\sigma}\cdot d\boldsymbol{\xi} = pA\,d\xi = \sum_e kT\left(\frac{\partial Z}{\partial\mathbf{r}_e}\right)\cdot d\boldsymbol{\xi}, \qquad (9.9\text{--}4)$$

where the pressure p is the component of $\boldsymbol{\sigma}$ normal to the surface.

---

* $\partial\phi/\partial\mathbf{r}$ is a short-hand symbol for the vector whose cartesian components are $\partial\phi/\partial r_x$, $\partial\phi/\partial r_y$, and $\partial\phi/\partial r_z$ where r_x, r_y, and r_z are the components of $\mathbf{r}$.

Now the partition function is the sum over all μ-space of the function $\ln (1 \mp e^{(\mu - \epsilon_j)/kT})$. Except for points very close to the surface of the system, this function is the same for all regions of configuration space. If the volume of the system is increased by an amount dV, then there will be a proportionate increase in the partition function. Thus the change in the partition function due to a uniform increase in the coordinates $\mathbf{r}_e$ by an amount $d\boldsymbol{\xi}$ will be the rate of change of partition function with volume times the increment of volume, $A\, d\xi$:

$$\sum_e \left(\frac{\partial Z}{\partial \mathbf{r}_e}\right) \cdot d\boldsymbol{\xi} = \left(\frac{\partial Z}{\partial V}\right)(A\, d\xi). \qquad (9.9\text{--}5)$$

As a consequence of Eqs. (9.9–4) and (9.9–5), the pressure is found to be

$$p = kT(\partial Z/\partial V)_{\mu,T}. \qquad (9.9\text{--}6)$$

For Boltzmann systems, the corresponding equation for the pressure is found by substituting Eqs. (8.7–3) and (8.7–10) into (9.9–6):

$$p = kTe^{\mu/kT}(\partial Q/\partial V)_T = NkT(\partial \ln Q/\partial V)_T. \qquad (9.9\text{--}7)$$

For long-range forces, no such simple statement can be made, since changes in the boundary of the system need not necessarily involve changes in the position of some particles in the environment interacting with the system via long-range forces. Consequently each such system must be treated as a separate case in accordance with the types of forces acting and the general motion of the boundaries. Nevertheless, the basic principle is contained in the statement of Eq. (9.9–2), which relates the force on a particle in the environment to the appropriate derivative of the partition function.

PROBLEMS

9.1 Show that the exact integral of the right-hand side of Eq. (9.3–5) over the volume V is given by the right-hand side of Eq. (9.3–6) multiplied by $1 - (A/V)\int_0^\infty (1 - e^{-\phi/kT})\, dn$, in which A is the surface area of the container and n is the distance from the surface. [*Hint:* Replace $e^{-\phi/kT}$ with $1 - (1 - e^{-\phi/kT})$.]

9.2 The molecules of a solid attract each other with a force $F = \mathfrak{F}(l/r)^5$. Two semi-infinite solids composed of n molecules per unit volume are separated by a distance d (i.e. solid fills the volume for $x \leq 0$ and $x \geq d$). Calculate the attractive force per unit area of surface.

9.3 A large parallel-plate capacitor has equal but opposite charge q/A per unit area on each plate, the plates being separated by a distance d. What is the attractive force between the plates per unit area of surface?

10

REVERSIBLE AND IRREVERSIBLE PROCESSES

10.1 Reversible and irreversible processes

A favorite trick of the makers of moving-picture comedies is to run a sequence of frames in reverse direction so that the characters in the film move backward. The picture of a high-diver erupting from a swimming pool and sailing feetfirst through the air to land on the diving board is sure to bring amusement to the audience because of the sense of ridiculousness of such an event. Everyone knows from experience that such events do not take place in nature. If we should make a motion picture of any process and then, playing the picture backward, observe that the reverse process cannot or does not occur in nature, we would term the original process *irreversible*. The flow of water over a waterfall, the breaking of waves against a beach, the hammering of a nail into a piece of wood are all irreversible processes which we have all observed.

Not all processes are irreversible. In the multiple-exposure photograph of Fig. 2.2, we are unable to determine from the picture alone which were the initial and which were the final positions of the two pucks. The law of momentum conservation does not permit us to distinguish the direction of time in such a picture since a reversal of the direction of motion constitutes a change in sign of all the momentum vectors and still conserves momentum. If we were to take similar pictures of an object falling through a vacuum or a pendulum swinging in a vacuum, we would again be unable to tell in which direction the object was moving or the pendulum swinging. We must therefore recognize that some processes are reversible in time; that is, the reverse of such a process can also be observed to occur.

In some instances the reverse of a reversible process can only be imagined. The motion of the planets about the sun is such a case. We cannot observe the reverse of their present motion, but our understanding of Newtonian mechanics enables us to describe what the motion must have been in the past, a description which can be checked against past observations. If we understand all about the behavior of a reversible process, it then becomes possible to recall past history as well as foretell future events (some aspects of astronomy are based upon this possibility). On the other hand, for irreversible processes it is not possible to determine under all circumstances the past or the future from an observation in the present. We have only to observe an object floating in a swimming pool to understand the impossibility of attempting to ascertain just how the object was placed in the pool.

The importance of the distinction between reversible and irreversible processes lies in their practical implications. The slowing down of an automobile by air resistance and friction in the wheel bearings is an irreversible process which makes the automobile a less satisfactory device than it would be if such processes were absent. The frictionless motion of a very high altitude earth satellite is a reversible motion, whose lack of attenuation makes it possible to dispense with the continuous propulsive force which is required of aircraft moving at low altitudes. The burning of a hydrocarbon fuel in air is an irreversible process, from which only a minor fraction of the chemical energy can be recovered in the form of electrical power. If this same reaction occurs reversibly in a fuel cell, however, all of the available chemical energy can be converted to useful electrical power. In a practical sense, therefore, reversible processes are much more desirable than irreversible ones.

10.2 Microscopic reversibility

A basic assumption underlying the theories of motion of microscopic particles is that the motion on this scale is reversible in time. There are assumed to be no such effects as friction and heating as are observed on a macroscopic scale. The forces acting on molecules and atoms are believed to be conservative and depend only on position. If there were friction between the molecules of a gas, for example, these molecules would eventually slow down, and the pressure would decrease to zero. Since this is not the case, it must be that no such forces can exist on the molecular level.

The time reversibility of motions governed by conservative forces follows directly from the equations of motion, either Newtonian or quantum-mechanical. If the algebraic sign of the momentum and time in Newton's law are both changed simultaneously, then the equation of motion is unchanged since the force depends only on position and not on momentum or time explicitly. For a conservative Newtonian system the instantaneous reversal of all the velocities would cause the system to retrace its past history. A similar result will also hold for Schrödinger's equation. If we simultaneously replace t with $-t$ and i with $-i$, the equation of motion is unchanged. All our descriptions of microscopic events assume reversible processes.

If all microscopic processes are reversible, how is it that some macroscopic ones are irreversible? This obvious question plagued scientists for many years, and no mathematically rigorous answer to it has yet been found. However, a physically satisfying answer can be proposed if we realize how much greater is the complexity of macroscopic systems compared with microscopic. An irreversible macroscopic process is simply a microscopically reversible one which proceeds in such a manner that its reverse would be extremely difficult to realize because of the exceedingly large number of favorable microscopic parameters which would have to prevail simultaneously in order for the reverse to happen.

Let us consider a simple example of this principle. Suppose we drop a block of wood into an initially smooth pond of water. The waves generated by the block of wood hitting the surface of the water will spread out radially from the point of contact, and after many reflections from the side of the pool the surface will be roughened by a random wave pattern which is more or less uniform over the whole surface of the pool. The decrease in potential energy of the block of wood will result in a corresponding increase in the energy of all the surface waves. Instead of being concentrated in the one degree of freedom (vertical motion) of the wood block, it will be spread over the very large number of degrees of freedom of the wave motion on the surface of the pond. Under favorable conditions, there will be very little damping of the waves so that the wave motion is essentially reversible. That is, any one wavelet could be reversed in direction and time simultaneously and still observe the same equation of motion. Yet we would call the process by which the energy of the block is transformed to wave energy an irreversible one because we have never observed the reverse of this process. It is not impossible that by a suitable stirring of the water we could produce a wave pattern which, at some time in the future, would miraculously converge upon the block, ejecting it from the pond and leaving the surface completely calm. The impossibility of performing such an experiment stems not from the irreversibility of wave motion but from the practical impossibility of determining the proper wave pattern which will produce this effect and then producing such a pattern at a given instant.

We must not conclude from this that every process in a macroscopic system is necessarily irreversible because of the large number of degrees of freedom of such systems. The distinction between reversible and irreversible processes in macroscopic systems arises from the ability or inability to produce the numerous microscopically favorable conditions for reversing the process with only a very few macroscopic constraints. A sound wave in a gas is a macroscopically reversible process, because it happens to be a type of motion in which the simple movement of a surface normal to itself is sufficient to so constrain the molecular motion that its reverse may also be achieved.

The study of reversible and irreversible macroscopic processes cannot be usefully pursued on a microscopic basis. In our study of macrostates, including the determination of the most probable macrostate, we have found a way to connect the microscopic and the macroscopic states of a system. We shall therefore attempt to relate reversible and irreversible processes to changes in the macrostates of a system.

10.3 Reversible and irreversible processes in thermodynamic systems

A possible means of connecting the changes in the macrostate of a system to the reversibility or irreversibility of the process is to describe the process in terms of the trajectory of the representative point in Γ-space. If we picture the surfaces of constant energy in Γ-space, as shown in Fig. 10.1, then a process in which the energy of the system is increased can be described by a line in Γ-space connecting the two energy surfaces, such as line AB in Fig. 10.1. Since a single point in Γ-space defines a microstate of the system, this process line or path defines the sequence of microstates through which the system passes in undergoing a change in thermodynamic state.

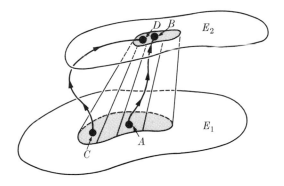

Fig. 10.1. The volume in Γ-space corresponding to the most probable macrostates having energies between E_1 and E_2 is indicated by a shaded base and top, joined by line segments, lying in these constant-energy surfaces. A reversible process (AB) has a path line lying within this volume while an irreversible process (CD) passes outside.

For each instantaneous value of the energy and volume of the system along this path, there is a class of microstates which forms the most probable macrostate. This class is indicated by the shaded area on the energy surfaces of Fig. 10.1. As the system undergoes changes in energy, this shaded area will sweep out a volume in Γ-space within which are all microstates corresponding to the sets of the most probable macrostates, and therefore thermodynamic equilibrium, for the given values of E and V. At thermodynamic equilibrium, for a fixed value of E and V, the representative point may move freely about the shaded area while the system remains in the most probable macrostate. Since there would appear to be no restriction on the direction of motion of the representative point in Γ-space, provided only that it remains within this shaded area, we can consider such changes as reversible. It is therefore proposed that a macroscopically reversible process is one for which the representative point in Γ-space always lies within the shaded volume of Fig. 10.1; that is, the system itself is always in a most probable macrostate corresponding to the instantaneous

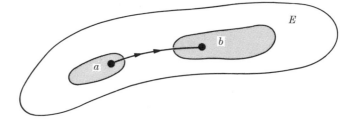

Fig. 10.2. The path of the irreversible process in which state a of Fig. 7.2 changes to state b upon removal of the diaphragm is indicated by the solid line on the energy surface E. The shaded areas represent the most probable macrostates of systems a and b.

values of E and V during a reversible process. Conversely, an irreversible process is one for which the instantaneous macrostate is different from the most probable macrostate. Such an irreversible process would be described by the curve CD in Fig. 10.1.

We might test this conjecture against the simple irreversible experiment of the free expansion of a gas into a vacuum, considered in Fig. 7.2. For the state a in which the gas is confined to the left half of the chamber, there will be a corresponding area of the energy surface (indicated by a in Fig. 10.2) which defines the most probable macrostate. For the state b, in which the gas is allowed to move freely throughout the whole volume, there will be a much larger area (indicated by b in Fig. 10.2) on the same energy surface since there is no change in energy upon removing the partition. These two areas will not overlap, because none of the microstates corresponding to the most probable macrostate of state b will be included among the corresponding microstates of state a. The path of the representative point in changing from a to b must necessarily move outside the limits of the most probable macrostate and pass through nonequilibrium thermodynamic states. This will therefore constitute an irreversible process, which we know empirically to be the case.

If we can identify irreversible processes with those in which the system can be found in a macrostate that is not the most probable macrostate, then we may be able to relate work and heat to changes in thermodynamic properties for both reversible and irreversible processes.

10.4 Changes in the most probable macrostate

Whether a process is reversible or irreversible, for each instantaneous value of E, V, and N, there is a most probable macrostate. A system undergoing an irreversible process may exist in a macrostate which is not the most probable one for its instantaneous value of E, V, and N. Since E, V, and N are quantities that can be determined even if the system is not at equilibrium, we can still determine the properties of the macrostate the system would be in if it were at equilibrium under these constraints. The thermodynamic equilibrium properties determined from our previous study of the most probable macrostate, such as temperature, entropy, pressure, and chemical potential, will correspond to the properties empirically measured in a reversible process. In an irreversible process, these properties cannot be measured. (For example, the temperature and pressure may be different in different parts of the system.) Nevertheless, we may still find the values of these properties which the system would have if it came to equilibrium with the instantaneous values of E, V, and N occurring in the irreversible process. In this sense, the changes in macrostate we are about to discuss are the actual changes in a reversible process but only hypothetical changes in an irreversible process.

In Section 8.5 we discussed changes in the most probable macrostate for a system of fixed volume in which the energy and number of particles were varied. According to Eq. (8.5–3), the corresponding change in entropy is

$$dS = \frac{1}{T} \, dE - \frac{\mu}{T} \, dN. \tag{10.4–1}$$

We wish to extend this to the case of systems whose volume is permitted to change. For the sake of clarity, we will assume that only short-range forces act between the system and its environment so that the only forces acting on the system are the surface stresses, or pressures, and that there are no body forces. Let us see how Eq. (10.4–1) would be modified under these circumstances.

If we insert the definition of the partition function Z given in Eq. (8.6–3) into Eq. (8.5–9), we obtain

$$S\{\mu, T, V\} = ((E - \mu N)/T) + kZ\{\mu, T, V\}, \tag{10.4–2}$$

where E, N, S, and Z are considered dependent functions of the independent variables, μ, T, and V. If we take the total derivative of both sides of this equation, we find

$$dS = \frac{1}{T} \, dE - \frac{\mu}{T} \, dN - \frac{E - \mu N}{T^2} \, dT - \frac{N}{T} \, d\mu + k \left\{ \frac{\partial Z}{\partial \mu} \, d\mu + \frac{\partial Z}{\partial T} \, dT + \frac{\partial Z}{\partial V} \, dV \right\}. \tag{10.4–3}$$

If we make use of Eqs. (8.6–5) and (8.6–6) and the definition of pressure given in Eq. (9.9–6), then Eq. (10.4–3) simplifies to

$$T \, dS = dE + p \, dV - \mu \, dN. \tag{10.4–4}$$

This equation is called *Gibbs' equation** and in classical thermodynamics is one of the consequences of the *second law of thermodynamics*. It relates the change

---

* Josiah Willard Gibbs (1839–1903), the most distinguished American mathematical physicist of his day, was the first to develop the thermodynamic principles of chemical equilibrium and to establish a general approach to statistical mechanics. He was also the originator of vector analysis.

in entropy to the changes in E, V, and N when the system remains at equilibrium. If we recall that entropy is proportionate to the logarithm of the acces-
sible volume $\mathcal{V}$ in Γ-space, then this equation relates the change in $\mathcal{V}$ due to
changes in total energy, volume, and number of particles in the system. For
example, if E is increased, then this volume increases because the average value
of the momentum coordinates increases. If the volume V is increased, the
maximum values of the position coordinates increase and thereby the phase
volume $\mathcal{V}$. If the energy and volume are fixed but new particles are introduced
into the system, the number of coordinates in Γ-space is increased. This has a
tendency to increase the volume $\mathcal{V}$ because of the increased number of dimensions, but since the same energy must be spread over more momentum coordinates, there is an opposite tendency to reduce the volume $\mathcal{V}$. Whether the
entropy increases or decreases when more particles are added to the system at
constant E and V depends on the algebraic sign of the chemical potential μ,
which can be determined only by a detailed investigation of the system at hand.
We may therefore consider Eq. (10.4–4) as relating the changes in phase volume
$\mathcal{V}$ with the changes in the macroscopic observables E, V, and N.

From another point of view, we can regard Eq. (10.4–4) as a compatibility
condition relating the changes in entropy to the intensive properties, p, T, and μ.
If we consider the extensive property S to be a function of the extensive properties E, V, and N, then the total differential dS would be

$$dS = \left(\frac{\partial S}{\partial E}\right)_{V,N} dE + \left(\frac{\partial S}{\partial V}\right)_{E,N} dV + \left(\frac{\partial S}{\partial N}\right)_{E,V} dN. \tag{10.4–5}$$

By comparing this with Eq. (10.4–4), we see that

$$\frac{1}{T} = \left(\frac{\partial S}{\partial E}\right)_{V,N}, \qquad \frac{p}{T} = \left(\frac{\partial S}{\partial V}\right)_{E,N}, \qquad \frac{\mu}{T} = -\left(\frac{\partial S}{\partial N}\right)_{E,V}. \tag{10.4–6}$$

Thus the macroscopically measurable intensive properties p, T, and μ are determined by how fast the entropy increases with E, V, and N and are therefore
themselves functions of E, V, and N. In other words, if we fix the values of
the three extensive variables E, V, and N, we thereby determine the values of
the dependent extensive variable S and the intensive variables p, T, and μ.

Before proceeding further, it is useful to note that there are further mathematical implications of Eq. (10.4–4). If S, T, p, and μ are considered functions
of the independent variables E, V, and N, then, since S is a single-valued function of the independent variables (the volume in phase space cannot have two
different values for the same E, V, and N),

$$\left\{\frac{\partial}{\partial V}\left(\frac{\partial S}{\partial E}\right)_{V,N}\right\}_{E,N} = \left\{\frac{\partial}{\partial E}\left(\frac{\partial S}{\partial V}\right)_{E,N}\right\}_{V,N}. \tag{10.4–7}$$

By substituting the appropriate partial derivatives from Eq. (10.4–6) into the above equation, we find

$$\left\{\frac{\partial}{\partial V}\left(\frac{1}{T}\right)\right\}_{E,N} = \left\{\frac{\partial}{\partial E}\left(\frac{p}{T}\right)\right\}_{V,N}. \tag{10.4-8}$$

This is one example of a set of restrictive conditions on the partial derivatives of thermodynamic properties which are called *Maxwell's relations*.

To show the usefulness of the above Maxwell relation, let us consider the perfect gas whose pressure was found to be (from Eq. 9.3–8)

$$p = \frac{NkT}{V}. \tag{10.4-9}$$

If we evaluate the derivative on the right-hand side of Eq. (10.4–8), we find

$$\left\{\frac{\partial}{\partial E}\left(\frac{p}{T}\right)\right\}_{V,N} = \left\{\frac{\partial}{\partial E}\left(\frac{Nk}{V}\right)\right\}_{V,N} = 0. \tag{10.4-10}$$

Therefore the derivative on the left-hand side of Eq. (10.4–8) must also be zero. Now T is in general a function of the independent extensive variables E, V, and N. If E and N are held fixed, and T is found not to vary when V is changed, which is the case when its partial derivative is zero, then T must be a function of E and N alone; that is,

$$T = T\{E, N\}$$

or

$$E = E\{T, N\}. \tag{10.4-11}$$

Thus a necessary consequence of the equation of state of a perfect gas, Eq. (10.4–9), is that the internal energy E depends only on the temperature and number of particles and not on the pressure or volume of the system.

There are further mathematical operations which may be utilized in applying Eq. (10.4–4). It is possible to consider S, V, and N the independent extensive variables and E, T, p, and μ the dependent variables and then continue the analysis of Eqs. (10.4–5) and (10.4–6). Such mathematical manipulations do not introduce any new physical consequences for these are all contained within the original statement of Eq. (10.4–4). However, they do provide us with practical relationships which might simplify the application of Eq. (10.4–4) to a particular problem or enable us to study changes in a system under conditions for which E, V, and N are not the controlling macroscopic variables. For example, in a laboratory experiment, it may very well be that p, T, and N can be held constant while other changes occur in E, V, and S. Equation (10.4–4) may then be rearranged to be in a more convenient form for discussing such a situation.

There are two processes involving changes in the most probable macrostate which are so common that they deserve special mention: the constant-volume and constant-pressure processes in a *closed system*, that is, a system having a fixed mass ($dN = 0$). Many laboratory experiments and industrial processes are carried out under conditions where either the pressure or volume is held fixed. It is therefore common to introduce additional thermodynamic properties, like the specific heats defined below, which may be measured easily in such experiments and from which the entropy and other thermodynamic properties may be subsequently calculated.

Let us first consider the constant-volume process ($dV = 0$) in a closed system ($dN = 0$). If a small amount of heat is added to the system, or a small amount of work is done on the system,* there will be a small temperature rise dT. Now we can compute the increase dE in energy from these measured heat or work quantities by using the first law of thermodynamics, Eq. (9.8–2), and can form the ratio dE/dT. Because the volume and number of molecules were held fixed in the process that the measurements were made for, this ratio equals the partial derivative $(\partial E/\partial T)_{V,N}$, for which the term *constant-volume specific heat C_v* is used:

$$C_v \equiv (\partial E/\partial T)_{V,N}. \tag{10.4–12}$$

In writing Eq. (10.4–12), we imply that E is a function of V, N, and T; that is, $E = E\{N, V, T\}$. While N, V, and T are variables which may be measured easily in the laboratory, they are not the best set of independent variables to be used in specifying E, because we cannot find all the remaining thermodynamic variables by partial differentiation of E with respect to V, N, and T. Thus $E\{V, N, T\}$ is not a thermodynamic potential function, as discussed in Section 8.6; nor is C_v a derivative of such a function.

If we multiply Eq. (10.4–12) by the first equality of Eq. (10.4–6), we find

$$C_v/T = (\partial E/\partial T)_{V,N}(\partial S/\partial E)_{V,N} = (\partial S/\partial T)_{V,N}, \tag{10.4–13}$$

in which $S = S\{V, N, T\}$. For a constant-volume change in a closed system the partial derivative of Eq. (10.4–13) is a total derivative, so that

$$dS = (C_v/T)\, dT \quad \text{if} \quad dV = 0 \quad \text{and} \quad dN = 0. \tag{10.4–14}$$

If C_v is known as a function of V, N, and T, as implied by Eq. (10.4–13), then Eq. (10.4–14) may be integrated to calculate the difference in entropy between two states at the same V and N but different temperatures:

$$S\{V_1, N_1, T_2\} - S\{V_1, N_1, T_1\} = \int_{T_1}^{T_2} (C_v/T)\, dT. \tag{10.4–15}$$

However, one cannot find from this equation alone the difference in entropy between states having different volumes.

---

* Even though the volume is held fixed, it may be possible to do work on the system. For example, a carbon resistor may be made hotter by holding it in a flame (i.e., adding heat) or by passing an electric current through it (i.e., doing electrical work on it).

For the constant-pressure process ($dp = 0$) in a closed system ($dN = 0$), we may follow a similar development. Measurement of the small amount of heat or work added to a system whose pressure is held fixed enables us to calculate the increase in internal energy dE from the first law, Eq. (9.8–2). If we also measure the increase in volume dV and temperature dT, we may determine the ratio $(dE + p\,dV)/dT$, which is really a partial derivative, and therefore define the *constant-pressure specific heat* C_p as the partial derivative:

$$C_p \equiv (\partial E/\partial T)_{p,N} + p(\partial V/\partial T)_{p,N} = (\partial\{E + pV\}/\partial T)_{p,N}. \qquad (10.4\text{–}16)$$

It is convenient to introduce a new extensive thermodynamic property called the *enthalpy H*:

$$H \equiv E + pV \qquad (10.4\text{–}17)$$

so that C_p may also be written as

$$C_p = \{\partial H/\partial T\}_{p,N}, \qquad (10.4\text{–}18)$$

in which it is implied that $H = H\{p, N, T\}$. Considered as a function of p, N, and T, the enthalpy H is not a thermodynamic potential function, for the reasons discussed above.

By adding $V\,dp$ to and subtracting it from the right-hand side, Gibbs' equation, (10.4–4), may be expressed in such a way that the enthalpy H replaces the internal energy E as a variable:

$$\begin{aligned}
T\,dS &= (dE + p\,dV + V\,dp) - V\,dp - \mu\,dN \\
&= d(E + pV) - V\,dp - \mu\,dN \\
&= dH - V\,dp - \mu\,dN. \qquad (10.4\text{–}19)
\end{aligned}$$

Now considering S as a function of H, p, and N, we may identify its partial derivatives in the same manner used to find Eq. (10.4–6), obtaining

$$1/T = (\partial S/\partial H)_{p,N}, \qquad V/T = -(\partial S/\partial p)_{H,N}, \qquad \mu/T = -(\partial S/\partial N)_{H,p}. \qquad (10.4\text{–}20)$$

Since these are all the remaining thermodynamic variables, we conclude that $S\{H, p, N\}$ (or similarly, $H\{S, p, N\}$) is a thermodynamic potential function.

If Eq. (10.4–18) is divided by the first equality of Eq. (10.4–20), the constant-pressure specific heat is found to be

$$C_p/T = (\partial H/\partial T)_{p,N}(\partial S/\partial H)_{p,N} = (\partial S/\partial T)_{p,N}. \qquad (10.4\text{–}21)$$

For the constant-pressure process in a closed system, since both p and N are fixed, the right-hand side of Eq. (10.4–21) is a total differential, so that

$$dS = (C_p/T)\,dT \qquad \text{if} \quad dp = 0 \quad \text{and} \quad dN = 0, \qquad (10.4\text{–}22)$$

which may be integrated to give the change in entropy between two states at the same pressure:

$$S\{p_1, N_1, T_2\} - S\{p_1, N_1, T_1\} = \int_{T_1}^{T_2} (C_p/T)\, dT. \qquad (10.4\text{--}23)$$

Taken together, Eqs. (10.4–15) and (10.4–23) enable us to find the change in entropy from a given reference state to a state at any other pressure and volume by integrating along successive paths at constant pressure or volume for which C_p and C_v are known.

10.5 Reversible work and heat in a closed system

If a closed system ($N = $ const, $dN = 0$) undergoes a reversible process, then the work and heat in such a process may be related to the change in thermodynamic properties in a simple way. Let us first determine what is the work in a reversible process for a closed system in which only short-range forces of interaction between the system and its environment are present. The work has previously been defined in Eq. (9.7–1) as the total force on the elements of the environment times the average displacement of the molecules of the environment. For a reversible process the system is always in the most probable macrostate so that the total force on an element of area of the confining surface of the environment is just the pressure p times the area. The work is therefore this force times the displacement $d\xi$ of the element of area, or the pressure times the increment in volume:

$$(dW)_{\text{rev}} = pA\, d\xi = p\, dV$$

or

$$W_{\text{rev}} = \int p\, dV. \qquad (10.5\text{--}1)$$

The total reversible work done in a reversible process can be determined only if we know how the pressure changes with volume in that particular process. For this reason, the integral sign is written with a horizontal line to emphasize this point.

The heat in a reversible process may now be determined from the first law of thermodynamics, Eq. (9.8–2):

$$(dQ)_{\text{rev}} = dE + (dW)_{\text{rev}} = dE + p\, dV. \qquad (10.5\text{--}2)$$

By comparing this with Eq. (10.4–4) for the particular case where dN is zero, we see immediately that

$$(dQ)_{\text{rev}} = T\, dS$$

or

$$dS = (dQ/T)_{\text{rev}}. \qquad (10.5\text{--}3)$$

In classical thermodynamics this becomes the definition of the change of entropy, namely, that it is the integral of the heat divided by the absolute temperature in a reversible process. In integral form this may be written:

$$Q_{rev} = \oint T \, dS,$$

$$S_2 - S_1 = \int_1^2 (dQ/T)_{rev}, \tag{10.5-4}$$

where again attention is drawn to the fact that the process in question must be defined in order to evaluate the two integrals written above.

Equations (10.5–1) and (10.5–4) are the basic equations for predicting the work and heat in a reversible process. Since reversible processes are often difficult to achieve, these equations will determine the best possible conditions that might be achieved in an actual process. For this reason, they form the basic working equations for a wide variety of thermodynamic problems. We shall make great use of them in subsequent chapters which discuss many such applications.

For the *reversible constant-volume process* in a closed system, the reversible heat dQ found from Eqs. (10.5–3) and (10.4–14) is

$$(dQ)_{rev} = T \, dS$$
$$= C_v \, dT \quad \text{if} \quad dV = 0 \quad \text{and} \quad dN = 0. \tag{10.5-5}$$

The origin of the term "specific heat" used for the derivative C_v defined by Eq. (10.4–12) is this relation between heat and temperature rise of Eq. (10.5–5). Only for a reversible constant-volume process will the ratio of heat dQ to temperature rise dT equal the constant-volume specific heat C_v.

For the *reversible constant-pressure process* in a closed system, Eqs. (10.5–3), (10.4–22), and (10.4–18) lead us to conclude that

$$(dQ)_{rev} = T \, dS = C_p \, dT$$
$$= dH \quad \text{if} \quad dp = 0 \quad \text{and} \quad dN = 0. \tag{10.5-6}$$

The increase in enthalpy is therefore equal to the heat added in a reversible constant-pressure process. Also, the constant-pressure specific heat C_p is the ratio of heat added to temperature rise for the same process.

10.6 Work and heat in irreversible processes

Irreversible processes are difficult to deal with because the system exists in macrostates that are different from the most probable macrostate. Since we have so far been able to develop only the properties of the most probable macrostate, we have no understanding of these other macrostates. Nevertheless, we can still determine something about the work and heat in an irreversible process.

Let us consider an irreversible process in which we very suddenly increase the volume of a system by moving outward the walls of the container. If the increment in volume dV is accomplished quickly enough, the molecules of the system will not move appreciably during this time interval. The short-range force between the molecules of the system and those of the container wall will very quickly become zero, so that very little or no pressure will be exerted by the system on the container walls during this sudden movement. If the system had remained at equilibrium during this expansion, it would have done a positive amount of work $p \, dV$. The actual work in the irreversible process is much less, since the normal stress was less than the equilibrium pressure p. For this particular case, then,

$$(dW)_{\text{irrev}} < p \, dV. \tag{10.6-1}$$

If this sudden change in volume were to be reversed, that is, if the container wall were suddenly moved inward, then the number of molecules near the surface would be greater than if equilibrium were maintained and the surface stress would necessarily be higher than the equilibrium pressure p. While the magnitude of the work of compression would be greater than the magnitude of $p \, dV$, this work of compression is negative and therefore the irreversible work would still observe the inequality of Eq. (10.6-1).

Let us now examine an irreversible heating process during which there is no macroscopic motion of the boundaries of the system. If heat is suddenly added at the surface of the system, the surface temperature T rises more rapidly than that in the interior. For a given amount of heat dQ added to the system, the surface temperature is higher and the ratio dQ/T is smaller than would have been the case if the same amount of heat were added so slowly that the temperature remained uniform within the system. For the latter process, the system would remain in the most probable macrostate for which $dQ/T = dS$ according to Eq. (10.5-3). Thus, for the very rapid irreversible heating process,

$$(dQ/T)_{\text{irrev}} < (dQ/T)_{\text{rev}} = dS. \tag{10.6-2}$$

On the other hand, for a very rapid cooling the surface temperature T would be lower and dQ/T larger in magnitude than for very slow cooling. However, dQ is negative for a cooling process, so that for irreversible cooling dQ/T is a larger negative number than dS, and Eq. (10.6-2) is still true.

In view of Eqs. (10.5-1) and (10.5-3), we may write for any process

$$dW \leq p \, dV, \tag{10.6-3}$$

$$dQ \leq T \, dS. \tag{10.6-4}$$

The second of these two relations, Eq. (10.6-4), is called the *inequality of Clausius*.

We can think of many examples which obviously conform to these inequalities. A system isolated so that neither heat nor work crosses its boundaries can increase in entropy and volume only if p is positive, or decrease in volume if p is negative, if there is any change possible at all. We can do work on a block of copper by hammering it without changing its volume. In such a case, dW is negative and $dV = 0$, which satisfies Eq. (10.6–3). Many other such examples may occur to the reader who will find them all in agreement with these inequalities.

It is not completely impossible to violate the inequalities in Eqs. (10.6–3) and (10.6–4) above. For example, a sphere of gas in which at one instant all the particles were located at the wall could be suddenly expanded to produce more work than the equilibrium pressure times the increment in volume. But such extreme situations do not in fact arise, and all practical irreversible processes are found to be in conformity with the above equations.

PROBLEMS

10.1 Derive Eq. (10.4–4) for a Boltzmann system by starting with the total differential of Eq. (8.7–12).

10.2 Show that the following are alternative forms of Eq. (10.4–4):

$$d(E - TS) = \mu\, dN - p\, dV - S\, dT,$$
$$d(H - TS) = \mu\, dN + V\, dp - S\, dT.$$

10.3 An equation of state of an imperfect gas is $P(V - V_0) = NkT$ in which V_0 is a constant. Show that the internal energy E is a function of temperature alone but that H is not.

10.4 Starting with Eq. (10.4–19), show that

$$\{\partial(1/T)/\partial p\}_{H,N} = -\{\partial(V/T)/\partial H\}_{p,N}.$$

10.5 If $pV = NkT$, show that $C_p = C_v + Nk$.

10.6 For the Boltzmann system of Problem 8.14, find the constant-volume specific heat C_v as a function of ϵ, T, and N. Plot a curve of C_v/Nk as a function of kT/ϵ.

10.7 In passing a current through a 1-kg coil of copper, 100 watts of electrical power is used. The temperature $\theta(°C)$ of the coil is measured as $0.263t - 9.6 \times 10^{-6}t^2$, in which t is the time in seconds elapsed since $\theta = 0°C$ was recorded. (a) Determine the specific heat of copper (kcal/kgm-C°) at 0°C and 200°C. (b) Is this a reversible process? (c) Determine the increase in entropy between 0°C and 200°C.

10.8 The volume V of helium gas in a cylinder fitted with a piston is increased by withdrawing the piston. The measured pressure p is found to equal $p_0(V_0/V)^{1.2}$ during this expansion of the volume, where p_0 and V_0 are the initial pressure and volume. For helium, $E = (\frac{3}{2})pV$. Does (a) the energy and (b) the entropy increase, remain constant, or decrease during the expansion process? (c) If the process is reversible, calculate the work done and heat added in doubling the initial volume when p_0 is 1 atm and V_0 is 1 m³.

10.9 Measurements (in identical units) of heat, work, and changes in thermodynamic properties are reported as follows for several processes in a closed system $(dN = 0)$:

Experiment	$\int_1^2 dQ$	$\int_1^2 dW$	$\int_1^2 T\, dS$	$\int_1^2 dE$	$\int_1^2 p\, dV$
1	100	0	125	100	25
2	0	0	100	0	100
3	50	−25	25	75	−25
4	−10	−50	10	35	−25
5	0	0	10	0	0
6	−30	50	−30	−80	50

For each case answer the following questions:
(a) Is the first law of thermodynamics satisfied?
(b) Is the second law of thermodynamics satisfied?
(c) If the answers to (a) and (b) are both yes, is the process reversible?

10.10 In Chapter 19, the speed of sound a in a fluid is shown to be $a^2 = (\partial p/\partial \rho)_{S,N}$ where the density $\rho \equiv Nm/V$ and m is the mass of a molecule. An alternative expression sometimes used is $a^2 = (C_p/C_v)(\partial p/\partial \rho)_{T,N}$. Show that $(\partial p/\partial \rho)_{S,N} = (C_p/C_v)(\partial p/\partial \rho)_{T,N}$ is a thermodynamic identity. [Hint: Make use of the mathematical identity $(\partial x/\partial y)_z(\partial y/\partial z)_x(\partial z/\partial x)_y = -1$.]

11

THE PERFECT GAS

11.1 The empirical perfect-gas law

The behavior of common gases at pressures and temperatures not too different from those of the atmosphere is embodied in the empirical laws of Boyle and Charles, which relate the changes in volume, pressure, and temperature of a fixed quantity of gas. According to Charles' law, for a fixed temperature the product of the pressure p and volume V is a constant. Boyle's law states that the pressure increases with increasing temperature if the volume is held fixed, so that one may define an empirical temperature θ which is proportional to the pressure. These two laws in combination permit us to define an *equation of state* for a gas of the form

$$pV/\theta = \text{const.} \qquad (11.1\text{--}1)$$

The empirical temperature θ is not necessarily the same as the absolute temperature T, for the former was derived from the simple behavior of a common gas while the latter is independent of the properties of any substance. If the two temperatures are identical (or proportional), this must be viewed as a coincidence arising from a particularly simple or ideal behavior of a gas. It is for this reason that a gas which observes the equation of state of the form of Eq. (11.1–1), with θ replaced by T, or

$$pV/T = \text{const} \qquad (11.1\text{--}2)$$

is called an *ideal* or *perfect* gas.

It is also a well-known fact that this equation of state does not agree accurately with the experimental measurements at high pressures and low temperatures. In fact, every gas condenses to a solid or a liquid at a sufficiently low temperature, in which case the perfect-gas law grossly fails to describe the condensed state. Under these conditions the gas is said to be imperfect, which should be understood to mean a nonideality or a failure to observe precisely the perfect-gas law. All gases are *imperfect gases* in the sense that a sufficiently precise experiment will reveal a departure from the perfect-gas law; on the other hand, many gases may be treated as perfect gases with good accuracy over a limited range of pressure and temperature which is characteristic of the gas in question and determinable by experiment. It is in this latter sense that we shall discuss the properties of perfect gases.

In addition to the simplified *equation of state*, Eq. (11.1–2), one might suspect that a perfect gas might also possess simple relationships between the other thermodynamic properties such as entropy S, internal energy E, and chemical potential μ. It will be found subsequently that this is the case and that what is called the *caloric equation of state*,

$$S = S\{E, V\}, \tag{11.1–3}$$

has a form in which the entropy is the sum of two parts—the first, a function of the internal energy alone, and the second, a function of the volume alone:

$$S = f\{E\} + g\{V\}. \tag{11.1–4}$$

The limits of pressure and temperature within which the perfect-gas equations of state, Eqs. (11.1–2) and (11.1–4), agree with experimental measurements to within any specified precision are essentially the same for either equation.

Equation (11.1–4) completely describes a perfect gas because $S\{E, V\}$ is a thermodynamic potential (see Section 8.6) from which all other thermodynamic functions may be derived, whereas this is not true of Eq. (11.1–2). However, since the entropy of a system cannot be measured directly, the $(p\text{-}V\text{-}T)$-equation of state is more accessible to simple experimental verification and therefore it exhibits more directly the relative importance of gas imperfections.

In the foregoing we have adopted the empirical definition of a perfect gas, which is the one most commonly assumed in the exposition of classical thermodynamics. However, it is our purpose to understand how this macroscopic behavior is a result of the motion of individual gas molecules and how to relate quantitatively the thermodynamic properties of a perfect gas to the motion of the gas particles. It was the possibility of showing this relationship that led Maxwell, Boltzmann, and Gibbs to develop the kinetic theory of gases and statistical mechanics and thereby to discover the more general applicability of these methods to systems other than gases. Therefore we shall return to a consideration of the motion of freely moving atoms or molecules.

11.2 The motion of gas molecules

The kinetic theory of gases is based on the supposition that the molecules of a gas move rapidly about inside the enclosing volume, colliding with one another and with the walls of the container and thereby giving rise to a pressure. Many of the consequences of this assumption are borne out by experiment. However, it is the simplicity of this motion which gives rise to the special properties of a gas. A gas is distinguished from a liquid by the fact that a gas molecule spends most of its time moving in a straight line, uninfluenced by the motion of the other molecules or the presence of a wall, while a liquid molecule always moves

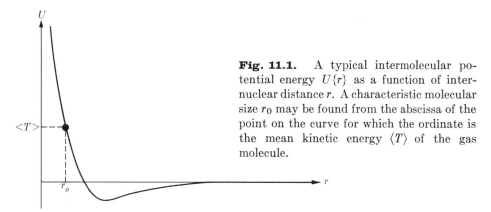

Fig. 11.1. A typical intermolecular potential energy $U\{r\}$ as a function of internuclear distance r. A characteristic molecular size r_0 may be found from the abscissa of the point on the curve for which the ordinate is the mean kinetic energy $\langle T \rangle$ of the gas molecule.

under the influence of the forces exerted by nearby molecules, changing direction and velocity every time it moves a molecular diameter. *A perfect gas is one in which the collisions between molecules can be ignored insofar as they affect molecular energy, even though it is by virtue of such collisions that energy and momentum are exchanged between molecules and equilibrium is achieved.*

To understand this paradox, it is best to consider the classical motion of two colliding particles which are subject to a conservative force directed along the line of centers and for which there exists a potential energy $U\{r\}$ such as is shown in Fig. 11.1. If the two particles in question, indicated by subscripts 1 and 2, have speeds v_1' and v_2' before colliding, then during the collision the conservation of energy requires that

$$\tfrac{1}{2}m_1 v_1^2 + \tfrac{1}{2}m_2 v_2^2 + U\{r\} = \tfrac{1}{2}m_1(v_1')^2 + \tfrac{1}{2}m_2(v_2')^2. \qquad (11.2\text{–}1)$$

Now if v_1 and v_2 are to be changed appreciably by the collision, then the molecules must approach each other closely enough for the potential energy to become comparable to the initial kinetic energy of the particles. For an "average" collision, we may define a distance r_0 at which the potential energy is equal to the average kinetic energy $\langle T \rangle$ of a gas particle:

$$U\{r_0\} \equiv \langle T \rangle, \qquad (11.2\text{–}2)$$

where r_0 is approximately the average distance of closest approach between two molecules undergoing a collision and is a measure of the molecular size.

If two molecules are found within a distance r_0 of each other at any instant, then we may consider them to be undergoing a collision. If the molecules of a gas are distributed at random in space, with an average density of N/V molecules per unit volume, then the probability of finding another molecule in a volume r_0^3 around a given molecule is Nr_0^3/V. Thus the fraction of molecules undergoing a collision at any instant, or the fraction of the time during which the motion of a given molecule is being changed by collisions, is approximately Nr_0^3/V. This same fraction is also the ratio of average potential to kinetic energy. Therefore, for the details of collisions to be thermodynamically unimportant it is necessary that

$$Nr_0^3/V \ll 1. \tag{11.2–3}$$

For a gas at normal temperature and pressure ($p = 1$ atmosphere, $T = 273°$K), N/V is 2.7×10^{19} molecules/cm^3. From what is known about intermolecular forces, r_0 is approximately 1 A (10^{-8} cm). Thus Nr_0^3/V is about 10^{-5}, and Eq. (11.2–3) is very well satisfied at room temperature and pressure. Only if the gas density N/V is increased greatly will the collisions become important. At densities normally associated with liquids ($N/V \simeq 10^{23}$ cm^{-3}), Nr_0^3/V becomes of the order of one and molecules are continually undergoing collisions with each other.

Despite the fact that a negligible fraction, Nr_0^3/V, of the molecules of a gas are undergoing collisions at any instant, collisions may occur very frequently on the laboratory time scale. As will be seen in Chapter 20, during one second each air molecule at room temperature and pressure undergoes about 10^{10} collisions of the type we have just described, i.e. a collision in which the kinetic energy and momentum of the colliding partners are considerably changed. It is therefore possible to exchange energy very rapidly among the gas molecules without having an appreciable fraction of the energy exist in the form of potential energy of the interacting pairs.* Thus thermodynamic effects, which are explicitly independent of time, and rate processes, which explicitly involve time, may be related to each other through the molecular size r_0. However, the latter affects the thermodynamic properties only to the extent of a gas imperfection but directly determines the rate processes, as discussed in Chapter 20.

11.3 The perfect-gas partition function

In the absence of external gravitational, electric, or magnetic fields a perfect-gas molecule moves in a straight line with constant momentum and energy, and upon collision with another molecule its energy and momentum are suddenly changed to new values. During its straight-line motion, the total energy of such an isolated molecule may be decomposed into two additive parts: (1) the kinetic energy of translation of the mass center ϵ_t and (2) the remaining kinetic and potential energies, which we shall call the molecular internal energy ϵ_i. The former depends only on the total mass m of the molecule and its total momentum p, while the latter depends on the state of rotation, vibration, and electronic excitation. According to the laws of quantum mechanics, the quantum states of translation, discussed in Section 5.8, are independent of those for internal

---

* An analogy with the financial economy can easily be drawn: the amount of currency in circulation need only be a small fraction of the economic wealth which is being redistributed through business transactions.

motions when the molecule is uninfluenced by external forces. We may therefore write the quantized energy of such a molecule as the sum of two quantized parts:

$$\epsilon_j = \epsilon_t + \epsilon_i, \tag{11.3-1}$$

in which the subscripts t and i respectively identify the discrete quantum states of translation and internal motion, while subscript j identifies the total energy state. The discrete values of ϵ_t are given by Eq. (5.8–5) as

$$\epsilon_t = \frac{h^2}{8mV^{2/3}} \, (n_x^2 + n_y^2 + n_z^2), \tag{11.3-2}$$

in which n_x, n_y, and n_z are any set of positive integers (excluding zero), each different set corresponding to a different t-value.

Although it is not generally true, it may be a good approximation that the internal energy ϵ_i can be considered to be the sum of the energies of vibration, rotation, and electronic excitation. While this approximation is pursued in Chapter 12, it is not necessary to the ensuing discussion of perfect gases.

It is customary to make the assumption, which will be justified *a posteriori*, that for a perfect gas the ratio μ/kT is a sufficiently large negative number that Boltzmann statistics may be used,* as discussed in Sections 8.4 and 8.7. The perfect-gas Boltzmann partition function Q, defined in Eq. (8.7–2), is

$$Q\{T, V\} \equiv \sum_j C_j e^{-\epsilon_j/kT}$$

$$= \sum_t \sum_i (e^{-\epsilon_t/kT})(e^{-\epsilon_i/kT}), \tag{11.3-3}$$

in which Eq. (11.3–1) has been used to factor the exponential into two terms and C_j has been taken as unity since t and i identify each quantum state. The double sum is to be taken over all possible pairs of translational and internal quantum states. Since t and i identify independent quantum states, so that all possible combinations of ϵ_t and ϵ_i appear in the sum of Eq. (11.3–3), it may be factored into the product of two sums:

$$Q = \left(\sum_t e^{-\epsilon_t/kT} \right)\left(\sum_i e^{-\epsilon_i/kT} \right) = Q_t Q_i, \tag{11.3-4}$$

where

$$Q_t \equiv \sum_t e^{-\epsilon_t/kT}, \tag{11.3-5}$$

$$Q_i \equiv \sum_i e^{-\epsilon_i/kT}. \tag{11.3-6}$$

---

* In the case where this is not true, such as an electron gas at high density or helium at low temperature, a gas may still be perfect in the sense of Section 11.2, but it is called a *degenerate* perfect gas.

Thus the partition function of the perfect gas is a product of two partition functions, one for the translational motion Q_t, called the *translational partition function*, and a second for the internal motion Q_i, called the *internal partition function*.

To evaluate Q_t, we substitute Eq. (11.3–2) into Eq. (11.3–5), obtaining

$$Q_t = \sum_{n_x=1}^{\infty} \sum_{n_y=1}^{\infty} \sum_{n_z=1}^{\infty} \left\{ \exp\left[- \frac{h^2(n_x^2 + n_y^2 + n_z^2)}{8mkTV^{2/3}} \right] \right\}. \tag{11.3–7}$$

Following the same procedure used in obtaining Eqs. (11.3–3) and (11.3–4), the exponential may be factored into three terms, each involving either n_x, n_y, or n_z in the exponent, and the sum may then be factored into the product of three infinite sums:

$$Q_t = \left[\sum_{n_x} \exp\left(- \frac{h^2 n_x^2}{8mkTV^{2/3}} \right) \right] \left[\sum_{n_y} \exp\left(- \frac{h^2 n_y^2}{8mkTV^{2/3}} \right) \right]$$
$$\times \left[\sum_{n_z} \exp\left(- \frac{h^2 n_z^2}{8mkTV^{2/3}} \right) \right] \tag{11.3–8}$$

since all possible combinations of n_x, n_y, and n_z are to be counted.

The sums may be replaced by integrals if the change in the exponent from one term to the next is sufficiently small:

$$\sum_{n_x=1}^{\infty} \exp\left(- \frac{h^2 n_x^2}{8mkTV^{2/3}} \right) = \int_0^{\infty} \exp\left(- \frac{h^2 n_x^2}{8mkTV^{2/3}} \right) dn_x \tag{11.3–9}$$

if

$$\frac{h^2}{8mkTV^{2/3}} \ll 1. \tag{11.3–10}$$

The integral of Eq. (11.3–9) is a definite integral, which may be evaluated from Table A–4:

$$\int_0^{\infty} \exp\left(- \frac{h^2 n_x^2}{8mkTV^{2/3}} \right) dn_x$$
$$= \left(\frac{8mkTV^{2/3}}{h^2} \right)^{1/2} \int_0^{\infty} \exp\left(- \frac{h^2 n_x^2}{8mkTV^{2/3}} \right) d\left(\frac{h^2 n_x^2}{8mkTV^{2/3}} \right)^{1/2}$$
$$= \left(\frac{2\pi mkT}{h^2} \right)^{1/2} V^{1/3}. \tag{11.3–11}$$

Since the series in Eq. (11.3–8) involving n_y and n_z are identical with that for n_x,

Table 11.1.   Evaluation of Q_t/N at the critical point*

Gas	T_c, °K	P_c, atm	$(V/N)_c$, 10^{-22} cm³	$\{2\pi mkT_c/h^2\}^{3/2}(V/N)_c$
He	5.3	2.26	0.96	1.8
Ar	151	48	1.25	11,200
H₂	33.3	12.8	1.08	6
O₂	154.4	49.7	1.23	8,000
H₂O	647.4	218	0.93	22,000

      * Critical-point data from Table 14.3.

by combining Eqs. (11.3–8), (11.3–9), and (11.3–11) the translational partition function is

$$Q_t = \left(\frac{2\pi mkT}{h^2}\right)^{3/2} V. \tag{11.3-12}$$

Before proceeding further, let us evaluate μ/kT from Eq. (8.7–10) in order to ascertain under what conditions it is sufficiently large and negative to justify the original assumption as to the applicability of Boltzmann statistics:

$$\frac{\mu}{kT} = \ln\left(\frac{N}{Q}\right) = -\ln\left[\left(\frac{Q_t}{N}\right)Q_i\right]$$

$$= -\ln\left(\frac{2\pi mkT}{h^2}\right)^{3/2}\left(\frac{V}{N}\right) - \ln Q_i. \tag{11.3-13}$$

Since Q_i is unity or greater, it is sufficient that

$$\left(\frac{2\pi mkT}{h^2}\right)^{3/2}\left(\frac{V}{N}\right) \gg 1 \tag{11.3-14}$$

in order for Boltzmann statistics to apply. Table 11.1 gives values of $Q_t/N = (2\pi mkT/h^2)^{3/2}(V/N)$ for several gases evaluated at the critical point,* which corresponds to the largest density and hence smallest value of V/N at which a fluid would be considered a gas rather than a liquid. It is readily seen that all gases except helium† and hydrogen condense to a liquid before the restrictions of Eq. (11.3–14) are violated. At temperatures higher than the critical temperature and pressures lower than the critical pressure, helium and hydrogen will also satisfy Eq. (11.3–14). Furthermore, the restriction of Eq. (11.3–10) will be more easily satisfied than that of Eq. (11.3–14), since $N \gg 1$.

---

    * For a discussion of the critical point, read Section 14.9.

    † For gaseous helium at a temperature below about 10°K, Bose-Einstein statistics must be used to determine the perfect-gas behavior. For a discussion of this system, see Mayer and Mayer, p. 416.

There is a simple quantum-mechanical interpretation of the restriction expressed by Eq. (11.3–14). If a gas particle has a kinetic energy equal to $3kT/2$, which will subsequently be shown to be the average energy, its momentum p is

$$p^2/2m = 3kT/2,$$
$$p = (3mkT)^{1/2}. \tag{11.3–15}$$

The de Broglie wavelength λ corresponding to this momentum is found from Eq. (5.3–1):

$$\lambda = h/p = (h^2/3mkT)^{1/2}. \tag{11.3–16}$$

In terms of the de Broglie wavelength, the restriction of Eq. (11.3–14) may be written as

$$\lambda \ll (V/N)^{1/3}. \tag{11.3–17}$$

Since $(V/N)^{1/3}$ is the average distance between particles in a gas, the use of Boltzmann statistics becomes invalid whenever the de Broglie wavelength of a particle of average energy becomes equal to the average distance between particles. In such a case, the wave function of a particle, which extends over a volume λ^3, overlaps the wave functions of nearby particles, so that it becomes likely that several particles will have the same wave function $\psi(\mathbf{r}, t)$, that is, exist in the same quantum state. When this occurs, the assumption underlying Boltzmann statistics, which is the improbability of two particles existing in the same quantum state at the same time, ceases to be valid.

Another system for which Boltzmann statistics fails to apply is the electron gas under the condition of high-number density found in metallic solids. Because of the small mass of the electron, Eq. (11.3–14) cannot be satisfied at moderate temperatures when V/N has the value corresponding to one free electron per atom of the solid. This particular case is discussed in Section 15.7.

11.4   Perfect-gas thermodynamic properties

The internal energy E, entropy S, chemical potential μ, and pressure p of a perfect gas may now be calculated from the general formulas for a Boltzmann system, Eqs. (8.7–10) through (8.7–12) and (9.9–7), by using the perfect-gas partition function given in Eqs. (11.3–4), (11.3–6), and (11.3–12). In all of these formulas either $\ln Q$ or its derivative appears. Since Q is the product of two factors, Q_t and Q_i, the thermodynamic properties will be the sum of two terms, one depending on Q_t and the other on Q_i. For example, the internal energy is

$$E = NkT^2 \left(\frac{\partial \ln Q}{\partial T}\right)_V = NkT^2 \left\{\frac{\partial \ln (Q_t Q_i)}{\partial T}\right\}_V$$

$$= NkT^2 \left\{\left(\frac{\partial \ln Q_t}{\partial T}\right)_V + \left(\frac{\partial \ln Q_i}{\partial T}\right)_V\right\}. \tag{11.4–1}$$

We may therefore define the first term in Eq. (11.4–1) as the internal energy component due to the translational motion E_t and the second term as the component due to internal motion with respect to the mass center of the molecule, E_i. Using this same scheme for all the properties, we find

$$E = E_t + E_i, \qquad S = S_t + S_i,$$
$$\mu = \mu_t + \mu_i, \qquad p = p_t + p_i,$$

(11.4–2)

in which

$$E_t = \tfrac{3}{2}NkT,$$

(11.4–3)

$$S_t = Nk\left[\frac{5}{2} + \ln\left\{\left(\frac{2\pi mkT}{h^2}\right)^{3/2}\frac{V}{N}\right\}\right],$$

(11.4–4)

$$\mu_t = -kT\ln\left\{\left(\frac{2\pi mkT}{h^2}\right)^{3/2}\frac{V}{N}\right\},$$

(11.4–5)

$$p_t = \frac{NkT}{V},$$

(11.4–6)

$$E_i = NkT^2\left(\frac{d\ln Q_i}{dT}\right),$$

(11.4–7)

$$S_i = \frac{E_i}{T} + Nk\ln Q_i,$$

(11.4–8)

$$\mu_i = -kT\ln Q_i,$$

(11.4–9)

$$p_i = 0.$$

(11.4–10)

In obtaining these equations, wherever the term Q/N or eQ/N appears, it has been factored into $(Q_t/N)Q_i$ or $(eQ_t/N)Q_i$. Furthermore, since the quantum states of internal motion are not affected by the size of the box which confines the gas, Q_i is independent of V and depends only on T. As a result, the derivative in Eq. (11.4–7) is a total derivative and the internal motion does not contribute to the pressure:

$$p_i = NkT\frac{\partial\ln Q_i}{\partial V} = 0.$$

(11.4–11)

The perfect-gas equation of state follows from Eqs. (11.4–2), (11.4–6), and (11.4–10),

$$pV = NkT,$$

(11.4–12)

and expresses the fact that the translational motion alone gives rise to the gas pressure. Unlike the other thermodynamic properties, the pressure does not depend on the internal degrees of freedom or the molecular mass but only on the number of molecules, N, in the volume V at the temperature T.

The relationship between entropy, energy, and volume can be put in the form of the caloric equation of state, Eq. (11.1–4), through use of the temperature as a parameter. For this purpose, we sum the contributions of translation and internal motion and obtain

$$S = Nk \left\{ \frac{3}{2} \ln T + T \frac{d \ln Q_i}{dT} + \ln Q_i \right\} + Nk \ln \left\{ \left(\frac{2\pi mk}{h^2} \right)^{3/2} \frac{e^{5/2} V}{N} \right\},$$

$$(11.4–13)$$

$$E = NkT \left\{ \frac{3}{2} + T \frac{d \ln Q_i}{dT} \right\}. \qquad (11.4–14)$$

It can be seen that Eq. (11.4–13) has the form of Eq. (11.1–4), since the first term is a function of T, which itself is a function of E, through Eq. (11.4–14), and the second term is a function of V alone.

It should be noted that Eq. (11.4–4) gives a value of minus infinity for S if T is set equal to zero, which is contrary to the original definition of entropy, Eq. (7.4–1), as being proportional to the logarithm of the number of microstates of the system and therefore always positive or at least zero. However, the restriction of Eq. (11.3–14) necessarily limits the range of validity of Eq. (11.4–4) to values of T and N/V which ensure that the entropy so computed will be positive and that μ/kT will be negative.

Finally, Eq. (11.4–14) shows that the internal energy of a perfect gas is a function of temperature alone and does not depend on the volume. This will also be true of the enthalpy H and the specific heats C_v and C_p defined in Eqs. (10.4–12), (10.4–16), and (10.4–17) as

$$H \equiv E + pV,$$

$$C_v \equiv \left(\frac{\partial E}{\partial T} \right)_V,$$

$$C_p \equiv \left[\frac{\partial (E + pV)}{\partial T} \right]_p = \left(\frac{\partial H}{\partial T} \right)_p.$$

Using Eqs. (11.4–2), (11.4–3), (11.4–7), and (11.4–12), the enthalpy and specific heats for a perfect gas become

$$H = \tfrac{5}{2} NkT + E_i, \qquad (11.4–15)$$

$$C_v = \tfrac{3}{2} Nk + dE_i/dT, \qquad (11.4–16)$$

$$C_p = \tfrac{5}{2} Nk + dE_i/dT. \qquad (11.4–17)$$

Thus the perfect-gas specific heats will change only with temperature due to the internal degrees of freedom of the molecule.

11.5   The perfect monatomic gas

At normal temperature and pressure, the noble gases (He, Ne, A, Kr, Xe) exist as monatomic gases. At somewhat higher temperatures, the vapors of the alkali metals (Li, Na, K, Ru, Cs) are also monatomic. At high temperatures and low pressures, diatomic gases such as H_2 or N_2 may be so greatly dissociated that almost all the gas particles are H or N atoms rather than molecules. In all these instances, the gases may be treated as perfect monatomic gases.

The only contribution to the internal motions of the monatomic gas particles comes from electronic and nuclear quantum states. Since the nuclear spin may be important only in the presence of a magnetic field, in determining the rotational states of a diatomic molecule, or in interactions between particles in a crystal, it is generally ignored in treating perfect monatomic gases. However, at high temperatures the electronic excitation of the atoms may make contributions to the thermodynamic properties which must be taken into account.

The major difficulty in calculating the internal partition function of atoms stems from the fact that the electronic quantum states cannot be expressed in terms of a simple formula, except for the hydrogen atom or any single electron atom such as the singly ionized helium atom. The energies and number of quantum states must be determined experimentally, and the calculation of thermodynamic quantities must be done numerically. The electronic partition function Q_e may be written as a series:

$$Q_e = \Sigma g_j e^{-\epsilon_j/kT} = g_0 + g_1 e^{-\epsilon_1/kT} + g_2 e^{-\epsilon_2/kT} + \cdots, \quad (11.5\text{--}1)$$

in which g_j is the number of quantum states of energy ϵ_j and ϵ_0 is taken to be zero for convenience. The corresponding values of E, S, and μ become

$$E_e = NkT^2 \frac{d \ln Q_e}{dT} = \frac{N}{Q_e} \sum_j g_j \epsilon_j e^{-\epsilon_j/kT}$$

$$= \frac{N}{Q_e} (g_1 \epsilon_1 e^{-\epsilon_1/kT} + g_2 \epsilon_2 e^{-\epsilon_2/kT} + \cdots), \quad (11.5\text{--}2)$$

$$S_e = \frac{E_e}{T} + Nk \ln Q_e, \quad (11.5\text{--}3)$$

$$\mu_e = -kT \ln Q_e. \quad (11.5\text{--}4)$$

A list of electronic energy states of some typical atoms is given in Table 11.2. The electronic energies have been divided by Boltzmann's constant k so that the exponent ϵ_j/kT may be more readily computed.* It can be seen that for

---

* Most tables list ϵ_j in the spectroscopist's unit of reciprocal wavelength, cm^{-1}. To obtain ϵ_j/k in units of K°, multiply by 1.4388 (see Table A–2). The source of this scale of measurement is the relationship between energy differences and frequency, or wavelength, of the light emitted, which is given in Eq. (5.2–2): $\epsilon_i - \epsilon_j = h\nu_{ij} = hc/\lambda_{ij}$, in which c is the speed of light. Thus $(\epsilon_i - \epsilon_j)/k = (hc/k)(1/\lambda_{ij})$, where λ_{ij} is the experimentally measured quantity but is reported as λ_{ij}^{-1}.

Table 11.2

Electronic energy states for which $\epsilon_e/k \leq 50{,}000\mathrm{K}°*$

Atom	Atomic weight	State†	ϵ_j/k, K°	g_j	ϵ_{ion}/k, K°	$(g_0)_{ion}‡$
H	1.008	^2S	0	2	158,000	1
He	4.003	^1S	0	1	285,500	2
C	12.01	^3P	0	9	130,800	6
		^1D	14,650	5		
		^1S	31,080	1		
		^5S	48,500	5		
N	14.01	^4S	0	4	169,000	9
		^2D	27,600	10		
		^2P	41,400	6		
O	16.00	^3P	0	9	158,200	4
		^1D	22,830	5		
		^1S	48,600	1		
Ne	20.18	^1S	0	1	250,000	6
Na	22.99	^2S	0	2	59,600	1
		^2P	24,400	6		
		^2S	37,000	2		
		^2D	41,950	10		
		^2P	43,600	6		
		^2S	47,700	2		
		^2D	49,600	10		
		^2F	49,700	14		
S	32.07	^3P	0	9	120,300	4
		^1D	13,300	5		
		^1S	27,400	1		
Cl	35.46	^2P	0	6	151,200	9
A	39.94	^1S	0	1	183,000	6
Xe	131.3	^1S	0	1	140,900	6

* Data from Moore.

† For an explanation of the term symbols in this column, see Davidson, p. 108. States of nearly equal energy have been put into groups, for which the total number of states is given in column under g_j.

‡ The number of quantum states of lowest electronic energy for the singly ionized atom.

gas temperatures below 1000°K, the contribution to Q, E, and S, is appreciable only for the lowest electronic state, called the ground state. Consequently Eqs. (11.5–2) through (11.5–4) may be approximated by

$$E_e \simeq 0, \tag{11.5–5}$$

$$S_e \simeq Nk \ln g_0, \tag{11.5–6}$$

$$\mu_e \simeq -kT \ln g_0. \tag{11.5–7}$$

With this approximation, the thermodynamic properties of a perfect monatomic gas may be obtained by substitution into Eqs. (11.4–2) through (11.4–17):

$$E \simeq \tfrac{3}{2} NkT, \tag{11.5–8}$$

$$S \simeq Nk \left[\frac{5}{2} + \ln \left\{ \left(\frac{2\pi mkT}{h^2} \right)^{3/2} \frac{g_0 V}{N} \right\} \right], \tag{11.5–9}$$

$$\mu \simeq -kT \ln \left\{ \left(\frac{2\pi mkT}{h^2} \right)^{3/2} \frac{g_0 V}{N} \right\}, \tag{11.5–10}$$

$$pV = NkT, \tag{11.5–11}$$

$$H \equiv E + pV \simeq \tfrac{5}{2} NkT, \tag{11.5–12}$$

$$C_v \simeq \tfrac{3}{2} Nk, \tag{11.5–13}$$

$$C_p \simeq \tfrac{5}{2} Nk. \tag{11.5–14}$$

A direct consequence of Eqs. (11.5–11) and (11.5–8) is that the energy and pressure of a monatomic gas are related by

$$p \simeq \tfrac{2}{3}(E/V). \tag{11.5–15}$$

In Chapter 20, it will be found that this proportionality between pressure and energy density (i.e., energy per unit volume) can be derived directly from the laws of motion of the gas particles and may also be true even if the gas is not at thermodynamic equilibrium. This serves to emphasize the fact that dynamical properties such as E, V, and p may be related through particle dynamics alone, while thermodynamical properties such as T, S, and μ can be determined only through the additional postulates and development of statistical mechanics.

11.6 The classical partition function

In Section 8.8, an alternative method of determining the Boltzmann partition function was given, based on the general relationship between a volume element in phase space and the number of quantum states corresponding to that volume element. We will rederive the formula for Q_t by using this approach.

In classical mechanics the translational energy ϵ_t of a freely moving particle is

$$\epsilon_t = (1/2m)(p_x^2 + p_y^2 + p_z^2). \tag{11.6-1}$$

Since we are considering translation in three directions, there are six dimensions to μ-space: x, y, z, p_x, p_y, and p_z. The partition function given by Eq. (8.8–2) becomes, for the case of translation,

$$Q_t = \frac{1}{h^3} \int \cdots \int \exp\left(-\frac{p_x^2 + p_y^2 + p_z^2}{2mkT}\right) dx\, dy\, dz\, dp_x\, dp_y\, dp_z. \tag{11.6-2}$$

The limits of integration on x, y, and z are the walls of the container, while those for the momentum components are $\pm\infty$. Since the integrand of Eq. (11.6–2) is independent of x, y, and z, these coordinates may be integrated first to give a factor V. The integrand may then be factored into three exponentials, each of which may be integrated to give

$$\int_{-\infty}^{\infty} e^{-p_x^2/2mkT}\, dp_x = (2\pi mkT)^{1/2}, \tag{11.6-3}$$

where the definite integral has been evaluated from Table A–4. Consequently, Q_t so evaluated is identical with that previously derived in Eq. (11.3–12).

The general limitations imposed on the use of the classical partition function, Eq. (8.8–2), are discussed in Section 8.8 and, for the translational motion of a perfect gas, become identical to those treated in Section 11.3.

11.7 The imperfect gas

It is not too difficult to determine the effect of intermolecular forces on the thermodynamic properties, provided that the gas is sufficiently dilute (i.e., its number density N/V is small enough) so that only two-body collisions need be considered. As estimated in Section 11.2, the probability that a given molecule will have a neighbor within a distance r_0 is Nr_0^3/V, a number which is much less than unity whenever our system is a gas rather than a liquid. If at any instant we select from our gas all those pairs of molecules undergoing a collision and ask what fraction of these would have a third molecule within a distance r_0, then this fraction would again be about Nr_0^3/V. Thus we see that the ratio of the probability of an N-body collision to an $(N - 1)$-body collision is just about Nr_0^3/V. If the gas is sufficiently dilute, i.e. if Nr_0^3/V is much less than one, then the corrections to the perfect gas law may be determined by considering each type of collision separately and then adding together the results. We should then expect that the equation of state, for example, would have the form

$$\frac{pV}{NkT} = 1 + B\left(\frac{Nr_0^3}{V}\right) + C\left(\frac{Nr_0^3}{V}\right)^2 + \cdots, \tag{11.7-1}$$

in which B and C are functions of temperature. As N/V approaches zero, the gas behaves exactly like a perfect gas since the right-hand side of Eq. (11.7–1) approaches one. An expansion of the equation of state of the form of Eq. (11.7–1) is called a *virial expansion*, and the coefficients of V^{-1}, V^{-2}, ... in the terms on the right-hand side are called the second, third, ... *virial coefficients*. Each such coefficient accounts for the intermolecular forces in collisions involving successively more molecules.

If we restrict ourselves to two-body collisions, we may determine the second virial coefficient, as well as the corresponding corrections to the perfect-gas thermodynamic properties due to two-body collisions, by making use of the classical partition function, Eq. (8.8–2). We first note that the total translational energy of a molecule is the sum of its kinetic and potential energies:

$$\epsilon_t = (1/2m)(p_x^2 + p_y^2 + p_z^2) + u\{r\}, \tag{11.7–2}$$

in which it is assumed that the potential energy $u\{r\}$ depends only on the distance r between the particle and its nearest neighbor. If we write the integral for the partition function as in Eq. (11.6–2), Q becomes

$$Q = \frac{1}{h^3} \int \cdots \int \exp\left(-\frac{p_x^2 + p_y^2 + p_z^2}{2mkT} - \frac{u}{kT}\right) dx\, dy\, dz\, dp_x\, dp_y\, dp_z. \tag{11.7–3}$$

Because the integrand can be factored into two exponentials, one of which explicitly depends on p_x, p_y, and p_z while the other implicitly depends on x, y, and z through the potential energy u, the first may be integrated on the momenta to give three identical factors, as in Eq. (11.6–3). Equation (11.7–3) thereby reduces to

$$Q = \left\{\frac{2\pi mkT}{h^3}\right\}^{3/2} \iiint e^{-u/kT}\, dx\, dy\, dz. \tag{11.7–4}$$

The integral in Eq. (11.7–4) can be rewritten in a different form by adding and subtracting unity from the integrand:

$$\iiint e^{-u/kT}\, dx\, dy\, dz = \iiint [1 - (1 - e^{-u/kT})]\, dx\, dy\, dz$$

$$= V - \iiint (1 - e^{-u/kT})\, dx\, dy\, dz. \tag{11.7–5}$$

If there are N particles in the gas, there are $N(N - 1)/2$ possible pairs of particles or, on the average, $N/2$ partners per particle. Thus there will be $N/2$ points within the volume V near which the potential energy is sufficiently large compared with kT to make $1 - e^{-u/kT}$ different from zero. Within each one of these small volumes, the integration on x, y, and z may be replaced by an integration on the radial distance r from the particle if the volume element $dx\, dy\, dz$ is replaced by a spherical shell of radius r and thickness dr, having a volume of $4\pi r^2\, dr$. The integral in Eq. (11.7–5) is therefore

$$\iiint (1 - e^{-u/kT})\, dx\, dy\, dz = \frac{N}{2} \int_0^\infty (1 - e^{-u\{r\}/kT})(4\pi r^2\, dr). \qquad (11.7\text{–}6)$$

By combining Eqs. (11.7–4) through (11.7–6), the partition function for the imperfect gas is

$$Q = \left\{\frac{2\pi m k T}{h^2}\right\}^{3/2} V \left\{1 - \frac{N}{V} b\{T\}\right\}, \qquad (11.7\text{–}7)$$

where

$$b\{T\} \equiv 2\pi \int_0^\infty (1 - e^{-u/kT}) r^2\, dr. \qquad (11.7\text{–}8)$$

Now $b\{T\}$ is essentially the molecular volume r_0^3 and thus Nb/V is much less than 1, according to our original assumption of a dilute gas. Making use of Eq. (11.3–12), the logarithm of Q then becomes

$$\ln Q = \ln Q_t + \ln \left(1 - \frac{Nb}{V}\right) = \ln Q_t - \frac{Nb\{T\}}{V} \qquad (11.7\text{–}9)$$

because $\ln (1 + x)$ is approximately x for $x \ll 1$ (see Table A–5).

It is now a simple matter to determine the additive contributions to E, S, p, and μ due to the additional factor in the partition function involving the integral $b\{T\}$. Making use of the relations developed in Section 11.4, we find

$$E = E_t - NkT^2 \left(\frac{N}{V}\right) \frac{db}{dT}, \qquad (11.7\text{–}10)$$

$$S = S_t - Nk \left(\frac{N}{V}\right) \left(T \frac{db}{dT} + b\right), \qquad (11.7\text{–}11)$$

$$\mu = \mu_t + kT \left(\frac{N}{V}\right) b, \qquad (11.7\text{–}12)$$

$$p = \frac{NkT}{V} \left(1 + \frac{Nb}{V}\right). \qquad (11.7\text{–}13)$$

By comparison with Eq. (11.7–1), we see that the second virial coefficient is Nb. The corrections to E and S involve db/dT, which is a function of temperature alone.

A very simple model of a gas is the *hard-sphere model* in which the molecules exert no force on each other until $r = d$, at which point the repulsive force becomes infinite. This is exactly the force law between two colliding rigid spheres of diameter d. The corresponding potential energy is zero for $r > d$ and positive

Table 11.3. Second virial coefficients at 300°K*

Gas	Nb (cm³/gm-mole)	Nb/V ($p = 1$ atm)
He	11.7	5.2×10^{-4}
Ne	10	4.5×10^{-4}
A	-15.2	-6.8×10^{-4}
H_2	14.3	6.4×10^{-4}
N_2	-4.4	-2.0×10^{-4}
CH_4	-49	2.2×10^{-3}
H_2O	-112	5.0×10^{-3}

* Data from Hirschfelder, Curtiss, and Bird, Chapter 3.

infinite for $r < d$. Using this model, it is easy to determine b from Eq. (11.7–8):

$$b = 2\pi \int_0^d r^2 \, dr = \frac{2\pi d^3}{3}, \qquad (11.7\text{–}14)$$

which is four times the volume of the hard-sphere molecule.

Table 11.3 gives selected values of Nb measured at 300°K for a mole of gas and the corresponding value of Nb/V at one-atmosphere pressure. Although $b\{T\}$ changes somewhat with temperature, it can be concluded from this table that the corrections for gas imperfections are less than one percent of the perfect-gas values for densities less than one hundred times normal density. The experimentally measured variation of b with temperature can be quite accurately reproduced by a suitable choice of intermolecular potential-energy function $u\{r\}$ and constitutes an indirect thermodynamic measurement of the intermolecular potential energy.*

11.8 Specific extensive properties

There are two generally useful ways of giving numerical values of the extensive properties such as energy and entropy. If the number of particles in the system is chosen to be Avogadro's number, $\widetilde{N} = 6.023 \times 10^{23}$, then the system contains one gm-mole of substance. The molar internal energy $\widetilde{E}$, the molar entropy $\widetilde{S}$, and the molar volume $\widetilde{V}$ so defined all contain the factor $\widetilde{N}k$, called the *universal gas constant*, for which the symbol $\widetilde{R}$ is used:

$$\begin{aligned} \widetilde{R} \equiv \widetilde{N}k &= 1.9872 \text{ cal/gm-mole K}° \\ &= 8.3143 \times 10^7 \text{ erg/gm-mole K}°. \end{aligned} \qquad (11.8\text{–}1)$$

* See Hirschfelder, Curtiss, and Bird, Chapter 3.

It is customary to specify $\widetilde{E}$ in cal/gm-mole, whereas the perfect-gas law, Eq. (11.4–12), requires cgs-units. In Eq. (11.8–1), $\widetilde{R}$ is given in both units for convenience.

If mks-units are used, $\widetilde{N}$ has the value of 6.023×10^{26} molecules per kgm-mole, and $\widetilde{R}$ becomes

$$\widetilde{R} = 1.9872 \text{ kcal/kgm-mole K}°$$
$$= 8.3143 \times 10^3 \text{ j/kgm-mole K}°. \tag{11.8–2}$$

Another method of specifying these properties is useful when considering the flow of fluids. Since fluid dynamics relates the forces and acceleration of a fluid, it is more convenient to specify the internal energy, entropy, or volume per unit mass of substance. These quantities are denoted by lower-case letters:

$$e \equiv E/Nm, \qquad s \equiv S/Nm,$$
$$\tag{11.8–3}$$
$$v \equiv V/Nm \equiv 1/\rho, \qquad h \equiv H/Nm = e + pv.$$

Here m is the mass of a molecule and ρ is the *mass density*, or mass per unit volume. Because E, S, and V all have the factor Nk, one sees that e, s, and v have the factor k/m, which is given the symbol $\mathcal{R}$:

$$\mathcal{R} \equiv k/m = (\widetilde{N}k)/(\widetilde{N}m) = \widetilde{R}/\widetilde{M}, \tag{11.8–4}$$

where $\widetilde{M}$ is the *molecular weight*, or mass of one mole of substance.

By virtue of Eqs. (11.4–16) and (11.4–17), the specific heats are related to the gas constant by

$$\widetilde{C}_p = \widetilde{C}_v + \widetilde{R}, \tag{11.8–5}$$

$$c_p = c_v + \mathcal{R}. \tag{11.8–6}$$

Tables A–2 and A–3 give factors for converting thermodynamic properties from one set of units to another.

PROBLEMS

11.1 At what temperature is the mean translational kinetic energy of a molecule equal to that of a singly charged ion that has been accelerated from rest through a potential difference of (a) 1 volt and (b) 1000 volts?

11.2 A mole of argon at 300°K and a mole of helium have equal volumes. What helium temperature is required if both gases are to have the same entropy?

11.3 (a) For a monatomic gas at low temperatures, show that the entropy may be written in the dimensionless form

$$S/Nk = S_0/Nk + c_1 \log (H/H_0) + c_2 \log (V/V_0),$$

in which c_1 and c_2 are dimensionless constants and S_0, H_0, and V_0 are evaluated at a reference state p_0, T_0. (b) If $p_0 = 1$ atm and $T_0 = 273.16$°K, calculate

S_0/Nk, c_1 and c_2 for helium.   (c) Plot lines of $V = 10^{-1}V_0$, $V = V_0$, and $V = 10V_0$ on a chart of log (H/H_0) versus $(S - S_0)/Nk$.   (d) Plot lines of $p = 10^{-1}p_0$, $p = p_0$, and $p = 10p_0$ on the same chart.   (e) Plot lines of $T = 10T_0$, $T = T_0$, and $T = 10^{-1}T_0$ on the same chart.   (f) Plot the line $\mu = \mu_0$.

11.4 According to the solution of the wave equation for a monatomic gas particle confined in a rectangular box of side dimensions L_x, L_y, and L_z, the translational energy ϵ_t is $h^2\{(n_x/L_x)^2 + (n_y/L_y)^2 + (n_z/L_z)^2\}/8m$, where n_x, n_y, and n_z are integers.   Show that the translational partition function Q_t is given by Eq. (11.3–12), independent of the shape of the box, i.e. the ratios L_y/L_x and L_z/L_x.

11.5 Helium gas in a high-altitude polyethylene balloon expands in volume by a factor of 10 while the balloon rises from sea level to its peak altitude.   During ascent the gas temperature was found to remain constant at a value of 300°K because of absorption of heat from the sun.   How much heat per mole of helium was absorbed during ascent?

11.6 A cylindrical vessel 1 m long and 0.1 m in diameter is filled with a monatomic gas at $p = 1$ atm and $T = 300°$K.   The gas is to be heated by an electrical discharge along the tube axis from electrodes at either end.   The discharge is supplied from a capacitor bank which stores 10^4 j.   What will be the gas temperature immediately after the discharge?

11.7 N perfect monatomic gas particles are contained in a rectangular box of base area A and height L.   The gas particles are subject to a downward gravitational force of magnitude mg, where m is the atomic mass and g is the gravitational acceleration.   (a) Find the partition function Q from Eq. (8.8–2) by integrating exp $\{-(\text{kinetic energy} + \text{potential energy})/kT\}$ over all of phase space, assuming that the potential energy is zero at the bottom of the box.   (b) By differentiating Q, show that $E = 3NkT/2 + mgLN/2$ if $mgL \ll kT$.

11.8 A balloon is so slowly inflated with air that the process is carried out at constant temperature.   Measurements of the pressure difference (Δp) between the air inside and outside the balloon are made as the volume increases beyond the initial value of 1 ft^3 and are as follows:

Δp, psi	0	2.1	3.1	3.7
V, ft^3	1	2	3	4

(a) Compute the work done on the balloon material alone.   (b) Compute the work required to inflate the balloon if the process is reversible.   (The atmospheric pressure is 14.7 psi.)

11.9 A force law sometimes used for imperfect gas calculations is the Sutherland model, for which $u = -\epsilon(\sigma/r)^6$ for $r > \sigma$ and $u = \infty$ for $r < \sigma$.   (a) Determine $b\{T\}$ when $T \gg \epsilon/k$.   (b) Find the corrections to the gas law and the internal energy (Eqs. 11.7–10 and 11.7–13).

11.10 At the boiling point of helium ($p = 1$ atm and $T = 4.22°$K) the vapor specific volume v is 0.06 m^3/kgm.   (a) Calculate v from the perfect-gas law.   (b) Assuming that Eq. (11.7–13) applies at this temperature and pressure, calculate the second virial coefficient Nb in the units used in Table 11.3.   (Compare this number with the volume of the liquid at the boiling point, 8 cm^3/gm.)

11.11 The speed of sound a in a perfect gas is $\{(c_p/c_v)\Re T\}^{1/2}$. Calculate the speed of sound in helium at 300°K.

11.12 How many cubic feet of helium at 1-atm pressure and 300°K are required to lift 2000 lb total weight of balloon material and payload of a high-altitude balloon? (For the atmosphere, $p = 1$ atm, $T = 300$°K, and $\widetilde{M} = 28.9$.)

11.13 A helium storage tank for a blowdown hypersonic wind tunnel has a volume of 10^4 ft³. During blowdown, the pressure decreases very suddenly from 50 atm to 40 atm, this process being adiabatic. (a) If the initial temperature is 300°K, what will be the gas temperature immediately after blowdown? (b) How much helium has left the tank? (c) A long time after blowdown, the helium temperature rises to 300°K. What will be the pressure?

11.14 (a) If a perfect monatomic gas is expanded adiabatically ($dQ = 0$) in a cylinder to twice its initial volume and *all* the work is that done on the moving piston, what is the ratio of final to initial pressure? (b) If the gas is expanded as above except that some heat is added, will the final pressure be higher or lower than that of part (a)? Prove your answer.

11.15 An atomic oxygen gas exists at a high temperature. (a) At what temperature would the number of atoms in the ^1D- and ^1S-states (see Table 11.2) be 1% of the number in the ^3P ground state? (b) At this temperature, what would be the ratio of the electronic energy E_e to the translational energy E_t of all the atoms?

12

POLYATOMIC PERFECT GASES

12.1 The rotation and vibration of polyatomic molecules

When in a state of minimum energy for internal motion, a molecule of n atoms is a fairly rigid structure in which the internuclear distances and directions are well determined. If the molecule rotates, its motion is that of a classical "rigid body," having in general three principal moments of inertia. If the molecule rotates at a very high angular velocity, the centrifugal forces will distort the structure, pulling the nuclei farther away from the mass center in the same manner as a weight swung in a circle from the end of a rubber band will move farther outward as its velocity is increased. Due to this stretching of the molecule, the moments of inertia will be increased when the rate of rotation, or rotational energy, is high.

In the absence of rotation, the nuclei can vibrate about their undisturbed positions with characteristic frequencies. If the amplitude of this motion is very large, then the molecule ceases to resemble very closely a rigid body, and the frequency of vibration is different from that for small-amplitude vibration. For large amounts of vibrational and rotational energy, these two motions are coupled since the rotation stretches the molecule and changes the vibrational frequency while the vibration alters the moment of inertia.

If it were not for the fact that the forces binding the atoms of a molecule were so strong, this coupling would have an important effect on the internal motion of a molecule. For most molecules the moments of inertia and the vibrational frequencies are only slightly changed when the internal energy (of either rotation or vibration) is less than half the *dissociation energy*, i.e. the energy which is required to break the molecule apart into its constituent atoms. Under the conditions of high gas temperature which are required to excite the vibration or rotation to such high energies, there will be so few molecules that the exact state of internal molecular motion is of little consequence to the thermodynamic properties of the gas as a whole. For this reason, it is generally a good approximation to consider the vibrational and rotational motions to be uncoupled and their energies to be additive.

The atoms of a molecule are bound together by the outermost electrons of each atom which interact with each other and with nearby atoms. If these

191

electrons are excited to a quantum state of higher energy, an excited electronic state of the molecule, analogous to that of an atom, is formed. As a result of this electronic excitation, the forces joining the atoms will be changed, and the internuclear separation and orientation and thereby the moments of inertia and vibrational frequencies may be different from those of the unexcited, or ground-state, molecule. Even though the vibrational and rotational motions are coupled to the electronic motion, it may be a useful approximation to disregard the change in moment of inertia and vibrational frequencies with electronic excitation. Assuming great accuracy is not required, it is possible to consider the internal energy ϵ_i of a molecule as the sum of rotational (ϵ_r), vibrational (ϵ_v), and electronic (ϵ_e) components:

$$\epsilon_i = \epsilon_r + \epsilon_v + \epsilon_e, \tag{12.1-1}$$

where each mode of motion is independent of the others, i.e. the quantum state of one mode is uninfluenced by the quantum state of another.

An immediate consequence of this assumption is the possibility of factoring the internal partition function Q_i into the product of partition functions for rotation (Q_r), vibration (Q_v), and electronic excitation (Q_e). From Eq. (11.3–6) for Q_i and Eq. (12.1–1), we find

$$Q_i = \sum_i e^{-\epsilon_i/kT} = \sum_r \sum_v \sum_e e^{-(\epsilon_r + \epsilon_v + \epsilon_e)/kT}$$

$$= \left(\sum_r e^{-\epsilon_r/kT} \right) \left(\sum_v e^{-\epsilon_v/kT} \right) \left(\sum_e e^{-\epsilon_e/kT} \right)$$

$$= Q_r Q_v Q_e. \tag{12.1-2}$$

For the same reason, the thermodynamic properties will be the sum of contributions from each type of motion, for example,

$$E_i = E_r + E_v + E_e,$$

where

$$E_r = NkT^2 \frac{d \ln Q_r}{dT}, \quad \text{etc.} \tag{12.1-3}$$

The rotational and vibrational motion of a molecule is the relative motion of the nuclei about the mass center of the molecule. Let us determine the number of pairs of conjugate coordinates (p, q) defining the phase space of this motion. For a molecule of n atoms, there are $3n$ position coordinates which determine the complete motion of the atoms. Since three of these are required to describe the motion of the mass center, there are but $3n - 3$ remaining to define the internal motion with respect to the mass center. Because we are considering the rotational motion to be that of a classical rigid body, three angular coordinates are needed to describe the relative angular position of a coordinate system fixed in the body and a coordinate system fixed in space. There remain $3n - 6$ coordinates to describe the $3n - 6$ vibrational modes of motion. The $3n - 3$ pairs of conjugate coordinates of rotation and vibration define the phase space of the internal motion and are said to constitute the $3n - 3$ *degrees of freedom* of the internal motion.

The foregoing determination of the rotational and vibrational degrees of freedom is incorrect in the degenerate case where the atomic nuclei of the molecule lie in a straight line, which is the case for *all* diatomic molecules and some polyatomic molecules such as CO_2, C_2H_2, and NO_2. For these *linear molecules*, there is no angular momentum of the nuclei about the molecular axis and therefore no corresponding angular coordinate measuring this rotation. Since there are but two rotational displacements remaining, these together with the three translational degrees of freedom leave $3n - 5$ vibrational degrees of freedom.

The degrees of freedom of atoms and molecules are summarized in Table 12.1. Diatomic molecules have two degrees of rotation and one of vibration, while triatomic molecules have two or three degrees of rotation and four or three modes of vibration, depending on whether or not they are linear.

Sketches of the shapes and internuclear distances of some polyatomic molecules are shown in Fig. 12.1. These shapes and dimensions are determined so that the moments of inertia and thereby the rotational quantum energies will agree with the measurements of the rotational spectrum.

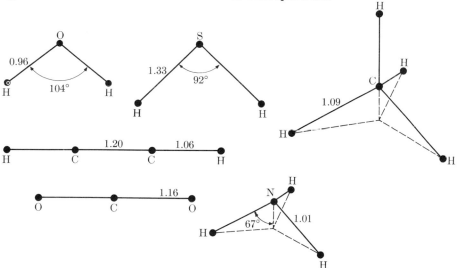

Fig. 12.1. Scale drawings of the polyatomic molecules listed in Table 12.3. For all molecules except CH_4 and NH_3, the atoms lie in the same plane. In the NH_3 molecule, the three hydrogen atoms form an equilateral triangle which is the base of a tetrahedron having a nitrogen atom at its apex. The hydrogen atoms in CH_4 form a regular tetrahedron with a carbon atom at the geometric center. The interatomic spacing is determined from spectroscopic measurements of the moments of inertia and is given in angstrom units (10^{-8} cm). (Data from Herzberg II.)

Table 12.1. Number of degrees of freedom of atoms and molecules

	Atom ($n = 1$)	Linear molecule	Nonlinear molecule
Translation	3	3	3
Rotation	0	2	3
Vibration	0	$3n - 5$	$3n - 6$
Total	3	$3n$	$3n$

12.2 Rotation of diatomic molecules

As explained in Section 5.10, the rotational quantum states of a diatomic molecule have the discrete energies

$$\epsilon_r = j(j + 1)h^2/8\pi^2 I, \qquad j = 0, 1, 2, \ldots \tag{12.2-1}$$

For each value of j there are $2j + 1$ quantum states of equal energy corresponding to motions with a component of angular momentum of $j\hbar$, $(j - 1)\hbar, \ldots,$ $\hbar$, 0, $-\hbar, \ldots, -j\hbar$. If we replace the quantum of rotational energy by introducing a characteristic rotational temperature θ_r defined by

$$\theta_r \equiv h^2/8\pi^2 I k, \tag{12.2-2}$$

then the rotational energies are

$$\epsilon_r = j(j + 1)k\theta_r \tag{12.2-3}$$

by virtue of Eqs. (12.2–1) and (12.2–2).

In summing the rotational partition function Q_r over all rotational states by collecting together the $2j + 1$ terms of equal energy, we find

$$Q_r = \sum_{j=0}^{\infty} (2j + 1)e^{-j(j+1)\theta_r/T}. \tag{12.2-4}$$

Except for H_2 (or its isotopes), the value of θ_r for all diatomic molecules is small compared with the lowest temperature at which it is still a gas (see Table 12.2), and it is therefore permissible to replace the sum of Eq. (12.2–4) by an integral:

$$Q_r = \int_0^{\infty} (2j + 1)e^{-j(j+1)\theta_r/T}\, dj = \int_0^{\infty} e^{-j(j+1)\theta_r/T}\, d[j(j + 1)]$$

$$= \frac{T}{\theta_r}, \qquad \text{if} \quad T \gg \theta_r. \tag{12.2-5}$$

Table 12.2.   Physical constants of diatomic molecules

(Data from Herzberg I, Table 39, and Gaydon, Chapter XII)

Molecule	Molecular weight	$\theta_r,$ K°	$\theta_v,$ K°	g_0†	$\epsilon_1/k,$‡ K°	$\epsilon^*/k = -\epsilon_d/k,$ K°
C_2	24.02	2.522	2572	6	27,700	−41,800
CH	13.02	20.80	4120	4	33,300	−40,300
Cl_2	70.92	0.351	813	1	26,400	−28,720
CN	26.02	2.735	2980	2	13,300	−88,200
CO	28.01	2.780	3122	1	93,500	−129,000
H_2	2.016	87.5	6325	1	132,000	−52,000
HCl	36.47	15.24	4300	1	112,000	−51,450
N_2	28.02	2.892	3393	1	100,000	−113,400
NO	30.01	2.453	2740	4	63,200	−75,300
O_2	32.00	2.080	2273	3	11,400	−59,000
OH	17.01	27.18	5370	4	47,100	−51,100
S_2	64.14	0.425	1045	3	45,700	−51,100
Na_2	45.98	0.223	229	1	21,130	−8,480

† Statistical weight of ground electronic state.
‡ Here ϵ_1 is the energy of the first excited electronic state.

For a homonuclear molecule (such as H_2, O_2, or N_2) only even or odd values of j are permitted, depending on the relative orientation of the nuclear spins along the axis of symmetry. This restriction is a consequence of the indistinguishability of two particles in the same quantum state and can be expressed in the overall requirement of even or odd symmetry of the rotational wave function for the nuclei. For temperatures larger than θ_r, this restriction is most easily thought of as a halving of the available volume in rotational phase space because the range of variation of the angle of rotation is halved as a result of nuclear symmetry. Therefore, for a homonuclear molecule only half of the terms in Eq. (12.2–4) are to be used, or only half of the volume in phase space, so that

$$Q_r = (\tfrac{1}{2})(T/\theta_r) \quad \text{(homonuclear).} \tag{12.2–6}$$

The corresponding contributions to the thermodynamic functions can now be found from Eqs. (11.4–7) through (11.4–9) to be

$$E_r = NkT^2(d/dT)[\ln (T/\gamma_s\theta_r)] = NkT, \tag{12.2–7}$$

$$C_r = dE_r/dT = Nk, \tag{12.2–8}$$

$$S_r = E_r/T + Nk \ln (T/\gamma_s\theta_r) = Nk \ln (eT/\gamma_s\theta_r), \tag{12.2–9}$$

$$\mu_r = -kT \ln (T/\gamma_s\theta_r), \tag{12.2–10}$$

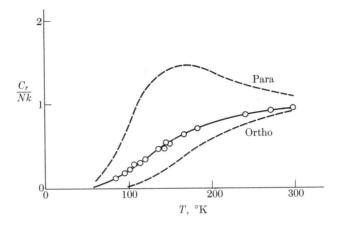

Fig. 12.2. A comparison of the measured (open circles) and calculated (solid line) rotational specific heat of diatomic hydrogen. The dashed curves are the specific heats of pure ortho- and parahydrogen, while the solid curve is the 3 : 1 mixture which is the equilibrium proportion at room temperature. (After Herzberg I, p. 470.)

in which γ_s, called the *symmetry number*, is either 2 or 1, respectively, depending on whether or not the molecule is homonuclear.

As mentioned above, for H_2, D_2, or HD, θ_r is not small compared with T when T is less than 300°K, and the partition-function sum in Eq. (12.2–4) cannot be replaced by the integral of Eq. (12.2–5). However, the sum can be determined numerically, and Fig. 12.2 shows a comparison of the calculated rotational specific heat C_r of H_2 with that determined from experiment. Additional calculated curves of specific heats of pure parahydrogen (antiparallel nuclear spins) and pure orthohydrogen (parallel nuclear spins) are also shown. The experimental measurements correspond to the 3:1 mixture of ortho- and parahydrogen which exists at normal temperature.[*]

12.3 Rotation of polyatomic molecules

For the general polyatomic molecule having three principal moments of inertia, there will be three characteristic rotational temperatures, θ_{r1}, θ_{r2}, and θ_{r3}, determined from the corresponding moments of inertia according to Eq. (12.2–2). When two of these moments of inertia are equal because of symmetry (that is, $\theta_{r1} = \theta_{r2}$) the molecule is called a "symmetric top" and its rotational energies are[†]

$$\epsilon_r = j(j + 1)k\theta_{r1} + K^2 k(\theta_{r3} - \theta_{r1}),$$

---

[*] For a more extensive discussion of ortho- and parahydrogen, see Hill, p. 367, or Mayer and Mayer, p. 172.

[†] See Herzberg II, p. 24, or Davidson, p. 172.

where

$$j = 0, 1, 2, 3, \ldots,$$

$$K = -j, -j+1, \ldots, j-1, j, \tag{12.3-1}$$

there being $2j + 1$ quantum states for each pair of values of j and K. The partition function may be summed by integrating in the manner of Eq. (12.2–5):

$$Q_r = \sum_{j=0}^{\infty} \left\{ \sum_{K=-j}^{K=j} (2j + 1) \exp\left[-\frac{j(j+1)\theta_{r1}}{T} - \frac{K^2(\theta_{r3} - \theta_{r1})}{T} \right] \right\}$$

$$= \int_{j=0}^{\infty} \int_{K=-j}^{K=j} \exp\left[-\frac{j(j+1)\theta_{r1}}{T} - \frac{K^2(\theta_{r3} - \theta_{r1})}{T} \right] dK \, d[j(j + 1)]. \tag{12.3-2}$$

Since the integration covers the Kj-plane for positive values of j but for K between $+j$ and $-j$, we can interchange the order of integration and integrate first on j from K to ∞ and then on K from $-\infty$ to $+\infty$:

$$Q_r = \int_{K=-\infty}^{K=+\infty} e^{-K^2(\theta_{r3}-\theta_{r1})/T} \left[\int_{j=K}^{\infty} e^{-j(j+1)\theta_{r1}/T} \, d[j(j + 1)] \right] dK$$

$$\simeq \frac{T}{\theta_{r1}} \int_{-\infty}^{\infty} e^{-K^2\theta_{r3}/T} \, dK$$

$$= \left(\pi \frac{T^2}{\theta_{r1}^2} \frac{T}{\theta_{r3}} \right)^{1/2} . \tag{12.3-3}$$

In the general case for which θ_{r1} does not equal θ_{r2}, the partition function can be determined from an integration over phase space by making use of the classical partition function, Eq. (8.8–2), to obtain*

$$Q_r = \frac{1}{\gamma_s} \left(\frac{\pi T^3}{\theta_{r1}\theta_{r2}\theta_{r3}} \right)^{1/2}, \tag{12.3-4}$$

which reduces to Eq. (12.3–3), when $\theta_{r1} = \theta_{r2}$, and in which γ_s is the symmetry number, i.e., the number of different rotational positions of the molecule which are indistinguishable by virtue of identical atoms. The value of γ_s must be determined from a knowledge of the spatial orientation of the atoms in the molecule. Values for common molecules are given in Table 12.3.

---

* For a derivation of Eq. (12.3–4) through this method, see Mayer and Mayer, p. 193.

Table 12.3

Properties of polyatomic molecules†

Molecule	Molecular weight, gm/mole	θ_r, K°	$\theta_v{}^m$, K°	γ_s	ϵ^*/k, K°
H_2O	18.02	13.37 20.87 40.0	2295 5255 5400	2	−110,300
H_2S	34.08	6.80 13.01 14.95	1857 3755 3865	2	−87,100
CO_2 (linear)	44.01	0.560	961 961 1923 3382	2	−192,100
C_2H_2 (linear)	26.04	1.692	880 880 1050 1050 2840 4735 4850	2	−195,500
NH_3	17.04	9.06 14.30 14.30	1365 2340 2340 4800 4915 4915	3	−139,600
CH_4	16.04	7.56 7.56 7.56	1880 1880 1880 2193 2193 4195 4345 4345 4345	12	−197,800

† Data from Herzberg II and Gaydon, Appendix II.

The rotational contribution to the thermodynamic properties of nonlinear polyatomic molecules can be determined from the partition function, Eq. (12.3–4):

$$E_r = \tfrac{3}{2} NkT, \tag{12.3–5}$$

$$C_r = \tfrac{3}{2} Nk, \tag{12.3–6}$$

$$S_r = Nk \ln \left[\frac{1}{\gamma_s} \left(\frac{\pi e^3 T^3}{\theta_{r1}\theta_{r2}\theta_{r3}} \right)^{1/2} \right], \tag{12.3–7}$$

$$\mu_r = -kT \ln \left[\frac{1}{\gamma_s} \left(\frac{\pi T^3}{\theta_{r1}\theta_{r2}\theta_{r3}} \right)^{1/2} \right]. \tag{12.3–8}$$

12.4   Vibration of diatomic molecules

In the discussion of Section 5.9, it was pointed out that the vibrational energies of the ideal harmonic oscillator, given by Eq. (5.9–4), are equally spaced, whereas the true vibrational energies of a diatomic molecule are more closely spaced as the vibrational energy approaches the dissociation energy.

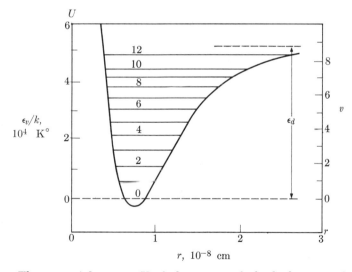

Fig. 12.3. The potential energy U of the atoms of the hydrogen molecule in its electronic ground state as a function of internuclear distance r. The true vibrational energy levels are shown by horizontal lines and are marked with the vibrational quantum number v. The evenly spaced vibrational levels of a harmonic oscillator which match the lowest levels of the molecule are shown on the scale at the right and are identified by the quantum number v; ϵ_d is the dissociation energy of the molecule. (After Herzberg I, p. 99.)

For example, Fig. 12.3 shows the true potential-energy curve and vibrational-energy levels of the H_2 molecule which can be compared with the ideal harmonic oscillator whose energy levels match the lowest of the H_2 molecule. This closer spacing of the high vibrational energy levels is a consequence of the reduction of the average force acting on the nuclei and the corresponding decrease in the frequency of the nonlinear motion at large amplitudes, as illustrated in Fig. 12.4. Because of the latter, the value of $h\nu$, which determines the difference between adjacent levels, is smaller at the large-amplitude motion associated with high vibrational energies (see Fig. 12.3).

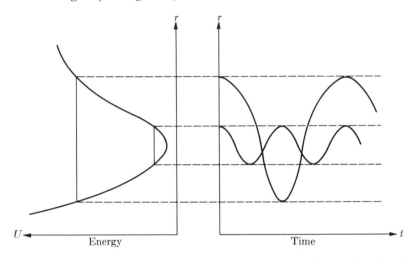

Fig. 12.4. The periodic motion of a classical anharmonic oscillator, showing how the frequency decreases as the amplitude of the motion increases. In the corresponding quantum-mechanical motion, the spacing $h\nu$ between levels decreases as the amplitude and energy of the vibration increases. (Compare with Fig. 12.3.)

Despite these differences between the ideal harmonic oscillator and a real diatomic molecule, it is usually a good approximation to use the harmonic-oscillator energy levels in computing the partition function and thermodynamic properties of a diatomic gas for the same reason that the vibration-rotation coupling can be ignored; namely, the number of molecules present in a gas at temperatures sufficiently high to excite high vibrational energies is so small that little error in the total gas thermodynamic properties results from approximating the true vibrational energies. On the other hand, if one wished to calculate this very small number of molecules in the high vibrational states in order to compare it with spectroscopic measurements of population densities, then the more accurate spacing of energy levels must be used.

There is no thermodynamic significance to the energy, $\frac{1}{2}h\nu$, of the lowest vibrational level, $v = 0$, which arises as a consequence of the uncertainty principle (see Section 5.9). Since the zero point of energy is arbitrary (see Section 8.5), it is customary to measure vibrational energies from the lowest level:

$$\epsilon_v = vh\nu, \qquad v = 0, 1, 2, \ldots \tag{12.4-1}$$

The dissociation energy is also measured from this level (see Fig. 12.3). In all that follows, this convenient choice has been made.

In calculating thermodynamic properties, it is convenient to replace the vibrational frequency ν by a characteristic vibrational temperature θ_v, defined by

$$\theta_v \equiv h\nu/k. \tag{12.4-2}$$

The vibrational partition function, Q_v, of the classical harmonic oscillator can now be found by substituting Eqs. (12.4-1) and (12.4-2) into (11.3-6) to obtain

$$
\begin{aligned}
Q_v &= \sum_{v=0}^{\infty} e^{-v\theta_v/T} \\
&= 1 + (e^{-\theta_v/T}) + (e^{-\theta_v/T})^2 + (e^{-\theta_v/T})^3 + \cdots \\
&= (1 - e^{-\theta_v/T})^{-1} \tag{12.4-3}
\end{aligned}
$$

by direct sum of the series, as given in Table A–5 of the Appendix. In contrast with the previous determination of Q_t and Q_r, the series can be summed in closed form without requiring that $T \gg \theta_v$ in order to replace the sum by an integral.

The corresponding thermodynamic properties may now be determined by differentiation:

$$
\begin{aligned}
E_v &= NkT^2 \frac{d}{dT} \{\ln (1 - e^{-\theta_v/T})^{-1}\} \\
&= \frac{Nk\theta_v}{(e^{\theta_v/T} - 1)}, \tag{12.4-4}
\end{aligned}
$$

$$(C)_v = \frac{dE_v}{dT} = \frac{Nk(\theta_v/T)^2 e^{\theta_v/T}}{(e^{\theta_v/T} - 1)^2}, \tag{12.4-5}$$

$$
\begin{aligned}
S_v &= \frac{E_v}{T} + Nk \ln (1 - e^{-\theta_v/T})^{-1} \\
&= Nk \left\{ \frac{\theta_v/T}{(e^{\theta_v/T} - 1)} - \ln (1 - e^{-\theta_v/T}) \right\}, \tag{12.4-6}
\end{aligned}
$$

$$\mu_v = kT \ln (1 - e^{-\theta_v/T}). \tag{12.4-7}$$

By applying Lhopital's rule when necessary, it can be found that all these properties approach zero as T approaches zero, whereas for $T \gg \theta_v$, they

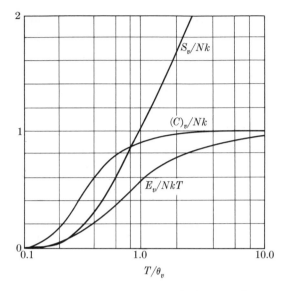

Fig. 12.5. The internal energy, specific heat, and entropy of the harmonic oscillator given by Eqs. (12.4–4) through (12.4–6). (Tables of these functions are given in Table A-6 of the appendix.)

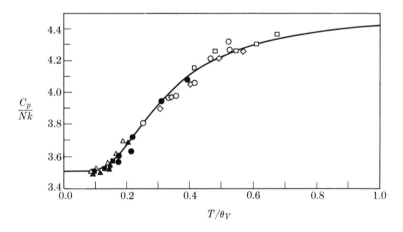

Fig. 12.6. A comparison of the measured constant-pressure specific heat C_p of diatomic gases with the values calculated from spectroscopic data. Only the vibrational motion causes the change in C_p with temperature. ($\bigcirc = O_2$; $\triangle = N_2$; $\square = CO$; $\lozenge = Cl_2$.) (By permission from R. Fowler and E. Guggenheim, *Statistical Thermodynamics*, Cambridge University Press, Cambridge, 1952, p. 102.)

approach the following high-temperature limits:

$$E_v \to NkT, \qquad (C)_v \to Nk,$$

$$S_v \to Nk \ln (eT/\theta_v), \qquad \mu_v \to -kT \ln (T/\theta_v),$$

when

$$T/\theta_v \to \infty. \tag{12.4–8}$$

These thermodynamic properties are plotted in Fig. 12.5 as a function of T/θ_v and are tabulated in Table A–6. The values of θ_v for some typical diatomic molecules are given in Table 12.2. It is interesting to note that there is some correlation between the dissociation energy ϵ_d and the vibrational-energy quantum; that is, molecules with small θ_v also have low dissociation energies. Furthermore, some molecules (such as Na_2) have such small values of θ_v that they have appreciable vibrational energy even at room temperature.

A comparison between the experimentally measured specific heats of several diatomic molecules and the theoretical calculation is shown in Fig. 12.6. The agreement is as good as the experimental uncertainty.

12.5 Vibration of polyatomic molecules

The $3n - 6$ vibrational modes of a polyatomic molecule (or $3n - 5$ modes for a linear molecule) will each have a discrete frequency, $\nu_1, \nu_2, \ldots, \nu_m, \ldots,$ ν_{3n-6}. The vibrational energy of the molecule when vibrating purely in the mth mode will be $(v_m + \tfrac{1}{2})h\nu_m$, where v_m is any integer, provided this energy is small compared with the dissociation energy so that the harmonic oscillator approximation is valid. For general vibratory motion of small energy, each of the $3n - 6$ modes is uncoupled from the others, and the energies are additive:

$$\epsilon_v = v_1 h\nu_1 + v_2 h\nu_2 + \cdots + v_m h\nu_m + \cdots + v_{3n-6} h\nu_{3n-6}, \tag{12.5–1}$$

in which the vibrational quantum numbers $v_1, v_2, \ldots v_m, \ldots, v_{3n-6}$ are any set of $3n - 6$ integers and in which the ground vibrational state energy $(\tfrac{1}{2})h(\nu_1 + \nu_2 + \cdots + \nu_m + \cdots + \nu_{3n-6})$ has been removed by measuring ϵ_v from this minimum level.

Following the same arguments previously used in Section 11.3 for the partition function of a system whose energy is the sum of independent parts, the vibrational partition function will become the product of partition functions of the type given in Eq. (12.4–3), in which the set of $3n - 6$ characteristic vibrational temperatures θ_{vm} are defined from the corresponding vibrational frequencies in accordance with Eq. (12.4–2). Thus we have

$$Q_v = \prod_{m=1}^{3n-6} (1 - e^{-\theta_{vm}/kT})^{-1}, \tag{12.5–2}$$

and the thermodynamic properties are the sums of the contributions from each vibrational mode as given by Eqs. (12.4–4) through (12.4–7) with the appropriate value of θ_{vm}:

$$E_v = \sum_m \left\{ \frac{Nk\theta_{vm}}{e^{\theta_{vm}/T} - 1} \right\}, \tag{12.5–3}$$

$$(C)_v = \sum_m \left\{ \frac{Nk(\theta_{vm}/T)^2 e^{\theta_{vm}/T}}{(e^{\theta_{vm}/T} - 1)^2} \right\}, \tag{12.5–4}$$

$$S_v = Nk \sum_m \left\{ \frac{\theta_{vm}/T}{(e^{\theta_{vm}/T} - 1)} - \ln(1 - e^{-\theta_{vm}/T}) \right\}, \tag{12.5–5}$$

$$\mu_v = kT \sum_m \ln(1 - e^{-\theta_{vm}/T}). \tag{12.5–6}$$

Table 12.3 shows that there are some polyatomic molecules for which the smallest value of θ_{vm} is close enough to 300°K that there would be a noticeable contribution to the specific heat at room temperature due to vibration. The more atoms a molecule contains, the more likely that there are low-frequency vibrational modes which will contribute to the thermodynamic properties at room temperature.   Furthermore, the many-atom molecule has more vibrational modes and hence greater ability to store energy at high temperatures than the few-atom molecule. In contrast, the rotational and translational contributions per molecule to the thermodynamic properties do not increase with increasing number of atoms per molecule.

12.6 Electronic states of molecules

The electronic states of molecules are generally more numerous than those of atoms. If an atom has g_1 electronic quantum states of the same energy, and a second atom has g_2 such states, then there may be as many as $g_1 g_2$ different ways in which these atoms can interact with each other when brought close together. In some of these interactions the internuclear forces* are attractive and can form a diatomic molecule while others are entirely repulsive. Of the attractive interactions, one has a potential minimum lower than all the others and forms the *ground electronic state* of the bound molecule, if the separated atoms are also in their ground electronic states.

To illustrate these points, the potential energy of two hydrogen atoms in their ground electronic states is shown in Fig. 12.7 as a function of the internuclear

---

* The internuclear force is not simply the force on one nucleus due to the other, which is always repulsive because both nuclei are positively charged. It is the sum of the contributions of both the nuclei and the electrons and can therefore be either attractive or repulsive. For a discussion of the theory of molecular binding, see Heitler, Chapter 8.

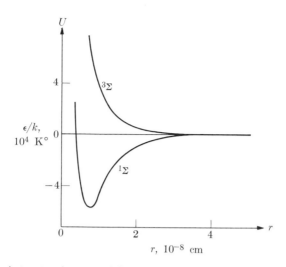

Fig. 12.7. The interatomic potential energy of the hydrogen molecule for the two electronic configurations of the molecule. The lower curve is the bound electronic ground state ($^1\Sigma$) and the upper curve is the repulsive excited electronic state ($^3\Sigma$). These potential energies apply to two atoms in the ground electronic state (^2S) at large separation distances. (After Herzberg I, p. 350.)

distance r. If the electron spins of the two electrons are oppositely directed along the internuclear axis, then the nuclei are attracted along the lower potential-energy curve and can form a bound molecule in the $^1\Sigma$ ground state.* If the electron spins are parallel, then there are three different ways the atoms can interact, but all have the same repulsive force indicated by the potential curve labeled $^3\Sigma$. Since this curve has no minimum with an energy lower than the energy of the two free atoms, the two atoms in this state cannot be bound together to form a molecule. Each hydrogen atom in its ground state (^2S) has a value of $g_0 = 2$, and there are four potential energy curves: one attractive and three (identical) repulsive curves.

There are no general rules as to how many of the possible potential curves are attractive, and hence can form stable molecules, and how many are repulsive. For example, Fig. 12.8 shows potential energy curves for the O_2 molecule. Two ground-state atoms (^3P-state) can interact in nine ways, giving rise to four attractive curves labeled $^3\Sigma$, $^1\Delta$, $^1\Sigma$, and $^3\Sigma$, of which the first is the ground electronic state with a degeneracy of 3 and the other three are excited states with degeneracies of 2, 1, and 3, respectively. Also shown is a potential energy curve for a ground state atom (^3P-state) interacting with an electronically excited atom (^1D-state). This attractive potential also constitutes an excited electronic state of the molecule.

---

* For a discussion of the notation used in specifying electronic states of molecules, see Davidson, p. 121.

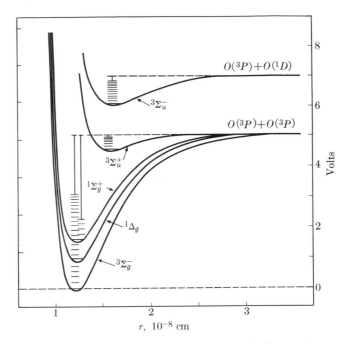

Fig. 12.8. The interatomic potential energy for several electronic states of the oxygen molecule. The molecular ground state ($^3\Sigma$) and three excited states ($^1\Delta$, $^1\Sigma$, and $^3\Sigma$), formed from two ground-state atoms (^3P), and an excited state ($^3\Sigma$), formed from a ground state (^3P) and an excited atom (^1D), are shown. Many other electronic states of higher energy are not shown. (By permission from G. Herzberg, *Molecular Spectra and Molecular Structure, I. Spectra of Diatomic Molecules*, 2nd Edition, D. Van Nostrand, Princeton, 1950, p. 446.)

Since the potential energy curves having entirely repulsive forces do not lead to bound molecules, they are of no importance to the thermodynamic properties of perfect gases. If one is concerned with the effects of collisions, as is necessary in the study of kinetic theory or imperfect gases (Section 11.7), then these repulsive forces may be more important than the attractive ones. For example, in the case of atomic hydrogen three out of four collisions, on the average, will be of the repulsive type since there are three repulsive states and only one attractive one.

The statistical weight g_0 of the ground electronic state and the energy ϵ_1 of the first excited electronic state of diatomic molecules are given in Table 12.2.

12.7 Thermodynamic properties of polyatomic molecules

Having determined the approximate separate additive contributions to the thermodynamic properties due to the translational, rotational, vibrational, and electronic quantum states of a molecule, we may now sum these to determine the total properties. For linear molecules, we combine Eqs. (11.5–8) through (11.5–11), (12.2–7) through (12.2–10), and (12.5–3) through (12.5–6) to obtain

$$Q = \frac{(2\pi m k T/h^2)^{3/2} V (T/\gamma_s \theta_r) g_0}{\prod_m (1 - e^{-\theta_{vm}/T})} ,$$ (12.7–1)

$$E = NkT \left\{ \frac{5}{2} + \sum_m \frac{(\theta_{vm}/T)}{e^{\theta_{vm}/T} - 1} \right\} ,$$ (12.7–2)

$$C_v = Nk \left\{ \frac{5}{2} + \sum_m \left[\frac{(\theta_{vm}/T)^2 e^{\theta_{vm}/T}}{(e^{\theta_{vm}/T} - 1)^2} \right] \right\} ,$$ (12.7–3)

$$S = Nk \left\{ \frac{7}{2} + \sum_m \left[\frac{\theta_{vm}/T}{(e^{\theta_{vm}/T} - 1)} \right] + \ln \left[\frac{(2\pi m k T/h^2)^{3/2} (V/N)(T/\gamma_s \theta_r) g_0}{\prod_m (1 - e^{-\theta_{vm}/T})} \right] \right\} ,$$ (12.7–4)

$$\mu = -kT \ln \left[\frac{(2\pi m k T/h^2)^{3/2} (V/N)(T/\gamma_s \theta_r) g_0}{\prod_m (1 - e^{-\theta_{vm}/T})} \right] ,$$ (12.7–5)

$$pV = NkT.$$ (12.7–6)

For a nonlinear polyatomic molecule, the corresponding expressions are obtained from Eqs. (11.5–8) through (11.5–11), (12.3–5) through (12.3–8), and (12.5–3) through (12.5–6):

$$Q = \frac{(2\pi m k T/h^2)^{3/2} V (\pi T^3/\gamma_s^2 \theta_{r1} \theta_{r2} \theta_{r3})^{1/2} g_0}{\prod_m (1 - e^{-\theta_{vm}/T})} ,$$ (12.7–7)

$$E = NkT \left\{ 3 + \sum_m \left[\frac{\theta_{vm}/T}{(e^{\theta_{vm}/T} - 1)} \right] \right\} ,$$ (12.7–8)

$$C_v = Nk \left\{ 3 + \sum_m \left[\frac{(\theta_{vm}/T)^2 e^{\theta_{vm}/T}}{(e^{\theta_{vm}/T} - 1)^2} \right] \right\} ,$$ (12.7–9)

$$S = Nk \left\{ 4 + \sum_m \left[\frac{\theta_{vm}/T}{(e^{\theta_{vm}/T} - 1)} \right] \right.$$
$$\left. + \ln \left[\frac{(2\pi m k T/h^2)^{3/2} (V/N)(\pi T^3/\gamma_s^2 \theta_{r1} \theta_{r2} \theta_{r3})^{1/2} g_0}{\prod_m (1 - e^{-\theta_{vm}/T})} \right] \right\} ,$$ (12.7–10)

$$\mu = -kT \ln \left[\frac{(2\pi m k T/h^2)^{3/2} (V/N)(\pi T^3/\gamma_s^2 \theta_{r1} \theta_{r2} \theta_{r3})^{1/2} g_0}{\prod_m (1 - e^{-\theta_{vm}/T})} \right] ,$$ (12.7–11)

$$pV = NkT.$$ (12.7–12)

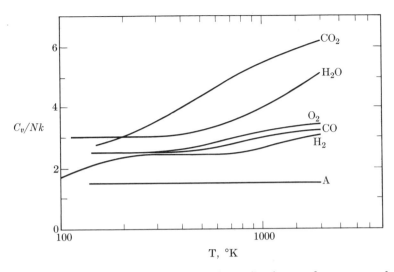

Fig. 12.9. The constant-volume specific heat C_v of several gases as a function of temperature, showing the increase of the vibrational contribution with temperature. (Data from Hilsenrath *et al.*)

The approximations used in determining the contribution of the internal degrees of freedom were the following:

(1) There is no coupling between vibration, rotation, and electronic excitation.
(2) T is much greater than any characteristic rotational temperature θ_r but much less than the dissociation energy divided by k.
(3) The difference in energy between the ground electronic state and the next higher excited electronic state is much greater than kT.

If greater accuracy is required than is permitted by these assumptions, the necessary modifications may be made as explained previously or in the references cited.

Referring to Eq. (12.7–9) for the nonlinear molecule, we observe that the constant-volume specific heat lies between $3Nk$ and $[3 + (3n - 6)]Nk$, or $(3n - 3)Nk$, since each vibrational mode, of which there are $3n - 6$, contributes at most Nk to C_v (see Eq. 12.4–8). For each degree of freedom of translation, of which there are three, and for each degree of freedom of rotation, also three, there is an additive contribution of $Nk/2$ for a total of $3Nk$. In contrast, each vibrational mode may contribute as much as Nk, or twice that for each degree of freedom of translation or rotation. This "double" contribution results from the fact that the total energy of vibration is the sum of both kinetic and potential energies whereas translational or rotational energy consists entirely of kinetic energy.

The variation of the specific heat with temperature for several polyatomic molecules is shown in Fig. 12.9. It can be seen that the limits of variation of C_v

are in accordance with the following values derived from Eqs. (12.7–3) and (12.7–9) and Table 12.1:*

$$\text{linear:} \quad \tfrac{5}{2} < C_v/Nk < 3n - \tfrac{5}{2},$$

$$\text{nonlinear:} \quad 3 < C_v/Nk < 3n - 3. \tag{12.7–13}$$

PROBLEMS

12.1 From a classical point of view, the rotational motion of a diatomic molecule may be considered the motion of a point mass (having a mass μ equal to the reduced mass of the molecule) moving on a spherical surface of radius d equal to the distance between the nuclei. Show that the partition function Q for this "two-dimensional" gas is T/θ_r. [*Hint:* Use Eq. (11.6–2) specialized to two dimensions.]

12.2 (a) Find an expression for Q_v when $T \gg \theta_r$ by replacing the sum of Eq. (12.4–3) by an integral. (b) Show that the same result is obtained for Q_v from Eq. (8.8–2) if the vibrational energy $\epsilon_v = \{p^2 + (\omega m q)^2\}/2m$ given by Eqs. (3.3–3) and (3.3–4) is used in the integrand.

12.3 A mechanical system of n identical masses (of mass m) connected in a straight line by identical springs (of stiffness K) has the natural vibration frequencies given by

$$\omega_r = 2\sqrt{\frac{K}{m}} \sin\left(\frac{r}{n} \cdot \frac{\pi}{2}\right), \qquad r = 1, 2, \ldots, n - 1.$$

A linear molecule of n identical atoms may be expected to have longitudinal vibration frequencies given by

$$\nu_r = \nu_m \sin\left(\frac{r}{n} \cdot \frac{\pi}{2}\right), \qquad r = 1, 2, \ldots, n - 1,$$

where ν_m is a characteristic vibrational frequency. (a) If $kT \gg h\nu_m$, show that the vibrational specific heat per molecule is $(n - 1)k$. (b) If $kT \ll h\nu_m$, show that the vibrational specific heat per molecule varies as T, if $n \gg h\nu_m/kT$.

12.4 The tables, "Thermodynamic Properties of Steam," give the measured value of c_p at 440°F and 1 psi as 0.465 Btu/lbm F°. Calculate the perfect-gas value of c_p in the same units for H_2O at this temperature.

12.5 Develop expressions for E_v, $(C)_v$, and S_v at high temperature in terms of a power series in the small parameter θ_v/T. Find terms up to the order of $(\theta_v/T)^2$.

12.6 From the dimensions given in Fig. 12.1, calculate the rotational moments of inertia of CO_2 and H_2O and show that they correspond to the values of θ_r given in Table 12.3.

12.7 Calculate the ratio S/Nk for H_2, O_2 and H_2O at 1-atm pressure and $T = 300°K$.

12.8 In the nozzle of an arc jet, undissociated N_2 is expanded isentropically from 4000°K to 400°K. What is the ratio of initial to final pressure?

---

* The sole exception is H_2, for which the decrease of C_v/Nk to below $\tfrac{5}{2}$ at temperatures below 300°K was discussed in Section 12.2.

12.9 A model for a vibrating diatomic molecule is constructed by cutting off an harmonic oscillator potential at the fifth vibrational level so that the dissociation energy is $5h\nu$, the remaining energy levels being $0, h\nu, \ldots, 4h\nu$. (a) Express the vibrational partition function and internal energy as functions of temperature. (b) At very high temperatures $(kT \gg h\nu)$, what are the vibrational internal energy and specific heat? (c) Sketch a rough curve showing how the variation of specific heat with temperature for this model compares with that for the classical harmonic oscillator.

12.10 By measuring the relative intensity of the lines in the spectrum of nitrogen which has been heated in an arc jet, the population (N_v) of the vibrationally excited molecules relative to that of the ground state (N_0) is determined (within experimental accuracy) to be

v	0	1	2	3
N_v/N_0	1.00	0.26	0.07	0.00

(a) Prove that the gas is in thermodynamic equilibrium with respect to the distribution of vibrational energy. (b) What is the gas temperature?

12.11 Calculate the constant-volume specific heat (cal/gm-mole K°) of CO_2 at 300°K, 1000°K, and 3000°K.

12.12 Make a plot of the following quantities for N_2 as a function of $\log T$ for $10^2 \leq T \leq 10^4$ °K. (a) $\ln Q_v$, (b) $\ln Q_i = \ln (Q_r Q_v Q_e)$, (c) S_i/Nk, (d) $E_i NkT$, (e) C_i/Nk.

12.13 Which gas will have the higher speed of sound $a = \{(c_p/c_v)\Re T\}^{1/2}$, water vapor or methane at (a) 300°K and (b) 1000°K?

13

MIXTURES OF PERFECT GASES

13.1 The homogeneous mixture of two perfect gases

A *mixture* of two gases consists of a spatially homogeneous* combination of N_a molecules of chemical species a and N_b molecules of species b coexisting in the same volume V. For example, if species a were argon and b were helium, then N_a and N_b would each be fixed by the mass of each substance introduced into the box of volume V. Alternatively, the species might be isotopes of the same chemical substance. On the other hand, if a were molecular hydrogen (H_2) and b were atomic hydrogen (H), then N_a and N_b would not necessarily be determined by the initial proportions of H and H_2 because it is possible for some H-atoms to recombine to form H_2 molecules after the species are mixed together. This latter mixture is often called a *reacting mixture* and its properties are discussed in Chapter 14. In this chapter we will consider only *nonreacting mixtures* for which N_a and N_b are fixed.

In Chapter 12 it was pointed out that the possible quantum states of a perfect-gas molecule are determined by the properties of a single molecule alone, such as its mass, moment of inertia, vibrational frequency, etc., and are independent of the presence of other molecules. In a mixture of two perfect gases, the possible quantum states of one species are therefore independent of the other species. For this reason we may mentally divide the μ-space of the gas into two sub-spaces, one of which is defined by the pairs of conjugate coordinates of the a-molecules (μ_a-space) and the other the b-molecule coordinates (μ_b-space). Following the arguments of Section 8.3, the μ_a-space may now be subdivided into cells of energy ϵ_{aj}, each of which contains C_{aj} quantum states and is filled with N_{aj} representative points, and a similar subdivision of μ_b-space is also possible. Because of the independence of the quantum states of the two species,

---

* By "spatially homogeneous" we mean that the number of a- and b-molecules per unit volume is the same everywhere within the total volume V (see Section 3.5).

the number of microstates w_a of the a-molecules is therefore given by Eq. (8.3–12),

$$\ln w_a = \pm \sum_j C_{aj}\{(1 \pm N_{a_j}/C_{a_j}) \ln (1 \pm N_{a_j}/C_{a_j}) \mp (N_{a_j}/C_{a_j}) \ln (N_{a_j}/C_{a_j})\} \tag{13.1–1}$$

and a similar expression exists for w_b. Since a possible microstate of the a-molecules is independent of a possible microstate of the b-molecules, the total number w of microstates of the mixture corresponding to a given distribution of representative points in μ-space is the product of w_a and w_b,

$$w = w_a w_b, \qquad \ln w = \ln w_a + \ln w_b. \tag{13.1–2}$$

To find the most probable macrostate of the mixture, we must maximize $\ln w$ subject to the restrictions that N_a and N_b are fixed, that is,

$$\sum_j N_{aj} = N_a, \qquad \sum_k N_{bk} = N_b, \tag{13.1–3}$$

and that the total energy E of the mixture is also fixed,

$$\sum_j \epsilon_{aj} N_{aj} + \sum_k \epsilon_{bk} N_{bk} = E, \tag{13.1–4}$$

in which the subscript k identifies the kth cell in μ_b-space.

Following the method of Section 8.4, we first determine the total differential of Eqs. (13.1–2) through (13.1–4):

$$d(\ln w) = \sum_j \ln (C_{aj}/N_{aj} \pm 1) \, dN_{aj} + \sum_k \ln (C_{bk}/N_{bk} \pm 1) \, dN_{bk}, \tag{13.1–5}$$

$$\sum_j dN_{aj} = 0, \tag{13.1–6}$$

$$\sum_k dN_{bk} = 0, \tag{13.1–7}$$

$$\sum_j \epsilon_{aj} \, dN_{aj} + \sum_k \epsilon_{bk} \, dN_{bk} = 0. \tag{13.1–8}$$

Multiplying Eqs. (13.1–6) through (13.1–8) by α_a, α_b and β, respectively, and then subtracting these from Eq. (13.1–5) results in

$$d(\ln w) = \sum_j \{\ln (C_{aj}/N_{aj} \pm 1) - \alpha_a - \beta\epsilon_{aj}\} \, dN_{aj}$$

$$+ \sum_k \{\ln (C_{bk}/N_{bk} \pm 1) - \alpha_b - \beta\epsilon_{bk}\} \, dN_{bk}. \tag{13.1–9}$$

If $\ln w$ is to be a maximum, then the coefficients of dN_{aj} and dN_{bk} must all be identically zero. The most probable distribution of the number of particles in each cell is therefore

$$N_{aj}^0 = \frac{C_{aj}}{e^{\alpha_a + \beta\epsilon_{aj}} \mp 1},$$

$$N_{bk}^0 = \frac{C_{bk}}{e^{\alpha_b + \beta\epsilon_{bk}} \mp 1}, \qquad (13.1\text{-}10)$$

which, on substitution into Eqs. (13.1–1) and (13.1–2), and use of the general definition of entropy $(S = k \ln w_0)$, gives

$$S = k \ln w_0 = k \left[\alpha_a N_a + \alpha_b N_b + \beta E \mp \sum_j C_{aj} \ln \left(1 \mp e^{-\alpha_a - \beta\epsilon_{aj}} \right) \right.$$

$$\left. \mp \sum_k C_{bk} \ln \left(1 \mp e^{-\alpha_b - \beta\epsilon_{bk}} \right) \right]. \qquad (13.1\text{-}11)$$

Following the same method used in Section 8.5, it is then possible to show that if V is constant,

$$dS = \beta k \, dE + \alpha_a k \, dN_a + \alpha_b k \, dN_b. \qquad (13.1\text{-}12)$$

Now for any system, even if it is not a perfect gas, S is a function of V, E, N_a, and N_b, and its total differential is therefore

$$dS = \left(\frac{\partial S}{\partial E} \right)_{V,N_a,N_b} dE + \left(\frac{\partial S}{\partial N_a} \right)_{V,N_b,E} dN_a$$

$$+ \left(\frac{\partial S}{\partial N_b} \right)_{V,E,N_a} dN_b + \left(\frac{\partial S}{\partial V} \right)_{E,N_a,N_b} dV. \qquad (13.1\text{-}13)$$

Using the definitions for absolute temperature and chemical potential given in Section 7.7, by a comparison of Eqs. (13.1–12) and (13.1–13) we find

$$\beta k = \left(\frac{\partial S}{\partial E} \right)_{V,N_a,N_b} \equiv \frac{1}{T}, \qquad (13.1\text{-}14)$$

$$\alpha_a k = \left(\frac{\partial S}{\partial N_a} \right)_{V,N_b,E} \equiv -\frac{\mu_a}{T}, \qquad (13.1\text{-}15)$$

$$\alpha_b k = \left(\frac{\partial S}{\partial N_b} \right)_{V,N_a,E} \equiv -\frac{\mu_b}{T}. \qquad (13.1\text{-}16)$$

It should be noted that the general arguments of Sections 7.5 through 7.7 imply that if the intensive properties T, μ_a, and μ_b are everywhere the same throughout the mixture, then the entropy of the isolated mixture is a maximum.

If Eqs. (13.1–14) through (13.1–16) are substituted into Eqs. (13.1–10), (13.1–11), (13.1–3), and (13.1–4), we find

$$N_a\{T, \mu_a; V\} = \sum_j \frac{C_{aj}}{e^{(\epsilon_{aj} - \mu_a)/kT} \mp 1}, \tag{13.1–17}$$

$$N_b\{T, \mu_b; V\} = \sum_k \frac{C_{bk}}{e^{(\epsilon_{bk} - \mu_b)/kT} \mp 1}, \tag{13.1–18}$$

$$E\{T, \mu_a, \mu_b; V\} = \sum_j \frac{\epsilon_{aj} C_{aj}}{e^{(\epsilon_{aj} - \mu_a)/kT} \mp 1} + \sum_k \frac{\epsilon_{bk} C_{bk}}{e^{(\epsilon_{bk} - \mu_b)/kT} \mp 1}, \tag{13.1–19}$$

$$S\{T, \mu_a, \mu_b; V\} = \frac{E - \mu_a N_a - \mu_b N_b}{T}$$

$$\mp k \sum_j C_{aj} \ln \left(1 \mp e^{(\mu_a - \epsilon_{aj})/kT}\right)$$

$$\mp k \sum_k C_{bk} \ln \left(1 \mp e^{(\mu_b - \epsilon_{bk})/kT}\right). \tag{13.1–20}$$

13.2 The Gibbs-Dalton laws

If we compare these equations with the corresponding Eqs. (8.5–7) through (8.5–9) for a single component gas, we can see that the thermodynamic properties of the mixture can be simply related to the properties each component would have if it existed by itself in the volume V at the temperature T. Denoting these *partial properties* by a superscript 0, we find that Eqs. (13.1–17) through (13.1–20) become

$$\mu_a = \mu_a^0, \tag{13.2–1}$$

$$\mu_b = \mu_b^0, \tag{13.2–2}$$

$$E = E_a^0 + E_b^0, \tag{13.2–3}$$

$$S = S_a^0 + S_b^0. \tag{13.2–4}$$

In Eqs. (13.2–1) and (13.2–2), we have inverted the relationships of Eqs. (13.1–17) and (13.1–18) by considering μ as a function of N, V, and T.

These equations express the *Gibbs-Dalton law for perfect-gas mixtures: The extensive properties (such as E, S, C_v) of a mixture of perfect gases are the sums of the properties each component would possess if it alone existed at the volume and temperature of the mixture, and the chemical potential of a component in the mixture is equal to its value when existing alone under the same circumstances.* Stating it this way, we have generalized the results of the two-component mixture by recognizing that the general argument of this section may be extended to any number of perfect-gas components. In arriving at this conclusion, we have not assumed that Boltzmann statistics necessarily applies. Since we now recognize the role of the partial properties, we may use Boltzmann statistics and perfect gas properties in what follows.

The pressure of the mixture is most easily related to the pressures of the components by differentiating Eq. (13.2–3) minus T times Eq. (13.2–4) with respect to V while holding N_a, N_b, and T fixed:

$$\left\{\frac{\partial}{\partial V}(E - TS)\right\}_{N_a, N_b, T} = \left\{\frac{\partial}{\partial V}(E_a^0 - TS_a^0)\right\}_{N_a, T} + \left\{\frac{\partial}{\partial V}(E_b^0 - TS_b^0)\right\}_{N_b, T}.$$

$$(13.2\text{--}5)$$

According to Eq. (10.4–4), the derivative $\{\partial(E - TS)/\partial V\}_{N,T}$ is

$$\{\partial(E - TS)/\partial V\}_{N,T} = (\partial E/\partial V)_{N,T} - T(\partial S/\partial V)_{N,T} = -p$$

so that

$$p = p_a^0 + p_b^0 = (N_a + N_b)kT/V. \qquad (13.2\text{--}6)$$

This is *Dalton's Law of partial pressures*, which states that *the pressure of a mixture of perfect gases is the sum of the (partial) pressures which each component would exert if it existed alone at the volume and temperature of the mixture.* Like a single component gas, the pressure of the mixture is determined only by the total number of molecules existing in the volume V at the temperature T and does not depend on the molecular mass or chemical composition of the molecules.

The Gibbs-Dalton laws enable us to determine the properties of mixtures of perfect gases when we are given the number of each species existing in a volume V at a temperature T by making use of the properties of each component as determined in Chapters 11 and 12. For example, the thermodynamic properties of air are determined by adding together the properties of N_2, O_2, CO_2, and A in the proportions in which they exist in air.

The proportions of the components are usually specified in either of two different ways. The *mole fraction* x_i of component i is defined as the ratio of the number N_i of i-molecules to the total number N of molecules:

$$x_i \equiv \frac{N_i}{N} = \frac{N_i}{\sum N_i}. \qquad (13.2\text{--}7)$$

By using the perfect-gas law, the mole fraction can also be expressed as the ratio of the partial pressure to the total pressure:

$$x_i = \frac{N_i}{N} = \frac{N_i kT/V}{NkT/V} = \frac{p_i^0}{p}. \qquad (13.2\text{--}8)$$

The *mass fraction* c_i is defined as the ratio of the mass $m_i N_i$ of the i molecules to the total mass of the system:

$$c_i \equiv \frac{m_i N_i}{\sum m_i N_i} = \frac{m_i x_i}{\sum m_i x_i}. \qquad (13.2\text{–}9)$$

The use of either the mole fraction or the mass fraction is usually determined by whether we wish to obtain the mixture properties for a unit mole or mass of mixture. For example, the entropy of the mixture is

$$S = \sum_i S_i^0. \qquad (13.2\text{–}10)$$

Using the definitions introduced in Section 11.8, the entropy of each component is

$$S_i^0 = \widetilde{S}_i^0(N_i/\widetilde{N}), \qquad (13.2\text{–}11)$$

which by virtue of Eq. (13.2–7) is

$$S_i^0 = x_i \widetilde{S}_i^0(N/\widetilde{N}). \qquad (13.2\text{–}12)$$

Multiplying Eq. (13.2–10) by $\widetilde{N}/N$ and using Eq. (13.2–12), we find that the molar entropy of the mixture is

$$\widetilde{S} = \sum_i x_i \widetilde{S}_i^0. \qquad (13.2\text{–}13)$$

By a similar development the entropy per unit mass of mixture becomes

$$s = \sum_i c_i s_i^0. \qquad (13.2\text{–}14)$$

Other specific extensive properties may be determined in a like manner.

Before proceeding further, it is worthwhile to consider the effect of gas imperfections on the validity of these mixture laws. For example, would the mixture of two imperfect gases also observe the Gibbs-Dalton laws? If we follow the reasoning of Section 11.7, which states that gas imperfections express the effect of the potential energy of colliding pairs of molecules, then the collisions of unlike molecules in a mixture cannot be determined from measurements of gas imperfections in the pure components, and the Gibbs-Dalton laws must in principle be inapplicable to imperfect gas mixtures in general. In some special cases, such as a mixture of noble gases, for a given interparticle force the distance of separation between unlike atoms is very nearly the average of the distance between the like pairs of each species while experiencing the same force. When this is so, then the Gibbs-Dalton laws apply also to the imperfect gas mixtures.*

---

* For a more extensive discussion, see Hirschfelder, Curtiss, and Bird, p. 222.

13.3 The entropy of mixing and Gibbs' paradox

If a container is subdivided by a partition into two parts of volumes V_1 and V_2, respectively, and each portion is filled with a different gas, say N_a molecules in V_1 and N_b molecules in V_2, both gases being at the same temperature (see Fig. 13.1), then the removal of the barrier separating the gases permits them to mix by molecular diffusion. After sufficient time, a uniform mixture of $N_a + N_b$ molecules will exist throughout the whole volume $V_1 + V_2$.

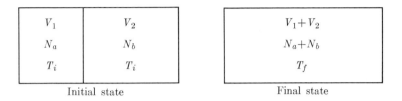

V_1	V_2
N_a	N_b
T_i	T_i

Initial state

| V_1+V_2 |
| N_a+N_b |
| T_f |

Final state

Fig. 13.1. The initial and final states of an isolated system in which unlike gases are permitted to mix at fixed total volume and energy. The entropy increase in the mixing of two perfect gases is given by Eq. (13.3–5).

If the system is insulated during the mixing process so that no heat is added to or given off by it, then by the first law of thermodynamics (Eq. 9.8–2), the internal energy does not change because neither heat nor work is added to the system. Denoting the initial and final states by subscripts i and f, respectively, the conservation of energy in this isolated system requires that

$$(E_a)_i + (E_b)_i = (E_a^0)_f + (E_b^0)_f, \qquad (13.3\text{–}1)$$

where the Gibbs-Dalton law has been used to determine the energy of the final state, and the extensive character of the internal energy has been used to determine the initial energy. According to Eq. (11.4–14), the internal energy of a perfect gas depends only on its temperature and number of molecules, and therefore Eq. (13.3–1) can be satisfied only if the initial and final temperatures are equal, since N_a and N_b are constant:

$$T_i = T_f. \qquad (13.3\text{–}2)$$

The system considered is an isolated system, and the entropy of the final state must equal or exceed that of the initial state in accordance with Eq. (7.4–6). This increase of entropy may be calculated by use of the Gibbs-Dalton law applied to the final entropy S_f:

$$\begin{aligned} S_f - S_i &= [(S_a^0)_f + (S_b^0)_f] - [(S_a)_i + (S_b)_i] \\ &= [(S_a^0)_f - (S_a)_i] + [(S_b^0)_f - (S_b)_i]. \end{aligned} \qquad (13.3\text{–}3)$$

For each component, the initial and final temperature and number of particles are the same, but the final volume is $V_1 + V_2$ whereas the initial volume is V_1 or V_2. According to Eq. (11.4–13), the difference between the final (partial) entropy and the initial entropy, which appears in Eq. (13.3–3), will be

$$
\begin{aligned}
(S_a^0)_f - (S_a)_i &= N_a k \ln \left[(V_1 + V_2)/N_a\right] - N_a k \ln (V_1/N_a) \\
&= N_a k \ln (V_1 + V_2) - N_a k \ln V_1 \\
&= N_a k \ln \left[(V_1 + V_2)/V_1\right]
\end{aligned}
\tag{13.3–4}
$$

and similarly for component b. The total entropy increase is therefore

$$
S_f - S_i = N_a k \ln (1 + V_2/V_1) + N_b k \ln (1 + V_1/V_2), \tag{13.3–5}
$$

which is always positive.

The increase of entropy in this mixing process is a result of the increase in the available volume of the Γ-space of the entire gas. For perfect gases, this increase in entropy (provided the internal energy is held fixed) is entirely due to the increased range of the position coordinates of the gas molecules, and therefore depends only on the volume increase for each component.

The separation of the components of a gas mixture is a practical process of great importance. Oxygen, nitrogen, and argon are separated from air by a liquefaction process. The separation of the isotopes of uranium and hydrogen is essential to the manufacture of fission or fusion fuels. The minimum amount of work required to effect this separation is related to the entropy difference of the mixed and unmixed state.

If we apply Eq. (13.3–5) to the degenerate case where a and b are identical species, then we would conclude that removing the partition would always result in an entropy increase even if the initial pressures on either side were equal. This latter conclusion, which violates our intuition, is called *Gibbs' paradox*. The reason for arriving at this erroneous conclusion lies in the assumption of Section 13.1 that the μ-space of the system can be divided into two parts, one for each of the species. Because of the principle of indistinguishability of molecules discussed in Section 5.7, the state of all identical molecules must be described by representative points in the same μ-space whose coordinates are those of a single molecule.

To determine the entropy increase associated with removing the partition between two samples of the same gas initially at different pressures but having the same temperature, with N_1 molecules in V_1 and N_2 molecules in V_2, we can use the perfect-gas thermodynamic properties directly. In accordance with the previous arguments concerning the conservation of internal energy for an isolated system, the temperature does not change because the energy and number of particles is fixed. The temperature-dependent portion of the perfect-gas entropy

(Eq. 11.4–13) is therefore unchanged in the process, and the increase in entropy becomes

$$S_f - S_i = S_f - [(S_1)_i + (S_2)_i]$$
$$= (N_1 + N_2)k \ln [(V_1 + V_2)/(N_1 + N_2)]$$
$$- N_1 k \ln (V_1/N_1) - N_2 k \ln (V_2/N_2)$$
$$= N_1 k \ln [(V_1 + V_2)N_1/(N_1 + N_2)V_1]$$
$$+ N_2 k \ln [(V_1 + V_2)N_2/(N_1 + N_2)V_2]. \qquad (13.3\text{–}6)$$

This entropy increase is generally not the same as that given by Eq. (13.3–5) with N_a and N_b replaced by N_1 and N_2, respectively. For the special case where the pressures in V_1 and V_2 are initially equal, the perfect-gas law requires that $N_1/V_1 = N_2/V_2$ because the initial temperatures are equal, so that the particle density N/V is initially equal in V_1 and V_2. The final molecule-number density $(N_1 + N_2)/(V_1 + V_2)$ must therefore equal the initial value, and the entropy change given by Eq. (13.3–6) is zero for the case of equal initial pressures. When V_2 is a vacuum, N_2 is zero, and the entropy increase is $N_1 k \ln (1 + V_2/V_1)$, in agreement with Eq. (7.4–5).

13.4 The perfect gas with constant specific heats

In many processes involving either pure gases or nonreacting mixtures, the changes in temperature may be moderate enough that the specific heat C_v does not change appreciably. When this is true, the changes in thermodynamic properties may be approximately related to one another, if we assume that C_v is exactly constant at some average value appropriate to the temperature range being considered. Because of the great usefulness of these approximate relations in many applications such as fluid flows and heat engine cycles, we will develop here the appropriate expressions for a perfect gas with constant specific heats.*

From the definition of the constant-volume specific heat C_v (Eq. 10.4–12), we can obtain E by direct integration since, for a perfect gas, E depends only on T:

$$\int \left(\frac{\partial E}{\partial T}\right)_V dT = \int C_v \, dT,$$
$$E = C_v T, \qquad (13.4\text{–}1)$$

in which the value of E at $T = 0$ is arbitrarily assumed to be zero. Since this relationship between E and T will be used only to determine changes in E when the temperature is changed, no error is introduced by assuming the most convenient constant of integration, namely, zero.

---

* Such a gas is sometimes called *calorically perfect*.

To determine the entropy S, we may start with Eq. (10.4–4) in the form suitable for a system of fixed number of particles $(dN = 0)$:

$$dS = \frac{1}{T} dE + \frac{p}{T} dV. \tag{13.4–2}$$

For a perfect gas, since E depends only on T, we may replace dE with $C_v \, dT$ in Eq. (13.4–2) and p/T with $R/V \equiv Nk/V$, because of the perfect-gas law, to obtain

$$dS = (C_v/T) \, dT + (R/V) \, dV, \tag{13.4–3}$$

which may be integrated to give

$$S - S_0 = C_v \ln (T/T_0) + R \ln (V/V_0). \tag{13.4–4}$$

The subscript 0 identifies the entropy S_0 of the gas when its temperature and volume are T_0 and V_0. In Eq. (13.4–4), we cannot specify the constant of integration by setting $S = 0$ when $T = 0$ because $\ln T$ approaches minus infinity when T approaches zero. This singular behavior is a result of our assuming that C_v is a constant even for $T = 0$, an assumption which violates the third law of thermodynamics (see Section 14.13).

Alternative expressions for the entropy may be obtained by substituting the perfect-gas law in the form

$$(p/p_0)(V/V_0) = (T/T_0) \tag{13.4–5}$$

into Eq. (13.4–4) to obtain

$$S - S_0 = C_p \ln (T/T_0) - R \ln (p/p_0) \tag{13.4–6}$$

$$= C_v \ln (p/p_0) + C_p \ln (V/V_0), \tag{13.4–7}$$

in which Eq. (11.8–5) has been used to relate R, C_p, and C_v.

The enthalpy H may be obtained directly from Eqs. (13.4–1) and (11.8–5):

$$H \equiv E + pV = C_v T + RT = C_p T. \tag{13.4–8}$$

An important process frequently encountered in fluid flows is the *isentropic* (or constant-entropy) change of state. If the subscript 0 identifies the initial state in such an isentropic process, then all further changes in p and V may be found from Eq. (13.4–7) by setting S equal to S_0, the constant value of the entropy in the process:

$$0 = C_v \ln (p/p_0) + C_p \ln (V/V_0)$$

or

$$pV^\gamma = p_0 V_0^\gamma, \tag{13.4–9}$$

where

$$\gamma \equiv C_p/C_v. \tag{13.4–10}$$

The ratio γ of the constant-pressure specific heat C_p to the constant-volume specific heat C_v must always exceed unity, because C_p exceeds C_v by the amount R. For a perfect monatomic gas, C_v is $3R/2$ and C_p is $5R/2$ so that γ is $\frac{5}{3}$. For polyatomic gases both C_v and C_p are larger and γ is therefore smaller than for the monatomic gas. Using this definition of γ, the specific heats C_p and C_v may be specified in terms of γ and R by suitably combining Eqs. (13.4–10) and (11.8–5):

$$C_v = R/(\gamma - 1), \tag{13.4–11}$$

$$C_p = \gamma R/(\gamma - 1). \tag{13.4–12}$$

Equations (13.4–4) and (13.4–6) may also be specialized for an isentropic process:

$$TV^{\gamma-1} = T_0 V_0^{\gamma-1}, \tag{13.4–13}$$

$$pT^{-\gamma/(\gamma-1)} = p_0 T_0^{-\gamma/(\gamma-1)}, \tag{13.4–14}$$

in which Eqs. (13.4–11) and (13.4–12) have been used in specifying the exponents.

The relations given above may be used to show the paths in the TS- and pV-planes of various thermodynamic processes. For example, in Fig. 13.2 are shown an isothermal process ($T = T_0$) and an isentropic process ($S = S_0$) in the pV-plane, as obtained from Eq. (13.4–5), with $T = T_0$, and Eq. (13.4–9), respectively. The constant-pressure process ($p = p_0$) and the constant-volume process ($V = V_0$) are plotted in the TS-plane by setting $p = p_0$ and $V = V_0$ in Eqs. (13.4–6) and (13.4–4), respectively. Of course, such curves may also be found for perfect gases with temperature-dependent specific heats, but then the simple relationships given above will no longer apply.

It should be emphasized that the assumption of constant specific heats is not generally true but is only a useful approximation for limited ranges of tem-

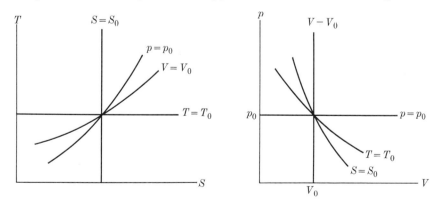

Fig. 13.2. Lines of constant T, p, V, and S for a perfect gas drawn in the TS- and pV-planes.

perature. For monatomic gases or their mixtures, the specific heat is very accurately constant up to high temperatures, where electronic excitation and ionization become important. For polyatomic gases, the vibrational contribution to the specific heat will increase with temperature, as shown in Fig. 12.9, so that the simplified equations developed above will not apply over a large range of temperature.

PROBLEMS

13.1 It is desired to duplicate the specific heat $(\text{cal/gm} \cdot \text{K}°)$ of neon by a mixture of helium and argon. (a) What should be the mole fraction of helium in the argon-helium mixture? (b) At 1-atm total pressure and 300°K temperature, which has the greater entropy, the mixture or the pure neon?

13.2 Considering air as a mixture having a N_2 mole fraction of 0.8 and an O_2 mole fraction of 0.2, calculate $\widetilde{E}$, $\widetilde{S}$, and $\widetilde{C}_v$ for air at 300°K and 1-atm pressure.

13.3 Four moles of N_2 and one mole of O_2 at $p = 1$ atm and 300°K are mixed to form air at the same pressure and temperature. What is the entropy of mixing per mole of air formed?

13.4 A mixture of two moles of H_2 and one mole of O_2 may react to form two moles of H_2O vapor. Which has the higher (a) entropy s and (b) specific heat c_v, the mixture or the water vapor, the comparison being made at the same temperature $T = 400°K$ and the same pressure $p = 10^{-2}$ atm?

13.5 A reversible isothermal process is found which will separate the mixed gases of the final state shown in Fig. 13.1 and return them to the initial state. (a) Show that the magnitude of the work required to unmix the gases is $T(S_f - S_i)$. (b) Calculate the cost of the work required to recover a ton of pure O_2 from the atmosphere if the isothermal process is reversible and electrical work costs \$0.005/kwh.

14

CHEMICAL AND PHASE EQUILIBRIUM

14.1 Changes in phase and chemical composition

A *phase* is defined as a spatially homogeneous portion of a thermodynamic system distinguishable from other phases by differences in physical or chemical properties. Liquid water is more dense than water vapor, while ice has a resistance to shear deformation that liquid water does not possess. Below the Curie temperature iron can be permanently magnetized, yet above this temperature it cannot. Such striking differences in properties, which are the result of quite different behavior on the molecular level in each phase, make the use of phases a convenient method of classifying the thermodynamic states of a substance.

The usual categories of solid, liquid, and gaseous phases are not the only possible subdivision even though they are the ones with which we have the most experience. In some cases a change in phase is marked only by subtle differences. There are at least seven phases of ice* distinguished principally by different crystallographic structure and small differences in density and specific heats. The detection of a change of phase is sometimes difficult and may depend on experimental finesse.

We can distinguish the *chemical species* in a phase by differences in their molecular structure. For example, oxygen may exist in the gas phase as O atoms, or O_2, or O_3 (ozone) molecules. Molecular O_2 or O_3 may also exist in the liquid or solid phase, there being marked differences between the liquids formed by condensing O_3 and O_2 (liquid ozone is highly explosive!). All of these we may consider as phases of chemically different species of oxygen.

So far we have considered only a phase composed of a single chemical species. If sugar is dissolved in water, we may consider the solution as a phase with two chemical components, sugar and water. The two components are said to coexist in the same phase; i.e., they occupy the same macroscopic volume at the same time.

---

* See Sears, p. 94, and Fig. 14.3.

A mixture of two gases, such as H_2 and O_2, is also a two-component phase. We know that each component maintains its molecular integrity as a chemical species, for by observing the absorption spectrum of the mixture we can detect all the lines of the H_2 and O_2 absorption spectra. Furthermore, we may combine the H_2 and O_2 in arbitrary proportions. On the other hand, H_2O vapor is not a two-component phase of H_2 and O_2, because the molecular structure is that of H_2O and not a mixture of H_2 and O_2 molecules. The criterion for determining the components of a phase is therefore the integrity of their molecular structure. Since the molecules can be mixed in different proportions, the proportions of the components of a phase are continuously variable, while the relative proportions of the atoms in each molecule are of course fixed.

A *change of phase* of a chemical species may occur when its thermodynamic state is changed. At atmospheric pressure, water cooled below 0°C becomes a solid, whereas when heated above 100°C, it becomes a vapor. These are physical changes brought about by the opposing effects of the attractive force between molecules, which tends to draw them together, and the mean momentum of the molecules, which tends to keep them apart. On the other hand, a *chemical change* involves the consumption of some chemical species and production of new species by the rearrangement of the atoms among the molecules. The dissociation of diatomic hydrogen at high temperatures to form atomic hydrogen is a chemical change, as is also the reaction of hydrogen with oxygen to form water vapor. In some instances a chemical change may be simultaneously accompanied by a change of phase, as when the solid fuel of a rocket burns to form the propellant gas.

Despite these differences, a change of phase and a chemical change in a system are thermodynamically similar, since they both are the result of a redistribution of the entire energy of a system among the atoms and molecules in a way that gives rise to the largest possible number of microstates. Since we initially adopted this point of view of a thermodynamic system in Chapter 7, there is no difficulty in treating these seemingly different changes by the same method.

The conditions under which a change of phase or of chemical species will occur may be of great practical importance. The invention of the steam engine was made possible by one of the physical properties of water, the fact that the boiling temperature increases with pressure. The difference in the boiling temperature of mercury and water, at a given pressure, is a difference which makes mercury a more attractive fluid for a space power system. The kinetic energy of the air moving with respect to a space vehicle determines what fraction of the air molecules will be dissociated and ionized upon flowing through the bow shock wave. All of these examples point out some practical consequences of the relationship between phase or chemical change and the thermodynamic restraints of pressure, temperature, energy, etc.

On the other hand, we cannot expect thermodynamics to tell us anything concerning the rates of such changes. For example, the energy change accompanying the burning of a candle is not much different from that involved in the detonation of a high explosive; it is the enormous difference in the rates of these changes which causes such destructive effects in an explosion. However, our thermodynamic studies can give us information about the pressure, temperature, and composition of these systems after the reaction has been completed. Furthermore, in many cases these reactions occur sufficiently rapidly to maintain the system at thermodynamic equilibrium. When this occurs, thermodynamics is very helpful in determining how the changes in pressure, temperature, and composition will be related to one another while the temporal rate of change of these quantities is governed by the constraints imposed on the system. Thus there is a fundamental difference between the rate at which the gas temperature rises in the cylinder of an automobile engine when the fuel is ignited and the rate at which it falls when the piston is subsequently withdrawn: the first is determined by a chemical reaction whose speed is intimately connected with the rearrangement of atoms among molecules and can be described only with difficulty, while the latter is proportionate to the speed of movement of the piston in a manner which can be precisely related to thermodynamic changes in the gaseous products of combustion.

14.2 Equilibrium in thermodynamic systems

In Chapter 7 the concept of the most probable macrostate was developed, and it was shown that under the constraints of fixed energy, volume, and number of particles, it was extremely unlikely that any state with macroscopically different properties would ever be observed. The most probable macrostate may therefore be called a *thermodynamic equilibrium state.*

In Section 7.4, the removal of an inhibition to the sharing of energy or particles among the parts of an isolated system was shown to result in the increase of $\ln w_0$ and hence of the entropy. In Sections 7.5 and 7.6, this principle of the increase of entropy on removal of an inhibition was used to show that the temperature T and chemical potential μ must be uniform throughout an isolated system in its most probable macrostate if energy and particles are permitted to be shared freely throughout the system. In this manner, the conditions for attainment of an equilibrium state could be posed in terms of thermodynamic properties alone. In classical thermodynamics, Eq. (7.4–6) is the starting point for the discussion of thermodynamic equilibrium.*

Because we wish to calculate the conditions for equilibrium in systems for which we are able to determine the partition function, it is sometimes easier to determine the most probable macrostate directly rather than to develop the conditions for equilibrium in the manner customarily followed in classical thermodynamics. In so doing, we make use of the microcanonical ensemble of systems whose particles interact only slightly, and therefore we are restricting

---

* See, for example, Keenan, Chapter 23, or Denbigh, Chapter 2.

ourselves to the simpler thermodynamic systems. To be completely general, we must use the canonical or grand ensemble* for which the argument is very similar to the one we shall use for the microcanonical ensemble.

In this chapter we consider several examples of thermodynamic equilibrium involving change of phase or a chemical change. In those cases where the results are generally true because they are derived directly from the principles discussed in Chapter 7, and are therefore not restricted to perfect gases or other simple systems, the equations are identified by a superscript +.

One other characteristic of the equilibrium state deserves to be reemphasized at this point, which is its microscopically dynamical character. Even though the proportions of liquid and vapor, for example, in a two-phase system at equilibrium are not changing, there is a continual interchange of the vapor molecules with the liquid molecules. That this is so is easily verified by an experiment in which one phase initially contains an isotope while the other does not; after sufficient time the isotopic component is uniformly distributed throughout both phases even though the proportions of the phases remain unchanged. This character of dynamical equilibrium is necessarily preserved in the argument which leads to the determination of the most probable macrostate and thereby the equilibrium thermodynamic properties. That argument was predicated on the possibility of the representative point in Γ-space moving freely about the surface of constant energy even while remaining within the volume in Γ-space corresponding to the most probable macrostate. From this point of view the constancy of thermodynamic properties on the macroscopic scale is perfectly compatible with the dynamical equilibrium on the microscopic scale, just as the constancy of total energy, linear momentum, and angular momentum of a system of particles is possible even though the corresponding properties of each particle are changing rapidly in time.

14.3 Chemical equilibrium in a multicomponent phase

In Section 13.1 we considered a nonreacting mixture of gases in which one molecular species did not (or could not) change into another by chemical reaction. In this section we shall determine the most probable distribution for a two-component mixture in which such a chemical change is possible and then consider the more general case of many components.

To describe the equilibrium between two chemical species a and b, it is customary to use the statement of dynamical equilibrium in the form

$$\nu_a X_a \rightleftarrows \nu_b X_b, \tag{14.3–1}$$

in which X_a and X_b are the molecular symbols of substances a and b, and ν_a is the number of a-molecules which can be rearranged to form ν_b-molecules of

---

* See Davidson, Chapter 14.

substance b. For example, the dissociation of N_2 would be described by

$$N_2 \rightleftarrows 2N, \tag{14.3-2}$$

in which $\nu_a = 1$, $\nu_b = 2$, $X_a = N_2$, and $X_b = N$. Equation (14.3–2) expresses the fact that at equilibrium two nitrogen atoms will recombine for every molecule which dissociates and therefore the number of atoms and molecules will not change with time. It does not determine the proportions of atoms and molecules.*

Strictly speaking, Eq. (14.3–1) is not an equation in the usual sense. However, it does express the conservation of atomic species in terms of the combining proportions of the molecules in which they are bound together. For example, in Eq. (14.3–2) the ratio ν_b/ν_a must be 2 if the number of nitrogen atoms is to be preserved in this reaction. A differential equation which expresses the combining proportions of Eq. (14.3–1) but makes use of the extensive thermodynamic variables N_a and N_b is

$$dN_a/\nu_a = -dN_b/\nu_b. \tag{14.3-3}$$

If N_a increases by an amount dN_a, this equation states that N_b must decrease by an amount $(\nu_b/\nu_a)\, dN_a$, which is in accordance with the scheme of Eq. (14.3–1).

It is now possible to determine the most probable macrostate of a two-component gas mixture by beginning with the arguments used in Section 13.1, which are applicable to perfect-gas mixtures. In the present case for which the number of a- and b-molecules is not fixed, Eqs. (13.1–6) and (13.1–7) must be replaced by Eq. (14.3–3), but with the total changes in N_a and N_b given in terms of the changes in N_{aj} and N_{bk}:

$$\sum_j dN_{aj}/\nu_a = -\sum_k dN_{bk}/\nu_b. \tag{14.3-4}$$

To find the maximum value of $\ln w$, we multiply Eq. (14.3–4) by ξ and Eq. (13.1–8) by β and subtract from Eq. (13.1–5) to obtain

$$d(\ln w) = \sum_j \{\ln (C_{aj}/N_{aj} \pm 1) - \xi/\nu_a - \beta\epsilon_{aj}\}\, dN_{aj}$$

$$+ \sum_k \{\ln (C_{bk}/N_{bk} \pm 1) - \xi/\nu_b - \beta\epsilon_{bk}\}\, dN_{bj}. \tag{14.3-5}$$

The most probable distribution may be obtained by equating the coefficients of the dN's to zero:

$$N^0_{aj} = \frac{C_{aj}}{e^{\xi/\nu_a + \beta\epsilon_{aj}} \mp 1}, \qquad N^0_{bk} = \frac{C_{bk}}{e^{\xi/\nu_b + \beta\epsilon_{bk}} \mp 1}. \tag{14.3-6}$$

---

* An obvious analogy: the bank teller's daily balance of deposits and withdrawals will not determine the total deposits on hand.

Adopting the same procedure used to determine α_a, α_b, and β in Eq. (13.1–10), we find that the exponent of the exponential in Eq. (14.3–6) may be related to the chemical potentials and temperature as in Eqs. (13.1–14) through (13.1–16), giving

$$\beta = 1/kT, \tag{14.3–7}$$

$$\xi/\nu_a = -\mu_a/kT, \tag{14.3–8}$$

$$\xi/\nu_b = -\mu_b/kT. \tag{14.3–9}$$

The Lagrange multiplier ξ may be eliminated between Eqs. (14.3–8) and (14.3–9) to give the general requirement for *thermochemical equilibrium:*

$$\nu_a\mu_a = \nu_b\mu_b. \tag{14.3–10$^+$}$$

We may arrive at this same result by using a general argument based on the discussion of Chapter 7. The entropy of the system is a function of the energy E, volume V, and numbers of molecules, N_a, N_b, because these variables determine the volume υ in Γ-space:

$$S = S\{E, V, N_a, N_b\}. \tag{14.3–11$^+$}$$

If the number of a- and b-molecules is changed while the energy and volume are held fixed (i.e., the system is isolated), then the change in entropy is

$$dS = \left(\frac{\partial S}{\partial N_a}\right)_{N_b,E,V} dN_a + \left(\frac{\partial S}{\partial N_b}\right)_{N_a,E,V} dN_b$$

$$= -\left(\frac{\mu_a}{T}\right) dN_a - \left(\frac{\mu_b}{T}\right) dN_b \tag{14.3–12}$$

by virtue of the definition of the chemical potential given in Eq. (7.7–3). Now the changes in N_a and N_b are related by Eq. (14.3–3) and, if this restriction is substituted into Eq. (14.3–12), then the condition that the entropy be a maximum (i.e., $dS = 0$) is just that of Eq. (14.3–10):

$$dS = -\left(\frac{\nu_a\mu_a}{T}\right)\left(\frac{dN_a}{\nu_a}\right) - \left(\frac{\nu_b\mu_b}{T}\right)\left(\frac{dN_b}{\nu_b}\right)$$

$$= -(\nu_a\mu_a - \nu_b\mu_b)\left(\frac{dN_a}{\nu_a T}\right)$$

$$= 0 \quad \text{if} \quad \nu_a\mu_a = \nu_b\mu_b. \tag{14.3–13}$$

We must therefore conclude that for an isolated system, Eq. (14.3–10) is a generally valid expression of the condition for thermochemical equilibrium in a two-component system.

It is relatively simple to extend this argument to a many-component phase. If the chemical change is expressed in the form

$$\nu_1 X_1 + \nu_2 X_2 + \cdots \rightleftarrows \nu_k X_k + \nu_{k+1} X_{k+1} + \cdots, \qquad (14.3\text{-}14)$$

in which X_1, X_2, ... are the molecular symbols and ν_1, ν_2 ... are the (positive) mole numbers determining the proportions in which they react, then by extension of Eq. (14.3-3) the possible changes in the number of molecules are related by

$$\frac{dN_1}{\nu_1} = \frac{dN_2}{\nu_2} = \cdots = \frac{-dN_k}{\nu_k} = \frac{-dN_{k+1}}{\nu_{k+1}} = \cdots \qquad (14.3\text{-}15)$$

This equation satisfies the requirement that the number of molecules must all change in proportion to the mole numbers. At constant volume and energy, the change in entropy is

$$dS = \sum_i \left(\frac{\partial S}{\partial N_i} \right)_{E,V,N_j} dN_i = -\sum_i \left(\frac{\mu_i}{T} \right) dN_i$$

$$= -\sum_i \left(\frac{\nu_i \mu_i}{T} \right) \left(\frac{dN_i}{\nu_i} \right), \qquad (14.3\text{-}16)$$

with the result that $dS = 0$ if

$$\nu_1 \mu_1 + \nu_2 \mu_2 + \cdots = \nu_k \mu_k + \nu_{k+1} \mu_{k+1} + \cdots \qquad (14.3\text{-}17)^+$$

This is the general condition for the chemical change described by Eq. (14.3-14) to be in equilibrium.

14.4 Thermochemical equilibrium of perfect gases

For perfect gases and their mixtures, the thermodynamic properties are readily calculated in accordance with the methods outlined in Chapters 11 and 12. If the components of the mixture can react with one another, the composition of the mixture may first be determined from the condition of Eq. (14.3-17) and then the properties can be found by applying the Gibbs-Dalton rule to the components, as will be discussed in Section 14.6.

For nondegenerate perfect gases the chemical potential of any species j in a mixture is given by Eq. (8.7-10):

$$\mu_j = -kT \ln (Q_j/N_j)$$
$$= -kT \ln (Q_j p_j^0 / N_j) + kT \ln p_j^0, \qquad (14.4\text{-}1)$$

in which the partial pressure p_j^0 of the species j in the mixture has been introduced for convenience. Multiplying Eq. (14.4-1) by ν_j/kT, and adding together the resulting equations for species on the right of Eq. (14.3-14) while subtracting the same for species on the left, we find

$$\nu_k \ln p_k^0 + \nu_{k+1} \ln p_{k+1}^0 + \cdots - \nu_1 \ln p_1 - \nu_2 \ln p_2 - \cdots$$

$$= \left\{ \nu_k \ln \left(\frac{Q_k p_k^0}{N_k} \right) + \nu_{k+1} \ln \left(\frac{Q_{k+1} p_{k+1}^0}{N_k} \right) + \cdots - \nu_1 \ln \left(\frac{Q_1 p_1^0}{N_1} \right) - \nu_2 \ln \left(\frac{Q_2 p_2^0}{N_2} \right) \cdots \right\}$$

$$+ \frac{\{\nu_k \mu_k + \nu_{k+1} \mu_{k+1} + \cdots\}}{kT} - \frac{\{\nu_1 \mu_1 + \nu_2 \mu_2 + \cdots\}}{kT}. \qquad (14.4\text{--}2)$$

The equilibrium criterion, Eq. (14.3–17), requires that the last two terms of Eq. (14.4–2) add to zero. Taking the antilogarithm of Eq. (14.4–2) and replacing p_k^0/N_k by kT/V according to Eq. (13.2–6), we determine the *equilibrium constant* K_p of a reacting perfect-gas mixture:

$$K_p \equiv \frac{(p_k^0)^{\nu_k}(p_{k+1}^0)^{\nu_{k+1}} \cdots}{(p_1^0)^{\nu_1}(p_2^0)^{\nu_2} \cdots} = \frac{(Q_k kT/V)^{\nu_k}(Q_{k+1} kT/V)^{\nu_{k+1}} \cdots}{(Q_1 kT/V)^{\nu_1}(Q_2 kT/V)^{\nu_2} \cdots}. \qquad (14.4\text{--}3)$$

In Section 11.3 it was shown that the partition function Q_j of any perfect-gas component may be factored into two terms, the first of which is the translational partition function given by Eq. (11.3–12) and the second of which is the partition function for internal motion of the molecule, $(Q_i^*)_j$. (The superscript $*$ denotes that an energy reference level common to all molecules is used in measuring the energies ϵ_i of internal motion of the molecules, as discussed further below.) Each factor of the right side of Eq. (14.4–3) can then be written as

$$Q_j kT/V = (2\pi m_j kT/h^2)^{3/2} kT(Q_i^*)_j \qquad (14.4\text{--}4)$$

and is a function of temperature alone since Q_i^* depends only on T. As a consequence, the equilibrium constant depends only on the temperature. Inserting Eq. (14.4–4) into Eq. (14.4–3) and replacing m_k by the molecular weight $\tilde{M}_k$ divided by Avogadro's number $\tilde{N}$, we can express the equilibrium constant as

$$K_p\{T\} = \left\{ \left[\left(\frac{2\pi}{\tilde{N}} \right)^{3/2} (kT)^{5/2} h^{-3} \right]^{\nu_k + \nu_{k+1} + \cdots - \nu_1 - \nu_2 - \cdots} \right\}$$

$$\times \left\{ \frac{(\tilde{M}_k)^{\nu_k}(\tilde{M}_{k+1})^{\nu_{k+1}} \cdots}{(\tilde{M}_1)^{\nu_1}(\tilde{M}_2)^{\nu_2} \cdots} \right\}^{3/2} \left\{ \frac{[Q_i^*]_k^{\nu_k}[Q_i^*]_{k+1}^{\nu_{k+1}} \cdots}{[Q_i^*]_1^{\nu_1}[Q_i^*]_2^{\nu_2} \cdots} \right\}. \qquad (14.4\text{--}5)^*$$

Before proceeding to some examples, we shall emphasize the necessity of using a common reference level from which the energies of the internal motion of all molecules must be measured. This necessity arises in the reacting mixture be-

---

* The factor $[(2\pi/\tilde{N})^{3/2}(kT)^{5/2}h^{-3}]$ has the dimensions of pressure. If T is the temperature in °K, then this factor is $2.56 \times 10^{-2} T^{5/2}$ atm.

cause we must conserve the energy of the isolated system even though we permit a variation in the proportions of the constituents. For example, it is possible for a diatomic molecule to be dissociated into two atoms, and we immediately recognize that two motionless atoms have more (potential) energy than the motionless molecule in its vibrational, rotational, and electronic state of least energy ($v = 0, j = 0$), i.e., its *ground* state of least internal motion. Thus the atoms have more energy than the molecule or, more conveniently, the molecule has less energy than the atoms. As we have already stressed in Section 8.5, it is immaterial which reference level is selected from which the energies are to be measured, provided that a consistent choice is made. For instance, it may be convenient to assume that all atoms have zero energy when in their lowest translational and electronic states. Thus all molecules will have an *energy of formation* ϵ^*, which is the energy to be supplied in order to form the molecule in its ground state from the constituent atoms in their ground states.

According to this convention the energy of formation of most molecules is negative since energy must usually be supplied to dissociate a molecule. On the other hand, an atomic ion will have a positive energy of formation since energy must be supplied to ionize the atom.

Whatever convention is adopted,† the quantized internal energy states of a k-molecule become

$$(\epsilon_i^*)_k = \epsilon_k^* + (\epsilon_i)_k, \tag{14.4-6}$$

in which $(\epsilon_i)_k$ is the energy measured from the ground internal state as was done in Chapter 12, and ϵ_k^* is the energy of formation of the molecule. The internal partition function $(Q_i^*)_k$ for species k therefore becomes

$$[Q_i^*]_k = e^{-\epsilon_k^*/kT}[Q_i]_k, \tag{14.4-7}$$

in which $[Q_i]_k$ is the usual internal partition function of Chapter 12, based on the energies ϵ_i.

If Eq. (14.4-7) is substituted into Eq. (14.4-5), the equilibrium constant can be expressed in terms of the ordinary internal partition function Q_i:

$$K_p \equiv \frac{(p_k^0)^{\nu_k}(p_{k+1}^0)^{\nu_{k+1}}\cdots}{(p_1^0)^{\nu_1}(p_2^0)^{\nu_2}\cdots} = \left\{\left[\left(\frac{2\pi}{\tilde{N}}\right)^{3/2}(kT)^{5/2}h^{-3}\right]^{\nu_k+\nu_{k+1}+\cdots-\nu_1-\nu_2-\cdots}\right\}$$

$$\times \left\{\frac{(\tilde{M}_k)^{\nu_k}(\tilde{M}_{k+1})^{\nu_{k+1}}\cdots}{(\tilde{M}_1)^{\nu_1}(\tilde{M}_2)^{\nu_2}\cdots}\right\}^{3/2}\left\{\frac{[Q_i]_k^{\nu_k}[Q_i]_{k+1}^{\nu_{k+1}}\cdots}{[Q_i]_1^{\nu_1}[Q_i]_2^{\nu_2}\cdots}\right\}e^{-\Delta\epsilon^*/kT}, \tag{14.4-8}$$

---

† One convention widely used is to consider as zero the energy of the elements in the molecular aggregation in which they are found at atmospheric pressure and 25°C. Since many elements exist in the solid phase under such conditions, the energy of formation of a compound will not simply be its dissociation energy but may also involve energies of phase change.

in which $\Delta\epsilon^*$ denotes the change in energy of formation:

$$\Delta\epsilon^* \equiv \nu_k \epsilon_k^* + \nu_{k+1}\epsilon_{k+1}^* + \cdots - \nu_1\epsilon_1^* - \nu_2\epsilon_2^* - \cdots \qquad (14.4\text{–}9)\dagger$$

The *net energy of formation for the reaction* $\Delta\epsilon^*$ determines the principal dependence of K_p on temperature. If $\Delta\epsilon^*/k$ is large compared with T, then K_p will vary very rapidly with temperature so that small temperature changes will produce large changes in the partial pressures of some of the constituents. The temperature dependence of the pre-exponential factors in Eq. (14.4–8) is more nearly proportional to a power of T.

Equation (14.4–8) by itself is insufficient to determine the partial pressures of all the species. In addition, one must specify that the total pressure is the sum of the partial pressures:

$$p = p_1^0 + p_2^0 + \cdots + p_k^0 + p_{k+1}^0 + \cdots, \qquad (14.4\text{–}10)$$

while additional statements must be made concerning the conservation of atoms. For example, if y_{ik} is the number of i-atoms in the k-molecule and there are initially N_i atoms in the mixture, then

$$\sum_k y_{ik} N_k = N_i. \qquad (14.4\text{–}11)$$

This restriction may be expressed in terms of the partial pressures of the molecules by replacing N_k with $p_k^0 V/kT$:

$$\sum_k y_{ik} p_k^0 = N_i kT/V. \qquad (14.4\text{–}12)$$

A set of equations of this type, together with Eqs. (14.4–8) and (14.4–10), is sufficient to permit finding the partial pressures p_k^0.

14.5 Some examples of gas-phase thermochemical equilibrium

As a simple example, consider the dissociation of a homonuclear diatomic molecule such as hydrogen:

$$H_2 \rightleftarrows 2H. \qquad (14.5\text{–}1)$$

If subscripts m and a denote the molecule and atom, respectively, the equilibrium constant may be determined directly from Eq. (14.4–8):

$$\frac{(p_a^0)^2}{p_m^0} = \left[\left(\frac{2\pi}{\widetilde{N}}\right)^{3/2} (kT)^{5/2} h^{-3} \right] \left(\frac{\widetilde{M}_a^2}{\widetilde{M}_m}\right)^{3/2} \times \left\{ \frac{g_a^2(1 - e^{-\theta_v/T})}{g_m(T/2\theta_r)} \right\} e^{-\epsilon_d/kT}. \qquad (14.5\text{–}2)$$

---

† The reader should assure himself that $\Delta\epsilon^*$ is independent of the choice of reference level from which the ϵ_k^* are measured.

Here Eqs. (12.2–6) and (12.4–3) were used for the molecular rotational and vibrational partition functions, the electronic partition functions were approximated by the ground state degeneracies g_a and g_m, and $\Delta\epsilon^*$ is found, from Eq. (14.4–9), to equal the (positive) dissociation energy ϵ_d by assuming zero energy of formation of the atoms:

$$\Delta\epsilon^* = 2(0) - (-\epsilon_d) = \epsilon_d. \tag{14.5–3}$$

If the total pressure of the mixture of atoms and molecules is p, then

$$p_a^0 + p_m^0 = p \quad \text{or} \quad \frac{p_m^0}{p} = 1 - \frac{p_a^0}{p}. \tag{14.5–4}$$

By dividing both sides of Eq. (14.5–2) by p, and using Eq. (14.5–4) to eliminate p_m^0, it is possible to solve for the mole fraction of atoms, $x_a \equiv p_a^0/p$:

$$\frac{x_a^2}{1 - x_a} = \left[\frac{(2\pi/\widetilde{N})^{3/2}(kT)^{5/2}}{h^3 p}\right]\left(\frac{\widetilde{M}_a}{2}\right)^{3/2}\left\{\frac{g_a^2(1 - e^{-\theta_v/T})}{g_m(T/2\theta_r)}\right\} e^{-\epsilon_d/kT}, \tag{14.5–5}$$

in which $\widetilde{M}_m$ has been replaced by $2\widetilde{M}_a$.

From the information in Tables (11.2) and (12.2), the mole fraction of atomic hydrogen has been plotted in Fig. 14.1 as a function of temperature for several pressures. For a given pressure, the degree of dissociation increases with temperature, the change from 10% to 90% mole fraction of atoms occurring over

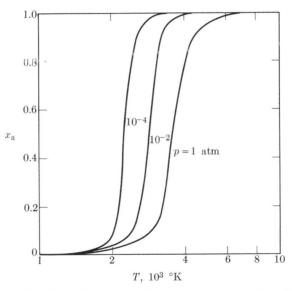

Fig. 14.1. The mole fraction of atomic hydrogen (x_a) as a function of temperature in an equilibrium mixture of atomic and molecular hydrogen at several pressures. Notice the opposing effects of increasing temperature and pressure on the fraction of atomic hydrogen which is formed in the dissociation equilibrium $H_2 \leftrightarrows 2H$.

a temperature interval which is quite small compared with ϵ_d/k. For a given temperature, the atom fraction decreases with increasing pressure, very large increases in pressure being required to depress the atom fraction from 90% to 10%. This is but a particular example of the opposing effects of temperature and pressure on all gas-phase equilibria: an increase in the former tends to cause the equilibrium to shift in the direction of forming more simple molecules whereas an increase in the latter causes a reverse trend.

While the solution of Eq. (14.5–5) gives a finite mole fraction for each species at all temperatures, the atom fraction is so small at low temperatures and the molecule fraction is so small at high temperatures that there is effectively only one component at either extreme, most of the change occurring in a small temperature interval. This behavior is somewhat similar to the change from a liquid to a vapor phase in which, as the temperature is raised, the dense component (analogous to the molecules) disappears and is replaced by the less dense component (analogous to the atoms).

As a second simple example we shall consider the equilibrium of an atomic species with its ion and a free electron:

$$A \rightleftarrows A^+ + e. \tag{14.5–6}$$

Denoting the atom, ion, and electron by subscripts a, i, and e, respectively, we find that the net energy of formation determined from Eq. (14.4–9) is

$$\Delta\epsilon^* = \epsilon_i - 0, \tag{14.5–7}$$

in which ϵ_i is the (positive) ionization energy. The equilibrium constant found from Eq. (14.4–8) is

$$p_i^0 p_e^0 / p_a^0 = [(2\pi/\tilde{N})^{3/2}(kT)^{5/2}h^{-3}](\tilde{M}_i\tilde{M}_e/\tilde{M}_a)^{3/2}\{g_i g_e / g_a\}e^{-\epsilon_i/kT}, \tag{14.5–8}$$

in which the electronic partition functions of the particles are approximated by their ground state degeneracies g. Since a free electron has two spin states, g_e is 2.

For a neutral plasma, i.e., one having zero net charge, the electron and ion number densities, and hence partial pressures, are equal:

$$p_i^0 = p_e^0. \tag{14.5–9}$$

If the total pressure is p, then

$$p_i^0 + p_e^0 + p_a^0 = p. \tag{14.5–10}$$

By use of Eqs. (14.5–9) and (14.5–10) to eliminate p_a^0 in Eq. (14.5–8), the mole fraction of electrons x_e, which is equal to the mole fraction of ions x_i, is found to be

$$\frac{x_e^2}{1 - 2x_e} = \left[\frac{2(2\pi\tilde{M}_e/\tilde{N})^{3/2}(kT)^{5/2}}{h^3 p}\right]\left(\frac{g_i}{g_a}\right)e^{-\epsilon_i/kT}, \tag{14.5–11}$$

in which the ratio of ion to atomic mass has been approximated by unity. This equation, called the *Saha equation*, describes the increase of the degree of ionization with increasing temperature. Because of its similarity to Eq. (14.5–5), the variation of x_e with p and T will be quite similar to that of Fig. 14.1, except that $0 \leq x_e \leq \frac{1}{2}$.

14.6 The thermodynamic properties of a reacting mixture

In applying the Gibbs-Dalton rules of Chapter 13 to the mixtures whose composition has been determined by the condition for thermochemical equilibrium, two precautions must be taken. First, the same energy reference level must be used for all species when determining the thermodynamic properties† and second, the specific heats of the mixture must be determined by differentiating the mixture internal energy rather than adding together the specific heats of the components. The first restriction is a consequence of energy conservation in the isolated system whose entropy was maximized in determining the equilibrium composition, while the second expresses the fact that any *derivatives* of thermodynamic properties of the mixture must include the effects of changing composition, which were excluded in the discussion of Chapter 13.

In accordance with these principles, we may write the internal energy E^* based on a common reference as the sum of the energies of the components:

$$\frac{E^*}{N} = \sum_k \frac{E_k^0 + N_k \epsilon_k^*}{N} = \sum_k x_k \left(\epsilon_k^* + \frac{E_k^0}{N_k} \right), \qquad (14.6\text{–}1)$$

in which E_k^0 is the internal energy as determined in Chapters 11 and 12, and x_k is the mole fraction N_k/N. The constant-volume specific heat C_v^* is obtained from Eq. (14.6–1) by differentiation at constant volume:

$$C_v^* \equiv \left(\frac{\partial E^*}{\partial T} \right)_V = \sum_k \left\{ \frac{\partial E_k^0}{\partial T} + \epsilon_k^* \left(\frac{\partial N_k}{\partial T} \right)_V \right\}$$

$$= \sum_k \left\{ (C_v)_k + \epsilon_k^* \left(\frac{\partial N_k}{\partial T} \right)_V \right\}, \qquad (14.6\text{–}2)$$

which clearly shows the additional contribution to C_v^* from the changing composition. The derivative $(\partial N_k/\partial T)_V$ must be obtained by appropriate differentiation of the equilibrium constant.

In Fig. 14.2 is plotted the constant-pressure specific heat C_p^* as a function of temperature for a fixed pressure of N_2O_4. The effect of dissociation in increasing the specific heat is plainly evident.

---

† As explained in Section 8.5, this restriction is *not* necessary in determining the entropy, provided E and Q in Eq. (8.7–12) are based on the same reference level for any species.

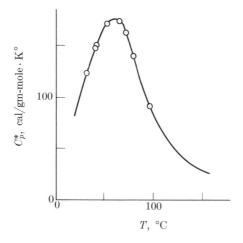

Fig. 14.2. The constant-pressure specific heat of N_2O_4, showing the increase due to its dissociation into NO_2, according to the equilibrium reaction $N_2O_4 \leftrightarrows 2NO_2$. The maximum in C_p occurs at the point where the rate of increase of the NO_2 fraction with temperature is greatest. The points are experimental measurements. (By permission from P. S. Epstein, *Textbook of Thermodynamics*, John Wiley, N. Y., 1937, p. 319)

The entropy and pressure of the mixture are

$$\frac{S}{N} = \frac{\sum S_k^0}{N} = \sum_k x_k \left(\frac{S_k^0}{N_k} \right) \tag{14.6-3}$$

and

$$pV = NkT. \tag{14.6-4}$$

If the pressure and temperature of the mixture are specified, then the mole fractions may be obtained from the equilibrium conditions, and the number density of molecules from Eq. (14.6–4).

For fluid flow problems, the specific properties per unit mass are usually desired. To obtain them, Eqs. (14.6–1) and (14.6–3) may be divided by the average mass per particle, $\sum x_k m_k$:

$$e^* = \frac{\{\sum x_k m_k (e_k^0 + \epsilon_k^*/m_k)\}}{\sum x_k m_k} = \sum_k c_k \left(e_k^0 + \frac{\epsilon_k^*}{m_k} \right), \tag{14.6-5}$$

$$s = \frac{\{\sum x_k m_k s_k^0\}}{\sum x_k m_k} = \sum_k c_k s_k^0, \tag{14.6-6}$$

in which e_k^0 and s_k^0 are the energy and entropy per unit mass discussed in Sections 11.8 and 13.2, and c_k is the mass fraction defined by Eq. (13.2–9).

As a simple example, let us determine the thermodynamic properties of a partially ionized monatomic gas. Denoting the right-hand side of Eq. (14.5–8), which is a function of temperature alone, by κ, we have from Eq. (14.5–11) the equilibrium condition for determining the mole fraction of electrons x_e:

$$x_e^2/(1 - 2x_e) = \kappa/p$$

or

$$x_e = (\kappa/p)\{(1 + p/\kappa)^{1/2} - 1\}. \tag{14.6-7}$$

The internal energy per mole of atoms is $\frac{3}{2}\widetilde{R}T$, while that of one mole of ions plus one mole of electrons is $2(\frac{3}{2})\widetilde{R}T + \widetilde{N}\epsilon_i$. The total energy for a mole of mixture is

$$\widetilde{E} = x_e\{3\widetilde{R}T + \epsilon_i\widetilde{N}\} + (1 - 2x_e)\tfrac{3}{2}\widetilde{R}T = \tfrac{3}{2}\widetilde{R}T + x_e(\widetilde{N}\epsilon_i) \qquad (14.6\text{--}8)$$

since there are $1 - 2x_e$ moles of atoms and x_e moles each of ions and electrons. In the same manner, using Eq. (11.5–9) for the entropy of each of the three components, we find the entropy of one mole of mixture from Eq. (14.6–3) to be

$$\frac{\widetilde{S}}{\widetilde{R}} = \frac{5}{2} + \ln\left\{\frac{(2\pi/h^2\widetilde{N})^{3/2}(kT)^{5/2}}{p}\right\}$$

$$+ (1 - 2x_e)\ln\left\{\frac{\widetilde{M}_a^{3/2}g_a}{1 - 2x_e}\right\} + x_e\ln\left\{\frac{(\widetilde{M}_i\widetilde{M}_e)^{3/2}2g_i}{x_e^2}\right\}. \qquad (14.6\text{--}9)$$

The molecular weight of the mixture, $\widetilde{M}$, is

$$\widetilde{M} = (1 - 2x_e)\widetilde{M}_a + x_e(\widetilde{M}_i + \widetilde{M}_e) = (1 - x_e)\widetilde{M}_a. \qquad (14.6\text{--}10)$$

For fluid-flow problems, the internal energy e and entropy s may be found by dividing Eqs. (14.6–8) and (14.6–9) by Eq. (14.6–10); and the density ρ, from the equation of state

$$\rho = p\widetilde{M}/\widetilde{R}T$$
$$= (1 - x_e)p/\Re_aT, \qquad (14.6\text{--}11)$$

in which $\Re_a$ is the gas constant $\widetilde{R}/\widetilde{M}_a$ for the pure atomic gas.

Considering p and T as the independent variables, Eqs. (14.6–7) through (14.6–11) permit our determining x_e, $\widetilde{E}$, $\widetilde{S}$, $\widetilde{M}$, and ρ for the equilibrium composition of the mixture.

14.7　The heats of reaction

The energy of formation ϵ_k^* of a molecule cannot always be obtained directly from spectroscopic measurement of the dissociation energy but often must be inferred from a measurement of the heat evolved in a chemical reaction. The basis for this inference lies in the experimental possibility of completely changing a fixed amount of *reactants* into *products* under controlled conditions of either constant volume or pressure. For example, if gaseous CO and O_2 are mixed together in a chamber in the mole proportions of $2:1$, and if this mixture (called the *reactants*) is then ignited with a small spark, the reactants burn to form very hot CO_2. If this fixed volume of CO_2 (called the *products*) is subsequently cooled, an amount of heat must be removed to bring its temperature back to the initial temperature of the reactants. Such a reaction is called *exothermic*, because heat is given off to the surroundings when the temperature of the products is brought back to the initial reactant temperature. An *endothermic* reaction requires heat addition to the system to bring the products back to the reactant temperature. According to the first law of thermodynamics (Section 9.8) and its convention as to the sign of heat, since there is no work done, the heat added to the system (which is negative for an exothermic reaction and positive for an endothermic reaction) is

$$Q^s = (E_p^s) - (E_r^s) \equiv \Delta E^s, \qquad (14.7\text{--}1)^+$$

where the superscript s identifies the *standard temperature and volume* at which the experiment is performed, and subscripts r and p identify the reactants and products, respectively. The quantity ΔE^s is called the *internal energy change of the reaction*† and is positive or negative, depending on whether the reaction is endothermic or exothermic.

This complete change from reactants to products may be described by the irreversible chemical reaction equation

$$2CO + O_2 \rightarrow 2CO_2, \qquad (14.7\text{--}2)$$

whose general form would be

$$\nu_1 X_1 + \nu_2 X_2 + \cdots \rightarrow \nu_k X_k + \nu_{k+1} X_{k+1} + \cdots \qquad (14.7\text{--}3)$$

This symbolism is in contrast with Eq. (14.3–14), which expresses the reversible change between reactants and products at equilibrium.

For a perfect-gas mixture it is possible to relate the energy change ΔE^s of the irreversible reaction of Eq. (14.7–3), as measured from a constant-volume experiment, to the net energy of formation of the molecules, $\Delta \epsilon^*$ of Eq. (14.4–9), for the same reaction. To develop this relationship, let us first determine the energy change of the reaction in terms of the internal energies of the reactants and products:

$$\Delta E \equiv E_p - E_r = (E_k^* + E_{k+1}^* + \cdots) - (E_1^* + E_2^* + \cdots). \qquad (14.7\text{--}4)$$

For each species j in a Gibbs-Dalton mixture,

$$E_j^* = E_j + N_j \epsilon_j^*, \qquad (14.7\text{--}5)$$

in which E_j is the perfect-gas internal energy determined in Chapters 11 and 12. Combining Eq. (14.7–5) with (14.7–4), we have

$$\Delta E = (E_k + E_{k+1} + \cdots) - (E_1 + E_2 + \cdots)$$
$$+ (N_k \epsilon_k^* + N_{k+1} \epsilon_{k+1}^* + \cdots - N_1 \epsilon_1^* - N_2 \epsilon_2^* - \cdots). \qquad (14.7\text{--}6)$$

---

† The term *constant-volume heat of reaction* is often applied to $-\Delta E^s$. It should be noted that the thermodynamic heat, Q^s in Eq. (14.7–1), has the *same* algebraic sign as ΔE^s.

Now the number of molecules of each reactant or product must be proportional to the mole numbers $\nu_1, \nu_2, \ldots$ appearing in Eq. (14.7–3) if all the reactants are to be consumed to form products:

$$N_1/\nu_1 = N_2/\nu_2 = \cdots N_k/\nu_k = N_{k+1}/\nu_{k+1} = \cdots \qquad (14.7\text{–}7)$$

With this restriction, the last term of Eq. (14.7–6) may be rewritten in terms of $\Delta\epsilon^*$, as defined in Eq. (14.4–9):

$$\Delta E^s = (E_k^s + E_{k+1}^s + \cdots) - (E_1^s + E_2^s + \cdots) + (N_1/\nu_1)\,\Delta\epsilon^*, \qquad (14.7\text{–}8)$$

in which the perfect-gas internal energies E_j^s are evaluated at the reference state s. Since the E_j^s are functions of temperature alone, only the reference-state temperature must be specified.

It is usual to specify the internal energy change of a reaction for an amount of reactants which consists of ν_1 moles of substance 1, ν_2 moles of substance 2, etc., so that $N_1 = \nu_1\widetilde{N}$, $N_2 = \nu_2\widetilde{N}$, etc. The *molar internal energy change* of the reaction, $\Delta\widetilde{E}^s$, is therefore related to $\Delta\epsilon^*$ by

$$\Delta\widetilde{E}^s \equiv (\nu_k\widetilde{E}_k^s + \nu_{k+1}\widetilde{E}_{k+1}^s + \cdots) - (\nu_1\widetilde{E}_1^s + \nu_2\widetilde{E}_2^s + \cdots) + \widetilde{N}\,\Delta\epsilon^*. \qquad (14.7\text{–}9)$$

A measurement of $\Delta\widetilde{E}^s$ therefore makes it possible to compute $\Delta\epsilon^*$ from Eq. (14.7–9).

The change of other thermodynamic properties which occurs in a chemical reaction of the type given by Eq. (14.7–3) can be found in a similar manner. For example, the change in enthalpy, ΔH^s, is

$$\Delta H^s \equiv H_p^s - H_r^s = (E + pV)_p^s - (E + pV)_r^s$$
$$= \Delta E^s + (p_k^0 V + p_{k+1}^0 V + \cdots)_p^s - (p_1^0 V + p_2^0 V + \cdots)_r^s, \qquad (14.7\text{–}10)$$

in which the total pressure of the gas mixture has been replaced by the sum of the partial pressures. By combining this with Eqs. (14.7–8) and (14.7–9), we find

$$\Delta H^s = (H_k^s + H_{k+1}^s + \cdots) - (H_1^s + H_2^s + \cdots) + (N_1/\nu_1)\,\Delta\epsilon^*, \qquad (14.7\text{–}11)$$

$$\Delta\widetilde{H}^s \equiv (\nu_k\widetilde{H}_k^s + \nu_{k+1}\widetilde{H}_{k+1}^s + \cdots) - (\nu_1\widetilde{H}_1^s + \nu_2\widetilde{H}_2^s + \cdots) + \widetilde{N}\,\Delta\epsilon^*, \qquad (14.7\text{–}12)$$

where H_j^s and $\widetilde{H}_j^s$ are the perfect-gas enthalpies, as determined in Chapters 11 and 12, which depend only on the reference-state temperature.

The ionization energies of some atoms and the dissociation energies of some diatomic molecules are given in Tables 11.2 and 12.2, respectively. These tabulated values can be used directly to calculate $\Delta\epsilon^*$ in equilibria involving atoms, ions, and diatomic molecules. Table 14.1 lists some common reactions involving polyatomic molecules for which $\Delta\widetilde{H}^0$ and $\Delta\epsilon^*$ are given directly. For other reactions, $\Delta\widetilde{H}^s$ is usually given, and $\Delta\epsilon^*$ may be computed from Eq. (14.7–12).

Table 14.1. Enthalpy change at 0°K and net energy of formation for some gas-phase reactions†

Reaction	$\Delta \widetilde{H}^0$, cal/gm-mole	$\Delta \epsilon^*/k$, K°
$O_2 + 2H_2 \rightarrow 2H_2O$	$-114,214$	$-57,500$
$O_2 + 2CO \rightarrow 2CO_2$	$-133,534$	$-67,200$
$O_2 + 2NO \rightarrow 2NO_2$	$-25,550$	$-12,870$
$S_2 + 2O_2 \rightarrow 2SO_2$	$-171,720$	$-86,500$
$2O_3 \rightarrow 3O_2$	$-69,026$	$-34,400$
$O_2 + 2C_{\text{solid}} \rightarrow 2CO$	$-54,404$	$-27,350$
$C_{\text{gas}} \rightarrow C_{\text{solid}}$	$-170,390$	$-85,800$

†Data from Lewis and von Elbe, p. 742.

While $\Delta \widetilde{H}^s$ depends on the temperature of the reference state s, it does not depend on the choice of the energy reference level, since only a change in enthalpy or energy is involved. Hence any consistent convention will always give the same value of $\Delta \widetilde{H}^s$ and $\Delta \epsilon^*$ for a given reaction.

An interesting relationship between the temperature derivative of the equilibrium constant and the enthalpy change of the reaction may be derived by differentiating the logarithm of Eq. (14.4–3) with respect to T. Since each factor on the right is a function of temperature alone, no loss in generality occurs if the volume is held fixed in differentiating this factor:

$$\frac{d}{dT}\left\{\ln\left(\frac{Q_j kT}{V}\right)\right\} = \left(\frac{\partial \ln Q_j}{\partial T}\right)_V + \frac{d \ln T}{dT}$$

$$= \frac{E_j^*}{N_j kT^2} + \frac{1}{T} = \frac{E^* + N_j kT}{N_j kT^2}$$

$$= \frac{E^* + p_j^0 V}{N_j kT^2} = \frac{H_j^*}{N_j kT^2}. \tag{14.7–13}$$

If this is now used when evaluating the derivative of the logarithm of Eq. (14.4–3), and Eq. (14.7–7) is also used, we find

$$\frac{d(\ln K_p)}{dT} = \frac{\nu_1}{N_1 kT^2}\{H_k^* + H_{k+1}^* + \cdots - H_1^* - H_2^* - \cdots\}$$

$$= \frac{\nu_1 \Delta H}{N_1 kT^2} = \frac{\Delta \widetilde{H}}{\widetilde{N} kT^2} = \frac{\Delta \widetilde{H}}{\widetilde{R} T^2}, \tag{14.7–14}$$

which is known as *van't Hoff's equation*.

For an exothermic reaction, such as the combustion of oxygen and hydrogen, $\Delta \widetilde{H}$ is negative and K_p decreases with increasing temperature. The proportions of products are therefore smaller as the temperature rises, so that not all the reactants are converted into products in high-temperature systems such as rocket-engine combustion chambers, and therefore not all the energy of the chemical reaction is available to produce thrust. For an endothermic reaction, such as the dissociation of nitrogen, the equilibrium constant increases with temperature and so also do the products of the dissociation, i.e., the atoms.

Another useful application of van't Hoff's equation is the determination of the enthalpy change of a reaction, $\Delta\widetilde{H}$, from measurements of the composition as a function of temperature. From the latter measurements K_p may be calculated and its temperature derivative determined, thereby permitting $\Delta\widetilde{H}$ to be found from Eq. (14.7–14).

14.8 Molecular structure of a phase

As pointed out in Section 14.1, the vapor, liquid, and solid phases of a single chemical species are only the most obvious phases which can be detected. Because of our everyday experience with them, however, they most clearly illustrate some of the properties of phase equilibrium. We will consider only these phases in our ensuing discussion.

From a molecular point of view, a liquid and solid closely resemble each other in that the motion of each molecule (or atom) is strongly affected by the forces exerted on it by its nearest neighbors. In a solid, these forces are so strong and directional in character that each particle is locked into position with respect to its neighbors. In this sense a solid is a gigantic molecule which resists distortion. While the forces in a liquid are strong enough to prevent particles from being compressed together or pulled apart very easily, their regular directional character has been lost and the particles are free to migrate past each other by the rotation of adjacent pairs of particles. It is the possibility of rotational motion on a molecular scale which differentiates a liquid from a solid. We might thus say that solid particles have vibrational motion whereas liquid particles have vibrational, rotational, and translational motion. A change in phase therefore consists in an alteration of the respective importance of each of these degrees of freedom.

A simple analog of this comparative motion of the molecules in a solid, liquid, or gas can be devised by placing a square picture frame on a table top. If the frame is packed solid with marbles in a regular pattern, no amount of translation or rotation of the frame on the table surface will disturb the relative location of the marbles. If one out of three or four marbles is removed in a random manner, the marbles can be made to change their respective locations by suitable movement of the frame. If all but a few of the marbles are removed, they mix quite freely with one another. The fact that for most substances the solid is more dense than the liquid, which is more dense than the gas, lends considerable substance to this analogy.

Table 14.2. Triple-point temperature and
pressure*

Substance	T, °K	p, atm
He	2.19	5.04×10^{-2}
Ne	24.57	0.426
A	84.0	0.675
H_2	13.84	6.94×10^{-2}
O_2	54.36	1.5×10^{-3}
N_2	63.18	0.124
CO_2	216.6	5.11
NH_3	194.3	0.60
H_2O	273.16	6.03×10^{-2}
Hg	234.2	1.63×10^{-9}

* Data from Zemansky, p. 203, and Allis
and Herlin, p. 29.

In Chapter 11 the properties of a dilute gas were discussed from the point of
view of the effect of intermolecular forces on the average behavior of the gas
molecules. It was shown that the average potential energy of the molecular
pairs was negligible provided the average distance between particles, $(V/N)^{1/3}$,
was small compared with the "size" of molecules, r_0. For this reason a vapor
is called a *dilute phase* while a liquid or solid is called a *condensed phase*, in
recognition of the fact that the molecules are packed so closely together that
they continually interact with each other and their potential energies are an
important part of the total internal energy of the phase. However, this distinction between a vapor and a liquid cannot always be made, for at a high enough
pressure a vapor can be compressed to a density for which the intermolecular
forces are no longer negligible, in which case it is unimportant whether it is
called a liquid or a vapor.

14.9 A phenomenological description of phase equilibrium

One of the remarkable facts about the simple phases is that it is possible to
find conditions under which two or more phases can coexist in equilibrium;
i.e., in an isolated system the proportions of the phases remain unchanged. For
example, water and its vapor, steam, can coexist at temperatures between 0°C
and 374°C, provided that for each temperature T_s in this interval, a proper
pressure, called the saturation pressure, $p_s\{T_s\}$, is maintained.* Water and ice
may coexist at a temperature of about 0°C, provided the pressure exceeds

---

* The *saturation temperature* T_s corresponding to a standard value of p_s is often
called the *boiling point*.

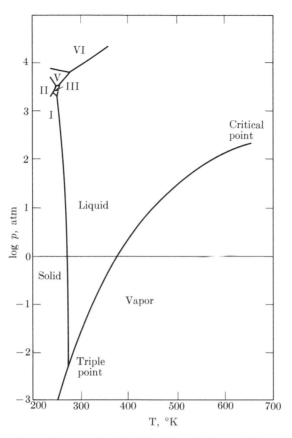

Fig. 14.3. The phase diagram for H_2O in the pT-plane. Lines show the pressure and temperature at which two phases may coexist in equilibrium. The intersection of two lines is a triple point at which three phases may remain in equilibrium. Roman numerals designate several solid phases. (Data from Allis and Herlin, p. 23, and Keenan and Keyes.)

4.6 mm Hg, but at very high pressures this *melting temperature* T_m may be greater or less than 0°C. Finally, at a single temperature and pressure, called the *triple point* (0°C and 4.58 mm Hg of pressure), ice, water, and steam may be in equilibrium. (Table 14.2 lists some triple-point temperatures and pressures for common gases.)

It is convenient to show graphically the relationship between temperature and pressure at which two phases are in equilibrium by lines in a pT-plane such as is shown in Fig. 14.3. Areas between lines give the conditions of pressure and temperature for which only a single phase can exist at equilibrium. The intersection of two lines defines a triple point of fixed p and T where three phases may be in equilibrium. Such a plot of the regions of variation of thermodynamic variables for which one or more phases may be present is called a *phase diagram*.

Note that the saturation curve in Fig. 14.3 (condition for coexistence of liquid and vapor) has a high pressure and temperature limit of 218 atm and 374°C, respectively, called the *critical point*. At higher pressures or temperatures it is impossible to observe a change of phase from liquid to vapor. For example, if liquid water at room temperature and 250-atm pressure is heated while the pressure is maintained constant, it does not "boil" but only expands in volume as the temperature is raised. Neither boiling nor droplet condensation can be observed in fluids having a temperature or pressure in excess of the critical temperature or pressure.

The values of the pressure, temperature, and molar volume at the critical point of several common gases are given in Table 14.3. The value of $p\tilde{V}/\tilde{R}T$ calculated at the critical point is also listed, showing how the vapor is substantially different from a perfect gas, for which $p\tilde{V}/\tilde{R}T$ is unity. (It is also remarkable that there is so little difference between the various gases in the value of $p_c\tilde{V}_c/\tilde{R}T_c$, a behavior which ultimately stems from the similarities in the shape of the intermolecular potential curves.*) In Table 11.3 are listed the room-temperature values of $\tilde{N}b$, the second virial coefficient of Eq. (11.7–13), which is a measure of the volume of the molecules of a dilute phase as discussed in Section 11.7. From a comparison of Tables 11.3 and 14.3, it can be seen that the critical-point molar volume is the same order of magnitude as the volume of the molecules, which is in agreement with our previous discussion of the lack of distinction between a dense vapor and a liquid.

Table 14.3.   Critical-point (p, V, T)-data†

	$T_c,$ °K	$\tilde{V}_c,$ cm³/gm-mole	$p_c,$ atm	$p_c\tilde{V}_c/\tilde{R}T_c$
He	5.3	57.8	2.26	0.300
Ne	44.5	41.7	25.9	0.296
A	151	75.2	48	0.291
Xe	289.8	120.2	57.9	0.293
H_2	33.3	65.0	12.8	0.304
O_2	154.4	74.4	49.7	0.292
N_2	126.1	90.1	33.5	0.292
CH_4	190.7	99.0	45.8	0.290
CO_2	304.2	94.0	72.9	0.276
H_2O	647.4	56.0	218.3	0.222
NH_3	405.5	72.5	111.3	0.243

† Values from Zemansky, p. 201, and Hirschfelder, Curtiss, and Bird, p. 245.

* For a detailed study of this relationship, see Hirschfelder, Curtiss, and Bird, Chapter 4.

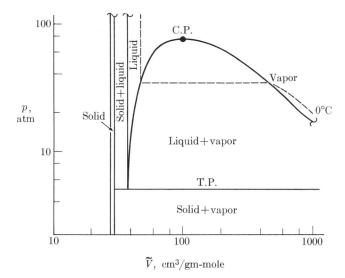

Fig. 14.4. The phase diagram for CO_2 in the $p\widetilde{V}$-plane. Lines separate areas of two phases from areas of a single phase, except for the triple point (T.P.). The critical point (C.P.) is the maximum pressure at which the liquid and vapor phases can be distinguished. A dashed line of constant temperature (isotherm) of 0°C is also shown. (By permission from W. P. Allis and M. A. Herlin, *Thermodynamics and Statistical Mechanics*, McGraw-Hill, New York, 1952, p. 47.)

Another remarkable fact about the equilibrium of two or more phases is that the proportions of the phases in equilibrium do not depend upon, nor do they determine, the temperature (or pressure) of the equilibrium mixture. To measure the melting temperature of ice, for example, we mix water and ice in any proportions and let the mixture come to equilibrium in a container. The proportions of the two phases do, of course, affect the volume and other extensive properties of the mixture. A 10% liquid–90% vapor mixture of water at 100°C and 1-atm pressure has a much larger volume than a 90% liquid–10% vapor mixture at the same pressure and temperature; it also has a greater internal energy and entropy. By using the volume as one coordinate and pressure as another, it is possible to distinguish different proportions of each of two phases in a phase diagram such as that of Fig. 14.4. In this diagram, the lines of Fig. 14.3 become areas while the triple point becomes a line and the critical point remains a point. There is a general rule, called the *phase rule*, which determines the number of extensive variables required to specify the thermodynamic state of a system with coexisting phases.*

An alternative method of portraying the relationship between pressure, volume, and temperature is to describe a surface in a three-dimensional space having as coordinates p, $\widetilde{V}$, and T. Figure 14.5 is a sketch of such a surface, showing its projection onto the pT- and $p\widetilde{V}$-planes.

---

* For a discussion of the phase rule, see Denbigh, Chapter 5, or Keenan, p. 476.

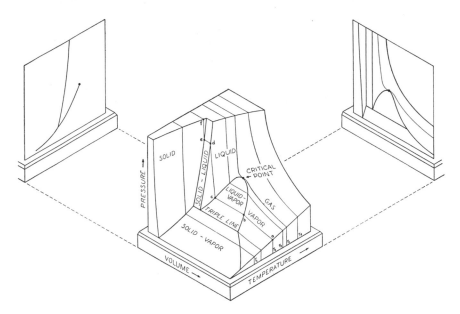

Fig. 14.5. A sketch showing how the $p\tilde{V}T$-surface projects onto the $p\tilde{V}$- and pT-planes.   (By permission from F. Sears, *Thermodynamics, The Kinetic Theory of Gases and Statistical Mechanics*, 2nd Edition, Addison-Wesley, Reading, Mass., 1953, p. 93.)

It is useful to summarize the differences between the equilibrium of two phases and the equilibrium of two chemical species in the gas phase. For the former

(1) the pressure and temperature cannot be changed independently of each other, but each is related uniquely to the other;

(2) the proportions of the phases may be varied independently of the temperature (or pressure);

(3) each phase occupies a different portion of the volume of the system; and

(4) each phase experiences the same pressure and temperature.

For two chemical species in equilibrium

(1) the temperature and pressure can each be varied independently of the other, both species being present in equilibrium at any given pressure and temperature;

(2) the proportions of the phases depend on the pressure and temperature but cannot otherwise be changed;

(3) both species occupy the same volume; and

(4) both species have the same temperature, while in general the partial pressures are different.

Despite these differences, the two kinds of equilibrium are closely related through the thermodynamic criterion for equilibrium. A simple change of phase such as that from liquid to vapor is called a *first-order transition* because the first partial derivatives of the extensive variable $H - TS$ with respect to the intensive variables are discontinuous. A *second-order* transition is one for which the corresponding second derivatives become discontinuous and is commonly observed in solid-phase transitions. For the chemical equilibrium discussed previously, *all derivatives* of extensive properties are continuous, and hence it is equivalent to an *infinite-order* transition.*

14.10 Thermodynamic properties of phases in equilibrium

It is well known that a change in phase, such as melting or boiling, is accompanied by the absorption of heat while the pressure and temperature remain fixed. Since there is usually a volume change accompanying melting or vaporization, the work done by the system will be the (constant) pressure times the increase in volume. According to the first law of thermodynamics, the difference in internal energies of two phases at the same equilibrium temperature and pressure is equal to the heat added to cause the change of phase minus the work done in the volume change. For example, for the melting of a mole of solid the internal energies of the liquid and solid, $\widetilde{E}_l$ and $\widetilde{E}_s$, respectively, have a difference given by

$$\widetilde{E}_l - \widetilde{E}_s = \widetilde{Q}_m - p_m(\widetilde{V}_l - \widetilde{V}_s), \qquad (14.10\text{--}1)^+$$

in which $\widetilde{Q}_m$ is the heat required to melt the solid completely and is called the *latent heat of fusion.*† By measuring the heat of fusion and the volume change we therefore determine the internal-energy difference between the solid and liquid phases at the melting point.

If we rearrange Eq. (14.10–1) in the form

$$\widetilde{Q}_m = (\widetilde{E}_l + p\widetilde{V}_l) - (\widetilde{E}_s + p\widetilde{V}_s) = \widetilde{H}_l - \widetilde{H}_s, \qquad (14.10\text{--}2)^+$$

we see that the *heat of fusion* measured in the experiment exactly equals the difference in enthalpy of the two phases. (This is simply another illustration of the equality of heat and enthalpy change in a constant-pressure reversible process, as was discussed in Section 10.5.) For the vaporization of a liquid or a solid we can measure respectively the *latent heat of vaporization* and *latent heat of sublimation* and, according to Eq. (14.10–2), each will equal the difference in enthalpies of the two phases involved.

---

* For a discussion of first- and second-order transitions, see Callen, Chapter 9.

† The similarity of Eq. (14.10–1) to Eq. (14.7–1) for a constant-volume chemical change would be more apparent if we wrote an equation for the melting process which would be equivalent to Eq. (14.7–2): $X_{\text{solid}} \to X_{\text{liquid}}$. Because there is no change in molecular structure accompanying a simple phase change, all the mole numbers of Eq. (14.7–3) are unity, and it is convenient to write Eq. (14.10–1) for the conversion of one mole of substance from one phase to another.

Table 14.4.   Melting and boiling at atmospheric pressure*

Substance	T_m, °K	$\widetilde{H}_l - \widetilde{H}_s$ cal/gm-mole	$\dfrac{\widetilde{S}_l - \widetilde{S}_s}{\widetilde{R}}$	T_b, °K	$\widetilde{H}_v - \widetilde{H}_l$, cal/gm-mole	$\dfrac{\widetilde{S}_v - \widetilde{S}_l}{\widetilde{R}}$
Molecular						
He				4.2	24.5	2.90
Ne	24.5	80.1	1.64	27.2	415	7.60
A	83.8	281	1.68	87.3	1560	8.90
H_2	14	28	1.0	20.5	220	5.45
N_2	63	218	1.73	77.3	1330	8.60
H_2O	273	1430	2.61	373	9717	13.0
CH_4	91.5	224	1.22	112	1955	8.71
C_2H_6	101	668	3.30	185	3517	9.50
Metal						
Na	370	630	0.85	1156	21,800	9.45
K	335	570	0.85	1030	18,600	9.00
Li	459	830	0.90	1599	30,800	9.60
Ag	1234	2700	1.10	2220	59,400	13.4
Au	1336	3180	1.19	2870	87,800	15.3
Cu	1356	2750	1.02	2570	114,000	22.4
Pt	2028	5300	1.31	4570	167,000	18.2
Pb	590	1120	0.95	1890	46,100	12.2
Hg	234	560	1.20	630	14,100	11.2
Ionic						
NaCl	1073	7220	3.4			
AgBr	703	2180	1.58			
NaOH	591	1600	1.37			
$AgNO_3$	583	6450	5.6			
Valence						
C				4000	140,000	17.5
SiO_2	1980			3200	148,000	23.3

* Data from Zemansky, p. 322–3, Allis and Herlin, p. 26, and Epstein, p. 119.

The entropy change accompanying a complete phase change of a mole of substance may also be determined by using Eq. (10.5–4) and recognizing that the temperature does not change during the reversible change of phase:

$$\widetilde{S}_l - \widetilde{S}_s = \int_s^l (d\widetilde{Q}/T) = \widetilde{Q}_m/T_m = (\widetilde{H}_l - \widetilde{H}_s)/T_m \qquad (14.10\text{–}3)^+$$

by virtue of Eq. (14.10–2), with similar relations for the processes of vaporization and sublimation.

In Table 14.4 the heats of fusion and vaporization are given for some substances classified according to the type of solid structure (see Section 15.2). It is interesting to note that the molar entropy change accompanying melting or vaporization does not differ greatly between substances. Thus, substances with high heats of melting or vaporization also have high melting and boiling temperatures.

In an equilibrium mixture of two phases, each occupies its own volume. The volume, like the other extensive properties, is therefore additive:

$$V = V_l + V_s, \qquad E = E_l + E_s, \quad \text{etc.} \qquad (14.10\text{--}4)^+$$

On the other hand, the intensive properties are *equal* for the two phases:

$$p_l = p_s, \qquad T_l = T_s, \qquad \mu_l = \mu_s, \qquad (14.10\text{--}5)^+$$

the equality of chemical potentials following from the criterion for equilibrium in a system composed of a single chemical species, as discussed in Section 7.6. These relations may be contrasted with the Gibbs-Dalton laws for a mixture of perfect gases discussed in Section 13.2.

We have pointed out that the pressure at which two phases may remain in equilibrium depends on the temperature in a way that is described by the curves $p = p\{T\}$ in a phase diagram such as Fig. 14.3. It is not difficult to show that the slope dp/dT of such a curve is a simple function of the thermodynamic properties of the phases. Equation (14.10–3) for the melting process, in the form

$$\widetilde{H}_l - T_m \widetilde{S}_l = \widetilde{H}_s - T_m \widetilde{S}_s, \qquad (14.10\text{--}6)^+$$

states that the quantity $\widetilde{H} - T\widetilde{S}$ is the same for both liquid and solid at the pressure p_m and temperature T_m for which the two may exist in equilibrium with each other. If the pressure and temperature of a mole of either phase are changed by an amount dp and dT, then the change in $\widetilde{H} - T\widetilde{S}$ would be

$$\begin{aligned}
d(\widetilde{H} - T\widetilde{S}) &= d(\widetilde{E} + p\widetilde{V} - T\widetilde{S}) \\
&= d\widetilde{E} + p\,d\widetilde{V} + \widetilde{V}\,dp - T\,d\widetilde{S} - \widetilde{S}\,dT. \qquad (14.10\text{--}7)^+
\end{aligned}$$

But according to Eq. (10.4–4), which expresses the restrictions of the second law of thermodynamics, the entropy change of a mole of substance (for which $dN = 0$) is

$$T\,d\widetilde{S} = d\widetilde{E} + p\,d\widetilde{V}. \qquad (14.10\text{--}8)^+$$

Combining this with Eq. (14.10–7), we find

$$d(\widetilde{H} - T\widetilde{S}) = \widetilde{V}\,dp - \widetilde{S}\,dT. \qquad (14.10\text{--}9)^+$$

Now consider a change from an equilibrium state p_m, T_m to a nearby state $p_m + dp_m$, $T_m + dT_m$ at which the two phases are still in equilibrium with each other. Since $\tilde{H} - T\tilde{S}$ is equal for both phases at either state, the change in $\tilde{H} - T\tilde{S}$ for one phase due to the change in state must equal that for the other phase. Hence, from Eq. (14.10–9),

$$\tilde{V}_l\, dp_m - \tilde{S}_l\, dT_m = \tilde{V}_s\, dp_m - \tilde{S}_s\, dT_m,$$

$$\frac{dp_m}{dT_m} = \frac{\tilde{S}_l - \tilde{S}_s}{\tilde{V}_l - \tilde{V}_s} = \frac{\tilde{H}_l - \tilde{H}_s}{{}_{\perp}{}_m(\tilde{V}_l - \tilde{V}_s)}. \qquad (14.10\text{–}10)^+$$

This equation, called the *Clausius-Clapeyron equation*, relates the rate of increase of pressure with temperature along a two-phase equilibrium curve to the heat of the phase change $(\tilde{H}_l - \tilde{H}_s)$ and the volume change $(\tilde{V}_l - \tilde{V}_s)$. Naturally, an equation of this type holds for vaporization and sublimation as well as melting.

At temperatures where the vapor pressure of a solid or liquid is very low, the vapor may be considered to be a perfect gas with a molar volume which is much larger than that of the condensed phase. Using the perfect-gas law and neglecting the volume of the condensed phase, the approximate Clausius-Clapeyron equation becomes

$$\frac{dp}{dT} = \frac{\tilde{H}_v - \tilde{H}_s}{T\tilde{V}_v} = \frac{p(\tilde{H}_v - \tilde{H}_s)}{\tilde{R}T^2}$$

or

$$\frac{d\ln p}{dT} = \frac{\tilde{H}_v - \tilde{H}_s}{\tilde{R}T^2} \qquad (14.10\text{–}11)$$

for either vaporization or sublimation. This is very similar to Eq. (14.7–14), the van't Hoff equation for the equilibrium between perfect-gas components of a reacting mixture.

There are many interesting applications of the Clausius-Clapeyron equation. Since ΔH, ΔV, and p are quantities easy to measure in an experiment, Eq. (14.10–10) may be integrated to find the ratio of absolute temperatures between any two equilibrium states:

$$\int_{p_1}^{p_2} \frac{(\tilde{V}_l - \tilde{V}_s)\, dp_m}{(\tilde{H}_l - \tilde{H}_s)} = \int_{T_1}^{T_2} \frac{dT_m}{T_m} = \ln\left(\frac{T_2}{T_1}\right), \qquad (14.10\text{–}12)^+$$

which is especially useful in establishing the absolute temperature of the boiling point of a substance.

Ice is a peculiar substance in that its volume decreases when it melts. According to the Clausius-Clapeyron equation, the melting temperature should therefore decrease with increasing pressure, as can be seen in Fig. 14.3 for ice I. For this reason, an increase in pressure causes ice to melt, a phenomenon quite essential to ice skating and detrimental to the construction of buildings in arctic regions.

14.11 Free energy

In determining the conditions for equilibrium of two phases, a combination of thermodynamic properties, $H - TS$, was found to be useful. This combination is called the *Gibbs free energy** and is denoted by F. We wish to show here some of the general properties of F which may be of further use in the study of equilibrium processes.

The total derivative of F is determined from its definition:

$$F \equiv H - TS = E + pV - TS,$$
$$dF = dE + p\,dV + V\,dp - T\,dS - S\,dT. \qquad (14.11\text{--}1)^+$$

For a system composed of N_1 molecules of species 1 and N_2 molecules of species 2, the entropy is a function of E, V, N_1, and N_2, and according to Eq. (10.4–4) its differential is

$$T\,dS = dE + p\,dV - \mu_1\,dN_1 - \mu_2\,dN_2, \qquad (14.11\text{--}2)^+$$

which, when substituted into Eq. (14.11–1), results in

$$dF = V\,dp - S\,dT + \mu_1\,dN_1 + \mu_2\,dN_2. \qquad (14.11\text{--}3)^+$$

We may therefore consider $F\{p, T, N_1, N_2\}$ as a *thermodynamic potential function* (see Section 8.6) from which V, S, μ_1, and μ_2 may be obtained by differentiation:

$$V = \left(\frac{\partial F}{\partial p}\right)_{T,N_1,N_2}, \qquad S = -\left(\frac{\partial F}{\partial T}\right)_{p,N_1,N_2},$$

$$\mu_1 = \left(\frac{\partial F}{\partial N_1}\right)_{p,T,N_2}, \qquad \mu_2 = \left(\frac{\partial F}{\partial N_2}\right)_{p,T,N_1}. \qquad (14.11\text{--}4)^+$$

The Gibbs free energy F is a useful property for describing the conditions for the attainment of equilibrium in a system maintained at constant pressure and temperature, restraints which are often readily achieved in the laboratory or in natural processes. In contrast with an isolated system, the entropy of the system whose temperature and pressure are maintained constant need not necessarily increase as equilibrium is approached. Instead, we shall find that F approaches an extremum under such conditions.

For an isolated system at equilibrium, dS, dV, and dE are all zero, and according to Eq. (14.11–2) the possible changes in N_1 and N_2 are related by

$$\mu_1\,dN_1 + \mu_2\,dN_2 = 0. \qquad (14.11\text{--}5)$$

---

* The term "free energy" is used because the decrease in F in any steady-flow process carried out at constant pressure and temperature is the maximum amount of work which may be obtained (see Denbigh, p. 68). It is therefore that portion of the energy which is available for the production of useful work under the constraints of constant pressure and temperature.

If the same equilibrium state is achieved while the system is maintained at constant pressure and temperature, the same condition for equilibrium given by Eq. (14.11–5) must also hold, for we have shown in Section 14.7 how this condition determines the equilibrium composition, which must be the same irrespective of the path by which equilibrium is approached. For fixed p and T, dp and dT are zero, and as a consequence Eqs. (14.11–3) and (14.11–5) yield the equilibrium condition for constant p and T:

$$dF = 0 \quad \text{if} \quad dp = dT = 0, \qquad (14.11\text{–}6)^+$$

which may readily be shown to correspond to a minimum of F.* Thus at fixed temperature and pressure, the free energy F is a minimum at equilibrium.

A simple example of this kind of equilibrium is that which exists between two phases, such as liquid and vapor. If a small amount of liquid is changed to vapor, while the pressure and temperature remain fixed, there is no change in F according to Eq. (14.10–6), while there is an increase in S since some heat must be added to cause the vaporization. Since the system is not isolated, the entropy may change without violating the second law of thermodynamics.

The most interesting property of F is that it can be expressed as the sum of the products of chemical potentials and number of particles. To show this, consider a process in which the pressure and temperature of a system are held fixed while its size is increased by an increase in N_1 and N_2, but in which the ratio N_2/N_1 remains constant. With the ratio N_2/N_1 defined by

$$\beta \equiv N_2/N_1, \qquad (14.11\text{–}7)$$

then

$$dN_2 = \beta \, dN_1. \qquad (14.11\text{–}8)$$

For such a process, with dp and dT zero, the free-energy change of (14.11–3) is

$$dF = \mu_1 \, dN_1 + \mu_2 \, dN_2 = (\mu_1 + \beta\mu_2) \, dN_1. \qquad (14.11\text{–}9)$$

The chemical potential is an intensive property which can be considered a function of the intensive properties pressure, temperature, and the molar ratio N_2/N_1; μ_1 or μ_2 cannot depend on N_1 or N_2 alone, for these are extensive properties. For example, if the system is doubled in size so that N_1 and N_2 are doubled, neither μ_1 nor μ_2 will change, for they are intensive properties and can be affected only by the composition through the proportions of N_1 and N_2. Since p, T, and β are held fixed in the process being considered, so will μ_1 and μ_2, and hence also the factor $\mu_1 + \beta\mu_2$. Equation (14.11–9) may therefore be integrated on the extensive variables F and N_1 to give

$$\int_0^F dF = (\mu_1 + \beta\mu_2)\int_0^{N_1} dN_1,$$

$$F = (\mu_1 + \beta\mu_2)N_1 = \mu_1 N_1 + \mu_2 N_2, \qquad (14.11\text{–}10)^+$$

---

* See Denbigh, p. 67.

by virtue of the definition of β in Eq. (14.11–7). It is easy to see that this equation may be extended to include any number of components. In particular, for a single species,

$$F = \mu N. \tag{14.11–11}^+$$

According to the last result, the general condition for equilibrium between two phases, which states that the chemical potentials of both phases are equal, implies that the Gibbs free energy per particle (or per mole) is also the same in each phase. The latter conclusion was reached in Eq. (14.10–6) by a more direct argument. Furthermore, in a two-phase system which is not at equilibrium, but in which the pressure and temperature are held fixed,* the tendency of the free energy to decrease as equilibrium is approached requires that the phase of higher free energy, and hence of higher chemical potential according to Eq. (14.11–11), should decrease while the other increases. Thus the substance tends to move from the phase of high to low chemical potential in order to achieve equilibrium. It is for this reason that the term "chemical potential" was originally devised.

The *Helmholtz free energy*, A, defined by

$$A \equiv E - TS, \tag{14.11–12}$$

is a useful thermodynamic potential function when the independent variables are chosen to be T, V, and N. By analogy with the Gibbs free energy, it is useful in treating the equilibrium of systems for which T and V are fixed, a situation which is also readily achieved in the laboratory. It can be shown that A *is a minimum under such conditions.†*

14.12 The equilibrium of a perfect-gas vapor and a condensed phase

At pressures well below the critical pressure, the vapor in equilibrium with the solid or liquid phase may be considered to be a perfect gas. If the chemical potential (or Gibbs free energy F) and the heat of vaporization of the condensed phase are known, then the vapor pressure may be calculated from the perfect-gas chemical potential, Eq. (12.7–5) or (12.7–11).

Before pursuing such a calculation, let us show how a vapor at a given pressure has a strong tendency to condense to a solid or a liquid when its temperature is lowered below the sublimation or boiling point. We shall show this by comparing the free energy of a condensed phase with that of the vapor.

---

* If the rates of phase change are slow enough, it is possible to temporarily maintain two phases which have the same p and T but are not at equilibrium. For example, the pressure of the vapor from a subliming solid may be held below the equilibrium vapor pressure by vacuum pumping, the required rate of pumping being determined by the rate of sublimation.

† See Denbigh, p. 80.

Let us consider the heating of a solid or liquid at constant pressure. For a single phase (N = const), Eq. (14.11–4) requires that the free energy F must decrease with increasing temperature since the entropy is positive:

$$\left(\frac{\partial F}{\partial T}\right)_{p,N} = -S. \tag{14.12–1}$$

Because the entropy increases with temperature when the pressure is held fixed, the free energy not only decreases with temperature, but decreases at a faster rate as the temperature increases. In Fig. 14.6 are sketched typical curves of F as a function of T for a constant pressure, illustrating their negative slope and curvature.

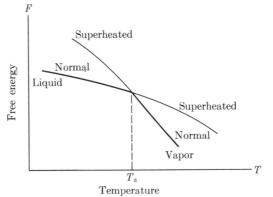

Fig. 14.6. A sketch of the Gibbs free energy F as a function of temperature T for a liquid and its vapor held at a fixed pressure. The intersection of the curves defines the saturation or boiling temperature because both phases have the same free energy. The upper branches of the curves define the superheated vapor or liquid which cannot exist at equilibrium but tends to condense or boil to the phase of lower free energy.

The entropy of a vapor will exceed that of a liquid or solid from which it can be formed because, at a given pressure, the condensed phase must be heated to be boiled or evaporated into the vapor phase. According to Eq. (14.12–1), the free energy F of the vapor will therefore decrease more rapidly than that of a condensed phase, as shown in Fig. 14.6. Where the two curves intersect, the free energies of the two phases are equal and they may remain in equilibrium at the boiling temperature T_s. At temperatures exceeding T_s the superheated liquid phase, having the higher free energy and chemical potential, cannot remain in equilibrium with the vapor and therefore tends to evaporate completely. Likewise, at temperatures below T_s the supercooled vapor phase tends to condense to a liquid which has the lower chemical potential. As a consequence, the free energy F for a single species at equilibrium is the lower of the two curves in Fig. 14.6. The discontinuity in $(\partial F/\partial T)_p$ at T_s is characteristic of a first-order transition.

Whenever the vapor may be considered a perfect gas, the vapor pressure may be calculated, provided the entropy and enthalpy of the condensed phase ($\widetilde{S}_c$ and $\widetilde{H}_c$) are known and the heat of vaporization has been measured at one temperature, T^+. To show how this is possible, the condition for equilibrium between two phases, Eq. (14.10–6), may be rearranged as follows:

$$\widetilde{H}_v - T\widetilde{S}_v = \widetilde{H}_c - T\widetilde{S}_c$$
$$= (\widetilde{H}_c - \widetilde{H}_c^+) - T\widetilde{S}_c + \widetilde{H}_v^+ - (\widetilde{H}_v^+ - \widetilde{H}_c^+), \qquad (14.12\text{–}2)$$

in which the superscript $+$ indicates the properties evaluated at the reference state of temperature T^+ at which the heat of vaporization, $\widetilde{H}_v^+ - \widetilde{H}_c^+$, has been measured.

For the condensed phase, $\widetilde{S}_c$ and $\widetilde{H}_c$ may be determined as follows. For a constant-pressure process, by integrating Eq. (10.4–18), we have

$$\int_{T^+}^{T} \left(\frac{\partial \widetilde{H}}{\partial T}\right)_p dT = \int_{T^+}^{T} \widetilde{C}_p \, dT,$$

$$\widetilde{H}_c - \widetilde{H}_c^+ = \int_{T^+}^{T} (\widetilde{C}_p)_c \, dT. \qquad (14.12\text{–}3)$$

For the same constant pressure process, by integrating Eq. (10.4–21), we find

$$\int_{0}^{T} \left(\frac{\partial \widetilde{S}}{\partial T}\right)_p dT = \int_{0}^{T} \left(\frac{\widetilde{C}_p}{T}\right) dT,$$

$$\widetilde{S}_c - \widetilde{S}_0 = \int_{0}^{T} \left(\frac{\widetilde{C}_p}{T}\right)_c dT, \qquad (14.12\text{–}4)$$

in which $\widetilde{S}_0$ is the entropy at $T = 0$.* These properties are only slightly dependent on pressure, because the constant-pressure specific heat $\widetilde{C}_p$ of a solid or a liquid is primarily a function of temperature alone.

For the vapor considered as a perfect gas, the enthalpy $\widetilde{H}_v^+$ is

$$\widetilde{H}_v^+ = \{\widetilde{E}^+ + p\widetilde{V}^+\} = \tfrac{5}{2}\widetilde{N}kT^+ + \widetilde{N}k(T^+)^2 \left(\frac{d \ln Q_i}{dT}\right)^+ \qquad (14.12\text{–}5)$$

from Eqs. (11.4–2), (11.4–3), (11.4–6), and (11.4–7). According to Eq. (14.11–11), the molar free energy of the vapor, $\widetilde{F}_v \equiv \widetilde{H}_v - T\widetilde{S}_v$, is equal to the chemical potential times $\widetilde{N}$:

$$\widetilde{H}_v - T\widetilde{S}_v = \widetilde{N}\mu_v = -\widetilde{N}kT \left\{\ln\left[\frac{(2\pi mkT/h^2)^{3/2}kT}{p}\right] + \ln Q_i\right\} \qquad (14.12\text{–}6)$$

by virtue of Eqs. (11.4–2), (11.4–5), (11.4–6), and (11.4–9).

---

* For a discussion of $\widetilde{S}_0$, see Section 14.13.

If Eqs. (14.12–3) through (14.12–6) are substituted into Eq. (14.12–2), the vapor pressure p is found to be

$$\ln p = \ln \left\{ \left(\frac{2\pi mkT}{h^2} \right)^{3/2} kTQ_i \right\} + \left(\frac{T^+}{T} \right) \left\{ \frac{5}{2} + T^+ \left[\frac{d \ln Q_i}{dT} \right]^+ \right\}$$

$$- \frac{\widetilde{H}_v^+ - \widetilde{H}_c^+}{\widetilde{R}T} + T^{-1} \int_{T^+}^{T} \left(\frac{\widetilde{C}_p}{\widetilde{R}} \right)_c dT - \int_0^T \left(\frac{\widetilde{C}_p}{\widetilde{R}T} \right)_c dT - \frac{\widetilde{S}_0}{\widetilde{R}}. \qquad (14.12\text{–}7)$$

Since condensed phases usually have a heat of vaporization $(\widetilde{H}_v - \widetilde{H}_c)$ which is large compared with $\widetilde{R}T$ (see Table 14.4), the entropy of the solid will be small enough that it may be neglected in Eq. (14.12–7), when a rough estimate of the vapor pressure is made. This approximation is especially useful in estimating the vapor pressures of refractory solids.

14.13 The third law of thermodynamics

In Chapter 7, entropy was defined as being proportional to the logarithm of the number of microstates of a system of N molecules confined to a volume V and having a total energy E. As the energy of the system is reduced, all the molecules lose energy and tend to exist in their quantum states of least energy. Since there is invariably some long-range attractive force between molecules and a short-range repulsive force, they tend to coalesce and form a condensed phase for which the potential energy has a minimum. Eventually a limit is reached at which the energy can be reduced no more, and for this condition there may be W_0 quantum states of the system, each with the same minimum energy. The entropy of this minimum energy state would therefore be

$$S_0 = k \ln W_0. \qquad (14.13\text{–}1)$$

If the system were a perfect gas, the molecules would not interact with each other, and there would be only one minimum-energy quantum state of the system. For a Bose-Einstein gas, this state would consist of all particles existing in the same quantum state of least energy. For this special case, S_0 would be zero. For liquids and solids in general it might be expected that the number W_0 of microstates of the system all of which have the same least energy is sufficiently small that $\ln W_0$ is much less than the number of molecules. As a consequence,

$$S_0 = k \ln W_0 \ll Nk$$

or

$$S_0 \simeq 0 \qquad (14.13\text{–}2)$$

since the entropy cannot be measured to an accuracy very much less than Nk.

Now, according to the discussion in Chapter 7 of the most probable macrostate, the number of molecules N_j having an energy ϵ_j decreases as ϵ_j/kT increases (see Fig. 8.2). Thus the proportion of low-energy molecules to high-energy molecules will increase as T decreases. At absolute zero of temperature ($T = 0$) the state of minimum energy will have been reached, provided the system remains at equilibrium, that is, it exists in its most probable macrostate.

These arguments may be summarized in a statement usually called the *third law of thermodynamics: a system which is at equilibrium under fixed constraints (such as pressure or volume) in its state of least energy has both zero absolute temperature and zero entropy.* The importance of the third law lies in its consequences for the behavior of systems at very low temperatures (cryogenics) and the quantitative aspects of chemical and phase equilibria.

The third law of thermodynamics cannot be tested directly because the absolute zero of temperature cannot be reached. The difficulty of reaching absolute zero stems from the fact that the entropy of a given system can be decreased only by removing heat from it, for according to Eq. (10.6–4), if dS is negative, so also must dQ be. But to remove heat from a body requires a heat sink at the same or lower temperature, so that the entropy of a sample can never be less than that corresponding to the temperature of the coldest heat sink available and must therefore be finite and irreducible to zero. Therefore, as a practical matter all tests of the third law require observing the behavior of systems as the temperature approaches, but never reaches, zero.

One consequence of the third law may be deduced from the limit of the Clausius-Clapeyron relation for the equilibrium of two phases, Eq. (14.10–10),

$$\lim_{T \to 0} \left\{ \frac{dp_m}{dT_m} \right\} = \lim_{T \to 0} \left\{ \frac{\tilde{S}_l - \tilde{S}_s}{\tilde{V}_l - \tilde{V}_s} \right\} = 0, \qquad (14.13\text{–}3)$$

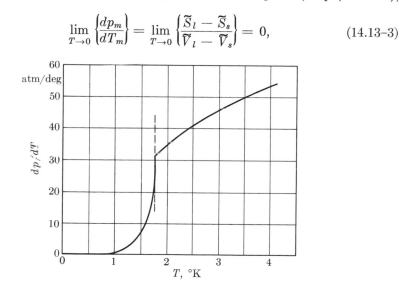

Fig. 14.7. The temperature derivative of the melting pressure of solid helium, showing how it approaches zero at zero temperature in accordance with the third law of thermodynamics as expressed in Eq. (14.13–3). The discontinuity in slope at 1.77°K occurs at a triple point where two liquid phases (Helium I and Helium II) and the solid phase are in equilibrium. Below this temperature, the solid melts to form Helium II which is a "superfluid." (After Mendelssohn, p. 372.)

since the entropy of all phases at $T = 0$ is zero. The value of dp/dT for the melting curve of solid helium at low temperatures is shown in Fig. 14.7, from which it can be seen that dp_m/dT_m does indeed approach zero. Furthermore, according to the limit of Eq. (14.10–6),

$$\lim_{T \to 0} \left\{ \frac{\tilde{H}_l - \tilde{H}_s}{T_m} \right\} = \lim_{T \to 0} \left\{ \tilde{S}_l - \tilde{S}_s \right\} = 0 \qquad (14.13\text{–}4)$$

so that the ratio of the heat of fusion to the melting temperature of solid helium must also approach zero at $T = 0$, which is in agreement with experiments. Thus at absolute zero the change from solid to liquid helium is accompanied by a volume change but no entropy change or heat of fusion.

Another consequence of the third law can be developed from Eq. (14.11–4) for a single species. By partial differentiation,

$$\left(\frac{\partial V}{\partial T} \right)_{p,N} = \left\{ \frac{\partial}{\partial T} \left(\frac{\partial F}{\partial p} \right)_{T,N} \right\}_{p,N},$$

$$\left(\frac{\partial S}{\partial p} \right)_{T,N} = - \left\{ \frac{\partial}{\partial p} \left(\frac{\partial F}{\partial T} \right)_{p,N} \right\}_{T,N}. \qquad (14.13\text{–}5)$$

Since the second partial derivatives are equal and since S cannot vary with p at $T = 0$,

$$\lim_{T \to 0} \left\{ \left(\frac{\partial V}{\partial T} \right)_p \right\} = 0; \qquad (14.13\text{–}6)$$

$V^{-1} (\partial V/\partial T)_p$, which is the volumetric coefficient of thermal expansion, must therefore approach zero at $T = 0$. This has also been confirmed by experiment, as shown in Fig. 14.8.

Another indirect test of the third law follows from a comparison of the equilibrium constants for a gas-phase chemical reaction measured in an experiment with those calculated according to the principles of Section 14.4. There is

Fig. 14.8. The volumetric coefficient of thermal expansion $(\partial \ln V/\partial T)_p$ of solid argon as a function of temperature T. This coefficient extrapolates to zero at zero temperature in accordance with the third law of thermodynamics. [After G. Pollack, "The Solid State of Rare Gases," *Rev. Mod. Phys.* **36**, 754 (1964).]

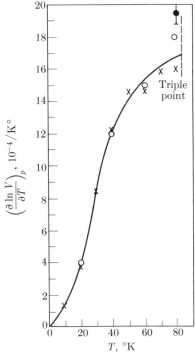

excellent agreement between the experiment and such calculations for many reactions. We can conclude that the entropies of all species would be zero at
$T = 0$ if they existed in the perfect-gas phase at that temperature, for that is
a consequence of the same principles by which the equilibrium constant was
calculated. Again, this is an extrapolation to zero temperature of a theoretical
result which is amply confirmed at higher temperatures for every substance for
which the experiments and calculations have been made.

A somewhat more direct but equally subtle test is that which involves the comparison of measured vapor pressures with those calculated from Eq. (14.12–7),
using the measured values of $\widetilde{C}_p$ for the solid. In making this comparison, it is
found that the agreement is within experimental error for most cases if $\widetilde{S}_0$, the
entropy of the solid at $T = 0$, is set equal to zero. In all other cases, agreement
is possible only if $\widetilde{S}_0$ has a positive value. This may be taken to indicate that
the solid used in the experiment in which $\widetilde{C}_p$ was measured did not remain in
equilibrium as it was cooled toward $T = 0$ but probably remained in a *metastable* state, having an energy higher than the minimum energy for equilibrium
at $T = 0$. Corresponding to this higher-than-minimum energy there is an energy
surface in the Γ-space of the system, a portion of which is a macrostate corresponding to the metastable state. The volume enclosed by this portion of the
energy surface can be called the entropy of the metastable state and is clearly
positive. For this reason, the entropy of all substances at absolute zero of
temperature must be limited by the inequality

$$\widetilde{S}_0 = \lim_{T \to 0} \{\widetilde{S}\} \geq 0. \qquad (14.13–7)$$

Where the tests have been made, this inequality has been found to be true.
Glassy solids or supercooled liquids are examples of metastable substances for
which the zero temperature entropy $\widetilde{S}_0$ can be of the order of $\widetilde{R}$.

Sometimes these consequences of the third law are stated in a form called
Nernst's heat theorem: the temperature derivative of the change in $F - H$ or
$A - E$ (both of which equal $-TS$) which occurs in a chemical reaction or a
phase change approaches zero at absolute zero temperature. Thus

$$\lim_{T \to 0} \left\{ \frac{d}{dT} [T \, \Delta S] \right\} = 0. \qquad (14.13–8)$$

By expanding the derivative and taking the limit, we obtain

$$\lim_{T \to 0} \{\Delta S\} = 0, \qquad (14.13–9)$$

in which ΔS is the entropy change of a chemical reaction or a change of phase.
This rule, empirically derived by Nernst, is in agreement with our previous discussion of the equality of entropy for all phases and substances in equilibrium
at absolute zero temperature.

PROBLEMS

14.1 An equimolar mixture of H_2 and Cl_2 is placed in a bomb at a pressure of 1 atm and at a temperature of 300°K. When the mixture is ignited, the temperature quickly rises to 1400°K because of the exothermic reaction

$$\tfrac{1}{2}H_2 + \tfrac{1}{2}Cl_2 \rightarrow HCl.$$

The equilibrium constant for this reaction is 250 at 1400°K. (a) What is the pressure in the bomb when the temperature is 1400°K? (b) What is the partial pressure of H_2 under these conditions?

14.2 Hydrogen and bromine combine to form hydrogen bromide according to the reaction: $H_2 + Br_2 \rightleftarrows 2HBr$. Stoichiometric proportions of hydrogen and bromine flow steadily into a reaction chamber. The gases leave the chamber in thermodynamic equilibrium at a temperature where the equilibrium constant K_p is 1. The total pressure is 1 atm. What are the partial pressures of all the constituents leaving the reaction chamber?

14.3 A kgm-mole of methane-oxygen mixture in a container occupies a volume of 22.4 m³ at 100°C. The mixture is ignited, and the temperature immediately rises to a high temperature. After some time, the mixture finally is cooled to 100°C by removing 14,000 kcal of heat. (a) Immediately after ignition, by how much has the internal energy changed compared with the internal energy before ignition? (b) What is the internal energy of the products at 100°C compared with the reactants at 100°C? (c) If a stoichiometric mixture of oxygen and methane ($CH_4 + 2O_2$) is ignited under the same conditions, 2×10^5 kcal of heat must be removed to return the products to the initial temperature. What was the molar ratio of methane to oxygen in the first experiment?

14.4 Work parts (a) and (b) of Problem 19.20.

14.5 Oxygen at 4000°K consists of an equilibrium equimolar mixture of atoms and molecules. What is the pressure?

14.6 (a) Find the mole fraction of N in an equilibrium mixture of N and N_2 for $T = 3,000, 6,000, 7,000, 8,000,$ and 10,000°K when the total pressure of the equilibrium mixture is 1 atm. (b) Determine the specific enthalpy h, cal/gm, for this mixture and plot log h as a function of log T from $T = 300$°K to $T = 10,000$°K. (c) On the scale for h, locate those points corresponding to the kinetic energy per unit mass of a body moving with a velocity of: (i) 3000 ft/sec, (ii) 10,000 ft/sec, and (iii) 25,000 ft/sec.

14.7 Calculate the specific heat c_p in cal/gm K° for O_2 at a pressure of 1 atm and a temperature of 4000°K.

14.8 Helium is to be used as a propellant in a plasma propulsion engine. If the pressure in the plasma motor is one atmosphere, (a) at what temperature would 1% of the helium be ionized, (b) at what temperature would 99% of the helium be doubly ionized, (c) at what temperature would the translational kinetic energy per particle equal the energy to doubly ionize the helium? (The first and second ionization potentials of helium are 24.6 and 54.4 ev, respectively, and the respective ground electronic state degeneracies of He, He^+, and He^{++} are 1, 2, and 1.)

14.9 Diatomic hydrogen and deuterium form HD according to the equilibrium: $H_2 + D_2 \rightleftarrows 2HD$. Find the equilibrium constant at 300°K if it is assumed that (1) the electronic structure of all the molecules and, hence, the internuclear forces are independent of the nuclear masses and (2) that the classical expression for the rotational partition function may be used. [*Hint:* Because of (1), the moment of inertia and the vibrational frequency will vary as μ and $\mu^{-1/2}$, respectively, where μ is the reduced mass of the molecule. Also, the sum of the dissociation energy ϵ_d plus the vibrational energy $h\nu/2$ of the ($v = 0$) ground vibrational state is the same for all three molecules.]

14.10 Monatomic gas particles adsorbed on the surface of a solid are held in a potential well which varies only with distance x from the surface (see Fig. 14.9). The motion parallel to the surface (yz-plane) is unhindered, so that the total energy is the sum of kinetic energies of motion in the y- and z-direction plus the kinetic and potential energy of the vibrational motion in the x-direction. (a) Determine the partition function for an adsorbed particle confined to a surface area A, assuming that Boltzmann statistics apply and that the potential well is characterized by a vibrational frequency ν. (b) At what surface concentration σ (particles/cm^2) would Boltzmann statistics no longer be applicable? (Evaluate for helium atoms at $T = 300°$K, assuming $h\nu \gg kT$.) (c) If the adsorbed atoms are in equilibrium with the surrounding monatomic gas, find an expression relating the surface concentration σ with the gas number density N/V.

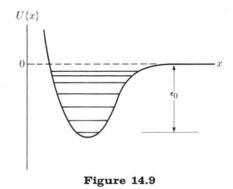

Figure 14.9

14.11 Small solid particles suspended in a high-temperature gas emit free electrons according to the phase equilibrium $e_{\text{solid}} \rightleftarrows e_{\text{gas}}$. The work required to remove an electron to infinity from a spherical particle of radius a and total positive charge Ze is $e(\phi + Ze/4\pi\epsilon_0 a)$, where ϕ is the work function of the solid, e is the magnitude of the electronic charge, and ϵ_0 is the electric permittivity. Assuming that the mixture of gas and particles is electrically neutral on a scale large compared with the average distance between solid particles, that the latter is large compared with a, and that the electron density between particles is uniform, derive an expression for the electron number density in terms of the above quantities, the gas temperature T, and solid-particle number density $\mathfrak{N}$.

14.12 For a slightly imperfect monatomic gas, the equation of state, Eq. (11.7–13), is given in terms of the integral $b\{T\}$ of Eq. (11.7–8). (a) If the gas particles are subject to an attractive force (of the type shown in Fig. 11.1) which can form stable diatomic molecules according to the equilibrium reaction $A_2 \rightleftarrows 2A$, show that for a small degree of association the equation of state of the mixture of atoms and molecules has the form given by Eq. (11.7–13), but in which $b\{T\} = (h^2/\pi mkT)^{3/2}(Q_m/Q_a^2)$, where m is the atomic mass and Q_m and Q_a are the molecular and atomic partition functions for internal degrees of freedom, respectively. (b) If the molecule is strongly bound, i.e., if the magnitude of the minimum potential energy $\gg kT$, show that the integral expression for $b\{T\}$ reduces to that given in (a) for the association reaction.

14.13 A tank of liquid H_2, having a diameter D of 1 m and a length L of 10 m, stores propellant for a space vehicle. If uninsulated, it will be heated by the sun, absorbing 0.1 kw/m^2 of projected area DL. If the density of the liquid hydrogen is 0.075 gm/cm^3 and its latent heat of vaporization is 108 cal/gm at the pressure at which it is stored, what fraction of the hydrogen will boil off in 1 hr?

14.14 Show that, at the triple point, the heat of sublimation equals the sum of the heats of melting and vaporization.

14.15 The following properties of water at the saturation point were measured in an experiment:

p, psi	$v_v - v_l$, ft^3/lbm	$h_v - h_l$, Btu/lbm
500	0.908	755
600	0.750	732
700	0.635	710
800	0.548	689

Find the ratio of the absolute temperatures at $p = 500$ and $p = 800$ psi.

14.16 Calculate $\widetilde{H}_v - \widetilde{H}_l$ at 300°K from Fig. 14.3 by assuming that the vapor is a perfect gas.

14.17 An insulated container of water having a temperature of 25°C is placed in a bell jar. A pump slowly reduces the pressure in the bell jar and the water boils under the reduced pressure. What fraction of the initial mass will have boiled away when ice begins to form on the surface of the water? (In the range of 0°C to 25°C, $c_p = 1$ cal/gm K° and $h_v - h_l = 540$ cal/gm.)

14.18 When water is introduced into a container of gas, some water will evaporate until the partial pressure of the vapor in the vapor-gas mixture rises to the saturation pressure of water at the temperature of the mixture. One gm-mole of N_2 at 300°K and 1-atm pressure and 0.1 gm-mole of water at the same temperature are placed together in an insulated container of fixed volume. After some time, a decrease in temperature and pressure is noted. Calculate the final (a) temperature and (b) pressure. (At $T = 300$°K, the properties at the saturation point of water are $p = 0.0345$ atm and $\widetilde{H}_v - \widetilde{H}_l = 10,520$ cal/gm-mole.)

14.19 Calculate the vapor pressure of monatomic calcium in equilibrium with a calcium crystal at 530°C. At 298°K, the latent heat of sublimation $\widetilde{H}_v - \widetilde{H}_s = 46.10$ kcal/gm-mole, the crystal entropy $\widetilde{S}_c = 9.95$ cal/gm-mole K°, and the crystal specific heat $\widetilde{C}_p = 6.28$ cal/gm-mole K°. The statistical weight of the ^2S ground electronic state of Ca is 2 and $\widetilde{M} = 40.08$. (Compare with the measured vapor pressure of 10^{-3} mm Hg at 530°C.)

15

CRYSTALS

15.1 The motion of atoms in a solid

Unlike a gas molecule, an atom in a solid always moves under the influence of its nearest neighbors. In contrast to a liquid, its orientation with respect to its neighbors is fixed; that is, it is not free to migrate easily throughout the volume of the solid. For that reason it is often useful to think of the atoms of a solid as having a vibratory motion about their average positions, the latter being determined by a balance between the mutual attractive and repulsive forces of the nearby particles. From this point of view, each atom moves under the influence of potential forces much like those which govern the vibratory motion of a diatomic molecule (see Fig. 12.3), except that motion in three dimensions, rather than one, is possible. In a solid, the equivalent of the dissociation energy of the diatomic molecule would be the energy of vaporization, while the compressibility of the solid would be related to the rate of change of interatomic force with position (see Section 4.3). Furthermore, in a crystal there are characteristic frequencies of vibration which are quite important to the interpretation of many observed phenomena such as x-ray and neutron scattering and the electrical properties of conductors and semiconductors.

There is another and complementary view which describes the motion of atoms in a solid in terms of wave propagation, as was discussed in Section 4.6. This description is useful in considering atomic motions correlated over distances which are very large compared with the interatomic spacing so that each atom does not move more or less independently of its neighbor. As we have pointed out in Chapter 4, this type of motion spreads energy and momentum throughout a medium at the group velocity of the waves. It is this correlated motion which determines the low-temperature thermodynamic properties of crystals, their thermal and electrical transport properties, and details of the x-ray and neutron scattering processes.

These complementary points of view are both necessary because they are each a simplified description of the same motion, various aspects of which are of consequence in different macroscopic behavior. In the case of the gas, an equivalent simplification was used: the motion was considered to be the sum of straight-line motion between collisions, from which the perfect-gas properties were calculated, plus the effects of collisions, from which the gas imperfections and transport properties could be determined. Of course, when using such simplifications we must be careful to realize the limitations imposed in their application and be aware of the conditions for which they cease to be valid approximations. Mindful of such caveats, we find it profitable to consider both aspects of the motion of solids in order to understand a behavior which would otherwise be inexplicable.

15.2 Binding forces in a solid

Most solids have approximately the same molar volume $\widetilde{V}$, about 10 cm^3/ gm-mole. If we calculate the average distance between atoms, r_0, by finding the cube root of the volume per atom, $(\widetilde{V}/\widetilde{N})^{1/3}$, it is found to be about 2×10^{-8} cm or 2 A. Thus r_0 is comparable to the dimensions of the simple molecules shown in Fig. 12.1. Although the forces which hold together the atoms or molecules of a solid are not necessarily the same as those which cause the formation of stable, isolated molecules, the internuclear distance at which the potential energy of these forces is a minimum is approximately the same.

A solid which possesses a regular periodic structure is called a crystal. We can distinguish four types of forces which produce the regular structure of a crystal:

(a) *Valence-bonded crystals* (such as diamond or quartz) are truly giant molecules in which the forces are of the same type as those which form simple molecules, namely, the interlocking of the unfilled outer electron shells of the atoms. Since these are very strong forces, such crystals are very hard and have high heats of vaporization.

(b) *Ionic crystals* (such as metallic halides) are held together by the Coulombic attraction of the positive and negative ions which are alternately distributed throughout the crystal. The molecule in the solid phase is effectively dissociated into a positive and negative ion.

(c) *Metallic crystals* consist of metallic ions in a sea of free electrons shared in common by all the atoms.

(d) *Molecular crystals* (such as helium or nitrogen) are held together by weak intermolecular attractive forces (van der Waals forces) due to induced dipole moments. It is the only crystal in which the electronic structure of the atom or molecule is left substantially unaltered.

Some thermodynamic properties of a crystal will reflect the type of bonding. Molecular crystals have the weakest bonds and therefore the lowest melting points and heats of vaporization, while the valence-bonded crystals are quite refractory (see Table 14.4). On the other hand, the molar specific heats of most crystals at moderate temperatures are nearly the same. This situation is quite analogous to the gas-phase properties of molecules: whereas the dissociation or ionization energies can be quite different, the room temperature specific heat depends only on the number of degrees of freedom of motion of the molecule. Since the binding energy of the molecules in a solid is a quantum-mechanical aspect of the motion which, like those discussed in Chapter 5, we accept as a starting point for the determination of thermodynamic properties, we will not be further concerned with the detailed nature of the binding forces.

Not all solids are crystals, of course, for many have an irregular structure which is more characteristic of liquids, so far as can be judged by x-ray diffraction measurements. Such glassy solids have the bulk properties of crystals, like resistance to shear deformation, but none of their symmetry. Also, they do not have clearly defined melting and boiling points. As discussed in Section 14.13, they are metastable systems in the thermodynamic sense.

15.3 Crystal structure and waves

A crystal *lattice* is a network of points defining the average location of the atoms of a crystal. A *cell* is the smallest unit of volume, enclosing an integral number of atoms, which can be surrounded by replicas of itself to form the crystal lattice. Several two-dimensional lattices are shown in Fig. 15.1, and the corresponding crystal cells have been drawn so that the lattice may be constructed by translating the cell in two directions (three directions for a solid), which are not necessarily orthogonal.

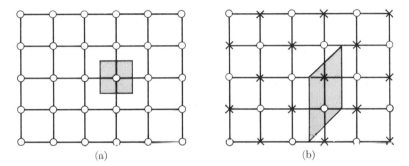

(a)   (b)

Fig. 15.1. A sketch of two-dimensional crystal lattices, showing the unit cell from which the lattice may be constructed by translating the cell parallel to its faces.

Every crystal lattice has several *planes of symmetry* passing through the lattice points which, if displaced normal to themselves by a distance l, will be identically located with respect to the lattice points. We may define a wave vector g_i, called a *lattice wave vector*,* whose magnitude is $2\pi/l$ and whose direction is normal to a plane of symmetry. The physical significance of g_i is that it defines the wave number of a wave in a crystal whose wave front is a plane of symmetry. If the symmetry properties of the crystal are to be incorporated into

---

* The term *reciprocal lattice vector* is commonly used to denote $g_i/2\pi$.

the quantum-mechanical description of the motion of the atoms of the crystal, they must appear in terms of the lattice wave vectors $\mathbf{g}_i$, which will define the characteristic wave numbers of the crystal.

It is helpful to think of the discrete crystal wave vectors $\mathbf{g}_i$ as defining a standing wave in the crystal for which all unit cells are in phase. The frequency of such a wave can thus be considered a natural frequency of the atoms in the unit cells, there being three such wave vectors and frequencies for each atom of the cell.

In Chapter 4, the concept of a plane wave was introduced. The wave vector κ was defined as a vector normal to the wave front, having a magnitude equal to 2π times the reciprocal of the wavelength (Eq. 4.2–3). The dynamical behavior of the medium through which the wave propagated was described by a dispersion equation in which the wave frequency ω was determined by the wave number κ. From this dispersion equation both the phase and group velocities could be found (Eqs. 4.2–6 and 4.5–5).

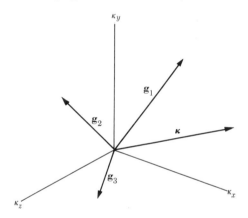

Fig. 15.2. A point in wave-number space defines a wave vector κ of a plane wave in a crystal. The discrete lattice vectors $\mathbf{g}$ define the wave number of the plane waves for which the atoms in each cell are exactly in phase with other atoms in neighboring cells.

To describe the kinds of waves which might propagate in a crystal, let us construct a *wave-number space* in which the three coordinates are the x-, y-, and z-components of the wave vector κ. The position vector of any point in this space defines a wave (number) vector and a possible plane wave in a crystal (see Fig. 15.2). In particular, those points whose position vectors are the reciprocal lattice vectors, $\mathbf{g}_i/2\pi$, are called the *reciprocal lattice points*. Any wave vector different from $\mathbf{g}_i$ describes a wave whose front does not coincide with the plane of symmetry of the crystal. For such a wave, the motion of atoms in adjacent cells along the wave front is not exactly in phase.

The concept of a wave arises from the observation of the macroscopic behavior of a *continuous medium* whose structural scale is so small compared with that of the wave phenomena under observation that it is of no significance to the wave propagation. However, we cannot extrapolate the characteristics of the propagation of sound waves in a crystal to wavelengths which are small compared to the interatomic distance, for in doing so we would be attempting to describe rapidly varying motion in the space between atoms, where no matter exists. We therefore recognize that a wave having a half-wavelength less than about the average distance between atoms normal to the wave front cannot exist and that only longer wavelengths, and thereby smaller wave numbers, are allowed. We can in principle determine a surface in wave-number space which encloses all possible crystal waves, excluding those which are impossible. It defines an allowed volume in wave-number space in the same way that the volume V of a box of gas particles defines the allowed volume in physical space. While this surface in κ-space is different for each crystal structure, it is roughly spherical in shape.

As already mentioned in Section 4.6, there are three ordinary modes of wave propagation in an atomic crystal: one longitudinal mode and two transverse modes. We should therefore distinguish three kinds of points in wave-number space corresponding to these three modes, since we wish to recognize the difference between a longitudinal wave carrying linear momentum and a transverse wave carrying angular momentum, both of which may have the same wave vector. In an ionic crystal there will also be optical modes which must be taken into account.

The dispersion equation, by which the frequency is related to the wave number, can be determined from experiments. At very low frequencies, say less than 100 kc/sec, the phase velocity for any mode is independent of frequency, and by Eq. (4.2–6), the angular frequency ω is simply proportional to κ:

$$\omega = c\kappa. \tag{15.3–1}$$

The theory of elasticity supplies a simple relationship between the phase velocities of the longitudinal (c_l) and transverse (c_t) waves in an isotropic medium and the static elastic constants:

$$c_l^2 = E/2(1 + \nu)\rho,$$

$$c_t^2 = (1 - \nu)E/(1 - 2\nu)(1 + \nu)\rho, \tag{15.3–2}$$

in which E is the longitudinal elastic modulus, or Young's modulus, ν is Poisson's ratio,* and ρ is the mass density. For an anisotropic solid, the phase velocity depends on the direction of κ and cannot be given so simply in terms of only two elastic constants. At higher frequencies and wave numbers near the limiting value, Eq. (15.3–2) no longer holds and the more direct experiments of x-ray or neutron diffraction must be used (see Section 15.4).

For ionic crystals with optical modes, the frequency varies only slightly with wavelength and can be measured by infrared absorption. This mode can be

---

* If a long thin bar is subjected to an axial tension, the ratio of the tensile stress to the longitudinal strain (fractional increase in length) is E, while the ratio of the fractional decrease in transverse dimension to the longitudinal strain is ν.

considered to be the vibration of adjacent pairs of atoms as though each pair were a separate diatomic molecule, with very little propagation of energy or momentum between molecules because of the small group velocity.

15.4 Quantum effects and Bragg reflection

The quantum-mechanical aspects of the motion of atoms in a solid can most easily be specified in terms of the universal relations which hold between energy and frequency on the one hand and momentum and wave number on the other, as given by Eqs. (5.2–1) and (5.3–1). The energy of a wave must be an integral multiple of $\hbar\omega$, and its momentum, a multiple of $\hbar\kappa$. Every elastic wave may be considered a group of elementary crystal excitations, called *phonons*, for which the quanta of energy and momentum are

$$\epsilon = \hbar\omega = \hbar\kappa c, \tag{15.4–1}$$

$$\mathbf{p} = \hbar\boldsymbol{\kappa}. \tag{15.4–2}$$

A group of phonons will travel with the group velocity given by Eq. (4.5–5), carrying with them the energy and momentum given in Eqs. (15.4–1) and (15.4–2).

Unlike particles, phonons do not possess the property of indestructibility, so that there is no conservation of the number of phonons in a system. Since they are the means by which momentum and energy propagate through a crystal lattice, we must of course account for the conservation of such momentum and energy in any interactions involving phonons, but we need not worry about the creation or destruction of phonons *per se*.

The increase in energy of a crystal above the minimum level which exists at absolute zero of temperature can be attributed to the presence of phonons in the crystal. The process of heating a crystal introduces more and more phonons of various frequencies, the energy which each phonon possesses being determined by its frequency according to Eq. (15.4–1). The total energy of the crystal can then be determined by summing the energies of all the phonons present. Because of the obvious analogy with the determination of the energy of a collection of perfect-gas particles, the crystal excitations are sometimes called a *phonon gas*.

The direct evidence for the existence of phonons, which comes from the scattering of x-rays or thermal neutrons by a crystal, is complicated by a phenomenon known as *Bragg reflection*. If a parallel beam of x-rays having a wavelength comparable to the distance between atoms in a crystal impinge on a small crystal, some x-rays are scattered only in particular directions, which can be made visible by placing a film normal to the beam axis at some distance behind the specimen. Figure 15.3 shows the strikingly regular array of scattered beams, in which the discreteness of the scattering angle is shown with the same clarity as that with which the discreteness in frequency of the light emitted

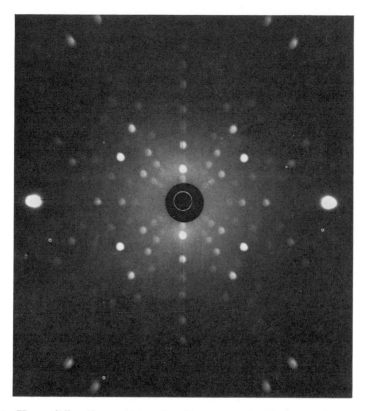

Fig. 15.3. X-ray diffraction pattern of a silicon crystal. The spots show the location at which photons struck the plane of the film after being scattered from the beam whose axis is normal to the film. (Photo courtesy J. T. Norton, M.I.T.)

from an atom appears in a spectrum. The explanation for the origin of this scattering pattern, due to W. L. Bragg, can be given in terms of the reciprocal lattice wave vectors $\mathbf{g}_i$ and the wave number and frequency of the x-rays, κ_x and ω_x, respectively. If a particular x-ray, having initially a wave vector κ'_x, is scattered through an angle θ and acquires a new wave vector κ''_x, then the intense scattering in the preferred directions observed is determined by the conditions

$$\kappa'_x = \kappa''_x + \mathbf{g}_i, \tag{15.4–3}$$

$$\omega'_x = \omega''_x. \tag{15.4–4}$$

The first of these equations expresses a momentum conservation, for it equates the momentum $\hbar\kappa'_x$ of the incoming photon (x-ray) with the sum of the momentum $\hbar\kappa''_x$ of the scattered photon and a characteristic momentum $\hbar\mathbf{g}_i$ of the lattice. The second equation expresses the conservation of energy for the photons, for $\hbar\omega_x'$ and $\hbar\omega_x''$ are the initial and final photon energies, respectively. Bragg reflection is an *elastic* scattering in which the energy of the photon is unchanged while its momentum is altered. As a consequence, momentum is added to the crystal, but there is no change in the energy of the crystal.

At this point it would appear paradoxical, in light of what we have said about phonons, which have both energy and momentum, that it is possible to add momentum in amount $\hbar g_i$ to a crystal without changing its energy. The explanation for this paradox lies in the fact that those few waves of very special symmetry (defined by the wave vectors g_i) describe motion which is completely correlated throughout the crystal, so that effectively the entire crystal participates in the reflection of the incoming photon. If the momentum $\hbar g_i$ is uniformly spread over the whole crystal, the corresponding kinetic energy, $(\hbar g_i)^2/2M$, is negligibly small compared with $\hbar\omega_x$, for the crystal mass M is exceedingly large and can be considered infinite.

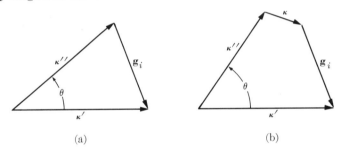

(a)   (b)

Fig. 15.4. The wave vector diagrams for (a) elastic scattering of an incident particle and (b) inelastic scattering due to the emission of a phonon having wave vector κ. These diagrams express the conservation of momentum for the particle (x-ray or neutron) and the crystal; κ' and κ'' are the incident particle wave numbers before and after scattering through the angle θ.

For x-rays, which have a constant phase velocity equal to the speed of light, the conservation of energy in a Bragg reflection implies that the magnitude of κ_x is unchanged, for by substituting Eq. (15.4–1) into Eq. (15.4–4), we find

$$\kappa_x' = \kappa_x'' \tag{15.4–5}$$

so that the superscript primes are no longer necessary. The conservation of momentum, Eq. (15.4–3), may then be plotted in a vector diagram as in Fig. 15.4(a), in which g_i is the base of an isosceles triangle of side κ_x and apex angle θ and is therefore related to κ_x by

$$g_i = 2\kappa_x \sin(\theta/2). \tag{15.4–6}$$

This may also be written in vector form by squaring Eq. (15.4–3):

$$(\kappa_x + g_i)^2 = \kappa_x^2,$$

$$2\kappa_x \cdot g_i + g_i^2 = 0. \tag{15.4–7}$$

The existence of phonons in a crystal can be detected by observing the much less intense scattering of x-rays at angles slightly different from those corresponding to Bragg reflection, or by measuring the scattering of a beam of thermal neutrons whose de Broglie wavelength is comparable to the atomic spacing in the crystal. In either experiment there is an *inelastic scattering* in which a phonon of wave number κ and frequency ω is created or destroyed and for which the conservation of momentum and energy can be stated as

$$\kappa'_x = \kappa''_x + \mathbf{g}_i + \kappa, \tag{15.4-8}$$

$$\omega'_x = \omega''_x + \omega, \tag{15.4-9}$$

where $\hbar\kappa_x$ is the momentum of the beam particle, either x-ray or neutron. The momentum vector diagram for Eq. (15.4-8) is shown in Fig. 15.4(b).

Equations (15.4-8) and (15.4-9) can be applied to the x-ray or neutron-beam experiments to determine the relationship between ω and κ for the phonons. The results of the analysis of some x-ray diffraction experiments are shown in Fig. 15.5, in which are plotted dispersion curves for one longitudinal and two transverse modes of phonon propagation in an aluminum crystal. For this particular case, the phase velocity is almost a constant, independent of wave number.

The crystal lattice vectors $\mathbf{g}_i$ are also important in the understanding of the motion of electrons in conductors and semiconductors, which is discussed in Section 15.6.

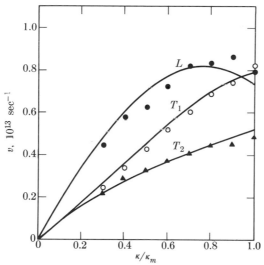

Fig. 15.5. Dispersion curves for elastic waves propagating along the [110]-axis of an aluminum crystal as measured by an x-ray diffraction experiment. The solid curves are a best fit to a theoretical model; T_1 and T_2 are transverse modes and L is a longitudinal mode. The abscissa is the ratio of wave number to maximum wave number for the mode being considered (κ/κ_m). [By permission from C. B. Walker, *Phys, Rev.*, A.I.P, N. Y., **103**, 551 (1956).]

15.5 Thermodynamic properties of a crystal

The first attempt to devise a theory for the thermodynamic properties of crystals was made by Einstein.* He suggested that each atom of a crystal could oscillate in three mutually perpendicular directions with the same frequency ν and for each of these three degrees of freedom the thermodynamic properties would be those of the ideal vibrating diatomic molecule. The constant-volume specific heat of a crystal would therefore be three times the value given by Eq. (12.4–5), or

$$C_v = \frac{3Nk(\theta_v/T)^2 e^{\theta_v/T}}{(e^{\theta_v/T} - 1)^2}, \tag{15.5–1}$$

in which θ_v is $h\nu/k$. At temperatures large compared with θ_v, C_v has the limiting value of $3Nk$, or 5.96 cal/gm-mole K°, a value which had previously been shown by Dulong and Petit to be empirically true for most solids. For low temperatures, $T \ll \theta_v$, the measured specific heats were higher than those predicted by Eq. (15.5–1), and a good fit to the experimental data over a wide range in temperature could not be made by choosing a suitable value of θ_v.

A major advance in the theory of crystals was made by Debye,† who suggested that the oscillations of the atoms in the crystal could best be described by standing waves of various natural frequencies, with the total number of such modes of oscillation equal to the $3N$ degrees of freedom possessed by the N atoms of the crystal. Invoking the concept of a phonon, we can consider that each standing wave consists of N_j phonons of frequency ω_j and has an energy $N_j\hbar\omega_j$, there being $3N$ discrete values of j. The quantum state of a phonon is identical to a vibrational mode of the crystal, the amplitude of this mode being determined by the number N_j of phonons. The thermodynamic properties of this phonon gas can therefore be derived from the properties of the elementary excitations, the phonons, following the development of Chapter 8.

The Debye theory of crystal properties is based on the following simplifying assumptions, concerning the nature of the crystal vibrations, which are listed below in order to emphasize the approximate nature of the ensuing development.

(1) The crystal vibrations are linear, so that the harmonic oscillator approximation is valid. This implies that the phonons, which are the quanta of

---

* Albert Einstein (1879–1955), the most widely known theoretical physicist of this century, could not find a teaching position at the time of receiving his Ph.D. degree in Zurich and worked on theoretical problems in physics in his spare time. At age 26 he published four monumental papers on the subjects of the special theory of relativity, the equivalence of mass and energy, the theory of Brownian motion, and the photon theory of light. Subsequently, he considered the specific heat of solids (1907), the emission and absorption of light (1917), and the quantum theory of a monatomic gas (1924).

† Peter J. W. Debye (1884–   ) is a physical chemist and Nobel laureate who contributed many ideas to the solid and liquid states, among which are theories of specific heats of crystals and electric polarization of ionic solutions.

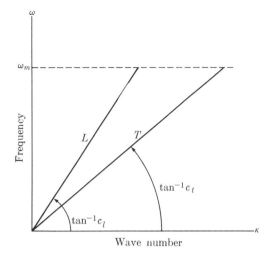

Fig. 15.6. The dispersion curves assumed in the Debye theory define a nondispersive, isotropic wave for one longitudinal and two transverse modes with a maximum frequency which is the same for all modes. The longitudinal and transverse phase (and group) velocities are c_l and c_t, respectively.

the harmonic oscillator, do not interact strongly with each other; that is, their interactions are negligible to the same degree as are two-particle collisions in a perfect gas. (Of course, the collisions of phonons will determine the rate of conduction of heat in a crystal just as molecular collisions determine heat conduction in a perfect gas.) We therefore consider the excitations in a crystal as constituting a *perfect phonon gas.*

(2) The phase velocity of any mode of wave propagation (either longitudinal or transverse) is constant for all frequencies and wave numbers independent of direction, so that the crystal is considered isotropic. Another consequence of isotropy is that both transverse modes have the same (straight line) dispersion curve. Furthermore, the maximum wave number is determined by assuming the maximum frequency to be the same for all modes of wave propagation. As a consequence of these assumptions, the simplified dispersion relation for the longitudinal or transverse waves in a crystal is

$$\omega = \kappa c, \qquad \omega \leq \omega_m,$$

$$d\omega/d\kappa = c, \tag{15.5–2}$$

which is plotted in Fig. 15.6. (This may be compared to a measured dispersion curve shown in Fig. 15.5.)

We shall determine the properties of a perfect phonon gas by first evaluating the partition function Z of Eq. (8.6–3) for the particular case of Bose-Einstein statistics [upper sign in Eq. (8.6–3)].* Since the Lagrange multiplier α, which equals $-\mu/kT$, was introduced into Eq. (8.4–6) to account for the conservation of species expressed by Eq. (8.4–1), we may take α and hence μ/kT to be zero for a phonon gas since no such species conservation law applies to phonons. Thus Z becomes

$$Z = -\sum_{j=0}^{3N} C_j \ln (1 - e^{-\epsilon_j/kT}).$$ (15.5–3)

According to the Debye assumption, the total number $\sum C_j$ of the vibrational frequencies ω_j of the crystal (or the number of phonon quantum states) is $3N$, an exceedingly large number. It is therefore reasonable to replace the sum in Eq. (15.5–3) with an integral,

$$Z = -\int_0^{3N} \ln (1 - e^{-\hbar\omega/kT}) \, dC,$$ (15.5–4)

in which the phonon energy was obtained from Eq. (15.4–1).

To determine the number of vibrational modes (or phonon quantum states) in a given frequency range $d\omega$, we can make use of the general relationship of Eq. (5.8–12) between the number of quantum states and the volume of phase space. A phonon of wave number κ has a momentum $\hbar\kappa$, and its phase space has the coordinates x, y, z, $\hbar\kappa_x$, $\hbar\kappa_y$, and $\hbar\kappa_z$. Through use of the volume element in phase space given by Eq. (5.8–9), the number of quantum states given by Eq. (5.8–12) becomes

$$dC = (1/h^3)\{4\pi V(\hbar\kappa)^2 \, d(\hbar\kappa)\} = (V\kappa^2/2\pi^2)\, d\kappa = (V\omega^2/2\pi^2 c^3)\, d\omega,$$ (15.5–5)

in which the dispersion relation of Eq. (15.5–2) has been used.

There are three classes of phonons corresponding to two transverse modes and one longitudinal mode of wave propagation. Equation (15.5–5) expresses the number of quantum states for each mode when c is the appropriate phase velocity. If we add the quantum states for the three modes of the same frequency, Eq. (15.5–5) becomes

$$dC = \frac{(1/c_l^3 + 2/c_t^3)V\omega^2 \, d\omega}{2\pi^2},$$ (15.5–6)

in which c_l and c_t are the longitudinal and transverse phase velocities. The maximum frequency ω_m may now be determined by integrating Eq. (15.5–6) over the $3N$ quantum states:

$$\{(1/c_l^3 + 2/c_t^3)V/2\pi^2\} \int_0^{\omega_m} \omega^2 \, d\omega = \int_0^{3N} dC,$$

$$\omega_m^3 = 18\pi^2 N/V(1/c_l^3 + 2/c_t^3).$$ (15.5–7)

---

* Bose-Einstein statistics apply to systems of waves when the waves can be superposed, i.e., when two or more phonons may exist in the same quantum state.

If Eq. (15.5–7) is used to eliminate the phase velocities in Eq. (15.5–6), the latter becomes

$$dC = 9N\omega_m^{-3}\omega^2\,d\omega \tag{15.5–8}$$

and the partition function, Eq. (15.5–4), is

$$Z = -9N\omega_m^{-3}\int_0^{\omega_m} \omega^2 \ln\left(1 - e^{-\hbar\omega/kT}\right) d\omega$$

$$= -9N(kT/\hbar\omega_m)^3\int_0^{\hbar\omega_m/kT} x^2 \ln\left(1 - e^{-x}\right) dx, \tag{15.5–9}$$

where

$$x \equiv \hbar\omega/kT. \tag{15.5–10}$$

The thermodynamic properties may be found from Eqs. (8.6–6) and (8.6–7) by setting $\mu = 0$ and differentiating Z with respect to T:

$$E = kT^2\left(\frac{\partial Z}{\partial T}\right)_V$$

$$= kT^2\left\{9N\omega_m^{-3}\int_0^{\omega_m}\left[\frac{\hbar\omega^3}{kT^2(e^{\hbar\omega/kT}-1)}\right]d\omega\right\}$$

$$= 3NkT\left\{3\left(\frac{T}{\theta_D}\right)^3\int_0^{\theta_D/T}\left[\frac{x^3}{(e^x-1)}\right]dx\right\}, \tag{15.5–11}$$

where

$$\theta_D \equiv \frac{\hbar\omega_m}{k}; \tag{15.5–12}$$

$$C_v = \left(\frac{\partial E}{\partial T}\right)_V$$

$$= 9Nk\left(\frac{\hbar^2}{k^2T^2\omega_m^3}\right)\int_0^{\omega_m}\left[\frac{\omega^4 e^{\hbar\omega/kT}}{(e^{\hbar\omega/kT}-1)^2}\right]d\omega$$

$$= 3Nk\left\{3\left(\frac{T}{\theta_D}\right)^3\int_0^{\theta_D/T}\left[\frac{x^4 e^x}{(e^x-1)^2}\right]dx\right\}; \tag{15.5–13}$$

$$S = \frac{E}{T} + kZ$$

$$= Nk\left\{9\left(\frac{T}{\theta_D}\right)^3\int_0^{\theta_D/T}\left[\frac{x^3}{(e^x-1)} - x^2\ln\left(1-e^{-x}\right)\right]dx\right\}. \tag{15.5–14}$$

In these differentiations, the volume is held fixed, thus requiring, from Eq. (15.5–7), that ω_m also be held fixed.

The characteristic temperature θ_D is called the *Debye temperature* of the crystal. The thermodynamic properties E, C_v and S depend on T/θ_D, through the definite integrals contained in the bracketed terms, and are plotted in

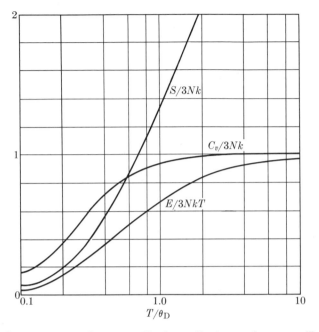

Fig. 15.7. The constant-volume specific heat C_v, internal energy E, and entropy S of a crystal as a function of temperature according to the Debye theory. Tables of these functions may be found in the *American Institute of Physics Handbook*.

Fig. 15.7. At very large temperatures, $T \gg \theta_D$, the specific heat approaches the Dulong and Petit value of $3Nk$. At temperatures very small compared with θ_D, the upper limit of the integral is effectively infinite, and the thermodynamic properties become

$$E = 3NkT \left\{ 3 \left(\frac{T}{\theta_D} \right)^3 \int_0^\infty \left[\frac{x^3}{e_x - 1} \right] dx \right\}$$

$$= \frac{(3\pi^4/5)NkT^4}{\theta_D^3}, \tag{15.5-15}$$

$$C_v = \left(\frac{12\pi^4}{5} \right) Nk \left(\frac{T}{\theta_D} \right)^3 = \frac{4E}{T}, \tag{15.5-16}$$

$$S = \left(\frac{4\pi^4}{5} \right) Nk \left(\frac{T}{\theta_D} \right)^3 = \frac{C_v}{3} = \frac{4E}{3T}, \tag{15.5-17}$$

in which the complete integrals of Appendix A–4 were used. Thus at very low temperatures the specific heat varies as T^3, in very close agreement with experiments.

By suitable choice of the Debye temperature, the specific heat calculated from Eq. (15.5–13) can be made to agree very well with the experimental

Table 15.1. Debye temperature and electronic specific heat of metals*

Substance	θ_D, °K	$\gamma_e \equiv (\tilde{C}_v)_e/T$ 10^{-4} cal/gm-mole (°K)^2
Be	1160	0.54
C (graphite)	391	0.074
C (diamond)	2000	
Na	158	4.3
Al	418	3.5
Fe	467	12
Cu	339	1.72
Ag	225	1.58
Pb	94.5	7.2
NaCl	300	
AgBr	144	
H₂O	315	
MgO	820	

*Data from Keesom and Pearlman, p. 302, and Zemansky, p. 268.

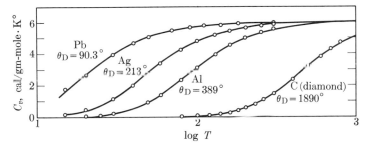

Fig. 15.8. The measured constant-volume specific heat (cal/gm-mole · K°) of several elements compared with the Debye theory. The Debye temperature θ_D was chosen for the best fit. (By permission from G. N. Lewis and M. Randall, *Thermodynamics*, 2nd Edition, revised by K. S. Pitzer and L. Brewer, McGraw Hill, New York, 1961, p. 56.)

measurements, such as is shown in Fig. 15.8. Table 15.1 lists the Debye temperatures for various substances which give the best fit to the experimentally measured specific heats.

The Debye temperature may also be calculated from Eqs. (15.5–7) and (15.5–12) in terms of the atomic-number density and phase velocities of the transverse and longitudinal waves, the latter being calculated from Eq. (15.3–2) through use of average elastic constants. Where this has been done,† the

† See Davidson, p. 361.

result has been found to agree closely with the value obtained from the best fit to the specific heat measurements.

Considering the approximations involved in the Debye theory, the close agreement with experimental measurements is surprising. While there have been many improvements suggested,* none have produced substantially better agreement with experiment.

15.6 Thermal expansion of crystals

The perfect phonon gas considered in Section 15.5 will have a pressure like that of an ordinary gas. The phonon pressure p_ϕ can be found from Eq. (9.9–6) by differentiating Eq. (15.5–9) with respect to the volume:

$$p_\phi = kT(\partial Z/\partial V)_T = kT(\partial \omega_m/\partial V)_T(\partial Z/\partial \omega_m)_T$$

$$= kT(\partial \omega_m/\partial V)_T\{-3Z/\omega_m - 9N\omega_m^{-1}\ln(1 - e^{-\hbar\omega_m/kT})\}. \qquad (15.6\text{–}1)$$

Integrating Eq. (15.5–9) by parts and replacing the integral by Eq. (15.5–11), we can express the partition function in the form

$$Z = -9N\omega_m^{-3}\left\{(\omega_m^3/3)\ln(1 - e^{-\hbar\omega_m/kT}) - (\hbar/3kT)\int_0^{\omega_m}[\omega^3/(e^{\hbar\omega/kT} - 1)]\,d\omega\right\}$$

$$= -3N\ln(1 - e^{-\hbar\omega_m/kT}) + E/3kT. \qquad (15.6\text{–}2)$$

If this is substituted into Eq. (15.6–1), the pressure is found to be

$$p_\phi = -\{\partial \ln \omega_m/\partial \ln V\}_T(E/V). \qquad (15.6\text{–}3)$$

This expression closely resembles Eq. (11.5–15) for the perfect monatomic gas pressure, which is $\frac{2}{3}$ of the energy per unit volume. According to the Debye theory, ω_m is proportional to $V^{-1/3}$, (Eq. 15.5–7), so that

$$\partial \ln \omega_m/\partial \ln V = -\tfrac{1}{3} \qquad (15.6\text{–}4)$$

and the phonon pressure is simply $\frac{1}{3}$ of the energy per unit volume.

The phonon pressure cannot be measured directly. However, the phonons are reflected from the faces of the crystal, so there must be a tensile stress in the crystal lattice that just balances the phonon pressure whenever the external pressure on the crystal face is zero. As the crystal is heated, the increased phonon pressure causes an expansion of the lattice which is resisted by the attractive forces between the atoms. (The elastic compressibility of the lattice is measured by the *isothermal volumetric compressibility*, $-(\partial \ln V/\partial p)_T$, which is the fractional decrease in volume per unit of increase in external pressure, p.) A small increase in temperature, dT, will cause a corresponding increase in

---

* See Ziman, Chapter 1.

Table 15.2. Grüneisen constant for crystals*

Substance	$\gamma_G \equiv -\dfrac{V(\partial \ln V/\partial T)_p}{C_v(\partial \ln V/\partial p)_T}$
Na	1.25
K	1.34
Cu	1.96
Ag	2.40
Al	2.17
NaCl	1.61

*Data from Leibfried, p. 277.

phonon pressure, $(\partial p_\phi/\partial T)_V\, dT$. There will be a correspondingly small fractional increase in volume equal to $-(\partial \ln V/\partial p)_T$ times the phonon pressure increase, so that the ratio of fractional volume increase to temperature increase is

$$\left(\frac{\partial \ln V}{\partial T}\right)_p = -\left(\frac{\partial \ln V}{\partial p}\right)_T \left(\frac{\partial p_\phi}{\partial T}\right)_V. \tag{15.6-5}$$

If Eqs. (15.6–3) and (15.6–4) are substituted into this, the thermal volumetric expansion coefficient $(\partial \ln V/\partial T)_p$ becomes

$$\left(\frac{\partial \ln V}{\partial T}\right)_p = -\left(\frac{C_v}{3V}\right)\left(\frac{\partial \ln V}{\partial p}\right)_T. \tag{15.6-6}$$

The measured values of the thermal expansion coefficient are considerably larger than the value given by the right-hand side of Eq. (15.6–6), but they are very nearly proportional to it. Grüneisen has found that the measured thermal expansion of crystals can be related to the isothermal compressibility by

$$\left(\frac{\partial \ln V}{\partial T}\right)_p = -\left(\frac{\gamma_G C_v}{V}\right)\left(\frac{\partial \ln V}{\partial p}\right)_T, \tag{15.6-7}$$

in which γ_G is a different constant for each substance. The values of γ_G listed in Table 15.2 are four to eight times the theoretical value of $\frac{1}{3}$ given in Eq. (15.6–6). This difference is believed to be due to the anharmonic or nonlinear character of the forces between atoms of the crystal. It is an effect very similar to that present in diatomic molecules, which was discussed in Section 12.1. As the average energy of the atoms increases, their average separation tends to increase because the attractive forces are less strong than the repulsive forces and the atoms spend more time where the forces are weaker. The empirical result of Grüneisen indicates that the mean atomic spacing increases in proportion to the energy per unit volume.

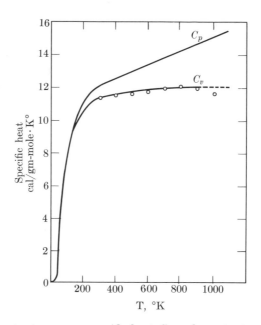

Fig. 15.9. The constant-pressure specific heat C_p and constant-volume specific heat C_v of NaCl. The difference between the two specific heats is proportional to $C_v^2 T$ according to Eq. (15.6–9). (By permission from M. Blackman, *Handbuch der Physik*, Vol. 7, Part 1, ed. by S. Flügge, Springer-Verlag, West Berlin, 1955, p. 370.)

The general thermodynamic relation between the specific heats is*

$$C_p - C_v = -TV\left(\frac{\partial \ln V}{\partial T}\right)_p^2 \left(\frac{\partial \ln V}{\partial p}\right)_T^{-1}. \tag{15.6–8}$$

If Eq. (15.6–7) is substituted into (15.6–8), the constant-pressure specific heat of a crystal is found to be

$$C_p = C_v\left\{1 - \left(\frac{\gamma_G^2 C_v T}{V}\right)\left(\frac{\partial \ln V}{\partial p}\right)_T\right\}. \tag{15.6–9}$$

According to Eq. (15.6–9), at temperatures small compared with the Debye temperature, C_p and C_v are nearly equal, while at high temperatures where C_v becomes constant, C_p increases linearly with temperature. Figure 15.9 shows C_p and C_v for NaCl as a function of temperature, illustrating this effect.

15.7 The motion of free electrons in a solid

In a metallic crystal, the atomic ions are immersed in a sea of electrons. While the electrons are not attached to particular ions and are free to move

---

* See Denbigh, p. 95.

about within the crystal, their motion is very strongly influenced by the presence of the ions. The potential energy of an electron and an ion which are separated by a distance equal to the average distance between ions in a crystal (about 10^{-8} cm) is approximately 1 ev, which is 10 times the average vibrational energy per atom of the crystal at room temperature. More important, the de Broglie wavelength of an electron which has an energy of $\frac{3}{2}kT$, as found from Eq. (11.3–16), is approximately 10 times the distance between ions when T is 300°K. An electron of this energy must therefore be considered to interact simultaneously with many nearby ions, and this interaction will necessarily be a strong one because of the large potential energy involved. Furthermore, according to Section 11.3, this is the same condition for which Boltzmann statistics becomes inapplicable and Fermi-Dirac statistics must be used. Because of the failure of Boltzmann statistics to apply, an electron gas in a metal is called a *degenerate* gas.

If an electron is to interact with only a single ion, its energy must be sufficiently great for its de Broglie wavelength, as given by Eq. (5.3–1), to be less than the interatomic spacing, $(V/N_a)^{1/3}$:

$$\lambda = h/p \leq (V/N_a)^{1/3}$$

or

$$p^2/2m_e \geq h^2/2m_e(N_a/V)^{2/3}. \qquad (15.7–1)$$

In a crystal for which there is one electron per atom, it will be subsequently found that the most energetic electrons approximately satisfy this equality. Thus there are some electrons which interact with the ions in a manner very similar to that of atoms in a dense gas or a liquid.

The peculiarities of the motion we are discussing arise from the very small value of $(V/N_a)^{1/3}$ for a solid or liquid metal. An ionized gas or plasma also contains free electrons, but unless its density approaches that of a solid (rarely achieved in the laboratory), it will behave like a mixture of nondegenerate perfect gases.

An electron will interact very strongly with a crystal lattice whenever its momentum $\hbar\kappa$ is such that it satisfies the condition for Bragg reflection given by Eq. (15.4–6). For momenta which are close to this value, the energy of the electron is no longer $p^2/2m_e$ but is higher or lower because of the interaction with the lattice. To illustrate this effect, consider a one-dimensional motion in the direction of the lattice vector $\mathbf{g}_i$, for which $\boldsymbol{\kappa}$ is parallel to $\mathbf{g}_i$ and $\boldsymbol{\kappa} \cdot \mathbf{g}_i$ is simply $\pm\kappa g_i$. The condition for reflection, Eq. (15.4–6) or (15.4–7), becomes

$$\kappa = \pm g_i/2 \qquad (15.7–2)$$

or

$$p = \hbar\kappa = \pm\hbar g_i/2.$$

Figure 15.10 shows a curve of the energy of the electron as a function of its

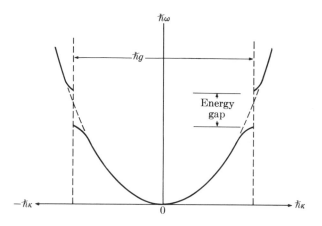

Fig. 15.10. A one-dimensional dispersion curve for an electron in a solid, showing the energy $\hbar\omega$ as a function of momentum $\hbar\kappa$. The parabolic dispersion curve for a free particle (Eq. 15.7–3) is distorted by the lattice atoms at $\hbar\kappa = \pm \hbar g/2$, causing an energy gap.

momentum. In the absence of any interaction, the energy would be the parabola

$$\epsilon = p^2/2m_e,$$
$$\hbar\omega = \hbar^2\kappa^2/2m_e. \qquad (15.7\text{--}3)$$

However, at $\kappa = \pm g/2$ the energy is discontinuous because of the strong interaction with the lattice, and an energy gap may exist as shown in Fig. 15.10. The presence of such energy gaps has a crucial influence on the electrical properties of semiconductors.

If we construct planes in wave-number space which are normal to and bisect the lattice vectors $\mathbf{g}_i$, we enclose a volume called the *Brillouin zone* (see Fig. 15.11). The surfaces of this volume define the wave vectors, and hence momenta, of the electrons for which the Bragg reflection condition is satisfied. If

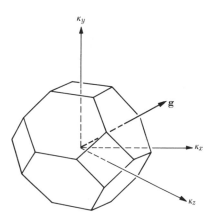

Fig. 15.11. The first Brillouin zone for a face-centered cubic lattice is the volume in κ-space enclosed by this figure (see Fig. 15.2). A lattice vector $\mathbf{g}$ is shown for which one hexagonal face of the surface is the perpendicular bisector. (After Ziman, p. 26.)

an energy gap exists, it will occur at the edge of the Brillouin zone. Inside the Brillouin zone, and near the origin, the electron energy will be given by Eq. (15.7–3) so that surfaces of constant electron energy are spheres in κ-space. Near the boundary of the Brillouin zone, constant energy surfaces are no longer spherical but tend to become parallel to the boundary. Where this happens, the group velocity (Eq. 4.5–5) of the electron,

$$v_g = d\omega/d\kappa = d(\hbar\omega)/d(\hbar\kappa) = d\epsilon/dp,$$ (15.7–4)

no longer is p/m_e because Eq. (15.7–3) is not correct. The ratio p/v_g, which may be called the *effective mass* of the electron in the crystal, is thus somewhat different from the mass of a free electron. This difference in mass must be taken into account when studying the transport properties of the electrons in a crystal.

15.8 The ideal Fermi gas

For electrons, which obey Fermi-Dirac statistics since no two electrons may exist in the same quantum state, the most probable distribution is given by Eq. (8.5–6):

$$N_j^0 = \frac{C_j}{e^{(\epsilon_j - \mu)/kT} + 1}.$$ (15.8–1)

In Fig. 15.12, N_j^0/C_j is plotted as a function of ϵ_j. When $\epsilon_j = \mu$, then $N_j^0 = C_j/2$. If $\epsilon_j \ll \mu - kT$, the number of particles per quantum state approaches one, but if $\epsilon_j \gg \mu + kT$, then the number of particles per quantum state is nearly zero. There is a band of energies near μ within which the number of electrons per quantum state changes rapidly from one to zero. The width of this band on the energy scale is about $2kT$.

At absolute zero of temperature, the width of this band is zero and the state of least energy consists in one particle per quantum state for all quantum states

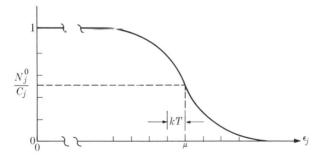

Fig. 15.12. The number of particles per quantum state (N_j^0/C_j) for a Fermi system as a function of energy ϵ_j. Most of the change in N_j^0/C_j occurs only where ϵ_j differs from the chemical potential μ by an amount of the order of kT. At $T = 0$, N_j^0/C_j changes discontinuously from 1 to 0 at ϵ equal to μ_0, the value of the chemical potential at zero temperature.

of energy equal to or less than μ_0. The chemical potential of the electrons at zero temperature, μ_0, is also called the *Fermi energy*. For a Fermi gas, the state of absolute zero of temperature and energy is a state for which there is considerable kinetic energy of the electrons. In this sense the "ground state" of the electron gas is similar to the ground electronic state of an atom: while they are both states of least energy, they are not states for which there is no motion.

An *ideal Fermi gas* is one for which the energy-momentum relationship is the same as that for a free particle, Eq. (15.7–3). The surfaces of constant energy in momentum space are spheres. In particular, the surface for which $p^2/2m_e$ is equal to μ_0 is a sphere in momentum space of radius $\sqrt{2m_e\mu_0}$ and volume $\frac{4}{3}\pi(2m_e\mu_0)^{3/2}$. A surface of energy μ_0 in phase space must enclose N_e quantum states of the electron because all cells are occupied at $T = 0$ by the N_e electrons. We may use Eq. (5.8–12) to determine the number of quantum states in this six-dimensional phase space by multiplying the volume V of configuration space times twice the above volume in momentum space and dividing by h^3:

$$N_e = \frac{2V[\frac{4}{3}\pi(2m_e\mu_0)^{3/2}]}{h^3}$$

or

$$\mu_0 = \left(\frac{h^2}{8m_e}\right)\left(\frac{3N_e}{\pi V}\right)^{2/3}. \tag{15.8–2}$$

The factor of 2 is introduced to account for the two spin states of the electron which exist for each translational quantum state.

If a metallic crystal has one free electron per atom and a molar volume $\tilde{V}$ of 10 cm³/gm-mole, then μ_0/k calculated from Eq. (15.8–2) is approximately 60,000K°. The Fermi energy is therefore very much larger than the average energy of a gas particle at room temperature. On the other hand, the average increase in internal energy per electron which will result from increasing the temperature from 0°K to T will be brought about only by the rearrangement of the electrons in quantum states of energy near to μ_0 and need not necessarily be comparable to μ_0 or even kT. To estimate this increase, we first compute the ratio of the volume in momentum space occupied by states whose energies lie between μ_0 and $\mu_0 + kT$ to the volume for states having energies less than μ_0:

$$\frac{\frac{4}{3}\pi(2m_e)^{3/2}\{(\mu_0 + kT)^{3/2} - \mu_0^{3/2}\}}{\frac{4}{3}\pi(2m_e\mu_0)^{3/2}} = \left\{1 + \left(\frac{kT}{\mu_0}\right)\right\}^{3/2} - 1 \simeq \frac{3}{2}\left(\frac{kT}{\mu_0}\right)$$

$$\tag{15.8–3}$$

since $\mu_0 \gg kT$ at solid temperatures. All the change in energy must be due to this same fraction of the entire number of electrons acquiring an energy of about kT per particle:

$$E - E_0 \approx \{\tfrac{3}{2}(kT/\mu_0)N_e\}kT.$$

Thus the constant-volume specific heat is

$$C_v \equiv \frac{\partial E}{\partial T}$$

$$\approx 3N_e k(kT/\mu_0). \tag{15.8-4}$$

Since $kT \ll \mu_0$, the specific heat of the electrons is much less than $N_e k$ but increases linearly with temperature. Because the electrons form a Fermi gas, their contribution to the total specific heat of a crystal is negligible at room temperature.

To obtain accurate expressions for the thermodynamic functions of a Fermi gas requires considerable mathematical development. If the partition function is written as an integral through use of Eqs. (8.6–3) and (5.8–8),

$$Z = \left(\frac{4\pi V(2m_e)^{3/2}}{h^3}\right) \int_0^\infty \epsilon^{1/2} \ln\left(1 + e^{(\mu-\epsilon)/kT}\right) d\epsilon, \tag{15.8-5}$$

in which the factor 2 is again introduced for the two spin states, then the thermodynamic functions may be expressed as integrals by suitable differentiation of Z. By further assuming that μ is small compared with kT, the functions are found to be*

$$E = (3N\mu_0/5)\{1 + (5\pi^2/12)(kT/\mu_0)^2 - \cdots\},$$
$$S = (Nk\pi^2/2)(kT/\mu_0)\{1 - (\pi^2/10)(kT/\mu_0)^2 + \cdots\},$$
$$C_v = (Nk\pi^2/2)(kT/\mu_0)\{1 - (3\pi^2/10)(kT/\mu_0)^2 + \cdots\},$$
$$p = 2E/3V,$$
$$\mu = \mu_0\{1 - (\pi^2/12)(kT/\mu_0)^2 - \cdots\}. \tag{15.8-6}$$

The specific heat is not greatly different from the approximation of Eq. (15.8–4).

The specific heat of the electrons in a metal may be measured by carefully fitting a curve of the form

$$C_v/Nk = (12\pi^4/5)(T/\theta_D)^3 + \gamma_e T/Nk \tag{15.8-7}$$

to the experimental data at very low temperatures. The first term is the phonon specific heat of Eq. (15.5–16), while the second, having the temperature dependence of Eq. (15.8–4), is that due to electrons. The values of γ_e so measured are given in Table 15.1.

While the experimental values of the electronic contribution to C_v are proportional to T, they do not have the exact value given in Eq. (15.8–6) if μ_0 is evaluated from Eq. (15.8–2), assuming an integral number of electrons per atom. The major cause of the difference lies in the assumption that the surface of constant energy which bounds the occupied quantum states at $T = 0$, called the *Fermi surface*, is a sphere in momentum (or wave-number) space. The true

---

* See Mayer and Mayer, p. 385.

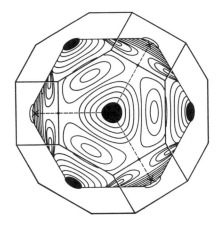

Fig. 15.13. The Fermi surface of copper (according to Pippard) in wave-number space. The Fermi surface lies within the Brillouin zone (shown by circumscribing truncated octahedron as in Fig. 15.11), touching the zone edge at the centers of the hexagonal faces. At zero temperature, the wave number vectors of all electrons lie within the Fermi surface. (By permission from J. Ziman, *Electrons and Phonons*, Clarendon Press, Oxford, 1960, p. 113.)

Fermi surface is distorted from a spherical shape because it tends to lie close to the bounding edge of the Brillouin zone (see Fig. 15.13). This is a direct consequence of the fact that electrons with a wave number comparable to the lattice vector g_i, and therefore a de Broglie wavelength approximately equal to the atomic spacing, must also have an energy approximately equal to μ_0 if there are one or more free electrons per atom [compare Eqs. (15.7-1) and (15.8-2)]. The proximity of the Fermi surface to the boundary of the Brillouin zone invalidates the relation between energy and momentum of Eq. (15.7-3) and thereby the numerical factors of Eq. (15.8-2) which were the result of this assumed spherical symmetry in momentum space.

15.9 Thermionic emission

If a solid is heated in a vacuum, free electrons are emitted and may be collected at another surface (anode) which has a higher electrical potential than the emitter (cathode). If there is no external circuit to permit the steady flow of electrons from cathode to anode, an "electron vapor" will form at the cathode surface which is in equilibrium with the electrons within the solid. Since the number density of the free electrons outside the solid is usually quite low, it is not a degenerate gas and can be described by Boltzmann statistics.

The equilibrium-number density of the electron gas outside the solid may be found from the general condition of equilibrium, which states that the chemical potential μ_s of the electrons in the solid equals that in the vapor, μ_v:

$$\mu_s = \mu_v. \tag{15.9-1}$$

Equation (11.5–10) can be used to determine the chemical potential of the electron vapor, provided a common reference level is selected from which to measure the electron energy both inside and outside the metal. If we choose as the zero of energy the energy of the electron in the solid having effectively zero translational energy, which is the reference level used in deriving the properties given in Section 15.8, then the energy of a stationary electron outside the solid will be higher by an amount we shall call ϕ. The energy ϵ_j of a gaseous electron would therefore be

$$\epsilon_j = \epsilon_t + \phi, \tag{15.9–2}$$

in which ϵ_t is the usual translational energy of a free particle. The partition function for the electron vapor is

$$Q_e = 2\left(\sum_j e^{-\epsilon_j/kT}\right) = 2e^{-\phi/kT}\left(\sum_t e^{-\epsilon_t/kT}\right)$$

$$= 2e^{-\phi/kT}(2\pi m_e kT/h^2)^{3/2}V, \tag{15.9–3}$$

in which the factor 2 derives from the two electron spin states, and the translational partition function is given by Eq. (11.3–12). The chemical potential of the gaseous electrons may now be found by substituting Eq. (15.9–3) into Eq. (8.7–10):

$$\mu_v = kT \ln (N_e/Q_e)$$

$$= \phi + kT \ln \{(N_e/2V)(2\pi m_e kT/h^2)^{-3/2}\}. \tag{15.9–4}$$

If this is substituted into Eq. (15.9–1), the gaseous electron number density becomes

$$N_e/V = 2(2\pi m_e kT/h^2)^{3/2}e^{-w/kT},$$

in which

$$w \equiv \phi - \mu_s. \tag{15.9–5}$$

The quantity w is called the *work function* of the metal. According to Eq. (15.8–6), the chemical potential μ_s of the electrons in the solid is negligibly different from the Fermi energy μ_0. The work function of a solid is nearly identical with the energy difference between a motionless electron outside the solid and the Fermi energy. It is effectively the ionization potential of the solid.

An upper limit to the amount of current which may flow to a cathode as a result of the emission of electrons from its surface may be deduced by applying the concept of detailed balance at the cathode surface. At the equilibrium condition, there is a flux of electrons from the gas toward the surface and an equal but opposite flux away from the surface, the momentum being carried by these particles giving rise to the pressure which the electron gas exerts on the surface of the cathode. The magnitude of this flux Γ_e of gas molecules per unit area and time is found in Section 20.4 to be

$$\Gamma_e = (N_e/V)(kT/2\pi m_e)^{1/2}. \tag{15.9-6}$$

Only a fraction f of these electrons impinging on the surface will actually enter the solid, the remaining fraction $(1 - f)$ being reflected from the surface. To maintain the equality of flux to and from the gas, an electron flux of $f\Gamma_e$ must be simultaneously emitted by the solid, if the number of electrons inside or outside the solid is to remain unchanged.

It is generally supposed that the application of a large potential difference between anode and cathode quickly sweeps away any electrons emitted by the solid, permitting none to return to the cathode. If this potential difference does not affect the electrons inside the solid, they will continue to be emitted at the same rate as previously, $f\Gamma_e$. The current j accompanying this electron flux is simply the flux times the electronic charge e:

$$j = ef\Gamma_e = \frac{4\pi f e m_e (kT)^2}{h^3} \exp{(-w/kT)} \tag{15.9-7}$$

by virtue of Eqs. (15.9–5) and (15.9–6).

The current given by Eq. (15.9–7), which is called *Richardson's equation*, is known as the *saturation current*. It is the maximum current which can be collected at a heated cathode no matter how great the difference in potential between anode and cathode. The experimental measurements of j as a function of temperature can be correlated by this equation with a value of f less than unity and with work functions which vary only slightly, if at all, with temperature.

The Richardson equation expresses the rate at which electrons leave a surface; it is not a purely thermodynamic statement. While the equilibrium electron density was used in order to arrive at the expression for the saturation current, the origin of the rate calculation lies in the kinetic theory arguments from which the particle flux to the wall was determined (Eq. 15.9–6). There are inherent uncertainties and inaccuracies in such arguments which render the conclusions drawn from them less reliable than those obtained in thermodynamics and statistical mechanics. Nevertheless, the simplicity of the treatment of thermionic emission and its fairly good agreement with experiment helps to emphasize at this point that equilibrium properties may be quite useful in the construction of theories of rate processes.

PROBLEMS

15.1 (a) The phase velocity of an elastic wave in a crystal is 5×10^5 cm/sec. Compute the quantum of energy $h\nu$ in a vibration mode of 1-cm wavelength. (b) For $T = 300°K$, compute the order of magnitude of stress in a wave of energy kT in a crystal of 1-cm^3 volume. (Young's modulus is 10^9 dyne/cm^2.)

15.2 Show that the de Broglie wavelength (Eq. 5.3–1) for a thermal neutron of energy kT (where $T = 300°K$) is comparable to the minimum wavelength of phonons in a crystal. (A typical value of V/N in a solid is 10^{-22} cm^3.)

15.3 The integral in Eq. (15.5–14) for the entropy S of a crystal replaces a sum over the $3N$ vibrational modes of the crystal. As $T \to 0$, the integral representation of S approaches zero as it should according to the third law of thermodynamics. Why is this behavior different from that of Eq. (11.4–4) for the translational motion of gas particles, which does not hold for low temperatures because the integral representation of the partition function sum is not valid as $T \to 0$?

15.4 Calculate the specific heat c_v and entropy s of Na, C (graphite) and Al at 300°K (see Table 15.1 and Fig. 15.7); $\widetilde{M}$ is 23, 12, and 27, respectively.

15.5 Develop expressions for E, C_v, and S for a crystal at high temperatures in terms of a power series in the small parameter θ_D/T, including terms of order $(\theta_D/T)^2$.

15.6 Using the relationship of Eq. (15.5–12), show that ω_m for an NaCl crystal (see Table 15.1) is the same order of magnitude as the frequency of an electromagnetic wave of infrared wavelength.

15.7 In an ionic crystal composed of N pairs of ions there are $3N$ optical modes of vibration. If all such modes have the same frequency ω_0 for all wave numbers κ between 0 and a maximum wave number κ_m, find the energy E of these modes as a function of T, ω_0, and N.

15.8 According to quantum mechanics, the minimum energy of vibration of each of the $3N$ modes of a crystal is $\hbar\omega/2$ above the classical minimum of the potential energy of the crystal. Show that the sum of $\hbar\omega/2$ over all the $3N$ modes of the Debye model is $9Nk\theta_D/8$.

15.9 Some of the thermal energy of a gas will consist of sound waves having a wavelength greater than a mean free path l. (a) Determine the fraction of the total energy invested in waves of this form by assuming that the maximum wave frequency ν_m is such that $h\nu_m/kT \ll 1$. (b) Evaluate this fraction for atmospheric air at $T = 300°K$ for which $c = 336$ m/sec and $l = 5 \times 10^{-8}$ m.

15.10 Find the average speed of electrons in a metal at $T = 0°K$. (Assume 10^{22} electrons/cm^3.)

15.11 From the measured electronic specific heat of Na (see Table 15.1), calculate (a) μ_0 from Eq. (15.8–6) and (b) the electron-number density N_e/V from Eq. (15.8–2). (c) Compare the latter with the atomic-number density. (For Na, $\rho = 0.954$ gm/cm^3 and $\widetilde{M} = 22.99$.)

15.12 (a) Calculate the maximum possible saturation current from a surface at 1000°K whose work function is 1.5 ev. (b) What would be the electron-number density N_e/V surrounding this surface when the net current leaving the surface is zero?

16

THERMAL RADIATION

16.1 The propagation of electromagnetic waves

An electromagnetic wave can propagate in a vacuum with a speed which is independent of frequency (or wavelength) and direction. These nondispersive waves carry energy and momentum because of the electric and magnetic fields that accompany them. For a plane wave in a vacuum, the amplitudes of the electric field E and the magnetic field H are related by*

$$E = \mu_0 cH, \qquad (16.1\text{--}1)$$

in which μ_0 is the magnetic permeability of free space and c is the phase velocity of light in a vacuum. The average energy per unit volume of the wave is $\mu_0 H^2/2$, and this equals c times the average momentum per unit volume, in accordance with the general wave relations of Eqs. (4.4–6) and (4.4–7).

Electromagnetic waves are transverse waves in that the electric and magnetic field vectors are each perpendicular to the wave vector κ and to each other. There are two possible waves of the same wave number, usually taken to be right and left circularly polarized waves,† both of which obey the same dispersion relation

$$\omega = \kappa c, \qquad (16.1\text{--}2)$$

in which c is the constant phase velocity and group velocity.

Electromagnetic waves can also propagate through a material medium. The nature of the interaction with the material medium is so varied that it is difficult to summarize. Generally speaking, for some portion of the electromagnetic spectrum the medium becomes dispersive, i.e., the phase velocity c of Eq. (16.1–2) depends on the frequency, which is the optical behavior of most transparent materials. For some frequencies the medium may become reflective to

---

* See Panofsky and Phillips, Chapter 11.

† A circularly polarized wave is one for which the electric (or magnetic) field vector at a point in space rotates in a clockwise (right) or counterclockwise (left) direction when viewed in the direction of propagation of the wave, that is, in the direction of κ.

incident radiation, permitting no transmission at all, like a metal reflecting a radar signal. At other frequencies the medium may transmit a wave while attenuating it in intensity by absorbing some of the wave energy. If the interaction of the radiation with the material medium is specified in terms of the dielectric and magnetic properties of the medium and its electrical conductivity, then the properties of the wave propagation in the medium may be determined. The interaction of the electromagnetic wave with the atoms and molecules of the medium is the source of the propagation properties of the medium and cannot be simply described. For these reasons we shall discuss only the radiation field in a vacuum and the special case of the interaction of radiation with a gas.

16.2 Black-body radiation

If a tungsten wire is heated by an electrical current, it emits radiation at all frequencies rather than at the discrete frequencies emitted by a gas. The character of this *continuous spectrum* of the emitted light may be described by measuring the *spectral intensity* of the radiation in a spectrometer or other instrument which can decompose the radiation into its component parts. The spectral intensity is proportional to the ratio of the energy flux entering the instrument per unit area and time in a frequency band between ν and $\nu + \Delta\nu$, divided by the bandwidth $\Delta\nu$. The energy flux is measured at the focal plane of the spectrometer by permitting the light within a small wavelength interval to fall upon a thermopile or other detector that will measure the rate at which energy is absorbed. Such measurements, while by no means simple to execute, make it possible to describe quantitatively the emission of radiation from heated solids.

A detailed study of the spectral intensity of the radiation from tungsten reveals what the human eye has qualitatively detected: there is a wavelength of maximum spectral intensity which, as the temperature of the tungsten is increased, moves from the red toward the blue, i.e., toward shorter wavelengths or higher frequencies. The spectral emission from different solids at the same temperature is similar, usually showing a maximum at comparable wavelengths. Thus the difference in color of the stars is attributable to the differences in their surface temperatures.

A more sophisticated experiment involves observing the radiation which exists in a nearly closed cavity inside a hot body. As shown in Fig. 16.1, the intensity of the radiation emitted through a small hole in the side of the box may be measured without a large loss of energy from the box. If the proper precautions are taken, the intensity so measured is found to be independent of the material from which the box is made and to depend only on the temperature of the box. This radiation is called *black-body radiation* because one cannot find a material at the same temperature which can radiate more intensely; i.e., there is nothing blacker than a black body!

The special character of black-body radiation was recognized in the latter half of the 19th century and was the cause of many attempts to explain it on

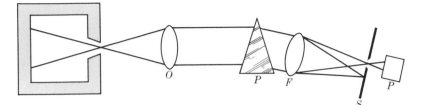

Fig. 16.1. The measurement of the spectral distribution of intensity of the light from a black-body enclosure. The light emitted from the small hole is made parallel by the objective lens O, is refracted by the prism P, and is refocused by the lens F. A slit S permits light of frequency only between ν and $\nu + \Delta\nu$ to pass through to the photocell P, which records the intensity in the band $\Delta\nu$.

the basis of thermodynamic arguments. In particular, Rayleigh* attempted to explain the variation of intensity with frequency by supposing that each standing electromagnetic wave which could be fitted into a box of volume V might have an average energy of $\frac{1}{2}kT$ just as a gas particle has an average energy of $\frac{1}{2}kT$ per degree of freedom. Since there is no limit to the frequency of an electromagnetic wave, there is an infinite number of such waves and therefore an infinite energy, according to Rayleigh's hypothesis. However, the calculated† spectral intensity at frequencies lower than that for maximum intensity was in reasonable agreement with the experimental measurements, even though the observed maximum in the intensity did not appear in the theory.

It was M. Planck‡ who suggested that the energy of the electromagnetic waves was quantized and showed how the measured black-body spectrum followed simply from such an hypothesis upon the introduction of a new empirical constant h. Not only did the new theory agree very closely with the experiments, giving a value of h and k which differed by only a small percent from the presently accepted values, but it also radically altered the course of thinking concerning the motion and structure of atomic systems, ushering in the era of modern quantum physics.

---

* John W. Rayleigh (Lord Rayleigh, 1842–1919), was elected a fellow of the Royal Society at age 31, and at age 37 succeeded J. C. Maxwell as head of the Cavendish Laboratory at Cambridge University. He published numerous papers on sound, wave theory, optics, electrodynamics, electromagnetism, scattering of light, hydrodynamics, capillarity, and elasticity.

† Rayleigh's calculation was corrected by Jeans, who added a factor of one-eighth. The corrected theory is called the Rayleigh-Jeans law.

‡ Max K. Planck (1858–1947) was a German physicist who studied under G. Kirchhoff in Berlin. His explanation in 1900 of the black-body energy spectrum, which required an entirely new approach to physical phenomena, was the foundation on which the theories of Einstein and Bohr, and the whole of quantum mechanics, were based. Planck's *Treatise on Thermodynamics* is a classic exposition of the subject.

16.3 The photon gas

The quantum of radiation is called a *photon*. Its energy and momentum can be given in terms of the frequency and wavelength of the radiation:

$$\epsilon = \hbar\omega = h\nu,$$

$$\mathbf{p} = \hbar\boldsymbol{\kappa} = (h/\lambda)(\boldsymbol{\kappa}/\kappa),$$

$$(16.3\text{–}1)$$

which are related by the dispersion equation (16.1–2). Like phonons, photons observe Bose-Einstein statistics, and the photon gas will have a partition function given by Eq. (15.5–4):

$$Z = -\int_{\omega=0}^{\omega=\infty} \ln\left(1 - e^{-\hbar\omega/kT}\right) dC, \qquad (16.3\text{–}2)$$

in which the upper limit of frequency is infinite. The number of quantum states, dC, for each mode will be given by Eq. (15.5–5), so that the total for the two modes of polarization is

$$dC = (V\omega^2/\pi^2 c^3)\, d\omega. \qquad (16.3\text{–}3)$$

By substitution of this into Eq. (16.3–2), the partition function is

$$Z = -(V/\pi^2 c^3) \int_0^\infty \omega^2 \ln\left(1 - e^{-\hbar\omega/kT}\right) d\omega, \qquad (16.3\text{–}4)$$

which can be converted into an integral on the total frequency $\nu \equiv \omega/2\pi$:

$$Z = -(8\pi V/c^3) \int_0^\infty \nu^2 \ln\left(1 - e^{-h\nu/kT}\right) d\nu$$

$$= -8\pi V(kT/hc)^3 \int_0^\infty x^2 \ln\left(1 - e^{-x}\right) dx,$$

$$(16.3\text{–}5)$$

where

$$x \equiv \frac{h\nu}{kT}. \qquad (16.3\text{–}6)$$

The definite integral in Eq. (16.3–5) has a value of $-\pi^4/45$ (see Table A–4), so that Z, E, S, and p may be found to be

$$Z = (8\pi^5 V/45)(kT/hc)^3, \qquad (16.3\text{–}7)$$

$$E = kT^2(\partial Z/\partial T)_V = (8\pi^5 V/15)(kT)^4/(hc)^3, \qquad (16.3\text{–}8)$$

$$S = \frac{E}{T} + kZ = 4E/3T, \qquad (16.3\text{–}9)$$

$$p = kT(\partial Z/\partial V)_T = E/3V. \qquad (16.3\text{–}10)$$

The *energy density*, E/V, of the photon gas is proportional to the fourth power of the temperature. The pressure of the phonon gas is one-third of the energy density, which is the same relationship for an ideal phonon gas (Debye theory), as discussed in Section 15.6. The photons exert a pressure on the surrounding solid surface because they are either reflected or absorbed and reemitted, thereby undergoing a change in momentum.

The distribution of the total energy among the photons of different frequency may be found by differentiating Eq. (16.3–5) with respect to T:

$$
\frac{\partial Z}{\partial T} = - \left(\frac{8\pi V}{c^3}\right) \int_0^\infty \nu^2 \left\{ \frac{(\partial/\partial T)(1 - e^{-h\nu/kT})}{(1 - e^{-h\nu/kT})} \right\} d\nu
$$
$$
= \left(\frac{8\pi V}{c^3}\right) \int_0^\infty \left\{ \frac{(h\nu^3/kT^2)}{e^{h\nu/kT} - 1} \right\} d\nu,
$$

(16.3–11)

so that the energy density becomes

$$
\frac{E}{V} = \left(\frac{kT^2}{V}\right)\left(\frac{\partial Z}{\partial T}\right)
$$
$$
= \int_0^\infty \left\{ \frac{8\pi h\nu^3}{c^3(e^{h\nu/kT} - 1)} \right\} d\nu.
$$

(16.3–12)

The integrand of the integral is called the *black-body spectral energy density* ϵ_ν,

$$
\epsilon_\nu \equiv \frac{8\pi h\nu^3}{c^3(e^{h\nu/kT} - 1)},
$$

(16.3–13)

and is the photon energy per unit volume and total frequency. The right-hand side of Eq. (16.3–13) is often called the Planck function. At very low frequencies, for which $h\nu \ll kT$, the limiting value of ϵ_ν may be found by noting that $e^{h\nu/kT} - 1$ is approximately $h\nu/kT$, giving

$$
\epsilon_\nu \to 8\pi\nu^2 kT/c^3,
$$

(16.3–14)

which is the *Rayleigh-Jeans* law. At very high frequencies, ϵ_ν decreases exponentially with ν; ϵ_ν has a maximum value at $h\nu/kT$ equal to 2.82.

A dimensionless plot of ϵ_ν as a function of ν is shown in Fig. 16.2. The ordinate is the dimensionless quantity

$$
\frac{(kT/h)\epsilon_\nu}{(E/V)} = \left(\frac{15}{8\pi^5 h}\right)\left(\frac{hc}{kT}\right)^3 \epsilon_\nu
$$
$$
= \left(\frac{15}{\pi^4}\right)\frac{(h\nu/kT)^3}{e^{h\nu/kT} - 1},
$$

(16.3–15)

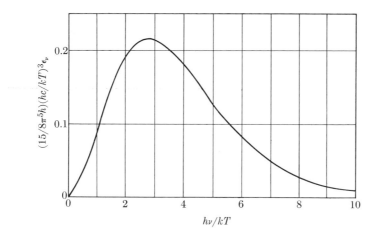

Fig. 16.2. The Planck black-body spectral energy density function ϵ_ν plotted as a function of frequency in the dimensionless manner given by Eq. (16.3–15). The area under this curve is unity.

while the abscissa is $h\nu/kT$. The area under the curve is unity. The maximum value of ϵ_ν not only increases as T^3, but the frequency at which this maximum occurs increases in proportion to T. There is a shift of the maximum toward the blue end of the spectrum as the temperature increases, which is the cause of the change in color of a solid which is heated to higher temperatures.

16.4 Black-body emission

The measurement of the properties of the black-body radiation field is accomplished in an experiment of the type illustrated in Fig. 16.1 rather than in the ordinary manner of calorimetric measurement of the internal energy of a gas. The latter type of measurement cannot be made on a photon gas, for the energy density is so minute at accessible temperatures that its change with temperature cannot be measured. On the other hand, the rate at which energy escapes through a small hole in an enclosed volume is great enough to be easily measured, but it must be shown how this energy flux is related to the properties of the phonon gas inside the volume if one is to accept this measurement as confirming the theory.

Consider the photon that escapes through the hole in the box of Fig. 16.1 with a velocity c and a direction of motion which makes an angle θ with the normal to the plane of the hole (see Fig. 16.3). At any point inside the box, the fraction df of photons moving in a direction such that their velocities make an angle between θ and $\theta + d\theta$ with the direction of the normal is just equal to the ratio of the solid angle $d\Omega$ which is included between two cones of apex angles θ and $\theta + d\theta$,

$$d\Omega = 2\pi \sin\theta \, d\theta, \qquad (16.4\text{–}1)$$

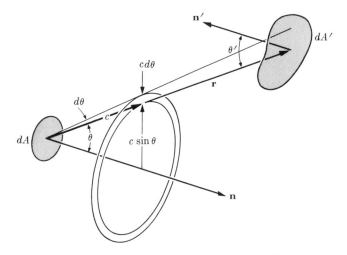

Fig. 16.3. The photons passing through the hole of area dA and lying within an angle θ to $\theta + d\theta$ from the normal **n** lie within the solid angle $d\Omega$ subtended by the ring of width $c\,d\theta$ and circumference $2\pi c \sin \theta$. Thus $d\Omega = 2\pi c \sin \theta\, d\theta$. The area dA', through which some of these photons pass, possesses a normal **n'**, which makes an angle θ' with respect to the direction of motion of photons incident upon it. The photons arriving at dA' from the area dA lie within a solid angle $d\Omega' = \cos \theta\, dA/r^2$.

to the solid angle of a sphere, 4π,

$$df = d\Omega/4\pi = \tfrac{1}{2} \sin \theta\, d\theta. \tag{16.4–2}$$

This follows from the fact that all directions of motion of the photons are equally probable at equilibrium, so the fraction moving in any direction within a solid angle $d\Omega$ is just $d\Omega/4\pi$.

These photons have a velocity component normal to the wall of $c \cos \theta$, and the average value $c_\perp$ of this component for $0 \leq \theta \leq \pi/2$ is

$$c_\perp \equiv \int (c \cos \theta)\, df,$$

$$c_\perp = \tfrac{1}{2} \int_0^{\pi/2} (c \cos \theta) \sin \theta\, d\theta \tag{16.4–3}$$

$$= c/4.$$

Since the rate at which photons impinge upon the wall (number per unit area per unit time) is the number per unit volume times the average component $c_\perp$ of velocity normal to the wall, the rate at which energy is transported to the wall is the energy density times the velocity component normal to the wall. If q is this energy flux per unit area and time, called the *total emissive power* or *radiancy*, then

$$q = c_\perp \int_0^\infty \epsilon_\nu\, d\nu. \tag{16.4–4}$$

Through use of Eqs. (16.3–12), (16.3–13), (16.3–8), and (16.4–3), q may be expressed as

$$q = (c/4)(E/V) = \{2\pi^5 k^4/15h^3 c^3\} T^4 \equiv \sigma T^4. \tag{16.4–5}$$

Equation (16.4–5) is the *Stefan-Boltzmann* law, which states that the power per unit area radiated from a black body is proportional to T^4. The constant of proportionality σ is called the *Stefan-Boltzmann* constant.

In the derivation just given, we have shown how the energy transported by the photons to a unit area of surface in unit time is equal to q. If the element of area is a small hole in a box, then this energy will escape through the hole at this same rate provided that the photons inside the box remain in equilibrium at a temperature equal to that of the box. This equilibrium will be maintained if the area of the hole is quite small compared with the total internal surface area of the box.

The *spectral emissive power* (or spectral radiancy) q_ν is defined as the energy transported to the surface per unit area and time by photons in a frequency range $d\nu$:

$$q \equiv \int_0^\infty q_\nu \, d\nu$$

or

$$q_\nu = c\epsilon_\nu/4 \tag{16.4–6}$$

by virtue of Eqs. (16.4–3) and (16.4–4). Thus q_ν, which is proportional to ϵ_ν, will have a variation with frequency, as shown in Fig. 16.2.

The spectral emissive power per unit solid angle (also called the spectral stearadiancy) $q_{\nu\Omega}$, in the direction θ, is defined by

$$q_\nu \equiv \int_0^{2\pi} q_{\nu\Omega} \, d\Omega = \int_0^{\pi/2} (2\pi \sin \theta) q_{\nu\Omega} \, d\theta, \tag{16.4–7}$$

so that

$$q_{\nu\Omega} = q_\nu \cos \theta/\pi = c\epsilon_\nu \cos \theta/4\pi \tag{16.4–8}$$

by virtue of Eqs. (16.4–3) through (16.4–5). This equation, known as *Lambert's law*, states that the power per unit solid angle radiated from an element of area of a black body varies as the cosine of the angle between the normal and the direction of the radiation.

The *spectral radiant intensity* $i_{\nu\Omega}$ is defined as the rate at which energy is carried across a surface per unit area normal to the direction of the photon motion, per unit of solid angle $d\Omega'$ about this direction, and per unit frequency. For example, at a distance $\mathbf{r}$ from the hole in the box of Fig. 16.3, a solid angle $d\Omega$ subtends an area $r^2 \, d\Omega$. The energy flux $i_{\nu\Omega} \, d\Omega'$ of the radiation at $\mathbf{r}$ from the area dA will be the ratio of the power emitted by the area dA into the solid angle $d\Omega$, or $dA(q_{\nu\Omega} \, d\Omega)$, to the subtended area $r^2 \, d\Omega$:

$$i_{\nu\Omega} \, d\Omega' \equiv \frac{dA(q_{\nu\Omega} \, d\Omega)}{r^2 \, d\Omega} = \left(\frac{q_{\nu\Omega}}{r^2}\right) dA, \tag{16.4–9}$$

provided that $r^2 \gg dA$, for we are considering only radiation moving in a direction very close to θ. By combining Eqs. (16.4–8) and (16.4–9), we find that

$$i_{\nu\Omega} = c\epsilon_\nu \left(\frac{\cos\theta\, dA}{4\pi r^2\, d\Omega'} \right). \tag{16.4–10}$$

Now the solid angle $d\Omega'$ subtended by the photons arriving at the point $\mathbf{r}$ is just $\cos\theta\, dA/r^2$, since $\cos\theta\, dA$ is the projection of the area dA on a plane normal to the direction of $\mathbf{r}$. Hence, the spectral radiant intensity is

$$i_{\nu\Omega} = c\epsilon_\nu/4\pi \tag{16.4–11}$$

and is independent of the distance or direction from the black body.

The human eye or a camera is sensitive to the intensity of a luminous source. Thus the apparent brightness of a candle does not depend on the distance from the observer to the source, provided the source is not too far away to be resolved into a recognizable image by the optical system.* The spectral distribution of the intensity of light from a black body is the same as that of the black-body radiation field and differs from the spectral emissive power q_ν only by the factor π^{-1} [compare Eqs. (16.4–6) and (16.4–11)]. Since ϵ_ν depends only on the temperature of the black body, a measurement of $i_{\nu\Omega}$ by an optical pyrometer enables one to determine the temperature of the body from a remote location. In this manner it is possible to measure the temperature of the surface of the sun from the earth or that of a steel furnace by viewing it through a window.

The *total spectral radiant intensity* i_ν is the integral of $i_{\nu\Omega}$ over the hemispherical solid angle available to a collector of incoming photons:

$$i_\nu \equiv \int_0^{2\pi} i_{\nu\Omega} \cos\theta'\, d\Omega', \tag{16.4–12}$$

in which θ' is the angle between the incoming photons and the normal to the collecting area (see Fig. 16.3). If one observes a black body of area A whose normal makes an angle θ to the line of sight and which is a distance r from the observer, then the small solid angle subtended by the black body is $A\cos\theta/r^2$ and Eq. (16.4–12), combined with Eqs. (16.4–11) and (16.4–6), integrates to

$$i_\nu = \frac{c\epsilon_\nu A \cos\theta \cos\theta'}{4\pi r^2} = \frac{q_\nu A \cos\theta \cos\theta'}{\pi r^2}. \tag{16.4–13}$$

An instrument, such as a photocell or bolometer, which measures the power collected over a range of incoming angles, has a signal proportional to i_ν. Thus the signal is proportional to the area of the black body and inversely propor-

---

* When an object such as a star cannot be resolved by the eye, then its apparent brightness is reduced in proportion to the true image area divided by the area of the receptor cell. The solid angle which can be resolved by the eye is approximately 10^{-6}, which is larger than that subtended even by the planets.

tional to the square of the distance. To measure the temperature of a black body with such an instrument, it is necessary to compare the intensities measured at two different frequencies, say $i_\nu\{\nu_1\}$ and $i_\nu\{\nu_2\}$, which must then be in the same proportion as the ϵ_ν evaluated at the same frequencies, according to Eq. (16.4–13). Since ϵ_ν is a known function of temperature as given in Eq. (16.3–13), the temperature must be determined from the transcendental equation

$$\frac{i_\nu\{\nu_1\}}{i_\nu\{\nu_2\}} = \left(\frac{\nu_1}{\nu_2}\right)^3 \frac{(e^{h\nu_2/kT} - 1)}{(e^{h\nu_1/kT} - 1)}. \qquad (16.4\text{–}14)$$

It is worth emphasizing the difference between the emissive power $q_{\nu\Omega}$ and the intensity $i_{\nu\Omega}$. The former measures the power emitted per unit area of emitter while the latter measures the power per unit area which could be collected. The former depends only on the temperature of the black-body emitter, varying with angle θ according to Lambert's law (Eq. 16.4–8), while the latter depends on the temperature of that portion of the emitter surface that is located along the line of sight from the collector. Unlike the emissive power, which is defined only at the surface of a black body and depends only on its local temperature, the intensity of the radiation field is determined at each point in space in terms of the surface temperatures of all surrounding black bodies. When a point in space is completely surrounded by a body of constant temperature, the intensity $i_{\nu\Omega}$ is isotropic; that is, it is independent of direction and equal to that of a black-body radiation field, namely $c\epsilon_\nu/4\pi$. Under these conditions, Eq. (16.4–12) may be integrated to show that $i_\nu = q_\nu$.

16.5 Emission from nonblack bodies

A mirror reflects most of the visible light incident upon it, so that the spectral distribution of the intensity of the light coming from the mirror is determined not by the mirror temperature but by the characteristics of this light. A perfect reflector might be called a white body in contrast to the black body which emits in a manner independent of any illumination falling on it. All opaque bodies fall within these extremes and may generally be termed nonblack bodies.

If electromagnetic radiation falls on a body, it may be in part reflected, in part transmitted, and the remainder absorbed. For an opaque body, the power of the incident wave must equal the sum of the power absorbed and the power reflected. Considering the electromagnetic wave as a stream of photons, an alternative statement would be that the fraction α_ν of incident photons of frequency ν absorbed plus the fraction reflected must add to unity. Such a statement implies that the energy $h\nu$ of a photon must appear either in the absorbing body or in the reflected wave. It is not a statement of conservation of the number of photons, which we know are not conserved.

If a nonblack body is brought into contact with a black-body radiation field by being placed, for example, in the wall of a large enclosure of fixed temperature, then the nonblack body will exchange energy with the radiation field until the former reaches the same temperature as the cavity giving rise to the radiation, i.e., the nonblack body and the radiation field will be in equilibrium with each other when their temperatures are equal.* Under this condition of equilibrium, or temperature equality, there must be one photon emitted by the nonblack body for each one absorbed from the radiation field, for otherwise the energy of the body would change and equilibrium would be destroyed.

The power q_ν^a absorbed by the nonblack body in the presence of any radiation field is just the fraction α_ν, called the *spectral absorptivity*, of the incident intensity i_ν at the surface:

$$q_\nu^a \equiv \alpha_\nu i_\nu. \qquad (16.5\text{-}1)$$

The power q_ν^e emitted by a nonblack body is said to be a fraction ε_ν, called the *spectral emissivity*, of the black-body emissive power q_ν:

$$q_\nu^e \equiv \varepsilon_\nu q_\nu. \qquad (16.5\text{-}2)$$

When the nonblack body is in equilibrium with a black-body radiation field, then $i_\nu = q_\nu$ and $q_\nu^a = q_\nu^e$, and we would conclude from Eqs. (16.5-1) and (16.5-2) that the spectral absorptivity and emissivity are equal:

$$\alpha_\nu = \varepsilon_\nu. \qquad (16.5\text{-}3)$$

This conclusion, called *Kirchhoff's law*,† is a result of the application of the concept of detailed balance of photon absorption and emission. A measurement of the absorption of an incident beam of light of known intensity i_ν, from which α_ν may be found in Eq. (16.5-1), and a measurement of the emissive power q_ν^e of the same nonblack surface in the absence of an incident beam, from which ε_ν may be calculated according to Eq. (16.5-2), always result in the confirmation of the equality of α_ν and ε_ν.

It should be emphasized that ε_ν is a function of both frequency ν and temperature T. Once it has been measured for different materials, the radiant heat transfer between nonblack bodies made of these materials may be calculated by a simultaneous solution of Eqs. (16.5-1), (16.5-2), and (16.4-12) applied to all surfaces, and Eq. (16.4-11) suitably modified to account for both emission and reflection from nonblack surfaces. Except for the simplest geometries, such problems are very difficult to solve.

---

* This follows from the simple considerations of Section 7.5, even though for the radiation field the number of photons is not a constant. It is sufficient that the radiation field entropy depend only on the energy and volume in order for the equality of temperature to be the necessary and sufficient criterion for equilibrium.

† Gustav R. Kirchhoff (1824–1887) developed the law for the distribution of currents in an electrical circuit as well as the statements concerning thermal radiation from bodies.

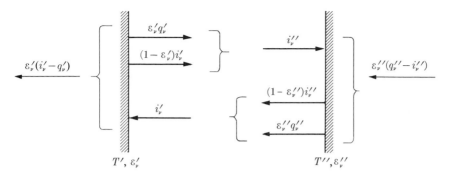

Fig. 16.4. Energy fluxes between two parallel nonblack surfaces of different temperatures and emissivities.

As a simple example of radiant heat transfer, consider two parallel surfaces having temperatures T' and T'' and surface emissivities of ε'_ν, and ε''_ν, respectively. If i'_ν and i''_ν are the intensities of the radiation incident upon the two surfaces (see Fig. 16.4), then the condition that the radiation incident upon one surface must be the sum of that reflected plus that emitted by the other surface may be written as

$$i'_\nu = (1 - \varepsilon''_\nu)i''_\nu + \varepsilon''_\nu q''_\nu,$$
$$i''_\nu = (1 - \varepsilon'_\nu)i'_\nu + \varepsilon'_\nu q'_\nu,$$

(16.5–4)

in which the superscripts identify the temperature T' or T'' at which ε_ν and q_ν are evaluated. The rate of heat transfer to the plate at temperature T' due to photons of frequency ν is the absorbed power $\varepsilon'_\nu i'_\nu$ minus the emitted power $\varepsilon'_\nu q'_\nu$. Solving Eq. (16.5–4) for i'_ν, we find this heat-transfer rate/unit frequency to be

$$\text{heat-transfer rate/unit frequency} = \varepsilon'_\nu(i'_\nu - q'_\nu)$$

(16.5–5)

$$= -\frac{(q''_\nu - q'_\nu)}{(1/\varepsilon'_\nu + 1/\varepsilon''_\nu - 1)}.$$

The total heat-transfer rate is the integral of Eq. (16.5–5) over all frequencies. In the particular case where ε_ν is independent of ν, called a *grey body*, this integration is readily performed to give

$$\text{heat-transfer rate} = \int_0^\infty \frac{(q''_\nu - q'_\nu)\,d\nu}{(1/\varepsilon' + 1/\varepsilon'' - 1)}$$

(16.5–6)

$$= \frac{\sigma[(T'')^4 - (T')^4]}{(1/\varepsilon' + 1/\varepsilon'' - 1)}$$

by virtue of Eqs. (16.4–4) through (16.4–6). Although most nonblack bodies are not grey, ε_ν may vary slowly enough with frequency that an average value may be used for the purpose of evaluating integrals of the type given in Eq. (16.5–6). If both $\mathcal{E}'$ and $\mathcal{E}''$ are unity, then it can be seen from Eq. (16.5–6) that the net heat-transfer rate is simply the difference between the black-body emissive powers of the two surfaces. On the other hand, if $\mathcal{E}'$ (or $\mathcal{E}''$) is very small compared with unity, then the net heat-transfer rate is reduced to a fraction $\mathcal{E}'$ of the black-body value. It is for this reason that the interior surfaces of a Dewar flask are silvered.

It is also worth noting that when $T' = T''$, as Eq. (16.5–5) states, no energy is transferred between the walls, irrespective of what $\mathcal{E}'_\nu$ and $\mathcal{E}''_\nu$ may be. This is, of course, a result of Kirchhoff's law that α_ν and $\mathcal{E}_\nu$ are equal.

16.6 The interaction of photons with a gas

The energy of a gas molecule can be changed not only by collisions with other molecules but also by absorption or emission of a photon. At high temperatures, this latter process may be an important means of bringing the gas to equilibrium. (Of course, the equilibrium state of the gas is independent of the process by which it is achieved.) Furthermore, there are many instances where the interaction between the photons and molecules may be important in processes for which the usual gas energy, pressure, and entropy are only slightly affected by the interaction. We shall therefore present a simple argument first proposed by Einstein concerning the rates of interaction between photons and molecules. Since this is a rate process, it will be necessary to introduce assumptions concerning the nature of the rates which are outside the scope of the statistical mechanics as we have developed it.

A molecule or an atom can emit a photon if its energy can change from a value of ϵ_u to a lower value of ϵ_l, where the energy difference $\epsilon_u - \epsilon_l$ may be due to changes in electronic, vibrational, and rotational motion. The frequency of the emitted photon is related to the energy difference by

$$h\nu = \epsilon_u - \epsilon_l. \tag{16.6–1}$$

This frequency has not a single value, for the energies ϵ_u and ϵ_l are not exactly fixed because of the uncertainty principle. However, the emitted radiation occurs within a narrow frequency interval $\Delta\nu$ on either side of the line center frequency ν_{ul}. Radiation of this type is called *spontaneous emission*, because the motion of the molecule or atom tends to cause the emission of radiation until the internal energy of the particle has reached its lowest state.

The rate of spontaneous emission of photons from a sample of gas is assumed to be proportional to the number N_u of particles in the upper state and to depend on the frequency in such a way that it is much more likely that a photon of frequency ν_{ul} would be emitted than one of slightly higher or lower frequency. If $A_{ul}\{\nu\}\, dt\, d\nu$ is the probability that a molecule in state u will emit a photon of frequency between ν and $\nu + d\nu$ in a time dt, then the change in the number

N_u of molecules in state u due to spontaneous emission would be

$$dN_u = - \left(N_u \int A_{ul} \, d\nu \right) dt,$$

$$dN_u/dt = -N_u \int A_{ul} \, d\nu.$$

$$(16.6\text{--}2)$$

It is also possible for a molecule in state l to absorb a photon which will raise the molecule to the state u. The rate at which this *absorption* occurs will be proportional to the number N_l of molecules in the lower state and to the number of photons or, more conveniently, to the photon energy density ϵ_ν of the proper frequency. If $\{B_{lu}\epsilon_\nu\} \, d\nu \, dt$ is the probability that a molecule in the lower state will absorb a photon of frequency between ν and $d\nu$ in the time dt, when it exists in a radiation field of energy density ϵ_ν, then the number of molecules in the upper state will increase by an amount

$$dN_u = \left(N_l \int B_{lu}\epsilon_\nu \, d\nu \right) dt,$$

$$\frac{dN_u}{dt} = N_l \int B_{lu}\epsilon_\nu \, d\nu.$$

$$(16.6\text{--}3)$$

It was further proposed by Einstein that a molecule will radiate more readily if a photon of the proper frequency disturbs it. He proposed that the rate of *induced emission* would be proportional to the energy density of the photons. If $B_{ul}\epsilon_\nu \, d\nu \, dt$ is the probability of induced emission, the number of upper-state molecules will decrease at the rate

$$\frac{dN_u}{dt} = -N_u \int B_{ul}\epsilon_\nu \, d\nu \qquad (16.6\text{--}4)$$

due to induced emission. The net rate of loss of molecules in the upper state may be determined by adding together Eqs. (16.6–2) through (16.6–4), giving

$$dN_u/dt = \int \{(N_l B_{lu} - N_u B_{ul})\epsilon_\nu - N_u A_{ul}\} \, d\nu. \qquad (16.6\text{--}5)$$

If the molecules are in equilibrium with a black-body radiation field at a temperature T, then the net growth in the number of upper-state molecules due to emission and absorption must be zero, for otherwise there would be energy exchanged between the molecules and the radiation. It is therefore necessary that the integrand of Eq. (16.6–5) be zero for all frequencies when ϵ_ν is the equilibrium (black-body) energy density of a photon gas:

$$\frac{N_u A_{ul}}{N_l B_{lu} - N_u B_{ul}} = \epsilon_\nu. \qquad (16.6\text{--}6)$$

However, at equilibrium the number of molecules in the upper and lower states is also related by the most probable distribution for a Boltzmann system, Eq. (8.7–13),

$$\frac{N_u^0}{N_l^0} = \frac{e^{-\epsilon_u/kT}}{e^{-\epsilon_l/kT}} = \left(\frac{g_u}{g_l}\right) e^{-(\epsilon_u - \epsilon_l)/kT}$$

$$= \left(\frac{g_u}{g_l}\right) e^{-h\nu/kT},$$

(16.6–7)

by virtue of Eq. (16.6–1), in which g_u and g_l are the number of quantum states of energy ϵ_u and ϵ_l. Combining this with Eqs. (16.6–6) and (16.3–13), we find

$$\frac{A_{ul}}{[(g_l/g_u)B_{lu}e^{h\nu/kT} - B_{ul}]} = \frac{8\pi h\nu^3}{c^3(e^{h\nu/kT} - 1)}.$$

(16.6–8)

If this is to be true for all frequencies, then

$$g_l B_{lu} = g_u B_{ul},$$

$$A_{ul} = \left(\frac{8\pi h\nu^3}{c^3}\right) B_{ul},$$

(16.6–9)

which means that all the transition probabilities are related to each other, for if one is known, then the other two may be found.

For line radiation, the Einstein probabilities are nonzero only near the line center. A mean lifetime τ_{ul} for spontaneous emission from the upper state may be defined by integrating A_{ul} over the width $\Delta\nu$ of the line:

$$\tau_{ul}^{-1} \equiv \int A_{ul}\, d\nu = \left(\frac{8\pi h\nu_{ul}^3}{c^3}\right) \int B_{ul}\, d\nu,$$

(16.6–10)

in which ν^3 may be taken outside the integral as ν_{ul}^3 because of the narrow range of integration. A typical value for τ is about 10^{-8} sec.

A *laser** is a nonequilibrium system in which the radiation energy density may grow to enormous values, provided there exists initially a population inversion; that is, $N_u > N_l$ and the radiation is trapped in the system by suitable reflecting surfaces. To demonstrate the principle on which it operates, consider a volume V of gas surrounded by a perfectly reflecting surface. The rate of increase of photon energy per unit volume and frequency, $d\epsilon_\nu/dt$, is equal to the photon energy $h\nu$ times the net rate of emission of photons. Since the latter is the negative of the net rate of depopulation of the upper state given by

---

* The word *laser* is an acronym for "light amplification by stimulated emission of radiation" and refers to devices which amplify optical or near-infrared frequencies. A *maser* is a similar device which amplifies microwaves.

Eq. (16.6–5), we have

$$
\begin{aligned}
\frac{d\epsilon_\nu}{dt} &= -h\nu\,\frac{d(N_u/V)}{dt} = \left(\frac{h\nu}{V}\right)\{N_u A_{ul} - (N_l B_{lu} - N_u B_{ul})\epsilon_\nu\} \\
&= A_{ul}\left\{\frac{[N_u - (g_u/g_l)N_l]c^3\epsilon_\nu}{8\pi\nu^2 V} + \frac{h\nu N_u}{V}\right\},
\end{aligned}
\tag{16.6–11}
$$

in which Eq. (16.6–9) has been used. If the second term in Eq. (16.6–11), that is due to spontaneous emission, is small, then the system will "lase" whenever $g_l N_u > g_u N_l$, for then ϵ_ν will increase exponentially in time, increasing by a factor of e in a time $8\pi\nu^2 V/A_{ul}[N_u - (g_u/g_l)N_l]c^3$. Such an increase cannot go on forever, since N_u will decrease by one for each photon created and N_l will thereby increase by one. Eventually much of the excitation energy originally in the excited upper-state particles will, in the absence of losses, appear as photons in the radiation field. If this radiation is allowed to escape or is "dumped," an extremely intense burst of radiation is emitted which, by virtue of its nonequilibrium origin, is not related to the black-body radiation at the temperature of the system.

The creation of the population inversion necessary for a lasing action is a complicated process which will not be discussed here. Whether the excited species exist in a solid, such as impurities in a ruby crystal, or in a gas discharge, the principle of operation is the same. Some lasers are operated intermittently, such as a ruby laser which is excited by absorption of light from a flash tube, or continuously, like a helium-neon gas laser which is excited by a continuous electrical discharge. In the latter case, the ultimate intensity of the laser light is determined by the rate at which the upper-state atoms may be excited.

Another aspect of laser operation deserves mention in light of the discussion in Section 16.5 concerning the spectral intensity $i_{\nu\Omega}$. If the laser volume is a right circular cylinder with optically plane parallel ends, only photons traveling parallel to the axis will remain in the volume for a sufficient number of reflections to be amplified. In other words, only a plane parallel light wave corresponding to a standing wave with wave front normal to the axis of the laser will be amplified. Thus the light emitted under these conditions will be a coherent electromagnetic wave of parallel light. The general argument which led to the conclusion of Eq. (16.6–11) is still valid if we replace ϵ_ν by the intensity $i_{\nu\Omega}$ and determine in which directions the intensity is amplified by reflecting surfaces.

16.7 Thermal noise in electrical circuits

An electrical amplifier is a device whose purpose is to generate an electrical signal greater in amplitude (or power) than the input signal which excites it. One usually desires an amplifier with a high gain (ratio of output to input amplitudes), which will faithfully reproduce the form of the input signal or will modify it in some known way. An arbitrary input signal may be decomposed into an infinite number of harmonic waves of different frequencies ν, and the amplifier may be required to amplify equally well any component having a frequency within the range between, say, ν_1 and $\nu_2 = \nu_1 + \Delta\nu$. The frequency interval $\Delta\nu$ is called the *bandwidth*, and it is frequently desired to have a constant gain within the bandwidth of the amplifier.

When a zero signal is fed into an amplifier, the output signal is not zero but is a randomly fluctuating signal, which is called the *noise* of the amplifier. The sources of this random signal are the components of the amplifier which generate random fluctuating voltages and currents even when no input signal is used. These random signals arise from thermal motion of the charged particles in the circuit elements and cannot be eliminated except by cooling the amplifier to absolute zero of temperature. The noise of this origin which is observed at the amplifier output is therefore called *thermal noise* to distinguish it from signals caused by the amplification of stray electromagnetic fields that might also be present. Because thermal noise is inherently generated by the materials from which the amplifier is made, and cannot therefore be eliminated by circuit design, there is a minimum input signal whose amplified output can barely be distinguished from the noise generated by the amplifier itself. Any weaker input signal cannot be detected at the output, while stronger signals, when amplified, will have superposed on them the noise generated by the amplifier. Since the noise reduces the fidelity with which the amplified output reproduces the character of the input, the ratio of noise amplitude to signal amplitude at the output is the measure of the accuracy with which the output (and hence input) signal is known. Thus a radar signal directed at the moon must be sufficiently intense that its reflection, when received back at the earth, has adequate power to exceed the noise level of the receiving amplifier if any information is to be obtained about the moon's surface from the returned signal. If this is not so, then the emitted signal must be strengthened or the thermal noise of the amplifier must be reduced.

Any element of an electrical circuit, such as a resistor, is a source of thermal noise. We may calculate the noise electrical power generated by such an element if we consider it to be a source of radiation of electrical signals of various frequencies just as a hot cavity is a source of black-body radiation. However, for electrical networks waves may propagate in one dimension only along the conductors connecting the elements, so that we should consider the electronic circuit elements as one-dimensional black bodies, and the electrical signals as photons propagating in a one-dimensional space.

If we adopt this point of view, then the electrical element may be thought of as a box of length L filled with photons of wave number κ. The phase space of the photons consists of the pair of conjugate coordinates x, $\hbar\kappa$ (position and momentum), and the number of photon quantum states dC in a volume element $L\,d(\hbar\kappa)$ of phase space is therefore

$$dC = (2/h)L\,d(\hbar\kappa), \tag{16.7-1}$$

in which the factor 2 arises from the two types of polarization of electromagnetic waves and the factor h is the unit of volume of a quantum state for a single degree of freedom. The partition function Z for a one-dimensional photon gas is found by substituting Eq. (16.7–1) into Eq. (16.3–2):

$$Z = -(2L/h) \int_{-\infty}^{\infty} \ln\,(1 - e^{-\hbar\omega/kT})\,d(\hbar\kappa)$$

$$= -(4L/c) \int_{0}^{\infty} \ln\,(1 - e^{-h\nu/kT})\,d\nu, \tag{16.7–2}$$

in which $h\nu = \hbar\omega = c\hbar\kappa$ has been substituted for ω and κ, c being the photon phase velocity. This is the one-dimensional equivalent of Eq. (16.3–5). The energy E of the photons may be found by differentiating Eq. (16.7–2):

$$E = kT^2(\partial Z/\partial T)_L = L \int_{0}^{\infty} \{4h\nu/c(e^{h\nu/kT} - 1)\}\,d\nu, \tag{16.7–3}$$

which is the equivalent of Eq. (16.3–12) for the three-dimensional case of black-body radiation.

The power radiated into the circuit from either end of the element must be one-half the energy per unit length E/L times the velocity c, for one-half the photons move to the right and the other half to the left. [This may be compared with the three-dimensional case for which the corresponding factor is one-fourth (Eq. 16.4–5).] The total power P from both ends must therefore be Ec/L:

$$P = Ec/L = \int_{0}^{\nu} \{4h\nu/(e^{h\nu/kT} - 1)\}\,d\nu. \tag{16.7\ 4}$$

The spectral power p_ν per unit frequency is defined by

$$P \equiv \int_{0}^{\infty} p_\nu\,d\nu \tag{16.7–5}$$

so that

$$p_\nu = 4h\nu/(e^{h\nu/kT} - 1). \tag{16.7–6}$$

This is the one-dimensional equivalent of the Planck black-body spectral energy density ϵ_ν (Eq. 16.3–13), and is plotted in Fig. 16.5 as a function of $h\nu/kT$. For low frequencies ($\nu \ll kT/h$), the denominator of Eq. (16.7–6) may be replaced by $h\nu/kT$ with the result that

$$p_\nu \simeq 4kT \quad \text{if} \quad \nu \ll kT/h. \tag{16.7–7}$$

At low frequencies the spectral power p_ν is independent of frequency, and the resulting electrical signal is called "white" noise.

If an amplifier will amplify a signal only within a bandwidth $\Delta\nu$, and if the maximum frequency limit of this band is much less than kT/h, then the noise power P is just

$$P = \int_{\nu_1}^{\nu_1 + \Delta\nu} p_\nu\,d\nu = 4kT\,\Delta\nu. \tag{16.7–8}$$

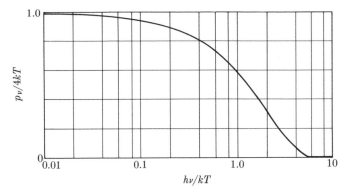

Fig. 16.5. The spectral power distribution p_ν of thermal noise emitted by an element of an electrical circuit.

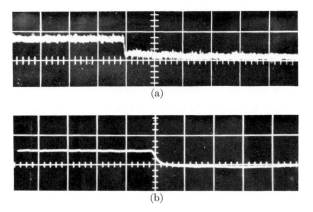

Fig. 16.6. The amplified response of an infrared photodetector to a step input of light intensity. Time moves from right to left, 20 μsec per major division. For the upper trace, a 1-Mc bandwidth amplifier was used, while a 100-kc bandwidth was used for the lower trace. The amplitude of the signal is identical for both traces. Note the greater noise of the upper trace (smaller ratio of signal to noise) as well as the faster response to the step input of light. The thermal noise easily visible in the upper trace is determined by the resistance of the photodetector crystal. (Photo by H. Freedman, M. I. T.)

If the circuit element is a resistor of Ω ohms resistance, then an instantaneous voltage difference ϕ across the resistor implies that a power ϕ^2/Ω is being generated by the resistor. The time average value of this power, $\langle\phi^2\rangle/\Omega$, must be equal to P: $\langle\phi^2\rangle/\Omega = 4kT\,\Delta\nu$ or

$$[\langle\phi^2\rangle]^{1/2} = \{4kT\Omega\,\Delta\nu\}^{1/2}. \tag{16.7–9}$$

Thus the root-mean-square average value of the fluctuating voltage across the resistor is given by the right-hand side of Eq. (16.7–9). The noise may be reduced by decreasing the amplifier bandwidth and/or the temperature of the element.

From Fig. 16.5 we see that the noise-power spectrum decreases drastically for frequencies greater than kT/h. For $T = 300°$, kT/h is about 10^9 cycles/sec, a frequency in the microwave range. It is therefore possible for microwave amplifiers to operate under conditions for which the spectral noise power of Eq. (16.7-6) is exponentially small.

An example of thermal noise generated by a resistor is shown in Fig. 16.6. The amplified response of a photodetector to a step input of light intensity is shown for amplifiers with two different bandwidths. The amplifier having the larger bandwidth shows a signal with a greater noise power, in agreement with Eq. (16.7-9).

PROBLEMS

16.1 Find the number of photons per cubic meter in a black-body radiation field at 300°K.

16.2 For a black-body radiation field show that (a) the pressure is a function of temperature alone, (b) $H = 4E/3$, (c) $C_v = 3S$, and (d) C_p is indeterminate.

16.3 From the thermodynamic potential function $S = S\{E, V\}$ all other properties may be found. Find $S\{E, V\}$ for the black-body radiation field.

16.4 At what temperature does the radiation pressure equal 1 atm?

16.5 At what temperature will the maximum energy density of the black-body radiation field occur at 6000 A?

16.6 (a) Calculate the emissive power (watts/m^2) from a black body at 1000°K. (b) Calculate the emissive power from the same body of the radiation with wavelength between 4000 and 7000 A.

16.7 The sun may be considered to be a black body having a temperature of 5800°K. Its diameter is 1.39×10^9 m, and its distance from the earth is 1.5×10^{11} m. (a) What is the total radiant intensity (watts/m^2) of sunlight at the surface of the earth? (b) What pressure would be exerted on a perfectly absorbing surface placed normal to the earth-sun line? (c) A flat surface on a satellite which faces the sun has an absorptivity of unity. If it radiates to space all the heat absorbed from the sunlight, what would be its temperature?

16.8 It is desired to measure the rapid rise in surface temperature of a black body by measuring the increase in radiation in the wavelength region between 3 and 5μ. A mirror (6-in. diameter) placed 1 ft from the surface focuses the radiation on an infrared photocell of 1-mm^2 aperture, the ratio of object to image size of the optical system being unity. The photocell is cooled to 70°K. (a) If the body increases in temperature from 300°K to 310°K, what will be the increase in infrared emissive power in the 3- to 5-micron band which passes through the photocell aperture? (b) If the bandwidth of the photocell amplifier is 10^5 cycles/sec, what will be the thermal noise power of the photocell?

16.9 In a solar furnace sunlight is focused by a mirror of 1-m diameter and 2-m focal length on a hole in the side of an insulated enclosure. The hole, located at the focal length of the mirror, is equal in diameter to the image of the sun. Assuming that the total intensity of sunlight is 1.4 kw/m², what is the maximum temperature inside the enclosure if the mirror is a perfect reflector?

16.10 Two parallel black surfaces at temperatures of 800°K and 300°K are separated by a vacuum. A sheet of metal foil of average emissivity of 0.2 is placed in the space between them. (a) What is the temperature of the metal foil? (b) By what fraction is the heat transfer from the hot to the cold wall reduced? (c) By what fraction is the heat transfer reduced if two layers of foil are placed between the black surfaces?

17

MAGNETIZATION

17.1 The magnetization of matter

In Section 9.2 we noted the distinction between short-range and long-range forces in determining the nature of the interaction of the molecules of a system with its surroundings. For short-range forces, such as van der Waals' attractive forces between molecules, the forces on the molecules of a system due to the molecules of the environment are exerted only on those system molecules lying in a very thin layer close to the surface. The average force could then be considered as a macroscopic surface stress, or pressure, acting on the system, and the resulting reversible work became the product of the surface stress times the displacement of the surface. For long-range forces, which are electrostatic, electromagnetic, or gravitational in origin, the environment molecules exert forces throughout the interior of the system. The work done in displacing the surface of the system is not only the product of the short-range surface force times the surface displacement but it also includes the effects of motion produced further in the interior of the system. For example, the dielectric material separating the conducting surfaces of a charged capacitor experiences an electric field due to the charged particles deposited on the capacitor plates. Because of this field, molecules throughout the volume of the dielectric will experience a force or a moment if they possess a net charge or electric dipole moment, respectively, and there will be an equal (but opposite) force or torque exerted on the charged particles on the plates. This long-range interaction between the system (dielectric) and its environment (charged conducting plates) is described in terms of an electrostatic field. The force on a molecule is determined by the local electric field while this field is in turn determined by the location and orientation of all the other molecules. In this way, the force on one molecule can be determined from a knowledge of the location of all other molecules. The concept of a field of force is introduced for convenience: if we are studying the motion of a molecule, which depends only on the local force field, we need not be concerned about the origin of the field; that is, it is convenient to separate the problem of the motion of a molecule subject to given forces from the problem of how such forces may arise.

311

Long-range forces, which are exerted throughout the volume of a system, are sometimes called body forces in contrast to the short-range forces, which are called contact forces or surface forces. Under ordinary conditions it is usually possible to exert much greater forces on macroscopic bodies by means of surface forces than by body forces and thereby to produce larger changes in energy by this method. For example, a surface pressure of 1000 atm will deform a 1-cm^3 block of copper, whereas the body force exerted on it by the gravitational attraction of the earth can be balanced by a pressure of only 0.01 atm on its lower face. The magnetic force on the conductors of an electromagnet which generate the very intense magnetic field of 10^5 gauss can be supported by a pressure of 400 atm, while pressure of millions of atmospheres can be generated in high-pressure testing devices. Since the total body force is proportionate to the volume of the body while the surface force is proportional to the area of the surface, body forces will become more important as the size of the system increases. (It is for this reason that magnetic and self-gravitational effects are important in astrophysical fluid dynamics, while they are usually insignificant in laboratory experiments.) Therefore, under ordinary conditions the amount of magnetic or electric work which can be done on a body will be small compared with the thermal energy at room temperature, so that electromagnetic effects tend to become more important at low temperatures where the thermal energy is equally small. In fact, we shall see in Section 17.4 how magnetic refrigeration processes are very effective means of cooling substances to extremely low temperatures.

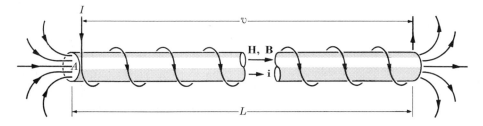

Fig. 17.1. A long cylindrical specimen magnetized by a superconducting solenoid of $\mathfrak{N}$ turns. $\mathcal{U}$ is the voltage difference between the coil leads. The unit vector in the axial direction is **i**.

In this chapter we shall be concerned with the thermodynamic properties of a substance which is subject to a uniform magnetic field whose strength may be varied at will. Suppose that a long cylindrical sample of the substance, having a length L and cross-sectional area A, is used as a core for winding a solenoidal electromagnet of $\mathfrak{N}$ turns, as shown in Fig. 17.1. If a current I is passed through the coil, a uniform magnetic field of intensity **H** will fill the volume AL. (We may neglect the fringing at the ends.) We shall assume for convenience that the solenoid winding is constructed from a superconducting material having

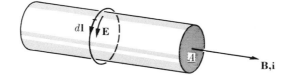

Fig. 17.2. Path of integration for Faraday's law, Eq. (17.1–1).

zero electrical resistance. As a consequence, if the current I is unchanging in time, the voltage difference υ between the coil leads will be zero and no power is required to maintain the current at this fixed value. On the other hand, if the current is changed, the time-varying magnetic induction **B** will cause a voltage difference υ to appear across the coil terminals, and electrical power will be absorbed. To determine this voltage, let us apply Faraday's law* to a single turn of the coil surrounding the core. If $d\mathbf{l}$ is the incremental length of coil winding measured in the azimuthal direction indicated in Fig. 17.2 and **E** is the electric field measured in the same direction, then Faraday's law states that

$$\oint \mathbf{E} \cdot d\mathbf{l} = -\int \frac{d\mathbf{B}}{dt} \cdot (\mathbf{i}\, dA)$$

or

$$\upsilon = -\mathfrak{N}\oint \mathbf{E} \cdot d\mathbf{l} = \mathfrak{N} A\mathbf{i} \cdot \frac{d\mathbf{B}}{dt}, \tag{17.1–1}$$

since $-\oint \mathbf{E} \cdot d\mathbf{l}$ is the voltage increase per coil turn in the direction of current flow. Here **i** is the unit vector in the axial direction, as shown in Figs. 17.1 and 17.2.

The electrical work dW_e required to maintain the current I for the time interval dt is just the power υI times the time:

$$dW_e = -\upsilon I\, dt$$
$$= -\mathfrak{N} A I \mathbf{i} \cdot d\mathbf{B} \tag{17.1–2}$$

because of Eq. (17.1–1). (We have invoked the thermodynamic convention that work done on the coil is negative.) The symbol dW_e is used to emphasize the fact that Eq. (17.1–2) cannot be integrated until the relationship between I and **B** is known.

For a uniformly wound solenoid, Ampère's law may be written for the closed curve of Fig. 17.3 to relate the line integral of the magnetic intensity **H** with the total current $\mathfrak{N}I$ linked by the closed curve:

$$\mathfrak{N}I = \oint \mathbf{H} \cdot d\mathbf{l} = \mathbf{H} \cdot \mathbf{i}L. \tag{17.1–3}$$

---

* For a discussion of the laws of magnetic induction, see Panofsky and Phillips, Chapters 7 and 9, or Feynman, Vol. II, Chapters 13–17.

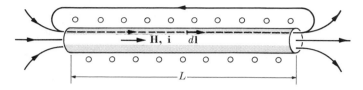

Fig. 17.3. Path of integration for Ampere's law, Eq. (17.1–3).

Substituting this into Eq. (17.1–2), we find that the electrical work is given by

$$dW_e = -(AL)\mathbf{H} \cdot d\mathbf{B}, \qquad (17.1\text{–}4)$$

in which we have replaced $(\mathbf{H} \cdot \mathbf{i})(\mathbf{i} \cdot d\mathbf{B})$ by $\mathbf{H} \cdot d\mathbf{B}$ because they are all parallel vectors.

It is important to note that the magnetic field intensity $\mathbf{H}$ given by Eq. (17.1–3) is the uniform value inside the solenoid windings, since the current enclosed by a continuous $\mathbf{H}$ field line is $\mathfrak{N}I$. The magnetic induction in Eq. (17.1–1) is the constant (average) value of $\mathbf{B}$ inside the core. It may be measured by integrating on time the voltage induced in a single turn coil wound around the core when the field coil is excited. We thus know $\mathbf{B}$ and $\mathbf{H}$ inside the core.

Let us integrate Eq. (17.1–4) for the simple case of a solenoid in a vacuum, for which $\mathbf{B}$ and $\mathbf{H}$ are related by

$$\mathbf{B} = \mu_0\mathbf{H}, \qquad (17.1\text{–}5)$$

where μ_0 is the vacuum magnetic permeability, having the value of $4\pi \times 10^{-7}$ weber/meter-ampere. Substituting Eq. (17.1–5) into Eq. (17.1–4) and integrating, the work W_e required to increase the magnetic intensity from zero to a value $\mathbf{H}$ is

$$W_e = -V \int_0^{\mathbf{H}} \mathbf{H} \cdot d(\mu_0\mathbf{H})$$
$$= -\mu_0 VH^2/2, \qquad (17.1\text{–}6)$$

in which V is the volume AL of the solenoid.

The quantity $\mu_0 H^2/2$ is often called the magnetic energy density of the vacuum magnetic field because it equals the work per unit volume which must be done on the coil to create the magnetic field $\mathbf{H}$. Since the work $-W_e$ is actually expended upon the moving charges in the superconducting coil, it would be equally appropriate to consider that $-W_e$ equals the increase in internal energy E of the superconducting charge carried in the coil, rather than the energy of the vacuum field. Whatever view we wish to adopt, the work $-W_e$ required to establish the vacuum field $\mathbf{H}$ will be denoted by E_v:

$$E_v \equiv V\mu_0 H^2/2. \qquad (17.1\text{–}7)$$

Now let us examine what happens when the same current I flows in the coil enclosing a material core. If we measure the magnetic induction $\mathbf{B}$ in the manner outlined above, we find that it no longer equals $\mu_0\mathbf{H}$, where $\mathbf{H}$ is known from the current I, through Eq. (17.1–3). Instead, $\mathbf{B}$ is larger than $\mu_0\mathbf{H}$ by an amount $\mu_0\mathbf{M}$, where $\mathbf{M}$ is the *magnetization:*

$$\mu_0\mathbf{M} \equiv \mathbf{B} - \mu_0\mathbf{H}$$

or

$$\mathbf{B} = \mu_0(\mathbf{H} + \mathbf{M}). \tag{17.1–8}$$

If $\mathbf{M}$ has the same direction as $\mathbf{B}$, the core material is called *paramagnetic,* otherwise it is called *diamagnetic* ($\mathbf{M}$ opposite to $\mathbf{B}$). A *ferromagnetic* material is one which may become permanently magnetized; that is, $\mathbf{B}$ may not return to zero when the current I, and hence $\mathbf{H}$, is reduced to zero.

If Eq. (17.1–8) is substituted into Eq. (17.1–4), the electrical work W_e may be found as a function of $\mathbf{H}$ and $\mathbf{M}$ rather than $\mathbf{H}$ and $\mathbf{B}$:

$$dW_e = -V\mathbf{H} \cdot (\mu_0\,d\mathbf{H} + \mu_0\,d\mathbf{M}) = -V\{d(\mu_0 H^2/2) + \mu_0\mathbf{H} \cdot d\mathbf{M})\}$$

$$= -\{dE_v + \mu_0 V\mathbf{H} \cdot d\mathbf{M}\}. \tag{17.1–9}$$

All the effects of the material core are contained in the second term on the right-hand side of Eq. (17.1–9). This term would be zero if there were no magnetization $\mathbf{M}$, that is, if there were no effect of the magnetic field on the material. We may therefore designate this term to be the reversible magnetic work dW_M; that is, the work expended on the core material which would thereby contribute to an increase in its internal energy:

$$dW_M \equiv -\mu_0 V\mathbf{H} \cdot d\mathbf{M}. \tag{17.1–10}$$

When the magnetization is a reversible process, the relationship between work, heat, and internal energy change given in Eqs. (10.5–2) and (10.5–3) becomes

$$T\,dS = dE - \mu_0 V\mathbf{H} \cdot d\mathbf{M}, \tag{17.1–11}$$

provided the volume V is fixed, so that no other work is involved.*

The macroscopic analysis of the magnetization experiment supplies no insight into the cause of the magnetization $\mathbf{M}$ but only relates the work done on the core material to the increase in magnetization. For an explanation of the magnetization we must propose a microscopic model in which the molecules of the core substance possess a magnetic dipole moment $\boldsymbol{\mu}$ caused by circulating charges within the molecule. If N/V magnetic dipoles per unit volume are

---

* For a more extensive development of the general thermodynamic relations for a magnetizable body, see Landau and Lifshitz, Vol. 8, Chapter IV.

aligned with the magnetic field, then the magnetization $\mathbf{M}$ is $N\boldsymbol{\mu}/V$;* that is, the net magnetic moment per unit volume. It is therefore the purpose of the microscopic theory to determine the magnetization in terms of the molecular properties.

17.2 The origin of the magnetic moment of a molecule

Molecules and atoms are composed of nuclei surrounded by orbiting electrons. Because of the orbital motion of the electrons, or the intrinsic motion (spin) of the electrons or nuclei, there may be a net circulation of charge, that is, a closed current loop which produces a dipole magnetic field of dipole strength $\boldsymbol{\mu}$. In the presence of an external magnetic field the dipole is subject to a torque $\boldsymbol{\mu} \times \mathbf{B}$, which is zero when $\boldsymbol{\mu}$ is parallel or antiparallel to $\mathbf{B}$ and a maximum when $\boldsymbol{\mu}$ is perpendicular to $\mathbf{B}$. For a rigid body, such a torque would cause an oscillatory or pendulumlike motion of the body, which prefers to align itself with the magnetic field. In atoms or molecules, the circulation of charge is related to the motion of mass, so that these particles also possess angular momentum about the dipole axis. When a magnetic field is applied, the particle precesses like a gyroscope about the applied magnetic field axis with an angular velocity ω which is proportional to the strength of the applied field.

Let us calculate the magnetic moment and precessional angular velocity of a rotating, charged rigid body whose rotational axis is inclined at an angle ψ

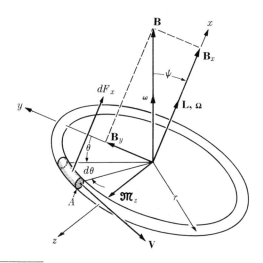

Fig. 17.4. Coordinate system for determining the moment $\mathfrak{M}_z$ which acts on a rotating charged ring in a uniform magnetic field.

---

* It is easy to see that this is dimensionally correct since the dimension of $\boldsymbol{\mu}$ is current times area and N/V is volume^{-1}, giving $\mathbf{M}$ the same dimensions as $\mathbf{H}$, current/length. The equivalence of M and dipole moment per unit volume may be shown by applying Ampère's law to a volume filled uniformly with small aligned current loops. (See, for example, Panofsky and Phillips, Chapter 7, or Feynman, Vol. II, Chapter 36.)

to a magnetic field $\mathbf{B}$. For simplicity let us take a thin ring of material of mass density ρ and charge density ρ_c, having the dimensions shown in Fig. 17.4. The ring has a mean radius r and a cross-sectional area A and rotates about the x-axis with an angular velocity $\boldsymbol{\Omega}$ while lying in the yz-plane. The angular position θ of any point on the ring is measured from the y-axis as shown. The magnetic field vector $\mathbf{B}$ is chosen to lie in the xy-plane.

The force on a charge q moving with a velocity $\mathbf{v}$ in a magnetic field $\mathbf{B}$ is $q(\mathbf{v} \times \mathbf{B})$. The force $d\mathbf{F}$ on an element of the rotating ring whose volume is $Ar\,d\theta$ is

$$d\mathbf{F} = (\rho_c Ar\,d\theta)(\mathbf{v} \times \mathbf{B}), \qquad (17.2\text{--}1)$$

where the peripheral velocity $\mathbf{v}$ has the magnitude $r\Omega$. For the magnetic field component $\mathbf{B}_x$ normal to the yz-plane of rotation, the component of $d\mathbf{F}$ in the direction of $\mathbf{v} \times \mathbf{B}_x$ is a radial force and has a total value of zero when summed over all values of θ. Thus the only component of force we need to consider is dF_x, which lies in the x-direction, that is, is normal to the plane of rotation,

$$dF_x = -\rho_c ArvB_y \cos\theta\,d\theta. \qquad (17.2\text{--}2)$$

The moment of the force dF_x about the z-axis is $-r\cos\theta\,dF_x$, which may be integrated to give the total moment $\mathfrak{M}_z$:

$$\mathfrak{M}_z = \int(-r\cos\theta\,dF_x) = \rho_c Ar^2 vB_y \int_0^{2\pi} \cos^2\theta\,d\theta = \pi\rho_c Ar^2 vB_y. \qquad (17.2\text{--}3)$$

The moment of the force about the y-axis is $r\sin\theta\,dF_x$, which integrates to zero. The angular momentum L of the rotating ring is the total mass $\rho A(2\pi r)$ times vr, or

$$L = 2\pi\rho Ar^2 v. \qquad (17.2\text{--}4)$$

Thus the moment $\mathfrak{M}_z$ of the magnetic force can be given in terms of the angular momentum L by combining Eqs. (17.2–3) and (17.2–4):

$$\mathfrak{M}_z = (\rho_c/2\rho)LB_y. \qquad (17.2\text{--}5)$$

In view of the coordinate system used in Fig. 17.4, this may be written in the vector form

$$\mathfrak{M} = (\rho_c/2\rho)(\mathbf{L} \times \mathbf{B}), \qquad (17.2\text{--}6)$$

in which $\mathbf{L}$ lies along the x-axis. If the magnetic moment $\boldsymbol{\mu}$ of the rotating ring is defined by $\mathfrak{M} \equiv \boldsymbol{\mu} \times \mathbf{B}$, then $\boldsymbol{\mu}$ may be given in terms of the angular momentum $\mathbf{L}$ and charge-to-mass ratio ρ_c/ρ:

$$\boldsymbol{\mu} = (\rho_c/2\rho)\mathbf{L}. \qquad (17.2\text{--}7)*$$

---

* If we substitute Eq. (17.2–4) into Eq. (17.2–7), we note that μ is the product of the current $\rho_c Av$ in the ring and the area πr^2 enclosed by the ring.

A single electron moving in a circle with an angular momentum $\hbar$ has a magnetic moment of magnitude μ_B which is called the Bohr magneton:

$$\mu_B \equiv e\hbar/2m_e, \qquad (17.2\text{--}8)$$

in which e/m_e is the charge-to-mass ratio of the electron. The Bohr magneton is a convenient unit to use when specifying the magnetic moment of a particle.

We have seen that the rotating ring of angular momentum $\mathbf{L}$ is subject to a torque $\mathfrak{M}$ which must be counterbalanced by an equal but opposite applied torque if the ring is to continue to rotate about the x-axis fixed in space. For a free body, the magnetic torque $\mathfrak{M}$ is unbalanced and the angular momentum changes at a rate which equals the applied torque:

$$d\mathbf{L}/dt = \mathfrak{M} = (\rho_c/2\rho)(\mathbf{L} \times \mathbf{B}). \qquad (17.2\text{--}9)$$

The motion produced by the torque $\mathfrak{M}$ is a precession in which the angular momentum vector $\mathbf{L}$ rotates about $\mathbf{B}$ with an angular velocity $\boldsymbol{\omega}$:

$$d\mathbf{L}/dt = \boldsymbol{\omega} \times \mathbf{L}$$

so that

$$\boldsymbol{\omega} = -\rho_c \mathbf{B}/2\rho \qquad (17.2\text{--}10)$$

in order to satisfy the equation of motion, Eq. (17.2–9). Here ω is called the Larmor frequency and for an electron has the value $eB/2m_e$.*

We shall now proceed to determine the change in kinetic energy of the rotating ring due to its precessional motion in the magnetic field.† Since the precessional angular velocity ω is very small compared with the rotational angular velocity Ω, we may add the component of $\boldsymbol{\omega}$ in the direction of the x-axis to determine the perturbed angular velocity Ω':

$$\Omega' = \Omega + \omega \cos \psi. \qquad (17.2\text{--}11)$$

The perturbed kinetic energy ϵ' of the rotation about the x-axis is one-half the mass times the square of the velocity $\Omega' r$:

$$\epsilon' = \tfrac{1}{2}\rho A(2\pi r)(\Omega' r)^2 = \pi \rho A r^3 (\Omega^2 + 2\Omega\omega \cos \psi + \omega^2 \cos^2 \psi) \qquad (17.2\text{--}12)$$

---

* The Larmor frequency ω is the precessional frequency of a "rigid" rotating body. The electron cyclotron frequency eB/m_e is the angular velocity of a free electron in a magnetic field, a motion which is also circular.

† In what follows, the angular velocity Ω or angular momentum L measured in the precessing coordinate system is assumed to be unchanged by the presence of the magnetic field. This assumption is necessary for microscopic systems because the angular momentum in the precessing coordinate system is quantized in the same manner as in the absence of a magnetic field. This quantum-mechanical requirement is the equivalent of the macroscopic theorem of Larmor (see Feynman, Vol. II, pp. 34 through 36 or Goldstein, p. 176), which relates the motion in the precessing coordinate system to that in the absence of a magnetic field.

by direct substitution of Eq. (17.2–11). Since $\omega \ll \Omega$, the last term on the right may be neglected and the second term becomes the change in kinetic energy ϵ_m due to the magnetic field:

$$\epsilon_m = 2\pi\rho A r^3 \Omega \omega \cos\psi = L\omega \cos\psi \tag{17.2–13}$$

according to Eq. (17.2–4). This may be written in vector form by use of Eqs. (17.2–10) and (17.2–7):

$$\epsilon_m = -(\rho_c/2\rho)\mathbf{L} \cdot \mathbf{B} = -\boldsymbol{\mu} \cdot \mathbf{B}. \tag{17.2–14}$$

The magnetic energy ϵ_m is the change in kinetic energy of the rotating body when the magnetic field $\mathbf{B}$ is applied. If the magnetic dipole $\boldsymbol{\mu}$ is aligned with $\mathbf{B}$, this energy is negative; that is, the body rotates more slowly. The opposite holds for $\boldsymbol{\mu}$ antiparallel to $\mathbf{B}$. When $\boldsymbol{\mu}$ is perpendicular to $\mathbf{B}$, there is no change in the kinetic energy ($\epsilon_m = 0$).

Because the dipole precesses about the field line $\mathbf{B}$, the time-averaged value $\langle\boldsymbol{\mu}\rangle$ of the dipole moment is its component in the direction of $\mathbf{B}$:

$$\langle\boldsymbol{\mu}\rangle = (\boldsymbol{\mu} \cdot \mathbf{B})\mathbf{B}/B^2$$

or

$$\langle\boldsymbol{\mu}\rangle = -\epsilon_m/B. \tag{17.2–15}$$

The time-averaged magnetic moment of a number of magnetic dipoles must also be in the direction of $\mathbf{B}$.

It is worth noting that there is no potential energy associated with the torque $\boldsymbol{\mu} \times \mathbf{B}$ exerted on a rotating molecular system, since the system does not deflect (i.e., rotate) in the direction of the applied torque but only in a direction $\mathbf{B}$ perpendicular to the torque. This situation is similar to that encountered by a charged particle moving in a magnetic field, for which the Lorentz force $q(\mathbf{v} \times \mathbf{B})$ is normal to $\mathbf{v}$ and can do no work on the moving particle. Thus there is no potential function whose spatial gradient gives the Lorentz force, and no potential energy is associated with this force.

For macroscopic magnetic dipoles, such as a compass needle, in a magnetic field, it is possible for the dipole to rotate in the direction of the torque $\boldsymbol{\mu} \times \mathbf{B}$ and thereby work is done in increasing the angular velocity of the dipole in the direction of the applied torque. However, any change in the direction of $\boldsymbol{\mu}$ causes a corresponding change in $\mathbf{M}$ and $\mathbf{B}$, with the result that electrical work must be expended if the exciting current I in the field coil producing the magnetic field is to be kept constant. As a consequence, electrical work must also be included in determining the change in potential energy.

In Eq. (17.2–13), $L\cos\psi$ is the component of L in the direction of the magnetic field $\mathbf{B}$. If a particle has an angular momentum component $\hbar$ in the field direction, then

$$\epsilon_m = \hbar\omega, \tag{17.2–16}$$

which is not a surprising result for a quantum system. We would therefore expect that the quantized magnetic energies would be proportional to the possible components of angular momentum along the B-axis and the Larmor frequency ω. This relation also explains why the electron quantum number m (see Section 5.11) is called the magnetic quantum number: it measures the component of L in units of $\hbar$.

For an atom whose ground electronic state has a total angular momentum L given by

$$L^2 = j(j+1)\hbar, \tag{17.2–17}$$

where $2j$ is an integer called the total angular momentum quantum number, the component of magnetic moment μ_m in the direction of **B** is

$$\mu_m = mg\mu_B, \tag{17.2–18}$$

and the quantized magnetic energy ϵ_m is

$$\epsilon_m = -\mu_m B = -mg\mu_B B, \tag{17.2–19}$$

where g is a factor greater than unity which depends on the relative contributions of electron spin and orbital momentum to the total angular momentum,* and m is the magnetic quantum number whose possible values are

$$m = -j, -j+1, \ldots, j-1, j. \tag{17.2–20}$$

The component of magnetic moment μ_m in the direction of B satisfies the classical relation of Eqs. (17.2–14) and (17.2–15).

The "unit" of magnetic energy $\mu_B B$ is not very large compared with kT at room temperature. In mks-units, $\mu_B B/k$ has the value $0.67B$ K°, which for a very strong field, such as $B = 10$ w/m², requires that $T = 6.7°$K in order for $\mu_B B$ to be equal to kT. On the other hand, the magnetization M produced by aligning N dipoles of magnetic moment μ_B in a solid of volume V is $N\mu_B/V$, for which $\mu_0 M$ has the value of 0.7 w/m² in an average solid. Thus the magnetization can be appreciable compared with the magnetic fields required to produce it, but these effects occur only at very low temperatures.

17.3 The perfect paramagnetic system

In analogy with the perfect gas discussed in Chapter 11, we may define a perfect paramagnetic system as one in which the magnetic energy of the atoms (or molecules) is determined only by the magnetic induction **B** according to Eq. (17.2–19) and is independent of the presence of nearby atoms or molecules. As we have discussed in Section 17.2, the magnetic energy is the result of an

---

* For a discussion of the factor g, see Mayer and Mayer, p. 344.

interaction of the applied magnetic field and the motion of the electrons in an atom or molecule and hence is part of the electronic energy. We are therefore concerned with the behavior of internal electronic degrees of freedom of the atoms in the presence of a magnetic field. If the electronic states of an atom are independent of the motion of the atom, or the positions or motions of nearby atoms, then they may be treated as were the internal degrees of freedom of the perfect gas and may be said to constitute a perfect magnetic system. Whether the atoms are in the gas, liquid, or solid phase is not important to the behavior of the paramagnetic system, except for the fact that the denseness of the phase may bring about a strong interaction between neighboring atoms which will cause the paramagnetism to become "imperfect." Because paramagnetism is important only at low temperatures, all of the atoms exist in their ground electronic state. We may therefore conclude that the properties of a perfect paramagnetic system are those of the ground electronic state of slightly interacting atoms in a solid, liquid, or gas.

Let us define a magnetic partition function Q_m by

$$Q_m \equiv \sum_m e^{-\epsilon_m/kT}, \tag{17.3-1}$$

which is actually the electronic partition function for an atom, for when $\mathbf{B} = 0$, the magnetic energies ϵ_m are also zero, and the sum in Eq. (17.3–1) will give the ground-state degeneracy. From the value of ϵ_m given in Eqs. (17.2–19) and (17.2–20), the partition function is

$$Q_m = \sum_{-j}^{+j} e^{mg\mu_B B/kT}. \tag{17.3-2}$$

For convenience in evaluating this sum, let us introduce the variable x defined by

$$x \equiv g\mu_B B/kT \tag{17.3-3}$$

so that the partition function may be rearranged as follows:

$$Q_m = \sum_{-j}^{+j} e^{mx} = e^{jx} \sum_{m=-j}^{m=+j} e^{(m-j)x} = e^{jx} \sum_{n=0}^{2j} e^{-nx}$$

$$= e^{jx} \left\{ \sum_0^{\infty} e^{-nx} - \sum_{2j+1}^{\infty} e^{-nx} \right\} = e^{jx} \left\{ \sum_0^{\infty} e^{-nx} - e^{-(2j+1)x} \sum_0^{\infty} e^{-nx} \right\}$$

$$= e^{jx} \{1 - e^{-(2j+1)x}\}/(1 - e^{-x})$$

$$= \{e^{(j+1/2)x} - e^{-(j+1/2)x}\}/\{e^{x/2} - e^{-x/2}\}$$

$$= \sinh \{(j + \tfrac{1}{2})x\}/\sinh (x/2). \tag{17.3-4}$$

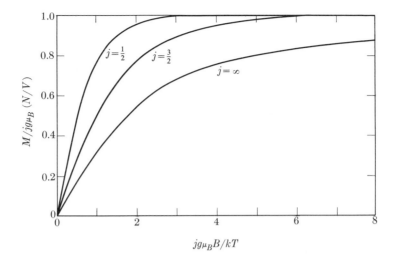

Fig. 17.5. The magnetization M as a function of the magnetic induction B and temperature T, as determined by Eq. (17.3–7) for several values of j. The maximum magnetic moment of an atom is $jg\mu_B$.

According to the usual rule for Boltzmann statistics, the internal energy E_m may be found from the partition function Q_m by differentiation according to Eq. (8.7–11):

$$E_m = NkT^2 \left\{\frac{\partial \ln Q_m}{\partial T}\right\}_B = NkT^2 \left(\frac{d \ln Q_m}{dx}\right)\left(\frac{\partial x}{\partial T}\right)_B$$

$$= -N(jg\mu_B B)\left[\left(1 + \frac{1}{2j}\right) \coth \{(j + \tfrac{1}{2})x\} - \left(\frac{1}{2j}\right) \coth \left(\frac{x}{2}\right)\right],$$

(17.3–5)

in which B is fixed when we differentiate Q_m with respect to T because ϵ_m depends on the external constraint B rather than on the volume V. The factor $(jg\mu_B B)$ in Eq. (17.3–5) is the maximum negative energy an atom may have and corresponds to a value of m equal to j. The function in brackets in Eq. (17.3–5), called the *Brillouin function*, varies monatonically from 0 to 1 as x varies from 0 to ∞. For very large values of j and small values of x it has the value $\coth (jx) - 1/(jx)$, called the *Langevin function*.*

The magnetization **M**, which has the direction of **B**, is the sum of the magnetic moments μ_m of the N atoms divided by the volume V:

$$M = \frac{\sum_{}^{N} \mu_m}{V} = -\frac{\sum_{}^{N} \epsilon_m/B}{V} = -\frac{E_m}{BV},$$

(17.3–6)

---

* In computing the partition function Q_m, if we replace the sum of Eq. (17.3–2) with an integration, we would obtain the Langevin function rather than the Brillouin function in the expression for E_m.

in which the relation between energy and magnetic moment is that of Eq. (17.2–19). Thus the magnetization becomes

$$M = jg\mu_B \left(\frac{N}{V}\right)\left[\left(1 + \frac{1}{2j}\right)\coth\left\{\frac{(j + \frac{1}{2})g\mu_B B}{kT}\right\} - \left(\frac{1}{2j}\right)\coth\left(\frac{g\mu_B B}{2kT}\right)\right].$$

(17.3–7)

This functional relationship is plotted in Fig. 17.5. For low temperatures or high magnetic fields such that $jg\mu_B B/kT$ is very large, the magnetization approaches $jg\mu_B$ per atom; that is, all the atoms are aligned in the direction of **B** and have the maximum component of μ_m possible in that direction. On the other hand, for high temperatures and low magnetic fields such that $jg\mu_B B/kT$ is very small compared with unity, we may expand the Brillouin function for small values of the argument $jg\mu_B B/kT*$ to obtain

$$M = jg\mu_B \left(\frac{N}{V}\right)\left\{\frac{(j + 1)g\mu_B B}{3kT}\right\}$$

or

$$M = \left\{\frac{j(j + 1)(g\mu_B)^2(N/V)}{3kT}\right\} B.$$

(17.3–8)

For the high temperatures for which this approximation holds, the magnetization is small compared with **H** so that **B** may be replaced by $\mu_0\mathbf{H}$ to give

$$\mathbf{M} = \left\{\frac{j(j + 1)(g\mu_B)^2\mu_0(N/V)}{3kT}\right\}\mathbf{H} \equiv \chi\mathbf{H},$$

(17.3–9)

in which the dimensionless coefficient χ is called the paramagnetic susceptibility.†

A comparison of experimental measurements for three paramagnetic salts with the theoretical magnetization of Eq. (17.3–7) is shown in Fig. 17.6. Other properties of these salts are given in Table 17.1.

The magnetic entropy S_m may also be determined from the partition function Q_m in accordance with Eq. (11.4–8) for internal degrees of freedom:

$$S_m = \frac{E_m}{T} + Nk\ln Q_m,$$

$$\frac{S_m}{Nk} = -jx\left[\left(1 + \frac{1}{2j}\right)\coth\left\{(j + \frac{1}{2})x\right\} - \left(\frac{1}{2j}\right)\coth\left(\frac{x}{2}\right)\right]$$

$$+ \ln\left\{\frac{\sinh\ (j + \frac{1}{2})x}{\sinh\ (x/2)}\right\},\qquad (17.3\text{–}10)$$

_____

* See Table A–5.

† Equation (17.3–9) is sometimes written in the form of Curie's law, $\mathbf{M} = C\mathbf{H}/T$, where C is called Curie's constant.

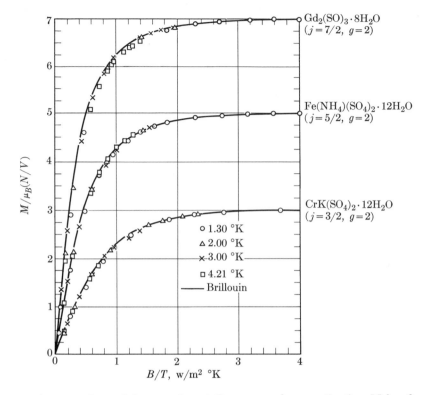

Fig. 17.6. A comparison of the experimentally measured magnetization M for three paramagnetic salts and the theory given by Eq. (17.3–7). N/V is the number of metallic ions per unit volume. (By permission from W. E. Henry, *The Physical Review*, **88**, p. 561, American Institute of Physics Inc., New York, 1952.)

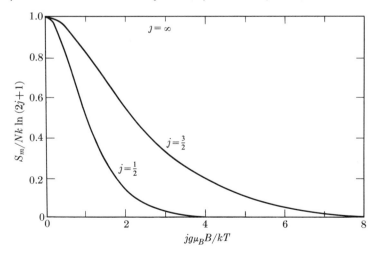

Fig. 17.7. The paramagnetic entropy S_m as a function of the magnetic induction B and temperature T, as determined from Eq. (17.3–10).

Table 17.1. Properties of paramagnetic salts at $T = 300°K$*

Salt	Molecular weight	Density, gm/cm^3	Susceptibility $(10^4\chi)$
Chromium potassium alum CrK(SO$_4$)$_2 \cdot$ 12H$_2$O	499	1.83	2.86
Ferric ammonium alum Fe(NH$_4$)(SO$_4$)$_2 \cdot$ 12H$_2$O	482	1.71	6.32
Gadolinium sulfate Gd$_2$(SO$_4$)$_3 \cdot$ 8H$_2$O	747	3.01	26.6

* *AIP Handbook*, p. 5–234.

in which Eqs. (17.3–4) and (17.3–5) have been used. For a fixed value of B, as T increases, x becomes very small, and the limiting value of S_m is

$$Nk \ln (2j + 1).$$

Again for a fixed value of B, as T becomes very small, x becomes very large, and the limiting value of S_m is zero as it should be, according to the third law of thermodynamics. For intermediate cases, the value of S_m is shown in Fig. 17.7.

It is interesting to note that B can never be zero at $T = 0$, because the limiting magnetization, $M = jg\mu_B N/V$, which is reached at $T = 0$, always contributes an amount $\mu_0 M$ to B even if H is zero. This remanent magnetization will not appear at higher temperatures, as discussed in Section 17.5.

The differential relation between entropy S_m, energy E_m, and magnetization M for a perfect paramagnetic system may be found by differentiating Eq. (17.3–10):

$$dS_m = \left(\frac{1}{T}\right) dE_m - \left(\frac{E_m}{T^2}\right) dT + Nk \left(\frac{\partial \ln Q_m}{\partial T}\right)_B dT + Nk \left(\frac{\partial \ln Q_m}{\partial B}\right)_T dB$$

or

$$T\, dS_m = dE_m + NkT \left(\frac{\partial \ln Q_m}{\partial B}\right)_T dB \qquad (17.3\text{–}11)$$

since $E_m = NkT^2 \{\partial \ln Q_m / \partial T\}_B$, by Eq. (17.3–5). However, the partition function Q_m depends only on the argument x so that the coefficient of dB in Eq. (17.3-11) becomes

$$NkT \left(\frac{\partial \ln Q_m}{\partial B}\right)_T = NkT \left(\frac{d \ln Q_m}{dx}\right)\left(\frac{\partial x}{\partial B}\right)_T. \qquad (17.3\text{–}12)$$

But from Eq. (17.3–3) we have

$$\left(\frac{\partial x}{\partial B}\right)_T = \frac{g\mu_B}{kT} = \left(\frac{T}{B}\right)\left(\frac{g\mu_B B}{kT^2}\right) = -\left(\frac{T}{B}\right)\left(\frac{\partial x}{\partial T}\right)_B. \qquad (17.3\text{–}13)$$

Upon substituting the above into Eq. (17.3–12), we find

$$NkT\left(\frac{\partial \ln Q_m}{\partial B}\right)_T = -\left(\frac{NkT^2}{B}\right)\left(\frac{d \ln Q_m}{dx}\right)\left(\frac{\partial x}{\partial T}\right)_B = -\frac{E_m}{B} = MV \quad (17.3\text{–}14)$$

through use of Eqs. (17.3–5) and (17.3–6).   Consequently, Eq. (17.3–11) becomes

$$T\,dS_m = dE_m + V\mathbf{M} \cdot d\mathbf{B}. \tag{17.3–15}$$

If we compare this with Eq. (17.1–11), we find that the term $V\mathbf{M} \cdot d\mathbf{B}$ appears in the place of $-\mu_0 V\mathbf{H} \cdot d\mathbf{M}$, which is the reversible work of magnetization. This does not mean that $V\mathbf{M} \cdot d\mathbf{B}$ is the whole work done in magnetizing a paramagnetic substance, because S_m and E_m are not the entire entropy S and internal energy E of the substance, which are related to each other through Eq. (17.1–11).   For example, a paramagnetic crystal has contributions to its entropy S and energy E from the phonon system as well as from its paramagnetic ions, and Eq. (17.1–11) describes the changes which may occur in the whole crystal, while Eq. (17.3–15) describes what occurs in the paramagnetic ions alone.   Thus an adiabatic reversible process in the paramagnetic crystal for which $dS = 0$ is not necessarily a process for which $dS_m = 0$, since there can be a corresponding change dS_p in the entropy of the "phonon gas" such that $dS_m + dS_p = 0$.   A process of this type is discussed in Section 17.4.

17.4 Magnetic cooling

The atoms of a paramagnetic crystal in a strong magnetic field have two types of motion which are not closely coupled with each other: the vibrational motion of the atoms in the crystal and the motion of the electrons in the atoms themselves. We can consider these nearly independent motions as distinct subsystems: the first we have called a phonon gas and the latter a paramagnetic system. When we say that the motions are not closely coupled, we mean that the photon quantum states and the magnetic quantum states are independent of each other even though energy of one kind of motion can be transformed into that of the other. This situation is quite analogous to that of a perfect diatomic gas in which the quantum states of vibration are independent of those of translation, but the energy of vibration may be exchanged with translational energy during a collision of two molecules. A perfect paramagnetic crystal at thermodynamic equilibrium will then have additive contributions to the extensive properties E and S, which are the sum of those for the phonon gas discussed in Chapter 15 and the perfect paramagnetic system considered in Section 17.3. For this reason it becomes possible to devise refrigeration cycles in which a paramagnetic crystal is the working medium and magnetic work is performed in lieu of the compression work which is ordinarily consumed in vapor-liquid cycles.

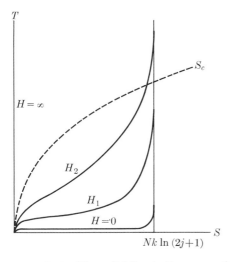

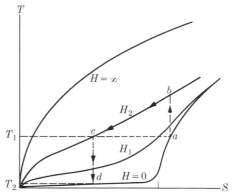

Fig. 17.8. The solid line is the magnetic entropy S_m of a perfect paramagnetic system as a function of temperature for different magnetic intensities, $0 < H_1 < H_2$. The dotted line is the entropy S_c of a perfect crystal, which varies as T^3.

Fig. 17.9. The solid lines are the sum of the crystal and magnetic entropies shown in Fig. 17.8. The process a-b-c-d is a magnetic process in which the crystal temperature is reduced from T_1 to T_2 by adiabatic demagnetization.

To illustrate the principle involved, let us construct a temperature-entropy diagram based on Eq. (17.3–10) for the paramagnetic system and Eq. (15.5–17) for the crystal. The paramagnetic system entropy S_m increases from 0 to $Nk \ln (2j + 1)$ as T increases from 0 to ∞ and is sketched in Fig. 17.8 for increasing values of magnetic field $H = 0, H_1, H_2, \ldots$ The crystal entropy S_c increases as T^3 for temperatures small compared with the Debye temperature; it is also sketched in Fig. 17.8. Adding these entropies, we may sketch total entropy curves for various magnetic field strengths, as shown in Fig. 17.9.

Let us suppose a paramagnetic salt is cooled in the absence of a magnetic field to a temperature T_1 by a large reservoir such as liquid helium at its boiling point (4.2°K). The crystal would then have an entropy to be found from Fig. 17.9 at the point a which is the intersection of the ($H = 0$)-curve and the horizontal line $T = T_1$. If the magnetic field is suddenly increased from 0 to H_2, a reversible adiabatic magnetization occurs along the isentrope from a to the point b. In this process the temperature increases just as it does in the isentropic compression of a gas. In the magnetization process $a - b$, the work of compression increases the energy of both the crystal (phonon gas) and the paramagnetic system since they are in equilibrium at the same temperature. (In compressing a diatomic gas, the average translational energy and average vibrational energy both increase.)

If the magnetized crystal is in contact with the reservoir at the temperature T_1, it will be cooled at constant H to the point c of Fig. 17.9, giving up heat to the reservoir while its entropy decreases. Now the crystal may be thermally isolated from the reservoir and the magnetic field decreased abruptly to zero. In this adiabatic demagnetization the temperature decreases from T_1 to that corresponding to the point d in Fig. 17.9, which lies at the intersection of the isentrope through c and the $(H = 0)$-curve. The crystal phonon gas and paramagnetic system have now been cooled to a temperature T_2 which is much lower than T_1 and may be used to cool other materials to temperatures between T_1 and T_2.

17.5 Negative temperatures

In some paramagnetic systems at very low temperature the magnetic moment is due to nuclear spin; that is, the motion of the nucleons gives rise to a magnetic moment in the same manner as that described in Section 17.2 for the motion of electrons. The magnitude of this moment is of the order of that given by Eq. (17.2–8) with the electron mass m_e replaced by the proton mass m_p:

$$\mu_n = e\hbar/2m_p, \tag{17.5–1}$$

where μ_n is called the nuclear magneton and is about a thousand times smaller than the Bohr magneton. The corresponding energies of nuclear magnetization are very small and at attainable magnetic fields are comparable to kT only when T is less than 10^{-3} °K. However, the nuclear Larmor frequencies are also low, compared with the electron Larmor frequency, and fall in the radio- or microwave-frequency range, so that nuclear precessional motion may be excited by an external electromagnetic wave in resonance at the Larmor frequency.

An interesting and useful aspect of nuclear magnetism is the very weak coupling between the crystal phonons and the nuclear precessional motions, so weak that it takes several minutes for a change in magnetic energy of the nuclei to be shared with the crystal phonons. On the other hand, the nuclear precessional motions are well coupled to each other and equilibrium is quickly established in about 10^{-5} sec in the paramagnetic system of the nuclei. As a consequence, the nuclear motions are comparatively isolated from the phonon gas and may be treated as a separate thermodynamic system.

If a nuclear paramagnetic system is magnetized in a strong field at low temperature, most of the nuclei have their magnetic dipole moments oriented in the direction of the applied field. If the applied field $\mathbf{H}$ is suddenly reduced to zero and then increased in the opposite direction, the nuclei tend to maintain the same total nuclear angular momentum and find themselves with their angular momentum, and hence also magnetic moment, now directed opposite to the applied field $\mathbf{H}$. This sudden reversal of the applied field thus converts a paramagnetic system ($\mathbf{M}$ and $\mathbf{H}$ parallel) to a diamagnetic system ($\mathbf{M}$ and $\mathbf{H}$ antiparallel). Because the magnetic energy ϵ_m of Eq. (17.2–19) is opposite in sign to μ_m, more of the nuclei now have high rather than low energies, and with respect to the distribution of magnetic energy the artificial diamagnetic system has a population inversion. In this situation the nuclear system may amplify a microwave of the appropriate frequency for the same reasons discussed in Section 16.6. Such an amplifier is called a *maser*.

An artificial diamagnetic nuclear system created in this way may be said to have a *negative absolute temperature*. To show how this may be considered a valid method of specifying the state of the system, let us replace T by $-T$, and therefore x by $-x$, in Eqs. (17.3–5), (17.3–6), and (17.3–10) for a paramagnetic system. Noting that $\coth(-x) = -\coth(x)$ and $\sinh(-x) = -\sinh(x)$, we find that

$$E_m\{-T\} = -E_m\{T\},$$
$$M\{-T\} = -M\{T\}, \tag{17.5–2}$$
$$S_m\{-T\} = S_m\{T\}.$$

Thus a system having a temperature $-T$ has the same entropy as a paramagnetic system of temperature T but has an energy and magnetization which are algebraically opposite to those of the corresponding paramagnetic system (i.e., $\mathbf{M}$ must be in a direction opposite to $\mathbf{B}$). Since this is the situation which exists in the artificial diamagnetic system discussed above, it is convenient to use negative temperatures in specifying its thermodynamic states.

In conclusion it should be noted that nuclear diamagnetic systems having negative temperatures cannot remain at equilibrium with ordinary systems having positive temperatures, such as the crystal phonon gas or a radiation field. Since the negative-temperature system has a higher energy ($E_m\{-T\} > 0$) than it would have at any positive temperature ($E_m\{T\} < 0$), it inevitably loses energy to its surroundings upon interacting with it and approaches equilibrium.

17.6 Ferromagnetism

In Section 17.2 we showed how each atom possesses an intrinsic magnetic dipole moment μ depending on its electronic (or nuclear) configuration. In Section 17.3 we considered a perfect paramagnetic system for which it was assumed that there were no forces exerted on any dipole by its nearest neighbors; that is, the short-range forces between nearby dipoles were neglected but the long-range forces which give rise to the magnetization $\mathbf{M}$ were not neglected since we used $\mathbf{B}$ rather than $\mu_0\mathbf{H}$ in determining the energy ϵ_m. When the short-range magnetic dipole forces are strong compared with the others we have considered, they tend to orient the dipole moments in a regular pattern even in the presence of a weak applied field $\mathbf{H}$. Furthermore, the magnetization $\mathbf{M}$ may remain after $\mathbf{H}$ is reduced to zero because the magnetic dipoles have been aligned in a pattern which maintains itself. This remanent magnetization is characteristic of *ferromagnets*.

There is a useful conceptual analogy between ferromagnetism and the condensation of a gas to form a solid. In the latter case, the attractive forces between molecules become strong enough to cause an ordered structure of a crystal to exist rather than the random structure of a gas, provided the temperature is not too high. A ferromagnet may therefore be considered the "condensed" or ordered phase of a paramagnet.

A simple model of a ferromagnet was first suggested by Weiss. He proposed that the energy of interaction between a magnetic dipole and its nearest neighbors is proportional to the magnetization $\mathbf{M}$, so that the magnetic energy ϵ_m may be given in terms of $\mathbf{H}$ and $\mathbf{M}$ by

$$\epsilon_m = -mg\mu_B\mu_0(H + \eta M), \tag{17.6-1}$$

which is the ferromagnetic analog of Eq. (17.2–19). If $\eta = 1$, then ϵ_m would have the paramagnetic value of Eq. (17.2–19). For ferromagnets the magnetization effect is much larger, so we would expect that $\eta \gg 1$.

The ferromagnetic magnetization M may be found from Eq. (17.3–7) if we replace B with $\mu_0(H + \eta M)$:

$$M = \left(\frac{jg\mu_B N}{V}\right)\left[\left(1 + \frac{1}{2j}\right)\coth\left\{\frac{(j + \frac{1}{2})g\mu_B\mu_0(H + \eta M)}{kT}\right\}\right.$$
$$\left. - \left(\frac{1}{2j}\right)\coth\left\{\frac{g\mu_B\mu_0(H + \eta M)}{2kT}\right\}\right]. \tag{17.6-2}$$

For the particular case of $H = 0$, Eq. (17.6–2) is a transcendental equation which determines the magnetization M for any given temperature T. By introducing a characteristic temperature T_c defined by

$$T_c \equiv \frac{j(j + 1)(g\mu_B)^2\mu_0\eta(N/V)}{3k} \tag{17.6-3}$$

and the saturation magnetization M_s defined by

$$M_s \equiv \frac{jg\mu_B N}{V}, \tag{17.6-4}$$

Eq. (17.6–2) may be rewritten as

$$\frac{M}{M_s} = \left(1 + \frac{1}{2j}\right)\coth\left\{\frac{3(j + \frac{1}{2})}{(j + 1)}\left(\frac{MT_c}{M_s T}\right)\right\} - \left(\frac{1}{2j}\right)\coth\left\{\frac{3}{2(j + 1)}\left(\frac{MT_c}{M_s T}\right)\right\}. \tag{17.6-5}$$

Now the right-hand side of Eq. (17.6–5), considered as a function of the argument $MT_c/M_s T$, has the shape shown in Fig. 17.5, i.e., a finite slope for $MT_c/M_s T = 0$ and a finite amplitude at $MT_c/M_s T = \infty$. The left-hand side of Eq. (17.6–5), considered as a function of the same argument $MT_c/M_s T$, is a

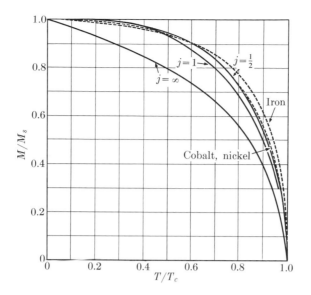

Fig. 17.10. The ferromagnetic magnetization M for $H = 0$ at temperatures less than the Curie temperature T_c. The solid lines are the theoretical magnetization given by Eq. (17.6–5) for the values of j indicated. The dotted lines are experimental measurements. (By permission from R. M. Bozorth, *Ferromagnetism*, p. 431, D. Van Nostrand, New York, 1951.)

straight line of slope T/T_c, which passes through the origin. The two curves will intersect at two points (one of which is the origin), provided T/T_c is not too large, giving a solution to the transcendental equation (17.6–5). By expanding the right-hand side for small values of the argument, it is easily found that nonzero solutions exist only for $T < T_c$. The solution $M = M\{T/T_c\}$ found in this manner is shown in Fig. 17.10 and is compared with some experimental measurements.

At temperatures greater than the temperature T_c, permanent magnetization of a ferromagnetic material is no longer possible, and the material behaves like a paramagnetic one; T_c is therefore the Curie temperature of the ferromagnetic substance. For temperatures sufficiently greater than T_c, the magnetization M found from Eq. (17.6–2) by expanding the right-hand side for small values of the argument is

$$\mathbf{M} = \{T_c/\eta(T - T_c)\}\mathbf{H}. \tag{17.6–6}$$

This is the *Curie-Weiss* law for the paramagnetic magnetization of a ferromagnetic material above its Curie temperature and may be compared with Eq. (17.3–9) for an ordinary paramagnetic material. Of course, Eq. (17.6–6) breaks down for $T \to T_c$.

The Curie temperature and saturation magnetization M_s for some ferromagnetic substances are given in Table 17.2.

Table 17.2.   Magnetic properties of ferromagnetic materials*

Substance	Fe	Co	Ni	Gd	FeCo	Fe$_3$Al	FeNi$_3$
$\mu_0 M_s,$ w/m^2	2.20	1.81	0.64	0.25	2.4	1.1	1.22
$T_c,$ $^\circ$K	1043	1404	631	289	1243	773	873

* AIP Handbook, pp. 5–170, 5–176.

17.7 Superconductivity

At very low temperatures many metals exhibit a property called *super-conductivity*, which is the absence of a measurable resistance to the flow of electrical current. Superconducting magnet coils, once excited, retain their magnetic field indefinitely so long as the necessary low temperature is maintained. Since there is no electrical power dissipated in a coil wound with superconducting wire, its behavior is just like that of a ferromagnetic material which may be permanently magnetized. A superconducting material exhibits on a macroscopic scale the perfect electrical behavior of microscopic atoms or molecules which is the origin of magnetic effects. Because a superconducting coil requires no electrical power to maintain its field strength constant in time, it has important practical advantages over normal electromagnetic coils.*

There are two types of superconducting materials called "soft" and "hard" superconductors. The former possess the simple properties which we shall describe below, while the latter have more complex properties associated with inhomogeneities of the material. "Hard" superconductors are practically more important because they remain superconducting at higher temperatures and magnetic field strengths and carry higher currents. However, their thermo-dynamic properties are not so well understood as those of the "soft" super-conductors, and we shall not treat them here.

A "soft" superconductor has the following properties which are experimentally measurable:

(a) The superconducting state is a phase of a solid conductor characterized by zero electrical resistance which occurs only at temperatures less than a critical temperature T_c and, for any $T < T_c$, only at magnetic field strengths H which are less than a critical field $H_c\{T\}$ which is a function of T. Using H and T as variables, the curve $H_c\{T\}$ in the phase diagram of Fig. 17.11 separates the superconducting from the normal state.

---

* In order to maintain the coil at low temperature, power must be expended to refrigerate the container enclosing the coil into which heat will "leak" from the surrounding atmosphere.

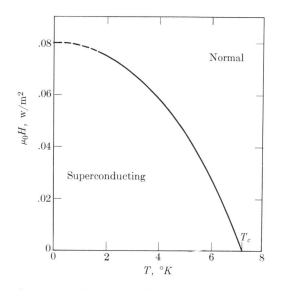

Fig. 17.11. Phase diagram of the superconducting and normal states of lead. (Dotted portion of curve is the extrapolation to 0°K.) The critical temperature T_c is 7.22°K.

(b) When $H = H_c\{T\}$, the normal and superconducting phases can coexist in arbitrary proportions just as the solid and liquid phases of a substance can coexist at the melting point. The transition from the superconducting to the normal phase as H is increased beyond H_c is accompanied by a heat of transition, i.e., heat must be added if the transition occurs at fixed temperature, as with the melting of a solid. Thus the transition from the superconducting phase to the normal phase is a first-order transition.*

(c) The superconducting phase is perfectly diamagnetic, i.e., $\mathbf{M} = -\mathbf{H}$ everywhere (Meissner effect) inside the superconductor and therefore $\mathbf{B} = 0$. The magnetic induction can be zero because currents flow on the surface of the superconducting sample in such a way as to maintain $\mathbf{B} = 0$ everywhere inside the superconductor.

(d) Although a superconducting wire has zero electrical resistivity, it cannot carry an indefinitely large current but has a limited capacity which, if exceeded, causes a transition to the normal state.

In what follows we will show how the experimentally measured critical field H_c is related to the measured heat of transition from the superconducting to the normal phase in a manner reminiscent of the Clausius-Clapeyron relation (Eq. 14.10–10) for a phase change. In order to do so, we shall assume that the normal phase, indicated by a subscript n, is nonmagnetic so that its entropy

---

* At the critical temperature T_c, the transition is second order. See Landau and Lifshitz, Vol. 5, Section 135.

change is that which normally obtains for a mole of substance as given by Eq. (10.4–4)

$$T \, d\widetilde{S}_n = d\widetilde{E}_n, \tag{17.7–1}$$

provided the volume changes in the processes we are considering can be neglected. For the superconducting phase, denoted by the subscript s, the corresponding entropy change is obtained from Eq. (17.1–11):

$$T \, d\widetilde{S}_s = d\widetilde{E}_s - \mu_0 \widetilde{V}_s \mathbf{H} \cdot d\mathbf{M}_s. \tag{17.7–2}$$

For a superconductor, $\mathbf{M}_s = -\mathbf{H}$ so that $\mathbf{H} \cdot d\mathbf{M}_s = -d(H^2/2)$ and Eq. (17.7–2) becomes

$$T \, d\widetilde{S}_s = d\widetilde{E}_s + \mu_0 \widetilde{V}_s \, d(H^2/2). \tag{17.7–3}$$

Let us now consider a process, similar to that discussed in Section 14.10, in which one mole of superconducting metal is changed to one mole of normal metal in a reversible process in which the temperature T and critical field H_c are held fixed. To accomplish this change, heat must be added in an amount equal to $T(\widetilde{S}_n - \widetilde{S}_s)$ because the process is reversible. At the same time, there will be some electrical work done on the system because the magnetic induction increases from $\mathbf{B} = 0$ to $\mathbf{B} = \mu_0 H_c$ (or the magnetic moment increases from $\mathbf{M} = -\mathbf{H}_c$ to $\mathbf{M} = 0$). The work done by the system is given by Eq. (17.1–10):

$$\int dW = -\mu_0 \widetilde{V}_s \int_{-H_c}^{0} \mathbf{H}_c \cdot d\mathbf{M} = -\mu_0 \widetilde{V}_s H_c^2 \tag{17.7–4}$$

since $\mathbf{H}_c$ is constant during the change of phase. We may now set the increase in internal energy $\widetilde{E}_n - \widetilde{E}_s$ equal to the heat added less the work done by the system:

$$\widetilde{E}_n - \widetilde{E}_s = T(\widetilde{S}_n - \widetilde{S}_s) - (-\mu_0 \widetilde{V}_s H_c^2)$$

or

$$\widetilde{E}_s + \mu_0 \widetilde{V}_s H_c^2 - T\widetilde{S}_s = \widetilde{E}_n - T\widetilde{S}_n, \tag{17.7–5}$$

which is the condition for equilibrium between the normal and superconducting phases.*

Let us now consider small changes dT and dH in temperature T and magnetic intensity H such that two phases continue to coexist, i.e., T and H are related by $H = H_c\{T\}$. For such changes, the differential of Eq. (17.7–5) must continue to be valid:

$$d\widetilde{E}_s + \mu_0 \widetilde{V}_s \, d(H_c^2) - T \, d\widetilde{S}_s - S_s \, dT = d\widetilde{E}_n - T \, d\widetilde{S}_n - \widetilde{S}_n \, dT. \tag{17.7–6}$$

---

* This is a particular example of a more general condition that, for fixed $\mathbf{H}$, the free energy $\widetilde{E} - T\widetilde{S} - \mu_0 \widetilde{V} \mathbf{H} \cdot \mathbf{M}$ is the same for two phases in equilibrium, as can easily be seen by setting $\mathbf{M}_s = -\mathbf{H}$ for the superconducting phase and $\mathbf{M}_n = 0$ for the normal phase.

By use of Eqs. (17.7–1) and (17.7–3) this condition reduces to

$$(\widetilde{S}_n - \widetilde{S}_s)\, dT = -\mu_0 \widetilde{V}_s \, d(H_c^2/2)$$

or

$$T(\widetilde{S}_n - \widetilde{S}_s) = -\mu_0 \widetilde{V}_s T H_c (dH_c/dT), \qquad (17.7\text{–}7)$$

where dH_c/dT is the slope of the curve $H_c\{T\}$ shown in Fig. 17.11. Since $T(\widetilde{S}_n - \widetilde{S}_s)$ is the heat of the phase change, we see by reference to Fig. 17.11 that it is positive for the superconducting-to-normal transition because dH_c/dT is negative. Furthermore, since $\widetilde{S}_n = \widetilde{S}_s$ at $T = 0$ because of the third law of thermodynamics (Section 14.13), dH_c/dT must also approach zero at $T = 0$, as shown in Fig. 17.11.

Equation (17.7–7) is the magnetic equivalent of the Clausius-Clapeyron equation, (14.10–10). It has been derived in a similar manner by considering first a change in phase under the conditions of fixed $\mathbf{H}$ and $\widetilde{V}^*$ and then a change in temperature along the coexistence line of the two phases. From a mathematical point of view, $\mu_0 \mathbf{H} \cdot \mathbf{M}$ plays the same role as the pressure p in the Clausius-Clapeyron derivation.

PROBLEMS

17.1 The strength of the magnetic field of the earth at its surface is of the order of 10^{-4} w/m². Compute the energy stored in a uniform vacuum field of this intensity in a cube of side dimension equal to the diameter of the earth, 8000 mi.

17.2 (a) By replacing the sum of Eq. (17.3–2) by an integration, find the partition function Q_m which is valid for $x \ll 1$. (b) Find E_m, M, and S_m for this same limiting case by differentiation of Q_m.

17.3 By using the series $\coth x = 1/x + x/3 + \cdots$, which is valid for small x, show that Eq. (17.3–8) is the limit of Eq. (17.3–7) for $jg\mu_B B/kT \ll 1$.

17.4 Using the molecular weight and density given in Table 17.1 in order to find N/V, and the values of g and j given in Fig. 17.6, calculate the paramagnetic susceptibility χ at 300°K from Eq. (17.3–9) and compare with the measured values of Table 17.1.

17.5 One gm-mole of $CrK(SO_4)_2 \cdot 12H_2O$ is placed in a magnetic field of 2 w/m² at 2°K. (a) What is the magnetization M? (b) If the crystal is maintained at 2°K while the magnetic field is slowly reduced to zero, how much heat is absorbed (or given up) by the crystal?

17.6 By using the series of Problem 17.3, show that there is no solution to Eq. (17.6–5) for $T > T_c$.

17.7 Show that Eq. (17.6–6) is obtained from Eq. (17.6–2) whenever

$$(j + \tfrac{1}{2})g\mu_B\mu_0(H + \eta M)/kT$$

is small.

---

* Experiments are performed at fixed pressure rather than volume, but for solids this is a negligible difference. For a more elaborate discussion, see Landau and Lifshitz, Vol. 8, p. 174.

17.8 Assuming that $j = g = 1$, compute the value of η for iron and nickel by using Eqs. (17.6–3) and (17.6–4) and the values of M_s and T_c given in Table 17.2.

17.9 The measured critical field $H_c\{T\}$ of a superconductor may usually be represented by the equation $H_c = H_{co}[1 - (T/T_c)^2]$ in which H_{co} is the critical field at $T = 0$. (a) Compare this simple expression with the experimental value shown in Fig. 17.11. (b) At what value of T/T_c will the heat of the phase change be a maximum? (c) Evaluate this maximum heat for lead for which $\tilde{V} = 18$ cm^3/gm-mole.

17.10 Make a sketch of the phase diagram in the TS-plane of a superconducting metal. Assume that the entropy of either phase is a function of temperature alone. For $H = 0$, assume the Debye law dependence of S on T. Show lines of constant H.

18

HEAT ENGINES

18.1 The production of work from heat

No one can doubt the essential importance to our industrial civilization of the inventions which have shown how to produce power from the combustion of fuel (or more recently, the fission of nuclei). Most nations have ceased to depend upon the wind, rainfall, and human or animal power to supply the need for power to cultivate crops, propel vehicles, or operate machinery. Many of the inventions were made at a time when little was understood concerning the physical limitations imposed on the processes by which power could be produced from combustion.* In fact, it was the incentive to understand better these processes that led a French engineer, Carnot,† to discover the second law of thermodynamics as applied to heat engines. (A more scientific statement of this law was subsequently given by Clausius‡ in 1850.) The desire of inventors to create perpetual-motion machines is so great and the economic consequences of power production so easily recognizable that the formulation of the laws of thermodynamics in terms of power-producing machines is often the preferred pedagogical approach even today.

---

*It is a fortuitous circumstance that even the crudest power plant produces more work per pound of fuel than that required to mine, transport, and process the fuel which is consumed. Thus the production of power by this means is not only technically possible but economically advantageous. At the present time, the corresponding advantage for nuclear fuels is usually less because the fuel processing is costly both in terms of energy and materials.

† Nicolas Leonhard Sadi Carnot (1796–1832) graduated from the École Polytechnique in 1814 and was commissioned in the army engineers. His paper, "Réflexions sur la puissance motrice du feu et sur les machines propres à développer cette puissance," published in 1824, contained a statement of the second law of thermodynamics as applied to heat engines but remained unrecognized for 25 years.

‡ Rudolf Julius Emmanuel Clausius (1822–1888), a German physicist, received his university degree in 1848 and in 1850 presented to the Berlin Academy his famous paper in which he formulated the second law of thermodynamics. He coined the word "entropy," and contributed many ideas to the kinetic theory of gases, such as that of the mean free path.

The theoretical understanding of the principles involved in the production of work from heat played little role in the early development of practical means to accomplish this end because the major obstacles were not thermodynamic in origin but mechanical. At the time of its invention the building of a steam engine was a greater feat than the discovery of the second law of thermodynamics. Burned at the best efficiency obtainable in a modern steam plant, one pound of fuel oil can produce enough electrical power to lift one thousand pounds a mile into the sky. The original developers of power machinery, who were pleased to achieve one percent of such performance, were more concerned with discovering the various schemes through which the chemical energy of coal and fuel oil could be utilized for practical purposes. Even today the new and sophisticated processes for producing electrical power, such as thermoelectric and thermionic devices and fuel cells, are usually attractive more for their special features of simplicity or size rather than for an intrinsic thermodynamic merit. Even so, the study of the limits imposed on the production of work from heat by the laws of thermodynamics is necessary both for an understanding of such processes and for an appreciation of those limitations which arise from the thermal properties of the materials used.

18.2   The heat reservoir and heat engine

Having discussed the laws of thermodynamics and some of their consequences, in Chapters 9 and 10, we wish to extend this study to the problem of "producing work from heat." We recognize that the combustion of a fossil fuel with air, or the exothermic reaction of any chemical compounds, can serve as a source of heat to be used for other purposes, whether it be heating a house or boiling water to drive a steam turbine. We do not claim that heat is stored in the fuel, nor for that matter is work, since these quantities are both qualitative and quantitative measures of the manner in which one system transfers some of its internal energy to another. Rather, we wish to avoid the problem of the detailed method by which the fuel is burned and to propose that it can be so consumed as to maintain a large mass of material, called a *heat reservoir*,* at a fixed temperature, say T_1. Whenever heat is supplied to another system from the heat reservoir, an equal amount may be added to the reservoir through the consumption of an appropriate amount of fuel, thereby maintaining the constancy of the temperature T_1. If the reservoir has a sufficiently large mass, moderate quantities of heat may be removed from or added to the reservoir without noticeably

---

* The reader is due an apology for the continued use of the traditional term "heat reservoir" so closely upon the previous assertion that heat is not stored in a system as is water in a reservoir. The term has its origin in the work of Carnot, who intuitively likened the flow of water from an elevated reservoir to a lower one to the flow of heat from a hot body to a cold one. So long as the reader understands the concept clearly, no great mischief ensues from the use of a traditional but misleading appellation.

changing its temperature, although the net amount removed must be replenished if the reservoir is to be used indefinitely while maintaining its temperature at T_1. The atmosphere or the ocean is a reservoir of this type which maintains its temperature nearly constant by absorbing heat from the sun and radiating heat to space.

A *heat engine* is a closed system which undergoes a cyclic process, exchanging heat with one or more reservoirs and producing work. In a *cyclic process* a system passes through a series of macrostates (not necessarily the most probable macrostates corresponding to thermodynamic equilibrium) in which the final and initial macrostates are identical. The heat engine is a *closed system*, exchanging no mass with its surroundings, and having its chemical composition unchanged upon return to its initial state after completing a cycle. The heat engine is primarily a model to which real machines may be compared and whose purpose is to elucidate the effect of the laws of thermodynamics on the possible operation of machines that can be constructed from available materials. Many machines, such as an aircraft gas turbine or rocket engine, produce useful work although they bear no clear resemblance to a heat engine as defined above: they are not closed systems; they do not undergo a cycle, etc. Nevertheless, the concept of a heat engine is very helpful in building models which enable us to understand more clearly how the physically realizable device operates.

In the following discussion we will assume that we have available a "hot" heat reservoir maintained at a temperature T_1 by the combustion of fuel and a "cold" heat reservoir, such as the atmosphere, having a temperature T_2. We also assume that we have heat engines of various kinds which can exchange heat with either or both of these reservoirs. (We might consider other reservoirs at temperatures T_3, T_4, etc., but we do not require such generality at this stage.) We defer until later the problem of relating the consumption of fuel to the maintenance of the temperature T_1 of the hot reservoir.

A schematic diagram of a heat engine exchanging heat with two reservoirs and producing work is shown in Fig. 18.1. In operating over a cycle, the heat Q_1 is absorbed by the heat engine from the hot reservoir, the heat Q_2 is absorbed from the cold reservoir, and the work W is done by the engine on some other system, although all these effects need not occur simultaneously nor in any particular sequence. According to the usual thermodynamic convention, Q_1, Q_2, and W shown in Fig. 18.1 are all positive.

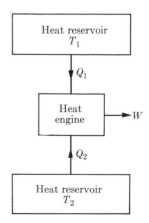

Fig. 18.1. A diagram of the operation of a heat engine which exchanges heat with a hot ($T = T_1$) and a cold ($T = T_2$) reservoir and produces work.

18.3 The performance of heat engines

Let us suppose that a heat engine operates in accordance with the scheme shown in Fig. 18.1. What restrictions on Q_1, Q_2, and W must there be in order that the laws of thermodynamics not be violated? Turning to the first law, Eq. (9.8–2), the change in internal energy E of the heat engine during an infinitesimal portion of the cycle is

$$dE = dQ - dW. \tag{18.3--1}$$

Upon integrating over the whole cycle, we obtain

$$\oint dE = \oint [dQ - dW],$$

$$0 = Q_1 + Q_2 - W,$$

or

$$W = Q_1 + Q_2, \tag{18.3--2}$$

in which the symbol $\oint$ indicates an integration over one cycle. Since the final and initial values of E are identical by the definition of a cycle, $\oint dE$ is zero. Equation (18.3–2) states that the work produced by the heat engine in one cycle is equal to the algebraic sum of the heats absorbed from the two reservoirs. (If heat were rejected to a reservoir, the corresponding Q would be negative.)

Let us now consider the process during which a small amount of heat, dQ, is added to the heat engine from the hot reservoir and during which dW and dQ_2 are fixed to be zero. For this infinitesimal process we may consider the reservoir and the heat engine to be constant-volume systems which exchange energy with each other but not with other systems. If heat flows from the reservoir to the heat engine, the internal energy of the reservoir decreases while that of the heat engine increases by an equal amount. According to the argument of Section 7.5, if this process is not to cause a decrease in the total entropy of the reservoir and the system, then the temperature T_e of the heat engine at the time when the heat dQ_1 is added to it must not exceed T_1. Thus we may conclude that

$$\frac{dQ_1}{T_e} \geq \frac{dQ_1}{T_1}, \tag{18.3--3}$$

which may be integrated over one cycle to give

$$\oint \frac{dQ_1}{T_e} \geq \oint \frac{dQ_1}{T_1} = \frac{Q_1}{T_1} \tag{18.3--4}$$

since the reservoir temperature T_1 is constant. By following a similar argument with respect to the absorption of heat from the reservoir having a temperature T_2, we would find

$$\oint \frac{dQ_2}{T_e} \geq \frac{Q_2}{T_2}, \tag{18.3--5}$$

which, when added to Eq. (18.3–4), results in

$$\oint \left(\frac{dQ_1 + dQ_2}{T_e} \right) \geq \frac{Q_1}{T_1} + \frac{Q_2}{T_2}. \tag{18.3–6}$$

Now for each infinitesimal change in the heat engine, its change in entropy must satisfy the inequality of Clausius, Eq. (10.6–4),

$$\frac{dQ}{T_e} = \frac{dQ_1 + dQ_2}{T_e} \leq dS_e, \tag{18.3–7}$$

which also may be integrated over one cycle, resulting in

$$\oint \left(\frac{dQ_1 + dQ_2}{T_e} \right) \leq \oint dS_e = 0, \tag{18.3–8}$$

where the equality follows from the fact that S_e is a property whose net change over a cycle must be zero. It therefore follows from Eqs. (18.3–6) and (18.3–8) that

$$\frac{Q_1}{T_1} + \frac{Q_2}{T_2} \leq 0, \tag{18.3–9}$$

which summarizes the restrictions that the second law places on the possible values of Q_1 and Q_2.

If we consider simultaneously the restrictions of the first law, Eq. (18.3–2), and those of the second law, Eq. (18.3–9), then we conclude the following:

(1) If $Q_2 = 0$, then $Q_1 \leq 0$ by Eq. (18 3–9), and it follows from Eqs. (18.3–2) and (18.3–9) that $W = Q_1 \leq 0$.

(2) If $Q_1 \geq 0$, then $Q_2 \leq -T_2Q_1/T_1 \leq 0$ by Eq. (18.3–9), and it subsequently follows from this and Eq. (18.3–2) that $W \leq Q_1(1 - T_2/T_1)$. Consequently, $T_2 < T_1$ if W is positive.

According to conclusion (1), *a heat engine which exchanges heat with one reservoir only* ($Q_2 = 0$) *cannot produce positive work* ($W \leq 0$) *but can only absorb work and add heat to the reservoir.* According to conclusion (2), *a heat engine which absorbs heat from one reservoir* ($Q_1 \geq 0$) *and must thereby reject heat to a second* ($Q_2 \leq 0$) *cannot produce positive work in excess of that absorbed from the first reservoir* ($W \leq Q_1$). Furthermore, positive work can be produced only if the first reservoir is hotter than the second ($T_2 > T_1$). Taken together, *these conclusions preclude the possibility of converting all the heat absorbed from a reservoir into work.*

A heat engine which converts all the heat absorbed from a single reservoir into work is called a *perpetual-motion machine of the second kind*. A *perpetual-motion machine (heat engine) of the first kind* would produce work without the extraction of heat from a reservoir. Both types of perpetual-motion machines are precluded by the laws of thermodynamics. However, it should be emphasized that these proscriptions extend only to heat engines as defined above and not to a closed system which undergoes a noncyclic change of state or to an open system that passes through a cycle. For example, the gas in a cylinder of an automobile engine may expand by pushing a movable piston, thereby doing work even if no heat is added to the gas. Alternatively, the fuel-air mixture in the cylinder of a gasoline engine may be compressed, ignited, expanded, and then replaced by a fresh charge, completing the cycle of events in the cylinder which produces useful work without absorbing heat from a reservoir. These latter are certainly interesting processes or cycles, but they must be explained on a basis other than that of a simple heat engine.

If we cannot convert all of the heat absorbed from a reservoir into work, then we must at least attempt to produce the maximum amount possible under the circumstances. By eliminating Q_2 between Eqs. (18.3–2) and (18.3–9), we find that

$$W/Q_1 \leq 1 - T_2/T_1. \tag{18.3–10}$$

The possibility of converting a larger fraction of the heat Q_1 into work W is improved as the ratio of T_2/T_1 becomes smaller. If the colder reservoir is the atmosphere, then the higher-temperature reservoir should be made as hot as possible. Alternatively, we might look for a colder reservoir than the atmosphere, such as the clear night sky into which we may radiate the heat Q_2. Either alternative has its practical limitations which will not be pursued further here. Rather, supposing that the two reservoirs are available, how do we go about achieving the maximum value of W given by the equality of Eq. (18.3–10)?

If we return to the origin of the inequality of Eq. (18.3–10), we see that it arose in the inequalities of Eqs. (18.3–3) and (18.3–7). The first inequality will disappear if the temperatures of the heat engine and either reservoir are identical whenever heat is being transferred between them. The second inequality stems from the irreversibility of the processes in the heat engine itself, irrespective of whether or not heat is actually being exchanged with a reservoir. If all the internal processes of the heat engine are reversible, and the exchange of heat with the reservoirs occurs at equal temperatures of the heat engine and reservoir, then the heat engine is said to be *reversible* and it produces an amount of work given by

$$(W/Q_1)_{\text{rev}} = 1 - T_2/T_1. \tag{18.3–11}$$

The ratio of work produced to heat absorbed from the hot reservoir is called the *thermodynamic efficiency* of the heat engine and is denoted by η_t:

$$\eta_t \equiv W/Q_1 = 1 + Q_2/Q_1. \tag{18.3–12}$$

In terms of efficiency, Eqs. (18.3–10) and (18.3–11) may be written as

$$\eta_t \leq (\eta_t)_{\text{rev}} = 1 - T_2/T_1. \tag{18.3–13}$$

From the inequality it follows that *the efficiency of any heat engine never exceeds that of a reversible heat engine operating between the same two reservoirs.* Furthermore, *the efficiency of the reversible heat engine depends only on the temperatures T_1 and T_2 and not on the details of the cycle or the nature of the material from which it is constructed.* That this is so surprises us at first, until we consider the fact that the statements of the first and second law which led to this conclusion were integrated in such a manner that the properties E and S disappeared and only T remained. As a result, only the reservoir temperatures could appear explicitly in the efficiency of the reversible heat engine.

18.4 Refrigeration

A reversible heat engine may be reversed in direction so that heat is absorbed from the low-temperature reservoir $(Q_2 > 0)$ and delivered to the high-temperature reservoir $(Q_1 < 0)$, which requires work to be supplied to the reversed heat engine $(W < 0)$. A heat engine operating in this reversed manner is called a heat pump (or refrigerator).* Like heat engines, all heat pumps are not reversible in the sense defined above for heat engines, but we would expect that a reversible heat pump would perform better than an irreversible one, i.e., would remove more heat from the low-temperature reservoir for a given amount of work delivered to the pump.

If we reconsider Eqs. (18.3–2) and (18.3–9), then if $Q_2 > 0$, it follows from Eq. (18.3–9) that $Q_1 < -T_1Q_2/T_2 < 0$ and thence from (18.3–2) that $W < -(T_1/T_2 - 1)Q_2 < 0$. *Thus if a heat pump removes heat $(Q_2 > 0)$ from a lower-temperature reservoir $(T_2 < T_1)$, it delivers heat to a higher-temperature reservoir $(Q_1 < 0)$ while absorbing work $(W < 0)$.*

The ratio of the heat removed from the cold reservoir (Q_2) to the magnitude of work required $(-W)$ is found by eliminating Q_1 between Eqs. (18.3–2) and (18.3–9):

$$\frac{Q_2}{(-W)} \leq \frac{T_2}{T_1 - T_2}. \tag{18.4–1}$$

The ratio $Q_2/(-W)$ is called the *coefficient of performance*, and Eq. (18.4–1) defines its upper limit which can be achieved only by a reversible heat pump.†

---

* The usual distinction is that a heat pump absorbs heat from a reservoir (such as the atmosphere) and delivers it to a finite system, such as a building to be heated in cold weather, while a refrigerator absorbs heat from a refrigerated space and delivers it to the atmosphere or other reservoir.

† A reversible heat pump is a reversible heat engine operated in the reverse direction! According to our definitions, a heat engine produces positive work and a refrigerator removes heat from the low-temperature reservoir. If a closed system operating for one cycle cannot accomplish either of these aims, it is not very interesting, even though it is possible to operate in such a manner $(Q_1 < 0, Q_2 < 0, W < 0)$. Some authors define the term "heat engine" to embody all three possibilities.

18.5 The Carnot cycle

While we can determine the best possible performance of a heat engine or
heat pump, which is obtainable only by reversible devices as defined above,
it remains to be seen whether we can invent a reversible cyclic process for which
it is possible to construct a reversible heat engine. Many such cycles have been
suggested, but it was Carnot who first discovered a cycle which would meet
these requirements.

Consider a cylinder fitted with a piston which encloses a fixed mass of gas.
The cylinder is brought into contact with a hot reservoir at a temperature T_1
and the piston is slowly withdrawn. For each increment in outward motion,
the temperature of the gas in the cylinder tends to fall but is immediately brought
back to the temperature T_1 by the flow of heat to the cylinder from the reservoir.
In this *isothermal expansion process* work is done by the system of cylinder,
piston, and gas while heat is transferred from the reservoir. Next the cylinder
is removed from contact with the reservoir, and a further expansion of the gas
in the cylinder occurs adiabatically (no heat transfer to the cylinder) by outward motion of the piston until the gas temperature is reduced to that of the cold
reservoir, T_2. During this *adiabatic expansion process* more work is done by
the system but no heat is added. Now the cylinder is brought into contact with
the cold reservoir while the gas is compressed isothermally. During this process
heat flows from the cylinder to the cold reservoir and work is absorbed. After

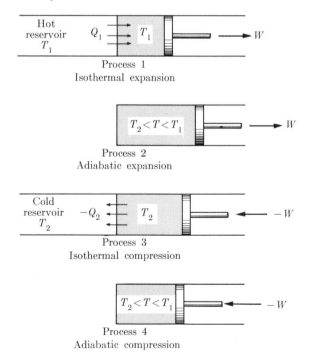

Fig. 18.2. The four processes of the Carnot cycle.

some compression, the cylinder is removed from contact with the reservoir, and a further *adiabatic compression* (during which additional work is absorbed) raises the gas temperature from T_2 to T_1, thereby completing the cycle of events and restoring the system to its initial state. This sequence of four processes, called the *Carnot cycle*, is summarized in Fig. 18.2.

When the isothermal and adiabatic processes described above are reversible, then the whole cycle is that of a reversible heat engine, for the reasons discussed in Section 18.3. A heat engine operating with this particular cycle must therefore have an efficiency determined solely by the temperatures T_2 and T_1, independent of the physical or chemical nature of the fluid in the cylinder or the amount of expansion of this fluid in the isothermal processes. (The amount of expansion in the adiabatic processes is determined by the temperatures T_2 and T_1 as well as by the nature of the fluid involved.)

Despite its simplicity, there are no practical heat engines designed to operate close to the theoretical Carnot cycle. The isothermal expansion process is difficult to achieve in practice, while the practical defects such as friction and heat losses which prevent our achieving reversible processes make other cycles more attractive. Therefore, from a practical point of view reversible heat-engine cycles such as the Carnot cycle may not necessarily serve as good models for useful heat engines, so that the design of practical devices may depend greatly on an understanding of the irreversible processes actually encountered.

While the ratio of work produced to heat absorbed from the hot reservoir in the Carnot cycle is just $1 - T_2/T_1$, the amount of work produced in one cycle by a cylinder of a certain size containing a given fluid cannot be determined without investigating the details of the process. To show how this may be done, let us suppose that the cylinder is filled with one mole of perfect gas of constant specific heat $\widetilde{C}_v$, for which the pressure p, internal energy $\widetilde{E}$, and entropy $\widetilde{S}$ are given by Eqs. (11.4–12), (13.4–1), and (13.4–4):

$$p = \widetilde{R}T/\widetilde{V}, \tag{18.5-1}$$

$$\widetilde{E} = \widetilde{C}_v T, \tag{18.5-2}$$

$$\widetilde{S} = \widetilde{S}_0 + \widetilde{C}_v \ln (T/T_0) + \widetilde{R} \ln (\widetilde{V}/\widetilde{V}_0). \tag{18.5-3}$$

Furthermore, we shall assume that the changes in energy and entropy of the piston and cylinder are very small compared with those of the gas and can therefore be neglected in computing the work and heat quantities involved in each step of the process.* For this reason the perfect-gas properties alone will determine the performance of the heat engine.

---

* This assumption, as well as that of the perfect gas, is made for the convenience of specifying the thermodynamic properties of the heat engine. It is extremely difficult to achieve in practice—but then no one attempts to build a reciprocating engine operating on the Carnot cycle. Since we are discussing the principle of operation of this engine, nothing is lost by this simplification.

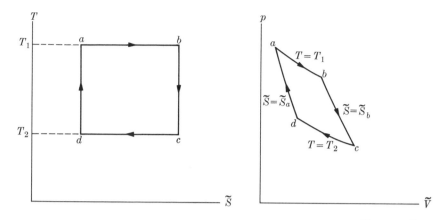

Fig. 18.3. The path of the processes of the Carnot cycle in the $T\widetilde{S}$- and $p\widetilde{V}$-planes. In the latter, the isentropic and isothermal processes are identified.

It will be found convenient to follow the changes in p, $\widetilde{V}$, T, and $\widetilde{S}$ throughout the cycle by describing the processes by curves in the $p\widetilde{V}$- and $T\widetilde{S}$-planes (see Fig. 18.3). If we denote by the subscripts a and b the state of the gas at the beginning and end of the isothermal expansion, then the change in entropy and pressure can be determined from Eqs. (18.5–1) and (18.5–3) in terms of the volume expansion ratio $\widetilde{V}_b/\widetilde{V}_a$:

$$\widetilde{S}_b - \widetilde{S}_a = \widetilde{R} \ln (\widetilde{V}_b/\widetilde{V}_a),$$

$$p_b/p_a = \widetilde{V}_a/\widetilde{V}_b, \tag{18.5–4}$$

since $T_a = T_b = T_1$. Thus the point b can be located in both planes. The isothermal process is of course a straight horizontal line in the $T\widetilde{S}$-plane and a hyperbola in the $p\widetilde{V}$-plane:

$$p\widetilde{V} = p_a\widetilde{V}_a. \tag{18.5–5}$$

The subsequent adiabatic expansion (process 2), because it is also reversible, must take place at constant entropy according to Section 10.5. Denoting the state at the end of this expansion by the subscript c, the volume change from b to c may be found from Eq. (18.5–3) by setting $\widetilde{S}_b - \widetilde{S}_c$ equal to zero:

$$0 = \widetilde{C}_v \ln (T_1/T_2) + \widetilde{R} \ln (\widetilde{V}_b/\widetilde{V}_c)$$

or

$$\widetilde{V}_b/\widetilde{V}_c = (T_2/T_1)^{1/(\gamma-1)} \tag{18.5–6}$$

since $T_b = T_1$ and $T_c = T_2$, and $\widetilde{R} = (\gamma - 1)\widetilde{C}_v$ by Eq. (13.4–11). The corresponding change in pressure may be found from Eqs. (18.5–1) and (18.5–6) to be

$$\frac{p_b}{p_c} = \frac{T_1\widetilde{V}_c}{T_2\widetilde{V}_b} = \left(\frac{T_1}{T_2}\right)^{\gamma/(\gamma-1)}, \tag{18.5–7}$$

thus locating the point c in the $p\widetilde{V}$-plane. This isentropic expansion is a vertical line in the $T\widetilde{S}$-plane and a hyperbola in the $p\widetilde{V}$-plane, determined from setting $\widetilde{S} - \widetilde{S}_b$ equal to zero in Eq. (13.4–7):

$$0 = \widetilde{C}_v \ln (p/p_b) + \widetilde{C}_p \ln (\widetilde{V}/\widetilde{V}_b)$$

or

$$p\widetilde{V}^\gamma = p_b\widetilde{V}_b^\gamma. \tag{18.5–8}$$

The state d at the end of the isothermal compression (process 3) is easily determined by noting that the volume ratio $\widetilde{V}_a/\widetilde{V}_d$ of the isentropic compression (process 4) must satisfy Eq. (18.5–6):

$$\widetilde{V}_a/\widetilde{V}_d = (T_2/T_1)^{1/(\gamma-1)} \tag{18.5–9}$$

because the temperature change must be the same as that for the isentropic expansion. It thus follows that the volume ratios in the isentropic processes are equal (that is, $\widetilde{V}_a/\widetilde{V}_d = \widetilde{V}_b/\widetilde{V}_c$). Because the change in volume in the complete cycle is zero, it is therefore necessary that the corresponding ratios in the isothermal processes are also equal, that is, $\widetilde{V}_b/\widetilde{V}_a = \widetilde{V}_c/\widetilde{V}_d$.*

Having determined the path of the Carnot cycle in the $p\widetilde{V}$-plane and the $T\widetilde{S}$-plane of a perfect gas,† we next wish to find the net work produced when the heat engine operates over one complete cycle. Since the net work produced is equal to the net heat added over one cycle (Eq. 18.3–2), we shall determine the latter for our reversible Carnot cycle by integrating Eq. (10.5–3) over one cycle:

$$\oint (dQ)_{\text{rev}} = \oint T \, d\widetilde{S}, \tag{18.5–10}$$

where the equality holds because the cycle is internally reversible. Now $\oint T \, d\widetilde{S}$ is simply the area enclosed by the rectangle in the $T\widetilde{S}$-plane, having a height $T_1 - T_2$ and a width $\widetilde{S}_b - \widetilde{S}_a$ given by Eq. (18.5–4). Thus the net work per cycle is

$$\oint (dW)_{\text{rev}} = \oint T \, d\widetilde{S} = \widetilde{R}(T_1 - T_2) \ln (\widetilde{V}_b/\widetilde{V}_a). \tag{18.5–11}$$

We can clearly see that the net work per cycle is increased by increasing the temperature difference between the reservoirs and also by increasing the volume ratio $\widetilde{V}_b/\widetilde{V}_a$ of the isothermal expansion. We also see that the amount of work

---

* This does not necessarily mean that $\widetilde{V}_b = \widetilde{V}_d$. We have chosen the first expansion ratio, $\widetilde{V}_b/\widetilde{V}_a$, to be given, as well as T_2/T_1, from which all other quantities are determinable in sequence by Eqs. (18.5–4) through (18.5–9).

† The Carnot cycle is always a rectangle in the $T\widetilde{S}$-plane, irrespective of the material from which the heat engine is constructed. This is a result of the nature of the cycle, which consists of isothermal and isentropic processes. The path of the cycle in the $p\widetilde{V}$-plane will of course be different from that shown in Fig. 18.3 if the fluid is not a perfect gas.

per cycle produced by one mole of monatomic gas will be the same for all gases since $\widetilde{R}$ is a universal constant. Most of all, it is readily apparent how the properties of the fluid, such as $\widetilde{R}$, and the details of the cycle, such as the volume expansion ratio $\widetilde{V}_b/\widetilde{V}_a$, affect the work produced in one cycle even though the efficiency is determined solely by the ratio T_1/T_2.

In examining the details of a heat-engine cycle, an additional fact of practical importance should be mentioned. In the Carnot cycle described above, expansion processes 1 and 2 produce work, some of which must be used subsequently in compression processes 3 and 4. For example, in a reciprocating engine some of the work done during the expansion of the gas in the cylinder is used to increase the kinetic energy of a flywheel, the remainder being delivered to the engine load. During the compression process the flywheel kinetic energy is reduced an equal amount in order to compress the gas in the cylinder. In an actual engine, where there will be losses due to friction and heat transfer, it is desirable that the net work produced not be a very small fraction of the work of expansion (or compression), for otherwise a small percentage loss of expansion work or increase of compression work would decrease severely the net work produced. It is primarily for this reason that practical heat engines make use, of cycles other than the Carnot, such as the Rankine and Brayton cycles discussed in Sections 18.6 and 18.7.

It is relatively easy to determine the work of compression for the Carnot cycle. For isothermal compression process 3, the reversible work is determined by integrating Eq. (10.5–1) with Eq. (18.5–1):

$$\int_c^d dW_{\text{rev}} = \int_{\widetilde{V}_c}^{\widetilde{V}_d} p \, d\widetilde{V} = \widetilde{R}T_2 \int_{\widetilde{V}_c}^{\widetilde{V}_d} d\widetilde{V}/\widetilde{V} = \widetilde{R}T_2 \ln\,(\widetilde{V}_d/\widetilde{V}_c). \qquad (18.5\text{–}12)$$

For adiabatic compression process 4, since there is no heat involved, the first law requires that the increase in internal energy equal the (negative) work done on the system:

$$\int_d^a dE = -\int_d^a dW$$

or

$$\int_d^a dW = E_d - E_a = \widetilde{C}_v(T_2 - T_1). \qquad (18.5\text{–}13)$$

Thus the total (negative) work of compression is the sum of these two parts, or

$$\int_c^a dW = \widetilde{C}_v(T_2 - T_1) + \widetilde{R}T_2 \ln\,(\widetilde{V}_d/\widetilde{V}_c). \qquad (18.5\text{–}14)$$

The ratio of the magnitude of this work of compression to the net work of the cycle given by Eq. (18.5–11) is

$$\frac{|\int_c^a dW|}{\oint dW} = \frac{(\widetilde{C}_v/\widetilde{R})}{\ln\,(\widetilde{V}_b/\widetilde{V}_a)} + \frac{T_2}{T_1 - T_2}, \qquad (18.5\text{–}15)$$

in which the equality of the volume ratios of the isothermal processes has been used. It can be seen that large volume ratios are favorable for reducing the ratio of compression work to net work.

Our examination of a reversible cycle, the Carnot cycle, has shown how the details of the cycle and the nature of the material used in constructing the heat engine must be known if the amount of the work and heat quantities involved is to be determined. While the efficiency is determined entirely by the temperatures T_1 and T_2 of the heat reservoirs, all other characteristics of the heat engine are determined by these other quantities. Furthermore, an analysis of the steps in any given cycle is usually very informative in understanding the operation of the irreversible heat engines, which are the only type that can be constructed in practice.

18.6 The Rankine cycle

The success of the steam engine, in a thermodynamic sense, stems from the fact that by employing a fluid which changes from liquid to vapor, the work-absorbing part of the cycle can be made very small compared with the work-producing part. Although the two-phase cycle does not equal the Carnot cycle in efficiency, it is widely used in the production of electrical power in central stations and propulsive power in ships, partly because of such practical aspects as the type of machinery involved, capital costs, reliability, etc. Improvements in steam power plant cycles based on thermodynamic principles have been so extensively developed that these plants are among the most efficient power-producing systems yet built.

The simplest two-phase cycle (liquid-vapor) for producing work is called the Rankine* cycle. Like the Carnot cycle, it consists of four successive processes, two of which are adiabatic while the others involve heating or cooling. The four processes, illustrated in Fig. 18.4 for a closed system, are (1) an adiabatic compression of a liquid from a pressure p_2 to p_1, (2) a constant-pressure evaporation, or boiling, of the liquid into a vapor, during which the volume increases as heat is added, (3) an adiabatic expansion of the vapor from the upper pressure p_1 to the lower pressure p_2, and (4) a constant-pressure condensation of the vapor to a liquid brought about by cooling and accompanied by a volume decrease.

These processes may be described by a closed curve in the $T\widetilde{S}$- or the $p\widetilde{V}$-plane, as shown in Fig. 18.5. In either plane the saturation curve separates the region of two phases coexisting in equilibrium from the region of a single phase (either vapor or liquid). In the $T\widetilde{S}$-plane are drawn two constant-pressure

---

* William J. M. Rankine (1820–1872), a Scottish engineer, contributed many ideas to the early development of thermodynamics, especially as related to steam engines. He wrote the *Manual of the Steam Engine* in 1859, the first treatise on applied thermodynamics.

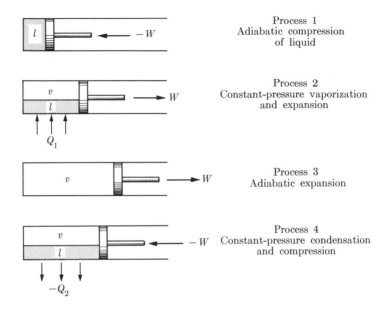

Fig. 18.4. The four processes of the Rankine cycle. The symbols v and l identify the vapor and liquid phases, respectively.

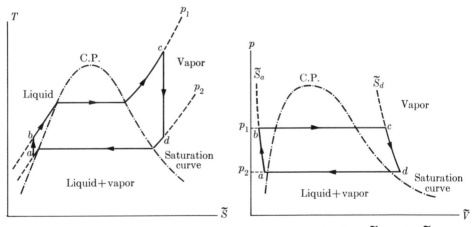

Fig. 18.5. The processes of the Rankine cycle plotted in the $p\widetilde{V}$- and $T\widetilde{S}$-planes. The critical point of the saturation curve is marked $C.P.$ (e.g. see Fig. 14.4).

lines (p_1 and p_2) which are horizontal in the two-phase region since temperature depends only on the pressure when two phases are present. In the $p\widetilde{V}$-plane are drawn two isentropes to show the path of an adiabatic reversible expansion and compression. If the processes are reversible, process 1 consists of an isentropic compression from a to b; process 2, a constant-pressure heating and expansion from b to c; process 3, an isentropic expansion from c to d; and process 4, a constant-pressure cooling and compression from d to a.

It can be seen from Fig. 18.5 that the temperature of the fluid changes during the constant-pressure processes for which heat is either added from a hot reservoir or rejected to a cold reservoir. It is therefore necessary that the hot reservoir have a temperature at least as great as T_c and that the cold reservoir have a temperature not more than T_a. Because the reservoir temperatures are not equal to the heat engine temperature during the heating and cooling processes, a heat engine operating on the Rankine cycle is not reversible and its thermodynamic efficiency will usually* be less than that of a reversible heat engine operating between T_c and T_a. Even if all the internal processes of the Rankine cycle are reversible, the heat engine cannot be operated in the reverse direction, causing heat to be removed from a reservoir at T_a and added to another at T_c.

Since the efficiency of the Rankine cycle is not determined solely by the temperatures T_c and T_a of the hot and cold reservoirs, we must examine the details of the processes in order to determine the work produced and heat supplied in each cycle. In order to do so, let us first consider process 2 in which heat is added at a constant pressure p_1. For such a constant-pressure process, Eq. (10.5–6) states that the heat Q_1 added is just the increase in enthalpy $\widetilde{H}$:

$$\int_b^c dQ = \int_b^c d\widetilde{H}, \qquad Q_1 = \widetilde{H}_c - \widetilde{H}_b. \tag{18.6–1}$$

For the same reason, the (negative) heat Q_2 rejected to the cold reservoir is

$$\int_d^a dQ = \int_d^a d\widetilde{H}, \qquad Q_2 = \widetilde{H}_a - \widetilde{H}_d. \tag{18.6–2}$$

The net work W produced by the heat engine in one cycle is, according to the first law (Eq. 18.3–2), equal to the sum of the heats Q_1 and Q_2:

$$\begin{aligned} W = Q_1 + Q_2 &= \widetilde{H}_c - \widetilde{H}_b + \widetilde{H}_a - \widetilde{H}_d \\ &= (\widetilde{H}_c - \widetilde{H}_d) - (\widetilde{H}_b - \widetilde{H}_a), \end{aligned} \tag{18.6–3}$$

in which the enthalpies have been regrouped to coincide with the enthalpy changes in the isentropic processes, for reasons which will be discussed below. The thermodynamic efficiency η_t is the ratio of the net work W to the heat Q_1 supplied from the hot reservoir,

$$\eta_t = \frac{W}{Q_1} = 1 - \frac{\widetilde{H}_d - \widetilde{H}_a}{\widetilde{H}_c - \widetilde{H}_b}, \tag{18.6–4}$$

and will therefore depend on the properties of the fluid used in the cycle.

---

* If the points a, b, c, and d all lie within the two-phase region of Fig. 18.5, then the Rankine and Carnot cycles would be identical.

Since all the processes in the cycle are reversible, the net work W, which equals the net heat $Q_1 + Q_2$, may be found to equal the net area in the $T\widetilde{S}$-plane, enclosed by the process path. By integrating Eq. (10.5–3) over one cycle, we obtain

$$\oint T \, d\widetilde{S} = \oint (dQ)_{\text{rev}} = Q_1 + Q_2 = W. \qquad (18.6\text{--}5)$$

Because of the shape of the constant-pressure curves, it is not so simple to evaluate this area as previously for the Carnot cycle. On the other hand, we can integrate Eq. (10.5–1) directly over one cycle to obtain

$$\oint p \, d\widetilde{V} = \oint (dW)_{\text{rev}} = W \qquad (18.6\text{--}6)$$

and see that the integral is the area of the $p\widetilde{V}$-plane enclosed by the cycle path in Fig. 18.5.

It is easy to show the equality of Eqs. (18.6–6) and (18.6–3) if we recognize that the enclosed area of the $p\widetilde{V}$-plane may be equally well evaluated by integrating on the variable p:

$$\oint p \, d\widetilde{V} = \oint \widetilde{V} \, dp$$
$$= \int_d^c \widetilde{V} \, dp - \int_a^b \widetilde{V} \, dp, \qquad (18.6\text{--}7)$$

in which the area has been determined from Fig. 18.5 in terms of integrals along isentropic processes 1 and 3 alone, since the constant-pressure processes do not contribute to the area with integration on p. Now for an isentropic process ($d\widetilde{S} = 0$) we find from Eq. (10.4–19) that

$$0 = d\widetilde{H} - \widetilde{V} \, dp$$

or

$$\widetilde{V} \, dp = d\widetilde{H}. \qquad (18.6\text{--}8)$$

Consequently the right-hand side of Eq. (18.6–7) may be integrated to give

$$\oint p \, d\widetilde{V} = \int_d^c d\widetilde{H} - \int_a^b d\widetilde{H} = (\widetilde{H}_c - \widetilde{H}_d) - (\widetilde{H}_b - \widetilde{H}_a), \quad (18.6\text{--}9)$$

which, by substitution into Eq. (18.6–6), gives Eq. (18.6–3).

Although we have determined the work and heat quantities for a Rankine cycle by considering the processes illustrated in Fig. 18.4, in which the fluid is contained within a cylinder and work is done on a moving piston, we have ignored an important technological fact: even the earliest steam engines used the piston motion only to expand the vapor, the heating and cooling of the fluid being accomplished outside the cylinder. In modern steam power plants the expansion and compression processes are carried out in a turbine and pump, respectively, rotating machines through which the fluid flows steadily. The

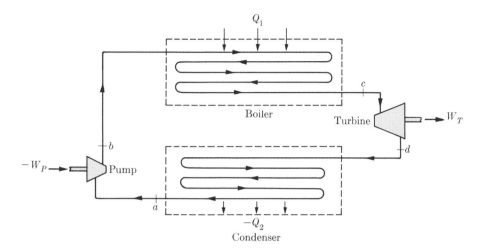

Fig. 18.6. Flow diagram of the processes in a steady-flow turbine power plant.

heating and cooling processes occur in a boiler and condenser (see Fig. 18.6). Nevertheless, the thermodynamic states through which the fluid passes is the same for the piston-cylinder engine illustrated in Fig. 18.4 as it is for the steady-flow steam plant illustrated in Fig. 18.6, and the processes shown in Fig. 18.5 apply equally well to both of them. The net work W and the cycle efficiency η_t are the same for either engine, but the work and heat involved in each process may be different. For example, in the steam plant of Fig. 18.6, work is produced by the turbine in the adiabatic expansion process and absorbed by the pump in the adiabatic compression process, and no work (but only heat) is involved in the heating and cooling processes in the boiler and condenser. On the other hand, in the piston-cylinder engine, each process produces or absorbs some work, since the volume $\widetilde{V}$ changes in each process.

It is clear from the foregoing discussion that the overall properties of a reversible cycle, such as the net work per unit mass of fluid and the thermodynamic efficiency, depend only on the thermodynamic path which the fluid follows. More detailed effects, such as the work and heat involved in each process, depend on the particular manner in which the process is carried out. Since some cycles involve steady-flow processes, a more detailed discussion of such effects must be deferred until Chapter 19.

18.7 Other cycles

The internal-combustion engine using a hydrocarbon or gas for fuel and air as an oxidant is not a heat engine as previously defined. However, there is a heat-engine cycle, called the Otto cycle, which duplicates reasonably well the history of pressure and volume changes in the cylinder of an internal-combustion engine. The processes of the reversible Otto cycle, plotted in the $p\widetilde{V}$-plane and

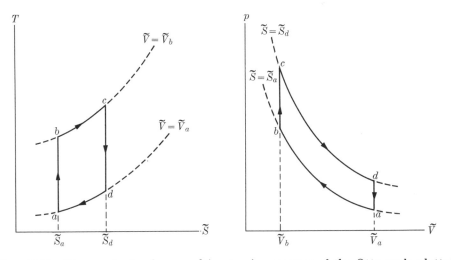

Fig. 18.7. The constant-volume and isentropic processes of the Otto cycle plotted in the $T\widetilde{S}$- and $p\widetilde{V}$-planes.

the $T\widetilde{S}$-plane in Fig. 18.7, consist of (1) an adiabatic (isentropic) compression from a to b, (2) a constant-volume heating from b to c, (3) an adiabatic (isentropic) expansion from c to d, and (4) a constant-volume cooling from d to a. Because the heating and cooling processes do not occur at constant temperature, the heat engine operating on this cycle will not be reversible and its efficiency will be less than that of a Carnot engine operating between reservoirs at temperatures T_c and T_a.

We may find the heat Q_1 added during the constant-volume heating process by noting from Section 10.5 that the heat must equal the increase in internal energy $\widetilde{E}$:

$$Q_1 = \int_b^c dQ = \int_b^c d\widetilde{E} = \widetilde{E}_c - \widetilde{E}_b. \qquad (18.7\text{–}1)$$

Similarly, the (negative) heat Q_2 lost in the cooling process is

$$Q_2 = \int_d^a dQ = \int_d^a d\widetilde{E} = \widetilde{E}_a - \widetilde{E}_d. \qquad (18.7\text{–}2)$$

Thus the net work W and the thermodynamic efficiency η_t may be determined:

$$W = Q_1 + Q_2 = \widetilde{E}_c - \widetilde{E}_b + \widetilde{E}_a - \widetilde{E}_d = (\widetilde{E}_c - \widetilde{E}_d) - (\widetilde{E}_b - \widetilde{E}_a),$$
$$(18.7\text{–}3)$$

$$\eta_t = \frac{W}{Q_1} = 1 - \frac{\widetilde{E}_d - \widetilde{E}_a}{\widetilde{E}_c - \widetilde{E}_b}. \qquad (18.7\text{–}4)$$

If the working fluid is one mole of perfect gas with constant specific heats, then the thermodynamic properties will be given by Eqs. (18.5–1) through

(18.5–3). The net work W of Eq. (18.7–3) may thus be written as

$$W = \tilde{C}_v\{(T_c - T_d) - (T_b - T_a)\}$$
$$= \tilde{C}_v\{T_c(1 - T_d/T_c) - T_b(1 - T_a/T_b)\}. \tag{18.7–5}$$

For the isentropic processes, the temperature ratios and volume ratios are related by Eq. (13.4–13):

$$T_a/T_b = (\tilde{V}_b/\tilde{V}_a)^{\gamma-1} = T_d/T_c \tag{18.7–6}$$

since the compression and expansion volume ratios are identical. On substituting Eq. (18.7–6) into Eq. (18.7–5), we find the work W to be

$$W = \tilde{C}_v(T_c - T_b)\{1 - (\tilde{V}_b/\tilde{V}_a)^{\gamma-1}\}. \tag{18.7–7}$$

Recognizing that the first factor in this expression is just Q_1, the thermodynamic efficiency η_t is simply

$$\eta_t = W/Q_1 = 1 - (\tilde{V}_b/\tilde{V}_a)^{\gamma-1}, \tag{18.7–8}$$

which depends only on the volume ratio of compression, $\tilde{V}_a/\tilde{V}_b$. It is easy to see that increasing the compression ratio will increase the thermodynamic efficiency, and it is for this reason among others that the diesel engine ($\tilde{V}_a/\tilde{V}_b \simeq$ 13) is more efficient than the gasoline engine ($\tilde{V}_a/\tilde{V}_b \simeq 8$). The amount of work W is also proportional to the temperature rise $T_c - T_b$ in the constant-volume heating process.

The analysis of the Otto cycle given above may be extended to determine the work of compression or expansion in a piston-cylinder type of engine, as was done for the Carnot cycle in Section 18.5. Because reciprocating internal-combustion engines also operate in this manner, they have a direct similarity with the Otto cycle even though they are not strictly heat engines as previously defined.

The Brayton cycle bears the same relationship to the gas turbine power plant as does the Rankine cycle to the steam power plant. It consists of the same processes as the Rankine cycle, but the working fluid is a noncondensing gas. The constant-pressure and isentropic processes are plotted in the $T\tilde{S}$- and $p\tilde{V}$-planes in Fig. 18.8, which differs from Fig. 18.5 only in the configuration of the process paths, that now follow those of a noncondensing gas such as the perfect gas with constant specific heats (Fig. 13.2). The steady-flow gas turbine power plant that is the equivalent of the steam power plant is shown in Fig. 18.9. It consists of a compressor which compresses the gas from p_2 to p_1, a heater which increases its temperature from T_b to T_c while the pressure remains fixed, a turbine which expands the hot compressed gas from p_1 to p_2 while delivering work, and a cooler which returns the temperature to T_a by cooling at constant

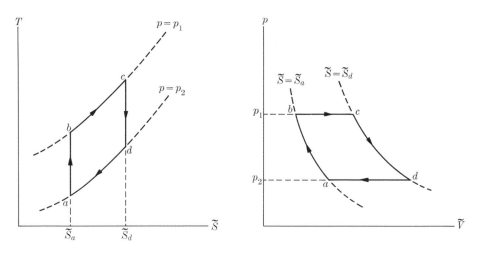

Fig. 18.8.   The constant-pressure and isentropic processes of the Brayton cycle plotted in the $T\widetilde{S}$- and $p\widetilde{V}$-planes.

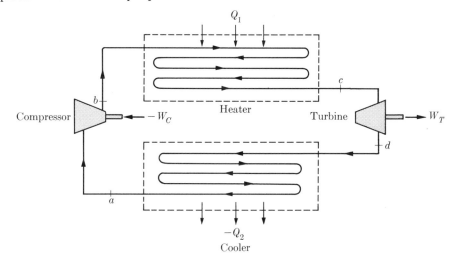

Fig. 18.9.   Flow diagram of the processes in a steady-flow closed-cycle gas-turbine power plant. The net work produced by the plant is the turbine work W_T minus the compressor work $-W_C$.

pressure. Net work is produced in the amount by which the turbine work exceeds that absorbed by the compressor.

The net work produced for each mole of gas which passes through the cycle and the efficiency with which this work is produced are given by the same expressions as those for the Rankine cycle, Eqs. (18.6–3) and (18.6–4), for the processes involved are the same. Since the Brayton cycle ordinarily makes use of a gas for the working fluid, we may evaluate W and η_t for a perfect gas with constant specific heats. Noting that $\widetilde{H} = \widetilde{C}_p T$ according to Eq. (13.4–8), the net work

W found from Eq. (18.6–3) is

$$W = \widetilde{C}_p(T_c - T_d) - \widetilde{C}_p(T_b - T_a)$$
$$= \widetilde{C}_p T_c(1 - T_d/T_c) - \widetilde{C}_p T_b(1 - T_a/T_b). \tag{18.7–9}$$

For the isentropic compression processes, the temperature ratios are related to the pressure ratio p_1/p_2 through Eq. (13.4–14):

$$p_1/p_2 = (T_b/T_a)^{\gamma/(\gamma-1)} = (T_c/T_d)^{\gamma/(\gamma-1)}. \tag{18.7–10}$$

With substitution of this into Eq. (18.7–9), the work W is found to be

$$W = \widetilde{C}_p(T_c - T_b)\{1 - (p_2/p_1)^{(\gamma-1)/\gamma}\}. \tag{18.7–11}$$

Since the first factor is just $\widetilde{H}_c - \widetilde{H}_b$, and thus the heat Q_1 added in the constant-pressure heating process, the efficiency η_t is simply

$$\eta_t = W/Q_1 = 1 - (p_2/p_1)^{(\gamma-1)/\gamma}, \tag{18.7–12}$$

which is similar to Eq. (18.7–8) for the Otto cycle.

18.8   Open cycles with chemical change

Internal-combustion engines (such as the aircraft gas turbine or gasoline engine) are not heat engines because the working fluid is not re-used over and over again, as is the water in a steam plant, but is exchanged for a new mixture of air and fuel which is subsequently burned in one stage of the cycle. We shall examine in this section the relation between this process involving chemical change and the heating processes previously discussed in connection with heat-engine cycles. While it is intuitively pleasing to suppose that the combustion process results in a heating of the fluid (that is, $Q_1 > 0$), the processes which actually occur are adiabatic or nearly so; hence the increase in temperature which is observed results from the change in chemical composition and not from heat addition from an external heat reservoir. For this reason it is necessary to distinguish clearly between the temperature rise brought about in the working fluid of a power plant because of chemical change and that which results from heating by an external source.

Suppose that a mixture of fuel and oxidant, called the *reactants*, is confined in a cylinder occupying a volume V_i at a pressure p_i and temperature T_i, the cylinder being closed with a movable piston. If the reactants are ignited and burn slowly to form *products* of combustion, while the piston is moved so as to maintain the pressure constant at the value p_i, then the first law of thermodynamics for this constant-pressure process may be written as

$$dQ = dE + p_i\,dV = d(E + p_iV) = dH \tag{18.8–1}$$

since the work done by the system is $p_i\,dV$.

Let us consider two different constant-pressure combustion processes of the type just described. In the first, let us cool the reacting mixture so that its final temperature is the same as the initial temperature T_i. The (negative) heat added to the system in this process is found by integrating Eq. (18.8–1):

$$\int_r^p dQ = H_p\{p_i, T_i\} - H_r\{p_i, T_i\} \equiv \Delta H^i, \qquad (18.8\text{–}2)$$

in which ΔH^i is defined as the enthalpy difference between products and reactants when both exist at the same temperature T_i and pressure p_i; $-\Delta H^i$ is often called the *constant-pressure heat of reaction*.*

Now consider an adiabatic constant-pressure process, in which the final temperature T_f is reached by the products when the reactants have all been consumed. Since no heat is involved, integration of Eq. (18.8–1) gives

$$0 = H_p\{p_i, T_f\} - H_r\{p_i, T_i\}. \qquad (18.8\text{–}3)$$

This latter adiabatic process is the one which actually occurs in a constant-pressure combustion process, and Eq. (18.8–3) may be rewritten by replacing $H_r\{p_i, T_i\}$ from Eq. (18.8–2):

$$H_p\{p_i, T_f\} = H_p\{p_i, T_i\} - \Delta H^i. \qquad (18.8\text{–}4)$$

Since the change in enthalpy in a constant-pressure reversible process is equal to the heat added, we may state as a conclusion from Eq. (18.8–4) that *the final state achieved in a constant-pressure process involving a chemical change is the same as would be reached by adding at constant pressure an amount of heat, $-\Delta H^i$, to the products which are initially at a temperature T_i and pressure p_i.*

It is therefore a useful concept to replace the constant-pressure combustion process by a constant-pressure heating of the products in which the heat Q_1 is set equal to $-\Delta H^i$. For any given mixture of reactants, ΔH^i must be determined experimentally or may be calculated for a perfect-gas mixture, as described in Section 14.7.

As a simple example of the latter case, consider the combustion of 2 moles of hydrogen with $(n + 1)$ moles of oxygen:

$$2H_2 + (n + 1)O_2 \rightarrow 2H_2O + nO_2, \qquad (18.8\text{–}5)$$

for which the value of $\Delta \widetilde{H}^0$ at $T = 0$ is given in Table 14.1 as $-114{,}214$ cal/gm-mole. To find ΔH^i at a temperature T_i we begin with Eq. (18.8–2):

$$\Delta H^i = H_p^i - H_r^i = (H_p^i - H_p^0) - (H_r^i - H_r^0) + (H_p^0 - H_r^0)$$
$$= (H_p^i - H_p^0) - (H_r^i - H_r^0) + \Delta H^0. \qquad (18.8\text{–}6)$$

---

* In Section 14.7 the constant-volume and constant-pressure heats of reaction were first introduced in determining the energy of formation of a Gibbs-Dalton mixture of perfect gases.

Now, the terms in parentheses are simply the difference in enthalpy for the products or reactants from the value which they have at $T = 0$ and hence are identical with the perfect-gas enthalpies denoted in Chapter 14 by $\widetilde{H}$ per mole. Thus each term may be given by

$$H_p^i - H_p^0 = 2(\widetilde{H}_{H_2O}^i) + n(\widetilde{H}_{O_2}^i),$$

$$H_r^i - H_r^0 = 2(\widetilde{H}_{H_2}^i) + (n + 1)(\widetilde{H}_{O_2}^i),$$

$\qquad$ (18.8-7)

which, upon combination with Eq. (18.8–6), results in

$$\Delta\widetilde{H}^i = \Delta\widetilde{H}^0 + 2(\widetilde{H}_{H_2O}^i) - 2(\widetilde{H}_{H_2}^i) - (\widetilde{H}_{O_2}^i). \qquad (18.8\text{-}8)$$

Although $\Delta\widetilde{H}^i$ is independent of n, the number of excess moles of oxygen, the final state f which is reached at the end of combustion will be affected by n, as can be seen by substituting Eq. (18.8–8) into (18.8–4):

$$2(\widetilde{H}_{H_2O}^f) + n(\widetilde{H}_{O_2}^f) = (n + 1)(\widetilde{H}_{O_2}^i) + 2(\widetilde{H}_{H_2}^i) - \Delta\widetilde{H}^0. \qquad (18.8\text{-}9)$$

Equation (18.8–9) may be used to determine the final state f from the initial state i and the enthalpy change at $T = 0$ for this reaction.

PROBLEMS

18.1 It is claimed that a substance at thermal equilibrium at a temperature T radiates in a frequency interval $\Delta\nu$ with a greater emissive power than a black body at the same temperature. Show how such a substance could be used to make a perpetual-motion machine of the second kind.

18.2 Two constant-volume heat reservoirs, each composed of a mass M of material having a constant value of c_v are initially at absolute temperatures T_{10} and T_{20}. A reversible heat engine operates between the two reservoirs, reducing the temperature of the warmer one and increasing the temperature of the colder one until both reach the same final temperature T_f. (a) What has been the change in the sum of the entropies of both reservoirs? (b) What is the final temperature? (c) How much work is done by the reversible engine?

18.3 A proposed fusion device requires a steady magnetic field for plasma containment. The field coil requires electrical power P_e to overcome the resistive loss in the windings and is kept at atmospheric temperature T_0 by an air cooling system. It is suggested that by cooling the coil with a refrigerator to a lower temperature T_L, the electrical power required to maintain the same magnetic field will be reduced to $P_e' = P_e(T_L/T_0)$ because the electrical resistivity of the coil winding is proportional to the absolute temperature T of the coil. However, some power P_R will be required to operate the refrigerator. If a reversible refrigerator cooled the coil at temperature T_L and rejected heat to the atmosphere at temperature T_0, would the total power $P_R + P_e'$ be less than, equal to, or greater than the power P_e required for the uncooled coil?

18.4 A building is to be heated to 70°F either directly by burning fuel or through use of a reversible heat pump. (a) If the cost of electrical work to operate the pump is ten times the cost of an equal amount of heat from a furnace, at what atmospheric temperature will the cost of the two methods be equal? (b) Which will be cheaper at colder atmospheric temperatures?

18.5 A magnetic refrigeration cycle makes use of $CrK(SO_4)_2 \cdot 12H_2O$ as the working substance. It consists of a reversed Carnot cycle operating between 2°K and 4°K. The cycle consists of (1) an adiabatic partial demagnetization from 4°K to 2°K, (2) a constant-temperature demagnetization at 2°K during which the magnetic field is reduced from 2 w/m² to zero and heat is absorbed, (3) an adiabatic magnetization from 2°K to 4°K, and (4) a constant-temperature additional magnetization during which heat is given off to the reservoir at 4°K. (a) Sketch these processes in the TS-plane, including lines of constant H (or B) as shown in Fig. 17.9. (b) Sketch the processes in the HM-plane. (c) What is the coefficient of performance of this reversible refrigerator? (d) What is the net work per cycle per gm-mole of salt?

18.6 Using the phase diagrams of Problem 17.10 and Fig. 17.11, describe a Carnot cycle which makes use of the normal-superconducting transition.

18.7 A steam power plant operates according to the ideal Rankine cycle as shown in Fig. 18.5. The enthalpy $h_a = 138.0$, $h_b = 138.7$, $h_c = 1527.4$, and $h_d = 1134.2$, all in units of Btu/lbm. (a) Find the efficiency of the cycle. (b) If the temperatures at c and a are 1000°F and 170°F, what fraction of the Carnot efficiency for this maximum and minimum temperature is actually achieved?

18.8 A reciprocating engine operates according to the ideal Brayton cycle, using as a fluid a perfect gas of constant $\gamma = 1.2$. If the ratio of maximum to minimum volume is 10, plot a curve of efficiency versus the logarithm of the pressure ratio.

18.9 A reciprocating engine operates according to the ideal Otto cycle, using as a fluid a perfect gas of constant $\gamma = 1.2$. If the ratio of maximum pressure to minimum pressure is 15, plot a curve of efficiency versus the logarithm of the ratio of maximum to minimum volume.

18.10 A heat engine is to be designed to operate between heat reservoirs at 600°K and 300°K, utilizing a perfect gas of constant $\gamma = 1.2$. The ratios of maximum to minimum volume and pressure should not exceed 10 and 20, respectively. (a) Which cycle is more efficient, a Brayton cycle or Otto cycle? (b) Which cycle will produce the greater work per cycle for a given amount of working fluid?

18.11 A mixture of 1 mole of H_2 and 10 moles of O_2 at 300°K reacts adiabatically at constant pressure to form a mixture of H_2O gas and O_2 at a higher temperature. (a) Estimate the final temperature by assuming that the specific heat C_p of the products is a constant. (b) Calculate the final temperature exactly by computing the enthalpy of the products accurately for temperatures in the neighborhood of the estimated one.

19

FLUID FLOW

19.1 The fluid continuum

A fluid, whether it be a gas or a liquid, is composed of molecules whose relative orientations with respect to each other continually change with time even when the fluid is stationary on the macroscopic, or laboratory, scale. In a gas the migration of one molecule from one point to another occurs easily, for even though its direction changes at random, its speed is about equal to the speed of sound. In a liquid the diffusion of a molecule occurs more slowly because its direction is altered more frequently. When a fluid flows from one point to another, e.g., air flowing over an airplane wing, this microscopic molecular motion occurs on a scale so small compared with the airplane wing that it can be ignored in comparison with the larger-scale macroscopic motion which we may observe easily by watching a wisp of smoke flow by. This does not mean that the molecular motion *per se* is unimportant, because we do know that such a motion in a gas determines its internal energy and pressure; this will subsequently be seen to be very important to the macroscopic motion. Rather, it is proposed that because of the great difference in scale between the molecular motion and the macroscopic flow, the former will be accounted for by averaging the molecular properties of a sample of fluid of small but macroscopic size and that this average will be incorporated into the macroscopic description.

At this point, this is by no means a novel proposal. In discussing the distinction between work and heat in Chapter 9, we found them to be different parts of the microscopic work when averaged over a macroscopically larger number of interacting particles. The thermodynamic properties previously treated were also macroscopic averages which could be used to understand the behavior of heat engines without the subsequent necessity of reconsidering the molecular quantum states in each instance encountered. It is the relationship between average quantities, such as heat, work, and energy, that is usually pertinent to the behavior of matter on a macroscopic scale and that can be successfully used in predicting and understanding the observable physical effects.

The usefulness of such an approach depends on our success in determining the appropriate average quantities and the manner in which they can be incorporated into a macroscopic description. For example, in Chapter 20 we shall study some simple situations in which the flow of heat or molecules is proportional to the change in temperature or molecular density. The proportionality constant relating these macroscopic quantities depends on the details of microscopic molecular collisions, but once these are understood, the macroscopic behavior of many flows in which heat conduction and diffusion are important may be readily described entirely on the macroscopic level.*

Not every type of flow can be treated from such a point of view. When a satellite flies through the atmosphere of the earth at an altitude of 100 mi, the air density is so low that the important microscopic scale, which is the mean free path of an air molecule, is no longer very small compared with the satellite. It is no longer very helpful in this case of rarefied-gas flow to adopt the point of view outlined above; instead, the microscopic and macroscopic scales become commensurate and phenomena on both scales must be considered simultaneously. Needless to say, such flows are usually difficult to treat both experimentally and theoretically.

The point of view outlined above is called the *continuum description of matter*. It is predicated upon the hypothesis that for any physical event to be described, one can isolate regions of space within which averages of molecular properties may be determined, regions which are so small compared with the scale of the event that these averages may be considered to be continuous functions of space and time but large enough to contain a very large number of particles (perhaps greater than 10^6). The usefulness of such a description will lie not only in our ability to relate the average quantities to each other, either theoretically or empirically, by means of *constitutive relations*,† but, more important, to permit the expression of the fundamental physical laws in terms of these average quantities. In this chapter, we shall be concerned mostly with statements of the conservation laws for a fluid.

19.2 Field properties

At any position **r** in space at the time t we may measure the mass ΔM of the molecules in a small volume ΔV and determine the ratio $\Delta M/\Delta V$, called the mass density ρ:

$$\rho\{\mathbf{r}, t\} \equiv \frac{\Delta M}{\Delta V}. \tag{19.2–1}$$

---

* Although we wish to deal here only with fluids, the point of view expressed above is commonly adopted in treating solids as well. In the latter case, the existence of microscopic defects such as dislocations must be incorporated into the macroscopic strength properties by an appropriate macroscopic averaging process.

† The relationship between stress and strain in a solid, or between heat flux and temperature gradient in a fluid, are examples of constitutive relations between average properties of the molecular motion which arise in the continuum description.

Other scalar extensive properties, such as internal energy ΔE and entropy ΔS, may also be measured, and the specific energy e and entropy s may be defined by

$$e\{\mathbf{r}, t\} \equiv \frac{\Delta E}{\Delta M} = \frac{1}{\rho} \frac{\Delta E}{\Delta V},$$

$$\hspace{6cm} (19.2\text{-}2)$$

$$s\{\mathbf{r}, t\} \equiv \frac{\Delta S}{\Delta M} = \frac{1}{\rho} \frac{\Delta S}{\Delta V},$$

in which Eq. (19.2-1) has been used. By virtue of this definition, the internal energy per unit volume and entropy per unit volume are ρe and ρs, respectively.

Of course, the volume ΔV must be small compared with the macroscopic volume V of the flow but large compared with the average volume per molecule, m/ρ,

$$V \gg \Delta V \gg m/\rho, \hspace{2cm} (19.2\text{-}3)$$

if this average is to be independent of the size of ΔV.

We can also define a mass velocity $\mathbf{v}$ by forming the ratio of the momentum $\Delta \mathbf{P}$ to the volume ΔV:

$$\mathbf{v}\{\mathbf{r}, t\} \equiv \frac{1}{\rho} \frac{\Delta \mathbf{P}}{\Delta V} \hspace{2cm} (19.2\text{-}4)$$

so that $\rho \mathbf{v}$ is the momentum per unit volume. Other vector properties of the fluid particles, such as magnetic dipole moment, could also be averaged in the same way, but we shall not be concerned here with these other possibilities.

Now let us consider a volume element ΔV of the fluid next to a boundary surface A which separates the fluid from its surroundings, as shown in Fig. 19.1. In the discussion of Section 9.7, it was shown that the microscopic work, dW_μ,

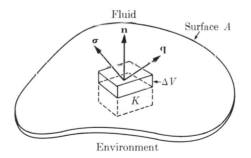

Fluid

Surface A

Environment

Fig 19.1. A section of the surface A separating a fluid (above) from its environment (below). On the fluid side of the surface the volume element ΔV contains those fluid molecules interacting with environment molecules in the cell K; $\mathbf{n}$ is the unit normal to the surface A directed inward toward the fluid; $\boldsymbol{\sigma}$ and $\mathbf{q}$ are the surface stress and heat-flux vector as defined by Eqs. (19.2-5) and (19.2-7), both considered positive when directed inward toward the fluid.

done on the environment external to the fluid was given by Eq. (9.7–1):

$$(dW_\mu)_K = \mathbf{F}_K \cdot d\boldsymbol{\xi}_K + \left\{ \sum_e \sum_j \mathbf{F}_{ej} \cdot (d\mathbf{r}_e - d\boldsymbol{\xi}_K) \right\}_K,$$

in which the subscript K denoted the small cell K of environment molecules acted upon by the average force $\mathbf{F}_K$ and undergoing an average displacement $d\boldsymbol{\xi}_K$. The force $\mathbf{F}_{ej}$ acts between an environment molecule e in the cell K and a system molecule j in the cell ΔV. The short-range forces $\mathbf{F}_{ej}$ act on those environment molecules so close to the surface A that we may consider them to be located on the surface. If we select a volume element ΔV which includes an area ΔA of the surface A, then we may define a surface stress $\boldsymbol{\sigma}$ by

$$\boldsymbol{\sigma} \equiv -\mathbf{F}_K/\Delta A, \tag{19.2–5}$$

which is the average force per unit area of surface exerted on the system molecules by those of the environment. The component of $\boldsymbol{\sigma}$ normal to the surface (whose unit inward normal is $\mathbf{n}$) is called the pressure p:

$$p \equiv \boldsymbol{\sigma} \cdot \mathbf{n}. \tag{19.2–6}$$

The second term on the right-hand side of Eq. (9.7–1) for the microscopic work may be replaced by defining a heat flux vector $\mathbf{q}$:

$$\Delta A (\mathbf{q} \cdot \mathbf{n}) \, dt \equiv - \sum_e \sum_j \mathbf{F}_{ej} \cdot (d\mathbf{r}_e - d\boldsymbol{\xi}_K) \tag{19.2–7}$$

so that $-\mathbf{q} \cdot \mathbf{n}$ is the heat lost by the system to the environment per unit time and area of surface. The vector $\mathbf{q}$ is positive in the thermodynamic sense; that is, $\mathbf{q}$ is positive whenever heat is gained by the molecules in the element ΔV. By combining Eqs. (19.2–5) and (19.2–7) with Eq. (9.7–1), we find

$$\begin{aligned} dW_\mu &= -\{\boldsymbol{\sigma} \cdot d\boldsymbol{\xi} + \mathbf{q} \cdot \mathbf{n} \, dt\} \, \Delta A \\ &= -\{\boldsymbol{\sigma} \cdot \mathbf{v} + \mathbf{q} \cdot \mathbf{n}\} \, \Delta A \, dt, \end{aligned} \tag{19.2–8}$$

in which the terms on the right are the macroscopic work dW and the heat $-dQ$ of Eq. (9.8–1), evaluated over the time interval dt during which the surface displaces an amount $d\boldsymbol{\xi} = \mathbf{v} \, dt$.

The surface A of Fig. 19.1 separates the fluid from its environment. However, the environment need not be a solid surface surrounding the fluid in order for Eq. (19.2–8) to be valid, for the environment could equally well be more fluid. The only requirement is that the surface A should be one across which there is no net flux of fluid particles.

There may also be long-range forces, such as a gravity force, acting on a fluid element, which must be taken into account. Since these will act throughout the volume of the fluid and not only at a surface, we may define a body force per unit mass, **a**, in terms of the body force $\Delta \mathbf{F}$ acting on the volume element ΔV:

$$\mathbf{a} \equiv \frac{1}{\rho} \frac{\Delta \mathbf{F}}{\Delta V}. \tag{19.2–9}$$

19.3   The conservation of mass, momentum, and energy

The mass, momentum, and energy of a system of particles are dynamical quantities which are constant in time if the system is isolated. Since a small volume of fluid is usually not isolated in the thermodynamic sense, we must develop the appropriate statements from dynamics and thermodynamics which describe what changes in the mass, momentum, and energy densities ρ, $\rho \mathbf{v}$, and ρe are possible in a fluid flow. We shall therefore use the field quantities defined in Section 19.2, but shall now consider a macroscopic volume V within which ρ, $\mathbf{v}$, and e are continuous functions of the variables $\mathbf{r}$ and t.

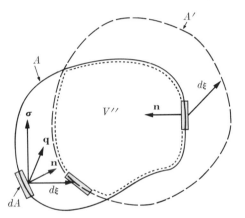

Fig. 19.2. The surface A (solid line), enclosing a volume V at a time t, distorts to a new surface A' (dashed line) which encloses a volume V' at a time dt later. The volume common to both V and V' is V'', enclosed by the dotted line. The displacement of each point on the surface A in the time dt is $d\boldsymbol{\xi} = \mathbf{v} \, dt$.

Consider the volume V, in Fig. 19.2, which is completely enclosed by the surface A at a time t. During a short time interval dt, each fluid element on the surface A undergoes a displacement $d\boldsymbol{\xi} = \mathbf{v} \, dt$ so that the surface now occupies a new position denoted by A' at the time $t' = t + dt$. During this time interval, each of the field quantities ρ, $\mathbf{v}$, and e at a point $\mathbf{r}$ change to the new values ρ', $\mathbf{v}'$, and e' given by

$$\rho' \{\mathbf{r}, t'\} = \rho \{\mathbf{r}, t\} + (\partial \rho / \partial t) \, dt,$$

$$\mathbf{v}' \{\mathbf{r}, t'\} = \mathbf{v} \{\mathbf{r}, t\} + (\partial \mathbf{v} / \partial t) \, dt, \tag{19.3–1}$$

$$e' \{\mathbf{r}, t'\} = e \{\mathbf{r}, t\} + (\partial e / \partial t) \, dt.$$

The *conservation of mass* may be expressed by the statement that the total masses of fluid enclosed by A and A' are equal:

$$\int \rho \, dV = \int \rho' \, dV', \tag{19.3–2}$$

where each integral is evaluated over the volumes V and V' at the times t and t', respectively. Now it is possible to write this statement in a different form if we notice from Fig. 19.2 that there is a volume V'' which is common to both V and V'. Also, the difference between V and V'' is a narrow strip whose volume element is $(\mathbf{n} \cdot d\boldsymbol{\xi}) \, dA$. We therefore write each side of Eq. (19.3–2) as the sum of two terms:

$$\int \rho(\mathbf{n} \cdot d\boldsymbol{\xi}) \, dA + \int \rho \, dV'' = \int \rho'(-\mathbf{n} \cdot d\boldsymbol{\xi}) \, dA + \int \rho' \, dV'', \tag{19.3–3}$$

the first terms on the left- and right-hand sides of this equation being integrated over the portions of the surface A lying outside and inside A', respectively. If we replace $d\boldsymbol{\xi}$ by $\mathbf{v} \, dt$ and $\rho' - \rho$ by $(\partial \rho / \partial t) \, dt$, then Eq. (19.3–3) becomes

$$\int (\partial \rho / \partial t) \, dV = \int \rho \mathbf{v} \cdot \mathbf{n} \, dA \tag{19.3–4}$$

in the limit of dt approaching zero, for which the integral over V'' may be replaced by the integral on V. The quantity $\rho \mathbf{v}$ is called the *mass flux per unit area*, and Eq. (19.3–4) states that its integral over the surface A must equal the rate of accumulation of mass in the volume V enclosed by A.

The *conservation of momentum* may be developed in a similar manner. The increase in momentum of the fluid in V' over that which existed in V must be caused by the surface force $\boldsymbol{\sigma}$ and body forces $\rho \mathbf{a}$ acting during the time interval dt:

$$\int \rho' \mathbf{v}' \, dV' - \int \rho \mathbf{v} \, dV = \left\{ \int \boldsymbol{\sigma} \, dA + \int \rho \mathbf{a} \, dV \right\} dt. \tag{19.3–5}$$

Again, the volume integrals may be decomposed into two parts, and the left-hand side written as

$$\int \rho' \mathbf{v}' \, dV' - \int \rho \mathbf{v} \, dV = -\int \rho \mathbf{v}(\mathbf{n} \cdot d\boldsymbol{\xi}) \, dA + \left(\int \{\partial(\rho \mathbf{v}) / \partial t\} \, dV'' \right) dt. \tag{19.3–6}$$

Again using $d\boldsymbol{\xi} = \mathbf{v} \, dt$, we may combine this with Eq. (19.3–5) to obtain

$$\int \{\partial(\rho \mathbf{v}) / \partial t\} \, dV = \int \{\boldsymbol{\sigma} + \rho \mathbf{v}(\mathbf{v} \cdot \mathbf{n})\} \, dA + \int \rho \mathbf{a} \, dV. \tag{19.3–7}$$

The quantity $\boldsymbol{\sigma} + \rho \mathbf{v}(\mathbf{v} \cdot \mathbf{n})$ is called the *momentum flux* and Eq. (19.3–7) states that the time rate of increase of momentum within the volume V is equal to the sum of the flux of momentum across the surface and the total body force acting on the fluid within the volume.

The equation of *conservation of energy* may be derived by applying the first law of thermodynamics to the fluid enclosed by the surface A. Before doing so, we should recall an elementary theorem of mechanics which states that the kinetic energy of a system of particles of total mass M, whose mass center moves with a velocity $\mathbf{v}_c$, is the sum of $Mv_c^2/2$ and the kinetic energy measured in a coordinate system fixed in the mass center. To prove this, let the velocity of particle i be given by

$$\mathbf{v}_i \doteq \mathbf{v}_c + \mathbf{v}_i', \tag{19.3-8}$$

in which $\mathbf{v}_i'$ is the velocity with respect to the mass center. Squaring Eq. (19.3–8) and multiplying by $m_i/2$, we find

$$m_i v_i^2/2 = m_i v_c^2/2 + m_i \mathbf{v}_c \cdot \mathbf{v}_i' + m_i(v_i')^2/2. \tag{19.3-9}$$

On summing over all the particles i, we find

$$\sum_i (m_i v_i^2/2) = Mv_c^2/2 + \sum_i m_i(v_i')^2/2 \tag{19.3-10}$$

since $\sum m_i \mathbf{v}_i' = 0$ because the total momentum measured with respect to the mass center is zero. Since the potential energy, which depends only on the relative positions of the particles, is the same in either coordinate system, we can conclude that the total energy of a moving system is the sum of its internal energy E as measured in the moving coordinate system plus its kinetic energy $Mv_c^2/2$. Consequently, the energy per unit volume of a moving fluid is $\rho(e + v^2/2)$.*

It is now possible to apply the first law of thermodynamics, Eq. (9.8–2), to the fluid within the surface A by noting that the increase in internal energy must be equal to the sum of the work done on the fluid volume by the surface forces and body forces in a displacement $d\boldsymbol{\xi}$ and the heat added to the volume in the time dt:

$$\int \rho'\{e' + (v')^2/2\}\,dV' - \int \rho\{e + v^2/2\}\,dV$$

$$= \int (\boldsymbol{\sigma} \cdot d\boldsymbol{\xi})\,dA + \int \rho(\mathbf{a} \cdot d\boldsymbol{\xi})\,dV + \left\{\int (\mathbf{q} \cdot \mathbf{n})\,dA\right\}dt. \tag{19.3-11}$$

Again subdividing the volume integrals on the left and dividing by dt, we find

$$\int \left\{\frac{\partial(\rho[e + v^2/2])}{\partial t}\right\}dV$$

$$= \int \left(\left\{\rho\left[e + \frac{v^2}{2}\right]\mathbf{v} + \mathbf{q}\right\} \cdot \mathbf{n} + \boldsymbol{\sigma} \cdot \mathbf{v}\right)dA + \int \rho\mathbf{a} \cdot \mathbf{v}\,dV. \tag{19.3-12}$$

---

* In fluid-flow problems, the thermodynamic properties e, h, etc., should be given in mechanical units (ergs/gm or joules/kgm) to be consistent with p (dynes/cm^2 or newtons/m^2) and v (cm/sec or m/sec).

The factor $\rho[e + v^2/2]\mathbf{v}$ may be called the *energy flux* and its integral over the surface A is one contribution to the rate of growth of energy within the volume V. The remaining terms on the right of Eq. (19.3–12) involving $\mathbf{q}$, $\boldsymbol{\sigma}$, and $\mathbf{a}$ are respectively the heat addition through the surface, work done in deforming the surface, and work done by the body forces throughout the volume.

It is usually convenient in many applications to consider the stress $\boldsymbol{\sigma}$ to be composed of two components: a pressure p normal to the surface, and hence in the direction of $\mathbf{n}$, and a shear stress $\boldsymbol{\tau}$ which is tangent to the surface:

$$\boldsymbol{\sigma} \equiv p\mathbf{n} + \boldsymbol{\tau},$$

where

$$\boldsymbol{\tau} \cdot \mathbf{n} = 0. \tag{19.3–13}$$

It is therefore possible to write

$$\rho e \mathbf{v} \cdot \mathbf{n} + \boldsymbol{\sigma} \cdot \mathbf{v} = (\rho e + p)\mathbf{v} \cdot \mathbf{n} + \boldsymbol{\tau} \cdot \mathbf{v}$$

$$= \rho h \mathbf{v} \cdot \mathbf{n} + \boldsymbol{\tau} \cdot \mathbf{v} \tag{19.3–14}$$

because the enthalpy h is defined as $e + p/\rho$.* On substituting Eq. (19.3–14) into Eq. (19.3–12), we may give the equation of conservation of energy in the form

$$\int \left\{ \frac{\partial(\rho[e + v^2/2])}{\partial t} \right\} dV$$

$$= \int \left(\left\{ \rho \left[h + \frac{v^2}{2} \right] \mathbf{v} + \mathbf{q} \right\} \cdot \mathbf{n} + \boldsymbol{\tau} \cdot \mathbf{v} \right) dA + \int \rho \mathbf{a} \cdot \mathbf{v}\, dV, \tag{19.3–15}$$

and the equation of motion in the form

$$\int \left\{ \frac{\partial(\rho \mathbf{v})}{\partial t} \right\} dV = \int \{ p\mathbf{n} + (\rho \mathbf{v} \cdot \mathbf{n})\mathbf{v} + \boldsymbol{\tau} \}\, dA + \int \rho \mathbf{a}\, dV. \tag{19.3–16}$$

Together with the equation of continuity,

$$\int \left\{ \frac{\partial \rho}{\partial t} \right\} dV = \int \rho \mathbf{v} \cdot \mathbf{n}\, dA, \tag{19.3–17}$$

they summarize the conservation of mass, momentum, and energy for a moving fluid.

In deriving these equations, we considered the motion of a fixed quantity of fluid enclosed within a surface which was displaced during a short time interval.

---

* We are assuming here that the normal component of the stress p is the same as the thermodynamic pressure. Only in exceptional cases, such as the interior of a shock wave, will there be a difference between these two quantities.

In letting the time interval approach zero, we determined the conservation relations in terms of integrals over a volume V or a surface A which bounds V, and these integrals are evaluated at a time t. If we wish, we may consider the surface A fixed in space and then integrate the conservation equations on time, thereby finding the change of mass, momentum, and energy within a fixed volume V, rather than within the moving volume illustrated in Fig. 19.2. The former is usually more convenient, and the fixed surface A is called a *control surface* surrounding the *control volume* V.

A *steady flow* is one in which all the field and surface variables (ρ, $\mathbf{V}$, σ, etc.) do not change with time and therefore depend only on $\mathbf{r}$. In a steady flow, the left-hand sides of the conservation equations (19.3-15) through (19.3-17) become identically zero since the respective integrands are zero. In some instances a flow is steady in one coordinate system but not in another. For example, for the observer seated in an airplane the flow over the wing is steady, but it is unsteady for the observer on the ground. Since the steady-flow description is simpler, it is usually desirable to select a coordinate system in which the flow is steady when analyzing a flow problem, provided such a choice is possible.

As stated above, the three conservation laws are insufficient to enable one to determine a flow field because there are only two scalar equations (continuity and energy) and one vector equation (momentum) in which the unknown scalar quantities ρ, e, and p and the unknown vector quantities $\mathbf{v}$, $\mathbf{q}$, and τ (the last being a two-dimensional vector) appear. It is therefore necessary to supply a scalar equation of state such as $p = p\{\rho, e\}$ and constitutive equations for $\mathbf{q}$ and τ in order to have sufficient information on hand to predict a fluid flow completely. If the fluid is a perfect gas, then the equation of state may be found from the information given in Chapters 11 through 13. Again for a perfect gas, the heat flux $\mathbf{q}$ and shear stress τ are shown in Chapter 20 to be related to e and $\mathbf{v}$. For other fluids more general constitutive relations and equations of state are necessary.

In this chapter we shall not deal with the study of fluid flows in general, which is called *fluid dynamics*. Instead we shall consider special cases for which a flow of simple geometry will be given (by virtue of our experience with such flows) and the consequences of the conservation laws will then be examined. Most of our examples will be selected from fluid-flow problems for which the conservation of energy enters as a crucial factor.

Because we shall study flows for which all the information (such as constitutive relations) is not known, we shall also require that the second law of thermodynamics not be violated by the flow in question. For example, if we hypothesized that the heat flux vector $\mathbf{q}$ was in the direction of increasing temperature, then heat would be flowing from a colder to a hotter region, in violation of the second law of thermodynamics. However, it is quite possible to satisfy mass, momentum, and energy conservation in a flow for which heat flows in the direction of increasing temperature. In order to eliminate the possibility of our considering such impossible flows, we shall derive a nonconservation law for entropy which has the form of the conservation equations previously derived but which is a statement of inequality rather than equality.

We begin by restating the inequality of Clausius, Eq. (10.6–4), in the form:

$$dS \geq dQ/T.$$

If we apply this statement to the fluid within the surface A of Fig. 19.2, we would conclude that its increase in entropy in the time interval dt must equal or exceed the integral of $\{(\mathbf{q} \cdot \mathbf{n})/T\}\, dt$ over the surface A:

$$\int (\rho s)'\, dV' - \int \rho s\, dV \geq \left(\int \left\{ \frac{\mathbf{q} \cdot \mathbf{n}}{T} \right\} dA \right) dt. \qquad (19.3\text{–}18)$$

Expanding the volume integrals as before, we obtain

$$\int \left\{ \frac{\partial (\rho s)}{\partial t} \right\} dV \geq \int \left(\rho s \mathbf{v} + \frac{\mathbf{q}}{T} \right) \cdot \mathbf{n}\, dA. \qquad (19.3\text{–}19)$$

The vector quantity $(\rho s \mathbf{v} + \mathbf{q}/T)$ may be called the entropy flux, and Eq. (19.3–19) states that the rate of increase of entropy within the volume V must equal or exceed the flux of entropy across the surface A. In the case of a steady flow, the left-hand side of Eq. (19.3–19) is zero and the right-hand side is zero or negative. We may therefore state that in a steady flow there is only an efflux of entropy (a net flux of entropy out of a volume) and never an inflow.

In comparison with the equations for conservation of mass, momentum, and energy (Eqs. 19.3–15 through 19.3–17), Eq. (19.3–19) is a statement of non-conservation of entropy, namely, that the increase of entropy in a volume exceeds the flux of entropy across the enclosing surface. This is not to say that the entropy of a fluid element never decreases, but only that the amount of the decrease will be less than the efflux of entropy as defined above. We shall find that the nonconservation of entropy will be useful in limiting the possible flow changes which might otherwise be considered.

19.4 The heating or cooling of fluids in ducts

One of the most common examples of fluid flow involving heating or cooling is the steady flow of a fluid through a duct in which heat is added or extracted from the fluid by virtue of a temperature difference between the fluid and duct wall. Such common processes as the generation of steam in a boiler, the condensation of water vapor in a condenser, or the cooling of water in the radiator of an automobile engine are examples of steady fluid flow with heat exchange. We shall consider what limitations are placed on such flows by the conservation laws previously derived.

Consider the flow shown in Fig. 19.3. A steady flow of fluid in a pipe is subject to a heating process in which heat is added between stations 1 and 2 that form

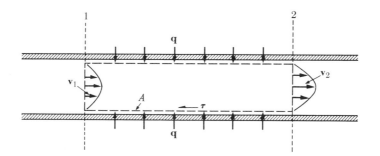

Fig. 19.3. The control surface A (dashed line) for the steady flow through a pipe of a fluid being heated. The shear stress τ acts on the fluid at the surface A in a direction opposite to $\mathbf{v}$.

the end surfaces of the control surface A. Denoting by the subscripts 1 and 2 the flow variables evaluated at these surfaces, the equation of mass conservation (Eq. 19.3–17) for a steady flow is

$$\int (\rho \mathbf{v} \cdot \mathbf{n})_1 \, dA_1 + \int (\rho \mathbf{v} \cdot \mathbf{n})_2 \, dA_2 = 0$$

or

$$\int \rho_1 v_1 \, dA_1 = \int \rho_2 v_2 \, dA_2 \equiv \dot{M}, \tag{19.4-1}$$

in which v_1 and v_2 are the magnitudes of the velocities $\mathbf{v}_1$ and $\mathbf{v}_2$, and $\dot{M}$ is the total mass flux, that is, the mass flow per unit time across the surface A_1 or A_2.

Now let us apply the equation of conservation of energy (Eq. 19.3–15) to the control volume and surface shown in Fig. 19.3. In the absence of body forces ($\mathbf{a} = 0$), the steady-flow energy equation becomes

$$\int (\{\rho[h + v^2/2]\mathbf{v} + \mathbf{q}\} \cdot \mathbf{n} + \boldsymbol{\tau} \cdot \mathbf{v}) \, dA = 0. \tag{19.4-2}$$

Now the shear stress $\boldsymbol{\tau}$ acts tangent to the control surface, so that $\boldsymbol{\tau} \cdot \mathbf{v}$ is zero on A_1 and A_2, which are normal to $\mathbf{v}$. On the tube walls $\boldsymbol{\tau} \cdot \mathbf{v}$ is also zero because $\mathbf{v}$ is zero where the fluid sticks to the wall. Consequently, we may write Eq. (19.4–2) in the form

$$\int \rho_2 v_2 (h_2 + v_2^2/2) \, dA_2 = \int \rho_1 v_1 (h_1 + v_1^2/2) \, dA_1 + \int \mathbf{q} \cdot \mathbf{n} \, dA, \tag{19.4-3}$$

in which the magnitudes of $\mathbf{v}$ have again been used.

For simple calculations it is often advantageous to make use of mass-averaged properties at the surface A_1 or A_2. For example, the mass-averaged enthalpy $\langle h \rangle$ is defined by

$$\langle h \rangle \equiv \frac{\int \rho h \mathbf{v} \cdot \mathbf{n} \, dA}{\int \rho \mathbf{v} \cdot \mathbf{n} \, dA} \tag{19.4-4}$$

and the mean-square velocity by

$$\langle v^2 \rangle \equiv \frac{\int \rho v^2 \mathbf{v} \cdot \mathbf{n}\, dA}{\int \rho \mathbf{v} \cdot \mathbf{n}\, dA}. \tag{19.4–5}$$

If we apply these definitions to Eq. (19.4–3), it becomes

$$\dot{M}\{\langle h_2 \rangle + \langle v_2^2 \rangle/2\} = \dot{M}\{\langle h_1 \rangle + \langle v_1^2 \rangle/2\} + \int \mathbf{q} \cdot \mathbf{n}\, dA. \tag{19.4–6}$$

The last term on the right is the total rate at which heat is being added to the flow, which we denote by $\dot{Q}$:

$$\dot{Q} \equiv \int \mathbf{q} \cdot \mathbf{n}\, dA. \tag{19.4–7}$$

The conservation of energy for the steady flow illustrated in Fig. 19.3 therefore becomes

$$\langle h_2 \rangle + \langle v_2^2 \rangle/2 = \langle h_1 \rangle + \langle v_1^2 \rangle/2 + \dot{Q}/\dot{M}. \tag{19.4–8}$$

The quantity $h + v^2/2$ is called the *stagnation enthalpy* because it equals the enthalpy which the fluid would possess if it were brought to rest ($v = 0$) in an adiabatic flow ($\dot{Q} = 0$). According to Eq. (19.4–8), the stagnation enthalpy will increase if heat is added to a fluid, or will decrease if it is cooled. Whether the increase (or decrease) in stagnation enthalpy consists in a change in $\langle h \rangle$, a change in $\langle v^2 \rangle/2$, or a change in both cannot be determined from energy considerations alone but must involve other aspects of the flow such as the conservation of mass or momentum.

We shall not apply the equation of conservation of momentum to the flow under consideration, for to do so requires some knowledge of the shear stress τ acting on the fluid. Since such a stress acts in a direction opposite to the flow, it must be balanced by a reduction in pressure p or a decrease in momentum ρv in the direction of the flow.

A *heat exchanger* is a device in which two streams of fluid exchange heat; i.e., the hotter one is cooled and the cooler one is heated. If the two fluids are separated by surfaces so that they do not mix (called a *closed heat exchanger*),

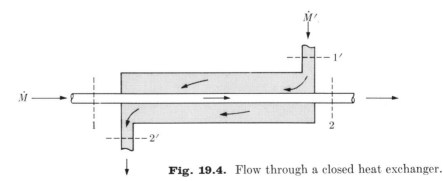

Fig. 19.4. Flow through a closed heat exchanger.

then the energy equation may be applied to each fluid separately. Denoting the inlet and outlet conditions for the two streams by 1 and 2, respectively, and the flow quantities of the second stream by superscript primes as shown in Fig. 19.4, then the energy equation for the second stream corresponding to Eq. (19.4–6) becomes

$$\dot{M}'\{\langle h_2'\rangle + \langle(v_2')^2\rangle/2\} = \dot{M}'\{\langle h_1'\rangle + \langle(v_1')^2\rangle/2\} + \dot{Q}'. \qquad (19.4\text{–}9)$$

Now the rate of heat addition $\dot{Q}$ to the first stream must equal the rate of heat loss $-\dot{Q}'$ from the second stream; that is, $\dot{Q} = -\dot{Q}'$ or $\dot{Q} + \dot{Q}' = 0$. Adding together Eqs. (19.4–9) and (19.4–6), we therefore find

$$\dot{M}\{\langle h_2\rangle + \langle v_2^2\rangle/2\} + \dot{M}'\{\langle h_2'\rangle + \langle(v_2')^2\rangle/2\}$$
$$= \dot{M}\{\langle h_1\rangle + \langle v_1^2\rangle/2\} + \dot{M}'\{\langle h_1'\rangle + \cdot\langle(v_1')^2\rangle/2\}, \qquad (19.4\text{–}10)$$

which states that the product of mass-flow rate $\dot{M}$ and stagnation enthalpy, summed over the entering streams, must equal the same quantity summed over the exiting streams. Of course, we could have arrived at the same conclusion by applying Eq. (19.3–15) directly to a control surface which enclosed the whole heat exchanger.

It is possible to satisfy Eq. (19.4–10) by having the colder fluid become colder and the hot fluid hotter because we have not considered the internal details by which the heat must flow locally from the hotter to the colder fluid. The nature of these processes and the rate at which heat can flow are the subject matter of the field of *heat transfer*, which we shall not consider. However, we do recognize that the nonconservation of entropy described in Eq. (19.3 19) requires that for the heat exchanger as a whole the efflux of entropy must be greater than the inflow because no net heat is added to the exchanger:

$$\dot{M}\langle s_2\rangle + \dot{M}'\langle s_2'\rangle \geq \dot{M}\langle s_1\rangle + \dot{M}'\langle s_1'\rangle. \qquad (19.4\text{–}11)$$

This condition therefore restricts the possible solutions of the energy equation, (19.4–10), to those which do not violate the second law of thermodynamics.

An *open heat exchanger* is one in which the incoming streams mix freely with each other and then emerge as a single stream. For example, if water is sprayed into a dry air stream, it evaporates and cools the air, and the resultant mixture of air and vapor has a lower temperature than either incoming stream. For this process Eq. (19.4–10) may be applied directly, if we evaluate $\langle h_2\rangle$ and $\langle h_2'\rangle$ at the single exit temperature T_2 and use the Gibbs-Dalton laws (Section 13.2) for the enthalpies of the components of the mixture.

19.5 Flow in rotating and reciprocating machines

There is a wide class of machines which operate in a cyclic manner and produce or absorb work while being supplied by a stream (or streams) of fluid. Reciprocating compressors, gasoline or diesel engines, centrifugal pumps and compressors, and turbines are examples of this class of rotating or reciprocating machines. The internal flow in such machines is not steady because at each point it changes with time. However, if the machine operates at a fixed rotational speed, then the internal flow is cyclic; that is, the history of the flow repeats itself in a period which is characteristic of the machine.* We may therefore integrate the conservation equations over one cycle during such constant-speed operation and obtain time-averaged statements of the conservation laws.

Let us illustrate the method of time-averaging by integrating the mass-conservation equation (19.3–17) over the period τ of the machine in question:

$$\int_0^\tau \{\int(\partial\rho/\partial t)\,dV\}\,dt = \int_0^\tau \{\int\rho\mathbf{v}\cdot\mathbf{n}\,dA\}\,dt. \qquad (19.5\text{--}1)$$

Now let us change the order of integration, integrating first on time and then on volume V or surface A:

$$\int \left\{\int_0^\tau (\partial\rho/\partial t)\,dt\right\}\,dV = \int \left\{\int_0^\tau \rho\mathbf{v}\,dt\right\}\cdot\mathbf{n}\,dA. \qquad (19.5\text{--}2)$$

The inner integral on the left may be integrated on time at any point to yield the change in density ρ that occurs in a cyclic time τ, which is necessarily zero everywhere in the volume V. Thus the left-hand side of Eq. (19.5–2) is identically zero. If we denote a time-averaged mass flow at any point by a superscript bar,

$$\overline{\rho\mathbf{v}} \equiv \tau^{-1}\int_0^\tau \rho\mathbf{v}\,dt, \qquad (19.5\text{--}3)$$

then the mass-conservation equation (19.5–2) will have the form

$$\int \overline{\rho\mathbf{v}}\cdot\mathbf{n}\,dA = 0. \qquad (19.5\text{--}4)$$

Applying this to the rotating machine shown in Fig. 19.5, which is supplied with a single stream entering across the surface A_1 and leaving across the surface A_2, we find

$$\int \overline{\rho_1 v_1}\,dA_1 = \int \overline{\rho_2 v_2}\,dA_2 \equiv \overline{\dot{M}}, \qquad (19.5\text{--}5)$$

which is the cyclic-flow analogue of Eq. (19.4–1). The time average of the mass-flow rate $\overline{\dot{M}}$ must be the same at entrance and exit.

In applying the energy conservation equation (19.3–15), we again will integrate over the period τ, causing the left-hand side to integrate to zero and

---

* In a four-cycle gasoline engine, the period covers two revolutions of the drive shaft. In a pump or turbine, the period is the time between passage of successive blades past a point. Thus periods usually range between 1 and 10^{-4} sec.

obtaining, in the absence of body forces ($\mathbf{a} = 0$),

$$\int_0^\tau \int \{(\rho\{h + v^2/2\}\mathbf{v} + \mathbf{q}) \cdot \mathbf{n} + \boldsymbol{\tau} \cdot \mathbf{v}\} \, dA \, dt = 0. \qquad (19.5\text{--}6)$$

Now let us choose the surface A to be the exterior surface of the rotating machine, including the surfaces A_1 and A_2, across which fluid enters and leaves, and the surface A_w, which is a cross section of the rotating shaft.* Recognizing that $\boldsymbol{\tau} \cdot \mathbf{v}$ is zero everywhere on A except on A_w, for which the torsional shear stress acting on the shaft is in the direction of the tangential velocity $\mathbf{v}$, we find that Eq. (19.5–6) becomes

$$\int \overline{\rho_1(h_1 + v_1^2/2)v_1} \, dA_1 - \int \overline{\rho_2(h_2 + v_2^2/2)v_2} \, dA_2$$
$$+ \int \overline{\mathbf{q} \cdot \mathbf{n}} \, dA + \int \overline{\boldsymbol{\tau} \cdot \mathbf{v}} \, dA_w = 0. \qquad (19.5\text{--}7)$$

Denoting the time-averaged rates of heat addition and work done by the system by $\bar{\dot{Q}}$ and $\bar{\dot{W}}$, respectively,

$$\bar{\dot{Q}} \equiv \int \overline{\mathbf{q} \cdot \mathbf{n}} \, dA, \qquad \bar{\dot{W}} \equiv - \int \overline{\boldsymbol{\tau} \cdot \mathbf{v}} \, dA_w, \qquad (19.5\text{--}8)$$

we may write the energy equation (19.5–7) in terms of combined mass- and time-averaged quantities:

$$\langle \bar{h}_2 \rangle + \overline{\langle v_2^2 \rangle}/2 = \langle \bar{h}_1 \rangle + \overline{\langle v_1^2 \rangle}/2 + (\bar{\dot{Q}} - \bar{\dot{W}})/\bar{\dot{M}}. \qquad (19.5\text{--}9)$$

Many high-speed rotating machines, e.g. turbines and compressors, have such small heat losses that they may be considered to be adiabatic, that is, $\mathbf{q} = 0$. If we apply the statement of nonconservation of entropy, Eq. (19.3–19), to an

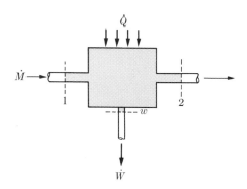

Fig. 19.5. A "black-box" control volume (shaded area) for a rotating machine.

---

* While the derivations given in Section 19.3 assumed that a single fluid was enclosed by the surface A, it can be seen that they apply equally well to a combination of fluid and solid in the volume V.

adiabatic rotating machine, we would find that

$$\langle \bar{s}_2 \rangle \geq \langle \bar{s}_1 \rangle \qquad \text{if} \quad \mathbf{q} = 0, \qquad (19.5\text{--}10)^*$$

since the entropy flux leaving the machine must equal or exceed that entering, $\mathbf{q}$ being zero everywhere. If we plot in the hs-plane the entering and leaving states 1 and 2 for a gas turbine as shown in Fig. 19.6, we would find point 2 lying lower and to the right of point 1. For a given pressure change from p_1 to p_2, Eq. (19.5–10) states that the minimum enthalpy h leaving the turbine would be that corresponding to point 3 in Fig. 19.6, where $s_3 = s_1$. State 3 would be the exit state for an adiabatic reversible turbine because its internal flow would thereby be isentropic. Since a reversible turbine would be a better machine than an irreversible one, we may define a figure of merit, called the *adiabatic turbine efficiency* η_a, by

$$\eta_a \equiv \frac{\langle \bar{h}_1 \rangle - \langle \bar{h}_2 \rangle}{\langle \bar{h}_1 \rangle - h_3}, \qquad (19.5\text{--}11)$$

which is less than unity but whose closeness to unity measures the approach

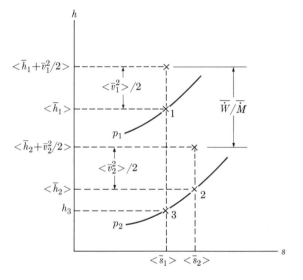

Fig. 19.6. The states (1) entering and (2) leaving an adiabatic turbine plotted in the hs-plane of the working fluid. The stagnation enthalpy $\langle h + v^2/2 \rangle$ at entrance and exit is also shown. The constant-pressure lines (solid curves) are drawn for the entering and leaving pressures p_1 and p_2.

---

* Note that it is not sufficient that $\overline{Q} = 0$ in order for this to be true. For example, we might add heat during the high-temperature part of the cycle and remove an equal amount of heat during a low-temperature portion, thereby making $\langle \bar{s}_2 \rangle < \langle \bar{s}_1 \rangle$ and $\overline{Q} = 0$.

to the ideal reversible machine. It should be emphasized that η_a is not a thermo-dynamic efficiency, which is the ratio of work to heat in a heat-engine cycle, but is a measure of performance of a component of a heat engine. The over-all thermal efficiency of a steam-turbine cycle will of course be influenced by the adiabatic turbine efficiency but not necessarily in exact proportion to it. In a similar manner one may define an adiabatic efficiency for a compressor.

For the reversible Rankine cycle discussed in Section 18.6, the corresponding steady-flow steam cycle is shown schematically in Fig. 18.6. We may calculate the thermodynamic efficiency of this cycle by applying our steady-flow energy equations to the boiler and condenser in order to calculate the net work done and the heat added. For the boiler, from Eq. (19.4–8), omitting average signs, we have

$$h_c + \frac{v_c^2}{2} = h_b + \frac{v_b^2}{2} + \frac{\dot{Q}_1}{\dot{M}}, \qquad (19.5\text{–}12)$$

where subscripts b and c denote the states entering and leaving the boiler and $\dot{Q}_1$ is the rate of heat addition. For the condenser, we have a similar energy equation,

$$h_a + \frac{v_a^2}{2} = h_d + \frac{v_d^2}{2} + \frac{\dot{Q}_2}{\dot{M}}, \qquad (19.5\text{–}13)$$

in which $-\dot{Q}_2$ is the rate of heat removal from the condenser. If the turbine and compressor are adiabatic, $\dot{Q}_1$ and $\dot{Q}_2$ are the only heats involved, and the thermodynamic efficiency defined by Eq. (18.3–12) becomes

$$\eta_t = 1 + \frac{\dot{Q}_2}{\dot{Q}_1} = 1 - \frac{h_d + v_d^2/2 - (h_a + v_a^2/2)}{h_c + v_c^2/2 - (h_b + v_b^2/2)} \qquad (19.5\text{–}14)$$

by use of Eqs. (19.5–12) and (19.5–13). If all the velocities are equal or are very small, then this efficiency is exactly the same as that given in Eq. (18.6–4) for the Rankine cycle as derived by assuming internally reversible processes. Nevertheless, Eq. (19.5–14) applies to a steady-flow Rankine cycle in which the processes are not necessarily reversible but for which the turbine and compressor are adiabatic, for these were the only assumptions involved in arriving at the expression for the efficiency.

In Fig. 19.6 are also plotted the stagnation enthalpies, $h + v^2/2$, for the entrance and exit conditions of an adiabatic turbine. From the energy equation (19.5–8), the work done by the turbine per unit mass of steam which flows through it is

$$\dot{W}/\dot{M} = h_1 + v_1^2/2 - (h_2 + v_2^2/2), \qquad (19.5\text{–}15)$$

which is the change in stagnation enthalpy across the turbine. This work may be determined graphically from Fig. 19.6 in the manner shown.

Because the hs-plane is so convenient for graphically representing processes involving steady flow, it is common to plot in the hs-plane the characteristics of the fluid being used, like the lines of constant T, p, and ρ as well as saturation curves for liquid-vapor equilibrium. Such a graphical representation of the thermodynamic properties is called a *Mollier diagram* and can be conveniently used in place of tabulated data for many engineering calculations.*

19.6 Steady flow of an ideal fluid

Many fluid flows occur under conditions for which the shear stress τ and the heat flux $\mathbf{q}$ are so small that they have little effect on the flow. An *ideal fluid* is one for which τ and $\mathbf{q}$ are identically zero, a condition that is not exactly satisfied by any real fluid but is approached very closely by many fluids under certain flow situations. We shall not here examine the physical conditions for which a flow of a real fluid may be approximated by the flow of an ideal fluid, a topic which is primarily the province of fluid mechanics, but shall only examine the thermodynamic consequences of assuming that $\tau = 0$ and $\mathbf{q} = 0$ in a steady flow.†

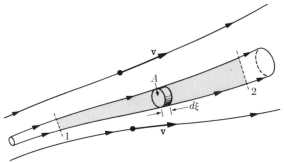

Fig. 19.7. The control volume (shaded area) enclosed by a stream tube has a cross-sectional area A and an incremental length $d\xi$ in the direction of $\mathbf{v}$.

In a steady flow, the trajectory of a fluid element, called a *streamline*, is a curve in space to which $\mathbf{v}$ is tangent everywhere. We shall determine the change in the thermodynamic variables between two points 1 and 2 which lie along the same streamline by applying the conservation laws to a control volume V enclosing a bundle of nearby streamlines, as shown in Fig. 19.7. The lateral surface of this volume, called a *stream tube*, is threaded with streamlines while the ends consist of two surfaces of areas A_1 and A_2 which are normal to the streamlines. On the lateral surface $\mathbf{v} \cdot \mathbf{n} = 0$, while on the end surfaces $|\mathbf{v} \cdot \mathbf{n}| = v$.

---

* A Mollier diagram for water, as well as tabulations of its thermodynamic properties, is given by Keenan and Keyes.

† The principal criterion for representing a real fluid by an ideal fluid is that the real fluid *Reynolds number* should be large. Even when this is so, the flow near a boundary surface or in a shock wave is far from ideal and must be treated separately.

If we apply the conservation-of-mass equation (19.3–17) to this steady flow, we find

$$\int \rho_1 v_1 \, dA_1 = \int \rho_2 v_2 \, dA_2$$

or

$$\rho_1 v_1 A_1 = \rho_2 v_2 A_2 \tag{19.6–1}$$

if we choose the areas A_1 and A_2 to be sufficiently small that ρ and $\mathbf{v}$ do not vary appreciably over the surfaces. Because of the way we have chosen the control surface, the inflow across A_1 must equal the outflow across A_2, there being no flow across the lateral surface which contains streamlines.

Now let us apply the equation of energy conservation, Eq. (19.3–15), to this steady flow of an ideal fluid for which $\tau = 0$ and $\mathbf{q} = 0$:

$$0 = \int \rho_1(h_1 + v_1^2/2)v_1 \, dA_1 - \int \rho_2(h_2 + v_2^2/2)v_2 \, dA_2 + \int \rho \mathbf{a} \cdot \mathbf{v} \, dV$$

or

$$\rho_1 v_1 A_1 \{h_1 + v_1^2/2\} = \rho_2 v_2 A_2 \{h_2 + v_2^2/2\} - \int \rho \mathbf{a} \cdot \mathbf{v} \, dV, \tag{19.6–2}$$

in which we again assume A_1 and A_2 are very small and in which we have retained the body force $\mathbf{a}$.

If the body force per unit mass $\mathbf{a}$ is a potential force such as gravity, then the work done in displacing a unit mass in this force field through a small displacement $d\boldsymbol{\xi}$ is the decrement in scalar potential ϕ per unit mass:

$$d\phi \equiv -\mathbf{a} \cdot d\boldsymbol{\xi}, \tag{19.6–3}$$

which is the differential form of Eq. (2.5–1) for the change of potential energy. To evaluate the integral on the right-hand side of Eq. (19.6–2), let us first replace $\mathbf{a} \cdot \mathbf{v}$ with $\mathbf{a} \cdot (d\boldsymbol{\xi}/dt)$, where $d\boldsymbol{\xi}$ is the increment in displacement of a fluid particle in the time dt. Next we shall replace the volume element dV with $A \, d\xi$, where A is the local cross section of the control volume and $d\xi$ is the increment in distance along the axis of this volume, as shown in Fig. 19.7. Making these substitutions, we find

$$\int \rho \mathbf{a} \cdot \mathbf{v} \, dV = \int_1^2 \rho \mathbf{a} \cdot \left(\frac{d\boldsymbol{\xi}}{dt}\right) A \, d\xi$$

$$= \int_1^2 \rho A \left(\frac{d\xi}{dt}\right) \mathbf{a} \cdot d\boldsymbol{\xi} = -\int_1^2 \rho A v \, d\phi, \tag{19.6–4}$$

in which Eq. (19.6–3) has been used. But the equation of mass conservation (19.6–1) shows that $\rho v A$ has the same constant value for any cross section along the stream tube, so that Eq. (19.6–4) may be written as

$$\int \rho \mathbf{a} \cdot \mathbf{v} \, dV = \rho_1 v_1 A_1 (\phi_1 - \phi_2). \tag{19.6–5}$$

By combining this with Eqs. (19.6–1) and (19.6–2), we obtain the energy equation for steady flow of an ideal fluid in a potential force field:

$$h_1 + v_1^2/2 + \phi_1 = h_2 + v_2^2/2 + \phi_2. \tag{19.6–6}$$

In a uniform gravitational field, such as that near the surface of the earth, the gravitational potential ϕ obtained from integrating Eq. (19.6–3) is

$$\phi = gz, \tag{19.6–7}$$

where g is the local acceleration due to gravity and z is the vertical distance above an arbitrary reference plane.

The equation for nonconservation of entropy, (19.3–19), may also be applied to the stream tube of Fig. 19.7. Since $\mathbf{q} = 0$ and the flow is steady, this statement reduces to

$$\int \rho_2 s_2 v_2 \, dA_2 - \int \rho_1 s_1 v_1 \, dA_1 \geq 0$$

or

$$(\rho_2 v_2 A_2)s_2 - (\rho_1 v_1 A_1)s_1 \geq 0. \tag{19.6–8}$$

By combining this with the conservation-of-mass equation, (19.6–1), we can conclude that the entropy cannot decrease in the flow direction along a streamline:

$$s_2 \geq s_1. \tag{19.6–9}$$

Now the flow of an ideal fluid is adiabatic since $\mathbf{q} = 0$; if it is also reversible, then it is isentropic along a streamline ($s_2 = s_1$). Whether or not the flow is reversible cannot be determined from considerations of mass and energy conservation alone but can be deduced only from a closer inspection of the detailed processes occurring in the fluid.

Let us apply the momentum conservation equation, (19.3–16), for an ideal fluid ($\tau = 0$) to a small volume $dV = A \, d\xi$, as shown in Fig. 19.7. If we denote the increase in the values of p, ρ, v, and A in the downstream direction by dp, $d\rho$, dv, and dA, respectively, then the conservation of momentum in the direction of flow requires that

$$(p + \rho v^2)A + p \, dA - \{(p + dp) + (\rho + d\rho)(v + dv)^2\}$$
$$\times (A + dA) + \rho \mathbf{a} \cdot (A \, d\xi) = 0, \tag{19.6–10}$$

in which $d\xi$ is the thickness of the volume element $A \, d\xi$ in the direction of motion. If we retain in Eq. (19.6–10) only those terms which are of first order in the differentials, we find that

$$\rho v^2 \, dA + A \, dp + Av^2 \, d\rho + 2\rho Av \, dv - \rho A\mathbf{a} \cdot d\xi = 0$$

or

$$A \{dp + \rho v \, dv + \rho \, d\phi\} = -v \, d\{\rho Av\}. \tag{19.6–11}$$

But the right-hand side is zero by virtue of mass conservation, so that the conservation of momentum requires the differential condition along a streamline:

$$(1/\rho) \, dp + d(v^2/2 + \phi) = 0. \qquad (19.6\text{--}12)$$

As it stands, this relationship between the changes in pressure and kinetic plus potential energy $v^2/2 + \phi$ cannot be integrated unless ρ is a constant or a function of p. Furthermore, Eq. (19.6–12) is a scalar equation of motion in the direction of flow and not a complete statement of the conservation of momentum, which requires one vector equation or three scalar equations. Nevertheless, we can draw an important conclusion from Eq. (19.6–12) by first writing the equivalent differential form of the energy equation (19.6–6):

$$d\{h + v^2/2 + \phi\} = 0. \qquad (19.6\text{--}13)$$

On subtracting Eq. (19.6–12) from the above, we find

$$dh - (1/\rho) \, dp = 0. \qquad (19.6\text{--}14)$$

According to Eq. (10.4–19), the left-hand side of this equation is equal to $T \, ds$ whenever the fluid remains at equilibrium with respect to variation of chemical composition, if any. For an ideal fluid at local thermodynamic equilibrium, we conclude that the entropy is constant along a streamline.* Consequently, we must use the equality of Eq. (19.6–9) rather than the inequality.

For an ideal fluid, the integral of the equation for conservation of momentum in the stream direction, Eq. (19.6–12), is identical to the integral form of the equation for conservation of energy, Eq. (19.6–6), because the entropy is constant along a streamline. In studying such ideal flows, we may therefore replace one or the other of these scalar conservation equations by the requirement that the entropy be constant along a streamline, a statement which may be more convenient to use than the one omitted. We shall use this approach in Section 19.7 when discussing flow in a nozzle.

An *ideal incompressible fluid* is one for which the density ρ does not vary along a streamline. For such an ideal fluid we may integrate Eq. (19.6–12) along a streamline to obtain *Bernoulli's equation:*

$$p_2/\rho + v_2^2/2 + \phi_2 = p_1/\rho + v_1^2/2 + \phi_1 \qquad \text{if} \quad \rho = \text{const.} \qquad (19.6\text{--}15)$$

It is important to notice that Bernoulli's equation follows directly from the conservation of momentum in the stream direction for a fluid having $\tau = 0$

---

* In Section 19.9 we shall consider the flow of an ideal fluid in which a chemical reaction occurs. For this flow the entropy may increase since the flow is not everywhere in thermodynamic equilibrium. In Section 19.8 we treat the case of a shock wave, for which the increase in entropy is partially the result of $\mathbf{q}$ and τ being nonzero in the shock front; i.e., the flow is not everywhere that of an ideal fluid.

and ρ equal to a constant along a streamline. The thermodynamic properties of the fluid do not affect the motion because the volume of a unit mass of substance cannot change, according to our hypothesis of an ideal incompressible substance, and there is thereby no mechanism for the internal energy of a fluid element to be transformed into kinetic energy, or vice versa. For this reason incompressible fluid flows may be studied independently of the thermodynamic properties of the fluid.

Like the ideal fluid, the ideal incompressible fluid is only a model which approximately describes the properties of real fluids in certain kinds of flows. The density of every fluid can be changed if it is subject to a high enough pressure, although it requires a much greater pressure increase to decrease the volume of water by 10% than to compress air by the same amount. For a fluid flow to be considered incompressible, we should therefore require that the fractional change in density along a streamline should be very small. According to Eq. (19.6–15), the order of magnitude of the changes in pressure in a flow might be about ρv^2, where v is a typical velocity in the flow. Since the rate of increase of density with pressure along a streamline is $(\partial\rho/\partial p)_s$, the condition that the fractional change in density is small is

$$(1/\rho)(\partial\rho/\partial p)_s(\rho v^2) \ll 1$$

or

$$v^2 \ll (\partial p/\partial \rho)_s. \tag{19.6–16}$$

The speed of sound in a fluid is $\{(\partial p/\partial\rho)_s\}^{1/2}$, so that the condition for considering a flow to be incompressible is that the flow velocity be small compared with the sound speed. Thus the low-speed flow of a gas, which we intuitively consider a compressible fluid, may be as close to an ideal incompressible flow as the flow of liquid water.

Our discussion of the steady flow of an ideal fluid was limited to the changes occurring along a streamline. The differences in fluid properties between nearby streamlines cannot be determined so easily because they depend on the two- or three-dimensional nature of the flow. Furthermore, we have not shown how the complete fluid-flow field is determined but have only derived statements relating the possible changes in flow variables which are consonant with the conservation laws. In some simple flow configurations these statements may suffice to determine the gross features of the flow, but for general flows we must have resort to the discipline of fluid dynamics in order to understand the phenomena in detail.

19.7 Flow in a convergent-divergent nozzle

One of the important inventions of the nineteenth century was the convergent-divergent nozzle developed by the Swedish engineer, De Laval, for use in steam turbines. Its importance stemmed from the fact that the peculiar shape of the nozzle was essential to the proper acceleration of the steam to a high velocity whenever a large pressure reduction was impressed across the nozzle. Although De Laval was more interested in high-speed rotating machines (such as cream separators) rather than interplanetary flight, he would undoubtedly have been pleased to observe that the nozzle of a rocket engine is not substantially different from those he invented for use with steam. De Laval nozzles are also used in supersonic wind tunnels and other devices which produce a steady supersonic flow of a gas.

The general shape of a De Laval nozzle is shown in Fig. 19.8. At the upstream end the duct decreases in cross-sectional area, reaches a point of minimum area called the throat, and then increases in area in the downstream direction. The nozzle may have a circular or a rectangular cross section. If the pressure decreases monotonically in the direction of flow, the velocity will increase as sketched in Fig. 19.8 because the flow will be accelerated.

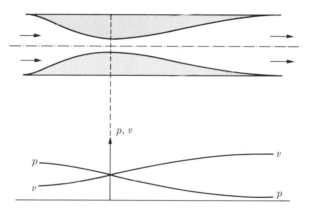

Fig. 19.8. A cross section of the convergent-divergent De Laval nozzle, and the distribution of pressure and axial velocity as a function of axial distance along the nozzle.

We will treat the flow in a De Laval nozzle as that of an ideal fluid in which the flow quantities ρ, v, p, etc., are uniform over a cross section of area A normal to the nozzle axis. The nozzle walls are streamlines, and each stream tube is supposed to undergo an identical change of area and other flow variables with axial distance. A flow of this type is called a quasi one-dimensional flow since all the variables approximately depend only on one dimension, i.e. axial distance. It is not truly one-dimensional because, for example, the flow velocities $\mathbf{v}$ at opposite sides of the channel are not exactly parallel but only approximately so. For more exact descriptions of the flow one must consider in greater detail these two-dimensional effects.

If we denote the conditions at the throat by a subscript t, then the conservation of mass and energy, Eqs. (19.6–1) and (19.6–6), and the condition of constant entropy, require that

$$\rho v A = \rho_t v_t A_t, \tag{19.7-1}$$

$$h + v^2/2 = h_t + v_t^2/2, \tag{19.7-2}$$

$$s = s_t. \tag{19.7-3}$$

If the quantities on the right-hand side of these equations are specified, then for any given A the values of ρ, v, and h may be obtained from these three equations, provided that the entropy s is a known function of ρ and h. (For example, on a Mollier chart we can locate the isentrope s_t and then determine ρ as a function of h for points along this isentrope.)

It is usually convenient to relate the thermodynamic variables to the *stagnation state*, denoted by the subscript s, which is defined as the state corresponding to $v = 0$. If the flow through the nozzle were supplied from a large tank of compressed gas, then the stagnation state would be the same as that of this reservoir. We may therefore write the energy equation, (19.7–2), in the alternative form

$$h + v^2/2 = h_s$$

or

$$v = \{2(h_s - h)\}^{1/2}. \tag{19.7-4}$$

The flow velocity v_t at the throat may be determined from these equations by first noting that small changes in v, ρ, and A must be related by the differential of the continuity equation (19.7–1),

$$\rho v \, dA + \rho A \, dv + A v \, d\rho = 0. \tag{19.7-5}$$

At the throat, $dA = 0$ because the nozzle cross-sectional area A is a minimum. Consequently the change in v and ρ is found by setting $dA = 0$, $v = v_t$ and $\rho = \rho_t$ in Eq. (19.7–5):

$$\rho_t \, dv = -v_t \, d\rho. \tag{19.7-6}$$

The equivalent differential of the energy equation (19.7–2), evaluated at the throat, is

$$dh + v_t \, dv = 0. \tag{19.7-7}$$

Eliminating dv between Eqs. (19.7–6) and (19.7–7), we find

$$v_t^2 = \rho_t(\partial h/\partial \rho)_s, \tag{19.7-8}$$

in which the ratio $dh/d\rho$ is evaluated at the throat conditions for an isentropic change in h and ρ, as required by Eq. (19.7–3). For an isentropic change, Eq. (10.4–19) requires that $(\partial h/\partial p)_s = 1/\rho$, so that the throat velocity v_t may also be expressed as

$$v_t^2 = \rho_t(\partial h/\partial p)_s(\partial p/\partial \rho)_s = (\partial p/\partial \rho)_s. \tag{19.7-9}$$

We shall subsequently see in Section 19.8 that $\{(\partial p/\partial \rho)_s\}^{1/2}$ is the speed of sound in a fluid, that is, the speed of propagation of a plane wave of small amplitude. Equation (19.7–9) therefore states that the flow velocity at the throat of a De Laval nozzle is equal to the speed of sound at that point. This flow is called *sonic* flow, while the terms *subsonic* and *supersonic* are used to denote flows for which v^2 is respectively less than or greater than the value of $(\partial p/\partial \rho)_s$ evaluated at the local flow conditions. We shall use the symbol a for the speed of sound,

$$a \equiv \{(\partial p/\partial \rho)_s\}^{1/2}, \tag{19.7–10}$$

which signifies that a is a thermodynamic property of a fluid since it is a derivative of thermodynamic properties, just as are the specific heats. The ratio M of the flow speed v to the local speed of sound a is called the *Mach number*,

$$M \equiv v/a, \tag{19.7–11}$$

and is therefore a function of both the flow field and the thermodynamic state.

To illustrate more clearly the nature of this nozzle flow, let us consider the fluid to be a perfect gas with constant specific heats. According to Eq. (13.4–8), the enthalpy h in Eq. (19.7–2) or (19.7–4) may be replaced by $c_p T$ and the condition of constant entropy by Eq. (13.4–13), resulting in

$$c_p T + v^2/2 = c_p T_t + v_t^2/2 = c_p T_s, \tag{19.7–12}$$

$$T\rho^{1-\gamma} = T_t \rho_t^{1-\gamma} = T_s \rho_s^{1-\gamma}, \tag{19.7–13}$$

since ρ varies inversely with the volume. The local speed of sound, defined by Eq. (19.7–10), may be found from the differential of the isentropic process described by Eq. (13.4–9):

$$c_v \, d\ln p - c_p \, d\ln \rho = 0 \quad \text{or} \quad (\partial p/\partial \rho)_s = \gamma p/\rho \tag{19.7–14}$$

so that

$$a^2 = \gamma p/\rho = \gamma \Re T = (\gamma - 1)c_p T, \tag{19.7–15}$$

in which the alternative forms derive from the perfect-gas law, $p = \rho \Re T$, and Eq. (13.4–12).

The relation between the stagnation state and that at the throat may be found from the energy equation (19.7–12) by setting v_t equal to a_t:

$$a_t^2/2 + c_p T_t = c_p T_s. \tag{19.7–16}$$

On substituting Eqs. (19.7–13) and (19.7–15) into this equation, we find

$$T_t/T_s = 2/(\gamma + 1), \qquad \rho_t/\rho_s = \{2/(\gamma + 1)\}^{1/(\gamma-1)},$$

$$p_t/p_s = \rho_t T_t/\rho_s T_s = \{2/(\gamma + 1)\}^{\gamma/(\gamma-1)},$$

$$v_t/a_s = a_t/a_s = \{T_t/T_s\}^{1/2} = \{2/(\gamma + 1)\}^{1/2}. \tag{19.7–17}$$

At other points in the flow, the thermodynamic variables p, ρ, and a and the flow speed v may now be found from Eqs. (19.7–12), (19.7–13), and (19.7–17) in terms of the temperature ratio T/T_s:

$$\frac{p}{p_s} = \left(\frac{T}{T_s}\right)^{\gamma/(\gamma-1)},$$

$$\frac{\rho}{\rho_s} = \left(\frac{T}{T_s}\right)^{1/(\gamma-1)},$$

$$\frac{a}{a_s} = \left(\frac{T}{T_s}\right)^{1/2},$$

$$\frac{v}{a_s} = \left\{\frac{2(1 - T/T_s)}{\gamma - 1}\right\}^{1/2},$$

$$M = \frac{v}{a} = \left\{\frac{2(T_s/T - 1)}{\gamma - 1}\right\}^{1/2}. \qquad (19.7\text{–}18)$$

The variation of these quantities is shown in Fig. 19.9 for the flow of a monatomic gas ($\gamma = \frac{5}{3}$). The throat conditions are those determined from Eq. (19.7–17). For very low temperature, the flow speed approaches the asymptotic value of $\{2/(\gamma - 1)\}^{1/2}a_s$, which equals $(2c_pT_s)^{1/2}$.

The corresponding area change may be determined by substituting Eqs. (19.7–17) and (19.7–18) into Eq. (19.7–1):

$$\frac{A_t}{A} = \frac{\rho}{\rho_t}\frac{v}{v_t} = \frac{\rho}{\rho_s}\frac{\rho_s}{\rho_t}\frac{v}{a_s}\frac{a_s}{v_t}$$

$$= \{(\gamma + 1)/2\}^{(\gamma+1)/2(\gamma-1)}\{2(1 - T/T_s)(T/T_s)^{2/(\gamma-1)}/(\gamma - 1)\}^{1/2},$$

$$(19.7\text{–}19)$$

which is also plotted in Fig. (19.9). It can be seen that A reaches a minimum at the throat (since A_t/A has a maximum there) and that a large increase in area downstream of the throat will accelerate the flow to a speed very close to its asymptotic value of $(2c_pT_s)^{1/2}$. For this reason not much of an increase in rocket thrust can be gained by increasing the ratio of exit area to throat area beyond about 20:1.

The change in flow variables for fluids other than a perfect gas with constant specific heats must be computed numerically from the available thermodynamic data and Eqs. (19.7–1) through (19.7–3) and (19.7–10). However, the variations with temperature will be similar to those shown in Fig. 19.9.

The nozzle flow we have described above is one for which the flow speed always increases in the direction of flow. Upstream of the throat the flow is subsonic ($v < a$) while downstream it is supersonic ($v > a$), as can be seen from Fig. 19.9. It is also possible for the flow in the same shape nozzle to be entirely subsonic, but in that case the flow speed in the diverging portion down-

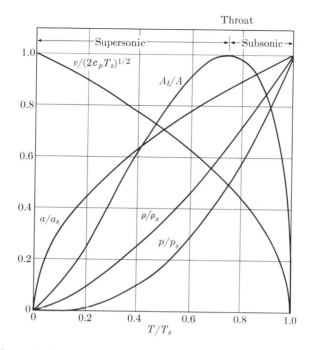

Fig. 19.9. The variation of p, ρ, a, v, and A with temperature in an isentropic quasi one-dimensional flow for a perfect monatomic gas ($\gamma = 5/3$). The area A is a minimum at $T/T_s = 0.75$. Compared with a, the scale for v is smaller by the ratio $(2c_pT_s)^{1/2}/a_s = \{2/(\gamma - 1)\}^{1/2} = 3^{1/2}$, so that $v = a$ at the throat.

stream of the throat will decrease in the flow direction, in contrast to the increase encountered in the De Laval nozzle.* In an entirely subsonic flow, the flow is accelerated upstream of the throat and decelerates downstream of the throat. The relation between the flow conditions at the throat and the stagnation conditions for a perfect gas with constant specific heats will not be that of Eq. (19.7–17) but will instead be determined by the mass flow of fluid through the nozzle.

In the De Laval nozzle, the mass flow for a perfect gas with constant specific heats is found by using Eq. (19.7–17):

$$\rho_t v_t A_t = \{2/(\gamma + 1)\}^{(\gamma+1)/2(\gamma-1)} \rho_s a_s A_t. \qquad (19.7\text{–}20)$$

---

* We have eliminated the possibility of such a flow in our previous treatment by insisting in Eq. (19.7–5) that $d\rho$ and dv are nonzero at the throat, that is, that the density and velocity continue to change with axial distance. The entirely subsonic flows arise from setting $d\rho = 0$ and $dv = 0$ in Eq. (19.7–5) evaluated at the throat ($dA = 0$), with the result that ρ and v reach a minimum and maximum, respectively, at the throat. For an incompressible fluid ($d\rho = 0$ everywhere), only flows of this latter type may occur, for then $dv = 0$ necessarily at the throat.

For given stagnation state density ρ_s and sound speed a_s, no greater mass flow can ever be passed through a channel of minimum area A_t than that given by Eq. (19.7–20), for every other flow condition arising from the same stagnation state requires a larger flow area to pass this maximum mass flow, as shown in Fig. 19.9. However, a lesser mass flow than that given by Eq. (19.7–20) is possible and gives rise to the entirely subsonic flows which we have been discussing. If the mass flow $\dot{M}$ and throat area A_t are specified, then the throat temperature T_t' for this subsonic flow may be found from Eq. (19.7–18) as follows:

$$\frac{\dot{M}}{A_t} = \rho_t' v_t' = \left\{ \frac{2(1 - T_t'/T_s)(T_t'/T_s)^{2/(\gamma-1)}}{(\gamma - 1)} \right\}^{1/2} \rho_s a_s, \qquad (19.7\text{–}21)$$

which may be solved numerically for T_t'/T_s, provided $T_t'/T_s \geq 2/(\gamma + 1)$.

19.8 Shock waves

When a body moves through a fluid at a speed which exceeds the speed of sound, it produces wave fronts in which the pressure, density, and temperature change very abruptly in a distance that is exceedingly small, being about a mean-free path. These wave fronts are called *shock waves* and can be thought of as

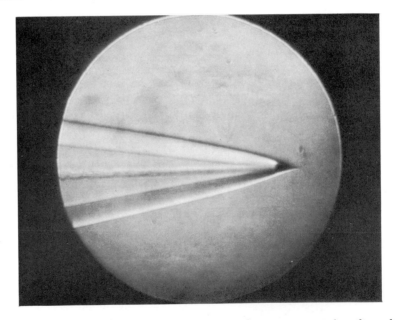

Fig. 19.10. A schlieren spark photograph of a 25-degree cone moving through air at a Mach number of 5.8. The cone was fired from a high-velocity gun and is moving to the right. The outermost disturbance is a shock wave, whose thickness is much smaller than would appear from the photographic image. (Courtesy R. Slattery, Lincoln Laboratory, M.I.T.)

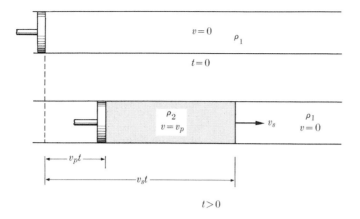

Fig. 19.11. A shock wave generated in a shock tube by the movement of a piston at constant velocity v_p into an initially stationary gas. The fluid moving at the piston speed v_p at a time t is shown by the shaded region.

surfaces in the macroscopic flow field across which there is a discontinuous change in the thermodynamic variables and the flow velocity. For an observer moving with the body at a constant velocity through the fluid, the oncoming flow is a steady supersonic flow and the shock wave is a surface fixed in space with respect to the body. For supersonic bodies, these shock-wave surfaces are generally curved and have tangent planes oblique to the oncoming flow (see Fig. 19.10).

Another method of producing a moving shock wave is to push a piston at a constant speed into a tube initially filled with stationary gas. As shown in Fig. 19.11, the moving piston is preceded down the tube, called a shock tube, by a shock wave of constant speed v_s which marks the front of the fluid that has been accelerated to the piston speed v_p. All the fluid between the shock wave and the piston, which occupies the volume $v_s t - v_p t$, is just that fluid that originally filled the volume $v_s t$. The density of the fluid behind the shock wave therefore exceeds that ahead by the ratio $v_s/(v_s - v_p)$; that is, the fluid is compressed by the shock wave.

To find the change in properties across this shock wave, it is more convenient to describe the flow as seen by an observer moving with the steady speed of the shock wave. Denoting the upstream and downstream conditions by subscripts 1 and 2, respectively, the steady-flow continuity, momentum, and energy equations (19.3–15) through (19.3–17) may be applied to the control surface shown in Fig. 19.12 for an ideal fluid ($\tau = 0$, $\mathbf{q} = 0$), resulting in

$$\rho_1 v_1 = \rho_2 v_2, \tag{19.8–1}$$

$$p_1 + \rho_1 v_1^2 = p_2 + \rho_2 v_2^2, \tag{19.8–2}$$

$$h_1 + v_1^2/2 = h_2 + v_2^2/2, \tag{19.8–3}$$

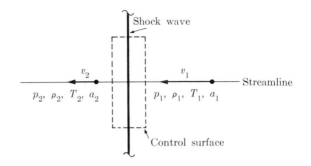

Fig. 19.12. The control surface for steady flow normal to a shock wave. Velocities are measured with respect to the shock wave.

while the nonconservation of entropy equation (19.3–19) requires that

$$s_2 \geq s_1. \tag{19.8-4}$$

Let us first consider a very weak wave for which $\rho_2 = \rho_1 + d\rho$, $p_2 = p_1 + dp$, etc., where the differential quantities are very small. To first order in these quantities, Eqs. (19.8–1) through (19.8–3) become

$$\rho_1 \, dv + v_1 \, d\rho = 0, \tag{19.8-5}$$

$$dp + 2\rho_1 v_1 \, dv + v_1^2 \, d\rho = 0, \tag{19.8-6}$$

$$dh + v_1 \, dv = 0. \tag{19.8-7}$$

By eliminating dv and $d\rho$ from Eqs. (19.8–5) through (19.8–7), we find that

$$dh - (1/\rho_1) \, dp = 0. \tag{19.8-8}$$

According to Eq. (10.4–19), this can be true only if $ds = 0$, i.e. if the wave compression process is isentropic. Eliminating dv between Eqs. (19.8–5) and (19.8–6), we obtain the flow velocity v_1,

$$v_1^2 = \{\partial p/\partial \rho\}_s, \tag{19.8-9}$$

where the specification of constant entropy follows from the previous equation. For a very weak shock wave, or *sound wave*, the propagation speed, or sound speed, into a stationary medium is $\{\partial p/\partial \rho\}_s^{1/2}$.

For stronger shock waves in a fluid, Eqs. (19.8–1) through (19.8–3) may be solved numerically for ρ_2, v_2, p_2, and h_2 if ρ_1, p_1, and v_1 are specified and if h is a known function of p and ρ. Solutions which satisfy the entropy limitation of Eq. (19.8–4) can be found only for values of v_1 which are greater than the local sound speed in the upstream flow; that is, the upstream flow is supersonic. For these solutions the downstream flow is subsonic. There is an increase in p_2, ρ_2, and h_2, and a decrease in v_2, across the shock wave.

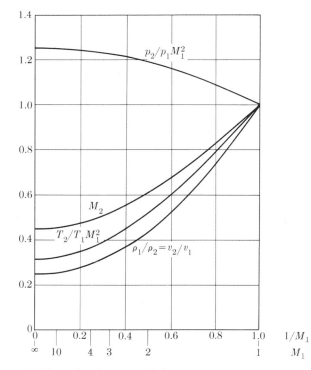

Fig. 19.13. Flow variables behind a normal shock wave in a perfect monatomic gas $(\gamma = 5/3)$.

For a perfect gas with constant specific heats, the energy equation (19.7–12) may be used in place of Eq. (19.8–3). In combination with the gas law, Eqs. (19.8–1), (19.8–2), and (19.7–12) may be solved simultaneously to yield

$$\frac{p_2}{p_1} = \frac{\{2\gamma M_1^2 - (\gamma - 1)\}}{\gamma + 1}, \qquad \frac{\rho_2}{\rho_1} = \frac{(\gamma + 1)M_1^2}{\{(\gamma - 1)M_1^2 + 2\}},$$

$$\frac{T_2}{T_1} = \frac{\{2\gamma M_1^2 - (\gamma - 1)\}\{(\gamma - 1)M_1^2 + 2\}}{(\gamma + 1)^2 M_1^2},$$

$$\frac{v_2}{v_1} = \frac{\rho_1}{\rho_2}, \qquad \frac{a_2}{a_1} = \left(\frac{T_2}{T_1}\right)^{1/2}, \qquad M_2^2 = \frac{\{(\gamma - 1)M_1^2 + 2\}}{\{2\gamma M_1^2 - (\gamma - 1)\}}, \qquad (19.8–10)$$

in which the upstream Mach number $M_1 = v_1/(\gamma \Re T_1)^{1/2}$ specifies the shock speed. These quantities are plotted in Fig. 19.13 for a shock wave in a perfect monatomic gas. It is interesting to notice that the pressure p_2 and temperature T_2 increase in proportion to M_1^2 at very high Mach number whereas the density ρ_2 approaches a fixed value of $\{(\gamma + 1)/(\gamma - 1)\}\rho_1$.

The increase of entropy across a shock wave arises from the shear stresses and heat conduction within the extremely thin shock front. Although τ and q are zero everywhere on the control surface of Fig. 19.12, the Bernoulli equation (19.6–12) does not correctly describe the momentum change within the shock front itself, and the entropy is therefore not constant for a fluid particle which passes through the shock wave.

19.9 Flow of an ideal fluid with chemical change

One can think of many examples of flows in which the fluid undergoes a change in chemical composition. A bunsen flame, rocket engine, gas turbine combustor, or reentering space vehicle exhibit important physical effects which are related to the chemical changes occurring in the fluid. We shall be content here to examine a few examples of such flows in which the fluid may be considered as ideal ($\tau = 0$, $q = 0$) but in which the chemical reactions cause appreciable changes in the flow properties.

At the outset, we recognize that a flow in which the chemical composition changes but in which the proportions of the species always remain in thermodynamic equilibrium at the local pressure and temperature can be treated by the methods previously outlined in Sections 19.1 through 19.8. In *equilibrium flows*, as they are called, the thermodynamic properties h, p, and ρ which appear in the conservation equations are related to each other through the condition for equilibrium, Eq. (14.3–17), which determines the local composition, and hence the extensive variables h and s, if p and ρ are initially specified. While the functional relationship may not be so simple as that for a perfect gas with constant specific heats, the thermodynamic properties of a fluid always at equilibrium may be determined by experiment or calculation and the properties presented in the form of a table or chart which can then be used in conjunction with the conservation laws to determine the flow variables. An example of an h vs. p chart for dissociated air in thermodynamic equilibrium is shown in Fig. 19.14.

As an example of this type of calculation, in Section 14.6 we considered the case of a partially ionized monatomic gas, for which the enthalpy h, entropy s, and density ρ can be written explicitly in terms of the pressure p, temperature T, and mole fraction of electrons x_e:

$$h = \frac{\{5\Re_a T/2 + x_e(\epsilon_i/m_a)\}}{(1 - x_e)},$$
(19.9–1)

$$s = \Re_a\left[\tfrac{5}{2} + \ln\left\{\frac{(2\pi/h^2\widetilde{N})^{3/2}(kT)^{5/2}}{p}\right\} + (1 - 2x_e)\ln\left\{\frac{\widetilde{M}_a^{3/2}g_a}{1 - 2x_e}\right\}\right.$$

$$\left. + x_e\ln\{(\widetilde{M}_i\widetilde{M}_e)^{3/2}2g_i/x_e^2\}\right]\Big/(1 - x_e),$$
(19.9–2)

$$\rho = \frac{(1 - x_e)p}{\Re_a T},$$
(19.9–3)

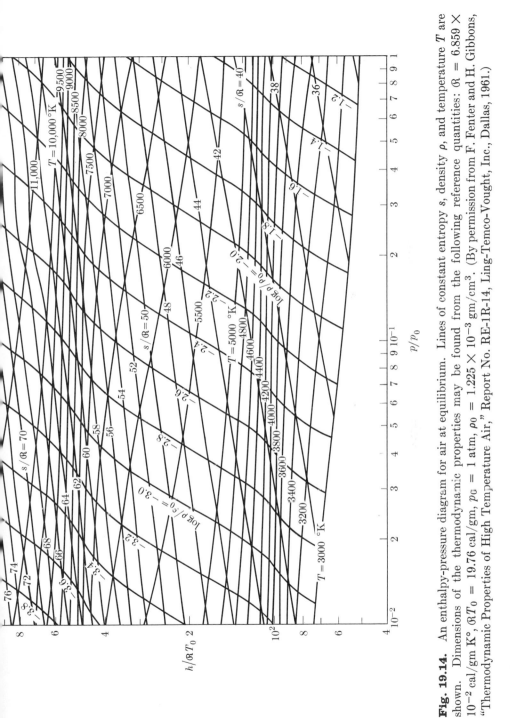

Fig. 19.14. An enthalpy-pressure diagram for air at equilibrium. Lines of constant entropy s, density ρ, and temperature T are shown. Dimensions of the thermodynamic properties may be found from the following reference quantities: $\mathfrak{R} = 6.859 \times 10^{-2}\,\mathrm{cal/gm\,K°}$, $\mathfrak{R}T_0 = 19.76\,\mathrm{cal/gm}$, $p_0 = 1\,\mathrm{atm}$, $\rho_0 = 1.225 \times 10^{-3}\,\mathrm{gm/cm^3}$. (By permission from F. Fenter and H. Gibbons, "Thermodynamic Properties of High Temperature Air," Report No. RE-1R-14, Ling-Temco-Vought, Inc., Dallas, 1961.)

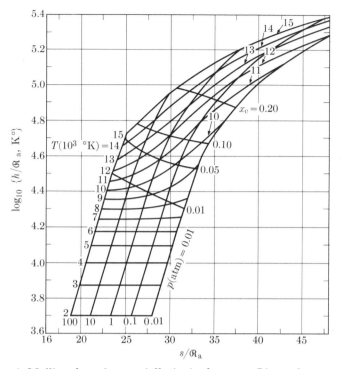

Fig. 19.15. A Mollier chart for partially ionized argon. Lines of constant temperature T, pressure p, and electron mole fraction x_e are shown. Enthalpy h and entropy s are divided by $\mathfrak{R}_a = 208.2 \; \text{j/kgm} \cdot \text{K}°$. The density may be found from Eq. (19.9–3). (By permission from R. J. Arave and O. A. Huseby, "Aerothermodynamic Properties of High Temperature Argon," Doc. No. D2-11238, p. 85, Boeing Co., Seattle, 1962.)

as previously derived in Eqs. (14.6–8) through (14.6–11). If the ionized gas is at thermodynamic equilibrium, then the mole fraction x_e may be found from Eq. (14.6–7):

$$x_e = (\kappa/p)\{(1 + p/\kappa)^{1/2} - 1\}, \qquad (19.9\text{–}4)$$

where

$$\kappa \equiv 2(2\pi m_e/h^2)^{3/2}(kT)^{5/2}(g_i/g_a)e^{-\epsilon_i/kT}. \qquad (19.9\text{–}5)$$

For any given p and T, we may then determine κ, x_e, h, s, and ρ for use in the equilibrium fluid flow equations. From inspection of the above equations we see that this is not an easy calculation, especially if we have an isentropic flow. It is sometimes convenient to plot graphically the solutions of these equations by drawing lines of constant p, x_e, and T in the hs-plane (Mollier chart), as shown in Fig. 19.15.

In some instances we may need to know only the change in enthalpy under conditions for which the enthalpy may be readily computed. In Fig. 19.16 is sketched an arc jet, a steady-flow device shaped like a rocket engine but in

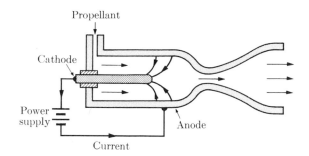

Fig. 19.16. A sketch of an arc jet.

which a monatomic propellant is heated in a direct-current arc to a temperature high enough to partially ionize the monatomic gas. If the stagnation point pressure p_s and temperature T_s are known, then the corresponding mole fraction $(x_e)_s$ may be calculated from Eqs. (19.9–4) and (19.9–5), and subsequently the stagnation enthalpy h_s from Eq. (19.9–1). If this gas is subsequently expanded through a convergent-divergent nozzle to a very low pressure, the temperature will decrease and the ions and electrons will recombine to form atoms; that is, x_e will become zero at the nozzle exit. The ideal fluid steady-flow energy equation (19.7–4) may then be used to calculate the velocity v_2 leaving the nozzle if Eq. (19.9–1) is used to determine the respective enthalpies:

$$v_2 = \{2(h_s - h_2)\}^{1/2}$$

$$= \left[\frac{\{5\mathcal{R}_a T_s + 2(x_e)_s \epsilon_i / m_a\}}{\{1 - (x_e)_s\}} - 5\mathcal{R}_a T_2 \right]^{1/2}, \qquad (19.9\text{–}6)$$

in which $(x_e)_2$ has been set equal to zero because T_2 is very low (see, for example, Fig. 19.15).

Under some conditions, the expansion of the plasma in the nozzle flow illustrated in Fig. 19.16 may be so rapid that the ions and electrons do not recombine as the temperature decreases, but their mole fractions remain "frozen" at the initial value $(x_e)_s$. This "frozen flow" is one for which the equilibrium composition is not maintained within the flow field but all changes in thermodynamic properties occur under the constraint of fixed composition; that is, x_e is a constant. Such a thermodynamic behavior is much like that of a mixture of oxygen and hydrogen at room temperature: the composition of the mixture is not that of true thermodynamic equilibrium (i.e. water vapor) but constitutes a state of metastable equilibrium, in which changes in composition take place too slowly to be of interest (at least in the absence of a spark!). For the steady flow being considered, the time of interest is the period required for an element of fluid to pass through the nozzle, which may be too short for the recombination of electrons and ions to occur. If this is so, the second term on

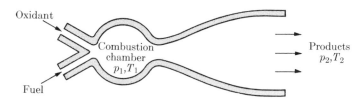

Fig. 19.17. A sketch of a combustion rocket engine.

the right-hand side of Eq. (19.9–1) for the enthalpy h is the same at the exit of the nozzle as at the entrance, so that the exit velocity v_{2f} for "frozen flow" determined from Eqs. (19.7–4) and (19.9–1) is

$$v_{2f} = \left\{ \frac{5 \Re_a (T_s - T_2)}{1 - (x_e)_s} \right\}^{1/2}. \tag{19.9–7}$$

On comparing this result with Eq. (19.9–6) for equilibrium flow, we find it to be smaller because none of the energy invested in ionization is recovered in the nozzle expansion. A similar situation may exist in the expansion of partially dissociated products of combustion in a rocket-engine nozzle.

As a second example of flow with a chemical change, let us consider the combustion of hydrogen and oxygen in a rocket engine as shown in Fig. 19.17. If no heat is lost from the rocket engine, then the steady-flow energy equation (19.6–6) may be used:

$$h_r\{p_1, T_1\} + v_1^2/2 = h_p\{p_2, T_2\} + v_2^2/2, \tag{19.9–8}$$

in which the subscripts r and p identify the reactants (oxygen and hydrogen) and products (water vapor and excess fuel or oxidant), respectively. The enthalpies are evaluated at the pressure and temperature existing at the inlet or outlet as indicated in the argument of h. At any given reference pressure p_i and T_i, the difference between the enthalpies of the reactants and products may be found in a constant-pressure experiment of the type described in Section 18.8, for which Eq. (18.8–2) may be written as

$$\Delta h^i \equiv h_p\{p_i, T_i\} - h_r\{p_i, T_i\}, \tag{19.9–9}$$

in which $-\Delta h^i$ is the constant-pressure heat of reaction per unit mass of reactants. Subtracting Eq. (19.9–8), we find

$$(v_2^2 - v_1^2)/2 = h_r\{p_1, T_1\} - h_r\{p_i, T_i\} - (h_p\{p_2, T_2\} - h_p\{p_i, T_i\}) - \Delta h^i, \tag{19.9–10}$$

from which the increase in velocity may be found by referring to the thermodynamic properties.

As a particular example, consider the reaction of oxygen with excess hydrogen:

$$O_2 + (n + 2)H_2 \rightarrow 2H_2O + nH_2. \tag{19.9–11}$$

If the entering and leaving streams are Gibbs-Dalton mixtures of perfect gases, and if we select the reference temperature T_i to be zero, then the terms on the right-hand side of Eq. (19.9–10) may be written as

$$h_r\{T_1\} - h_r\{0\} = \frac{\{\widetilde{H}_{O_2} + (n+2)(\widetilde{H}_{H_2})\}_{T=T_1}}{\widetilde{M}_{O_2} + (n+2)\widetilde{M}_{H_2}},$$

$$h_p\{T_2\} - h_p\{0\} = \frac{\{2\widetilde{H}_{H_2O} + n\widetilde{H}_{H_2}\}_{T=T_2}}{2\widetilde{M}_{H_2O} + n\widetilde{M}_{H_2}}, \qquad (19.9\text{--}12)$$

$$\Delta h^0 = \frac{\Delta \widetilde{H}^0}{\widetilde{M}_{O_2} + (n+2)\widetilde{M}_{H_2}},$$

in which the perfect-gas molar enthalpies $\widetilde{H}$ are those given in Chapter 12 and $\Delta\widetilde{H}^0$ is the enthalpy change of $-114,214$ cal/gm-mole $= -4.79 \times 10^5$ kj/kgm-mole for the reaction in question, as given in Table 14.1.

For a rocket engine, v_1 is much smaller than v_2, so that the exhaust velocity v_2 may be found by substituting Eq. (19.9–12) into (19.9–10).

19.10 The fuel cell

A fuel cell is a steady-flow device which consumes a fuel and oxidant and produces electrical power.* Unlike many of the previous examples of fluid flow, the kinetic energy of the moving fluid is unimportant, whereas the change in chemical composition and phase is the principal means of producing electrical power. Even so, we shall find it most convenient to treat the operation of the fuel cell as a steady-flow problem.

A hydrogen-oxygen fuel cell is shown diagrammatically in Fig. 19.18. An electrolyte, such as a solution of KOH in water, is contained between two porous metallic electrodes. (Because of surface tension, the solution will not leak through the very fine pores of the electrodes.) When hydrogen gas is introduced on the outside of one electrode and oxygen gas at the other, the electrostatic potential of the hydrogen electrode becomes negative with respect to the oxygen electrode. If the two electrodes are connected to a load through an external electrical circuit, as shown in Fig. 19.18, a current will flow externally from the positive (oxygen) electrode to the negative (hydrogen) electrode, while hydrogen and oxygen are absorbed at the two electrodes and water vapor is evolved at the positive (oxygen) electrode. At the same time, heat is given off by the fuel cell, which must be cooled to maintain its temperature at a fixed value.

The detailed processes by which the fuel and oxidant are consumed while electrical work is done may be understood by considering the flows shown in

---

* The storage battery is not a fuel cell because it consumes its electrodes and must be recharged with electrical work.

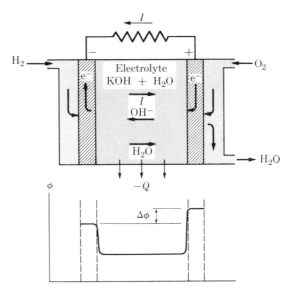

Fig. 19.18. A sketch of the hydrogen-oxygen fuel cell, showing the flow of various chemical species and the distribution of electric potential ϕ within the cell.

Fig. 19.18. The electrolyte consists of K^+ positive ions and OH^- negative ions in solution. Only the OH^- ions participate in the fuel cell process. A flux of OH^- ions diffusing through the electrolyte from the positive to the negative electrode carries negative charges to the hydrogen electrode and hence a positive current I to the positive electrode.* At the hydrogen electrode a gaseous H_2 molecule is dissolved in the electrolyte filling the pores of the electrode, reacts with an OH^- ion to form an H_2O molecule in solution, and injects an electron into the solid. This reaction may be summarized by the chemical change equation

$$2\{H_2\}_g + 4\{OH^-\}_l \rightarrow 4\{e^-\}_s + 4\{H_2O\}_l, \qquad (19.10\text{--}1)$$

in which the subscripts g, l, and s identify the gaseous, liquid, and solid phases in which the molecule indicated is found. The electron moves into the solid, where the electrostatic potential is higher than in the liquid.

The H_2O formed at the hydrogen electrode then diffuses toward the oxygen electrode, carrying no current (since it is uncharged) but providing, in conjunction with the opposite counterflow of OH^- ions, a net flux of hydrogen toward the oxygen electrode. (Note that there is no net flux of oxygen due to these countercurrent streams.) At the oxygen electrode, some of this H_2O is oxidized by O_2 dissolved in the electrolyte while absorbing an electron from the electrode,

---

* For this reason the hydrogen electrode is called the anode and the oxygen electrode the cathode.

and the remainder is evolved as a vapor according to the reaction:

$$4\{H_2O\}_l + \{O_2\}_g + 4\{e^-\}_s \rightarrow 4\{OH^-\}_l + 2\{H_2O\}_g. \qquad (19.10\text{--}2)$$

The net result of both of these two electrode reactions is obtained by summing Eqs. (19.10–1) and (19.10–2):

$$2\{H_2\}_g + \{O_2\}_g \rightarrow 2\{H_2O\}_g, \qquad (19.10\text{--}3)$$

which describes the conversion of reactants (fuel and oxidant) to products.

In the external circuit, the electrons collected at the negative hydrogen electrode pass through the load, arriving at the positive oxygen electrode where they are attached again to the electrolyte ions. This flux of electrons is an electric current passing from the positive to negative electrodes through the load, thereby doing electrical work on the load.

The change in electrostatic potential in the fuel cell is sketched in Fig. 19.18. The potential difference between the two electrodes arises at the surface of the electrode and not within the electrolyte itself. The presence of hydrogen at one electrode and oxygen at the other causes a potential difference between electrode and electrolyte which is not the same at both electrodes but is higher at the oxygen electrode. The net potential difference $\Delta\phi$, which appears across the electrodes in the external circuit, is thus the difference between these two electrode potential changes since there is a negligible potential change within the electrolyte.

Neglecting the kinetic energy of the moving fluids, the steady-flow energy equation may be applied to the fuel cell considered as a control volume, resulting in

$$\dot{M}_{H_2O}h^*_{H_2O} = \dot{M}_{H_2}h^*_{H_2} + \dot{M}_{O_2}h^*_{O_2} + \dot{Q} - I\,\Delta\phi, \qquad (19.10\text{--}4)\dagger\ddagger$$

in which the rate of electrical work $I\,\Delta\phi$ done by the fuel cell is the product of the current I and the electrode potential difference $\Delta\phi$. The conservation of mass requires that

$$\dot{M}_{H_2O} = \dot{M}_{H_2} + \dot{M}_{O_2} \qquad (19.10\text{--}5)$$

since no electrolyte is consumed. The nonconservation of entropy may be expressed as

$$\dot{M}_{H_2}s_{H_2O} \geq \dot{M}_{H_2}s_{H_2} + \dot{M}_{O_2}s_{O_2} + \dot{Q}/T \qquad (19.10\text{--}6)$$

---

† We here consider the flux of electrons out of the control volume at the negative electrode and into the control volume at the positive electrode at a higher potential as electrical work done on the environment by the fluid in the control volume. Alternatively, we can consider a resistive load as part of our control volume, in which case $I\,\Delta\phi$ is the heat removed from the control volume to maintain the temperature of the resistor at a fixed value. The resulting energy equation is the same in either case.

‡ As in Chapter 14, the superscript * denotes a property calculated on the basis of a common energy scale.

because the entropy (carried by the stream) leaving the control volume must exceed that entering by not less than $\dot{Q}/T$.

If we multiply Eq. (19.10–6) by T and subtract this from Eq. (19.10–4), we find that

$$I \, \Delta\phi \leq \dot{M}_{H_2}(h^* - Ts)_{H_2} + \dot{M}_{O_2}(h^* - Ts)_{O_2} - \dot{M}_{H_2O}(h^* - Ts)_{H_2O}.$$

$$(19.10–7)$$

Since $h^* - Ts$ is the Gibbs free energy per unit mass (see Section 14.11), we see that the electrical work per unit mass of reactants cannot exceed the reduction in free energy when the reactants are changed to products. We may therefore define the *thermochemical efficiency* of a fuel cell as the ratio of the actual power $I \, \Delta\phi$ to the maximum possible value given by the right-hand side of Eq. (19.10–7).

A *reversible fuel cell* is one for which the equality of Eq. (19.10–7) obtains because all the internal processes are reversible. For the reversible oxygen-hydrogen fuel cell, the reversible current I_R is related to the mass flux $\dot{M}_{H_2}$ of hydrogen in accordance with Eq. (19.10–1), which states that two electrons are liberated for each hydrogen molecule that reacts:

$$I_R = \frac{2e\dot{M}_{H_2}}{m_{H_2}} = \frac{2(\widetilde{N}e)\dot{M}_{H_2}}{\widetilde{M}_{H_2}}, \tag{19.10–8}$$

in which e is the magnitude of the electronic charge.† For the reversible cell, the reactants are consumed in stoichiometric proportions so that

$$\frac{\dot{M}_{H_2O}}{2\widetilde{M}_{H_2O}} = \frac{\dot{M}_{H_2}}{2\widetilde{M}_{H_2}} = \frac{\dot{M}_{O_2}}{\widetilde{M}_{O_2}}. \tag{19.10–9}$$

By combining Eqs. (19.10–7) through (19.10–9) for the reversible cell, and noting that the free energy per mole $\widetilde{F}^*$ is just $\widetilde{M}(h^* - Ts)$, we find

$$\Delta\phi_R = \frac{\{2\widetilde{F}^*_{H_2} + \widetilde{F}^*_{O_2} - 2\widetilde{F}^*_{H_2O}\}}{4(\widetilde{N}e)}, \tag{19.10–10}$$

in which $\Delta\phi_R$ is the potential difference between the electrodes of a reversible cell.

A well-constructed fuel cell may operate in a reversible manner when the current I is very small. As more power is generated in the cell, the potential $\Delta\phi$ becomes less than $\Delta\phi_R$ and the cell operates in an irreversible manner, the power being less than the ideal amount given by the right-hand side of Eq. (19.10–7). Even so, the electrical work may still exceed that which would be obtained by burning the same fuel in a combustion cycle such as a gas turbine or internal-combustion engine.

---

† The product of the electronic charge e and Avogadro's number $\widetilde{N}$ is called the Faraday and has the value of 9.6487×10^7 coul/kgm-mole.

PROBLEMS

19.1 If ρ_c is the electric charge density per unit volume of a fluid, develop an equation for conservation of charge, similar to Eq. (19.3–4) for conservation of mass.

19.2 Natural gas (CH_4), compressed to a pressure of 60 atm and a temperature of 300°K, flows through a long pipeline, emerging at the other end at 10-atm pressure. The velocity entering the pipeline is 45 m/sec. (a) If no heat is added to (or removed from) the pipeline, find the temperature leaving the pipeline. (b) Show that your answer satisfies the entropy equation for steady flow.

19.3 In an experimental magnetohydrodynamic power plant argon gas is to be heated from 25°C to 1500°C in a closed heat exchanger by a stream of N_2 which enters at 3000°C and leaves at 1000°C. The nitrogen is heated in an arc jet from 25°C to 3000°C. (a) If 1 lbm/sec of argon is to be heated, what mass flow of N_2 is needed? (b) If 80% of the electrical power to the arc jet is available for heating the nitrogen, what electrical power is required?

19.4 The exhaust gases from a coal-fired furnace, having a composition of 0.80 mole fraction of N_2 and 0.20 mole fraction of CO_2, are to be reduced in temperature from 600°F to 300°F by mixing with air initially at 70°F. What is the required ratio of the mass flow of air to exhaust gas?

19.5 Oxygen is compressed from a pressure of 1 atm to a pressure of 10 atm in a reciprocating compressor. The oxygen enters at 70°F and leaves at 300°F. The compressor is cooled by a flow of water of 1.5 lbm/sec, which enters at 70°F and leaves at 115°F. The power required to operate the compressor is 100 kw. (a) How many lbm/sec of oxygen is compressed? (b) Show that the net entropy flux from the compressor is positive.

19.6 In a closed-cycle gas turbine power plant helium enters the adiabatic turbine at 8-atm pressure and 1500°F and leaves at 1-atm pressure and 650°F. (a) What is the adiabatic turbine efficiency? (b) How much work does the turbine deliver per pound of helium flowing through the turbine?

19.7 In the adiabatic compressor of a supersonic aircraft, air enters at $p = 0.1$ atm, a temperature of 20°F, and a velocity of 2000 ft/sec. The air leaves the compressor at $p = 0.5$ atm, a temperature of 1050°F, and a velocity of 1000 ft/sec. How much compressor work is required per pound of air?

19.8 Water is compressed in a centrifugal pump from a pressure of 1 atm to a pressure of 50 atm. How much work is required per pound of water if the compression is a reversible adiabatic process?

19.9 A hot, high-velocity air stream leaves a stack at a temperature of 200°F, at a pressure of 1 atm, and an upward velocity of 300 ft/sec. Assuming an ideal fluid flow, determine how high the air stream will rise before its upward velocity becomes zero. (The atmospheric pressure $p = e^{-z/28,000}$ atm, in which z is the altitude in feet above sea level.)

19.10 Estimate the speed of sound in a mixture of water containing 20% by volume of small air bubbles. The mixture temperature is 300°K and the pressure is 1 atm.

19.11 In a steady-flow supersonic wind tunnel, air stored at 10-atm pressure and 70°F is passed adiabatically through a convergent-divergent nozzle and exhausts as a supersonic stream at atmospheric pressure. Assuming a constant $\gamma = 1.4$, (a) determine the Mach number of the flow at the nozzle exit, (b) its temperature,

(c) the ratio of exit area to throat area required, (d) the mass flow (lbm/sec) if the throat area is one square inch.

19.12 It is desired to design a hypersonic wind tunnel using helium, in which the test section will operate at a Mach number of 20. (a) What stagnation temperature is required if the test-section temperature is 10°K? (b) What stagnation pressure is required if the test-section pressure is 10^{-4} atm? (c) What is the ratio of test-section area to throat area?

19.13 For a shock wave in a perfect gas with constant specific heats, find the values of

$$\frac{p_2}{\rho_1 v_1^2} \quad \text{and} \quad \frac{2c_p T_2}{v_1^2}$$

for the limit of $M_1 \to \infty$.

19.14 For the shock tube experiment illustrated in Fig. 19.11, find p_2, ρ_2, T_2, and v_p for a shock wave of velocity $v_s = 10^3$ m/sec moving into argon at an initial temperature of 25°C and 1-atm pressure.

19.15 The pressure at the stagnation point of a blunt hypersonic vehicle flying at 7000 m/sec in air is 0.2 atm. (a) Determine the stagnation temperature from Fig. 19.14. (b) At a point farther along the same streamline, the pressure is 0.02 atm. What are the temperature and flow velocity at this point?

19.16 Find the pressure, density, and temperature behind a shock wave in air moving with a velocity of 1500 m/sec. The upstream air temperature and pressure are 300°K and 5×10^{-4} atm. Use Fig. 19.14 for the equilibrium thermodynamic properties.

19.17 In a laboratory experiment argon is heated in an arc jet to a stagnation temperature of 12,000°K and a pressure of 1 atm. It is then expanded adiabatically in a convergent-divergent nozzle to a pressure of 0.01 atm. Assume that the expansion is that of an ideal fluid at equilibrium. (a) What would be the argon temperature at the arc jet exit? (b) What would be its velocity? (c) What would be its temperature? If during the expansion the composition were unchanged from that existing in the stagnation chamber, (d) what would be the exit temperature and velocity? (Use the equilibrium thermodynamic data of Fig. 19.15.)

19.18 In a steady-flow rocket engine to be used for space propulsion, hydrogen is heated in a nuclear reactor to 3000°K at 300 psi. The gas then expands adiabatically and reversibly in the rocket nozzle to zero pressure. What will be the exhaust velocity?

19.19 On a rocket-engine test stand gaseous O_2 and H_2 at 25°C are supplied to the rocket in the ratio of 4 moles of H_2 to 1 mole of O_2. The fuel and oxidant react adiabatically at high pressure and then are accelerated in the rocket nozzle to a high velocity. The exhaust temperature is spectroscopically measured to be 1000°K. What is the exhaust velocity?

19.20 A magnetohydrodynamic steady-flow propulsion engine is supplied from an arc jet with helium at 15,000°K which is 10% ionized (i.e., 10% of the helium supplied to the jet has been ionized) and enters the accelerator with a velocity of 10,000 m/sec. The helium leaves the accelerator at the same temperature but has been accelerated to 30,000 m/sec while its pressure has decreased to 1% of the entrance pressure. If the helium is at equilibrium at both the entrance and exit of the accelerator, (a) what is the fraction of ionization at exit, (b) what is the change in enthalpy (j/kgm) between exit and entrance? (c) For a mass flow of 1 gm/sec, how much power is added to the stream in the accelerator, assuming no heat loss?

19.21 An oxygen-hydrogen fuel cell operating at 100°C is supplied with H_2 at $p = 2$ atm and O_2 at $p = 1$ atm while H_2O at $p = 1$ atm is evolved. Calculate the potential ϕ_R of the reversible cell, assuming that H_2O vapor under these conditions is a perfect gas.

20

COLLISIONS IN A GAS

20.1 Transport and other rate processes

It has been repeatedly stressed that time does not enter explicitly into the laws of thermodynamics or the arguments of statistical mechanics. If changes occur in a system with the passage of time, then through the laws of thermodynamics we are able to relate the changes in thermodynamic properties to the heat and work quantities involved, but we can make no general statements concerning how rapidly such changes may take place. In the mixing process discussed in Section 13.3, for instance, we were able to calculate the increase in entropy caused by the thorough mixing of two different perfect gases, but no conclusion was reached concerning the length of time required for this mixing to be accomplished. Indeed, to calculate the rate at which the entropy of the system increases with time is much more difficult than to determine the total increase which occurs in the mixing process. Paradoxical as this situation may seem, it is not very different from that encountered in particle dynamics, where a knowledge of the total energy and angular momentum of a system of particles permits us to place certain limits on the possible motion even though we may not be able to solve for the detailed motion as a function of time. For example, a ball thrown vertically upward with a given initial velocity cannot exceed the height at which the increase in its potential energy equals its initial kinetic energy. However, the time required to reach this maximum height can be determined only from an integration of the equations of motion, which in general is a difficult calculation. As in the case of dynamical systems, a description of the temporal behavior of a thermodynamic system requires more detailed information concerning its behavior than a knowledge of thermodynamic properties alone.

The temporal behavior of a thermodynamic system is describable on the macroscopic scale in terms of *rate processes*. A rate process is one in which the change with time of a conserved* thermodynamic property such as mass, momentum, or energy may be related to the thermodynamic properties of the

---

* By a conserved thermodynamic property we mean one for which a continuum-type conservation law may be derived from the laws of thermodynamics or dynamics, as was done for a fluid in Chapter 19. Other properties, such as entropy and the free energies, have nonconservation laws involving inequalities, as illustrated by Eq. (19.3–19).

system. For example, the rate at which a gaseous mixture of hydrogen and oxygen is being converted to water vapor may be measured in an experiment, and the manner in which this rate depends on the temperature and pressure of the mixture describes macroscopically the rate process of *chemical reaction*. If a hot and a cold metal block are brought into contact with either side of a sheet of paper, the rate of increase of temperature (and hence of internal energy) of the cold block may be found to be related to the temperature difference between the blocks and the thickness of the paper separating them. This is the rate process of *heat conduction*, in which changes in internal energy occur at a rate determined by spatial differences in temperature. In the case of heat conduction, the rate process is called a *transport process* because internal energy is "transported" from the hot to the cold block; i.e., the internal energy of the hot block decreases while that of the cold block increases by an equal amount. In a similar manner, in a fluid momentum and mass may be "transported" from one point to another whenever differences in velocity or mass density exist between nearby fluid elements.

In rate processes in which mass, momentum, or energy moves from one point in a system to another, it is customary to define a mass, momentum, or energy *flux* by determining the rate at which the corresponding quantity appears to move across an imaginary unit surface in the system because of a decrease in the conserved quantity on one side of the surface and a corresponding increase on the other. In a gas, these fluxes are easy to specify because the mass, momentum, and energy carried by gas molecules crossing an imaginary unit surface in a unit time may be readily determined in terms of the velocities and masses of the molecules, as will be discussed in Section 20.4. In an undeformed solid, where the internal energy of the solid is changed only by the addition of heat and where no work is done, the energy flux is simply called the *heat flux*. In a fluid, in which work may also be accomplished in deforming a fluid element, as discussed in Section 19.3, part of the energy flux across the surface of a moving element may be considered a heat flux and the remainder is called the viscous work of dissipation. When mass transport is also present in a fluid, the components of the energy flux are more difficult to identify.

Transport and other rate processes in gases are often of great practical importance. Heat conduction in a gas will determine the rate of heating of a space vehicle entering the atmosphere of the earth as well as the amount of radiator surface required to cool an automobile engine. Momentum transport in the air partially determines the frictional drag exerted on an airplane wing, thereby affecting the power required to propel it. The transport of water vapor in dry air will influence the rate of drying of a wet surface exposed to an air flow. The reaction rate of fuel with air will affect the performance of a gasoline engine. Any one of these aspects alone could hardly be treated in a book of this size, so that we shall be forced to consider only the most elementary aspects of the transport effects. We shall therefore show how the transport of mass, momentum, and energy proceeds at a rate which depends on the properties of colliding gas molecules.

20.2 The velocity distribution function

In Chapter 8, in discussing the statistical description of a system of independent particles, we introduced the phase space (called μ-space) composed of the pairs of conjugate momentum and position coordinates describing the motion of each of the independent particles. A macrostate of the system was described by enumerating the number N_j of representative points in each cell j into which μ-space was divided in an arbitrary manner. The most probable macrostate of a system of N particles contained in a volume V and having a total energy E was then determined by a variational method.

In treating the translational motion of perfect-gas molecules in Chapter 11, it was also found convenient to decompose μ-space into configuration space having cartesian coordinates x, y, and z and momentum space having cartesian coordinates p_x, p_y, and p_z. For our study of the kinetic theory of gases we wish to adopt this description but shall use instead the velocity coordinates v_x, v_y, and v_z, which are the components of the velocity $\mathbf{v}$ in the x-, y-, and z-directions, to define a *velocity space* to replace the momentum space previously used. Since we shall be concerned with a perfect gas for which $\mathbf{p} = m\mathbf{v}$, this constitutes a change in the dimensions of a unit volume of μ-space and is introduced only to bring our description into accordance with the traditional description introduced by Maxwell* and Boltzmann.† Thus the coordinates of our new phase space are the pairs of position and velocity components x, v_x; y, v_y; and z, v_z, that is, the pair of vectors $\mathbf{r}$, $\mathbf{v}$ (see Fig. 20.1). The dimensions of a volume element in this space are therefore (velocity $\times$ length)^3.

To describe a macrostate of the gas we shall replace the discrete description used in Chapter 8, in which phase space was divided into numerous small cells, by a continuous description. We define the number density f of representative points in phase space as the ratio of the number of points in a cell to the volume of that cell in the same manner as we define the number density n of gas molecules in physical space. At any instant, the number density f, also called the *distribution function*, will depend on the position in phase space at the time t; that is, it is in general a function $f\{\mathbf{r}, \mathbf{v}, t\}$ of $\mathbf{r}$, $\mathbf{v}$, and t.

---

* James Clerk Maxwell (1831–1879) is best known for his contributions to electromagnetic theory, begun as a Cambridge undergraduate and completed in 1873 in his treatise *Electricity and Magnetism*. He wrote his first technical paper at age 15 and thereafter contributed many outstanding ideas in solid mechanics, color perception, astronomy, and kinetic theory of gases. His books, *Theory of Heat* (1871) and *Matter and Motion* (1876), are classic expositions of these subjects.

† Ludwig Boltzmann (1849–1906) laid the foundation for modern developments in the kinetic theory of gases. He introduced what is now called the Boltzmann equation to explain the link between the reversible mechanics of molecules and irreversible processes in gases. His *Lectures on Gas Theory* (see Bibliography) is still eminently readable. Subjected to vitriolic criticism for his work, which today is the starting point of such a newly emerging field as plasma physics, Boltzmann prematurely ended his own life.

Fig. 20.1. The phase space used in the kinetic-theory description of a perfect gas has the cartesian components x, y, z, v_x, v_y, and v_z, of which x, y, and z locate a point $\mathbf{r}$ in configuration space, and v_x, v_y, and v_z locate a point $\mathbf{v}$ in velocity space. The components in the direction x, y, and z of the velocity $\mathbf{v}$ of a molecule are, respectively, v_x, v_y, and v_z.

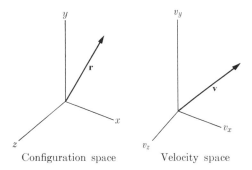

Configuration space   Velocity space

Because of the way we have defined the distribution function f, we can see that the number N of molecules in the system must be the integral of f:

$$N = \int_{-\infty}^{\infty} \ldots \int f\{\mathbf{r}, \mathbf{v}, t\} \, dx \, dy \, dz \, dv_x \, dv_y \, dv_z, \qquad (20.2\text{–}1)$$

in which the sixfold integral extends over all of phase space, that is, over both velocity space and configuration space. Equation (20.2–1) expresses the restriction that the number of representative points in phase space must equal the number of molecules in the system being considered. Dynamical properties of the system, such as translational energy E_t and linear momentum $\mathbf{P}$, may also be determined from a knowledge of the distribution function f by multiplying the translational energy $mv^2/2$ or momentum $m\mathbf{v}$ of a particle by the number $f \, dx \, dy \, dz \, dv_x \, dv_y \, dv_z$ of particles in a volume element $dx \, dy \, dz \, dv_x \, dv_y \, dv_z$ of phase space and then integrating over all of phase space:

$$E_t = \int_{-\infty}^{\infty} \ldots \int (mv^2/2) f \, dx \, dy \, dz \, dv_x \, dv_y \, dv_z, \qquad (20.2\text{–}2)$$

$$\mathbf{P} = \int_{-\infty}^{\infty} \ldots \int m\mathbf{v} f \, dx \, dy \, dz \, dv_x \, dv_y \, dv_z. \qquad (20.2\text{–}3)$$

In Chapter 19 we discussed the motion of a fluid, beginning in Section 19.2 by defining macroscopically the mass, momentum, and energy densities of a fluid. In each case, we found the ratio of the quantity being considered to the volume of a small fluid element located at the point $\mathbf{r}$ in (configuration) space at the time t. To find the corresponding expressions in terms of the distribution function f, we first note that we find the number density $n\{\mathbf{r}, t\}$ of molecules per unit volume of configuration space at a point $\mathbf{r}$ at the time t by summing over all of velocity space the representative points which are located at $\mathbf{r}$ in phase space:

$$n\{\mathbf{r}, t\} = \int_{-\infty}^{\infty} \!\!\! \int \!\! \int f\{\mathbf{r}, \mathbf{v}, t\} \, dv_x \, dv_y \, dv_z. \qquad (20.2\text{–}4)$$

The mass density $\rho\{\mathbf{r}, t\}$ is therefore

$$\rho\{\mathbf{r}, t\} = mn\{\mathbf{r}, t\} = \int\!\!\!\int\!\!\!\int_{-\infty}^{\infty} mf\{\mathbf{r}, \mathbf{v}, t\}\, dv_x\, dv_y\, dv_z. \tag{20.2-5}$$

The momentum density of the fluid, that is, the momentum per unit volume, will be denoted by $\rho\langle\mathbf{v}\rangle$, where $\langle\mathbf{v}\rangle$ is the average translational velocity of the gas molecules. The momentum density is found by summing the momentum $m\mathbf{v}$ of a molecule over all the molecular velocities:

$$\rho\langle\mathbf{v}\rangle \equiv \int\!\!\!\int\!\!\!\int_{-\infty}^{\infty} m\mathbf{v}f\{\mathbf{r}, \mathbf{v}, t\}\, dv_x\, dv_y\, dv_z. \tag{20.2-6}$$

The momentum density $\rho\langle\mathbf{v}\rangle$ is a vector quantity so that Eq. (20.2–6) is a vector equation which is equivalent to the three scalar equations for the components of the momentum per unit volume in the x-, y-, and z-directions. In Eq. (20.2–6) both ρ and $\langle\mathbf{v}\rangle$ are functions of $\mathbf{r}$ and t. By combining Eqs. (20.2–4) and (20.2–5) with Eq. (20.2–6), we find that the average velocity $\langle\mathbf{v}\rangle$, which is a function of $\mathbf{r}$ and t, is given by the integral

$$\langle\mathbf{v}\rangle = (1/n)\int\!\!\!\int\!\!\!\int_{-\infty}^{\infty} \mathbf{v}f\{\mathbf{r}, \mathbf{v}, t\}\, dv_x\, dv_y\, dv_z. \tag{20.2-7}$$

Finally, the kinetic energy density, which we shall denote by $\rho\{e_t + \langle\mathbf{v}\rangle^2/2\}$, to conform with the notation introduced in Section 19.3, is found by summing the kinetic energy $mv^2/2$ over all possible velocities:

$$\rho\{e_t + \langle\mathbf{v}\rangle^2/2\} \equiv \int\!\!\!\int\!\!\!\int_{-\infty}^{\infty} (mv^2/2)\, f\{\mathbf{r}, \mathbf{v}, t\}\, dv_x\, dv_y\, dv_z, \tag{20.2-8}$$

in which the translational energy e_t is also a function of $\mathbf{r}$ and t.

From the preceding derivation we can see how a knowledge of the distribution function $f\{\mathbf{r}, \mathbf{v}, t\}$ makes it possible to find not only the total mass, momentum, and translational energy of a gas but also the distribution of these quantities throughout configuration space, that is, the mass, momentum, and energy densities as a function of position $\mathbf{r}$ and time t. Since the latter description is the one adopted in the study of fluid dynamics, the distribution function f is a possible starting point for developing the fluid dynamics of gases.

The fundamental problem of the kinetic theory of gases is to determine the distribution function $f\{\mathbf{r}, \mathbf{v}, t\}$ which will exist in a gas in a given macroscopic situation such as the flow over an airplane wing or the conduction of heat between two surfaces separated by a layer of gas. This is in general an insoluble problem but one which has been successfully treated in special cases. We shall not consider the kinetic theory of gases from this fundamental point of view but shall instead seek to develop heuristic arguments which lead to a qualitative and quantitative understanding of transport processes. In so doing we shall refer to the results obtained from the more comprehensive treatment of transport processes which determines the distribution function from first principles. The simple derivation we shall use is approximately correct, while the mathematical development to improve on it is exceedingly great. Because the simple kinetic theory incorporates all the important physical principles and is very helpful in understanding physical and chemical phenomena in gases, it has great practical utility even though it does not possess the accuracy which is typical of statistical mechanics.

20.3 The Maxwellian velocity distribution

For a stationary gas at thermodynamic equilibrium we may find the equilibrium distribution function f^0, also called the *Maxwellian distribution function*, by using Eq. (8.7–13) for the most probable macrostate of a Boltzmann system. Let us consider a volume element of the phase space illustrated in Fig. 20.1, having a volume $dx\,dy\,dz\,dv_x\,dv_y\,dv_z$. If there are N_j^0 representative points in this volume element, then

$$N_j^0 = f^0\,dx\,dy\,dz\,dv_x\,dv_y\,dv_z. \qquad (20.3–1)$$

To determine the number of quantum states C_j in this same element, we multiply the volume $dx\,dy\,dz\,dv_x\,dv_y\,dv_z$ by m^3 to form a volume element

$$dx\,dy\,dz\,d(mv_x)\,d(mv_y)\,d(mv_z) = dx\,dy\,dz\,dp_x\,dp_y\,dp_z$$

which, when divided by h^3, gives the number of translational quantum states C_j in the cell j:

$$C_j = \frac{dx\,dy\,dz\,dp_x\,dp_y\,dp_z}{h^3} = \left(\frac{m}{h}\right)^3 dx\,dy\,dz\,dv_x\,dv_y\,dv_z. \qquad (20.3–2)$$

Substituting Eqs. (20.3–1) and (20.3–2) into Eq. (8.7–13), we find

$$\frac{N_j^0}{C_j} = \frac{h^3 f^0}{m^3} = \frac{N}{Q}\,e^{-\epsilon_j/kT}. \qquad (20.3–3)$$

The translational energy ϵ_j is $mv^2/2 = m(v_x^2 + v_y^2 + v_z^2)/2$, while the translational partition function $Q = (2\pi mkT/h^2)^{3/2}V$, as given by Eq. (11.3–12). Making these substitutions into Eq. (20.3–3), we find the Maxwellian distribution function f^0 to be

$$f^0 = n(m/2\pi kT)^{3/2}e^{-m(v_x^2+v_y^2+v_z^2)/2kT}, \qquad (20.3–4)$$

in which $n = N/V$ is the uniform number density of the molecules.

It is easy to show that Eq. (20.2–1) is identically satisfied by this choice of f^0. If we substitute Eq. (20.3–4) into (20.2–1), we find

$$N = \left\{\iiint n \, dx \, dy \, dz\right\} \left\{(m/2\pi kT)^{1/2} \int_{-\infty}^{\infty} e^{-mv_x^2/2kT} \, dv_x\right\}$$

$$\times \left\{(m/2\pi kT)^{1/2} \int_{-\infty}^{\infty} e^{-mv_y^2/2kT} \, dv_y\right\} \left\{(m/2\pi kT)^{1/2} \int_{-\infty}^{\infty} e^{-mv_z^2/2kT} \, dv_z\right\}.$$

$$(20.3\text{–}5)$$

Now, the first factor on the right-hand side of Eq. (20.3–5) is the integral of the uniform number density n over the volume V and hence is equal to N. Each of the additional factors, when integrated with the help of Table A–4, is unity:

$$(m/2\pi kT)^{1/2} \int_{-\infty}^{\infty} e^{-mv_x^2/2kT} \, dv_x = (1/\pi)^{1/2} \int_{-\infty}^{\infty} e^{-mv_x^2/2kT} \, d\{(m/2kT)^{1/2} v_x\}$$

$$= 2(1/\pi)^{1/2} \int_{0}^{\infty} e^{-x^2} \, dx = 1. \qquad (20.3\text{–}6)$$

By a similar integration of Eq. (20.2–2), it can be shown that the translational energy E_t of the equilibrium system is $3NkT/2$, in agreement with Eq. (11.4–3). Substituting Eq. (20.3–4) into Eq. (20.2–2) and performing the integration over the volume V of configuration space gives

$$E_t = (Nm/2)(m/2\pi kT)^{3/2} \iiint_{-\infty}^{\infty} (v_x^2 + v_y^2 + v_z^2) e^{-m(v_x^2+v_y^2+v_z^2)/2kT} \, dv_x \, dv_y \, dv_z.$$

$$(20.3\text{–}7)$$

To integrate over velocity space, let us replace the volume element $dv_x \, dv_y \, dv_z$ by a thin spherical shell of radius $v = (v_x^2 + v_y^2 + v_z^2)^{1/2}$ and thickness dv, having a volume $4\pi v^2 \, dv$. Equation (20.3–7) thereby reduces to the single integration on v from 0 to ∞:

$$E_t = (Nm/2)(m/2\pi kT)^{3/2} \int_{0}^{\infty} v^2 e^{-mv^2/2kT} (4\pi v^2 \, dv)$$

$$= (4NkT/\pi^{1/2}) \int_{0}^{\infty} (mv^2/2kT)^2 e^{-mv^2/2kT} \, d[mv^2/2kT]^{1/2}$$

$$= 3NkT/2 \qquad (20.3\text{–}8)$$

through use of Table A–4.

Since the average kinetic energy per molecule is $(3/2)kT$, the average value $\langle v^2 \rangle$ of the square of the velocity is found to be

$$\langle mv^2/2 \rangle = 3kT/2$$

or

$$\langle v^2 \rangle = 3kT/m. \qquad (20.3\text{–}9)$$

The *mean speed* $\langle v \rangle$ of a molecule is the average value of the magnitude v of the velocity:

$$\langle v \rangle \equiv (1/n) \int vf \, dv_x \, dv_y \, dv_z. \tag{20.3–10}$$

For the Maxwellian distribution given by Eq. (20.3–4), we may calculate this to be

$$\langle v \rangle = (m/2\pi kT)^{3/2} \iiint\limits_{-\infty}^{\infty} (v_x^2 + v_y^2 + v_z^2)^{1/2} e^{-m(v_x^2+v_y^2+v_z^2)/2kT} \, dv_x \, dv_y \, dv_z$$

$$= (m/2\pi kT)^{3/2} \int_0^{\infty} v e^{-mv^2/2kT} (4\pi v^2 \, dv)$$

$$= 4(2kT/\pi m)^{1/2} \int_0^{\infty} (mv^2/2kT)^{3/2} e^{-mv^2/2kT} \, d[mv^2/2kT]^{1/2}$$

$$= (8kT/\pi m)^{1/2} \tag{20.3–11}$$

by use of Table A–4 in evaluating the definite integral. For a monatomic gas, the speed of sound a given by Eqs. (19.7–15) and (13.4–10) is $(5kT/3m)^{1/2}$, which is smaller than the mean speed $\langle v \rangle$ by the factor $(5\pi/24)^{1/2} = 0.809$. Nevertheless, it can be seen that a sound wave propagates at a speed comparable to the mean speed of the molecules. The root-mean-square speed $\{\langle v^2 \rangle\}^{1/2}$ is larger than the mean speed by the factor $(3\pi/8)^{1/2} = 1.083$.

20.4　The fluxes of mass, momentum, and energy

The molecules of a gas are in rapid motion, moving with a mean speed which is approximately equal to the speed of sound. If we wish to treat a gas as a fluid, as was done in Chapter 19, by considering the motion of a macroscopic element of volume, then we must be careful to account for the fact that there is a flow of molecules across the surface of such a volume element. At any point on the surface of the element there will be some molecules having velocities directed outward and others with inwardly directed velocities. Even though such molecules may suffer a collision after moving a short distance, at any instant there are many molecules which, within a very short time, will cross the surface of the volume element in either direction. In this section we will be concerned with the flow of such molecules, and with the "flow," or *flux*, of momentum and energy carried by the molecules crossing an imaginary surface in a gas.

Let us consider a macroscopic control volume V in a stationary gas enclosed by a surface A, as shown in Fig. 20.2. We wish to determine the rate at which molecules at a point $\mathbf{r}$ on the surface A cross the unit area ΔA, whose inwardly directed unit normal is $\mathbf{n}$. To calculate this quantity we will first select a group of molecules at the point $\mathbf{r}$ having a velocity $\mathbf{v}$ which lies within a volume element

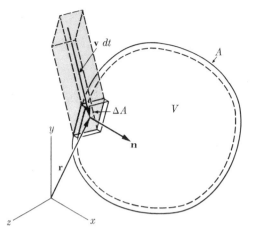

Fig. 20.2. The molecules of velocity **v**, which flow in the time dt across the unit elemental area ΔA of the control surface A, lie within the volume of the parallelepiped shown by dotted lines. The unit vector **n** is normal to the surface element ΔA.

$dv_x \, dv_y \, dv_z$ in velocity space, for which there are $f\{\mathbf{r}, \mathbf{v}, t\} \, dv_x \, dv_y \, dv_z$ such molecules per unit volume of configuration space. In a short time dt all such molecules within the parallelepiped of slant height **v** dt and base area ΔA, lying outside the surface A as shown in Fig. 20.2, will move inward across the area ΔA. Since the volume of the parallelepiped is $(\mathbf{v} \, dt) \cdot \mathbf{n}(\Delta A)$ and there are

$$f\{\mathbf{r}, \mathbf{v}, t\} \, dv_x \, dv_y \, dv_z$$

molecules per unit volume, the corresponding number flow of molecules per unit area and time is just $\mathbf{v} \cdot \mathbf{n} \, f\{\mathbf{r}, \mathbf{v}, t\} \, dv_x \, dv_y \, dv_z$. If we denote the net number flux [molecules/(unit area)(unit time)] by Γ_n, then by summing over all velocities we find

$$\Gamma_n\{\mathbf{r}, t\} \equiv \int\!\!\!\int\!\!\!\int_{-\infty}^{\infty} \mathbf{v} \cdot \mathbf{n} \, f\{\mathbf{r}, \mathbf{v}, t\} \, dv_x \, dv_y \, dv_z. \tag{20.4–1}$$

If we should choose the x-axis to coincide with the direction of **n**, then $\mathbf{v} \cdot \mathbf{n} = v_x$ and the number flux Γ_x in the positive x-direction is

$$\Gamma_x\{\mathbf{r}, t\} = \int\!\!\!\int\!\!\!\int_{-\infty}^{\infty} v_x \, f\{\mathbf{r}, \mathbf{v}, t\} \, dv_x \, dv_y \, dv_z. \tag{20.4–2*}$$

---

* Here Γ_x may be regarded as the x-component of a number flux vector $\boldsymbol{\Gamma}$ defined by $\boldsymbol{\Gamma} \equiv \int\!\!\int\!\!\int_{-\infty}^{+\infty} \int \mathbf{v} f \, dv_x \, dv_y \, dv_z$ so that $\Gamma_n = \boldsymbol{\Gamma} \cdot \mathbf{n}$. Since we shall consider only one-dimensional problems, we shall not adopt this more general notation. However, it is worth emphasizing that the number flux Γ_n depends on **n**, that is, on the orientation of the surface element ΔA.

In a stationary gas at equilibrium, Γ_x is zero because there can be no net motion of the gas molecules.† However, of equal practical interest is the flux of molecules in one direction only, called the *efflux*. For example, the efflux Γ_x^+ in the x-direction would be given by

$$\Gamma_x^+ \{\mathbf{r}, t\} \equiv \iint \left[\int_0^\infty v_x f\{\mathbf{r}, \mathbf{v}, t\} \, dv_x \right] dv_y \, dv_z \qquad (20.4\text{-}3)$$

and that in the $(-x)$-direction is defined as

$$\Gamma_x^- \{\mathbf{r}, t\} \equiv \iint \left[\int_{-\infty}^0 (-v_x) f\{\mathbf{r}, \mathbf{v}, t\} \, dv_x \right] dv_y \, dv_z, \qquad (20.4\text{-}4)$$

so that the net flux Γ_x would be

$$\Gamma_x = \Gamma_x^+ - \Gamma_x^-. \qquad (20.4\text{-}5)$$

In a gas at equilibrium, the efflux Γ_x^+ would not be zero but would equal Γ_x^- so that the net flux Γ_x would be zero.

As a simple example of the usefulness of this concept, consider a container of gas surrounded by a vacuum. If there is a small hole in the surface of this container, as shown in Fig. 20.3, the rate at which the gas escapes into the vacuum may be found by calculating the efflux Γ_x^+ at the hole, for no molecules will enter the hole from the vacuum side; i.e., at the hole $\Gamma_x^- = 0$. At any other point on the surface of the container, Γ_x^+ and Γ_x^- will be equal because the solid surface reflects as many molecules as are incident upon it.

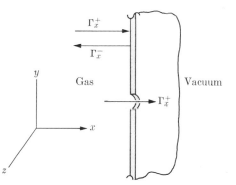

Fig. 20.3. The flow of gas through a small hole in a container surrounded by a vacuum may be found from the efflux Γ_x^+ of molecules moving in one direction across a plane in a stationary gas equilibrium.

---

† In this case $f\{\mathbf{r}, \mathbf{v}, t\}$ is an *even* function of v_x; that is, $f\{-v_x\} = f\{v_x\}$. As a consequence $\int_{-\infty}^\infty v_x f \, dv_x$ must be zero and so also must Γ_x as determined from Eq. (20.4-2). There can be no net flux Γ_x unless the distribution function f is an asymmetric function of the velocity components v_x, v_y, or v_z. Such a distribution function is called *skewed*.

Let us calculate the efflux Γ_x^+, assuming that $f\{\mathbf{r}, \mathbf{v}, t\}$ is the equilibrium Maxwellian distribution given by Eq. (20.3–4).* On substituting Eq. (20.3–4) into Eq. (20.4–3) for Γ_x^+, we find

$$\Gamma_x^+ = \iint \left[\int_0^\infty v_x n (m/2\pi kT)^{3/2} e^{-m(v_x^2 + v_y^2 + v_z^2)/2kT} \, dv_x \right] dv_y \, dv_z$$

$$= n \left[\int_{-\infty}^\infty (m/2\pi kT)^{1/2} e^{-mv_y^2/2kT} \, dv_y \right] \left[\int_{-\infty}^\infty (m/2\pi kT)^{1/2} e^{-mv_z^2/2kT} \, dv_z \right]$$

$$\times \left[(2kT/\pi m)^{1/2} \int_0^\infty (mv_x^2/2kT)^{1/2} e^{-mv_x^2/2kT} \, d(mv_x^2/2kT)^{1/2} \right]$$

$$= n(kT/2\pi m)^{1/2} \tag{20.4–6}$$

through use of Table A–4 and Eq. (20.3–6). In terms of the mean speed $\langle v \rangle$ given by Eq. (20.3–11), the number efflux Γ_x^+ can be conveniently written as

$$\Gamma_x^+ = n\langle v \rangle/4 \tag{20.4–7}$$

so that the average value of v_x for the $n/2$ particles per unit volume moving toward $+x$ is one-half of the mean speed $\langle v \rangle$.

Each molecule which passes across the surface element ΔA possesses a mass m, a momentum $m\mathbf{v}$, and a kinetic energy $mv^2/2$ which are transported across the surface by the moving molecule. Because these quantities are conserved by isolated systems of molecules, it is of interest to compute the flux (and efflux) of mass, momentum, and energy† in a manner similar to that used above to determine the number of molecules. Of course, the mass flux (or efflux) is simply obtained by multiplying Γ_n or Γ_x^+ by the molecular mass m. However, to find the momentum and energy fluxes we must multiply the number flow $\mathbf{v} \cdot \mathbf{n} f\{\mathbf{r}, \mathbf{v}, t\} \, dv_x \, dv_y \, dv_z$ of molecules having a velocity $\mathbf{v}$ by $m\mathbf{v}$ or $mv^2/2$ before integrating over all velocities.

If we denote by $\mathbf{P}_n$ the flux of momentum across the element of unit area ΔA in Fig. 20.2; that is, the momentum carried by the molecules whose number flux is Γ_n, then $\mathbf{P}_n$ is

$$\mathbf{P}_n\{\mathbf{r}, t\} \equiv \iiint_{-\infty}^{\infty} m\mathbf{v}(\mathbf{v} \cdot \mathbf{n}) f\{\mathbf{r}, \mathbf{v}, t\} \, dv_x \, dv_y \, dv_z. \tag{20.4–8}$$

---

* This assumption is valid if the diameter of the hole is small compared with the distance between molecular collisions (mean free path as discussed in Section 20.5) in the gas near the hole. When this is so, the flow through the hole is said to be a *free-molecule flow*. If the hole is much larger than the mean free path, then the flow is properly treated by the method of fluid dynamics discussed in Chapter 19.

† If the molecules carry an electric charge, as do the free electrons in a solid, then the current, or flux of charge (which is also conserved), would be of interest, as discussed in Section 20.8.

The momentum flux $\mathbf{P}_n$ is a vector quantity since it is the product of the vector momentum $m\mathbf{v}$ of a particle times the number flux $\mathbf{v} \cdot \mathbf{n} \, f\{\mathbf{r}, \mathbf{v}, t\} \, dv_x \, dv_y \, dv_z$.* If we choose the x-axis to coincide with the unit normal $\mathbf{n}$ so that $\mathbf{v} \cdot \mathbf{n} = v_x$, then the momentum flux vector $\mathbf{P}_x$ would be

$$\mathbf{P}_x\{\mathbf{r}, t\} \equiv \iiint\limits_{-\infty}^{\infty} m\mathbf{v}v_x f\{\mathbf{r}, \mathbf{v}, t\} \, dv_x \, dv_y \, dv_z. \qquad (20.4\text{-}9)$$

The components of the vector $\mathbf{P}_x$ in the x- and y-directions, denoted by P_{xx} and P_{xy}, would thus be

$$P_{xx} \equiv \iiint\limits_{-\infty}^{\infty} mv_x^2 f \, dv_x \, dv_y \, dv_z, \qquad (20.4\text{-}10)$$

$$P_{xy} \equiv \iiint\limits_{-\infty}^{\infty} mv_x v_y f \, dv_x \, dv_y \, dv_z \qquad (20.4\text{-}11)$$

and similarly for the z-component.

In a stationary gas at equilibrium, the momentum flux P_{xx} may be found by substituting the Maxwellian distribution of Eq. (20.3-4) into (20.4-10):

$$P_{xx} = mn(m/2\pi kT)^{3/2} \iiint\limits_{-\infty}^{\infty} v_x^2 e^{-m(v_x^2+v_y^2+v_z^2)/2kT} \, dv_x \, dv_y \, dv_z$$

$$= (2nkT/\pi^{1/2}) \int_{-\infty}^{\infty} (mv_x^2/2kT)e^{-mv_x^2/2kT} \, d[mv_x^2/2kT]^{1/2}$$

$$= nkT \qquad (20.4\text{-}12)$$

through use of Table A-4 and Eq. (20.3-6). According to the perfect-gas law, the equilibrium gas pressure p is equal to $NkT/V = nkT$. Thus the momentum flux P_{xx} at equilibrium is equal to the pressure p,

$$P_{xx} = p, \qquad (20.4\text{-}13)$$

and the momentum fluxes P_{xy} and P_{xz} are zero because the integrand of Eq. (20.4-11) is an odd function of v_x (or v_y).

The efflux of momentum, that is, the momentum carried by those molecules moving in one direction only, may be found by integrating over half of velocity space:

$$\mathbf{P}_x^+ \equiv \iint\limits_{-\infty}^{\infty} \left[\int_0^{\infty} m\mathbf{v}v_x f \, dv_x \right] dv_y \, dv_z. \qquad (20.4\text{-}14)$$

---

* The vector $\mathbf{P}_n$ is not necessarily parallel to $\mathbf{n}$. Since the dimensions of momentum flux are the same as pressure, $\mathbf{P}_n$ may be regarded as the *stress* in a gas. Like the stress in a solid, it is a tensor quantity.

For a gas at equilibrium, the x-component of $\mathbf{P}_x^+$ is one half of P_{xx}:

$$P_{xx}^+ = P_{xx}/2 = p/2. \tag{20.4–15}$$

The momentum flux of all the molecules approaching a wall is therefore $p/2$, as is that of all those leaving the wall after reflection. Thus the force per unit area of wall is twice $p/2$ or p. It is this change in momentum of the gas molecules reflected from a wall which was used in Section 1.6 to compute the pressure of a perfect gas.

The flux of kinetic energy carried by molecules crossing the surface ΔA is found by multiplying the number flux $\mathbf{v} \cdot \mathbf{n}\, f\{\mathbf{r}, \mathbf{v}, t\}\, dv_x\, dv_y\, dv_z$ by $mv^2/2$ and integrating over all velocities. Denoting this energy flux by Q_n, we have

$$Q_n\{\mathbf{r}, t\} \equiv \int\!\!\!\int\!\!\!\int_{-\infty}^{\infty} \left(\frac{mv^2}{2}\right) \mathbf{v} \cdot \mathbf{n} f\{\mathbf{r}, \mathbf{v}, t\}\, dv_x\, dv_y\, dv_z \tag{20.4–16}$$

or, for the energy flux Q_x in the x-direction,

$$Q_x\{\mathbf{r}, t\} \equiv \int\!\!\!\int\!\!\!\int_{-\infty}^{\infty} \left[\frac{m(v_x^2 + v_y^2 + v_z^2)v_x}{2}\right] f\{\mathbf{r}, \mathbf{v}, t\}\, dv_x\, dv_y\, dv_z. \tag{20.4–17}$$

In a stationary gas at equilibrium, f is the Maxwellian distribution, and the integrand of Eq. (20.4–17) is an odd function of v_x, so that $Q_x = 0$. However, at equilibrium the kinetic energy efflux Q_x^+ carried by the molecules moving in the $+x$-direction only is not zero:

$$Q_x^+ = \int\!\!\!\int_{-\infty}^{\infty}\left\{\int_0^{\infty}\left[m(v_x^2 + v_y^2 + v_z^2)\frac{v_x}{2}\right]\left[n\left(\frac{m}{2\pi kT}\right)^{3/2}\right]e^{-m(v_x^2+v_y^2+v_z^2)/2kT}\, dv_x\right\} dv_y\, dv_z$$

$$= \int_0^{\infty}\left(\frac{mnv_x^3}{2}\right)\left(\frac{m}{2\pi kT}\right)^{1/2} e^{-mv_x^2/2kT}\, dv_x + \int_0^{\infty}\left(\frac{mnv_x}{2\pi}\right)e^{-mv_x^2/2kT}$$

$$\times \left\{\int_{-\infty}^{\infty}\left(\frac{mv_y^2}{2kT}\right)e^{-mv_y^2/2kT}\, dv_y + \int_{-\infty}^{\infty}\left(\frac{mv_z^2}{2kT}\right)e^{-mv_z^2/2kT}\, dv_z\right\} dv_x$$

$$= nkT\left(\frac{2kT}{\pi m}\right)^{1/2}\int_0^{\infty}\left(\frac{mv_x^2}{2kT}\right)^{3/2}e^{-mv_x^2/2kT}\, d\left[\frac{mv_x^2}{2kT}\right]^{1/2}$$

$$+ \left(\frac{nkT}{\pi}\right)\left(\frac{2kT}{m}\right)^{1/2}\int_0^{\infty}\left(\frac{mv_x^2}{2kT}\right)^{1/2}e^{-mv_x^2/2kT}\, d\left[\frac{mv_x^2}{2kT}\right]^{1/2}$$

$$\times \left\{2\int_{-\infty}^{\infty}\left(\frac{mv_y^2}{2kT}\right)e^{-mv_y^2/2kT}\, d\left[\frac{mv_y^2}{2kT}\right]^{1/2}\right\} = nkT\left(\frac{2kT}{\pi m}\right)^{1/2}, \tag{20.4–18}$$

where the definite integrals have been evaluated from Table A–4. Since the mean speed $\langle v \rangle$ equals $(8kT/\pi m)^{1/2}$, the equilibrium efflux Q_x^+ of kinetic energy could also be written as

$$Q_x^+ = \left(\frac{nkT}{2} \right) \langle v \rangle = \Gamma_x^+(2kT) \qquad (20.4\text{--}19)$$

through use of Eq. (20.4–7). Thus the average kinetic energy transported by the molecules moving in the $+x$-direction is $2kT$ per molecule rather than $3kT/2$, which is the average kinetic energy per molecule. The reason for this paradoxical result is that we have averaged the kinetic energy over the flux of molecules, rather than the number of molecules, of a given velocity. Since the flux is proportional to the number times the velocity, the flux-averaged kinetic energy places greater weight on the high-velocity molecules than does the number-averaged kinetic energy and is therefore greater than the latter.

In this section we have determined the relationship between the distribution function $f(\mathbf{r}, \mathbf{v}, t)$ and the fluxes and effluxes of mass, momentum, and energy. For a stationary gas at equilibrium, the flux of mass and energy is zero because of the symmetry of the distribution function, while the flux of momentum component normal to a surface is equal to the gas pressure. The effluxes of mass, momentum, and energy carried by molecules moving in one direction only were also computed for a stationary gas at equilibrium. These latter quantities, which are useful in determining the transfer of mass, momentum, and energy in simple free-molecule flows, will also be used in Sections 20.6 and 20.7.

20.5 Binary collisions in a gas

If two gas molecules approach close enough to each other, there will be sufficient force exerted to deflect both molecules from their original straight lines of flight. When this happens, the two molecules are said to undergo a *binary collision*. Even when the force between two molecules is directed along the line joining their mass centers (i.e., it is a central force), the change in motion of the molecules in a binary collision is not easy to compute. For the sake of simplicity in discussing the effects of collisions, we shall use the *hard-sphere model* of a perfect gas: the molecules exert no force on each other until their mass centers are a distance d apart, at which point there arises an infinite repulsive central force which causes an instantaneous change in their velocities. If the molecules were macroscopic, hard, frictionless spheres of diameter d, then the force between them would be of this type. For this simplest of models, the dynamics of a collision is readily determined.

Let us consider two hard-sphere molecules, denoted by subscripts 1 and 2, having position vectors $\mathbf{r}_1$ and $\mathbf{r}_2$ and velocities $\mathbf{v}_1$ and $\mathbf{v}_2$ at a given instant, as shown in Fig. 20.4(a). According to Section 2.7, because the two molecules are subject only to central forces, the relative motion of 2 with respect to 1

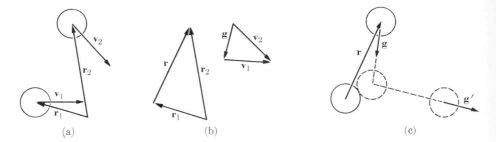

Fig. 20.4. Two hard-sphere molecules with positions r_1 and r_2 and velocities v_1 and v_2 undergo a binary collision for which the relative motion is shown in (c). The relative position r and the relative velocity g are determined as in (b).

is the same as that of a single particle having a reduced mass m_{12} given by

$$1/m_{12} \equiv 1/m_1 + 1/m_2 \qquad (20.5\text{--}1)$$

and moving with the relative position $r \equiv r_2 - r_1$ and the relative velocity $g \equiv v_2 - v_1$ but subject to the same force of repulsion upon collision (i.e., when $r = d$). We can therefore determine r and g as shown in Fig. 20. 4(b) and plot them in the usual way for the motion of a single particle, as shown in Fig. 20.4(c). Following this motion in the plane of r and g, the two molecules will collide when their centers are a distance d apart as illustrated. The relative velocity g will be changed instantaneously to the value g', such that the change in momentum $m_{12}(g' - g)$ is in the direction of the line of centers, and hence of the repulsive force, at the instant of collision. While the relative velocity g is changed in direction to g', there is no change in its magnitude because the kinetic energy $m_{12}g^2/2$ is conserved in the collision since the repulsive force is conservative. As a consequence the change in relative motion in the collision may be found and, by inverting the construction of Fig. 20.4(b) and (a), so may the absolute motion also be determined.

Let us next compute the rate at which a given molecule 1 is struck by other molecules 2 which approach it from various directions with various relative velocities g. Figure 20.5 shows the relative motions of several type-2 molecules which collide with molecule 1. Whenever the mass center of a type-2 molecule reaches a distance d from the mass center of molecule 1, a collision occurs. If we draw an imaginary sphere of radius d about the mass center of molecule 1, then the number of collisions ν_{12} per unit time between molecule 1 and all molecules 2 is equal to the rate at which the mass centers of molecules 2 reach the surface of this sphere of area $4\pi d^2$. In Section 20.4 we found that the rate Γ_n^+ at which molecules crossed a fixed surface of unit area was equal to $n\langle v \rangle/4$. In the space of relative motion, the rate at which type-2 molecules will cross a unit area will therefore be $n_2\langle g \rangle/4$, where $\langle g \rangle$ is the average relative speed. Thus the collision frequency ν_{12} of molecule 1 with molecules 2 will be the product

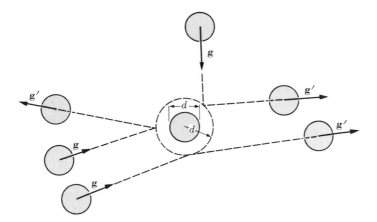

Fig. 20.5. The relative motion of "hard-sphere" molecules undergoing collision with a given molecule of diameter d. The relative velocities $\mathbf{g}$ and $\mathbf{g}'$ before and after collision, respectively, are shown to indicate the direction of travel.

of the area $4\pi d^2$ of the spherical surface and the efflux of molecules $n_2\langle g\rangle/4$:

$$\nu_{12} = \pi d^2 n_2\langle g\rangle. \tag{20.5-2}$$

The factor πd^2, which is the projected area of the sphere of radius d, is usually called the *collision cross section*.

The average value $\langle g\rangle$ of the relative speed g is not the same as the average speed $\langle v\rangle$ of either molecule 1 or molecule 2, but in a gas at equilibrium it is found to be* the same as the average speed of a molecule having a reduced mass m_{12},

$$\langle g\rangle = (8kT/\pi m_{12})^{1/2}, \tag{20.5-3}$$

which is not surprising since the relative motion involves only the reduced mass of the colliding molecules and not their separate masses.

In a single component gas, for which all molecules have the same mass m, the reduced mass $m_{12} = (1/m + 1/m)^{-1} = m/2$, and $\langle g\rangle = \sqrt{2}\,\langle v\rangle$. The collision frequency ν, given in Eq. (20.5-2), therefore becomes

$$\nu = \sqrt{2}\,\pi d^2 n\langle v\rangle, \tag{20.5-4}$$

where we have dropped all subscripts since all molecules are identical.

If a molecule undergoes ν collisions per unit time while moving with an average speed $\langle v\rangle$, then the average distance l between collisions, called the *mean free path*, would be the product of the average speed $\langle v\rangle$ and the average time ν^{-1} between collisions:

$$l \equiv \langle v\rangle/\nu = 1/\sqrt{2}\,\pi d^2 n, \tag{20.5-5}$$

---

* For a derivation of the mean relative speed, see Chapman and Cowling, p. 89.

where we have used Eq. (20.5–4) to determine the mean free path l in terms of the molecular diameter d and number density n. Thus the mean free path varies inversely with the number density n of the molecules and the collision cross section πd^2.

Let us calculate approximately the collision frequency ν and mean free path l of an "air" molecule in air at atmospheric pressure and a temperature of $300°K$. We shall assume that air has a molecular weight of 29 and that the molecular diameter is 4×10^{-8} cm (see, for example, Fig. 12.8). Using the constants given in Table A–1, we find $n = 2.45 \times 10^{19}$ cm^{-3} and $m = 4.85 \times 10^{-23}$ gm, while from Eqs. (20.3–11), (20.5–4), and (20.5–5) we compute that $\langle v \rangle = 4.67 \times 10^4$ cm/sec, $\nu = 8.08 \times 10^9$ sec^{-1}, and $l = 5.75 \times 10^{-6}$ cm. Because of this very small mean free path and the very large collision frequency, air behaves like a fluid continuum in most macroscopic processes. Only at very high altitudes where l becomes large would the flow of air over a vehicle become a free-molecule flow rather than a classical continuum flow.

It is worth noting that the mean free path in a gas is always larger than the average distance between molecules, $n^{-1/3}$. In the numerical example considered above, $l = 5.75 \times 10^{-6}$ cm while $n^{-1/3} = 3.45 \times 10^{-7}$ cm. In general, the ratio $l/n^{-1/3}$ may be found from Eq. (20.5–5) to be

$$\frac{l}{n^{-1/3}} = \frac{1}{\sqrt{2}\,\pi(dn^{1/3})^2}. \tag{20.5–6}$$

Since $dn^{1/3}$ is the ratio of the diameter d of a molecule to the average distance $n^{-1/3}$ between molecules, it must therefore be very small if the system is a gas rather than a liquid or solid, as discussed in Section 11.2. As a consequence, $l \gg n^{-1/3}$.

20.6 Viscosity

When one solid slides over another, like a book sliding on a table, a steady external force is required to maintain the motion. This applied force is equal and opposite to the *frictional force* exerted by the table on the book. The frictional force is found to depend on the normal force between the surfaces, the speed of the motion, and the nature of the materials involved.

If the two surfaces are separated by a layer of fluid, such as lubricating oil or even a gas, then the corresponding frictional force τ per unit area of surface, called the *friction stress* or *shear stress*, is found from experiment to be proportional to the relative speed U divided by the thickness δ of the fluid film separating the two surfaces, the constant of proportionality μ being called the *viscosity*:

$$\tau = \mu U/\delta. \tag{20.6–1}$$

The viscosity μ is not the same for all fluids, but for any one fluid it does not

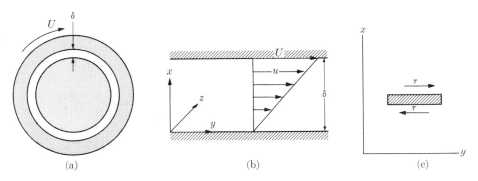

Fig. 20.6. Plane Couette flow (b) may be approximately achieved experimentally by rotating the outer of two concentric cylinders with a peripheral speed U while maintaining the inner one stationary (a). If the radial spacing is very small compared with the cylinder radius, then the fluid moves as though contained between two infinite plane-parallel surfaces separated by a distance δ, one being stationary and the other moving with a speed U, as in (b). The tangential shear stresses acting on a thin fluid element shown in (c) must add to zero since there is no tangential acceleration.

depend on U or δ; it depends only on the thermodynamic state of the fluid, that is, its temperature, density, etc.

Figure 20.6(a) illustrates a simple viscous flow contained between concentric rotating cylinders in which, because of the small spacing, the flow is nearly the same as that between two infinite-plane parallel surfaces, as shown in Fig. 20.4(b). In this experiment the frictional force per unit area of cylinder surface may be measured and the viscosity may be found from Eq. (20.6–1). Also, the tangential velocity u may be measured, and it is found to vary linearly with the distance x from the inner surface, as shown in Fig. 20.6(b):

$$u = Ux/\delta. \qquad (20.6\text{–}2)$$

If we consider the y-component of forces acting on a fluid element, as shown in Fig. 20.6(c), then we can see that the shear stress τ must be constant throughout the fluid, for there is no acceleration of the fluid in the y-direction and no other forces are acting on the fluid. If we differentiate Eq. (20.6–2) to obtain

$$du/dx = U/\delta \qquad (20.6\text{–}3)$$

and substitute it into Eq. (20.6–1), we find that

$$\tau = \mu \, du/dx \qquad (20.6\text{–}4)$$

for plane Couette flow. Although we have not shown it to be so, Eq. (20.6–4) is generally found to hold empirically for other simple steady flows of viscous fluids; it was first suggested by Newton. In other words, if we measure the velocity distribution in a flow, then the motion calculated from the viscous force computed from Eq. (20.6–4) together with the other forces exerted on the fluid will be found to agree with the motion which is measured.

We shall now calculate approximately the shear stress τ in a gas in plane Couette flow by making use of the simple mean-free-path ideas discussed above in Section 20.5. This shear stress should equal the net flux P_{xy} of the momentum in the y-direction carried across a unit area of fluid surface normal to the x-axis. Because the gas is not in equilibrium, we shall calculate this flux by adding algebraically the two effluxes P_{xy}^{+} and P_{xy}^{-}.

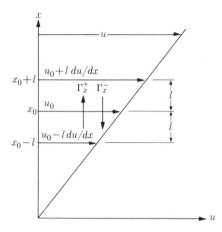

Fig. 20.7.   The distribution of fluid velocity u in a plane Couette flow.

In Fig. 20.7 is shown the fluid velocity distribution in a plane Couette flow. If u_0 is the velocity at $x = x_0$, then the velocity in any other plane normal to the x-axis is $u_0 + (x - x_0)\,du/dx$. In particular, the fluid velocities at the planes $x = x_0 \pm l$ are $u = u_0 \pm l\,du/dx$, respectively. The efflux of particles across the $(x = x_0)$-plane are Γ_x^{+} and Γ_x^{-}, as shown in Fig. 20.7. To estimate the efflux of momentum P_{xy}^{+} we shall multiply the number efflux Γ_x^{+} by the average y-momentum $m(u_0 - l\,du/dx)$ of the particles at the plane $x = x_0 - l$, which is, on the average, the location at which the molecules whose efflux is Γ_x^{+} experienced their last collision. Therefore, our basic assumption is that the molecules moving in one direction possess the mean characteristics of the fluid at a distance l in the direction from which they are moving. We thus find P_{xy}^{+} to be

$$P_{xy}^{+} = \Gamma_x^{+} m(u_0 - l\,du/dx) \tag{20.6–5}$$

and P_{xy}^{-} to be

$$P_{xy}^{-} = \Gamma_x^{-} m(u_0 + l\,du/dx). \tag{20.6–6}$$

Subtracting the second of these equations from the first, and noting that

$\Gamma_x^+ = \Gamma_x^- = n\langle v\rangle/4$, we find the net flux P_{xy} of the y-component of momentum to be

$$P_{xy} = P_{xy}^+ - P_{xy}^- = -(\Gamma_x^+ + \Gamma_x^-)ml\,\frac{du}{dx}$$

$$= -\left(\frac{mnl\langle v\rangle}{2}\right)\frac{du}{dx}.$$

(20.6–7)

Since the shear stress τ given by Eq. (20.6–4) is equal to $-P_{xy}$, we find that the viscosity μ is

$$\mu = \rho l\langle v\rangle/2$$
(20.6–8)

in which $\rho = mn$ is the mass density of the gas. In terms of the molecular diameter d, the viscosity μ is found from substituting Eq. (20.5–5) into (20.6–8) to be

$$\mu = m\langle v\rangle/8^{1/2}\pi\,d^2$$
(20.6–9)

and is therefore independent of the number density of the gas.

The more exact kinetic theory of a monatomic hard-sphere gas* gives the following expression for the viscosity:

$$\mu = (5\pi/32)\rho l\langle v\rangle,$$
(20.6–10)

which is only 2% less than the approximation of Eq. (20.6–8). This agreement is fortuitous, because our approximate method provides only an estimate of the shear stress rather than an exact calculation. However, the dependence of the viscosity on the mean speed $\langle v\rangle$ and molecular diameter d is properly accounted for by the approximate theory based on the mean-free-path concept.

For a gas composed of hard-sphere molecules, the viscosity as given by Eq. (20.6–9) will be proportional to the mean speed $\langle v\rangle$, and hence to $T^{1/2}$, but will not vary with gas density or pressure at a given temperature T. Measurements of the viscosity of a gas show indeed that it varies only with the temperature, but in general it is not proportionate to $T^{1/2}$. To explain the measured temperature dependence we must resort to more sophisticated models for the intermolecular potential energy than that of the hard sphere, such as the attractive-repulsive potential shown in Fig. 11.1. In using this model, the dynamics of a binary collision are more difficult to calculate but, on the average, can be considered the same as that between hard spheres whose diameter d is a function of the temperature T; that is, $d = d\{T\}$. The reason that the effective size of the molecules in a collision changes with temperature is that an increase in temperature and hence an increase in the average kinetic energy of a colliding pair of molecules will require that they approach closer to each other, that is, experience a greater repulsive force, in order to be deflected in the col-

---

* See Chapman and Cowling, p. 218.

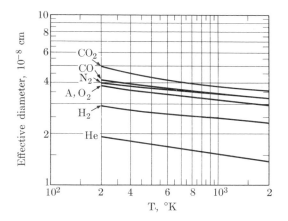

Fig. 20.8. The effective hard-sphere diameter d of several gases as a function of temperature. (Data from Hilsenrath et $al.$ and Hirschfelder, Curtiss and Bird.)

lision. As a result, the molecules appear to be smaller spheres as the temperature increases. In Fig. 20.8, in which are plotted the effective hard-sphere diameters of several gas molecules as a function of temperature, this trend can easily be seen. It is also evident that there is not a great difference in size between common molecules.

Another example of the usefulness of the mean-free-path concept is the determination of the fluid velocity u_s at a solid surface. In macroscopic fluid dynamics, the velocity of a viscous fluid flowing past a solid surface is considered to be zero at the surface (that is, $u_s = 0$) because the fluid "sticks" to the surface of the solid. In a gas the velocity u_s is not exactly zero and the gas is said to "slip" along the solid surface with a speed $u_s \geq 0$. Under most circumstances the *slip velocity* u_s is very small compared with the bulk velocity of the fluid and may be considered zero for all practical purposes. However, at very low densities the phenomenon of *fluid slip* must be taken into account.

To compute the slip velocity u_s at a wall, consider the plane Couette flow illustrated in Fig. 20.6(b). At the wall ($x = 0$), there will be an efflux Γ_x^+ of molecules away from the wall, which carries no y-component of momentum ($P_{xy}^+ = 0$) because these molecules leave from a stationary surface. There will be an equal efflux Γ_x^- toward the wall of molecules having an average momentum of $m\{u_s + l(du/dx)_{x=0}\}$ acquired by collisions about one mean free path away from the surface, that is, at $x = l$, where the fluid velocity is $u_s + l(du/dx)_{x=0}$. Thus the net y-momentum flux $(P_{xy})_{x=0}$ would be

$$(P_{xy})_{x=0} = -\Gamma_x^- m\{u_s + l(du/dx)_{x=0}\}$$

$$= -\frac{\rho\langle v\rangle\{u_s + l(du/dx)_{x=0}\}}{4},$$

(20.6–11)

in which the efflux Γ_x^- has been replaced by $n\langle v \rangle / 4$. Now the shear stress at the wall, which equals $-(P_{xy})_{x=0}$, should also equal $\mu(du/dx)_{x=0}$:

$$\rho\langle v \rangle \{u_s + l(du/dx)_{x=0}\} / 4 = \mu(du/dx)_{x=0}$$

or

$$u_s = \{4\mu/\rho\langle v \rangle - l\} (du/dx)_{x=0}$$
$$= l(du/dx)_{x=0}, \tag{20.6-12}$$

in which Eq. (20.6–8) has been used to eliminate μ. The fluid velocity u_s at a surface is therefore not generally zero.

In the Couette flow illustrated in Fig. 20.6, the velocity gradient du/dx is U/δ, so that the slip velocity u_s at the inner stationary wall is $U(l/\delta)$ and would therefore be very small whenever the mean free path l is small compared with the gap δ. At very low densities for which l becomes large compared with δ the slip velocity may be an appreciable fraction of U.

In the study of fluid dynamics there arises a dimensionless similarity parameter $\rho U \delta / \mu$, called the *Reynolds number*, where U and δ are a characteristic velocity and length of the flow. This parameter is a measure of the ratio of the inertial force to the viscous force on a fluid element. Using Eq. (20.6–8) for the viscosity, we find that the Reynolds number of a flowing gas would be $2(U/\langle v \rangle)(\delta/l)$. Since the factor δ/l is necessarily large for a continuum flow (as compared with a free-molecule flow), and the fact $U/\langle v \rangle$ is approximately equal to the Mach number, the Reynolds number of a continuum gas flow tends to be large, especially for supersonic flow.

20.7 Thermal conductivity

In the absence of fluid motion, the transport of energy through a gas by molecular collisions is called *heat conduction*. If parallel hot and cold surfaces are separated by a thin layer of gas, as shown in Fig. 20.9, then it is found empirically that the heat $-Q_n$ leaving the hot plate per unit area and time is proportional to the temperature difference $T_h - T_c$ between the two plates and inversely proportional to the distance δ between them, with a constant of

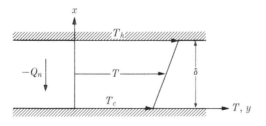

Fig. 20.9. The one-dimensional flow of heat between plane-parallel hot and cold surfaces is the thermal equivalent of plane Couette flow of a viscous fluid.

proportionality λ called the *thermal conductivity:*

$$Q_n = -\lambda(T_h - T_c)/\delta, \tag{20.7-1}$$

where λ, like μ, is a transport property of the gas. For this simple one-dimensional heat conduction, the gas temperature is found to increase linearly with x in the space between the surfaces, as shown in Fig. 20.9, with the result that the heat flux Q_n may be written as

$$Q_n = -\lambda \, dT/dx, \tag{20.7-2}$$

which is known as *Fourier's law of heat conduction.* The analogy between Eqs. (20.7-1) and (20.7-2) for heat conduction and Eqs. (20.6-1) and (20.6-4) for viscous stress was first exploited by Prandtl in the study of heat transfer in a moving fluid—a complication we shall avoid in our simple treatment.

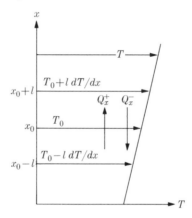

Fig. 20.10. The temperature distribution in the one-dimensional heat flow shown in Fig. 20.9.

We shall now calculate λ approximately for the hard-sphere model of a perfect monatomic gas, deferring until later the added complications encountered in polyatomic gases. The procedure will be analogous to that used in Section 20.6 in determining the transport of momentum. We shall first find the efflux Q_x^+ of kinetic energy crossing the plane $x = x_0$, at which $T = T_0$, by assuming that it can be found from Eq. (20.4-19) with the temperature T evaluated at the plane $x = x_0 - l$, where $T = T_0 - l \, dT/dx$, as shown in Fig. 20.10:

$$Q_x^+ = 2k\{T_0 - l \, dT/dx\}\Gamma_x^+. \tag{20.7-3}$$

Similarly, we can determine Q_x^- by assuming that the molecules moving in the $(-x)$-direction across the $(x = x_0)$-plane are characterized by the temperature $T = T_0 + l \, dT/dx$ at the plane $x = x_0 + l$, in which, on the average, they experienced their last collision:

$$Q_x^- = 2k\{T_0 + l \, dT/dx\}\Gamma_x^-. \tag{20.7-4}$$

By noting that $\Gamma_x^+ = \Gamma_x^- = n\langle v\rangle/4$, we find that the net kinetic energy flux $Q_x = Q_x^+ - Q_x^-$ is

$$Q_x = 2k\left\{T_0 - l\frac{dT}{dx}\right\}\Gamma_x^+ - 2k\left\{T_0 + l\frac{dT}{dx}\right\}\Gamma_x^-$$

$$= -2kl\left\{\frac{dT}{dx}\right\}(\Gamma_x^+ + \Gamma_x^-) \tag{20.7-5}$$

$$= -nkl\langle v\rangle\frac{dT}{dx},$$

so that the thermal conductivity λ is found by comparison with Eq. (20.7-2) to be

$$\lambda = nkl\langle v\rangle. \tag{20.7-6}$$

This may be compared with the exact value* for a hard-sphere monatomic gas:

$$\lambda = (75\pi/128)nkl\langle v\rangle, \tag{20.7-7}$$

which is larger than the approximate calculation by the factor 1.84. This discrepancy is more representative of the approximate nature of the mean-free-path approach than was the corresponding comparison for the viscosity μ.

For a monatomic gas, the constant-volume specific heat c_v determined in Chapter 11 is $3k/2m$, and Eq. (20.7-7) may alternatively be written as

$$\lambda = (25\pi/64)\rho c_v l\langle v\rangle \tag{20.7-8}$$

or, through use of Eq. (20.6-10) for the viscosity μ, as

$$\lambda = \tfrac{5}{2}\mu c_v. \tag{20.7-9}$$

For a monatomic gas, c_v is a constant independent of temperature, so that λ, like μ, depends only on the temperature and not on the density or pressure of a gas. Furthermore, the variation of λ with temperature is the same as that of μ. The simple equality of Eq. (20.7-9) has been found to be in excellent agreement with the experimental measurements of λ and μ for monatomic gases.

The foregoing approximate theory does not take into account the energies of vibration and rotation which may be exchanged in collisions between polyatomic molecules and may therefore contribute to the transport of energy in a polyatomic gas. If the energy associated with the internal degrees of freedom of a molecule were transferred as rapidly as the kinetic energy of translation, then we would expect Eq. (20.7-9) to hold also for polyatomic gases, provided c_v were the entire constant-volume specific heat, that is, the sum of the translational specific heat $3k/2m$ and the specific heat c_i due to the internal degrees of freedom:

$$c_v = 3k/2m + c_i. \tag{20.7-10}$$

---

* See Chapman and Cowling, p. 235.

Experimental measurements of λ and μ for polyatomic gases show that such is not the case, for the experimental values of λ are less than $(\frac{5}{2})\mu c_v$. It was suggested by Eucken that the transport of vibrational and rotational energy was slower than that of translational energy and that Eq. (20.7–9) should be written as

$$\lambda = \mu\{\tfrac{5}{2}(3k/2m) + c_i\} \tag{20.7–11}$$

for all gases, certainly being correct for monatomic gases for which $c_i = 0$. This empirical expression is in very good agreement with experimental measurements of λ and μ for all polyatomic gases.

A more convenient form of Eq. (20.7–11) may be found by using Eqs. (11.8–4), (11.8–6), and (13.4–10) to replace k/m by

$$k/m = \Re = c_p - c_v = c_v(\gamma - 1). \tag{20.7–12}$$

On substituting Eqs. (20.7–12) and (20.7–10) into (20.7–11), we find

$$\lambda = \{(9\gamma - 5)/4\}\mu c_v. \tag{20.7–13}$$

In the study of heat transfer in flowing fluids, an important dimensionless similarity parameter is the Prandtl number $c_p\mu/\lambda$. According to the Eucken relation of Eq. (20.7–13), the Prandtl number of a gas is $4\gamma/(9\gamma - 5)$. For a monatomic gas ($\gamma = \frac{5}{3}$), the Prandtl number is $\frac{2}{3}$, while for polyatomic gases ($\frac{5}{3} \geq \gamma > 1$), it lies between $\frac{2}{3}$ and 1.

20.8 Diffusion

The diffusion of molecules through a gas is a physical phenomenon with which we are very familiar. Our acute sense of smell enables us to detect such minute concentrations of organic molecules that we can easily detect, for example, the spread of carbon tetrachloride vapor from an uncovered container placed in the far corner of a room. Although the mixing of gases in many instances is aided by bulk motion of the fluid, careful tests show that the diffusion of one gas through another, in the absence of bulk motion, proceeds about as rapidly as does the spread of heat.

A typical molecular diffusion experiment is illustrated in Fig. 20.11. Two large flasks of equal volume V, connected by a small diameter tube of comparatively small volume, are initially filled with only species 1 in the left flask and only species 2 in the right, the gas pressure and temperature being uniform throughout. As time proceeds, some of the type-1 molecules diffuse through the tube into the right-hand flask while some type-2 molecules diffuse in the opposite direction. At any instant the number densities n_1 and n_2 are uniform throughout either flask, but vary linearly along the diffusion tube, as shown in Fig. 20.11. By measuring the rate dn_1/dt at which the number density n_1 of species 1 increases in the right-hand flask, the number flux Γ_{z1} of species 1

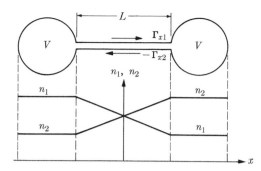

Fig. 20.11. A simple binary diffusion experiment.

through the tube of cross-sectional area A may be found:

$$A\Gamma_{x1} = V \, dn_1/dt. \qquad (20.8\text{--}1)$$

Since the pressure p and temperature T are the same throughout the system, so also will be the total number density n:

$$n \equiv n_1 + n_2 = p/kT. \qquad (20.8\text{--}2)$$

Because the number density of molecules is constant everywhere, there must be a number flux Γ_{x2} of species 2 into the left-hand flask which is equal but opposite to that of species 1 into the right-hand flask:

$$\Gamma_{x2} = -\Gamma_{x1}. \qquad (20.8\text{--}3)$$

From such experiments it is found empirically that the number flux Γ_{x1} of species 1 is related to the other measured quantities by

$$\Gamma_{x1} = \frac{D_{12}\{(n_1)_L - (n_1)_R\}}{L}, \qquad (20.8\text{--}4)$$

in which $(n_1)_L$ and $(n_1)_R$ are the uniform values of n_1 in the left and right flasks, respectively, and D_{12} is a proportionality constant called the *binary diffusion coefficient*. Like λ and μ, D_{12} is a transport property of the gas mixture composed of species 1 and 2. Because n_1 varies linearly with x in the diffusion tube as sketched in Fig. 20.11, Eq. (20.8–4) could also be written in the form

$$\Gamma_{x1} = -D_{12} \, (dn_1/dx). \qquad (20.8\text{--}5)$$

This equation for the diffusion of one species through another is known as *Fick's law*. Because n is a constant, $dn_1/dx = -dn_2/dx$, and it follows from Eq. (20.8–5) and (20.8–3) that

$$\Gamma_{x2} = -D_{12} \, (dn_2/dx), \qquad (20.8\text{--}6)$$

which expresses the flux of species 2 in terms of the rate of change of n_2 with x.

To calculate approximately the binary diffusion coefficient D_{12} from the mean-free-path approach, we will consider the motion of the n_1 molecules of species 1 in a unit volume of the diffusion tube. These molecules have an average velocity in the $+x$-direction of Γ_{x1}/n_1 and are impeded in their motion down the tube by a counterflow of species 2 molecules having a mean velocity of Γ_{x2}/n_2. Thus the average velocity of a species-1 molecule relative to the average of a species-2 molecule is $\Gamma_{x1}/n_1 - \Gamma_{x2}/n_2$. As a result of the collisions between unlike species of molecules, the average momentum of either species is destroyed by scattering collisions with the other species and the mean velocity tends to decrease. On the other hand, there is a decrease of the partial pressure $p_1 = n_1kT$ in the direction of Γ_{x1}, so that the species-1 molecules are accelerated in that direction by the pressure, just as in a fluid flow. The steady diffusion of species 1 is therefore a balance between the acceleration due to the decrease in pressure p_1 and the loss of momentum by collisions with species 2.

Let us first determine the rate at which momentum is lost by the n_1 molecules in a unit volume. Because we are considering the relative motion of species 1 and 2, we will assume that the average momentum lost per collision is the product of the reduced mass m_{12} and the average relative velocity $\Gamma_{x1}/n_1 - \Gamma_{x2}/n_2$. If ν_{12}, as given by Eq. (20.5–2), is the rate at which a species-1 molecule is hit by species-2 molecules, then there will be $n_1\nu_{12}$ binary collisions per second between unlike molecules in a unit volume, and the n_1 molecules will lose momentum at a rate equal to $n_1\nu_{12}m_{12}\{\Gamma_{x1}/n_1 - \Gamma_{x2}/n_2\}$.

The net x-component of force on the n_1 molecules in a unit volume due to the difference in partial pressure p_1 is just $-dp_1/dx$, which must equal the rate of increase of momentum. Setting the rate of loss minus the gain of momentum per unit volume equal to zero, we find

$$n_1\nu_{12}m_{12}\left\{\frac{\Gamma_{x1}}{n_1} - \frac{\Gamma_{x2}}{n_2}\right\} - \left(-\frac{dp_1}{dx}\right) = 0. \qquad (20.8\text{–}7)$$

Replacing Γ_{x2} with $-\Gamma_{x1}$ and dp_1/dx with $kT\,dn_1/dx$, we may solve Eq. (20.8–7) for Γ_{x1}, obtaining

$$\Gamma_{x1} = -\left(\frac{n_2kT}{nm_{12}\nu_{12}}\right)\frac{dn_1}{dx}. \qquad (20.8\text{–}8)$$

If we use Eqs. (20.5–2) and (20.5–3), this may be written alternatively as

$$\Gamma_{x1} = -\left\{\frac{\langle g\rangle}{8nd^2}\right\}\frac{dn_1}{dx}, \qquad (20.8\text{–}9)$$

in which the average relative velocity $\langle g\rangle$ is given by Eq. (20.5–3). By comparison with Eq. (20.8–6), the binary diffusion coefficient is

$$D_{12} = \langle g\rangle/8nd^2. \qquad (20.8\text{–}10)$$

The exact kinetic-theory value for a mixture of hard-sphere molecules* is

$$D_{12} = 3\langle g \rangle / 32nd^2, \tag{20.8–11}$$

which is $\frac{3}{4}$ of the approximate value given in Eq. (20.8–10).

Unlike the thermal conductivity λ and viscosity μ, the binary diffusion coefficient D_{12} depends on the total number density n. The product $n\,D_{12}$, or $p\,D_{12}$, is found experimentally to depend only on the temperature, in agreement with Eq. (20.8–10).

If species 1 and 2 are two isotopes of a heavy element, so that m_1 is approximately equal to m_2, then D_{12} is called the *self-diffusion coefficient* because the molecular properties of both species are nearly identical. Setting $m_1 = m_2 = 2m_{12}$ in Eq. (20.8–11), we find by comparison with Eq. (20.6–10) for the viscosity μ that

$$D\rho = 6\mu/5, \tag{20.8–12}$$

in which D is the coefficient of self-diffusion. While the factor $\frac{6}{5}$ is correct only for hard-sphere molecules, it is not greatly different for more realistic intermolecular potentials.

The molecular diameter d in Eq. (20.8–11) defines the effective cross section πd^2 for the collision of molecules of dissimilar species 1 and 2. In Fig. 20.8 the molecular diameter d defines the cross section for collision between molecules of the same species. In the absence of more detailed information, the collision diameter for unlike molecules may be taken as the arithmetic mean of the self-collision diameters of each species.

As an additional example of diffusion of one species through another, we will consider the drift of charged particles in a gas caused by the application of an electric field For example, when a gas is heated to a temperature at which it is ionized, then the positively charged species will drift in the direction of an applied electric field and the negatively charged species will move in the opposite direction. Since the motion of charged particles constitutes a current, the gas (or more correctly, the plasma) is an electrical conductor The *electrical conductivity* σ of the plasma is defined as the ratio of the *current density j* (amp/m²), which is the flux of charge, to the electric field E (volts/m) and therefore has the dimensions of amp-volt/m or (ohm-m)$^{-1}$:

$$j \equiv \sigma E. \tag{20.8–13}$$

This is the form of Ohm's law for a continuum.

The simplest case to consider is that of a binary mixture of oppositely charged particles which is electrically neutral; that is, the total charge density is zero:

$$n_1 q_1 + n_2 q_2 = 0, \tag{20.8–14}$$

---

* See Chapman and Cowling, p. 245.

in which q_1 and q_2 are the electric charge per molecule of species 1 and 2, respectively. When an electric field E_x is applied in the x-direction, a body force of $n_1 q_1 E_x$ per unit volume is applied to the species-1 molecules, tending to accelerate them in the direction of the force. This drift is retarded by collisions with the other molecules, and the balance of momentum loss and gain is given by Eq. (20.8–7), with the acceleration force per unit volume $(-dp_1/dx)$ replaced by $n_1 q_1 E_x$:

$$n_1 \nu_{12} m_{12} \{ \Gamma_{x1}/n_1 - \Gamma_{x2}/n_2 \} - n_1 q_1 E_x = 0. \tag{20.8–15}$$

The total current j_x is the sum of the products of the number fluxes times the charge per molecule:

$$j_x \equiv q_1 \Gamma_{x1} + q_2 \Gamma_{x2}. \tag{20.8–16}$$

Because the gas is electrically neutral, the current j_x may be written in the alternative form

$$j_x = \frac{n_1 q_1 \Gamma_{x1}}{n_1} + \frac{n_2 q_2 \Gamma_{x2}}{n_2} = n_1 q_1 \left\{ \frac{\Gamma_{x1}}{n_1} - \frac{\Gamma_{x2}}{n_2} \right\} \tag{20.8–17}$$

through use of Eq. (20.8–14). By substitution of Eq. (20.8–15) into (20.8–17), Ohm's law for the binary mixture is

$$j_x = \left\{ \frac{n_1 q_1^2}{\nu_{12} m_{12}} \right\} E_x, \tag{20.8–18}$$

so that the electrical conductivity σ becomes

$$\sigma = \frac{n_1 q_1^2}{\nu_{12} m_{12}} \tag{20.8–19}$$

or, through use of Eq. (20.5–2) for the collision frequency ν_{12},

$$\sigma = \frac{n_1 q_1^2}{\pi d^2 n_2 \langle g \rangle m_{12}}. \tag{20.8–20}$$

If species 1 is an electron and species 2 is a singly charged ion, then $q_1 = -e$, $q_2 = e$, $n_1 = n_2$, $m_1 = m_e \ll m_2$, and therefore

$$m_{12} = (1/m_e + 1/m_2)^{-1}$$

is very nearly the same as m_e. As a consequence, $\langle g \rangle$ is practically the same as the mean speed $\langle v_e \rangle$ of the electron, and Eq. (20.8–20) becomes

$$\sigma = \frac{e^2}{\pi d^2 m_e \langle v_e \rangle}, \tag{20.8–21}$$

in which πd^2 is the collision cross section for ion-electron collisions. Since the conductivity σ involves only the electron mass, all the current is carried by the drift of electrons, which, due to their very small mass, diffuse more easily than the ions.

If a gas is only slightly ionized, say one ion-electron pair per thousand molecules, then the drift of charged particles will be retarded by collision with the neutral molecules. Although the mixture is ternary, i.e., it has three components, the current due to either charged component may be recovered from Eq. (20.8-17) by letting species 2 be the neutral molecules and passing to the limit of $n_2 \gg n_1$ and $q_2 \ll q_1$, that is $n_2 = n$ and $q_2 = 0$. As a consequence, the electrical conductivity due to the free electrons, as given by Eq. (20.8-20), becomes

$$\sigma = \frac{n_e}{n} \frac{e^2}{\pi d^2 m_e \langle v_e \rangle}, \qquad (20.8\text{-}22)$$

in which πd^2 is the cross section for electron-neutral molecule collisions. Therefore, in a slightly ionized gas the electrical conductivity is proportional to the mole fraction n_e/n of electrons.

20.9 The Boltzmann equation

In the foregoing discussion of transport properties we have used the mean-free-path approach in order to understand the basic physical principles and to determine the principal parameters which are important in each process. By utilizing the concept of the collision of two hard-sphere molecules and assuming that the distribution function was nearly Maxwellian, we were able to determine approximately the transport coefficients. As indicated earlier, to proceed to a more comprehensive and exact theory involves such an increase in mathematical difficulty as to be beyond the scope of this book. Instead, we shall discuss here only the first step in this more difficult route, namely the derivation of a master equation called the *Boltzmann equation*, from which the more exact solutions are eventually found. As a further illustration of the usefulness of the Boltzmann equation, we shall derive the general fluid-dynamics equations of conservation of mass and energy for a monatomic gas.

Let us begin by recalling the description of the state of a gas adopted in Section 20.2. Each molecule of the gas was represented by a point in the cartesian phase space whose coordinates are x, y, z, v_x, v_y, and v_z, and the density of such points in phase space was denoted by $f\{\mathbf{r}, \mathbf{v}, t\}$; that is, at any time t, f depends on the position $\mathbf{r}$, $\mathbf{v}$ in phase space. The acceleration, or force per unit mass, being the time rate of change of velocity, determines the "velocity" of the representative point in velocity space just as the velocity, which is the time rate of change of position, determines the velocity in configuration space. Therefore, each representative point moves along a trajectory in phase space, the components of the "velocity" in phase space in the directions x, y, z, v_x, v_y, and v_z being v_x, v_y, v_z, a_x, a_y, and a_z, respectively, where a_x, a_y, and a_z are the components of the acceleration of the molecule in the x-, y-, and z-directions, respectively. It is therefore profitable to consider the motion of representative points in phase space as though it were a six-dimensional fluid of number density f moving with a velocity whose components are v_x, v_y, v_z, a_x, a_y, and a_z.

For the time being, let us assume that there are no collisions between molecules so that the only forces acting on a molecule are conservative forces depending only on the position $\mathbf{r}$. Thus the acceleration will also depend on $\mathbf{r}$, that is, $a_x = a_x\{\mathbf{r}\}$, $a_y = a_y\{\mathbf{r}\}$, and $a_z = a_z\{\mathbf{r}\}$. For example, this force may be an electric or gravitational force exerted by molecules outside the system. Let us now determine the equation for the conservation of the number of points in phase space, which expresses the fact that each molecule of the system must be represented by a point in phase space. Selecting a volume element $dx\, dy\, dz\, dv_x\, dv_y\, dv_z$, we find that the five-dimensional differential area normal to the x-axis is $dy\, dz\, dv_x\, dv_y\, dv_z$. The flux of representative points into the volume across this area is the product of the density f, the normal component of phase-space velocity v_x and the area, or a total of $v_x f\, dy\, dz\, dv_x\, dv_y\, dv_z$. The excess of the outflow at $x + dx$ over the inflow at x is $[\partial\{v_x f\, dy\, dz\, dv_x\, dv_y\, dv_z\}/\partial x]\, dx = [\partial\{v_x f\}/\partial x]\, dx\, dy\, dz\, dv_x\, dv_y\, dv_z$, or $\partial\{v_x f\}/\partial x$ per unit volume of phase space. Repeating this operation for the other five dimensions, we find that the net outflow of points minus the inflow of points per unit volume would be

$$\text{(outflow − inflow)/unit volume} = \frac{\partial(v_x f)}{\partial x} + \frac{\partial(v_y f)}{\partial y} + \frac{\partial(v_z f)}{\partial z}$$

$$+ \frac{\partial(a_x f)}{\partial v_x} + \frac{\partial(a_y f)}{\partial v_y} + \frac{\partial(a_z f)}{\partial v_z}. \qquad (20.9\text{–}1)$$

Since f is the number of points per unit volume, $-\partial f/\partial t$ is the rate at which points are passing out of a unit volume of phase space. Setting $-\partial f/\partial t$ equal to the right-hand side of Eq. (20.9–1), we find

$$\frac{\partial f}{\partial t} + \frac{\partial(v_x f)}{\partial x} + \frac{\partial(v_y f)}{\partial y} + \frac{\partial(v_z f)}{\partial z} + \frac{\partial(a_x f)}{\partial v_x} + \frac{\partial(a_y f)}{\partial v_y} + \frac{\partial(a_z f)}{\partial v_z} = 0. \qquad (20.9\text{–}2)$$

Since v_x, v_y, and v_z are independent variables, they are constant in the partial differentiations with respect to x, y, and z. Also, since a_x, a_y, and a_z depend only on $\mathbf{r}$, they are constant in the partial differentiations with respect to v_x, v_y, and v_z. We may therefore write Eq. (20.9–2) in the form

$$\frac{\partial f}{\partial t} + v_x \frac{\partial f}{\partial x} + v_y \frac{\partial f}{\partial y} + v_z \frac{\partial f}{\partial z} + a_x \frac{\partial f}{\partial v_x} + a_y \frac{\partial f}{\partial v_y} + a_z \frac{\partial f}{\partial v_z} = 0, \qquad (20.9\text{–}3)$$

which expresses the conservation of points in phase space for a system of gas molecules which do not collide with each other.

We may recognize that Eq. (20.9–3) is a form of Liouville's equation (see Section 3.5) because the system of noncolliding molecules acted upon by conservative forces is a microcanonical ensemble of molecules. So long as molec-

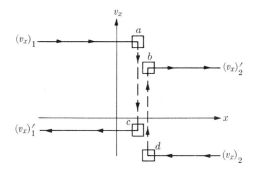

Fig. 20.12. The trajectories of colliding particles 1 and 2 in the $v_x x$ phase plane.

ular collisions do not occur very rapidly, as in interstellar or interplanetary gases, Eq. (20.9–3) may be used as a starting point for studying the behavior of a collisionless gas.

Where binary collisions are important, as in the cases of the transport effects we have discussed, Eq. (20.9–3) must be modified to take them into account. To see how this may be done, let us consider the binary collision of two hard-sphere molecules of equal mass and diameter d, in which the initial velocities $\mathbf{v}_1$ and $\mathbf{v}_2$ are changed into the velocities $\mathbf{v}_1'$ and $\mathbf{v}_2'$ by the collision. If we consider only the components of velocity in the x-direction, then the components $(v_x)_1$ and $(v_x)_2$ are changed into $(v_x)_1'$ and $(v_x)_2'$. (Because of conservation of momentum, $(v_x)_1 + (v_x)_2 = (v_x)_1' + (v_x)_2'$.) The result of such a collision may be plotted in the (x, v_x)-phase plane, as shown in Fig. 20.12, in which the trajectories of particles 1 and 2 undergo a discontinuous jump in phase space upon collision. It therefore appears that a collision removes some points from a volume element in phase space, like a and d in Fig. 20.12, and introduces an equal number into other volume elements, like b and c. The effect of collisions may therefore be accounted for by a source term in Eq. (20.9–3), denoted by $(\partial f/\partial t)_c$, which is the number of points per unit volume that appear at the point $\mathbf{r}$, $\mathbf{v}$ in phase space in a unit time because of collisions, in the manner illustrated in Fig. 20.12. Repeating the derivation of Eq. (20.9–3), but with the addition of a source term $(\partial f/\partial t)_c$, we arrive at the *Boltzmann equation:*

$$\frac{\partial f}{\partial t} + v_x \frac{\partial f}{\partial x} + v_y \frac{\partial f}{\partial y} + v_z \frac{\partial f}{\partial z} + a_x \frac{\partial f}{\partial v_x} + a_y \frac{\partial f}{\partial v_x} + a_z \frac{\partial f}{\partial v_z} = \left(\frac{\partial f}{\partial t}\right)_c. \qquad (20.9\text{–}4)$$

To determine the collision term $(\partial f/\partial t)_c$ is not an easy task, but it is found to be an integral of a function of f. For this reason, the Boltzmann equation is exceedingly difficult to solve. However, some properties of the term $(\partial f/\partial t)_c$ may readily be determined by noting that the mass, momentum, and kinetic energy of each colliding pair of molecules is unchanged in a collision. For example, as a result of a collision two representative points move abruptly from one location in velocity space to another; that is, they disappear at $\mathbf{v}_1$, $\mathbf{v}_2$ and appear at $\mathbf{v}'_1$, $\mathbf{v}'_2$. The integral of $(\partial f/\partial t)_c$ over all of velocity space must therefore be zero in order to preserve the number of representative points of the colliding pairs:

$$\iiint\limits_{-\infty}^{\infty} \left(\frac{\partial f}{\partial t}\right)_c dv_x\, dv_y\, dv_z = 0. \tag{20.9-5}$$

Because the momentum of the colliding pairs is conserved, that is, $\mathbf{v}_1 + \mathbf{v}_2 = \mathbf{v}'_1 + \mathbf{v}'_2$, the product of $m\mathbf{v}$ and $(\partial f/\partial t)_c$ integrated over velocity space must also be zero:

$$\iiint\limits_{-\infty}^{\infty} m\mathbf{v} \left(\frac{\partial f}{\partial t}\right)_c dv_x\, dv_y\, dv_z = 0. \tag{20.9-6}$$

And because of conservation of kinetic energy in collisions,

$$\iiint\limits_{-\infty}^{\infty} \left(\frac{mv^2}{2}\right)\left(\frac{\partial f}{\partial t}\right)_c dv_x\, dv_y\, dv_z = 0. \tag{20.9-7}$$

These properties of the collision term may be put to good use in deriving what are called the *equations of change*, namely, the general equations for conservation of mass, momentum, and energy. To illustrate how this is done, let us first integrate the Boltzmann equation (20.9–4) over all of velocity space:

$$\iiint\limits_{-\infty}^{\infty} \left\{\frac{\partial f}{\partial t} + v_x\frac{\partial f}{\partial x} + v_y\frac{\partial f}{\partial y} + v_z\frac{\partial f}{\partial z} + a_x\frac{\partial f}{\partial v_x} + a_y\frac{\partial f}{\partial v_y} + a_z\frac{\partial f}{\partial v_z}\right\} dv_x\, dv_y\, dv_z$$

$$= \iiint\limits_{-\infty}^{\infty} \left(\frac{\partial f}{\partial t}\right)_c dv_x\, dv_y\, dv_z. \tag{20.9-8}$$

According to Eq. (20.9–5), the right-hand side of Eq. (20.9–8) is always zero. The first term on the left-hand side may be integrated as follows:

$$\iiint\limits_{-\infty}^{\infty} \left(\frac{\partial f}{\partial t}\right) dv_x\, dv_y\, dv_z = \frac{\partial\left\{\iiint\limits_{-\infty}^{\infty} f\, dv_x\, dv_y\, dv_z\right\}}{\partial t} = \frac{\partial n}{\partial t} \tag{20.9-9}$$

because of Eq. (20.2–4). The next term becomes

$$\iiint\limits_{-\infty}^{\infty} v_x\left(\frac{\partial f}{\partial x}\right) dv_x\, dv_y\, dv_z = \frac{\partial\left\{\iiint\limits_{-\infty}^{\infty} v_x f\, dv_x\, dv_y\, dv_z\right\}}{\partial x} = \frac{\partial\{n\langle v_x\rangle\}}{\partial x} \tag{20.9-10}$$

by means of the x-component of Eq. (20.2–7). The next two terms may be similarly integrated. Since f must approach zero for infinite velocities, the following term involving a_x is found to be zero:

$$\iiint_{-\infty}^{\infty} a_x \left(\frac{\partial f}{\partial v_x}\right) dv_x \, dv_y \, dv_z = a_x \iint_{-\infty}^{\infty} [f]_{v_x=-\infty}^{v_x=+\infty} dv_y \, dv_z = 0. \qquad (20.9\text{–}11)$$

Thus the two remaining terms are zero, and Eq. (20.9–8) becomes, when multiplied by m,

$$\frac{\partial \rho}{\partial t} + \frac{\partial(\rho\langle v_x\rangle)}{\partial x} + \frac{\partial(\rho\langle v_y\rangle)}{\partial y} + \frac{\partial(\rho\langle v_z\rangle)}{\partial z} = 0, \qquad (20.9\text{–}12)$$

which is the differential form of the equation of continuity or conservation of mass whose integral form is given in Eq. (19.3–4). If we multiply Eq. (20.9–12) by $dx \, dy \, dz$ and integrate over the volume of the gas, we would obtain Eq. (19.3–4).

To obtain the equation of conservation of energy, we multiply the Boltzmann equation by $mv^2/2$ and integrate over velocity space. The collision term integrates to zero by Eq. (20.9–7), while typical terms on the left become

$$\iiint_{-\infty}^{\infty} \left(\frac{mv^2}{2}\right)\left(\frac{\partial f}{\partial t}\right) dv_x \, dv_y \, dv_z = \frac{\partial\{\iiint (mv^2/2)f \, dv_x \, dv_y \, dv_z\}}{\partial t}$$

$$= \frac{\partial\{\rho[e_t + \langle\mathbf{v}\rangle^2/2]\}}{\partial t} \qquad (20.9\text{–}13)$$

by Eq. (20.2–8);

$$\iiint_{-\infty}^{\infty} \left(\frac{mv^2}{2}\right) v_x \left(\frac{\partial f}{\partial x}\right) dv_x \, dv_y \, dv_z = \frac{\partial Q_x}{\partial x} \qquad (20.9\text{–}14)$$

by Eq. (20.4–17); and by integration by parts,

$$\int_{-\infty}^{\infty} v^2 \left(\frac{\partial f}{\partial v_x}\right) dv_x = [v^2 f]_{v_x=-\infty}^{v_x=\infty} - \int_{-\infty}^{\infty} f\left(\frac{\partial v^2}{\partial v_x}\right) dv_x$$

$$= 0 - 2\int_{-\infty}^{\infty} v_x f \, dv_x, \qquad (20.9\text{–}15)$$

the integral involving a_x becomes

$$\iiint_{-\infty}^{\infty} \left(\frac{ma_x v^2}{2}\right)\left(\frac{\partial f}{\partial v_x}\right) dv_x = -ma_x \iiint_{-\infty}^{\infty} v_x f \, dv_x \, dv_y \, dv_z \qquad (20.9\text{–}16)$$

$$= -\rho a_x \langle v_x\rangle.$$

The equation of energy conservation therefore becomes

$$\frac{\partial\{\rho[e_t + \langle\mathbf{v}\rangle^2/2]\}}{\partial t} + \frac{\partial Q_x}{\partial x} + \frac{\partial Q_y}{\partial y} + \frac{\partial Q_z}{\partial z}$$

$$- \rho\{a_x\langle v_x\rangle + a_y\langle v_y\rangle + a_z\langle v_z\rangle\} = 0. \qquad (20.9\text{--}17)$$

This is the differential form of Eq. (19.3–12), provided we identify the heat flux $\mathbf{q}$ in Eq. (19.3–12) by

$$q_x = \int\!\!\!\int\!\!\!\int_{-\infty}^{\infty} \left\{\frac{m(\mathbf{v} - \langle\mathbf{v}\rangle)^2}{2}\right\} [v_x - \langle v_x\rangle] f\, dv_x\, dv_y\, dv_z \qquad (20.9\text{--}18)$$

and similarly for the other components, and the stress $\boldsymbol{\sigma}$ by

$$\sigma_x = \int\!\!\!\int\!\!\!\int_{-\infty}^{\infty} m(\mathbf{v} - \langle\mathbf{v}\rangle)(v_x - \langle v_x\rangle) f\, dv_x\, dv_y\, dv_z. \qquad (20.9\text{--}19)$$

In other words, $\mathbf{q}$ and $\boldsymbol{\sigma}$ are the energy flux and momentum flux measured in a coordinate system translating with the velocity $\langle\mathbf{v}\rangle$. When this is done, Eqs. (19.3–12) and (20.9–17) are identical.

The equation of motion for a fluid may be found by multiplying the Boltzmann equation by $m\mathbf{v}$ and integrating over all of velocity space. When this is done, the equation of motion which results is the differential form of Eq. (19.3–16). Thus the statements of the conservation of mass, momentum, and energy on a macroscopic scale may be derived from the single scalar equation for the conservation of representative points in phase space as expressed in the Boltzmann equation.

PROBLEMS

20.1 Write an integral expression for the total angular momentum $\mathbf{L}$ of a gas in terms of the distribution function f.

20.2 Show that Eq. (20.2–8) is identically satisfied if the translational energy e_t is defined by $e_t \equiv (1/n)\int\!\!\int\!\!\int_{-\infty}^{\infty} \int \{[\mathbf{v} - \langle\mathbf{v}\rangle]^2/2\} f\, dv_x\, dv_y\, dv_z$.

20.3 The distribution function f of a monatomic gas of N molecules contained in a volume V is a constant everywhere in that portion of phase space lying within the configuration space volume V and within a spherical volume in velocity space of radius v_m but is zero elsewhere in phase space. (a) Within this volume, find the distribution function f in terms of N, V, and v_m. (b) Find the total energy E and momentum $\boldsymbol{P}$ of the system. (c) Find the mean speed $\langle v\rangle$.

20.4 Make a sketch of the Maxwellian distribution function f^0 as a function of the molecular speed v. (a) What is the maximum value of f^0? (b) At what value of v does f^0 equal one-half its maximum value?

20.5 In a stationary gas at equilibrium, the number of molecules per unit volume having a speed between v and $v + dv$ is the number of representative points inside a thin spherical shell in velocity space of radius v and thickness dv, namely, $4\pi v^2 f^0\, dv$. For a given increment dv of velocity, at what value of v will this number be a maximum?

20.6 If the distribution function f of a gas is isotropic; that is, it depends only on the speed v and not on the direction of the velocity $\mathbf{v}$, show (a) that the number efflux $\Gamma_x^+ = n\langle v \rangle / 4$ and (b) the momentum flux P_{xx} equals two-thirds of the kinetic energy per unit volume, even though f is not necessarily a Maxwellian distribution. [*Hint:* Use polar spherical coordinates to describe velocity space, so that $v_x = v\cos\theta$, $v_y^2 + v_z^2 = v^2\sin^2\theta$ and $dv_x\, dv_y\, dv_z = 2\pi v^2 \sin\theta\, dv\, d\theta$].

20.7 Find the thrust on the box of gas illustrated in Fig. 20.3 which is caused by the free molecule flow through a hole of area A.

20.8 A polyethylene balloon at an altitude of 100,000 ft is filled with helium gas at a pressure of 10^{-2} atm and a temperature of 300°K. The balloon has a diameter of 10 m. If the balloon has numerous pinholes of 10^{-3} cm in diameter, how many such pinholes per square meter of surface are there if 10% of the helium leaks out in 10 hr?

20.9 A spherical satellite 1 ft in diameter moves through the atmosphere of the earth with a speed of 25,000 ft/sec at an altitude of 500,000 ft, where the atmospheric density is 10^9 molecules/cm³. (a) How many air molecules will strike the satellite in 1 sec? (b) If the molecules which strike the satellite rebound with a speed of 3×10^4 cm/sec, what will be the drag force on the satellite?

20.10 A flowing gas has the distribution function

$$f = n(m/2\pi kT)^{3/2} e^{-m\{(v_x - u)^2 + v_y^2 + v_z^2\}/2kT},$$

in which n, T, and u are constants. (a) Show that the mean velocity $\langle \mathbf{v} \rangle$ is a constant, u, having the direction of $+x$; that is, the gas is flowing in the $+x$-direction at a uniform speed u. (b) Find the fluxes Γ_x, P_{xx}, and Q_x, and compare them with the flux of mass, momentum, and energy of a flowing perfect gas as found in Chapter 19.

20.11 Using the collision diameters given in Fig. 20.8, calculate the viscosity μ (gm/cm-sec), thermal conductivity λ (cal/cm-sec K°), and Prandtl number $c_p\mu/\lambda$ of argon, hydrogen, and nitrogen at 300°K and 2000°K.

20.12 The thermal diffusivity is the name given to the ratio $\lambda/\rho c_p$. Compute the thermal diffusivity of hydrogen and helium at $T = 300$°K and a pressure of 1 atm.

20.13 Two parallel plates having temperatures of 300°K and 310°K are separated by a gap of 1 mm filled with nitrogen. (a) At what rate (cal/cm²-sec) is heat conducted through the gas from the hot to the cold plate? (b) If the gap is filled with hydrogen instead of nitrogen, by what factor will the heat transfer be increased, or decreased?

20.14 The characteristic time for the mixing by diffusion of two gases in a container of dimension L is L^2/D_{12}. Calculate this time in seconds for the mixing of hydrogen and oxygen at $T = 300$°K and 1-atm pressure if $L = 1$ m.

20.15 Calculate the electrical conductivity σ (ohm-m)$^{-1}$ of argon at 7000°K and 1-atm pressure if 0.1% of the argon is ionized and the effective cross section for electron-argon atom collisions is 5×10^{-16} cm².

20.16 Find an expression for the electrical conductivity of a neutral mixture of positive and negative ions of equal but opposite charge in which the negative ion mass is equal to the positive ion mass.

440

REFERENCES

ALLIS, W. P., and M. A. HERLIN, *Thermodynamics and Statistical Mechanics*, McGraw-Hill, New York, 1952.

ARAVE, R. J., and O. A. HUSEBY, "Aerothermodynamic Properties of High Temperature Argon," Doc. No. D2-11238, Boeing Co., Seattle, 1962.

BLACKMAN, M., "The Specific Heat of Solids," *Handbuch der Physik*, S. Flügge, ed., Vol. 7, Part 1, pp. 325 through 381, Springer-Verlag, Berlin, 1955.

BOZORTH, R. M., *Ferromagnetism*, D. Van Nostrand, New York, 1951.

CALLEN, H. B., *Thermodynamics*, Wiley, New York, 1960.

CHAPMAN, S., and T. G. COWLING, *The Mathematical Theory of Non-Uniform Gases*, Cambridge University Press, Cambridge, 1953.

DAVIDSON, N., *Statistical Mechanics*, McGraw-Hill, New York, 1962.

DENBIGH, K., *The Principles of Chemical Equilibrium*, Cambridge University Press, Cambridge, 1955.

DOLE, M., *Introduction to Statistical Thermodynamics*, Prentice-Hall, New York, 1954.

EPSTEIN, P. S., *Textbook of Thermodynamics*, Wiley, New York, 1937.

FENTER, F., and H. GIBBONS, "Thermodynamic Properties of High Temperature Air," Report No. RE-1R-14, Ling-Temco-Vought, Inc., Dallas, 1961.

FEYNMAN, R. P., et al, *Lectures on Physics, II*, Addison-Wesley, Reading, Mass., 1964.

FOWLER, R., and E. A. GUGGENHEIM, *Statistical Thermodynamics*, Cambridge University Press, Cambridge, 1952.

GAYDON, A. G., *Dissociation Energies and Spectra of Diatomic Molecules*, Dover Publications, New York, 1950.

GOLDSTEIN, H., *Classical Mechanics*, Addison-Wesley, Reading, Mass., 1950.

GRAY, D. E. (ed.), *American Institute of Physics Handbook (2nd Edition)*, McGraw-Hill, New York, 1963.

HEITLER, W., *Elementary Wave Mechanics*, Clarendon Press, Oxford, 1945.

HENRY, W. E., "Spin Paramagnetism of Cr^{+++}, Fe^{+++}, and Gd^{+++} at Liquid Helium Temperatures in Strong Magnetic Fields," *Phys. Rev.*, **88,** 559 through 562 (1952).

HERZBERG, G., *Molecular Spectra and Molecular Structure I. Spectra of Diatomic Molecules*, 2nd Edition, D. Van Nostrand, Princeton, 1950.

HERZBERG, G., *Molecular Spectra and Molecular Structure II. Infrared and Raman Spectra of Polyatomic Molecules*, D. Van Nostrand, Princeton, 1945.

HILL, T. L., *Introduction to Statistical Thermodynamics*, Addison-Wesley, Reading, Mass., 1960.

HILSENRATH, J., et al., *Tables of Thermal Properties of Gases*, National Bureau of Standards Circular 564, U.S. Government Printing Office, Washington, 1955.

HIRSCHFELDER, J. O., C. F. CURTISS, and R. B. BIRD, *Molecular Theory of Gases and Liquids*, Wiley, New York, 1954.

KECK, J., J. CAMM, B. KIVEL, and T. WENTINK, "Radiation from Hot Air," *Ann. Phys.*, **7,** 1 through 38 (1959).

KEENAN, J. H., and F. G. KEYES, *Thermodynamic Properties of Steam*, Wiley, New York, 1936.

KEENAN, J. H., *Thermodynamics*, Wiley, New York, 1941.

KEESOM, P., and N. PEARLMAN, "Low Temperature Heat Capacity of Solids," *Handbuch der Physik*, S. Flügge, ed., Vol. 14, pp. 282 through 344, Springer-Verlag, Berlin, 1956.

LANDAU, L. D., and E. M. LIFSHITZ, *Statistical Physics*, (Vol. 5 of *Course of Theoretical Physics*), Addison-Wesley, Reading, Mass., 1960.

LANDAU, L. D., and E. M. LIFSHITZ, *Electrodynamics of Continuous Media*, (Vol. 8 of *Course of Theoretical Physics*), Addison-Wesley, Reading, Mass., 1960.

LEIBFRIED, G., "Gittertheorie der mechanischen und thermischen Eigenschaften der Kristalle," *Handbuch der Physik*, Vol. 7, Part 1, pp. 104 through 324, S. Flügge, ed., Springer-Verlag, Berlin, 1955.

LEWIS, B., and G. VON ELBE, *Combustion, Flames and Explosions of Gases*, Academic Press, New York, 1951.

LEWIS, G. N., and M. RANDALL, *Thermodynamics*, 2nd Edition, revised by K. S. Pitzer and L. Brewer, McGraw-Hill, New York, 1961.

MACDONALD, D. K. C., *Noise and Fluctuations: an Introduction*, Wiley, New York, 1962.

MAYER, J. E., and M. G. MAYER, *Statistical Mechanics*, Wiley, New York, 1940.

MENDELSSOHN, K., "Liquid Helium," *Handbuch der Physik*, S. Flügge, ed., Vol. 15, pp. 370 through 458, Springer-Verlag, Berlin, 1956.

MOORE, C. E., *Atomic Energy Levels* (Vol. I), National Bureau of Standards Circular 467, U.S. Government Printing Office, Washington, 1949.

PANOFSKY, W., and K. H. PHILLIPS, *Classical Electricity and Magnetism*, 2nd Edition, Addison-Wesley, Reading, Mass., 1962.

POLLACK, G., "The Solid State of Rare Gases," *Rev. Mod. Phys.*, **36,** 749 through 791 (1964).

SEARS, F. W., *An Introduction to Thermodynamics, The Kinetic Theory of Gases, and Statistical Mechanics*, Addison-Wesley, Reading, Mass., 1950.

WALKER, C. B., "X-Ray Study of Lattice Vibration in Aluminum," *Phys. Rev.*, **103,** 547 (1956).

ZEMANSKY, MARK W., *Heat and Thermodynamics*, McGraw-Hill, New York, 1957.

ZIMAN, J. M., *Electrons and Phonons*, Oxford University Press, Oxford, 1960.

BIBLIOGRAPHY

ASTON, J. G., and J. J. FRITZ, *Thermodynamics and Statistical Thermodynamics*, Wiley, New York, 1959.

BOLTZMANN, L., *Lectures on Gas Theory*, translated by S. G. Brush, University of California Press, Berkeley, 1964.

BORN, M., *Natural Philosophy of Cause and Chance*, Clarendon Press, Oxford, 1949.

COX, RICHARD T., *Statistical Mechanics of Irreversible Change*, The Johns Hopkins Press, Baltimore, 1955.

CRAWFORD, F. H., *Heat, Thermodynamics, and Statistical Physics*, Harcourt-Brace and World, New York, 1963.

FRENKEL, J., *Kinetic Theory of Liquids*, Dover Publications, New York, 1955.

HARRIS, L., and A. L. LOEB, *Introduction to Wave Mechanics*, McGraw-Hill, New York, 1963.

HERCUS, E. O., *Elements of Thermodynamics and Statistical Mechanics*, University Press, Melbourne, 1950.

HERZBERG, G., *Atomic Spectra and Atomic Structure*, Dover Publications, New York, 1944.

HILDEBRAND, J. H., *An Introduction to Molecular Kinetic Theory*, Reinhold, New York, 1963.

HILL, L., *Statistical Mechanics*, McGraw-Hill, New York, 1956.

HUANG, K., *Statistical Mechanics*, Wiley, New York, 1963.

INGARD, U., and W. L. KRAUSHAAR, *Introduction to Mechanics, Matter and Waves*, Addison-Wesley, Reading, Mass., 1960.

JEANS, SIR JAMES, *An Introduction to the Kinetic Theory of Gases*, Cambridge University Press, Cambridge, 1959.

KHINCHIN, A. I., *Mathematical Foundations of Statistical Mechanics*, Dover Publications, New York, 1949.

KING, L., *Thermodynamics*, W. H. Freeman and Co., San Francisco, 1962.

KIRKWOOD, J. G., and I. OPPENHEIM, *Chemical Thermodynamics*, McGraw-Hill, New York, 1961.

KITTEL, J., *Elementary Solid State Theory*, Wiley, New York, 1962.

LANDAU, L. D., and E. M. LIFSHITZ, *Mechanics* (Vol. 1 of *Course of Theoretical Physics*), Addison-Wesley, Reading, Mass., 1960.

LEE, J. F., F. W. SEARS, and D. L. TURCOTTE, *Statistical Thermodynamics*, Addison-Wesley, Reading, Mass., 1963.

MacDONALD, D. K. C., *Introductory Statistical Mechanics for Physicists*, Wiley, New York, 1963.

MENDELSSOHN, K., *Cryophysics*, Interscience Publishers, New York, 1960.

MORSE, P. M., *Thermal Physics*, W. A. Benjamin, New York, 1964.

PENNER, S. S., *Quantitative Molecular Spectroscopy and Gas Emissivities*, Addison-Wesley, Reading, Mass., 1959.

REYNOLDS, W. C., *Thermodynamics*, McGraw-Hill, New York, 1965.

RUSHBROOKE, G. S., *Introduction to Statistical Mechanics*, Clarendon Press, Oxford, 1955.

RUTGERS, G., "Temperature Radiation of Solids," *Handbuch der Physik*, S. Flügge, ed., Vol. 26, pp. 129 through 170, Springer-Verlag, Berlin, 1958.

SCHIFF, L. I., *Quantum Mechanics*, McGraw-Hill, New York, 1949.

SCHRÖDINGER, E., *Statistical Thermodynamics*, University Press, Cambridge, 1952.

SOMMERFELD, A., *Thermodynamics and Statistical Mechanics*, Academic Press, Inc., New York, 1956.

TOLMAN, C., *The Principles of Statistical Mechanics*, Oxford University Press, London, 1938.

TRIBUS, M., *Thermostatics and Thermodynamics*, D. Van Nostrand, Princeton, 1961.

WILSON, A. H., *Thermodynamics and Statistical Mechanics*, Cambridge University Press, Cambridge, 1960.

APPENDIX

Table A–1. Physical constants and defined units*

Constant	Symbol	Value	Unit (mks)	Unit (cgs)
Speed of light in vacuum	c	2.9979	10^8 m/sec	10^{10} cm/sec
Elementary charge	e	1.6021	10^{-19} coul	
Electron mass	m_e	9.1091	10^{-31} kgm	10^{-28} gm
Proton mass	m_p	1.6725	10^{-27} kgm	10^{-24} gm
Hydrogen atom mass	m_H	1.6734	10^{-27} kgm	10^{-24} gm
Proton mass/electron mass	m_p/m_e	1836.1		
Elementary charge/electron mass	e/m_e	1.7588	10^{11} coul/kgm	
Planck's constant	h	6.6256	10^{-34} j · sec	10^{-27} erg · sec
	$\hbar \equiv h/2\pi$	1.0545	10^{-34} j · sec	10^{-27} erg · sec
Boltzmann's constant	k	1.3805	10^{-23} j/K°	10^{-16} erg/K°
Avogadro's number	$\tilde{N}$	6.0225	10^{26} (kgm-mole)$^{-1}$	10^{23} (gm-mole)$^{-1}$
Gas constant	$\tilde{R} \equiv \tilde{N}k$	8.3143	10^3 j/kgm-mole · K°	10^7 erg/gm-mole · K°
		1.9872	kcal/kgm-mole · K°	cal/gm-mole · K°
Faraday	Ne	9.6487	10^7 coul/kgm-mole	

Quantity	Definition	Value	Units	Units
Stefan-Boltzmann constant	$\sigma \equiv 2\pi^5 k^4/15h^3c^2$	5.6697	10^{-8} watts/m$^2 \cdot$ (K°)^4	10^{-5} erg/cm^2 sec $\cdot$ (K°)^4
Radiation constant	hc/k	1.4388	10^{-2} m $\cdot$ K°	cm $\cdot$ K°
Bohr magneton	$\mu_B \equiv e\hbar/2m_e$	9.2732	10^{-24} amp/m^2 (j-m^2/weber)	
Magnetic permeability of vacuum	μ_0	4π	10^{-7} kgm-m/coul^2 (h/m)	
Electric permittivity of vacuum	$\epsilon_0 \equiv (\mu_0 c^2)^{-1}$	8.8543	10^{-12} (coul·sec)^2/kgm·m^3 (farad/m)	
Standard atmosphere	(atm)	1.01325	10^5 n/m^2	10^6 dyne/cm^2
Loschmidt's number (p/kT evaluated at $p = 1$ atm and $T = 273.16$ °K)		2.6869	10^{25} m^{-3}	10^{19} cm^{-3}
Standard acceleration	g_0	9.8066	m/sec^2	10^2 cm/sec^2
Thermochemical calorie	(cal)	4.1840	j	10^7 erg
British thermal unit	(Btu)	1.0551	10^3 j	10^{10} erg
		2.5216	10^{-1} kcal	10^2 cal
Pound mass	(lbm)	4.5359	10^{-1} kgm	10^2 gm
Pound force	(lbf)	4.4482	n	10^5 dyne
Inch	(in)	2.54	10^{-2} m	cm

* Values taken from *NBS Technical News Bulletin*, October, 1963.

Table A–2.   Conversion of units of energy per molecule*

	$\dfrac{\text{cal}}{\text{gm-mole}}$, $\dfrac{\text{kcal}}{\text{kgm-mole}}$	$\dfrac{\text{j}}{\text{kgm-mole}}$	ev	K°	cm⁻¹	sec⁻¹	erg
1 cal/gm-mole or 1 kcal/kgm-mole =	1	4.1840×10^3	4.3363×10^{-5}	5.0323×10^{-1}	3.4976×10^{-1}	1.0485×10^{10}	6.9473×10^{-17}
1 j/kgm-mole =	2.3901×10^{-4}	1	1.0364×10^{-8}	1.2027×10^{-4}	8.3595×10^{-5}	2.5061×10^{6}	1.6604×10^{-20}
1 ev =	2.3061×10^4	9.6487×10^{7}	1	1.1605×10^4	8.0658×10^3	2.4180×10^{14}	1.6021×10^{-12}
1 K° =	1.9872	8.3143×10^3	8.6170×10^{-5}	1	6.9503×10^{-1}	2.0836×10^{10}	1.3805×10^{-16}
1 reciprocal wavelength in cm⁻¹ =	2.8591	1.1963×10^4	1.2398×10^{-4}	1.4388	1	2.9979×10^{10}	1.9863×10^{-16}
1 unit frequency in sec⁻¹ =	9.5370×10^{-11}	3.9903×10^{-7}	4.1356×10^{-15}	4.7993×10^{-11}	3.3356×10^{-11}	1	6.6256×10^{-27}
1 erg =	1.4394×10^{16}	6.0225×10^{19}	6.2418×10^{11}	7.2435×10^{15}	5.0347×10^{15}	1.5093×10^{26}	1

* Constants taken from Table A–1. Denoting the unit of energy per molecule by [ ], the energy, measured in joules, is 4.184×10^3 $\tilde{N}^{-1}$[kcal/kgm-mole], $\tilde{N}^{-1}$[j/kgm-mole], e[ev], k[K°], $10^2 hc$[cm⁻¹], h[sec⁻¹], and 10^{-7}[erg], where $\tilde{N}$, e, k, h, and c have the mks values given in Table A–1.

Table A–3. Conversion of units of energy/mass*

	$\dfrac{\text{Btu}}{\text{lbm}}$	$\dfrac{\text{ft-lbf}}{\text{lbm}}$	$\dfrac{\text{cal}}{\text{gm}} , \dfrac{\text{kcal}}{\text{kgm}}$	$\dfrac{\text{erg}}{\text{gm}}$	$\dfrac{\text{j}}{\text{kgm}}$
$1\,\dfrac{\text{Btu}}{\text{lbm}} =$	1	7.7821×10^2	5.5595×10^{-1}	2.3261×10^7	2.3261×10^3
$1\,\dfrac{\text{ft-lbf}}{\text{lbm}} =$	1.2850×10^{-3}	1	7.1441×10^{-4}	2.6035×10^4	2.6035
$1\,\dfrac{\text{cal}}{\text{gm}}$ or $1\,\dfrac{\text{kcal}}{\text{kgm}} =$	1.7987	1.3998×10^3	1	4.1840×10^7	4.1840×10^3
$1\,\dfrac{\text{erg}}{\text{gm}} =$	4.2990×10^{-8}	3.3455×10^{-5}	2.3901×10^{-8}	1	10^{-4}
$1\,\dfrac{\text{j}}{\text{kgm}} =$	4.2990×10^{-4}	3.3455×10^{-1}	2.3901×10^{-4}	10^4	1

* Constants taken from Table A–1.

Table A–4.   Definite integrals

$\int_0^\infty e^{-x^2}\,dx = \dfrac{\pi^{1/2}}{2}$	$\int_0^\infty x^3 e^{-x^2}\,dx = \dfrac{1}{2}$	$\int_0^\infty \dfrac{x^4 e^x\,dx}{(e^x - 1)^2} = \dfrac{4\pi^4}{15}$
$\int_0^\infty x e^{-x^2}\,dx = \dfrac{1}{2}$	$\int_0^\infty x^4 e^{-x^2}\,dx = \dfrac{3\pi^{1/2}}{8}$	$\int_0^\infty x^2 \ln (1 - e^{-x})\,dx = -\dfrac{\pi^4}{45}$
$\int_0^\infty x^2 e^{-x^2}\,dx = \dfrac{\pi^{1/2}}{4}$	$\int_0^\infty \dfrac{x^3\,dx}{(e^x - 1)} = \dfrac{\pi^4}{15}$	$\int_0^\infty \dfrac{x^2\,dx}{(e^x - 1)} = 2\displaystyle\sum_{n=1}^\infty n^{-3} = 2.4041$

Table A–5.   Series

$$(1 - x)^{-1} = 1 + x + x^2 + x^3 + \cdots, \qquad x^2 < 1,$$

$$e^{-x} = 1 - x + \frac{x^2}{2!} - \frac{x^3}{3!} + \cdots, \qquad x^2 < \infty,$$

$$\ln (1 + x) = x - \frac{x^2}{2} + \frac{x^3}{3} - \frac{x^4}{4} + \cdots, \qquad x^2 < 1,$$

$$\sinh x = x + \frac{x^3}{3!} + \frac{x^5}{5!} + \cdots, \qquad x^2 < \infty,$$

$$\coth x = \frac{1}{x} + \frac{x}{3} - \frac{x^3}{45} + \cdots, \qquad x^2 < \pi^2,$$

Asymptotic Series
$(x \to \infty)$

$$\ln (x!) = x \ln x - x + (\tfrac{1}{2}) \ln x + (\tfrac{1}{2}) \ln 2\pi + \frac{1}{12x} + \cdots$$

Table A–6. Thermodynamic functions of the harmonic oscillator*

θ_v/T	$(C)_v/Nk$	E_v/NkT	$\ln Q_v$	S_v/Nk	θ_v/T	$(C)_v/Nk$	E_v/NkT	$\ln Q_v$	S_v/Nk
0.00	1.0000	1.0000	∞	∞	1.60	0.8114	0.4048	0.2255	0.6303
0.05	0.9998	0.9752	3.0206	3.9958	1.70	0.7904	0.3800	0.2017	0.5817
0.10	0.9992	0.9508	2.3522	3.3030	1.80	0.7687	0.3565	0.1807	0.5372
0.15	0.9981	0.9269	1.9712	2.8981	1.90	0.7466	0.3342	0.1620	0.4962
0.20	0.9967	0.9033	1.7078	2.6111	2.00	0.7241	0.3130	0.1454	0.4584
0.25	0.9948	0.8802	1.5087	2.3889	2.20	0.6783	0.2741	0.1174	0.3915
0.30	0.9925	0.8575	1.3502	2.2077	2.40	0.6320	0.2394	0.0951	0.3345
0.35	0.9898	0.8352	1.2197	2.0549	2.60	0.5859	0.2086	0.0772	0.2858
0.40	0.9868	0.8133	1.1096	1.9229	2.80	0.5405	0.1813	0.0627	0.2440
0.45	0.9833	0.7918	1.0151	1.8069	3.00	0.4963	0.1572	0.0511	0.2083
0.50	0.9794	0.7708	0.9328	1.7036	3.20	0.4536	0.1360	0.0416	0.1776
0.55	0.9752	0.7501	0.8603	1.6104	3.40	0.4129	0.1174	0.0340	0.1514
0.60	0.9705	0.7298	0.7959	1.5257	3.60	0.3743	0.1011	0.0277	0.1288
0.65	0.9655	0.7100	0.7382	1.4482	3.80	0.3380	0.0870	0.0226	0.1096
0.70	0.9602	0.6905	0.6863	1.3768	4.00	0.3041	0.0746	0.0185	0.0931
0.75	0.9544	0.6714	0.6394	1.3108	4.25	0.2652	0.0615	0.0144	0.0759
0.80	0.9483	0.6528	0.5966	1.2494	4.50	0.2300	0.0506	0.0112	0.0618
0.85	0.9419	0.6345	0.5576	1.1921	4.75	0.1986	0.0414	0.0087	0.0501
0.90	0.9352	0.6166	0.5218	1.1384	5.00	0.1707	0.0339	0.0068	0.0407
0.95	0.9281	0.5991	0.4890	1.0881	5.50	0.1264	0.0226	0.0041	0.0267
1.00	0.9207	0.5820	0.4587	1.0407	6.00	0.08968	0.01491	0.00248	0.01739
1.10	0.9050	0.5489	0.4048	0.9537	6.50	0.06371	0.00979	0.00151	0.01130
1.20	0.8882	0.5172	0.3584	0.8756	7.00	0.04476	0.00639	0.00091	0.00730
1.30	0.8703	0.4870	0.3182	0.8052	7.50	0.03115	0.00415	0.00055	0.00470
1.40	0.8515	0.4582	0.2832	0.7414	8.00	0.02148	0.00269	0.00034	0.00303
1.50	0.8318	0.4308	0.2525	0.6833	9.00	0.01000	0.00111	0.00012	0.00123

* More complete tables may be found in Dole, p. 223.

LIST OF SYMBOLS

Italic numerals following the entry give the chapter in which the quantity is defined. In cases where the symbol has two or more meanings, standard numerals indicate the other chapters in which it is found. A few symbols, used only locally in a derivation, are not listed.

A	Area
A	Wave function amplitude, 5
A	Helmholtz free energy, 14
$A\{\kappa\}$	Amplitude function of wave pulse, 4
A_t	Area of nozzle throat, 19
A_{ul}, B_{ul}, B_{lu}	Einstein transition probabilities, 16
ΔA	Element of surface area
$\mathbf{a}$	Body force per unit mass, 19
a	Distance from semi-infinite solid, 9
a	Speed of sound, 19
a_t	Sound speed at nozzle throat, 19
a_x, a_y, a_z	Component of acceleration in the x-, y-, z-direction, 20
$\mathbf{B}$	Magnetic induction, 17
B	Magnitude of magnetic induction $\mathbf{B}$, 17
b	Configuration integral, 11
C	Number of quantum states of phonons or photons, $15, 16$
C_{aj}, C_{bk}	Number of quantum states of a-, b-molecule in cell j, k, 13
C_j	Number of particle or wave quantum states in cell j, 8
C_p	Constant-pressure specific heat, 10
$\tilde{C}_p$	Constant-pressure specific heat of one mole of substance, 11
$(\tilde{C}_p)_c$	Constant-pressure specific heat of condensed phase, 14
C_r	Rotational specific heat, 12
C_v	Constant-volume specific heat, 10
$(C)_v$	Vibrational specific heat, 12
$\tilde{C}_v$	Constant-volume specific heat of one mole of substance, 11
$(C_v^0)_k$	Constant-volume specific heat of component k in a perfect-gas mixture, 14

C_v^*	Constant-volume specific heat of a reacting mixture, *14*
c	Phase velocity, *4*, 15, 16
c	Speed of light, 11, 16
c_i	Mass fraction of component i, *13*, 14
c_i	Specific heat per unit mass due to internal motion, 20
c_l, c_t	Phase velocity of longitudinal, transverse wave in a solid, *15*
c_p	Constant-pressure specific heat of unit mass of substance, *11*
c_v	Constant-volume specific heat of unit mass of substance, *11*
$c_\perp$	Component of c perpendicular to wall, *16*
D	Self-diffusion coefficient, *20*
D_{12}	Binary diffusion coefficient, *20*
d	Molecular diameter, 1, 11, 20
d	Internuclear equilibrium separation, 2, 4, 5
d	Grating spacing, 5
d	Capacitor plate spacing, 9
$\mathbf{E}$	Electric field, *9*
E	Total energy, *1*, 7–18
E	Young's strain modulus, *4*, 15
E	Energy density of a wave, *4*
E	Magnitude of electric field, 16, 20
$\widetilde{E}$	Energy per mole, *11*
E^*	Energy of a reacting mixture, based on common-reference energy level, *14*
E_e	Energy of electronic states, *11*
E_i	Energy of internal motion, *11*
E_i^0	Energy of component i in a perfect-gas mixture, *13*
E_m	Magnetic energy, *17*
$E_k^s, \widetilde{E}_k^s$	Energy, molar energy, of species k at reference state s, *14*
$\widetilde{E}_n, \widetilde{E}_s$	Molar energy of normal, superconducting phase, *17*
E_p^s, E_r^s	Energy of products, reactants at standard state s, *14*
E_r	Energy of rotational motion, *12*
$\widetilde{E}_s, \widetilde{E}_l, \widetilde{E}_v$	Molar energy of solid, liquid, vapor phase, *14*
E_t	Energy of translational motion, *11*
E_v	Energy of vibrational motion, *12*
E_v	Energy of vacuum field, *17*
ΔE^s	Energy change of a constant-volume reaction at reference state s, *14*
$\Delta\widetilde{E}^s$	Molar energy change of constant-volume reaction at state s, *14*
e	Magnitude of electronic charge, 5, 15, 17, 19, 20
e	Base of natural logarithm
e	Energy per unit mass, *11*, 19
e^*	Energy per unit mass of reacting mixture, based on common-reference energy level, *14*
e_k	Energy per unit mass of species k, 14
e_t	Translational energy per unit mass, *20*
ε_v	Spectral emissivity, *16*
$\mathbf{F}$	Force vector, *2*
F	Force, 1

F	Gibbs free energy, *14*
$\widetilde{F}$	Gibbs free energy per mole of substance, *14*
F_i	Component of force in the direction of q_i, *3*
$\mathbf{F}_{ij}$	Force acting on particle i caused by particle j, *2*
$\mathbf{F}_j^0$	Total force acting on particle j caused by particles outside the system, *2*
$\mathfrak{F}$	Repulsive force between particles a distance l apart, *9*
f	Number of degrees of freedom of molecular motion, *5, 7, 8*
f	Fraction of incident electrons which is absorbed, *15*
f	Number density of points in phase-space, *20*
f^0	Maxwellian distribution function, *20*
$\mathbf{g}$	Relative velocity of one particle with respect to another, *2*
g	Magnitude of relative-velocity vector $\mathbf{g}$, *2, 5, 20*
g	Acceleration of gravity, *4, 19*
g	Magnetic-moment factor, *17*
g_0	Standard acceleration, *1*
g_0	Degeneracy (statistical weight) of ground electronic state, *12*
$\mathbf{g}_i$	Lattice wave vector, *15*
g_i	Number of quantum states of energy ϵ_i, *5, 11*
g_i	Degeneracy of ground electronic state of species i, *14*
g_i	Magnitude of lattice wave vector $\mathbf{g}_i$, *15*
g_u, g_l	Statistical weights of upper, lower state, *16*
$\mathbf{H}$	Magnetic-intensity vector, *17*
H	Enthalpy, *10, 11, 13*
H	Magnitude of the magnetic intensity, *16, 17*
$\widetilde{H}$	Enthalpy per mole of substance, *18*
H_c	Critical magnetic intensity for a superconductor, *17*
$H_k^s, \widetilde{H}_k^s$	Enthalpy, molar enthalpy, of species k at reference state s, *14*
H_p, H_r	Enthalpy of products, reactants, *18*
$\widetilde{H}_s, \widetilde{H}_l, \widetilde{H}_v, \widetilde{H}_c$	Molar enthalpy of solid, liquid, vapor, condensed phase, *14*
ΔH^s	Enthalpy change in a constant-pressure reaction at reference state s, *14*
$\Delta \widetilde{H}^s$	Molar enthalpy change in constant-pressure reaction at reference state s, *14*
$\mathfrak{IC}$	Hamiltonian function, *3*
h	Planck's constant, *5–20*
h	Enthalpy per unit mass, *11, 19*
$\hbar$	Planck's constant/2π, *5*
h_r, h_p	Enthalpy per unit mass of reactants, products, *19*
h_s	Stagnation enthalpy per unit mass, *19*
Δh^i	Enthalpy difference between unit mass of products and reactants at state i, *19*
I	Mass moment of inertia, *5, 12*
I	Total electric current, *17, 19*
I_{rev}	Total electric current in reversible fuel cell, *19*
i_ν	Total spectral radiant intensity, *16*
$i_{\nu\Omega}$	Spectral radiant intensity, *16*
j	Rotational quantum number, *5, 12*

j	Electric current per unit area 15, 20
K	Spring constant, *2*, *4*, *5*
K	Rotational quantum number for symmetric top molecule, *12*
$K°$	Degree on kelvin scale of absolute temperature, *1*
K_{21}	Ratio of masses of particles 2 and 1, *1*
K_p	Equilibrium constant, *14*
k	Boltzmann's constant, *7*
$\mathbf{L}$	Angular-momentum vector, *2*
L	Side dimension of cubical box, 3, 5, 7, 16
L	Magnitude of angular momentum of rotating body, 5, 17
L	Length of solenoid, 17
L_z	Component of angular momentum, *5*
l	Orbital quantum number, *5*
l	Scale of forces, *9*
l	Mean free path, *20*
$\mathbf{M}$	Magnetization vector, *17*
M	Magnitude of magnetization vector $\mathbf{M}$, *17*
M	Mass of a system, 7
M	Mach number, *19*
$\widetilde{M}$	Molecular weight, *1*
$\dot{M}$	Mass flow rate, *19*
$\widetilde{M}_k$	Molecular weight of species k, *14*
M_n, M_s	Magnetization of normal, superconducting phase, *17*
M_s	Saturation magnetization, *17*
$\mathfrak{M}$	Moment of forces, *17*
$\mathfrak{M}_z$	Moment of forces about z-axis, *17*
m	Mass of molecule or particle, 1–20
m	Magnetic quantum number, *5*
m_{12}	Reduced mass of molecular species 1 and 2, *20*
m_a	Mass of atom
m_e	Mass of electron
$m_i, m_j, m_k, \ldots$	Molecular mass of component $i, j, k, \ldots$, *13*
N	Number of molecules in a system
$\widetilde{N}$	Avogadro's number, *1*
N_a	Number of atoms in a solid, *15*
$N_a, N_b, N_k, \ldots$	Number of molecules of species $a, b, k, \ldots$, *14*
N_e	Number of electrons in a solid, *15*
N_i	Number of molecules in the quantum state i, *5*
N_i	Number of molecules of species i in a mixture, *13*
N_j	Number of molecules having representative point in cell j of μ-space, *8*
N_j	Number of phonons of angular frequency ω_j, *15*
N_j^0	Value of N_j for the most probable macrostate, *8*
N_u, N_l	Number of atoms in the upper, lower electronic state, *16*
N_{aj}, N_{bk}	Number of a, b molecules in the cell j, k of μ-space, *13*
N_{aj}^0, N_{bk}^0	Value of N_{aj}, N_{bk} for the most probable macrostate, *13*
$\mathfrak{N}$	Number of coil turns, *17*
$\mathbf{n}$	Unit normal vector, *3*

n	Number density of molecules, 1, 5, 9, 20
n	Radial distance in $n_x n_y n_z$-space, 5
n	Principal quantum number, 5
n	Number of atoms in a molecule, 12
n_1, n_2	Number density of molecular species 1, 2, 20
n_e	Number density of electrons, 20
n_x, n_y, n_z	Translational quantum numbers, 5
$\mathbf{P}$	Wave momentum-density vector, 4
$\mathbf{P}$	Total momentum, 20
P	Wave momentum density, 4
P	Noise power, 16
$\mathbf{P}_n$	Momentum flux across unit area whose normal is $\mathbf{n}$, 20
P_i	Probability of selecting a molecule in a quantum state i, 6
$\mathbf{P}_x$	Momentum flux across unit area normal to x-axis, 20
$\mathbf{P}_x^+$	Efflux of momentum across unit area normal to x-axis, 20
P_{xx}	x-component of $\mathbf{P}_x$, 20
P_{xx}^+	x-component of $\mathbf{P}_x^+$, 20
P_{xy}	y-component of $\mathbf{P}_x$, 20
$\mathbf{p}$	Momentum vector, 2, 5, 20
$\mathbf{p}$	Phonon or photon momentum vector, 15, 16
p	Pressure, 1, 4, 9–20
p	Magnitude of momentum vector $\mathbf{p}$, 2, 5, 7, 11, 15
p_c	Critical pressure, 14
$\mathbf{p}_i, \mathbf{p}_i'$	Momentum of particle i before, after collision, 2
p_i	Generalized momentum coordinate, 3
p_i, q_i	Conjugate coordinates, 3
p_i^0, p_j^0, p_k^0	Partial pressure of components $i, j, k, \ldots$ in a perfect-gas mixture, 13
p_m	Pressure at melting point, 14
p_m, q_m	Maximum values of p, q for the harmonic oscillator, 5
p_s	Saturation pressure, 14
p_s	Stagnation pressure, 19
p_t	Pressure at nozzle throat, 19
p_x, p_y, p_z	Components of $\mathbf{p}$ in x-, y-, z-directions, 5
p_ν	Spectral noise power, 16
p_ϕ	Phonon pressure, 15
p_θ	Angular momentum, 3
Δp	Wave-pressure amplitude, 4
Δp	Momentum increment, 5
Q	Partition function, 8, 9, 11, 20
Q	Heat, 9, 10, 18
$\dot{Q}$	Total rate of heat addition, 19
Q_{cl}	Classical partition function, 8
Q_e	Partition function for electronic states, 11, 12
Q_e	Partition function of electrons, 15
Q_i	Partition function for internal motion, 11
$(Q_i)_k$	Internal partition function of species k, 14

$(Q_i^*)_j,\ (Q_i^*)_k,\ \ldots$	Internal partition function of species $j,\ k,\ \ldots$ based on common energy reference level, *14*
$Q_j,\ Q_k,\ \ldots$	Partition function of components $j,\ k,\ \ldots$ in a mixture, *14*
Q_m	Magnetic partition function, *17*
Q_n	Kinetic energy flux across unit area normal to **n**, *20*
Q_{rev}	Heat in reversible process, *10*
Q_r	Partition function for rotation, *12*
Q_t	Translational partition function, *11*
Q_v	Partition function for vibration, *12*
Q_x	Kinetic energy flux across unit area normal to x-axis, *20*
Q_x^+	Kinetic energy efflux in $+x$-direction, *20*
$Q_1,\ Q_2$	Heat added from hot, cold heat reservoir, *18*
q	Position vector in configuration space, *5*
q	Heat-flux vector, *19*
q	Total emissive power, *16*
q	Electrical charge, *17*
q_i	Generalized position coordinate, *3, 5*
q_i	Electric charge of particle i, *9, 20*
q_ν	Spectral emissive power, *16*
$q_{\nu\Omega}$	Spectral stearadiancy, *16*
R	Gas constant, Nk, for system of N molecules, *13*
$\tilde{R}$	Universal gas constant, $\tilde{N}\mathrm{k}$, *11*
$\Re$	Gas constant for a unit mass of gas, *11*
$\Re_a$	Gas constant for a unit mass of atoms, *14*
r	Position vector, *2, 5, 9, 19, 20*
r	Relative position of one particle with respect to another, *2*
r	Magnitude of position vector **r**, *2*
r_e	Equilibrium internuclear separation of rotating diatomic molecule, *2*
r_0	Range of intermolecular force, *11*
S	Entropy, *7*
$\tilde{S}$	Entropy per mole, *11*
S_e	Entropy contribution from electronic states, *11*
S_e	Entropy of heat engine, *18*
S_i	Entropy contribution from internal motion, *11*
S_i^0	Entropy of component i in a perfect-gas mixture, *13*
$\tilde{S}_i^0$	Entropy per mole of component i in a mixture, *13*
S_m	Magnetic entropy, *17*
$\tilde{S}_n,\ \tilde{S}_s$	Molar entropy of normal, superconducting phase, *17*
$\tilde{S}_0$	Molar entropy of phase at zero temperature, *14*
S_r	Contribution to entropy from rotational motion, *12*
$\tilde{S}_s,\ S_l,\ \tilde{S}_v,\ \tilde{S}_c$	Molar entropy of solid, liquid, vapor, condensed phase, *14*
S_t	Entropy contribution from translational motion, *11*
S_v	Contribution to the entropy from the vibrational motion, *12*
s	Spin quantum number, *5*
s	Entropy per unit mass, *11, 19*
s_i^0	Entropy per mass of component i in a mixture, *13*

T	Absolute temperature, 1, 7, 8–20
T	Kinetic energy, 2, 9, 11
T_c	Temperature at critical point, 14
T_c	Curie temperature, 17
T_c	Critical temperature for a superconductor, 17
T_e	Temperature of heat engine, 18
T_h, T_c	Temperature of hot, cold surface, 20
T_m	Melting temperature, 14
T_s	Saturation temperature, 14
T_s	Stagnation temperature, 19
T_t	Temperature at nozzle throat, 19
T_1, T_2	Temperature of hot, cold heat reservoir, 18
t	Time
U	Potential energy or potential function, 2, 9, 11
U	Relative speed of parallel surfaces, 20
u	Component of velocity in x direction, 1
u	Velocity of fluid element, 4
u	Two-body intermolecular potential energy, 11
u_s	Slip velocity at wall, 20
V	Volume
$\tilde{V}$	Volume per mole, 11
$\tilde{V}$	Molar volume at the critical point, 14
$\tilde{V}_n, \tilde{V}_s$	Molar volume of normal, superconducting phase, 17
$\tilde{V}_s, \tilde{V}_l, \tilde{V}_v$	Molar volume of solid, liquid, vapor phase, 14
$\mathcal{V}$	Phase-space volume between energy surfaces E and $E + \delta E$, 7, 8, 10, 14
$\mathcal{V}$	Voltage, 17
$\mathcal{V}_e$	Phase-space volume enclosed by energy surface E, 7
$\mathbf{v}$	Velocity vector, 2
v	Speed, 1, 9, 19, 20
v	Component of velocity parallel to wall, 1
v	Vibrational quantum number, 5, 12
v	Volume in phase space corresponding to a macrostate, 8
v	Specific volume (volume per unit mass), 11
$\langle v_e \rangle$	Mean speed of electrons, 20
v_g	Group velocity, 4
$\mathbf{v}_i, \mathbf{v}_i'$	Velocity of particle i before, after collision, 2
v_m	Vibrational quantum number for mth mode, 12
v_t	Speed at nozzle throat, 19
v_x, v_y, v_z	Components of velocity in x-, y-, z-direction, 20
W	Thermodynamic probability, 7, 8
W	Macroscopic work, 9, 10, 18
$\dot{W}$	Rate of macroscopic work, or power, 19
W_e	Electrical work, 17
W_m	Magnetic work, 17
W_{rev}	Work in reversible process, 10
W_μ	Microscopic work, 9
w	Component of velocity parallel to wall, 1

w	Thermodynamic probability of a macrostate, *8, 12, 13*
w	Work function, *15*
w_a, w_b	Number of microstates of a-, b-molecules, *13*
w_0	Thermodynamic probability of the most probable macrostate, *8*
$X_a, X_b, \ldots$	Chemical symbol of species $a, b, \ldots, 14$
x	Cartesian position coordinate, 1, 4, 5, 9, 20
x	$\hbar\omega/kT$, *15*, 16
x	$g\mu_B B/kT$, *17*
x, y, z	Cartesian position coordinates, 1–20
x_i	Mole fraction of component i, *13*
y_{ik}	Number of i-atoms in molecule k, *14*
Z	Partition function, *8*
α	Lagrange multiplier, *8*
α_a, α_b	Lagrange multipliers for a mixture of a- and b-molecules, *13*
α_ν	Spectral absorbtivity, *16*
β	Lagrange multiplier, *8*
Γ_e	Number flux of electrons, *15*
Γ_i	Flux of points in phase space in the direction of i, *3*
Γ_n	Net number flux of molecules per unit area, *20*
Γ_x	Net number flux of molecules in the direction of x-axis, *20*
Γ_x^+, Γ_x^-	Efflux of molecules in the direction of $+x$, $-x$, *20*
Γ_{x1}, Γ_{x2}	Values of Γ_x for species 1, 2, *20*
γ	Ratio of specific heats, C_p/C_v, *13*
γ_s	Symmetry number, *12*
γ_e	Coefficient of electronic specific heat, *15*
γ_G	Grüneisen constant, *15*
δ	Separation distance between surfaces, *20*
ϵ	Energy of a molecule, 1, 5, 9, 15
ϵ	Strain, *4*
ϵ	Energy of a phonon, *15*
ϵ	Energy of a photon, *16*
ϵ^0	Additive constant on energy scale, *8*
$\epsilon_{aj}, \epsilon_{bk}$	Energy of a-, b-molecule in cell j, k, *13*
ϵ_d	Dissociation energy, *12*
ϵ_e	Electronic energy of a molecule, *5*
ϵ_i	Energy of molecule in the quantum state i, *5, 8, 9*
ϵ_i	Energy of molecular motion with respect to mass center, *11*, 12
ϵ_i	Ionization energy, 14, 19
ϵ_j	Energy of molecules having representative point in cell j of μ-space, *8*
ϵ_k^*	Energy of formation of molecule of species k, 12, *14*
ϵ_m	Magnetic energy, *17*
ϵ_p	Phonon energy, *5*
ϵ_r	Rotational energy of a molecule, *5*
ϵ_t	Translational energy of a molecule, *5*
ϵ_u, ϵ_l	Electronic energy of upper, lower state in a transition, *16*
ϵ_v	Vibrational energy, *5*
ϵ_0	Electric permittivity of a vacuum, *5*

ϵ_ν	Black-body spectral energy density, *16*
$\Delta\epsilon$	Energy increment, *5*
$\Delta\epsilon^*$	Net energy of formation in a reaction, *14*
η	Ferromagnetic factor, *17*
η_a	Adiabatic turbine efficiency, *19*
η_t	Thermodynamic efficiency, *18*
θ	Angular displacement, 3, 9, 16, 17
θ	Empirical temperature, *10*
θ	Scattering angle, *15*
θ_D	Debye temperature, *15*
θ_r	Rotational temperature, *12*
$\theta_{r1}, \theta_{r2}, \theta_{r3}$	Rotational temperatures for nonlinear polyatomic molecule, *12*
θ_v	Vibrational temperature, *12*, *15*
$\boldsymbol{\kappa}$	Wave vector, *4*
κ	Wave number; magnitude of wave vector $\boldsymbol{\kappa}$, *4*, 5, 15, 16
κ	Equilibrium constant for ionization, *14*, 19
$\kappa_x, \kappa_y, \kappa_z$	Components of $\boldsymbol{\kappa}$ in the x-, y-, z-directions, *5*
$\boldsymbol{\kappa}'_x, \boldsymbol{\kappa}''_x$	Wave vector of incident, reflected x-ray, *15*
λ	Wave length, *4*, 16
λ	de Broglie wave length, *5*, 7, 11, 15
λ	Thermal conductivity, *20*
$\boldsymbol{\mu}$	Magnetic dipole moment, *17*
μ	Reduced mass, *2*, 5
μ	Chemical potential, *7–15*
μ	Viscosity, *20*
$\mu_a, \mu_b, \mu_k, \ldots$	Chemical potential of component $a, b, k, \ldots$ in a mixture, *13*
μ_B	Bohr magneton, *17*
μ_e	Chemical potential contribution from electronic states, *11*
μ_i	Chemical potential contribution from internal motion, *11*
μ_i^0	Chemical potential of component i in a perfect-gas mixture, *13*
μ_m	Average component of $\boldsymbol{\mu}$ in the direction of $\mathbf{B}$, *17*
μ_n	Nuclear magneton, *17*
μ_r	Contribution to the chemical potential from rotational motion, *12*
μ_s	Chemical potential of electrons in solid, *15*
μ_t	Chemical potential contribution from translational motion, *11*
μ_v	Contribution to the chemical potential from the vibrational motion, *12*
μ_v	Chemical potential of electron vapor, *15*
μ_0	Fermi energy, *15*
μ_0	Magnetic permeability of free space, 16, 17
ν	Total frequency, *4*, 5, 15, 16
ν	Vibrational frequency, *5*, 12
ν	Poisson's ratio, *15*
ν	Collision frequency of single species, *20*
$\nu_a, \nu_b, \nu_k, \ldots$	Mole number of species $a, b, k, \ldots$, *14*
ν_{ul}	Frequency of spectral line, *16*
ν_m	Vibrational frequency of mth mode, *12*

ν_{12}	Collision frequency of a species-1 molecule with species-2 molecules, *20*
$\Delta\nu$	Band width, *16*
ξ	Displacement vector of system environment, *9*
ξ	Position vector of control surface, *19*
ξ	Displacement of fluid element, *4*
ξ	Lagrange multiplier, *14*
$\Delta\xi$	Amplitude of displacement of fluid element in a wave, *4*
ρ	Density of representative points in phase space, *3*
ρ	Mass density, 4, *11*, 14, 15, 17, 19, 20
ρ_c	Charge density, *17*
ρ_t	Mass density at nozzle throat, *19*
ρ_s	Stagnation mass density, *19*
$\boldsymbol{\sigma}$	Surface stress, *9*
σ	Stress magnitude, *4*
σ	Electrical conductivity, *20*
σ	Stefan-Boltzmann constant, *16*
$\boldsymbol{\tau}$	Shear stress vector, *19*
τ	Period of cycle, *19*
τ	Shear stress, *20*
τ_{ul}	Lifetime for spontaneous emission, *16*
ϕ	Potential energy, 1, 8, 9, 19
ϕ	Potential energy of forces acting between particles inside and outside of a system, *2*, 9
ϕ	Potential energy difference between an electron outside and inside a solid, *15*
ϕ	Voltage difference, *16*
ϕ_j	Interaction potential energy of molecules in cell j, *9*
$\Delta\phi$	Potential difference between fuel-cell electrodes, *19*
$\Delta\phi_{\mathrm{rev}}$	Electrode potential difference for a reversible fuel cell, *19*
χ	Paramagnetic susceptibility, *17*
ψ	Wave function, *5*, 11
ψ	Angular displacement, *17*
ψ^*	Complex conjugate of ψ, *5*
$\boldsymbol{\Omega}$	Angular velocity vector, *17*
Ω	Magnitude of $\boldsymbol{\Omega}$, *17*
Ω	Solid angle, *16*
Ω	Electrical resistance, *16*
$\boldsymbol{\omega}$	Angular velocity vector of precessional motion, *17*
ω	Angular velocity or frequency, *2*, *4*
ω_j	Number of ways of assigning C_j quantum states to N_j particles, *8*
ω_j	Angular frequency of crystal vibrational mode j, *15*
ω_m	Maximum angular frequency of crystal vibration, *15*
ω'_x, ω''_x	Angular frequency of incident, reflected x-ray, *15*

ANSWERS TO EVEN-NUMBERED PROBLEMS

Chapter 2

2.2 2.18×10^{-3} 2.6   (a) 3.16×10^9 j   (b) 4.74×10^8 j

Chapter 3

3.2   B, D, and E

Chapter 4

4.4   (b) $(G/\rho)^{1/2}$ 4.6 7.8×10^6 m

Chapter 5

5.2 $p/2m,\ p/m$ 5.4   (a) eB/m_e (b) $n\hbar\omega/2$ 5.6 $3\epsilon_m/5$
5.8   (a) 7.42×10^{-9} cm   5.12   (b) $6(\epsilon_0/m)^{1/2}/\pi d$
       (b) 1.04×10^{-8} cm   (c) 5.5×10^{14} sec^{-1}

Chapter 6

6.2   (a) 67ϵ (b) 66.7ϵ

Chapter 7

7.2   (b) $(4\pi e m E/3N)^{3N/2}$ 7.4   (b) $3k \ln 2$ 7.6 $(\mu_a T_b - \mu_b T_a)/(T_b - T_a)$

Chapter 8

8.2   (a) $\sum_j \{C_j \ln (1 + N_j/C_j) + N_j \ln (1 + C_j/N_j) + (\tfrac{1}{2}) \ln [(C_j + N_j)/N_j C_j]\}$
       (b) $\sum_j \{N_j \ln C_j - N_j \ln N_j + N_j - (\tfrac{1}{2}) \ln N_j\}$
8.6   (a) $N_j^0/C_j = e^{-(\alpha + \beta \epsilon_j + \boldsymbol{\gamma} \cdot \mathbf{p}_j)}$
8.12 $\mp h^{-f} \int \cdots \int \ln \{1 \mp e^{(\mu - \mathcal{H}(q_1 \cdots p_f))/kT}\}\, dq_1\, dp_1 \cdots dq_f\, dp_f$
8.14   (a) $Q = 1 + e^{-\epsilon/kT}, \qquad E = N\epsilon/(e^{\epsilon/kT} + 1)$
       (b) $E/N\epsilon = 1 - 1/N(e^{-\mu/kT} - 1)$

Chapter 9

9.2 $(\pi/4)\mathfrak{F}(l/d)^5(nd^3)^2$

Chapter 10

10.6 $C_v/Nk = (\epsilon/kT)^2 e^{\epsilon/kT}/(e^{\epsilon/kT} + 1)^2$
10.8   (a) Decrease   (b) Increase   (c) 6.6×10^4 j, 4.62×10^4 j

Chapter 11

11.2   2990°K   11.6   2840°K   11.8   (a) -1020 ft-lbf
                                                   (b) -1264 ft-lbf
11.10   (a) 8.65×10^{-2} m^3/kgm   11.12   31,600 ft^3 11.14   (a) 0.33
        (b) -88 cm^3/gm-mole   (b) Higher

Chapter 12

12.2   (a) T/θ_v 12.4   0.465 btu/lbm F°   12.8 10^4 12.10   (b) 2500°K

Chapter 13

13.2   1490 cal/gm-mole, 47.5 cal/gm-mole K°, 4.97 cal/gm-mole K°

13.4   (a) Mixture   (b) Mixture

Chapter 14

14.2   All partial pressures equal $\frac{1}{3}$ atm.   14.4   (a) 0.708   (b) 4×10^8 j/kgm

14.6   (a) 0.00, 0.202, 0.595, 0.885, 0.994

       (b) 860, 2750, 5690, 9100, 11,600 cal/gm

14.8   (a) 14,600°K   (b) 72,000°K   (c) 204,000°K

14.10   (a) $2\pi mkTA/h^2(1 - e^{-\theta_v/T})$ (b) $2\pi mkT/h^2 = 5 \times 10^{16}$ cm^{-2}

      (c) $(N/V)(h^2/2\pi mkT)^{1/2}e^{\epsilon_0/kT}/(1 - e^{-\theta_v/T})$

14.16   458 cal/gm   14.18   (a) 281°K   (b) 0.949 atm

Chapter 15

15.4   0.252, 0.520; 0.45, 0.54; 0.194, 0.221 cal/gm K°   15.10 5.8×10^7 cm/sec

15.12   (a) 3×10^4 amp/m^2 (b) 4.06×10^{12} cm^{-3}

Chapter 16

16.4   141,000°K   16.6   (a) 5.67×10^4 watts/m^2

                                 (b) 7.6×10^{-2} watts/m^2

16.8   (a) 9.35×10^{-7} watts   16.10   (a) 675°K   (b) 0.1   (c) 0.0526

       (b) 3.85×10^{-16} watts

Chapter 17

17.2   (a) $(2/x) \sinh (jx)$ (b) $E_m = NkT\{1 - jx \coth (jx)\}$, $M = E_m/BV$,

                               $S_m = Nk\{1 - jx \coth (jx) + \ln [(2/x) \sinh (jx)]\}$

17.8   1060, 2210

Chapter 18

18.2   (a) Zero   (b) $(T_{10}T_{20})^{1/2}$ (c) $MC_v[(T_{10})^{1/2} - (T_{20})^{1/2}]^2$

18.4   (a) 10°F   18.10   (a) Both are equally efficient

       (b) Direct heating   (b) Otto cycle

Chapter 19

19.2   (a) 285°K   19.4   1.34   19.6   (a) 0.765   (b) 8.2×10^5 ft-lbf/lbm

19.8 -1.64×10^3 ft-lbf/lbm   19.10   29.4 m/sec

19.12   (a) 1340°K   (b) 20.8 atm   (c) 1600

19.14   11.85 atm, 5 kgm/m^3, 1260°K, 675 m/sec

19.16   0.1075 atm, 6.5×10^{-3} kgm/m^3, 4450°K   19.18 1.01×10^4 m/sec

19.20   (a), (b) See Problem 14.4   (c) 8.1×10^5 watts

Chapter 20

20.4   (a) $n(m/2\pi kT)^{3/2}$ (b) $\{(2 \ln 2)kT/m\}^{1/2}$ 20.8   187 m^{-2}

20.12   1.52, 2.68 cm^2/sec   20.14 1.41×10^4 sec   20.16 $(2)^{1/2}q^2/\pi d^2 <v>$

INDEX

Absolute temperature, 111, 129
Absolute value, of energy, 131
  of entropy, 131
Absolute zero of temperature, 257
Absorption, 303
Absorptivity, spectral, 300
Adiabatic turbine efficiency, 376
Arc jet, 395
Avogadro's number, 14

Bernoulli's equation, 381
Binary collisions, 417
Black-body emission, 295
  radiation, 291
  spectral energy density, 294
Body force, 365
Bohr, N., 60
  magneton, 318
Boiling point, 242, 248
Boltzmann, L., 3, 172, 406
  constant, 105
  equation, 435
  partition function, 133
  statistics, 178
  system, 127
Bose-Einstein, distribution, 127
  statistics, 83
Bragg reflection, 268, 281
Brayton cycle, 355
Brillouin, function, 322
  zone, 282, 286
British thermal unit, 16

Calorically perfect gas, 219
Calorie, 14
Canonical ensemble, 226
Canonical equations of motion, 33
Carnot, N., 2, 337
  cycle, 344
Cell in μ-space, 117
Chemical change, 224
Chemical potential, 113, 114, 129, 253
Chemical species, 223

Classical partition function, 135, 185
Clausius, R., 2, 337
  -Clapeyron equation, 250, 257
  inequality, 168
Closed system, 163, 339
Coefficient, binary diffusion, 429
  of performance, 343
  self-diffusion, 431
Collision, broadening, 66
  cross-section, 419
  frequency, 418
Condensed phase, 242
Conductivity, electrical, 431
  thermal, 426
Configuration space, 36
Conjugate coordinates, 3
Conservation, of angular momentum, 21, 28
  of atomic species, 227, 232
  of energy, 23, 28, 367
  of mass, 366
  of momentum, 19, 27, 366
Constant-pressure heat of reaction, 358
Constant-pressure specific heat, 165
  of a crystal, 280
Constant specific heats, 219
Constant-volume heat of reaction, 238
Constant-volume specific heat, 164
Constitutive relations, 362
Continuous medium, 266
Control surface and volume, 369
Convergent-divergent nozzle, 383
Couette flow, 421
Coulomb force, 146
Coupling of vibration and rotation, 191
Critical point, 177, 244
Critical temperature for
    superconductivity, 332
Crystal, cell, 265
  lattice, 265
  structure, 264
Curie's constant, 323
Curie's law, 323

Curie temperature, 331
Curie-Weiss law, 331
Cycle, Brayton, 355
    Carnot, 344
    open, 357
    Otto, 353
    Rankine, 349, 377
Cyclic process, 339
Cyclotron frequency, 318

Dalton's law, 215
de Broglie, L., 63
    wavelength, 63, 178, 281, 286
Debye, P., 272
    temperature, 275, 277
    theory of specific heats, 272, 277
Degenerate perfect gas, 175, 281
Degenerate states, 71, 79
Degree, of freedom, 193
    of temperature, 15, 16
De Laval nozzle, 383
Density, energy, 51, 363
    magnetic energy, 314
    mass, 362
    momentum, 50, 363
    phase-space, 39
Detailed balancing, 4, 287
Deviation, 100
Diffraction, 62, 268
Diffusion, binary, 429
Dilute phase, 242
Discrete distribution function, 91
Dispersion relation, 53, 267, 271, 273, 282
Dispersive medium, 47
Dissociation, energy, 191, 195
    equilibrium, 232
Distribution, 89
    Bose-Einstein, 127
    continuous, 93
    discrete, 91
    energy, 89
    Fermi-Dirac, 127
    function, 91, 406
    probability, 92
    velocity, 406
Dulong and Petit, 272
Dynamical variables, 90
Dynamics, 5

Efficiency, adiabatic turbine, 376
    thermochemical, 400
    thermodynamic, 342
Efflux, 413
Einstein, A., 272, 302
    transition probability, 302
    theory of specific heat, 272
Electrical conductivity, 431
Electromagnetic waves, 290
Electron volt, 15
Electronic energy states of atom, 182
Electronic excitation, 192
Electronic partition function, 181
Electronic states of molecule, 204
Emission of radiation, induced, 303
    spontaneous, 302
Emissive power, spectral, 297
    total, 296
Emissivity, 300
Empirical temperature, 171
Endothermic reaction, 238
Energy, 149
    conservation of, 23, 367
    dissociation, 191, 195
    electronic, 80
    Fermi, 284
    interaction, 150
    internal, 139
    ionization, 182, 234
    nuclear, 82
    potential, 22
    rotational, 78
    translational, 75
    vibrational, 75
Energy density, 51
    magnetic, 314
Energy of formation, 198, 231
    net, 232, 238, 240
Energy reference level, 230, 235
Engine, heat, 339, 342
    internal combustion, 357
    rocket, 396
Ensemble, 37
    average, 100
    canonical, 38, 226
    grand, 38, 226
    microcanonical, 38, 98

state of, 96
stationary, 41, 100
Enthalpy, 165
  change in a reaction, 239
  stagnation, 372
Entropy, 105, 128
  increase of, 110
  magnetic, 323
  of mixing, 217
  nonconservation of, 110, 370
Environment, 29
Equation, of change, 436
  of state, 171
  caloric, 172
Equilibrium, constant, 230
  dissociation, 232
  flow, 392
  ionization, 234
  thermochemical, 228
  thermodynamic, 90, 225
  variables, 90
Ergodic hypothesis, 102
Eucken, 428
Exothermic reaction, 237
Extensive property, 106

Faraday, 313, 400
Fermi-Dirac, distribution, 127
  statistics, 83, 283
Fermi, energy, 284
  surface, 285
Ferromagnetism, 315, 329
First law of thermodynamics, 153
First-order transition, 247, 333
Fluctuation theory, 101
Fluid dynamics, 139, 188, 236, 369
Flux, 405, 411
Force, 20
  body, 365
  central, 21
  conservative, 22
  field, 143
  short- and long-range, 140
Fourier's law, 426
Free energy, Gibbs, 251
  Helmholtz, 253
Frequency, angular, 26, 47
  collision, 418

cyclotron, 318
  Larmor, 318
  total, 26, 47
Frozen flow, 395
Fuel cell, 397

Gas, degenerate, 175, 281
  Fermi, 284
  ideal, 143, 171
  imperfect, 171, 184, 206, 216
  perfect, 143, 171
  phonon, 273
  photon, 293
Gibbs, -Dalton law, 214, 216, 23
  free energy, 251
  W., 2, 172
Gibbs' equation, 161
Gibbs' paradox, 218
Gram-calorie, 14
Gram-mole, 14
Grand ensemble, 38, 226
Grey body, 301
Ground state, 231
Group velocity, 52
Grüneisen constant, 279

Hamiltonian function, 34
Hard-sphere model, 186, 417
Harmonic oscillator, 74, 77, 199
Heat, 140, 152
  of fusion, 258
  in irreversible process, 168
  of reaction, 237
    at constant pressure, 358
    at constant volume, 238
  reversible, 167
Heat engine, 339
  reversible, 342
Heat exchanger, 372
Heat pump, 343
Heat reservoir, 338
Helmholtz free energy, 253
Homonuclear molecule, 79, 195

Ideal Fermi gas, 284
Ideal fluid, 378
Ideal gas, 143, 171
Ideal incompressible fluid, 381
Imperfect gas, 171, 184, 206, 216

Independent particles, 116
Indistinguishability, 58, 69
Induced emission, 303
Inequality of Clausius, 168
Inhibition, 107, 109, 110
Intensive property, 111
Interaction energy, 150
Internal-combustion engine, 357
Internal energy, 139
  change in a reaction, 238
Internal partition function, 176, 192, 230
Ionization, energy, 182, 234
  equilibrium, 234
Irreversible process, 156, 159
Isentropic process, 220

Kelvin scale of temperature, 112
Kilocalorie, 13
Kilogram-mole, 14
Kinematics, 17
Kinetic theory of gases, 3, 11
Kirchhoff's law, 300

Lagrangian multipliers, 126
Lambert's law, 297
Langevin function, 322
Larmor frequency, 318
Laser, 304
Latent heat, of fusion, 247, 248
  of sublimation, 247
  of vaporization, 247, 248
Lattice wave vector, 265
Linear molecule, 80, 193
Liouville's theorem, 35, 38, 99, 434
Long-range force, 140, 146

Mach number, 385
Macroscopic scale, 4
Macrostate, 89
  most probable, 117, 124
  probability of, 118
  stationary, 99
Magnetic cooling, 326
Magnetic dipole moment, 315
Magnetic energy density, 314
Magnetic entropy, 323
Magnetic partition function, 321
Magnetic work, 315
Magnetization, 315

Maser, 304, 329
Mass, 19
  conservation of, 366
  density, 188, 362
  fraction, 216
  reduced, 25, 418
Maxwell, J. C., 3, 172, 406
  relations, 163
  velocity distribution, 409
Mean free path, 56, 419
Mean speed, 411
Mechanics, statistical, 3, 6, 101
Meissner effect, 333
Metastable state, 259
Microcanonical ensemble, 38, 98
Microscopic reversibility, 157
Microscopic scale, 4
Microscopic work, 364
Microstate, 88
Mixture of perfect gases, 211
Molar properties, 187
Molecular size, 173
Molecular structure of a phase, 241
Molecular weight, 188
Molecule, polyatomic, 77
Mole fraction, 215
Mole numbers, 229, 239
Mollier diagram, 378, 394
Moment, of inertia, 78, 196
  magnetic, 315
Momentum, angular, 21
  conservation of, 366
  density, 50
  linear, 19
  space, 36
Most probable macrostate, 117, 124
  changes of, 161
Multicomponent phase, 229

Negative temperature, 328
Nernst's heat theorem, 259
Noise, thermal, 306
Nonblack body, 299
Nonconservation of entropy, 110, 370
Nonlinear molecule, 194
Nonreacting mixture of gases, 211
Nuclear magneton, 328
Nuclear spin, 181, 195

Occupation number, 120
Open cycle, 357
Optical mode, 267
Orthohydrogen, 196
Oscillator, harmonic, 74, 77
Otto cycle, 353

Parahydrogen, 196
Paramagnetic susceptibility, 323
Paramagnetism, 315
Partial pressure, 215, 232
Partial property, 214
Partition function, 131, 133
    Boltzmann, 133
    electronic, 181
    internal, 176, 192, 230
    magnetic, 321
    perfect-gas, 174
    rotational, 194, 197
    translational, 176
    vibrational, 201, 203
Pauli exclusion principle, 82
Perfect gas, 143, 171, 173
    caloric equation of state, 180
    equation of state, 179
    monatomic, 181
    polyatomic, 191
    thermodynamic properties, 178
Perfect paramagnetic system, 320
Perfect phonon gas, 273
Perpetual-motion machine, 341
Phase, 223
    change of, 224
    condensed, 242
    diagram, 243, 245
    dilute, 242
    multicomponent, 229
    rule, 245
Phase space, 34
Phase velocity, 47, 367
Phonon, gas, 268
    pressure, 278
Photoelectric effect, 62
Photon, 60, 293
    gas, 293
Physical constants of molecules, 195, 198
Planck, M., 3, 292
    function, 294

Planck's constant, 60
Polarized wave, 290
Polyatomic molecule, 80
Polyatomic perfect gas, 191
Position vector, 17
Postulate of statistical mechanics, 101
Potential, 131
    function, 131, 199, 251
Prandtl number, 428
Pressure, 143, 155
    in a gas, 8, 415
    phonon, 278
    saturation, 242
Probability density, 68, 94
    energy, 68
    momentum, 68
Probability distribution function, 92
Probability, of a macrostate, 118
    thermodynamic, 103
Products, 237, 357
Properties of molecules, 195, 198
Property, extensive, 106
    intensive, 111
    molar, 187
    thermodynamic, 90

Quantum mechanics, 58
Quantum number, magnetic, 61, 81
    nuclear spin, 82
    orbital, 81
    principal, 80
    rotational, 78
    spin, 61, 81
    translational, 71
    vibrational, 75
Quantum statistics, 83

Radiant heat transfer, 301
Rankine, J., 349
    cycle, 349, 377
Rate process, 404
Ratio of specific heats, 221
Rayleigh-Jeans law, 294
Rayleigh, Lord, 292
Reactants, 237, 357
Reacting mixture of gases, 211, 235
Reciprocal lattice points, 266
Refrigeration, 343

Representative point, 34
Reversible heat, 167
Reversible heat engine, 342
Reversible process, 156, 159
  constant-pressure, 167
  constant-volume, 167
Reversible work, 166
Reynolds number, 425
Richardson's equation, 288
Rocket engine, 396
Rotation, of diatomic molecule, 194
  of polyatomic molecule, 191, 196
Rotational partition function, 194
  of polyatomic molecule, 197
Rotational temperature, 194, 196

Saha equation, 235
Saturation current, 288
Saturation pressure, 242
Schrödinger wave equation, 67
Second law of thermodynamics, 161
Second-order transition, 247
Self-diffusion coefficient, 431
Shear stress, 368, 371, 420
Shock tube, 389
Shock wave, 388
Short-range force, 140
Slip velocity, 424
Sound, speed, 390
  wave, 390
Space, configuration, 36
  momentum, 36
  phase, 34
  quantum number, 72
  velocity, 406
  Γ, 37, 88
  μ, 37, 82, 88
Specific heat, constant, 219
  constant-pressure, 165, 280
  constant-volume, 164
  of monatomic gas, 222
  of polyatomic gas, 208
  ratio, 221
Specific property, 14
  extensive, 187
Spectral absorptivity, 300
Spectral emissive power, 297
Spectral emissivity, 300

Spectral radiant intensity, 291, 297, 298
Spontaneous emission, 302
Stagnation, enthalpy, 372
  state, 384
Standing wave, 72
State, metastable, 259
  quantum, 60
  stagnation, 384
  stationary, 72
  thermodynamic, 90
Statistical average, 100
Statistical mechanics, 3, 6, 101
Statistical weight, 206
Stationary ensemble, 41, 100
Stationary macrostate, 99
Stationary state, 72
Steady flow, 369
Stefan-Boltzmann, constant, 297
  law, 297
Stirling's formula, 124
Stream tube, 378
Stress, 142, 143, 154, 364, 415
  shear, 368, 371, 420
Superconductivity, 332
Supercooled vapor, 254
Superheated liquid, 254
Symmetric-top molecule, 196
Symmetry number, 196, 197
System, thermodynamic, 87

Temperature, 111
  absolute, 111, 129
  Debye, 275, 277
  empirical, 171
  Kelvin scale, 112
  melting, 243
  negative, 328
Thermal conductivity, 426
Thermal expansion of crystal, 278
Thermal noise, 306
Thermionic emission, 286
Thermochemical efficiency, 400
Thermochemical equilibrium, 228
  perfect gas, 229
Thermodynamic efficiency, 342
Thermodynamic equilibrium, 90, 225
Thermodynamic potential function, 132,
  251

Thermodynamic probability, 103
Thermodynamic properties, 90
    crystal, 275
    ideal Fermi gas, 285
    perfect monatomic gas, 183
    polyatomic gas, 207
    rotation, 195
    vibration, 201, 204
Thermodynamics, 1
    classical, 1, 5
    first law of, 153
    molecular, 2
    phenomenological, 1
    second law of, 161
    third law of, 257
Thermodynamic state, 90
Thermodynamic system, 87
    state of, 88
Thermodynamic variables, 90
Total emissive power, 296
Total spectral radiant intensity, 298
Trajectory, 17, 34
Transition, first-order, 247, 333
    second-order, 247
Transition probability, 302
Translational partition function, 176
Transport process, 405
Triple point, 242, 243

Uncertainty principle, 58, 64
Units, 13
Universal gas constant, 187

van't Hoff's equation, 240
Velocity, 17
    distribution function, 406
    group, 52
    phase, 47, 267
    relative, 25
    space, 406
Vibrational partition function, 201, 203

Vibrational temperature, 195, 198, 201
Vibration, of molecules, 74
    of polyatomic molecules, 191, 203
Virial coefficient, 185, 187
Virial expansion, 185
Viscosity, 420
Volume in phase space, 73, 98, 104
Volumetric coefficient of thermal
    expansion, 258, 279

Wave, 44
    electromagnetic, 290
    longitudinal, 47, 267
    plane, 46
    polarization, 290
    sound, 390
    standing, 72
    transverse, 45, 267, 290
Wave equation, 48
Wave function, 66
Wave mechanics, 69
Wave number, 47
    angular, 64
    space, 266
Wave-particle duality, 58, 62
Wave vector, 47
    lattice, 265
Weiss, 330
White noise, 307
Work, 140, 147
    irreversible, 168
    macroscopic, 152
    magnetic, 315
    microscopic, 149, 364
    reversible, 166
Work function, 287

X-ray diffraction, 268

μ-space, 37

Γ-space, 37, 98